The New Natura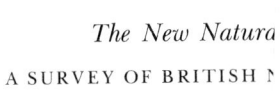
A SURVEY OF BRITISH

FRESHWATER FISHES
OF THE BRITISH ISLES

Editors
Max Walters, ScD, VMH
Professor Richard West, ScD, FRS
David Streeter, FIBiol
Sarah A. Corbet

The aim of this series is to interest the general reader in the wildlife of Britain by recapturing the enquiring spirit of the old naturalists. The editors believe that the natural pride of the British public in the native flora and fauna, to which must be added concern for their conservation, is best fostered by maintaining a high standard of accuracy combined with clarity of exposition in presenting the results of modern scientific research.

The New Naturalist

FRESHWATER FISHES OF THE BRITISH ISLES

Peter S. Maitland and
R. Niall Campbell

With 21 colour photographs and
over 200 black and white
photographs and diagrams

HarperCollins*Publishers*

HarperCollins*Publishers*
London · Glasgow · Sydney · Auckland
Toronto · Johannesberg

First published 1992

© Peter S. Maitland & R. Niall Campbell

ISBN 0 00 219380 9 (Paperback)
ISBN 0 00 219383 3 (Hardback)

Printed and bound by Butler & Tanner, Frome, Somerset, UK

Contents

Editors' Preface	7
Authors' Preface	9
1. Introduction	11
2. Fish Form and Function	21
3. Investigating Fish	37
4. Distribution and Habitat	46
5. Fish Conservation	61
6. Fish Identification	69
7. Lampreys	79
8. Sturgeon	90
9. Shads	93
10. Salmon, Trout and Charr	98
11. Whitefish	145
12. Grayling	158
13. Smelt	163
14. Pike	167
15. Carps	177
16. Loaches	230
17. Catfishes	238
18. Eels	241
19. Sticklebacks	250

20. Cods	262
21. Bass	266
22. Sunfish	270
23. Perch	279
24. Gobies	293
25. Mullets	296
26. Sculpins	304
27. Flatfish	308
28. The Future	312
Appendix 1: Distribution Maps	323
Appendix 2: The Names of British Freshwater Fishes	330
Appendix 3: Growth Curves	333
References	344
Bibliography	347
Index	361

Editors' Preface

The New Naturalist series has, up to now, almost completely ignored Britain's freshwater fish. Not one of the 74 volumes produced since 1945 has dealt specifically with them. Sea fish have fared slightly better, having been the subject of Sir Alister Hardy's second volume *The Open Sea: Fish and Fisheries*. Fresh water as a habitat was described in the admirable volume *Life in Lakes and Rivers* by T.T. Macan and E.B. Worthington, which first appeared in 1951 and had many further editions, but this devoted most of its attention to plants and invertebrates, and fish only receive a brief mention. Many of the volumes describing different parts of Britain, for instance *Natural History in the Highlands and Islands* by F. Fraser Darling and J. Morton Boyd and *The Broads* by E.A. Ellis, include some notes on fish, but no comprehensive account of these important animals has appeared in our series up till now.

With *Freshwater Fish* we believe that we have fully restored the balance. This new volume comprehensively covers its subject. The first five chapters and the last (the 28th) chapter deal with the wider problems concerning the natural history of fish. Their anatomy and physiology is briefly but succinctly described, as is their behaviour and development. Techniques for studying fish are given. Chapter Four is a useful account of distribution and habitat, and Chapter Five discusses the important and timely topic of fish conservation. Chapter 28 deals with the future and draws attention to the problems facing our fresh water and our fish, arising from industrialisation, population growth and agriculture. It paints a relatively optimistic picture of the future, provided that we can safeguard existing habitats and provide new ones in our changing countryside

The remaining 22 chapters deal systematically with the different families of fish found in British fresh waters. Every species is described, including information on its behaviour, distribution and biology. The longest chapters are those on the *Salmon, Trout and Charr*, which obviously include our 'game' fish, and on *Carps*, which include many 'coarse fish' (including Tench, Chub, Rudd and Bream, and the Minnow which many of us captured and cherished in our childhood). This part of the book extends the information found in field guides which have proved so valuable in making identification of specimens possible.

Angling today is the most popular sport in Britain, with over 4,000,000 devotees who regularly fish. We hope that this book will appeal to these anglers and add to the interest of their pastime by allowing them to see how the restricted number of species they catch fit into the whole picture of freshwater ecology. Anglers as a whole have done much to preserve our fresh waters, and the species of fish in them, but unfortunately some individuals have been responsible for unfortunate introductions of fish into new, unsuitable habitats. The wider knowledge this book gives should discourage such practices in the future.

Fish are known to be efficient detectors of water pollution and the actions of the Anglers' Cooperative Association, using the common law, in prosecuting polluters has made an important contribution to preserving many streams and rivers. Today we have more comprehensive legislation to control pollution and to preserve our environment. Here fish will continue to act as 'indicator species' and so make their contribution to seeing that the laws are enforced and that all forms of freshwater life continue to flourish.

Authors' Preface

Natural history has a strong tradition in the British Isles, sending down very deep roots during the nineteenth century in particular. During the latter half of that century and the beginning of the twentieth century a number of excellent volumes on the natural history of fish in these islands were produced, among them the notable works by Day, Houghton, Jenkins, Maxwell and Regan. However, over the last 50 years there has been a dearth of publications on this subject, probably due to a variety of factors – the intervention of two world wars, the demise of the old 'amateur naturalist' (usually a person of means with time to devote to his interests) and the increase in the number of modern biologists (often looking down somewhat on old-fashioned 'natural history') among them. A new comprehensive work on the natural history of our freshwater fishes has been sadly needed for several decades and the authors – both professional biologists, but always self-confessed natural historians of freshwater fish from boyhood days – have attempted to fill this gap with the present book.

The authors hope that this book will give pleasure to those readers already interested in the freshwater fish of the British Isles and perhaps stimulate them to observe more of their natural history. It is our hope that other readers of the book, who perhaps have only a passing interest in the subject, may go beyond the illustrations to delve into some aspect of the text. We fervently wish also that more of our anglers will consider a broader view of their hobby, taking an interest, not only in the natural history of the species they fish for, but in the other members of our fish fauna also. The strength of the angling lobby in this country is very great and all our native fish need support if they are to survive into future centuries. Finally, we acknowledge the pleasure and excitement that fish have given us during our working and our private lives. We would like to think that some of this enjoyment will be apparent in the following pages and give the reader some satisfaction too.

In preparing this book, we have received a great deal of help from a wide variety of people all over the British Isles and in particular would like to acknowledge the following:

Colin and Mary Allsebrook, Alastair Barbour, David and Alex Barbour, Jon Bass, Fiona Bowles, T. Burrey, Bruce Campbell, Margaret Campbell, Ronald Campbell, David Charlton, James Chubb, Andrew Currie, Christine Dickson-Barr, Maurice de Bunsen, Emlyn Evans, Andrew Ferguson, Alan Frake, Patrick Fitzmaurice, Ross Gardiner, Ronald Greer, Elaine Hamilton, John Hardie, Phil Hickley, Donald Hoy, Ian Hynd, Anthony Irvine, Andrew Jones, Clive Kennedy, Mike Ladle, David Le Cren, Fergus Leveson-Gower, Sarah Lorimer, Alex Lyle, Pat Noble, Hugh MacCrimmon, David Mackay, Mick Marquis, Jean McCormack, I. A. Duncan Millar, Ray Milton, Finbar McCormick, John Mitchell, Chris Moriarty, Peter Nicholson, Ken O'Hara, Margaret Palmer, Mike Pawson, J. C. L. Phillips, David Piggins, Paul Raven, Barry Rickards, Graham Scobie, David Shaughnessey, William Shearer,

Richard Shelton, Iain Thornber, John Thorpe, Eileen Twomey, Brian and Jane Twelves, Andrew Walker, Kenneth Wheelan, Alwyne Wheeler, R. G. Weaver, Paul Wilkins, Gordon Williamson.

Anglian Water Authority, Bridgewater Angling Association, Central Fisheries Board (Dublin), DAFS Freshwater Fisheries Laboratory, Department of the Environment for Northern Ireland Conservation Service, Fisheries Conservation Board for Northern Ireland, Freshwater Biological Association, Ministry of Agriculture, Fisheries & Food (England), Nature Conservancy Council, Roinn Na Mara, Severn Trent Water Authority, Wessex Water Authority.

We are particularly grateful to Sheila Adair for her help with references and to Ann Henty for reading the entire manuscript and making many useful suggestions for its improvement.

Since the text of this book was completed several statutory bodies have been reorganised and have changed their designations. The Department of Agriculture and Fisheries for Scotland (DAFS) is now the Scottish Office Agriculture and Fisheries Department (SOAFD). The North of Scotland Hydro-Electric Board (NSHEB) is now Scottish Hydro-Electric (SHE) and the Nature Conservancy Council (NCC) has split in to three country bodies for Scotland, England and Wales. The new Nature Conservancy Council for Scotland will merge in 1992 with the Countryside Commission for Scotland to form Scottish Natural Heritage. Soon, if current proposals for the Environmental Protection Agencies are implemented, there will be other changes involving the National Rivers Authority and the Scottish River Purification Boards. The reader is asked to bear all these changes in mind when reading any text involving such organisations

1
Introduction

The Importance of Fish

It is a surprising fact that fish are the most abundant and yet, overall, the least known of the vertebrate classes. Well over 35,000 species have been described so far and it is likely that eventually the real totals will indicate that three out of every five vertebrate species are fish. Every year about 100 new species are described, so the final total of species world-wide must be near 40,000. They live in virtually all kinds of aquatic habitats and have developed a wide variety of form and function.

Fish occur in both marine and freshwater environments, but although fresh waters occupy only a minute fraction of the earth's surface and only 0.0093% of the total water found on earth, it has been estimated that 33% of all fish belong to primary freshwater species (i.e. fish entirely restricted to fresh water), mainly carps, characins and catfishes. Because of the fragile nature of freshwater habitats and the pressures from human activities in all parts of the world, it is this section of the fish fauna which is under greatest threat.

Apart from aesthetic and many other conservation considerations, there is no doubt that fish form an extremely important part of the human diet throughout the world. In recent years, over 60 million tonnes of fish have been harvested annually from aquatic environments. Over 20% of the total commercial catch moving into human consumption normally comes from fresh waters, and in addition there is a widespread subsistence fishery for which there are no data (though it is estimated at c. six million tonnes). (Subsistence fisheries are distinct from commercial ones in that local people are going out regularly and catching fish for their own food and not to sell commercially.) Furthermore, there is in many countries an important sport fishery. Taking all these sources into account it is estimated that freshwater fish provide human food in a quantity not far below the registered ocean catch of fish.

The importance of conserving this resource – both marine and freshwater – for the future in virtually all continents and countries is clearly imperative. The size of the task is vast, however, taking into account the enormous number of species involved over almost the whole globe, and the problem must be tackled in a variety of ways and by many individuals and organisations if any measure of success is to be achieved.

Habitats

Though its fish fauna is rather impoverished, for reasons which are discussed in another chapter, the British Isles is richly endowed with a wide variety of freshwater habitats. Flowing waters range from numerous small and several large estuaries, through lowland rivers, to many upland rivers and streams.

Table 1 Checklist of the fresh water fishes of the British Isles.

LAMPREYS Family Petromyzonidae
Sea Lamprey *Petromyzon marinus* Linnaeus 1758
River Lamprey *Lampetra fluviatilis* (Linnaeus 1758)
Brook Lamprey *Lampetra planeri* (Bloch 1784).

STURGEON Family Acipenseridae
Common Sturgeon *Acipenser sturio* Linnaeus 1758

SHADS Family Clupeidae
Allis Shad *Alosa alosa* (Linnaeus 1758)
Twaite Shad *Alosa fallax* (Lacepede 1803)

SALMON, TROUT AND CHARR Family Salmonidae
Atlantic Salmon *Salmo salar* Linnaeus 1758
Brown Trout *Salmo trutta* Linnaeus 1758
Rainbow Trout *Oncorhynchus mykiss* (Walbaum 1792)
Pink Salmon *Oncorhynchus gorbuscha* (Walbaum 1792)
Arctic Charr *Salvelinus alpinus* (Linnaeus 1758)
Brook Charr *Salvelinus fontinalis* (Mitchill 1815)

WHITEFISH Family Coregonidae
Houting *Coregonus oxyrinchus* (Linnaeus 1758)
Powan *Coregonus lavaretus* (Linnaeus 1758)
Vendace *Coregonus albula* (Linnaeus 1758)
Pollan *Coregonus autumnalis* (Pallas 1776)

GRAYLING Family Thymallidae
Grayling *Thymallus thymallus* (Linnaeus 1758)

SMELT Family Osmeridae
Smelt *Osmerus eperlanus* (Linnaeus 1758)

PIKE Family Esocidae
Pike *Esox lucius* Linnaeus 1758

CARPS Family Cyprinidae
Common Carp *Cyprinus carpio* Linnaeus 1758
Crucian Carp *Carassius carassius* (Linnaeus 1758)
Goldfish *Carassius auratus* (Linnaeus 1758)
Barbel *Barbus barbus* (Linnaeus 1758)
Gudgeon *Gobio gobio* (Linnaeus 1758)
Tench *Tinca tinca* (Linnaeus 1758)
Silver Bream *Blicca bjoerkna* (Linnaeus 1758)
Common Bream *Abramis brama* (Linnaeus 1758)
Bleak *Alburnus alburnus* (Linnaeus 1758)
Minnow *Phoxinus phoxinus* (Linnaeus 1758)
Bitterling *Rhodeus sericeus* (Bloch 1782)
Rudd *Scardinius erythrophthalmus* (Linnaeus 1758)
Roach *Rutilus rutilus* (Linnaeus 1758)
Chub *Leuciscus cephalus* (Linnaeus 1758)
Orfe *Leuciscus idus* (Linnaeus 1758)
Dace *Leuciscus leuciscus* (Linnaeus 1758)

LOACHES Family Cobitidae
Spined Loach *Cobitis taenia* Linnaeus 1758
Stone Loach *Noemacheilus barbatulus* (Linnaeus 1758)

CATFISHES Family Siluridae
Danube Catfish *Silurus glanis* Linnaeus 1758

EELS Family Anguillidae
European Eel *Anguilla anguilla* (Linnaeus 1758)

STICKLEBACKS Family Gasterosteidae
Three-spined Stickleback *Gasterosteus aculeatus* Linnaeus 1758
Nine-spined Stickleback *Pungitius pungitius* (Linnaeus 1758)

CODS Family Gadidae
Burbot *Lota lota* (Linnaeus 1758)

BASS Family Serranidae
Sea Bass *Dicentrarchus labrax* (Linnaeus 1758)

SUNFISH Family Centrarchidae
Largemouth Bass *Micropterus salmoides* (Lacepede 1802)
Pumpkinseed *Lepomis gibbosus* (Linnaeus 1758)
Rock Bass *Ambloplites rupestris* (Rafinesque-Schmaltz 1817)

PERCH Family Percidae
Perch *Perca fluviatilis* Linnaeus 1758
Ruffe *Gymnocephalus cernua* (Linnaeus 1758)
Pikeperch *Stizostedion lucioperca* (Linnaeus 1758)

GOBIES Family Gobiidae
Common Goby *Pomatoschistus microps* (Kroyer 1840)

MULLETS, Family Mugilidae
Thick-lipped Mullet *Chelon labrosus* (Risso 1826)
Thin-lipped Mullet *Liza ramada* (Risso 1826)
Golden Mullet *Liza aurata* (Risso 1810)

SCULPINS Family Cottidae
Bullhead *Cottus gobio* Linnaeus 1758

FLATFISH Family Pleuronectidae
Flounder *Platichthys flesus* (Linnaeus 1758)

INTRODUCTION

Fig 1 The River Tay, Britain's largest river by flow and an important Salmon river, as well as home to a variety of other fish species (Peter Maitland).

Standing waters too are abundant, from small and large lowland lakes to numerous small and medium-sized upland ones. There are many artificial water bodies as well, especially canal systems, gravel pits and reservoirs. The varied geology and topography found throughout these islands is reflected in these waters and brackish, alkaline and acid systems are found in many areas.

The actual number of water bodies occurring in the British Isles is surprisingly large. A study of Ordnance Survey maps has shown that in Great Britain as a whole there are over 10,000 individual river systems entering the sea, while inland there are over 81,000 ponds, lakes and reservoirs. The latter have a total surface area of 2404km^2, which represents 1.04% of Great Britain.

The major single cause of the extinction of populations of fish (and indeed most other species of both plants and animals) throughout the world is the destruction of habitat. Some years ago, the Nature Conservancy Council in Great Britain carried out a massive review of natural habitats and produced a clear statement of conservation criteria, and a list of major sites all over the country which should be protected. These were of three categories: Grade 1 Sites (the most valuable), Grade 2 Sites (not quite so important but valuable as replacements to Grade 1 Sites) and Sites of Special Scientific Interest (not so important as the previous two categories, but with at least one important feature requiring protection of some kind). A review of freshwater systems was included within this project and data on over one thousand different sites were collected and reviewed. Though the status of fish was not an integral part of this study, the fact that so many important freshwater habitats of all kinds were set aside for conservation inevitably meant considerable protection for their fish faunas. More recently, special consideration has been given to the conservation of sites which are particularly important for their fish communities and criteria for the definition of these have been produced.

The Fish Fauna

This book is about all freshwater fishes in the British Isles – in the broadest sense. Thus, it includes animals belonging to both Cyclostomes and Pisces. Technically, since the Cyclostomes belong to the Agnatha and have no proper jaws, only the Pisces are true fishes. However, throughout the book, for convenience sake, we categorise both Cyclostomes and Pisces as fish. The species considered in this book are all those which occur in fresh water for a significant period of their lives and which are known to have breeding populations established somewhere in or around the British Isles. Native species, as well as successfully introduced foreign species, come into this category. Also included are a few species which may have occurred here at one time, or at least appeared regularly as vagrants. However, not included are a number of species which have been introduced unsuccessfully on one or more occasions, or which have established themselves somewhere only with continued artificial help from humans, e.g. tropical species in the vicinity of heated effluents.

Identification

There are a number of books whose main concern is the identification of freshwater fish. Some of these guides deal with the whole of Europe whereas others deal only with the British Isles. The more important of these works are included in the bibliography at the end of this volume. Each of these has strengths and weaknesses (as no doubt this one has) and may in turn contain other references to studies of interest. The identification of many of the species of fish found in the British Isles is often possible using certain of these publications, simply by reference to and comparison with the various illustrations in them. This is, however, often a slow and inaccurate method of identification and, moreover, the older works include no reference to many of those species introduced relatively recently (e.g. Brook Charr and Pumpkinseed). Thus, in addition to the account of the natural history for each of the species, which forms the bulk of this book, it is hoped that the identification keys (in combination with the illustrations) will prove to be a straightforward way of identifying any fish found in fresh water in these islands.

Casual Species

Many people have been tempted at various times over the last few centuries to introduce various foreign fish species to the British Isles but only 12 of them, discussed later in this book, have been successful in establishing permanent populations. Many more species have been introduced unsuccessfully and these have included the Danube Salmon *Hucho hucho* and Mud Minnow *Umbra krameri* from Europe, and the Brown Bullhead *Ictalurus nebulosus*, Black Bullhead *Ictalurus melas*, Walleye *Stizostedion vitreum* and Smallmouth Bass *Micropterus dolomieu* from North America.

More recently, a number of semi-tropical American, African and Asian species have been introduced. The Guppy *Poecilia reticulata*, a common tropical aquarium fish, was found to be breeding successfully and thriving a number of years ago in the vicinity of a heated effluent outlet running into the River Lee in Essex. Similarly, near a warm-water effluent supplying the Church Street Canal in St Helens, Lancashire, a population of *Tilapia zillii* managed to establish itself successfully over several years. More recently there have been widespread introductions of the Chinese Grass Carp (sometimes called the White Amur) *Ctenopharyngodon idella* into several lakes in various parts of the British Isles for the purposes of weed control and limited angling. Though it seems unlikely that this species will ever breed successfully in this country, no doubt specimens will appear from time to time. Apart from the Grass Carp none of these casual specimens is dealt with in detail in this book.

Threats to Fish and their Habitats

Humans have used water from earliest times, not only for drinking, but also for an increasing number of other purposes as civilisations became more sophisticated. There has also been a close association between humans and fish populations for thousands of years and in many cases it is now difficult to separate the effects of human impact from those of more natural processes. However, over the last two hundred years, in the developed countries, and only the last few decades in developing regions, many new and intensive pressures have been applied to fish habitats and to fish populations.

Pollution

The influence of polluting substances on natural waters and their fish populations can be very variable, according to the substances themselves and the conditions and fish species in the water concerned. Most pollution comes from domestic, agricultural or industrial wastes or from the results of these activities on land use and run-off in the catchment area. Pollution can be either completely toxic, thereby eliminating all the fish species present, or selective, killing off only a few sensitive species or altering the environment so that some species are favoured and others are not.

Many polluting effluents are directed into rivers in order that the offending substances may be carried away from the polluter and eventually to the sea. As a result, many of the world's finest rivers have become grossly polluted and have lost most or all of their fish populations. Migratory species may be especially affected in such systems, for it is normally the lowest reaches of rivers and their estuaries that are most seriously polluted and such fish must pass through them at two stages in their life history. Thus, one extreme belt of pollution in the lower part of a river can have a major effect on fish communities in the whole system.

Habitat Destruction

The extraction of water for human use varies in its impact on aquatic habitats. Where total abstraction takes place, the results are obvious and disastrous. The dry and lifeless river beds below major abstraction points around the world bear witness to this. More often there is only partial abstraction. Here, the continual variations in water levels or flows lead to unstable habitats and communities, and the shorelines of such systems are often virtually devoid of plants or animals.

Land drainage has often affected freshwater fish populations. The canalisation of a river course to prevent flooding is usually carried out in a very drastic manner and the river bed frequently remains in an unstable condition. Plants and animals do recolonise from other areas but the simplification of the channel environment leads to a general biological impoverishment and the habitat rarely returns to its original condition. Land drainage works of many kinds lead to faster run-off in wet weather and little reserve in dry weather, so leading to more extreme conditions in the aquatic systems into which they drain. There has been widespread destruction, by draining or filling-in, of many thousands of small ponds, ox-bow lakes and other small waters all over the world. Such habitats are of major importance to many species of small fish (as well as being important aquatic habitats in their own right), but often there is little outcry about their destruction. The economic and social claims of those destroying them are well known (cheap dumping grounds for garbage, reclamation of land for agriculture, removal of a potential nuisance and danger to children, etc.) and rarely opposed.

Commercial Fishing

The commercial harvesting of fish varies in its impact on the aquatic communities concerned. Indeed, because it is in their interests to keep water as natural and uncontaminated as possible, fishermen can act as a strong force against pollution and other dangers. However, considerable harm can be done to target species by overfishing and even to non-target species where these are taken in significant numbers as a by-catch. With some specialised forms of fishing, such as poisoning, extensive damage can be done to all the species present in the water concerned. An efficient fishery based on cropping the sustainable yield is what should be aimed at both for the long-term good of the fishery and also to have the least impact on the aquatic community as a whole.

Table 2 Some of the main dangers facing freshwater fish and their habitat in the British Isles.

Danger	Effect
Industrial and domestic pollution	Elimination of stocks. Blocking of migratory species.
Land use (farming and forestry)	Eutrophication, acidification, sedimentation.
River obstructions (dams)	Blocking of migratory species.
Acid deposition	Elimination of fish stocks in poorly buffered waters.
Drainage and canalisation	Loss of habitat, shelter and food supply.
Industrial development (including roads)	Sedimentation, obstructions, transfer of species.
Eutrophication	Algal blooms, de-oxygenation, changes in fish species.
Fish farming	Eutrophication, introductions, diseases, genetic changes.
Fishery management	Elimination by piscicides, introductions.
Introduction of new species	Elimination of native species, diseases, parasites.
Fluctuating water levels (reservoirs)	Loss of habitat, spawning and food supply.
Warm water discharge	De-oxygenation, temperature gradients.
Water abstraction	Loss of habitat and spawning grounds.

Sport Fishing

There are a number of major conflicts between angling and wildlife conservation in fresh waters. The problems which have arisen in recent years in the British Isles relate to the use of lead weights, litter disposal, disturbance, habitat alteration, the use of pesticides and the elimination of predators, and the introduction and translocation of exotic fish species. On the other hand, anglers are said to be very beneficial in supporting controlled multi-purpose use of waters and acting as a powerful lobby for pollution prevention.

New and specialised forms of sport fishing are also a threat in many areas. In tropical shallow seas and in some temperate waters an increasing number of tourists have been attracted to snorkelling and SCUBA diving and have armed themselves with spear guns. Many of the fish in these waters are large and confiding and make easy targets for such fishermen. Their beauty and colour have resulted in their own destruction and they have become rare in some waters as a result.

Aquarium Trade

The conservation significance of the world-wide aquarium trade in fish is now considerable and though British fish are not affected directly (except by species introduced through this source) aquarists in this country have created an important demand for many rare foreign species. In spite of the interest shown by zoos in the captive breeding of threatened mammals, birds and reptiles, little interest has been shown by public aquaria in the breeding of threatened or rare fish species. A few public aquaria do hold species of conservation interest and these fall into two categories. Firstly, small species, which although threatened in the wild are readily bred. In most cases these fish originated from captive-bred specimens and are maintaining their own populations in captivity. Secondly, large, more spectacular fishes, mainly caught in the wild, have a tendency to mature at a large size and to require specialised conditions for breeding. Thus, in order to maintain their exhibits, aquaria have to procure specimens from the wild regularly and this could have a deleterious effect on some wild stocks.

Enormous numbers of fish, both freshwater and marine, are now handled by the aquarium trade world-wide. A considerable proportion of these are caught in the wild and then flown to various countries for sale. The annual international retail value of ornamental fish has been estimated at 1.5 billion US dollars. In the United States alone there are about 20 million fish hobbyists, who import each year over 125 million fish comprising 450 different species. The impact of all this on wild stocks is uncertain but there is some concern about a number of populations in various parts of Africa and South America where the collecting pressures are intense.

Conservation

The European fish fauna is distinctly poor – especially in the north and west. There are a few endemic species (i.e. fish which are found only in this area of the world) and some relict groups in the south-east. In the south numbers are also increased by the presence of various peripheral fish (i.e. which have close links with the sea) of Mediterranean origin. Northern Europe shares the greater part of the widely distributed northern Asiatic fish fauna. A number of individual countries in Europe have developed conservation measures for their fish but there has been little concerted activity.

In general, where there is exploitation of a threatened species it is essential that it is monitored and control exerted. The pollution of fresh waters is probably the single most significant factor in causing major declines of many species in Europe but engineering works, land use and various other human pressures have also given rise to problems. Each country must develop rational conservation-orientated policies for the management of its own fish stocks. Too often, however, the basic information necessary for this is lacking. Europe as a whole has little to be proud of in the way it has treated its stocks of freshwater (and marine) fish, but fortunately none is yet extinct and there may still be time to retain an intact, diverse and economically very valuable fish fauna if action is taken soon.

The conservation of both freshwater and marine fishes, so long neglected, has at last started to become a focus for attention on a world-wide basis. Compared to the attention given to and the progress made with the conservation of birds and mammals the effort devoted in the past to fish in most countries has been shameful – this in spite of the facts, discussed above, that they are the world's most abundant vertebrates, have more species than all the other vertebrates put together and are a major source of protein for humans in many areas of the world.

In many countries, not too much attention has previously been paid to fish conservation other than in relation to a few species of concern to anglers or commercial fishermen, and to a variety of species which have been introduced from other continents. However, for most countries there are a number of accounts of some aspects of the fish fauna which can form an initial basis for a conservation approach. The convening of a workshop on the threatened freshwater fish of any country can be an important milestone for its fish fauna, representing a major initiative in the thinking and organisation of a programme for the active conservation of fish in that country.

Information for Conservation

Information on the current distribution and status of all the species of fish concerned in any area is fundamental in producing a conservation policy. Even in the British Isles, where the distribution of most species of freshwater fish was thought to be quite well known, it was felt necessary to instigate a scheme to produce up-to-date information on the general distribution of all species. This mapping scheme continues.

Distribution

The development of a sophisticated mapping scheme should be promoted very strongly in every area where it is hoped to initiate sound fish-conservation management policies. It is recommended that any group which is involved in setting it up obtains advice from successful specialist groups elsewhere. Among the important principles involved in such schemes is the establishment of a standard method of recording and data retrieval. For each region: a) there should be task forces covering specialised problems; b) the data should be centralised (using an appropriate computing system); c) it should be possible to produce distribution maps of many different kinds easily (e.g. on fish diseases, feral fish, etc.).

Fish Abundance

In many general geographical studies of fish there has been relatively little discussion concerning the ways of looking at the actual status of each fish species in any area. Sometimes, detailed population dynamics (concentrating entirely on the numbers of fish in the various age groups) are given too much emphasis as, to some extent, the actual numbers of individuals within a single system do not really mean too much in conservation terms. This is because, unlike most terrestrial – or even marine – systems, the entire population of fish in a lake or a river is vulnerable to a single incident of disease or pollution. Thus it is safer to have fewer fish in several lakes or rivers than an enormous population at one site. Also there will be great variation among different species – smaller, fecund, fast-growing species can be present in enormous numbers whereas the larger, slow-growing ones may be relatively few in number. Each is vulnerable to different pressures in its own way. Large numbers do not mean safety for the species, and the fact that there are ten million of one species in a lake does not mean that it is any safer than another species with a population of one million when a pollution incident occurs. Another point for consideration is that in most situations it is extremely difficult and usually time-consuming and expensive to obtain quantitative values for populations of fish.

A much more realistic approach to the problem in relation to conservation is to concentrate on: a) any changes in the distribution of a species over time, and b) the numbers of discrete populations of each species. Accurate distribution maps produced at different times will indicate whether or not a species is spreading or contracting and it is usually more important to know this than the actual total numbers involved. Species with very limited distributions and only one or two discrete populations are extremely vulnerable and in such cases it is suggested that management of some kind is called for. In the British Isles, any species with less than five discrete populations is considered under some threat and efforts are now being made to establish additional populations of such species in new waters. A code of conduct has been developed for the procedures to be followed in such situations.

Pisciculture

As an alternative to habitat protection, fish may be taken into 'captivity' and bred in ponds or aquaria. This can sometimes be an important part of the conservation strategy for any threatened species, but it can really only be considered as a short-term policy. However, the topic is so important in relation to the conservation of several fish species in the wild that there is a need for a popular illustrated account of the problems and their solutions for general distribution to fish farmers, fishery managers and others. This should emphasise the importance of the numbers of fish which should be used as well as the need to maintain a genetic diversity similar to that found in the wild.

It is, however, gratifying to see many of these important genetic principles already being followed in fishery development in a number of countries. The philosophy has important implications not only for wild populations of angling or commercial species but also for smaller species kept by aquarists and zoos. The role of zoos and public aquaria in this area has been negligible in the past but such institutions could have an important and positive role to play in fish conservation in the future.

Literature

This book has relied heavily on the work of others. The foundation of the knowledge of both the authors was based on several of the classical works on British freshwater fish, and this, together with lifetime careers associated with fish ecology and access to the many individual scientific publications dealing with various species, is the background on which the text was written. Of major importance in this country in the last two decades has been the establishment of the Fisheries Society of the British Isles and the numerous papers appearing in its publication, the Journal of Fish Biology. However, in order to make the text more readable and keep the narrative flowing, reference to individual works has been largely avoided, but all of those drawn from and used in the book are referred to in the bibliography at the end. In doing so we acknowledge our debt to all those concerned.

2

Fish Form and Function

Anatomy

The most obvious external sense organs of fish are located on the head; a pair of eyes, nostrils (normally paired) and sometimes barbels (or feelers) which may vary in number, size and position according to species. The head anterior to the mouth is normally called the snout; the position of the mouth itself varies; it may be terminal, superior (opening above) or inferior (opening below). In a few species the mouth is modified to form a sucker.

The mouth has several bones which may be important in the identification of some species − maxillary, premaxillary, vomer, hyoid, palatine, etc. Several of these may carry teeth − long or short, permanent or deciduous. In adult lampreys, the oral discs have supra-oral and infra-oral areas bearing teeth. The mouth opens into a pharynx and some fish have, at the back of this, bones which are specialised for chewing and crushing, known as pharyngeal bones; the shape of these is important in identifying members of the carp family (Cyprinidae).

From the sides of the pharynx, cavities lead past the main respiratory organs known as gills; together these form the branchial region. Each gill has a strong supporting arch, with a set of comb-like rakers on one side, whose function is to strain out food in some species and to prevent food material passing from the mouth into the delicate blood-filled respiratory lamellae, aligned on the other side of the gill arch. Normally there are four gills on each side of the pharynx, the passages between them leading to the outside through gill openings. In most species of fish these are protected by a single flattened bony gill cover on either side, called the operculum.

Fig. 2 The main external features of a typical fish.

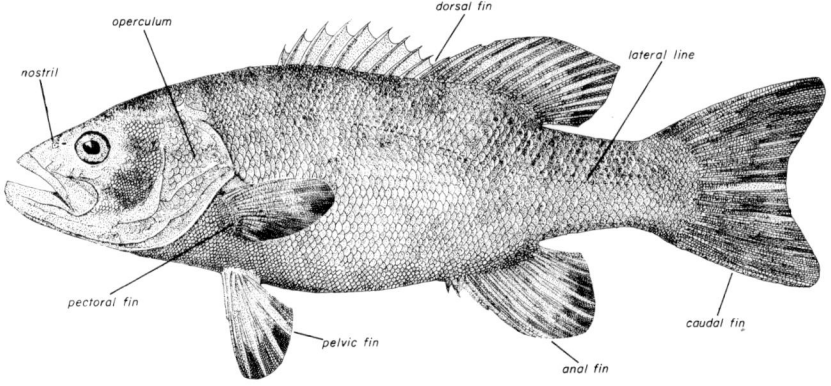

Fig. 3 A close-up view of the head of a Powan (Peter Maitland).

The body is enclosed in skin; in most fish, small bony plates known as scales lie embedded in this, forming a protective but extremely flexible covering over everything except much of the head – which is already well protected by various bones. The scales vary in shape and number from species to species and they are often useful for identification. Some species have no scales; in others the scales are replaced by isolated bony scutes which project from the skin. Within the skin too, are a number of pigment cells which are responsible for much of the variable colouration of the fish. Though colour is useful in distinguishing fish it should be regarded with caution, for even within one species colour can vary greatly with age, sex, season, time of day, emotional state, etc.

Fish biologists see scales as something more than a simple part of fish anatomy. The structure of scales and the way each is laid down in the fishes' skin means that each records in the lines within the scale, or circuli, the growth of its bearer in the same way as the rings in the trunks of trees. Given a single scale from a mature fish a competent biologist can often identify the species, establish its age, calculate its rate of growth throughout its life and say how often it has spawned. In migratory fish it is often possible to establish the time spent in fresh water and in the sea, or in its nursery stream and in its parent lake. Thus, a detailed knowledge of scale development and anatomy is indispensable to any competent ichthyologist.

The important features of fish scales are shown in the accompanying figure. Although a few families of fish have no scales at all, most fish do and in these there are normally differences between scales from different parts of the body – those near the head, the lateral line and areas adjacent to the fins usually showing some modification of shape. Most identification keys refer to typical body scales (the great majority) found above and below the lateral line

FISH FORM AND FUNCTION

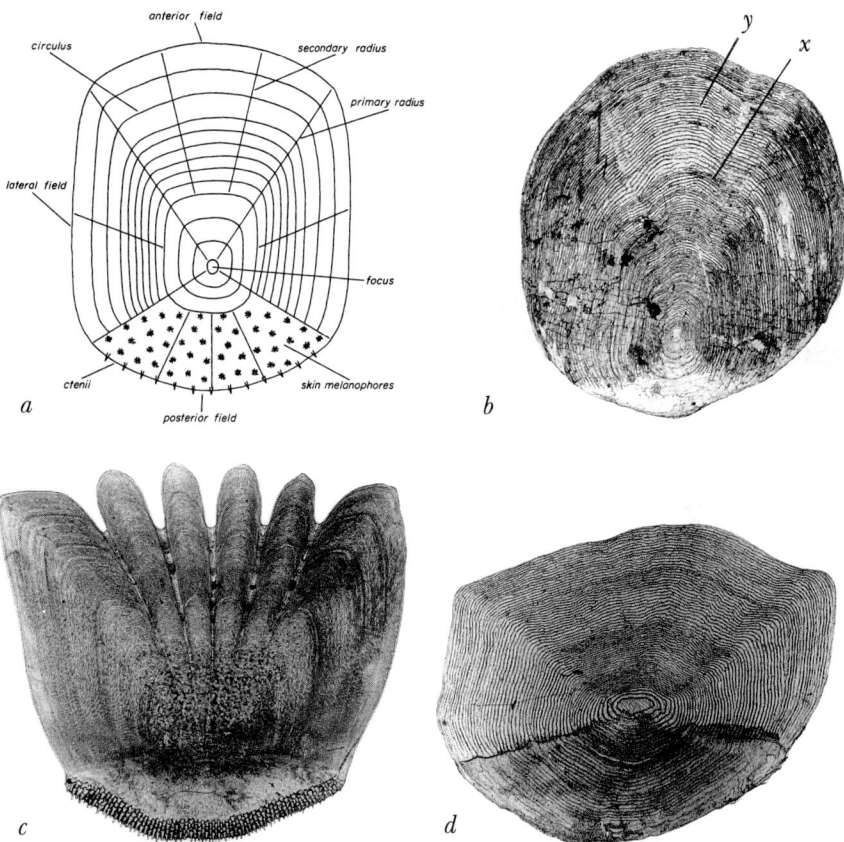

Fig. 4 a, General characteristics of a fish scale; *b*, a scale from a Loch Rannoch ferox trout 78cm in length, 5.4kg in weight and 13+ years old: *x* indicates point at which 'ferox growth' began at 8+ years of age (approx. 34cm long) when the trout began feeding on fish, *y* indicates the point at which the first year of 'ferox growth' ended (Niall Campbell); *c*, a typical ctenoid scale from a Perch (FBA); *d*, a typical cycloid scale from a Powan (FBA).

between head and tail. The scales overlap on the body of the fish like tiles on a roof, but unlike tiles much less than half of each scale is normally exposed. The width of circuli and the numbers laid down are related to growth of the fish; wide circuli indicate good (fast) growth (which usually takes place in summer); narrow circuli indicate poor (slow) growth (which normally occurs in winter). Bands of narrow circuli are usually formed each winter and are called annuli. In addition to scales, other bony parts of the body are also of use for ageing; among the most important are opercular bones, fin rays and otoliths.

Along each side of the body in many species of fish is a lateral line; this is a thin sensory canal just underneath the skin and connected to the exterior through a series of pores. These often pierce individual scales. Branches of the system run on to the head. The main function of the lateral line is sensory – the fine detection of all kinds of changes in water pressure and vibrations in the water.

The characteristic position of fins on a fish is indicated in the figure. There are two sets of paired fins, both usually positioned ventrally – the pectoral fins (normally anterior) and the pelvic fins (normally posterior). In some of the more advanced fish, the pelvics can actually be in front of the pectorals. These pairs of fins are more or less equivalent to the fore and hind legs of terrestrial vertebrates. On the fishes' back is a dorsal fin; this can consist of two distinct parts, or be divided into two (occasionally three) separate fins, or have the anterior fin only as a number of isolated spines. Some fish have a small fleshy rounded fin with no rays, known as the adipose fin behind the dorsal fin. In European fish this occurs only in the Salmonidae and related families (Coregonidae, Osmeridae, Thymallidae). That part of the body posterior to the anus is known as the caudal region. Ventrally (just behind the anus) this carries the single anal fin, while posteriorly, where the body ends in the caudal peduncle, is the single caudal (or tail) fin. The supporting structures of the mainly membranous fins are known as rays; these may be branched (and rather soft) or unbranched (and hard – these are usually referred to as spiny or bony) and are often useful taxonomic characters. In many fish the sharp fin spines, which can be erected at will, are used as weapons of aggression or defence.

Internally are many structures which it is also important to understand in order to appreciate how fish function. As in other vertebrates, the body is mainly supported by a strong bony but flexible vertebral column. To this are linked the head and fins, and the numerous blocks of muscle (often interspersed with fine bones, which may be attached or unattached to the spinal column) occurring along either side of the body. These muscles, the flesh of the fish, are its means of propulsion and are also the part most sought after by its predators, including, of course, humans.

Below the vertebral column is the main body cavity of the fish, containing many of its vital organs; these can really be examined properly only by dissection and are normally cleaned out entirely when the fish is gutted prior to cooking.

The pharynx leads into an oesophagus which opens into the stomach. Any food eaten by the fish is held in the stomach for some time before passing into the intestine where it is digested; any undigested materials move on into the rectum, from which they are evacuated periodically through the anus as faeces. Associated with the gut is the liver, itself often used by humans as a rich source of oil and vitamins. Dorsal to the gut lie the paired sexual organs – quite simple in most fish and consisting of two elongated bags whose contents, eggs (ova) in the female and milt (sperm) in the male, exit through a common genital duct and papilla beside the anus. The sex of many fish can be determined only by examination of these gonads; the female ovaries usually contain what are obviously globular eggs (often white or yellowish in colour) whilst the male testes are smooth and white. Immediately below the vertebral column (lying along the 'ceiling' of the body cavity) are the kidneys and the swimbladder. The latter maintains neutral buoyancy by changes in its volume as gases move into or out of solution in the blood. In some species it is also directly connected to the pharynx for active pumping of air in and out via the mouth. This means that the fish does not have to expend any muscular effort in maintaining its level at any depth in the water column. Fish which have no swimbladder, such as lampreys, rays and sharks, often live on the sea or river bed, and must swim constantly to maintain their position; when they stop swimming, they simply sink to the bottom.

Behind the head, just posterior to the gills is the chambered muscular heart, which pumps blood, firstly through the gills to be oxygenated (and rid itself of carbon dioxide) and then through the body to carry these dissolved gases to and from the tissues.

In fish the brain is well protected inside the bony skull and, though simpler than in birds and mammals, is nonetheless a complex lobed organ. At the back of the head, also enclosed in bone, are the semicircular canals or inner ears, which are important in helping the fish to maintain its balance. Within a chamber inside each canal are secreted loose pieces of calcium carbonate, known as otoliths. These, like scales, grow in proportion to the size of the fish and can often be used when ageing specimens. They help the fish maintain its balance in the water by a system of nerves which respond to the position of the otolith, and hence gravity, and enable the fish to orientate itself.

Physiology

One of the most important features of fish physiology is that, unlike birds and mammals (which are warm blooded), fish – like amphibians and reptiles and all invertebrates – are cold blooded. This means that, except where there are special adaptations, they assume the same temperature as their environment. This may be below freezing in cold climates or above the temperature of warm- blooded animals in the tropics.

Food and Growth

Fish, like all organisms, require food to live and grow. This food is produced in the first instance by photosynthetic plant life and may come to the fish indirectly via herbivorous invertebrates or a more complex food chain of some kind. Fish biologists have been able to discover the feeding behaviour and type of food eaten as well as explore the nutritional value of the different foods by observation in the field and experiments there and in the laboratory. Much of this work is recent and relates to developments in fish farming.

The mouth and gut of a fish have been described above, but it should be realised that not only is the mouth adapted to the kind of food eaten but also the gut is modified in this respect. Thus, the oesophagus and stomach are very distensible in carnivorous fish, allowing them to swallow whole fish which may be very large relative to their own size. The main purpose of the digestive system is to break down foods (by mechanical and biochemical means) into soluble materials which can be absorbed through the gut wall and subsequently used for metabolism and growth. After food has been swallowed it is acted upon by enzymes secreted by the gut and organs associated with it. Important among these is the liver, which secretes bile, an important aid to digestion; the liver also acts as a storage and processing organ for food products after absorption.

Food is moved down the gut by waves of contraction of the gut wall. In some fish a little absorption takes place in the stomach, but it is in the intestine that most food material passes into the bloodstream as soluble fats, proteins and carbohydrates. These then provide energy for movement, materials for replacing or regenerating cells or for growth. Since the body temperature of a fish is controlled by its environment, all these processes are fast at high ambient temperatures and slow at low ones. The efficiency of fish in converting foods is variable, but it is known that in hatchery conditions, for instance, Rainbow Trout can have a conversion efficiency of about 3.5 or less (i.e. for every 3.5kg of food eaten, they increase in weight by 1kg). The conversion ratios in fish can be very high as, unlike birds and animals, they do not have to use energy to maintain a high body temperature so a larger proportion of the food can go to body building. In the wild, Brown Trout probably have an average conversion ratio of 7:1 throughout the seasons.

Fish growth is closely related to the quantity and quality of food eaten, though other factors (space, temperature, health, etc.) are also involved. One of the outstanding features of fish is their phenomenal plasticity as far as growth is concerned. When food and other conditions are suitable many species are able to grow very fast. But in adverse circumstances, perhaps with no food, or very cold conditions for long periods, they are able to survive, but will not grow at all. This is in contrast to most warm-blooded birds and mammals, which are less tolerant and usually die after a short period without food – unless they are able to hibernate or go into some other kind of torpor. Unlike birds and mammals also, fish continue to grow throughout their lives and do not stop on reaching sexual maturity. Many species of small fish – especially in the tropics – live for only one or two years but some large species (e.g. Sturgeon) may live for 30 years or longer.

The Blood System

The circulatory blood-supply links digestion, respiration and excretion. Its main function is to carry oxygen and carbon dioxide, cell wastes and products of excretion, minerals and dissolved foods around the body. The blood of fish, as of other vertebrates, is a fluid plasma with various materials in solution and in which the solid blood cells are carried. These cells are of two types; white lymphocytes and leucocytes, and red erythrocytes. Red haemoglobin in the latter aids oxygen transport in the blood. The amount of blood present in the body is quite low; usually only about 2.3% of the body weight, compared to more than 6% in mammals.

The circulatory system of fish is relatively simple, consisting of a rather tubular heart, arteries, capillaries and veins. The heart (containing one-way valves) pumps blood forward into the gills where it passes through fine capillary vessels, usually in close contact with the water outside. Blood then collects in arteries, which transport it to the tissues, where it again passes through capillaries. It then flows into veins which pass through the liver and kidneys (yet another capillary system) before going back to the heart. Blood pressure is highest on leaving the heart, drops considerably after passing through each capillary system and is low by the time it passes through the final major veins back into the heart.

Respiration and Excretion

Respiration in fish, as in other animals, concerns the intake of oxygen and elimination of carbon dioxide, one of the main products of metabolism. Gills are equivalent to the lungs of many terrestrial animals and are the site where oxygen from the water in which the fish is living enters the blood and carbon dioxide leaves it. In a number of adult fish and in many fish fry, some respiration takes place through the skin. It will be obvious that respiration in fish is closely linked with the circulatory system – particularly in the gill region.

Two main types of gills occur in fish. In the pouch-like gills of lampreys, each pouch has an internal opening to the pharynx and an external one to the environment. The branchial gills of higher fishes however, are carried on arches on either side of the pharynx and connect to the outside through a series of gill slits (as in sharks and rays) or through a single opening protected by the gill cover or operculum (as in most other fish). In a few unusual types of fish, particularly those which may have to withstand drought regularly, there are specialised organs of respiration involving the gut or swimbladder. In all gill systems the main objective is the same; to allow the maximum proximity of the blood in the gill capillaries (enclosed in thin epithelial tissue) to the water moving past the gills.

Water passing over the gills is kept in constant unidirectional motion by the fish – except in lampreys where it is pumped in and out of the same openings by movements of the pharynx (because the mouth is used as a sucker). With other fish, when the mouth opens, water is sucked inside and fills the whole of the mouth and buccal cavity, on either side of which are the gills. The mouth then closes and water is forced between the gills and out past the opercula, which are opened at this point. Thus the mouth and opercula are in constant alternative motion at a rate dependent on the oxygen requirements of the fish. The respiratory system of fish is made even more efficient by the fact that the passage of blood within the gills and of water without are in opposite directions, blood passing from the heart forwards, water passing from the mouth backwards so that there is a maximum difference in concentration of oxygen and carbon dioxide in the water and blood at all points.

Most oxygen taken up in the blood is carried in red cells, which allow far larger amounts to be carried than would be contained in the same volume of water. As oxygen is taken up, carbon dioxide is released, and when blood finally passes from the gills to the tissues it is rich in the former but low in the latter.

A further important function of the gills of fish is that of uptake and excretion of salts. Fish excrete their body wastes in various ways: partly through the gills, partly into the gut (to pass out with faeces), but mainly, as in other vertebrates, through the kidneys, from which waste products pass to the exterior through special ducts, whose openings are linked closely to those of the gonads. In fish, kidneys have the dual function of eliminating body wastes and helping to control the water/salt balance. Fish blood is kept in equilibrium with its surroundings by the process known as osmosis, in which water in solutions separated by a semi-permeable membrane will pass from the more dilute solution into the other until they are at the same concentration. In sea water, which is more concentrated than blood, water tends to pass out from the fish mainly through the gills and fish have to drink water regularly to compensate. In fresh water, water tends to pass into the fish through the gills and must constantly be discharged via the kidneys to compensate. The difference in ability to control the quality of the blood in relation to the outside salt concentration is the main factor preventing freshwater fish from living in the sea and vice versa. Fish which are able to pass from fresh to salt water and back have special excretory abilities. In the sea (like marine fish) they must be able to get rid of excess salt that they take in by drinking to replace water.

The kidneys of fish are made of numerous small tubules. These act, under the pressure of blood, as minute filters which take out various, mainly nitrogenous, salts and pass them (together with excess water) to the outside via the renal ducts. These open close to the anus of the fish.

Behaviour

The behaviour of fish, like that of other vertebrates, is made up of two components – instinct and learning. Much of the life of a fish is dominated by the former but the learning process should not be underestimated as a visit to a modern fish farm will show. Here, fish such as Rainbow Trout and Atlantic Salmon quickly learn to assemble at particular places to be fed, or even to feed themselves from automatic dispensers which release food when the fish press a lever or some other triggering mechanism.

A simple type of behaviour is shown by shoaling species, such as Roach. Though many species of fish are solitary virtually all of their lives (except at spawning time), others spend most of their lives in the company of their own species, forming shoals which may number many thousands of individuals. Most purely solitary species are predatory and often large; the Pike is a good example. Other than on the spawning grounds, members of this species are rarely found together; one of the reasons for this is that large Pike regularly eat small ones and there are certain situations, when suitable food species are rare or absent, where they eat little else.

Shoaling species, in contrast, tend to be smaller, herbivorous, planktivorous or more commonly omnivorous fish which keep together in packs – the density of which usually depends on the activity in which they are engaged. Shoaling fish often, but by no means always, tend to be silvery in colour, living in open areas of water. Many of the carp family (e.g. Roach, Dace, Minnows) are typical examples. Almost immediately after hatching, the young start to congregate together and move about as one unit. This is at its most dispersed at night or sometimes when feeding, but when moving about, especially if danger threatens, a very tight pack is formed. Such shoals may break up to form smaller units or join together to form larger ones, but many of the fish may remain together all their lives. Spawning is likewise a communal shoaling activity, often preceded by a migration in which enormous shoals move to one part of a lake, or upstream into running water, to reproduce.

Shoaling behaviour is usually thought to be for mutual protection and advantage; it is much more difficult for predators to approach unseen, while a new source of food discovered by one member of the shoal is very soon likely to be engaging the attention of most of its other members. Occasionally, fish are found together in considerable numbers and the term shoal is applied, but the congregation here is one of chance and there is no interplay or reaction among fish as there is in a true shoal. Thus, during winter, certain fish (e.g. Carp and Chub) may congregate in deep holes in lakes or rivers and remain together in a rather torpid state for many weeks.

An important aspect of fish behaviour which has received considerable attention from fish biologists and others is migration. Many more fish undertake migrations than is commonly supposed, but the movements are often of a local nature and do not involve the spectacular distances or homing problems solved by better known species. A good example of small-scale migration is found in Brown Trout, populations of which are common in lakes all over northern and highland Europe. Adult Brown Trout in these lakes are territorial and often occupy one relatively small area of the lake for most of the year. In the autumn, however, they move to the mouths of streams entering the lake and migrate upstream to their spawning grounds.

Both Atlantic and Pacific Salmon have similar patterns of migratory behaviour, and as with many salmonids, they migrate to the natal stream and the distances travelled and obstacles surmounted are spectacular. It is now known that many Atlantic Salmon reach maturity in the seas off Greenland. In order to reach the European (or North American) coast, these fish have to migrate in a particular direction for many hundreds of kilometres and then locate the mouth of the river from which they originally emigrated. They then have to swim through the estuary with its violent changes of salinity (and in modern times often significant pollution) and then upstream to the headwaters, sometimes leaping waterfalls over 3 metres in height. In contrast, the migration of the few adult fish which survive spawning and return to the sea, or of the descending smolts (as the young are called) seems a much simpler and more passive affair, though the same problems of pollution and salinity are involved. Although much studied, the behaviour involved in the migration of these fish is still not clearly understood. It is generally felt that orientation over long distances, say in the sea, is related to physical features (e.g. water currents) but that in the recognition of natal rivers, chemistry is more important.

Migratory fish such as Atlantic Salmon which move into fresh water to spawn but whose progeny then pass down into the sea to grow to maturity are called anadromous. Lampreys, Common Sturgeon, Twaite Shad, Smelt and several other species come into this category. Catadromous species, on the other hand, show the opposite type of behaviour, growing up in fresh water but migrating downstream to the sea to spawn. Eels and some populations of Flounders are good examples of this type of life history.

The behavioural aspects of fish biology reach their most complicated and bizarre at breeding time. In many species, only then is it possible to distinguish the sexes externally, sometimes simply because the female is plump with eggs, but more often because the male has become brightly coloured or has developed tubercles. These are small white nodules which appear on the head and sometimes the fins and bodies of sexually mature fish during the spawning season. They are most common among the carp family (Cyprinidae), but occur in some other families too, for example, the whitefishes (Coregonidae). Many types of behaviour are shown by fish during the breeding season; apart from the spawning act itself, these range from aggression towards males of the same species or predators of the eggs and young, through complicated nest-building activities to fanning the eggs in the nest and actively 'herding' the young fish until they can fend for themselves.

The carp family (Cyprinidae) as a whole show relatively little in the way of sophisticated spawning behaviour; a distinct exception to this is the Bitterling, a small, unobtrusive fish which lives in ponds, canals and slow-flowing rivers. Its complex spawning behaviour is described on page 211, and involves the development of bright colours, the selection of territory around a large freshwater mussel and a complex inter-relationship with that mussel, within which the eggs are eventually laid and develop. Another fish which becomes very colourful at spawning time is the male Three-spined Stickleback. The reproductive behaviour of this species has been studied intensively, and there are many complex interactions between the males and females and their environment.

The behaviour of fish in relation to feeding is also of considerable interest to biologists, fish farmers, anglers and others. It is in relation to feeding that fish seem to exhibit their greatest potential for learning, and the opportunistic nature of many species has led to their considerable success in some waters. The feeding patterns of some species, mainly fish predators (e.g. Pikeperch) on the one hand and filter feeders (e.g. lamprey larvae) on the other, are very instinctive and stereotyped. Other fish are more adaptable. Thus, Trout in a river may be feeding very actively on benthic invertebrates on the bottom one day, but ignoring these completely the next day to feed on mayflies which have started to emerge at the edge of the river. On the third day, both these sources may not appear in the diet which might then consist entirely of terrestrial insects that are being blown on to the water surface and are thus very easily available. Opportunist fish species in changing circumstances like these prefer the food source which is most easily available to them for the least expenditure of energy.

Development

All British freshwater fish are oviparous, i.e. the sperm and eggs are ejected close together in the water and after fertilisation the egg undergoes development quite independently of its parents, though they may protect it in some way, or keep it clean. This is in contrast to the many live-bearing species found in the tropics, e.g. the Mosquito Fish (*Gambusia affinis*) where the anal fin of the male is modified as an elongated penis. This is used to fertilise the eggs inside the female, where they remain protected until hatching. The young are then born live. However, unlike mammals, they do not receive any food materials from the female subsequent to fertilisation.

In oviparous fish, the reproductive systems are essentially similar, consisting of paired gonads (ovaries in the female, testes in the male) and their ducts to the exterior. In the testes a complex series of cell divisions known as spermatogenesis gives rise to sperm – specialised sex cells which carry the hereditary characters of the father and are produced in huge numbers. Each sperm has a long whip-like tail which enables it to swim about in the seminal fluid secreted by the sperm ducts and subsequently ejected into the water at spawning. Oogenesis in the female parallels spermatogenesis and leads to the development of varying numbers of eggs within her ovary. Like sperm, each egg carries the hereditary characteristics of its parent, but the cell itself is very much larger as it also contains large quantities of yolk and fat. The number of eggs produced by a female fish usually increases with size and varies tremendously among species. Thus, small fish like Bitterling and Three-spined Stickleback, whose eggs and early fry are afforded considerable protection after laying, produce relatively few (50–100) eggs at each spawning. Larger species, however, whose eggs are shed directly into the open water and given no further protection lay very large numbers each year (e.g. up to

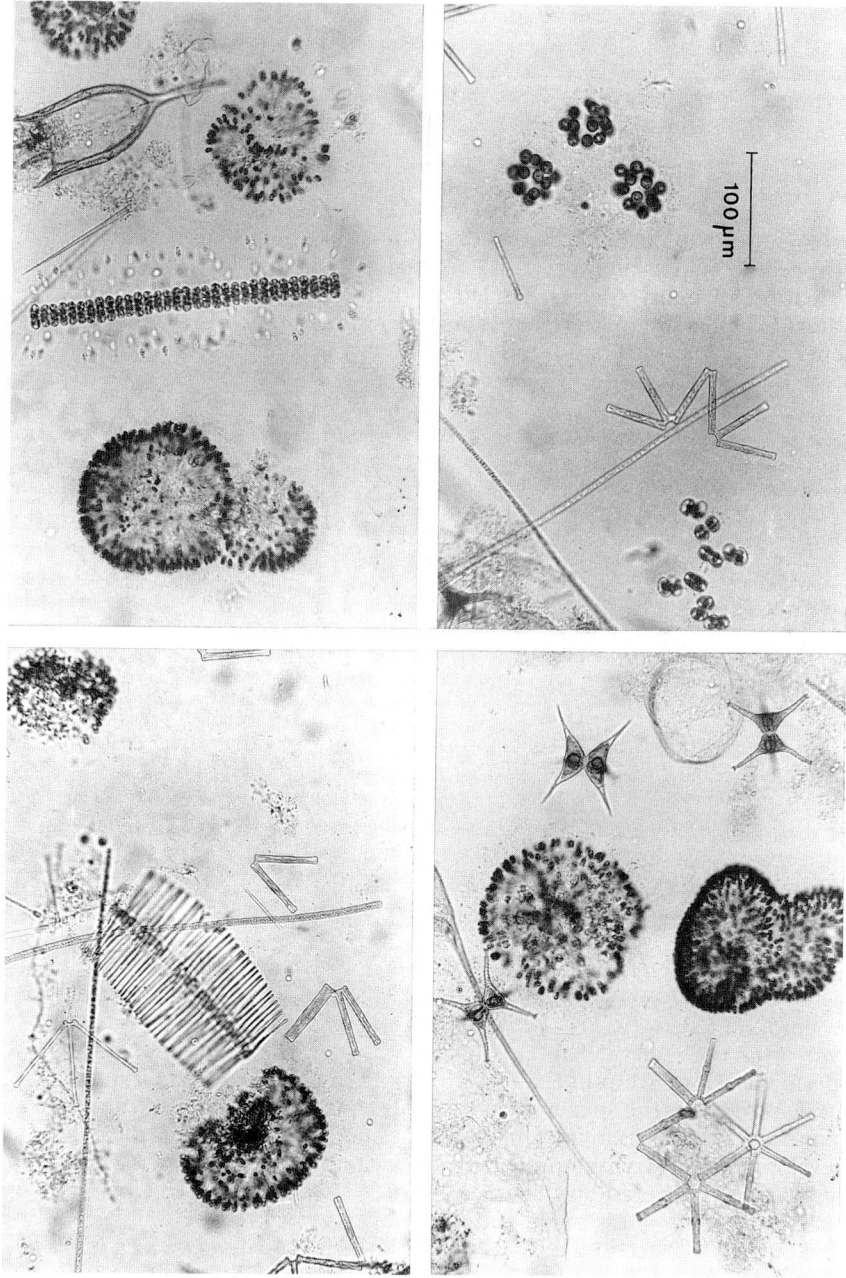

Fig. 5 Examples of various phytoplankton (x150), the start of the food chain in many fresh waters (Tony Bailey-Watts).

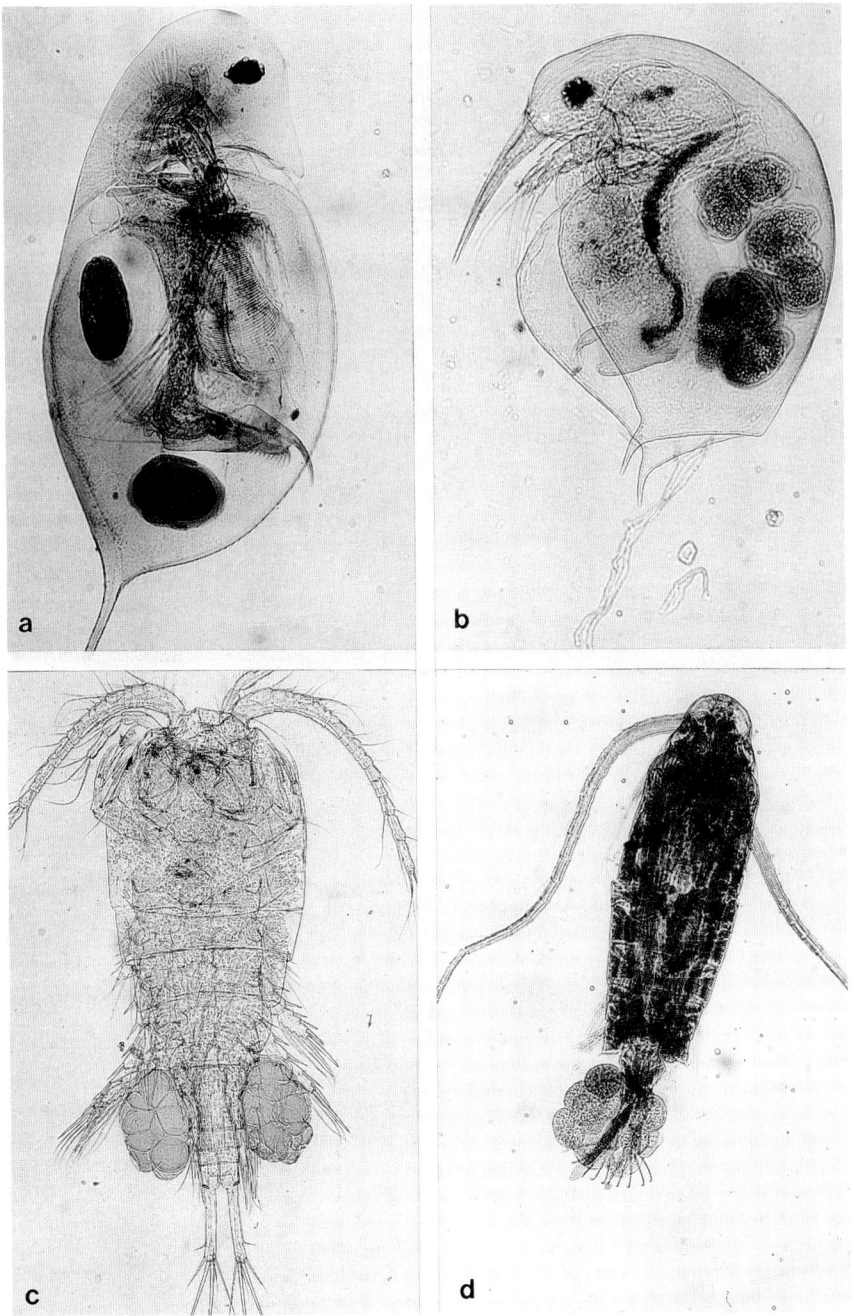

Fig. 6 Examples of various zooplankton (x50), many of which graze phytoplankton and are themselves essential food for various fish: **a**, *Daphnia*; **b**, *Bosmina*; **c**, *Cyclops*; **d**, *Diaptomus* (Ann Chapman).

one million per female in the Burbot and in the Flounder). The number of eggs produced by a female is referred to as her fecundity.

In almost all British fish, reproduction is a cyclic process related to the seasons of the year. It is controlled by reproductive hormones whose secretion is in turn dependent on environmental factors (e.g. temperature and daylength). The gonads, particularly the ovaries, may undergo considerable changes in size and appearance over the year, starting at their smallest just after the spawning season when the sexual products are shed. The actual spawning period for any population of a species is short (usually a few weeks); the time of year at which different species spawn can vary tremendously. Thus, in the British Isles, some fish are spawning somewhere in virtually every month of the year.

After spawning, the eggs of different fish find themselves in very varying situations. Many species construct a nest of some kind to give the eggs protection during development. This 'nest' may be simply an open depression in the substrate (e.g. Sea Lamprey); a similar hole in which the eggs are laid but then covered over with adjacent gravel (e.g. Atlantic Salmon); a space cleared out underneath a rock (e.g. Bullhead); or a much more complicated structure created from pieces of weed (Three-spined Stickleback). Some species protect the eggs and often the young fish in these nests (e.g. sticklebacks and Rock Bass); others leave immediately after spawning (e.g. Brown Trout).

Eggs which are spawned without the protection of a nest of some kind can be laid in various ways. A few fish lay long strings of eggs which tangle up among vegetation (e.g. Perch). Many others lay adhesive eggs which may stick to stones (Sturgeon), to plants (e.g. Carp and Pike), or to sand and plants (e.g. Gudgeon and Spined Loach). The complicated spawning pattern of Bitterling, where the eggs end up inside a freshwater mussel, is described elsewhere. Finally, many species simply spawn in the open water and the eggs may then just float (e.g. Flounder) or sink to the bottom and lie in crevices there (e.g. Vendace).

Egg development time varies greatly among species, and within a species it is very dependent on temperature. Usually the eggs of fish which spawn in the spring and, especially, the summer hatch quickly, the incubation period lasting about 14 days in the spring for Three-spined Sticklebacks and only 3.5 days for Carp in the summer. In fish which spawn in the autumn and winter, on the other hand, the eggs may take up to 150 days to hatch (e.g. Atlantic Salmon).

The egg itself undergoes profound changes during incubation. Most of its volume is occupied by yolk, the cell resulting from the original union of the sperm and ovum being very small. This cell, however, undergoes a process known as cleavage to give two cells, then 4, then 8, 16, 32 and so on, each group of cells gradually differentiating and growing into a different part of the embryo fish. The yolk is gradually used up during this process and eventually the egg consists of a spherical membrane inside which is curled up a small fish. The pigmented eyes and the rapidly beating heart can usually be seen quite clearly at this stage.

Upon hatching, the young fish may start swimming immediately and continue to do so for virtually the rest of its life (e.g. whitefish) or, more commonly, it may rest in a protected place for some time until the remains of the yolk sac are fully absorbed. Atlantic Salmon and Brown Trout lie among

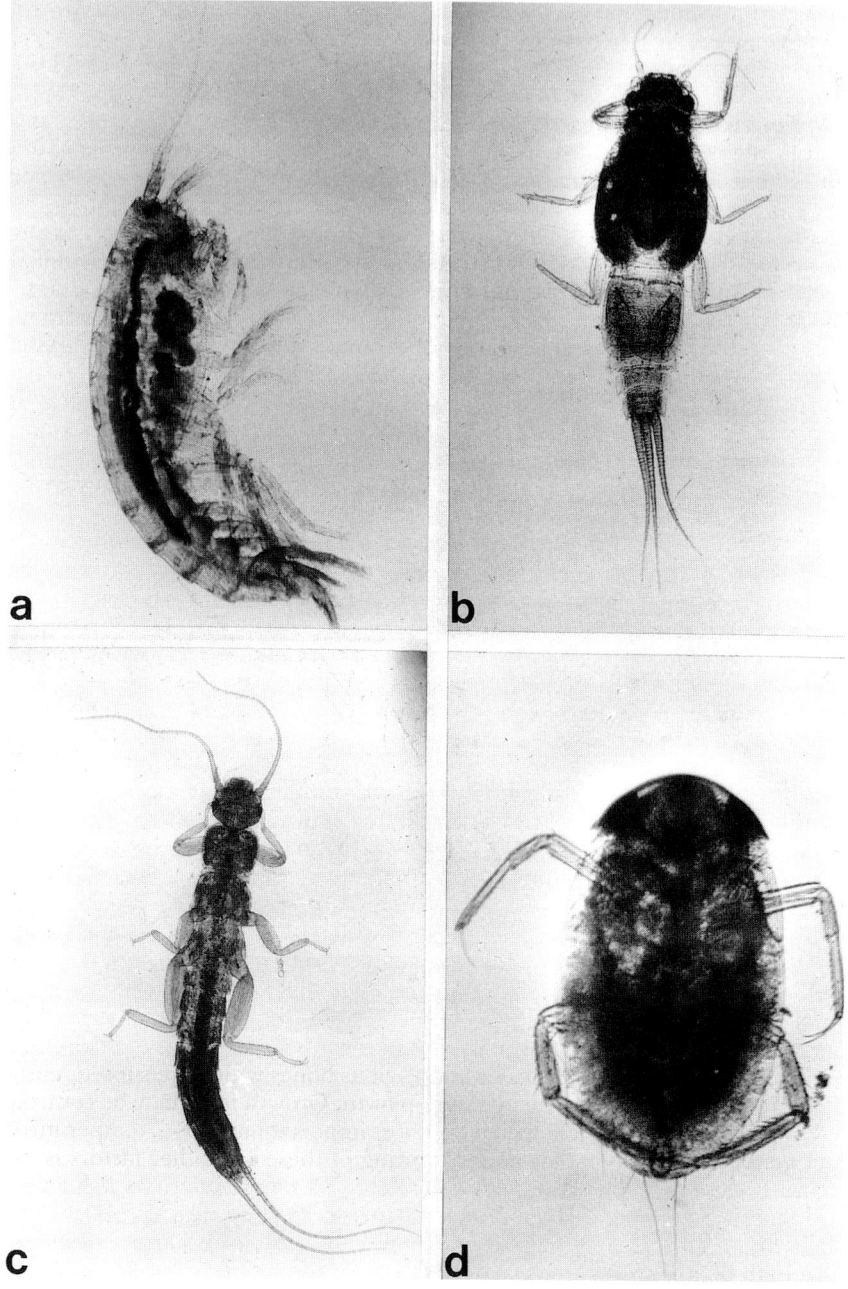

Fig. 7 Examples of some bottom-living invertebrates (x10), important as food for fish. **a**, Freshwater shrimp; **b**, Mayfly larva; **c**, Stonefly larva: **d**, Aquatic bug (Peter Maitland).

gravel in their nest (redd) during this period, while Pike have a temporary adhesive organ by means of which they hang, resting, attached to vegetation. During this period, most fry make a rapid visit to the water surface to fill the swimbladder with air.

Various names, often used rather imprecisely, are given to the young stages of fish. In general, the term larva is used to describe the stage from hatching until the fish is a miniature adult. This may take only a few days (Carp), or up to a year or more (Sea Lamprey and Eel). In some cases, including the two just mentioned, the two stages are so different that they were originally described by taxonomists as two different species. The larval stage itself is sometimes divided into prolarval, where the yolk sac is still present, and postlarval, when it has disappeared. In general, larvae are characterised by transparency, absence of scales, presence of large pigment cells and embryonic, undifferentiated fins. Beyond the larval stage, fish tend to look very much more like the adults although many features, particularly colouration and sexual differences, are not evident until full maturity is attained. Most identification keys refer to mature specimens of the species concerned and some difficulty may be met with if only young fish are available. If it is necessary to identify larval specimens, specialist keys must be used.

Age at maturation (i.e. when fish are able to reproduce) varies very much among different species and even among different populations of the same species. In general, sexual maturity is related to size, which in turn is dependent on growth. Thus, fish in fast-growing populations tend to become mature earlier than those in slow-growing ones. Both food and temperature affect growth; fish at higher latitudes mature later than those at lower ones. In Finland, Roach do not mature until they are 5–6 years old, whereas in southern Europe the same species may be mature at 2–3 years.

Small species of fish tend to mature and die early. The Three-spined Stickleback, for instance, normally matures and dies within two years, whereas the massive Sturgeon does not mature until it is 15–20 years old and may live for ten or more years beyond that. Some fish spawn only once; the Atlantic Salmon usually spends 2–6 years in fresh water and a further 1–2 years in the sea before it is mature and comes back to fresh water to spawn; very few fish live beyond this to spawn a second time. In the case of the Pink Salmon and Eel there appears to be complete mortality after the first spawning. Other species, such as Brown Trout, may spawn several times during their lives.

The growth of most British fish takes place in annual spurts – usually during the warmer months of the year. These seasonal variations lead to physical and chemical differences in scales and various bones which are subsequently of great value in determining age and growth. Growth itself may be controlled by many factors, among which the most important are food, temperature and genetic constitution. An understanding of these and other factors is essential to the successful management of fish stocks, particularly in fish farms and small closed sport fisheries, where success may be determined by the ability of the fish stock to achieve optimum growth.

In both benthic (bottom) and pelagic (open water) feeding fish, growth is usually related to the amount of food available. Thus, populations of Carp in ponds with a high production of invertebrates grow faster than those in ponds with poor production. The growth of the latter fish may be improved by reducing the number of fish, fertilising the pond to improve invertebrate production or feeding the fish directly with manufactured fish food. Changes in the quality and quantity of food can very quickly affect growth rates. In Atlantic Salmon, a dramatic increase in growth takes place immediately after migration from fresh water to the sea. For their first few years, anadromous Sea Trout and sedentary Brown Trout may live together in the same streams and grow at identical rates. As soon as Sea Trout move into salt water where more food is available and winter temperatures are milder, they start to grow at a very much faster rate than the Brown Trout, which have remained in fresh water.

3

Investigating Fish

Fish are difficult to observe in their natural environment and this is probably the main reason why they are a neglected element of our native wildlife. This has also led to some wild and erroneous items of fish lore! For instance, one of the authors was brought up by informed riverside locals to believe that the large kype on the lower jaw of the male spawning Salmon was used by the fish to dig the redd for his mate to lay her eggs in; also that these highly coloured, hook-jawed cock fish were very old and better 'out of the way'. Both seemed very feasible beliefs but, of course, are just not true.

Only in recent times has it been possible, thanks to sophisticated diving equipment, to go beneath the surface and observe fish in their natural surroundings. However, most of our native fishes react nervously to the presence of divers, who, because of poor light penetration and the lack of clarity in our fresh waters (compared to those of the sea along our west coast), are usually too close to the fish for the latter to behave normally.

There are some exceptions to this, of course. Some fish are very obvious in shallow waters, especially when they are engrossed in spawning activities. Lampreys and Minnows are good examples of this, and both authors have spent many enjoyable hours sitting quietly in the sunshine on river banks watching the fascinating natural behaviour of these and various other species.

However, excellent observations can be made through the viewing panels of artificial river sections and fish passes (salmon ladders) and if human observers are not available all the time to record what is going on, then video cameras can take over. Detailed observations of the spawning of Salmon and Trout have been made in this manner, while the behaviour of other species has been studied using aquaria of a size suitable to the fish being studied. For instance, the complicated and ritualised breeding sequence of sticklebacks, from nest building to the dispersal of fry, can be watched in minute detail in a small well-lit aquarium.

Some information on fish biology can be obtained by marking or tagging fish in the wild and then releasing them to study daily movements or long migrations. With some fish, it is possible to study their food by evacuating the stomachs in some way (by 'spooning' or pumping them out) and then returning the fish to its habitat, retaining the stomach contents for examination.

Although the behaviour of some of our freshwater species can be observed during spawning, their activities throughout the rest of the annual life cycle can only be followed circumstantially by comparatively crude methods, often involving the fish being caught and killed (e.g. for examination of the stomach contents in feeding studies). Once a dead fish is available, a number of important factors can be determined. Its breeding status can be ascertained – whether it is immature or mature, and possibly whether it has spawned previously or is ripening to spawn again. If the fish is a female, the number of eggs in the ovaries can be counted or estimated to provide data on fecundity. The degree of infestation by external and internal parasites can also be noted and some of these organisms preserved for identification, if necessary.

Catching Fish for Research Purposes

Fish may be caught in a variety of ways, many of which are illegal unless a permit is available for the specimens to be used for research purposes. Some species, especially their young stages, can be captured in shallow water with a simple hand net used from the bank or when wading. Larger fish may be caught by netting – either sweep netting (seining) from the shore or by setting gill nets (hang nets) in open water. The former involves encircling shoals of fish with the net and gradually directing them towards the shore as the net is pulled in. With gill nets, as the name implies, fish become entangled by the gills in the mesh of the net, usually set overnight.

Sweep netting is suitable for some rivers and lake shallows but cannot be used everywhere, as a smooth bottom, free of obstructions, is essential for the sole, or bottom rope, to sweep smoothly over the substrate, without becoming snagged. Most species of fish in the area are liable to be caught, providing they are not small enough to escape through the mesh. Occasionally, large and active fish may jump to freedom over the floating head rope. The method is, however, partly selective and has the disadvantage of requiring a boat and a trained crew of netsmen. It may also cause considerable damage to the shallow water habitat over which the net is dragged. However, the fish are collected alive (in contrast to many captured in gill nets) and this is one of the standard ways of catching fish for tagging and subsequent release and for other purposes for which live undamaged fish are required.

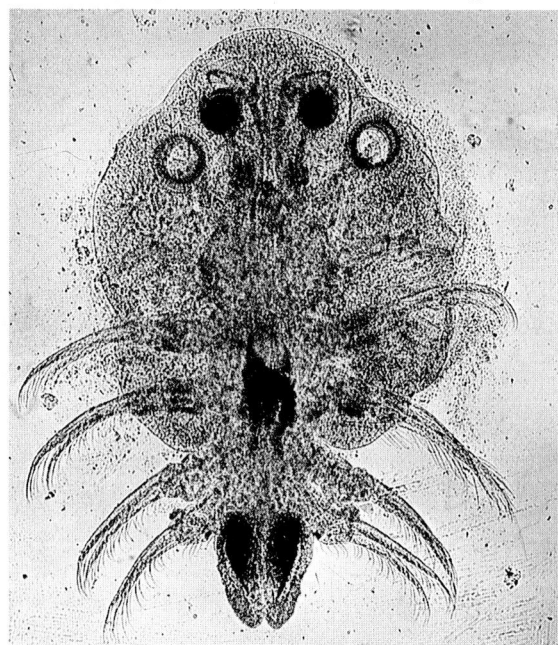

Fig. 8 The fish louse *Argulus* (x15), a common ectoparasite of fish in the British Isles (Peter Maitland).

INVESTIGATING FISH

Fig. 9 Catching fish with a hand net, a simple but effective method in some waters (Peter Maitland).

In gill netting, the fish become entangled while trying to push their way through the mesh and, as the name of the net implies, become caught by the gills if they try to wriggle out backwards. Larger predatory fish may often be caught up by their teeth. Gill netting is particularly size selective and to overcome the biasing of samples, either a series of nets of different meshes is set

Fig. 10 Removing a Roach from a gill net (Kathleen Maitland).

Fig. 11 Seine netting fish (Brown Trout, Pike and Perch) at Loch Leven (Niall Campbell).

at the same time or a single net made up of a series of mesh sizes is used. Gill nets can be set in any depth of water and in general are much more versatile and less demanding in manpower than sweep nets.

Shortly after World War II, fine synthetic threads (either monofilament or

Fig. 12 An echo-sounding from Loch Lomond, showing the dense numbers of fish, mainly Trout and Powan, in the upper waters (Peter Maitland).

Fig. 13 A barrier with traps for collecting Atlantic Salmon (for egg production) on the River Garry system, Inverness (Niall Campbell).

finely braided or twisted nylon thread) were used for making gill nets. These are much more deadly than the previous nets (of linen or cotton thread) as they are much less visible to the fish and effective even in daylight. Also, synthetic nets have little bulk when not in use, so that a lone fisherman can operate a very long length of netting on his own. Monofilament net is now used almost universally by commercial fishermen and, in conjunction with sophisticated echo-sounders, is so efficient that serious overfishing has resulted in many regions. Fish caught in gill nets are very often found dead or are killed during extraction from the net.

Angling is a slow and usually selective method of sampling fish. It is especially selective for species, size and feeding behaviour, but has its uses in certain special circumstances, where other methods cannot be employed for legal, social or physical reasons. Normal angling methods do not usually cause too much damage to the fish and those caught can often be kept alive or marked and released. Barbless hooks can be used for most species, but the use of set lines with many baited barbed hooks, set over the bottom or at any level up to the surface, results in most of the fish being taken dead or having to be killed. This is a particularly effective method for catching fish that feed mainly during darkness or where nets cannot be used.

Trapping is a method usually used in rivers to catch fish that are migrating, e.g. returning adult Salmon or Sea Trout as they move upstream to their spawning grounds or Salmon smolts or silver Eels heading downstream to the sea. Trapping is a traditional method for catching salmonids for food, with its origins lost in the mists of antiquity. The method exploits fish when

Fig. 14 Emptying a trap set for adult lampreys (Ken East).

they are at their maximum vulnerability, i.e. when they are passing in large numbers through narrow waters. In a few parts of the British Isles, Salmon are still harvested commercially by trapping; elsewhere on salmonid rivers trapping may take place to catch ripe fish to provide fertilised eggs for hatcheries or to provide data on stock levels or migration patterns.

Traps, usually in the form of tunnel or fyke nets, can also be used to catch feeding fish such as Eels during their nightly prowling for food. These traps are tethered in shallow water and the fish captured alive, although when large numbers accumulate in the final compartment of the trap net mayhem may arise, as the larger fish start to eat their smaller captive brethren. Such trap nets can be modified for research purposes to catch most of the species that come into shallow water. Even tiny elvers are caught in this way in specially designed fyke nets. Recently it has been shown that baited traps set on the bottom in deep water will even take such fish as Arctic Charr.

Electric fishing is a method where, when a current is passed through water between two electrodes, a large proportion of the fish within the electrical field are attracted towards the anode and become stunned, so that they can be lifted out with a hand net. A small proportion of the fish (especially the smaller ones) may become completely stunned and remain under stones or entangled among thick vegetation. With equipment working well under optimum conditions as much as 75% of the fish population can be caught during the first fishing of a length of stream. Much of the remainder can be captured at second and third fishings and the numbers from the three fishings can be used to estimate the original total population in the section of the stream being fished.

There are problems with electric fishing, however, and it is usually only useful in small and medium-sized rivers. Very small fish, such as Salmon fry, may not be so strongly affected by the electric current as larger fish and so may escape. If the correct voltage is used fish will recover completely once the current is switched off and the fish netted and transferred to a container. Although the reaction of fish when within an electric field has been known for a long time, it is only within the last few decades that this collecting technique has been developed and widely used. Originally the electric fishing of a stream required the use of a portable petrol generator, but battery backpack shocking units have now been developed and allow the operator great mobility so that isolated waters in rough terrain can now be reached and sampled in this way.

Electric fishing is more effective in streams because fish cannot escape from the electric field when it approaches them – as they can in large rivers or lakes. The strength of the electric field is strongest in high conductivity alkaline waters and least in low conductivity acid peaty waters. In still waters, electric-shocking equipment especially designed for use from boats can be employed.

Poisoning is a somewhat drastic but highly effective method of collecting fish. The advantage of this method is that the total stock and all the age groups of a fish population can be counted and invaluable data obtained on all aspects of the biology of the species concerned – information that can be applied to the management and conservation of stocks elsewhere. Opportunities to use poison can arise when fishery managers decide to eradicate 'unwanted' species of fish so that new populations of 'desirable' species can be established. For example, the management aim might be to eradicate Pike and perhaps other coarse fish species from a lake so that a trout fishery could be established. If the correct amount of selective fish poison (piscicide) is used all the fish would be killed, but the invertebrates and plant life little affected. After application of the poison, many fish rise to the water surface and if they are netted at this stage and placed in clean water, the majority will recover.

However, most piscicides also kill all stages of amphibians, so great care has to be taken over the timing of the operation, the conduct of which should be based on a thorough survey conducted beforehand. A common piscicide is based on an extract of derris root (also used as a horticultural pesticide), the active principle of which has been known to jungle-dwelling South American Indians for centuries as a means of collecting fish. It is harmless to mammals and birds. The product is usually marketed as 'Rotenone' and where the law allows, spot applications of Rotenone can be used by fishery scientists to collect samples of fish from small areas of streams and lakes. In the British Isles the use of piscicides is strictly controlled by governments, which only issue licences for its application after consulting environmental agencies and other organisations.

Obtaining Data from Fish Samples

Fish taken alive for experiments based on tagging or marking are usually marked and released as soon as possible or retained in specially designed tanks or floating cages. Fish taken dead or which have to be killed, are ideally examined fresh, but for logistical reasons they are often deep frozen or preserved in 4% formaldehyde or 70% alcohol. If the fish are large, a slit should be made along the ventral surface to allow the preservative to penetrate the body cavity. It is worth noting that in an emergency, fish can also be preserved by immersing them in ordinary table salt, in methylated spirits well mixed with 50% water, in table vinegar or even sun-dried. If money is no object, or the fish is extraordinarily important, any proprietary drinking spirit (e.g. whisky, brandy, gin, vodka) will do splendidly!

Length may be measured in three ways. 'Fork length' is the distance from the tip of the snout to the end of the middle tail fin ray, and is the way in which salmonid fish are usually measured. 'Total length' is the distance from the tip of the snout to the end of the longest ray of the tail fin (the tail fin is usually squeezed together to provide this measurement. 'Standard length' is the distance from the tip of the snout to the point at which the body of the fish ends and the tail fin begins (i.e. the end of the caudal peduncle). The exact position of this point is sometimes difficult to identify. The authors favour fork length as the simplest and most accurate measurement of length. The girth of fish is also sometimes recorded and is taken to be the circumference of the body at its point of maximum depth.

Fish can be aged in a variety of ways. The examination of scales and opercular or other bones is the most common method (depending on species); broadly speaking, scales are used in salmonid fish and operculars in Perch, Pike and some other coarse fish. In some cases otoliths are of value, perhaps where a fish without scales is involved (e.g. Bullhead), or because the scales are very small (e.g. Eel), or (especially with old fish) evidence is required to confirm scale or opercular readings. The extraction of otoliths requires some skill, for they are located in the semi-circular canal pits in the skull behind the eyes. They may have to be cleared, polished or sectioned before becoming readable.

The best scales for age determination are usually those obtained from either the 'shoulder' of the fish or further along its back above the lateral line. The age and growth pattern of many fish is recorded on the scales (and other bony parts) by alternate zones of fast and slow growth, representing summer and winter growth respectively. Thus a zone of fast growth plus an adjacent one of slow growth represents an annual increment. In some fish, such as salmonids, erosion marks on the scales can be recognised, indicating that the fish has spawned. As the growth of a scale is broadly proportional to the increase in length of a fish, its rate of growth over its lifetime can be calculated, assuming erosion has not been too drastic.

However, snags do exist, such as the appearance of false year marks (perhaps when food was scarce during the middle of the summer and growth was checked), or the absence of a recognisable winter zone. Thus, a fair degree of experience and skill is necessary in the interpretation of scales, operculars or otoliths from some populations. In addition, it is important to examine several scales and to have them cleaned and mounted properly (or to have celluloid impressions made) before magnifying the image for reading.

Fish Tagging

The marking or tagging of fish provides data on many aspects of their biology, including growth, as well as migration behaviour. Isaac Walton refers to an experiment carried out in the seventeenth century when Salmon smolts were marked; these returned to the same river as mature Salmon, proving the relationship between parr and adults – something that had not been certain until then. In recent years, vast programmes of fish marking and tagging have been carried out world-wide on a variety of fish, principally important commercial or subsistence species. However, a permanent dilemma faces fish taggers; either the tag has to be large and conspicuous enough for a fisherman or fish processor to notice it on a captured fish (in which case it may affect the chances of survival by affecting behaviour or attracting predators), or small and inconspicuous so that it does not affect survival but can then only be recognised by a trained expert, perhaps using an electronic metal-sensing device. The success of any marking programme depends on recapturing as many of the marked fish as possible.

A wide variety of types of fish tags have been used. Most are attached to the back of the fish by a non-corrodible wire or plastic thread, which is passed through the gristle in front of the dorsal fin. Other types are made to be clipped on to the opercular bone, while the most inconspicuous kinds are inserted out of sight beneath the skin or within the cartilage of the snout. Most tags bear a serial number or code, together with the name of the tagging agency and an offer of reward. In recent years very sophisticated tags have been developed, some of them emitting sonar or other signals. Such tags are used to track the movements of individual fish (e.g. Salmon entering a river from an estuary) or to monitor other features such as activity, etc.

The simpler marking of fish is usually carried out by injecting a vital dye into the skin, which is actively taken up by the tissue and so remains visible for a long time. With this method a limited number of colour and position codes can be used for recognition and the method is often used simply to follow the fate of a batch of fish (perhaps from a hatchery) rather than individual fish. Another simple method of marking fish is by fin clipping. This is usually done either by clipping off the top third of a fin, which will regenerate leaving a scar, or in the case of the adipose fin (which is unimportant in swimming) the whole fin – which does not regenerate. Again only a limited number of combinations is possible. Research has shown – somewhat surprisingly perhaps – that the effect of fin clipping on the survival of individual fish is minimal.

In some species (e.g. Grayling and Pike) the pattern and shape of individual marks or scars on each fish can be used to recognise them and record their personal histories if they are recaptured regularly enough.

From the above it can be seen that to carry out meaningful studies of even quite simple aspects of fish biology, a considerable input of manpower, equipment and time is required – at a level usually outside the resources of the most enthusiastic amateur. Thus, as pointed out at the beginning of this chapter, in contrast to the ease of making observations on many other forms of wildlife, the study of fish is difficult and this is probably the main reason why our freshwater fish fauna has tended to have been ignored by the general naturalist.

4

Distribution and Habitat

The Origin of the British Fish Fauna

For most parts of the British Isles, the history of the freshwater fishes begins during the final stages of the last ice age, about 13–15,000 years ago, when the great ice cap that had covered all of Scotland and all but the most southern parts of England, Wales and Ireland was melting and retreating northwards. At that time, and for about the next 3000 years, a land connection existed between England and the Continent, from just north of the River Humber southwards to the River Thames. Both humans and much of our terrestrial wildlife recolonised the country, sterilised by the ice cap, via this land bridge. Through it flowed rivers which were either tributaries of the River Rhine, or at least shared a flood plain with this large continental river, giving them a common fish fauna.

There is also evidence, though less definite, that a similar land connection linked some river systems in the south of England with others in France. The

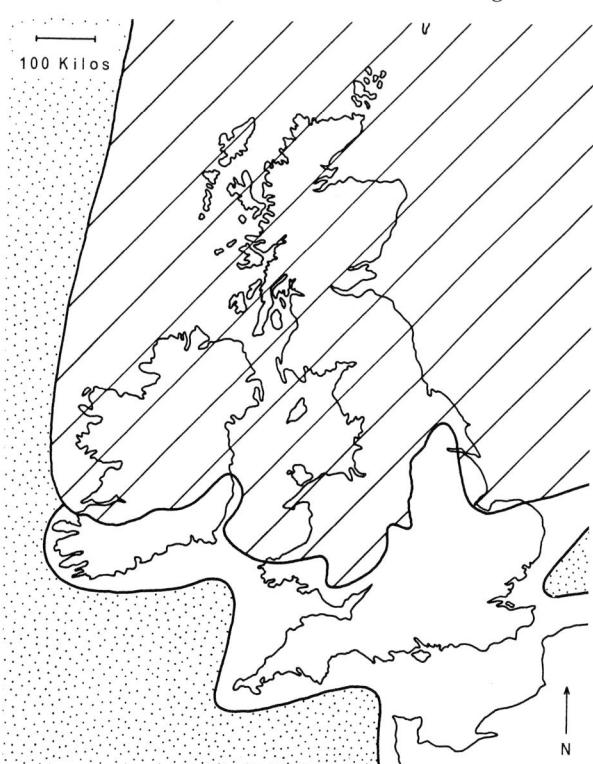

Fig. 15 Generalised map of the British Isles to show the approximate extent of the ice sheet at the height of the last glaciation and the probable British coastline and connections to continental Europe immediately after the last ice age.

Table 3 The origins of the freshwater fish fauna of the British Isles.

Indigenous species		Introduced species	
Via the sea (Euryhaline)	Via land bridge (Stenohaline)	From Europe	From N America
Sea Lamprey	Grayling	Common Carp	Rainbow Trout
River Lamprey	Pike	Crucian Carp	Pink Salmon
Brook Lamprey	Barbel	Goldfish	Brook Charr
Sturgeon	Gudgeon	Bitterling	Largemouth Bass
Allis Shad	Tench	Orfe	Pumpkinseed
Twaite Shad	Silver Bream	Danube Catfish	Rock Bass
Atlantic Salmon	Common Bream	Pikeperch	
Brown Trout	Bleak		
Arctic Charr	Minnow		
Houting	Rudd		
Powan	Roach		
Pollan	Chub		
Vendace	Dace		
Smelt	Spined Loach		
Eel	Stone Loach		
Three-spined Stickleback	Burbot		
Nine-spined Stickleback	Perch		
Sea Bass	Ruffe		
Common Goby	Bullhead		
Thick-lipped Mullet			
Thin-lipped Mullet			
Golden Mullet			
Flounder			

finding of Dace bones in an excavation site near the River Stour in Dorset suggests that this species was present there about 500 BC. Such an hypothesis would account for the wide distribution of a number of species in the south of England, such as Dace, Gudgeon, Pike, Bream, Minnow, Roach, Chub, Stone Loach and Perch, all of which are common in northern France.

The indigenous British freshwater fish fauna can be divided into two groups according to their origin: (i) those fishes which could live in both salt and fresh water, known as euryhaline species and (ii) those fishes which could live only in fresh water, known as stenohaline species. As the ice melted, euryhaline fishes were able to follow the coastline northwards and colonise any new ice-free fresh waters that were accessible from the sea. Surviving ice dams must have provided refuge lakes for many of these colonisers for a period until the ice melted. For example, in Scotland, the great Loch of Glen Roy must have been accessible up the Spey valley from the North Sea and successively drained down at different periods (leaving the famous Parallel Roads) until only Lochs Laggan, Roy and Treig were left, draining to the west. Stenohaline species, on the other hand, being unable to move round the coasts, were restricted to the English tributaries of continental rivers. It is possible that, during the last inter-glacial phase, most of the euryhaline species were able to exist in the southern, ice-free areas of the British Isles, living in a post-glacial environment similar to that found at present in southeast Iceland and southern Greenland, close to the ice cap – but this is by no means certain. However, most of the stenohaline fishes require much higher summer water temperatures for successful breeding than those found in such areas, but it is possible that at least some of the original stenohaline species may have colonised south-east England from the Continent during earlier inter-glacial periods and survived successfully in this ice-free refuge until the final retreat of the ice. Again, this is not certain.

As the number of euryhaline species is not great, the number of species truly native to northern England, Wales, Scotland and Ireland is comparatively small. Also, the comparatively short length of time that the land bridge with the Continent existed did not allow a full representation of the north-west European fish fauna to reach Britain (this is also true of other elements of the fauna and flora), while later introductions from Europe and elsewhere were selective and not comprehensive. Thus, the present freshwater fauna of the British Isles is an impoverished one (55 species) when compared with that of north-west Europe (c. 80 species) and Europe as a whole (c. 215 species).

Thus, the fish faunas of England, Wales, Scotland and Ireland are, respectively, examples of the phenomenon known as the 'island effect', i.e. the further islands are from their parent continent the more impoverished are their floras and faunas in terms of species diversity. It can be seen, therefore, that the poorest fish faunas occur in western Ireland and the Western Isles of Scotland.

Considerable information is available on the recent development of the freshwater fish fauna of Scotland from the descriptions of the fishes of the parishes found in the Old Statistical Account and elsewhere. Likewise, it is known that Pike, Carp, Gudgeon, Tench, Roach, Rudd, Bream, Dace, Minnow, Stone Loach and Perch were all introduced into Ireland. Of course, not all introductions resulted in successful self-sustaining populations and it is known that at least 12 other species which were introduced to Scotland failed to become established there.

Distribution

Much of the present day distribution of freshwater fishes in the British Isles is the result of redistribution by humans, for many reasons, intentional and otherwise. However, some natural redistribution must have taken place as a result of post-glacial changes in land levels, melting of ice dams and by river capture – though the latter would probably only have affected those stenohaline species living in fast-flowing head-waters, such as Minnows, Stone Loach and Bullhead. Presumably, at times, great natural catastrophes must have taken place, such as flooding on a massive scale, resulting in the formation of temporary lakes, which might have allowed the colonisation of hitherto isolated river systems across low watersheds.

However, certainly in recent years, humans have been the main agents of redistribution. They imported several fish species as food from the Continent, such as Carp, and translocated several native species within the British Isles, presumably for the same reason – e.g. Pike and Perch to Ireland and parts of Scotland and Wales and areas in west and northern England previously without them. By tradition, the clergy have been held responsible for much of the redistribution of Pike and Perch. These two species were ideal for small ponds, moats and lakes, where they could easily be gathered, assuring a dependable supply of fish for Fridays.

There is another factor too concerning these two species: both travel very well, especially in cool weather, just wrapped in damp sacking or wet moss, etc. Like this they will stay alive for long periods. Many an angler's family has been startled by the sudden coming to life of a Pike when dumped into the kitchen sink after being hours in a damp fishing bag! Thus, their transport would have been a relatively simple matter even by pack animal or slow boat. Carp and Tench also travel well out of water, but their scarcity in the north suggests that either they were not used as much as the former two species, or the northern climate did not suit them. Certainly in Scotland, at any rate, the distribution of Pike and Perch fits in well with what is known about the locations of early medieval ecclesiastical settlements. In Ireland, no written record of their first introduction has so far been uncovered, but shipments of Pike were being exported to southern English ports from Ireland at the end of the fifteenth century and some authorities believe that they were first introduced during the fourteenth century. Perch were certainly there at the end of the sixteenth-century. References to their presence in Scotland suggest that Pike were well established locally by the mid-seventeenth century and that they were certainly present at the end of the previous century. Perch were known to be present at that time too. However, results from archaeological excavations carried out at several Scottish burghs have so far not revealed bones of Pike or Perch, although bones of other species were present. At Perth, for instance, bones of these two species were not found during excavations covering the period 1200–1400 AD, a time when they were commonly used as food in English towns. Pike were certainly used as food during the reign of James VI, as the palace accounts of 1649 reveal. These fish probably came from the Lake of Menteith.

Humans have also introduced and redistributed fish for sport, particularly those fish which provide both sport and food, such as Brown and Rainbow Trout, Brook Charr, Grayling, Pike, Carp, Tench and Pikeperch. In Scotland, during the last century and the early years of the present, nearly every body of water larger than one hectare was stocked with Brown Trout, often from private estate hatcheries, which proliferated during that period. Estate staff were sent out with buckets of young Trout to the most isolated lochs – some at altitudes of 600–900m – which fish were unlikely ever to reach by natural means.

As an indirect result of developing sport fisheries, several other species have become widely redistributed too. These comprise the bait species such as Gudgeon, Minnow, Roach, Dace and Stone Loach. The Gudgeon and Stone Loach were once popular natural spinning baits for Salmon in northern rivers, as were Minnow and Loach for Trout. Dace and Roach were more often used as live or dead bait for Pike. The end result in many cases was that unused live bait was (and still is) released at the end of the fishing expedition – for convenience and to 'improve' the food available to the local predatory fishes. Also, anglers were keen to build up a stock of their favourite bait fish locally so that they could collect them on the spot in future. As the railway system moved northwards last century so southern anglers extended the range of their activities. The process continues to this day; Ruffe, hitherto unknown in Scotland, were first caught by one of the authors in Loch Lomond in 1982, probably released by anglers from the south. It is now one of the commonest species in the loch. Recently, both Chub and Dace have suddenly appeared in the same system.

Table 4 Scottish freshwater fish and their occurrence at different times since the last ice-age.

Original Colonisers	By 1790	Later arrivals By 1880	By 1970	By 1985
Sea Lamprey	Pike	Brook Charr	Rainbow Trout	Ruffe
River Lamprey	Roach	Grayling	Pink Salmon	
Brook Lamprey	Stone Loach	Tench	Common Carp	
Atlantic Salmon	Perch	Common Bream	Goldfish	
Brown Trout	Minnow	Chub	Gudgeon	
Arctic Charr		Crucian Carp	Rudd	
Powan			Orfe	
Vendace			Dace	
Eel			Bullhead	
Three-spined Stickleback				
Nine-spined Stickleback				
Sea Bass				
Common Goby				
Thick-lipped Mullet				
Thin-lipped Mullet				
Golden Mullet				
Flounder				

As a result of such activities, Roach, Gudgeon, Stone Loach and Minnow appeared many years ago in several of the great east-coast Scottish Salmon rivers as far north as the River Don, while the River Tweed contains Dace as well. Also in Scotland, the practice of using live Minnows for trout bait has been responsible, particularly in the years since World War II, for their steady advance northwards, and they now occur in river systems draining to the Pentland Firth. The practice of releasing live bait has also resulted in the establishment of Roach and Dace populations in Ireland.

As well as Minnows, Three-spined Sticklebacks were sometimes introduced into trout-angling waters to improve the availability of food. Conversely, Pike were introduced to upland lakes to thin out dense populations of stunted Trout – in the hope that a sparser population of larger Trout would result. Evidence of this practice is fairly common in Scotland, where lochs completely isolated from any source of Pike contain populations of that species only. The Trout have usually been long since completely eliminated while the Pike survive, presumably by eating their own young. In North America too there is evidence of Pike being redistributed as a fish-population control measure.

Fish have also sometimes been relocated for amenity purposes due to the desire to diversify the local fish fauna. Such a practice, understandable as it is, is thoughtless and potentially dangerous ecologically. Several originally pristine communities of native fishes in Scottish lochs have been put at risk because of this practice. Those mainly responsible are newly settled incomers from the south who, like the original British settlers in New Zealand, wish to angle for a familiar fish species. Recently, an increasing number of Scottish anglers too have turned to coarse fishing and have moved several species about, especially in the Midland Valley.

In Ireland, Roach are being redistributed unofficially to provide more winter angling for visiting coarse fishermen, as the previously established Rudd are neither so satisfactory nor so attractive for this purpose. Angling with live bait is now banned in Ireland in an effort to control the unplanned spread of coarse fish species. A recent attempt in Ireland to import Grayling was thwarted promptly by Irish Customs.

In Great Britain, unsuccessful attempts have been made over the years to introduce at least another 12 species, while temporary populations of a number of tropical species have existed from time to time in sections of rivers and canals warmed by hot-water effluents from factories and power-stations. These are assumed to have originated from surplus fish released by aquarists.

While the above introductions can all be classed as intentional, humans have, of course, been responsible for many unintentional introductions. In England, Wales and Ireland and to a lesser extent in Scotland, the construction of navigational canals has been a major factor in the redistribution of species from one river system to another. In Scotland, relatively recently, previously separate catchments have been linked by tunnels for hydroelectric generating purposes and it is known that Charr, Pike, Minnows, Three-spined Sticklebacks and Perch have all been redistributed in this way.

Another anthropogenic factor responsible for the redistribution of fish might possibly be called the 'end of vacation' factor, and one of the authors (in his early youth) has been guilty of introducing fish species to waters hitherto without them under this heading! The term is fairly self-explanatory; many parents are not willing to look after fish (or amphibians and reptiles) in bowls and jam jars that their children may have purchased or collected elsewhere during the holidays. Once term has started, the fortunate denizens of the jars and bowls are taken to the nearest water and released. Unfortunately, such releases are seldom recorded so that the origin of a new fish (or amphibian or reptile) which has mysteriously appeared in a place where it was hitherto unknown can never be traced, nor can any possible ecological repercussions be monitored.

Of course, in the great majority of releases established populations do not result – but some do. One of the authors has come to the conclusion, after a contemporary study of the present status of the non-feathered vertebrates of the Inner and Outer Hebrides, that the main factor responsible for the recent increase in introductions (successful and otherwise) of small animals – mostly Amphibia – to the islands is the movements of the human inhabitants (i.e. expatriate islanders returning home on vacation and the new generation of residents of southern origin returning from vacation), coupled with the advent of the 'roll-on/roll-off' vehicle ferries and the plastic bag. It appears that much of the motivation stemmed from the prominence now given to wildlife conservation by the media and by the teaching of biology at primary level in local schools – a comparatively recent advance.

However, it is known that no alien fish species have become established in the Outer Hebrides and only three species (i.e. Brook Charr, Pike and Perch), very locally, in the Inner Hebrides. Unfortunately, further introductions can be expected and these might have a disruptive effect on some of our original, pristine, fish communities. It is also the case that races of the same fish species from geographically isolated areas have been redistributed on a very large scale. For example, there may now be extremely few populations of Brown Trout that have not been genetically adulterated by the introduc-

Fig. 16 The high (30m) waterfall on the River Endrick near Fintry – a complete barrier to fish migrating upstream (Kathleen Maitland).

tion of races from other areas of the British Isles or from the Alpine regions of central Europe.

Ever since the artificial rearing of Trout was developed, that is, from about the middle of the last century, hatchery-produced Trout have been added to many natural Trout populations – even in the most remote areas. For many decades, the famous race of Loch Leven Trout was spread over the British Isles and far beyond. The fallacious concept on which this stocking activity was (and still is!) based, is that 'new blood' is needed to improve and maintain a trout fishery. For example, at the turn of the century, ova from Bavarian lake trout were widely advertised for hatchery and, subsequently, stocking purposes. Even within the last few years, an angling club on the island of Mull, off the west coast of Scotland, has been importing young Brown Trout for stocking purposes from a hatchery in north-east England. Polish Sea Trout and Norwegian Salmon and Sea Trout strains are regularly introduced to our native populations. Also, several species of angler's coarse fish, mostly members of the carp family, are similarly being redistributed to bolster existing, long-established populations.

One agency that some believe is responsible for introductions and redistribution is the transport of fish eggs on the feet of waterfowl. It is argued that if this was a very regular occurrence our fishes would have a much more even distribution by now than they do. Also, one would tend not to find similar neighbouring water bodies with quite different fish faunas. Nevertheless, it is relevant to note that one of the most widely distributed of the stenohaline fish in the British Isles at the moment – the Perch – lays eggs in shallow water in long ribbons, and it is perfectly conceivable that at least some of its dispersion since the last ice age was via the feet of migrating waterfowl. One of the authors knows of a new private pond (near an established population of Perch) where young Perch suddenly appeared – much to the surprise of the owner!

Live freshwater and marine fish (and other organisms) have been rained from the skies at times. For example, Merthyr Tydfil was subjected to a rain of sticklebacks in 1858, indicating that they were probably caught up in a water spout. Similar incidents have been reported in the British Isles within the last decade. Though rare, even one such event each century since the last ice age could have had a considerable effect on the dispersion of some species.

A phenomenon associated with the colonisation of fresh waters by several euryhaline species is the establishment of land-locked, completely freshwater populations, which have lost their anadromous behaviour. Or, rather, the anadromous habit has become suppressed, as individuals of land-locked populations do not seem to have lost their tolerance of sea water. The species involved in the British Isles are River Lamprey, Brook Lamprey, Brown Trout, Arctic Charr, Powan, Pollan, Vendace, Smelt, Twaite Shad and Three-spined and Nine-spined Sticklebacks. Of these, River Lampreys, Trout, Smelt, Twaite Shad and Three-spined Sticklebacks also exist as anadromous populations in Britain. Anadromous populations of Arctic Charr and Nine-spined Sticklebacks exist elsewhere in the world.

The term 'land-locked' is actually a popular misnomer and is most misleading. It should really be applied only when a population of anadromous fishes is physically cut off from the sea (e.g. by a waterfall or dam). Some fish have stopped migrating although not physically barred. Arctic Charr are sometimes found not far above the estuaries of rivers with clear access to their natal lake above and the sea below, while, for example, the Powan of Lochs Lomond and Eck, the Pollan of Loughs Neagh and Erne, the Goureen of Lough Leane and innumerable populations of Three-spined Sticklebacks would face no physical barriers to maintaining their once anadromous behaviour.

With fish, as with other animals, the top priority in the life cycle is to breed. Temperate fresh waters are less productive than the coastal marine environment but they support fewer predators. Some originally marine fish, like the lampreys, salmonids, smelts and sticklebacks, have come to protect their young by leaving the relatively dangerous coastal waters and spawning in fresh water, evolving special adaptations for living in this environment at that time. But this is a compromise, because the relative scarcity of food in fresh water limits growth opportunities. If the young fish grow fast enough to mature there they will stay in fresh water, but if they cannot they will move back to the richer marine world until they are ready to spawn.

This choice of strategy, apparently dependent on rate of development at a critical spring season, gives rise to both migratory and land-locked forms in these species. As rates of development are dependent on both genetic capacities and the environmental opportunities to express them, it is not surprising to find that land-locking varies both in time and in space. Characteristically it is most evident at the extremes of a species' range – where the physiologically (i.e. genetically) most specialised forms have evolved. So, for example, Arctic Charr populations at their southernmost latitudes are now all land-locked, achieving maturity before smolting, and so not emigrating to what is now, presumably, a sea too warm for their existence.

Both life cycles may co-exist among salmonids in the centre of their ranges, but their relative expression may vary from year to year. Females, whose reproductive energy needs are more difficult to meet in the freshwater environment, dominate the migratory component, and males the resident one. Even though much smaller than the females at spawning, these resident males are fully potent and can induce females to spawn. In mixed migratory and resident populations, large migratory males dominate at spawning, but the small males may still contribute by dashing in on one side of the female and fertilising some of the eggs while the large male is spawning on the other side.

Emigration of young to the sea occurs in the spring, and is chiefly a passive displacement of animals for whom life in fresh water is becoming stressful due to complex physiological changes (smolting). Their marine adaptations are 'switched on' when they arrive in the sea. The return migration into fresh water occurs at (and presumably in response to) maturation, and the fish reassert their freshwater adaptations at this time. The residents, which are beginning to mature, do not lose their freshwater adaptations, and so are not displaced to sea. Maturation and smolting are thus contradictory processes.

The situation with Trout is complex, as it is the case that a varying proportion (which may alter from year to year) of individuals (mostly female) from largely non-migratory 'Brown Trout' populations may go to sea and become 'Sea Trout'. Land-locked populations of Atlantic Salmon are not present in the British Isles, but are found in Norway and are common in north-east North America. Some years ago, one of the authors examined some Salmon from Loch Glashan in Argyll which had been unable to migrate to sea as smolts (because of hydro-electric works) and had continued to grow in the fresh water to a size of over 40cm. This shows that smolting is a temporary phase and that in the presence of good feeding, failure to reach the sea does not necessarily have fatal consequences.

In the case of Arctic Charr, the land-locked behaviour is almost certainly controlled by temperature, as further north, in northern Norway, Iceland, Greenland and Canada, for instance, there are anadromous as well as the purely resident populations that occur in the British Isles and other parts of Europe. Modification in the behaviour of Three-spined Sticklebacks has also been observed between anadromous northern and resident southern populations in Europe. The general explanation, however, for the presence of land-locked populations of originally anadromous fishes is based on the fact that salmonids (salmon, trout and charr) currently show anadromy only in the northern and therefore cooler part of their range. With a southern extension of the arctic and cooler conditions it is likely that the anadromous habit would move south too, and during the last ice age there were anadromous populations of Salmon and Trout in the Mediterranean and Adriatic Seas.

The repetitive process of euryhaline populations periodically being forced southwards by the advancing ice of a new ice age and moving back north again as it retreats is the background against which these fish have evolved, their behaviour being dictated by the inescapable necessity to breed in fresh water. The loss of the anadromous habit and the establishment of wholly land-locked populations is of great evolutionary significance, as this can lead to species radiation, where the isolated populations evolve subspecies, and later species, as fish become adapted to the ecological niches offered by their

Fig. 17 The River Colne near Uxbridge – an SSSI and a good example of a rich lowland river suitable to many species of fish (Peter Wakeley, NCC).

differing freshwater environments as long as another ice age does not halt this process. However, in the long term future environmental conditions are extremely uncertain as 'global warming' seems set to modify the advent of a future ice age.

Habitats in the British Isles

The British Isles are renowned for the great variety of landscapes they contain within a relatively small land area. This quality reflects the wide range of basic conditions fundamental to the evolution of contrasting land forms such as high and low ground, hard and soft rocks, rich and poor soils, high and low rainfalls, a highly convoluted coastline and a history of various intensive land uses. It follows therefore that this land has also produced a wide variety of natural freshwater habitats, to which must be added the considerable number of artificial water bodies, such as the canal networks in the lowlands and numerous reservoirs of all shapes and sizes, mostly in the uplands.

The range of our natural freshwater habitats encompasses the high corrie lochs of the Cairngorm plateau in the Central Highlands of Scotland at around 900m in altitude, with their clear green-tinted waters, ice-free for less

Fig. 18 Left, Woodwalton Fen National Nature Reserve – a man-made canalised system, but very suitable for many species of fish, especially the carp family (Peter Wakeley, NCC); *Right*, The River Severn near Hampton Lode – an SSSI and an extremely important water for a large variety of fish species (Peter Wakeley, NCC).

than half the year; the large, deep and elongated, glaciated lake basins of mountainous areas in Scotland and north-west England, with their acid, biologically poor (oligotrophic) waters; the great shallow biologically rich (eutrophic) limestone loughs of Ireland; the acid peat-stained pools, the source of upland rills, becks and burns; the swift flowing chalk and marl streams of southern England and parts of Ireland, with dense vegetation waving in their clear waters; the turbid lower reaches of large rivers, whose systems include tributaries of various characteristics, but whose original natures are now largely masked by the run-off from agricultural land and the discharge of domestic and industrial effluents (but most of which are not polluted to the extent that fish life is excluded); the many lovely estuaries with full ranges of salinity from fresh to salt water; the less common habitats such as the mildly saline water bodies impounded by storm beaches around the coast, or found in basins at the heads of Hebridean tidal systems; and the immense variety of ponds, ditches and marshy pools throughout the land.

The most important qualities of freshwater habitats that, in theory, dictate the density and species composition of the fish present are water velocity, level of dissolved oxygen, summer temperatures and the level of chemical, and therefore biological, richness and degree of pollution.

Many of the large rivers which rise in upland areas gradually progress from being fast-flowing and oligotrophic to slow-flowing and eutrophic. There are many classic examples on the Continent (e.g. the Rivers Rhine and Gironde) where the species composition of the fish fauna is closely related to the habitat provided by each particular section of the river. However, in the British Isles, with its short rivers, its impoverished fauna and flora and spe-

DISTRIBUTION AND HABITAT 57

Fig. 19 Loch Flemington, an example of a eutrophic northern loch with typically dense marginal vegetation (Niall Campbell).

Fig. 20 Loch Awe and Cruachan Reservoir. Arctic Charr along with other species have been accidentally pumped up from Loch Awe into Cruachan Reservoir, so creating a new population (North of Scotland Hydro-electric Board).

Fig. 21 Above, Loch Morar, the deepest loch in the British Isles and home to a salmonid community of Atlantic Salmon, Brown and Sea Trout and Arctic Charr, as well as European Eel and Three-spined Stickleback (Kenneth Morris); *Left*, Loch Ness: an aerial view looking south-west down the loch. This enormous loch contains more water than all the lakes and reservoirs in England and Wales put together and its fish community is dominated by salmonids – Atlantic Salmon, Brown and Sea Trout and Arctic Charr (Aerofilms Ltd).

cialised history of fish colonisation, redistributions and introductions, this type of correlation is only approximate.

However, there are some features and relationships characteristic of the communities found in fresh waters in the British Isles. In the mountainous regions the mainly hard insoluble rocks and poor soils mean that the acid waters of their streams and lakes are poor in the minerals required to promote growth and can therefore only support a low level of biological productivity. Their invertebrate life is poor in species and dominated by insects. These habitats, though, favour salmonid fishes, and Atlantic Salmon, Brown

Fig. 22 The lower reaches of the River Endrick before it enters Loch Lomond (Peter Maitland).

Trout and Arctic Charr thrive in the cool, clean, well-oxygenated waters and clear silt-free gravels, which are so important for the survival of their eggs and young stages. Such habitats are the most vulnerable to the impact of 'acid rain', as they have insufficient buffering capacity to neutralise the acids being deposited from the atmosphere. Some coarse fish also inhabit such waters but they seldom dominate the salmonids, for most coarse species do not tolerate the environmental poverty or low summer temperatures.

At the other extreme there are typical lowland river systems flowing over soluble mineral-rich strata and influenced by run-off from the rich agricultural soils in the catchment. This results in high-pH 'alkaline' waters and a biologically rich, eutrophic, environment. The turbid waters of these systems usually support much aquatic vegetation and a rich and diverse invertebrate fauna, with molluscs and crustaceans as important members. Being at a low altitude, the relatively high summer water temperatures provide the conditions essential to so many coarse fish species for successful ova hatching and fry survival. Such habitats are suitable for most members of the carp family and many other stenohaline fishes. However, where these fish (especially Pike) are absent, salmonid fishes will thrive as long as there are tributaries with good spawning and nursery areas to provide an adequate recruitment to maintain their populations further downstream. Apropos of this, it is interesting to speculate on the immense production of Salmon and Trout that must have taken place in, for instance, the rich and very extensive low-lying River Shannon system in Ireland before Pike and other coarse fish became established there. This is yet another example of the well-intended, but ultimately ecologically disastrous actions of humans.

Through the passage of time, fresh waters naturally tend to become silted up and more eutrophic, but this process has been greatly accelerated by human activities. This applies even to some water bodies in highland areas due to the ever increasing afforestation that is now taking place. This involves a considerable amount of ploughing and drainage and the application of chemical fertilisers to land newly prepared for tree planting, while the rehabilitation and reclamation of hill land for pasture also results in substantial amounts of fertiliser run-off into feeder streams. An early sign of eutrophication is the appearance of green algae on rocks and stones in or near the stream and along the shores of lakes where this has never been seen before. Slight eutrophication probably has little effect on the fishes of these upland areas, but the accumulation of nutrients, along with those from other human sources in the lower reaches, can and does produce conditions lethal to fish, especially due to low oxygen levels during hot dry weather and low water flows.

In concluding this chapter we would like to refer to what must be a novel and unusual freshwater fish habitat – the artificial upper reservoir of an hydroelectric pumped-storage scheme operating at Loch Awe in Argyll. Here, in the small high (300m) reservoir created by the North of Scotland Hydro-Electric Board when they built the Cruachan Scheme in 1964, there are populations of Brown Trout, Arctic Charr, Eels, Minnows, Perch and Three-spined Sticklebacks. All these fish must originally have been pumped up through the turbines from Loch Awe and they survive precariously the twice-daily risk of being sucked down again when the station at the loch side is generating!

5

Fish Conservation

In the British Isles in recent times we have tended to take our freshwater fish fauna for granted. Naturalist authors of the eighteenth, nineteenth and early twentieth centuries showed a keen interest in our fishes, but now the emphasis of popular natural history is very much on plants, butterflies, birds and mammals. Some excellent guidebooks on the identification of our freshwater (and marine) fishes, with notes on their biology, have been produced but the last true natural history was probably that of Travis Jenkins, first published in 1925. There may well be a simple explanation for this shortcoming: plants, butterflies, birds and our larger mammals are photogenic and can be easily observed in the wild but most fishes cannot. They are normally seen alive only in aquaria or struggling in anglers' keep nets, but are more usually seen dead in anglers' bags, on fishmongers' slabs or preserved or cast in glass cases in the local hostelry or museum.

This state of affairs has resulted in low 'fish appeal'; fish are just things that anglers sit on stools in the rain to catch or commercial fishermen harvest callously in large numbers! Thus, in recent times the study of fishes and their conservation has been left mainly to scientists supporting commercial fisheries, or the management of sport fisheries; to biology teachers; to a small proportion of anglers; to the relatively few professional and amateur ichthyologists and to children with nets and jam jars. All this adds up to a sad lack of general awareness of an important element of our native fauna and no effective country-wide policy for fish conservation can emerge from such relative

Fig. 23 Loch Eck, where an important fish community, including Arctic Charr and and Powan, is found (Peter Maitland).

Table 5 The rarer species of native freshwater fish in the British Isles.

Species	Occurrence
Sturgeon	An increasingly rare vagrant around our coasts.
Allis Shad	Now uncommon around our coasts. No certain breeding sites.
Twaite Shad	Less common than formerly around our coasts. Breeds in only a few rivers. Land-locked race in the Lough Leane.
Arctic Charr	Fewer populations than formerly. Many in Scotland and Ireland, a few in Wales and England.
Houting	A former visitor around our coasts. Now extinct in the British Isles.
Powan	Only six populations altogether
Vendace	Only two populations left. Two others extinct this century.
Pollan	Only five populations in large Irish loughs.
Smelt	Much less common than formerly in our estuaries. Only a few breeding populations left in about ten rivers.
Burbot	Formerly in only a few rivers in eastern England. Probably now extinct in the British Isles.

apathy. How different is the present attitude to the conservation of many other forms of wildlife, especially plants and birds.

It is essential, therefore, for the survival of our rare native fish species and communities that this state of affairs should not be allowed to continue. Apart from the aesthetic and scientific reasons for fish conservation, there are other important reasons: commercial value (i.e. conservation is synonymous with 'wise exploitation'), sporting value (often with direct and indirect financial and social implications), reservoirs of important genes (of potential value in the future), amenity and education. Freshwater fish are also important as food for many waterside birds and waterfowl, including some rare and threatened species such as Black-throated Divers, while for Otters, whose survival in much of Britain is still in the balance, a good fish fauna is essential.

However, with the scientific research which has been carried out in the British Isles in recent years, particularly since World War II, we now know much more about the ecology and status of many of our freshwater fishes – enough on which to base an effective conservation policy, if the interest and willingness to carry it out are there.

There have been several recent reviews of the status of our rarer freshwater fishes and their vulnerability. Original fish communities are also under threat – indeed there are probably very few left now. Certainly, this is the case with original communities of stenohaline species and we are uncertain if there are any pure ones left. Some fully representative euryhaline communities are still intact, or only slightly adulterated, such as in Loch Eck in Argyll, where Salmon, Trout (Brown and Sea), Arctic Charr, Powan, Three-spined Stickleback, Eel, Minnow and Flounder occur. Minnows and some Rainbow Trout (which are not self-sustaining) are probably legacies from visiting anglers and fish farming respectively. These two alien species, however, do not seem to have disrupted the original community. Other good examples

FISH CONSERVATION 63

Table 6 Examples of important communities of freshwater fish in the British Isles.

System	Species
River Avon	Sea & Brook Lamprey, Atlantic Salmon, Trout, Rainbow Trout, Grayling, Smelt, Pike, Common & Crucian Carp, Goldfish, Barbel, Gudgeon, Tench, Silver & Common Bream, Bleak, Minnow, Roach, Rudd, Chub, Orfe, Dace, Stone Loach, Eel, Three-spined Stickleback, Sea Bass, Perch, Thick- & Thin-lipped & Golden Mullet, Bullhead, Flounder
Lough Corrib	Sea & Brook Lamprey, Atlantic Salmon, Trout, Arctic Charr, Pike, Common Bream, Minnow, Rudd, Roach, Stone Loach, Eel, Three- & Nine-spined Stickleback
Loch Eck	Sea Lamprey, Atlantic Salmon, Trout, Rainbow Trout, Arctic Charr, Powan, Minnow, Eel, Flounder
Lough Erne	Atlantic Salmon, Trout, Rainbow Trout, Arctic Charr, Pollan, Pike, Common Bream, Minnow, Rudd, Roach, Stone Loach, Eel, Three-spined Stickleback, Perch
River Great Ouse	Brook Lamprey, Trout, Smelt, Pike, Common & Crucian Carp, Barbel, Gudgeon, Tench, Silver & Common Bream, Bleak, Minnow, Bitterling, Rudd, Roach, Chub, Dace, Spined & Stone Loach, Danube Catfish, Eel, Three- & Nine-spined Stickleback, Sea Bass, Perch, Ruffe, Pikeperch, Bullhead, Flounder
Haweswater	Trout, Arctic Charr, Powan (Schelly), Minnow, Eel, Three-spined Stickleback, Perch.
Lough Leane	Twaite Shad, Atlantic Salmon, Trout, Arctic Charr, Gudgeon, Tench, Perch, Eel, Three-spined Stickleback
Loch Lomond	Sea, River & Brook Lamprey, Atlantic Salmon, Trout, Powan, Pike, Gudgeon, Minnow, Roach, Chub, Dace, Stone Loach, Eel, Three- & Nine-spined Stickleback, Perch, Ruffe, Flounder
River Severn	Sea, River & Brook Lamprey, Allis & Twaite Shad, Atlantic Salmon, Trout, Rainbow Trout, Brook Charr, Grayling, Pike, Common & Crucian Carp, Goldfish, Barbel, Gudgeon, Tench, Silver & Common Bream, Bleak, Minnow, Rudd, Roach, Chub, Orfe, Dace, Stone Loach, Danube Catfish, Eel, Three- & Nine-spined Stickleback, Sea Bass, Perch, Ruffe, Pikeperch, Common Goby, Thick-lipped Mullet, Bullhead, Flounder
River Skealtar	Atlantic Salmon, Trout, Arctic Charr, Eel, Three- & Nine-spined Stickleback, Common Goby, Thick-lipped Mullet, Flounder
Llyn Tegid	Brook Lamprey, Atlantic Salmon, Trout, Powan (Gwyniad), Grayling, Pike, Gudgeon, Minnow, Rudd, Roach, Stone Loach, Eel, Three-spined Stickleback, Perch, Ruffe, Bullhead.
River Thames	Sea, River & Brook Lamprey, Twaite Shad, Atlantic Salmon, Trout, Rainbow Trout, Grayling, Smelt, Pike, Common & Crucian Carp, Goldfish, Barbel, Gudgeon, Tench, Silver & Common Bream, Bleak, Minnow, Rudd, Roach, Chub, Orfe, Dace, Stone Loach, Eel, Three- & Nine-spined Stickleback, Sea Bass, Perch, Ruffe, Thick- and Thin-lipped Mullet, Bullhead, Flounder

of original euryhaline communities occur at Llyn Tegid, Dyfed and Haweswater in Cumbria, but predatory and/or competitor species (i.e. Pike, Perch and Ruffe in Llyn Tegid, and Perch in Haweswater) are now in these waters and may represent a current or potential danger.

Some of the rich rivers of eastern and southern England, such as the Great Ouse, Severn and Hampshire Avon, contain almost full representations of the original stenohaline fishes, although these are now well mixed with later introductions. Such populations should be kept under observation, and if possible safeguarded. The rarer fishes, including some which may have become extinct in recent times, mainly due to habitat changes, are listed in the accompanying table.

As well as rare species, rare varieties of fish also deserve more attention: for example, the various local races of Arctic Charr, the spine-deficient Three-spined Stickleback populations that have been found recently at a few sites in the Western Isles and northern Scotland and the unique land-locked River Lamprey found in Loch Lomond. Also in the north of Scotland, recent biochemical work has indicated that there are possibly two distinct races of Brown Trout with quite separate origins.

A provisional list of some important original fish communities and a summary of the dangers which individual communities and their habitats face have been tabulated. It should be remembered that while none of our native fish species is endemic – for they all occur elsewhere in north-western Europe – they have been isolated from their common stock since the end of the last great ice age and some have developed into distinct local races. This is more than can be said, say, for the great majority of our native birds whose populations are, in the main, continuous with those of mainland Europe.

The main human pressures on our fish stocks are those resulting from exploitation, pollution, loss of habitat and the irresponsible redistribution of disruptive fish species from other parts of the country. In recent years there has been a marked trend in the British Isles away from natural mixed fish populations towards artificially maintained unstable stocks of a few species for sporting and commercial interests.

Legislation

What protection is currently available against these dangers? In Great Britain, the Wildlife and Countryside Act (1981), (WACA), can afford protection to listed endangered species (e.g. the Burbot, which may actually be extinct now in Britain) and lists some disruptive fish species (such as the non-indigenous Pikeperch and Danube Catfish) which must not be allowed to escape to the wild or be deliberately redistributed, without a licence issued by the Ministry of Agriculture Fisheries & Food (MAFF) in England and Wales, or, in Scotland, by the Department of Agriculture & Fisheries for Scotland (DAFS), after consultation with the Nature Conservancy Council. However, there is no ban on the redistribution of equally disruptive native species; the recent introduction and rapid establishment of the Ruffe in Loch Lomond (which now poses a threat to the Powan there) is discussed below, and is an example of this type of problem.

Under the WACA, the owners and occupiers of Sites of Special Scientific Interest (SSSIs), which have been notified by the NCC, are provided by the latter with a list of 'Potentially Damaging Operations' which could damage or destroy the interest of the site. In cases where the site has been notified wholly or partly for its freshwater interest the list would include those operations that might damage the fish community, directly or indirectly. Before any such operations can be carried out the owners or occupiers have to advise the NCC in writing of their intentions. The NCC then enters into negotiations with them and if the parties do not arrive at a mutually satisfactory outcome, a compulsory 'stop' order can be applied for by the NCC to allow time for arbitration. However, of the 3000 or so SSSIs in Britain, although many contain elements of open-water habitat, comparatively few have actually been notified for freshwater interest and fewer still of these for their fish interest. A review of all sites which contain open water, from the fish conservation aspect, might be extremely rewarding and an important step forward.

The NCC are, however, reviewing the level of statutory protection presently afforded to our freshwater fish fauna under the WACA. In 'A Nature Conservation Review' (NCR) published by the NCC in 1977 there is a list of key conservation sites in Great Britain. The open-water section contains details of 99 freshwater sites, mostly selected according to physical, chemical, botanical and ornithological criteria. In only 48 cases are fish referred to and very few were partly or wholly set up to protect a fish species or community.

Since the publication of the NCR, the NCC have, however, laid down guidelines for the selection of fish SSSIs. These can be summarised as follows:

i) It appears that, in general, the occurrence of a rare species of fish alone does not rate the establishment of an SSSI but additional justification is required, i.e. the presence of other rare species of plants or animals and/or the representativeness of the site as a prime example of a certain habitat type.

ii) The best communities of representative native fish populations might qualify for SSSI notification.

iii) Waters which contain outstanding assemblages of fish species (both native and introduced) might qualify for notification, e.g.

   a) Southern waters (below the line from the Humber to the Mersey, but excluding Wales) with 20 or more breeding species.

   b) Waters in Wales with 15 species breeding.

   c) Waters in northern England and southern Scotland with ten or more breeding species.

   d) Waters in northern Scotland, north of the Great Glen, with six or more breeding species.

   e) Water with unusual communities.

   f) Waters containing rare or unique varieties of fish.

All these criteria would no doubt be subject to further revision as more information on our fish stocks becomes available.

As an additional safeguard central government's permission is required before fish poisons are used for fishery management purposes and if a wetland SSSI was involved the NCC would be consulted.

The control of pollution legislation, administered by the former Water Authorities (now the National Rivers Authority) in England and Wales and the River Purification Boards in Scotland, and supported by EC directives, has resulted in the rehabilitation of many polluted waters and the maintenance of high standards in others. But there are still 'grey areas' where pollution cannot be controlled in spite of legislation, because of the 'national interest', and/or lack of public funds. Moreover, there is recent evidence that after the Water Authorities were formed in England and Wales, with dual control for pollution prevention and the treatment of sewage (which is the main cause of pollution), many rivers have deteriorated. This is not the case in Scotland where these functions are exercised by separate authorities. However, there are encouraging examples of what can be achieved – in the cleaning up of the River Thames, which now supports at least 25 species of freshwater fish and has been optimistically stocked with young Salmon, while in Scotland Salmon have returned to the River Clyde, until recently lethally polluted in its lower reaches.

In Ireland, freshwater fish legislation is aimed at conservation of fish as an exploitable resource rather than as elements of the native fauna. However, in both the Irish Republic and Northern Ireland sections of current legislation are also potentially effective in the latter role and in some respects possibly more effective than those in force in Great Britain. For example, the importation of all cold water fish and their eggs into any part of Ireland without a licence is prohibited, while a licence is also required for the transportation of any live fish within the Irish Republic. The use of live bait (the source of many harmful introductions) is also banned. Also in the Republic, if interesting fish communities and their habitats came under threat, they could be protected, in theory, by application of the Planning and Wildlife Acts, under which, respectively, Amenity and Nature Reserves can be set up. The Water Pollution Act is implemented by the Department of the Environment, while the Department of the Marine has important powers under the Fisheries Acts.

In Northern Ireland, the Department of Agriculture, under the Prohibition of Introduction of Fish Order, can prohibit the introduction of any species of freshwater fish into any waters where it considered that this would be detrimental to the existing fishery. This order also contains the names of certain 'undesirable' fish species which are banned from Northern Ireland, viz. Coho Salmon, Pink Salmon, Brook Charr, Grayling, Barbel, Bleak, Chub, Crucian Carp, Dace, Silver Bream, Pikeperch, Largemouth Bass and Smallmouth Bass. (Dace is present locally in Eire and Pink Salmon as a vagrant to the British Isles, while Smallmouth Bass occur sparsely in Europe as an introduction from North America.)

Also implemented by the Department of Agriculture is the Diseases of Fish Act, which controls the importation or distribution of any species, dead or alive, which may be considered to constitute a health hazard to Northern Ireland's fish stocks. The Fisheries Conservation Board for Northern Ireland acts as an agent for the Department of the Environment in detecting, reporting on and giving evidence in pollution cases. Current problems affecting native fish species in Ireland arise from land drainage, eutrophication, fish farming and the adverse ecological repercussions resulting from the rapid spread of undesirable species (in spite of legislation).

Fish species, communities and their habitats in Northern Ireland can now be protected under the Nature Conservation, Amenity, Lands and Wildlife Orders of 1985 and 1987 (which parallel the Wildlife and Countryside Act (1981) in force in Britain) and are administered by the Nature Conservation Branch of the Department of the Environment. An Area of Special Scientific Interest (ASSI) or a Nature Reserve could be designated or set up to protect a wetland site and its fauna. As in Britain, owners or occupiers of ASSIs or NNRs must give prior notice of any proposed activities that could damage the interest of a site. The Department of the Environment (NI) can also establish National Parks with bye laws protecting the wildlife they contain.

Future Efforts

What can be done to further the cause of freshwater fish conservation in the British Isles as a whole? An essential step must be to inform and interest that large and influential section of the public already interested in natural history and the conservation of wildlife. It must be generally realised that the conservation of the freshwater fish element of our native fauna has been and still is neglected in comparison with the more popular elements of our wildlife and that a number of our original fish communities and individual rare species are also endangered. While there is much scientific information already available on the biology and ecology of many of our freshwater fish species, this is spread widely over a range of sources, only readily obtainable by fishery scientists. There is a need for a summary of such information to be found within one cover. We hope that this book will make some contribution towards these goals. Also there are a great many anglers and angling organisations in the British Isles and their co-operation should be sought by, for instance, the NCC, the County Naturalist Trusts in England and Wales and the Scottish Wildlife Trust in Scotland. After all, fish conservation should, in the long term at least, be in the anglers' best interests, but it is our experience that the majority of anglers are not primarily interested in the natural history or ecology of their quarry and even less in fish species which are not angled.

However, many more basic data are required and another survey should be carried out of the freshwater fish of the British Isles by the combined efforts of all interested individuals and parties to provide information on the distribution of all species and their current status. The results of such a survey could be reviewed against the list of SSSIs in Britain and equivalent sites in Ireland, and any gaps in the 'official' list of fish conservation sites could be filled as appropriate. The results could be stored so as to be available to the public, and all statutory and private bodies with control over freshwater sites would be made aware of any potential for fish conservation under their aegis and their co-operation sought.

Obviously the conferring of National Nature Reserve (NNR) or SSSI status on a water body cannot guarantee that the rare fish species or community therein will be safe from the deliberate introduction of a disruptive species for selfish motives – indeed such cases have already occurred. Thus, in certain cases it might well be safer not to confer any official status to a site, thus avoiding the usual publicity. This is a sad commentary on the times we live in! In some cases the redistribution or even reintroduction from abroad of rare or newly extinct species might be justified. There are, currently, precedents involving other animals; NCC have reintroduced the White-tailed Sea Eagle to the west coast of Scotland by importing young birds from Norway over a period of years and other agencies are involved in re-establishing Otters in areas now devoid of them, where habitat conditions have improved over recent years. Fish redistributions and introductions should be at or near original sites, using the nearest suitable stocks, but as a last resort, stock from abroad could be used.

One of the authors is currently involved in a programme to establish new populations of threatened fish species in the British Isles. For instance, attempts are being made to re-establish Arctic Charr in southern Scotland, where several populations have disappeared this century leaving only one population – at present threatened by acidification – in Loch Doon. So far, two introductions have been made, both in large artificial reservoirs in the Borders Region, but it is too early to know whether these have been successful or not.

Other species involved in the programme include the Burbot, which might have to be reintroduced from abroad, and Vendace, which is being reintroduced to Scotland from English sources. The establishment of land-locked populations of Smelt (such as once occurred at Rostherne Mere) is also under consideration. In some cases, captive breeding may be necessary so that a significant stock of the species is available for release. Newly made artificial lakes (e.g. worked-out gravel pits or quarries) could be used for stocking with rare species or original communities to increase their representation throughout the country, and possibly even be opened to controlled angling. On the other side of the coin, the spread of dangerous or disruptive species might be halted by their elimination through the careful use of fish poisons or their numbers controlled by less drastic methods such as trapping or netting. For example, in this context, Pike and Perch might be alien species in some small water body and pose a potential threat to existing rare species or the original euryhaline community there. The early discovery of the presence of any of these species could help greatly with their subsequent control.

6
Fish Identification

Every species of fish which is known to be established in fresh water somewhere in the British Isles is included in this book. A few other fish are also included, the most important of which are brackish water forms that, though basically marine, occur regularly in fresh water during part of their life cycle. Many purely marine species also occur regularly in brackish water (but never in fresh water) and these are only mentioned occasionally.

Native forms make up the bulk of the British freshwater fauna, but there are also about a dozen introduced species which have thrived and bred, sometimes establishing populations over wide areas; all such species are included here. Other freshwater species of doubtful status in the British Isles have not been included (though mention may be made of them in places). Among these are various tropical species, widely kept in aquaria, associated with heated effluents (e.g. the Guppy *Poecilia reticulata*), the Chinese Grass Carp *Ctenopharyngodon idella* which has been introduced to a number of waters to control vegetation but does not breed here in the wild, and odd records of various temperate species brought into the country for aquarium purposes for which there is no evidence of an established population – e.g. the Black Bullhead *Ictalurus melas*.

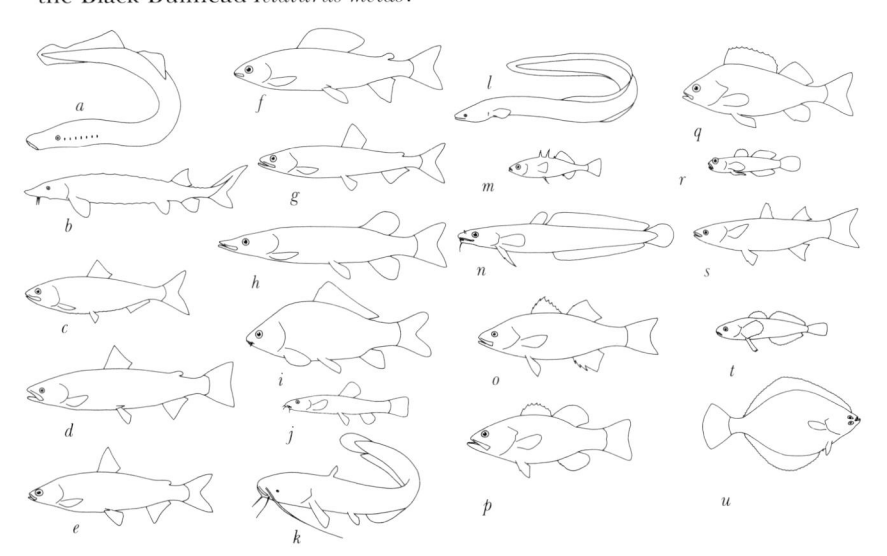

Fig. 24 Outline diagrams of representative types of each family: a, Petromyzonidae; b, Acipenseridae; c, Clupeidae; d, Salmonidae; e, Coregonidae; f, Thymallidae; g, Osmeridae; h, Esocidae; i, Cyprinidae; j, Cobitidae; k, Siluridae; l, Anguillidae; m, Gasterosteidae; n, Gadidae; o, Serranidae; p, Centrarchidae; q, Percidae; r, Gobiidae; s, Mugilidae; t, Cottidae; u, Pleuronectidae (from Maitland 1972b).

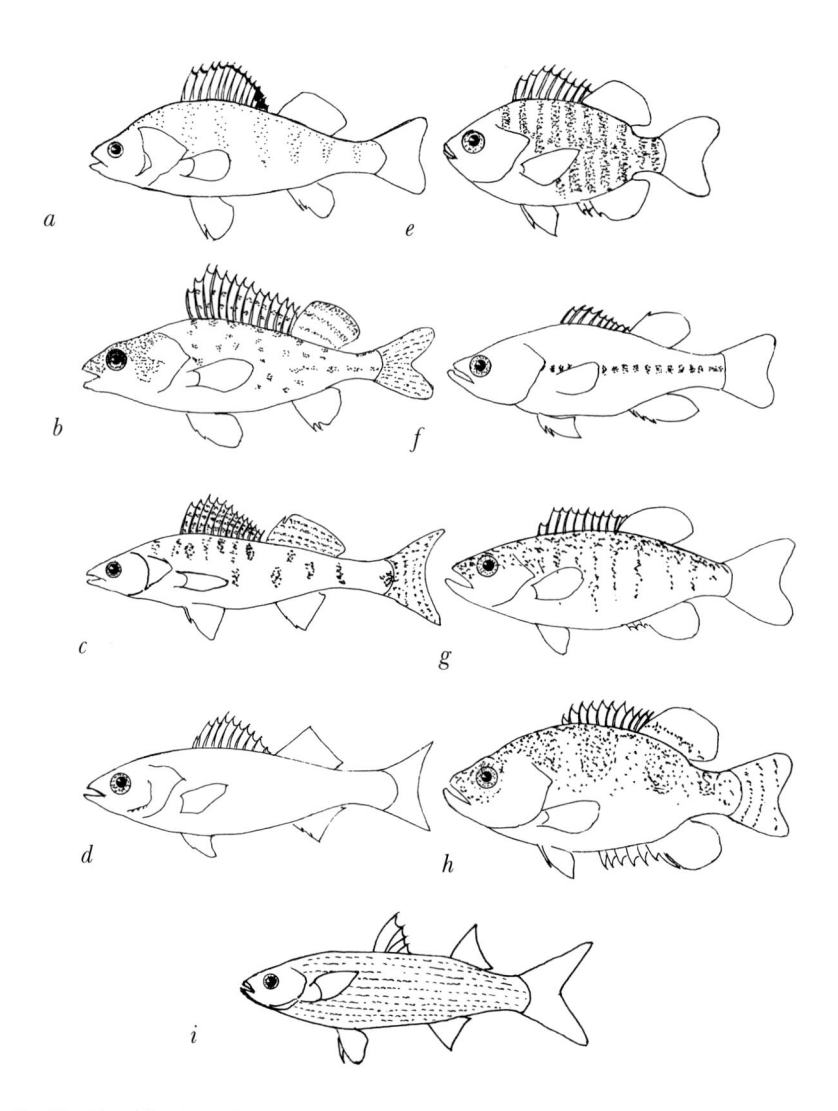

Fig. 25 Identification of the young stages of some fish with spiny front dorsal fins can be confusing. Thus, the presence of a species in waters hitherto without it may go undetected until the adult stages are found, by which time it may be firmly established. For example, small Ruffe or Pumpkinseeds (both normally undesirable species) may be confused with young Perch of the same size. In this figure, sketches of the most similar species are contrasted – the main diagnostic features being the relationship between the first and second dorsal fins followed by colouration; a, Perch (gap between dorsals, pale olive-green overall with 5–8 pale or indistinct vertical bars on body, black spot at rear of first dorsal, fronts of pelvic and anal fins faintly yellow); b, Ruffe (high first dorsal which is joined to second, marks on both dorsals and tail fin, iris mainly dark, conspicuous dark freckling over most of body); c, Pikeperch (elongate body, gap between dorsals, markings on membranes of dorsals and tail fin, greeny olive-silver overall); d, Sea Bass (gap between dorsals, no markings on fins or body, silvery overall); e, Pumpkinseed (dorsals joined, 10–11 bars along body and a broken horizontal line, no black spot at rear of gill cover in adult, pearly iridescence on gill cover below eye, olive-brown overall); f, Largemouth Bass (first dorsal only just joined to second); g, Smallmouth Bass; h, Rock Bass (dorsals joined, very deep and flat body, patchy brownish overall with no distinct markings); i, mullet.

Identification Keys

The identification keys which appear in the following pages follow the dichotomous pattern common to many wildlife guides. Where possible, several distinguishing characters have been used at each point in the key and these should be used in combination with each other. Every species is figured, and after preliminary identification from the text, the relevant figure and photograph (if present) should be consulted. Due consideration must always be given to the possibility of any specimen being very young, malformed, aberrant or a hybrid.

The most common numerical features used in the key are counts of fin rays and of scales. In all the fin-ray counts mentioned, the number for each fin includes both the hard unbranched spiny rays and the soft branched rays, unless otherwise stated. The main scale counts are taken along the lateral line starting at the first scale behind the operculum and ending at the last scale before the caudal fin. Some diagonal scale counts may also be used: these are normally counted from the lateral line up to the adipose fin (where present) and from the lateral line down to the anal fin. Occasionally counts are made from the lateral line up to the dorsal fin or down to the pelvic fin.

Where colours are used in the key they refer to the condition in the fresh fish and should be true irrespective of size (above the larval and fry stages), sex and condition, unless otherwise stated. With many species it is possible to determine the sex accurately only by dissection of the genitalia; this is especially true outside of the breeding season. With others there are constant external sexual differences. These have not been included in the keys.

Hybrids

Various species of freshwater fish in the British Isles hybridise quite frequently with one another in the wild. Such hybrids are obviously rather difficult to identify with a normal dichotomous key and their characters are usually intermediate between those of the two parent species. Unfortunately, due to the very nature of speciation, it is often those species which are most alike (and thus difficult to distinguish from each other in the first place) which are most likely to hybridise. Quite a number of hybrids have been recorded from the wild in the British Isles – most of them among the carp family Cyprinidae.

The list of natural hybrids recorded from the British Isles to date is as follows: TroutxSalmon, TroutxBrook Charr, CarpxCrucian Carp, BreamxOrfe, BreamxRudd, RoachxRudd, RoachxBream, RoachxBleak, ChubxBleak, DacexBleak, DacexRudd.

Use of the Key

The identification keys to the families (in this chapter) and to species (in other relevant chapters) are based on a standard dichotomous pattern, where at each point in the key the reader who is trying to identify a fish is presented with two alternatives. The one to follow is that which fits the specimen best – where possible, characters which are clear-cut and unambiguous have been given. Having selected one alternative, the reader is then led to another couplet, and so on until the identity of the family is reached. This can then be confirmed by reference to outline diagrams of all the groups involved. Later in the book there are guides to the individual species, family by family. Having identified the family of any fish from the first key, the reader should then go to the similar type of key within each family section to make the final identification of the species. This can then be confirmed by the relevant illustration and distribution map – though it should always be borne in mind that fish are continually being moved around by humans and turning up in new places.

Formal identification using the whole set of keys is often not necessary, especially with the more unusual or obvious species. Thus, if the reader wishes to identify an eel-like fish with one pair of fins it will be seen immediately from the family outline diagram that this must be in the family Anguillidae. On looking up the relevant family section it will be found that if it is from fresh water in the British Isles it can really be only one species – the European Eel *Anguilla anguilla*.

The common names in this book are mostly those in most widespread use, and each is followed by the appropriate scientific name. This consists of two parts: the genus (equivalent to a human surname in Europe) and the specific name (equivalent to a christian name). Occasionally, the common name most used previously has been so misleading that the authors have used alternative, but much more meaningful, names (e.g. for *Salvelinus fontinalis* we use Brook Charr – for this is a charr – instead of the more common name Brook Trout).

For each species there is also a listing of alternative common names used in different parts of the British Isles. There is also a an appendix of the most commonly used Gaelic names in Ireland and Scotland and also of the common Welsh names.

For each species there is a full description of its physical appearance, colour variation and a distribution map and illustration. The text has been standardised to some extent to facilitate comparisons and includes information on the size, habitat, distribution, breeding habits, age and growth, the food and economic value of each species. The maps show the general distribution in the British Isles. It must be remembered that each species occurs only in suitable types of water within the areas shown and not everywhere.

Problem Fish

Although it is theoretically possible, with the aid of the keys in this book, to identify to species level all fish known to occur in fresh water in the British Isles, a few species (especially some juveniles) are rather difficult to identify accurately without experience. There is also always the possibility of a hybrid or of a species new to the country turning up. In cases of doubt, a live specimen should be shown to some local expert before being returned to its habitat. Where this is not feasible, however, one or more specimens of the species concerned should be killed humanely, and preserved as described below. The specimen(s) should then be sent to a competent ichthyologist for examination, together with relevant details of where and when it was caught, etc. It is not normally advisable to send fresh fish by post as they deteriorate too rapidly. When sending preserved fish, they should first be drained of preservative, wrapped in damp muslin and then sealed into a plastic bag before being packed firmly in a box. In this form the fish will travel for many days in perfect condition.

The keys in this book are intended to be as useful as possible in the field, so that it is possible to return fish to the water after capture, examination and identification. During this process, specimens should always be kept damp and cool. The features used to differentiate families and species are mainly external ones; characters which are as objective and absolute as possible have been selected where feasible. Nevertheless, it is sometimes necessary to resort to characters which involve killing the fish; the characters concerned here are mainly found in the region of the head – gills in the shad family, mouth bones in the salmonids, pharyngeal bones in the carp family, etc.

Collection and Preservation

As described in a previous chapter, fish may be captured by a wide variety of methods, depending on the species concerned, its size, its habitat, etc. In the British Isles, among the commonest methods of capture in fresh water are angling for larger fish and the use of a hand net for smaller fish. There are many other methods of capture (some of them much more efficient, but illegal in most situations) which can be used; e.g. electric fishing, gill nets, seine nets, trawl nets, traps, etc. Most methods of fishing are highly selective and may often capture only one size group of one species and sometimes even one sex. For example, gill nets used in Loch Lomond in January in shallow water over gravel may only catch adult male Powan and nothing else – in spite of the fact that 18 other species of fish occur in this water. This is because most fish are in deeper water at this time of the year, but it is spawning time for Powan and the males congregate in large numbers over gravel beds waiting for ripe females to come in to spawn. In carrying out any detailed study of a mixed fish population it is therefore normally advisable to use several different methods of capture.

Unfortunately, the general keys in this book will not serve to identify the very small specimens (larvae and fry) of most species. For a short time after hatching, the young of most fish change very rapidly in form, and features characteristic of the species do not appear for some time. Unlike many invertebrates, adult fish, because of their large size, can mostly be identified in the field and there is no need to take them away for this purpose. Thus, in many instances it is possible to identify specimens correctly immediately after capture and return them alive to the water. It is pointless to kill such fish unless they are required for food, research or some other purpose. In the case of species which are difficult to identify accurately in the field it may be necessary to take them away for detailed examination, although a good colour photograph would be a suitable alternative. It is preferable that specimens are always kept alive, but this is sometimes not possible, especially with large or delicate specimens, and most of these must be killed humanely. Clearly where dissection is essential for their accurate identification, all specimens must be killed.

Apart from asphyxiation, one of the best methods of killing fish without damaging them is to use a liquid anaesthetic of some kind. Specimens dropped into an appropriate solution are narcotised very quickly and can then either be frozen or transferred to a suitable fixative. Fish should be examined as fresh as possible, ideally within 48 hours, or sooner in warm weather. If they cannot be examined within this time they should either be frozen or fixed in some way. Frozen fish keep their colours better than fixed ones; the best procedure is to place each specimen in a polythene bag with a little water and a label and freeze the whole as quickly as possible. The fish should be kept straight during this process and care must be taken not to damage its fins.

Even frozen fish will not keep indefinitely, however, if they have to be subjected to periodic thawing for examination purposes and normally specimens to be stored must be fixed in some way. The fixative most commonly used in the past is 4% formaldehyde, but this must be used with extreme care. Each fish should be preserved by placing it flat on its side in a shallow dish with its fins spread as much as possible, and then pouring enough of this solution over it to cover it completely. Specimens should be left for several days to ensure complete fixation. With large fish (more than 30cm long) it is advisable to make a small slit in the ventral body wall, or to inject the body cavity with a small amount of 40% formaldehyde to ensure complete fixation internally. The fish can then be stored temporarily in polythene bags or permanently in suitable sealed jars, either in 4% formaldehyde solution or in more pleasant preservatives such as 70% alcohol or 1% propylene phenoxetol. Each jar should have inside it a label, written in pencil or indelible ink, with a note of the species concerned, the water where it was collected, the date and name of the collector and who carried out the identification.

In situations where the suggested preservatives are not available, quite good results can be had with more easily obtained material such as: methylated spirits (diluted 7 parts of spirits to 3 parts of water), salt (1 part of salt to 2 parts of water), or vinegar (acetic acid), as used as a condiment. Preservation can be carried out in polythene bags, keeping the fish as straight as possible.

Eggs or larvae can be preserved and stored in small tubes containing either 4% formaldehyde or 70% alcohol. Labels (preferably written in soft pencil) with the relevant data (species, locality, date, colour of eggs when fresh, exact habitat, name of collector, etc.) should be placed inside each tube. In the case of eggs a reasonable number should be taken where possible, especially if the eggs are adhering to each other, for the form of attachment may be important in identification. This type of material is exceedingly scarce in this country, especially for some species.

Some species of fish can be identified from their scales alone, and in addition it is often possible with several good scales taken from the sides of the body to establish the specimen's age and certain features of its past history. When scales are available from specimens, they should be placed inside a small envelope which is then flattened and allowed to dry; they will keep indefinitely in this way. The envelope should bear on the outside the following information: species, locality, date, name of collector, and length (total, fork or standard), weight and sex of the specimen concerned. The length of a fish can be read in a number of different ways; the most useful method (fork length) is to record the exact distance between the tip of the snout and the end of the middle ray of the tail fin. For identification, the scales should be cleaned and mounted on glass slides, either dry or in glycerine jelly.

As with other vertebrates, bones are often very useful in the identification of fish, and in some cases (e.g. the pharyngeal bones of Cyprinidae or the vomer bones of Salmonidae) they may be virtually essential for final identification. Certain bones are also of major importance in providing information on the age and growth of some species, perhaps where the scales are unreliable for this purpose (as in Perch and Pike), or are very small with close rings (e.g. Arctic Charr), or the species does not possess scales at all (e.g. catfish). Preparation of all such bones for examination and subsequent preservation is a relatively simple task; frozen or fresh material should be used, not material which has been previously fixed. The relevant bones should be cut out from the fish concerned along with their attached tissues (muscle, etc.). Each bone should be dropped into very hot water for a few minutes and then scrubbed gently with a small stiff brush (an old toothbrush is ideal) to clean away soft tissue. The process should be repeated until the bone is completely clean. It can then be placed on clean paper and allowed to dry out slowly in a warm (but not hot) atmosphere. Details concerning the fish from which the bone was removed (species, locality, date, name of collector, length, weight and sex) should be written either on a small stiff label attached to the bone by strong thread or on the outside of an envelope or small box in which the bone is kept. Bones cleaned and dried in this manner will keep more or less indefinitely.

A great many of the species of freshwater fish which occur in the British Isles can be kept quite successfully in captivity, either indoors in aquaria or outdoors in ponds. The provision of adequate living conditions for such species is a relatively simple matter, the main requirements being reasonable space (with as large a surface area as possible), cool, clean water, sufficient cover (in the form of aquatic plants or stones) and appropriate food for the species concerned. Details are not given here but there are several admirable books (some listed in the Bibliography) dealing specifically with the subject of fish-keeping.

Fish and Pain

The question of how sensitive fish are to pain is a vexed one and something that most fishery workers and anglers must ask themselves from time to time. It is a topic that is also given publicity in the media due to statements issued by animal rights organisations and their associated anti-angling lobbies. The latter regard the hooking of fish as a barbarous act of cruelty. One of the authors, a life-long angler, came to the conclusion early in his angling career that fish do not feel pain with anything like the intensity felt by higher mammals – including humans. This conclusion was based on an incident witnessed as a teenager: in his tropical community aquarium at feeding time an Angel Fish (a name which is a wild misnomer as any tropical aquarist will know) plucked out the eye of a Black Widow tetra. The latter just kept on feeding as if nothing had happened and lived for many months more.

Later angling experiences, involving several species of fish including Salmon, Trout and Pike confirmed this initial impression. For example, on several occasions, Trout that had escaped due to the cast snapping came back to be caught again a short time later. On one occasion, a Trout was caught less than 15 minutes after its initial escape, still with the original fly hook in its mouth. Pike are notorious for returning almost immediately to seize a lure after having just shaken free of it. On another occasion, a substantial Trout was caught and released after tagging it by threading the tag wire by hypodermic needle through the gristle in front of the dorsal fin. A week later, the same Trout was caught again and released once more – only to be caught again three weeks later.

There is other evidence of the apparent insensitivity of fish to pain, as humans know it, including the sight of fish dreadfully injured by seal attack or by accidents at hatcheries or fish farms, but apparently behaving quite normally and feeding. The wounds involved would normally completely incapacitate and cause great pain in a mammal. However, these incidents should in no way be regarded as carte blanche for treating fish callously. The integrity of 'put and take' fishing needs to be examined carefully (would we release chickens or lambs in a field and then catch them again by dragging them towards us by barbed hooks caught in their mouths?), both in relation to cruelty and the ecological problems raised. Barbless hooks should always be used where fish are to be released after capture. Where fish are to be killed, humane methods must be implemented immediately. A sharp blow on the back of the head with a hard object is probably the most efficient way for larger fish. The use of fish as live bait should be banned.

Key to the Families

In the following key, where a couplet is not reached directly from the preceding couplet, the number of the couplet from which the direction came is given in parenthesis.

1. No paired fins. Seven pairs of gill openings. No lower jaw – mouth in adults a sucking disc. A single median nostril between the eyes.
 PETROMYZONIDAE (p.79).
 One or two pairs of fins. One pair of gill openings, each protected by an operculum. Lower jaw present – mouth never a sucking disc. Paired nostrils anterior to the eyes. **2.**

2. Upper lobe of caudal fin much longer than the lower (heterocercal). Five longitudinal rows of large bony plates on the body. Snout greatly elongated. **ACIPENSERIDAE (p.90).**

 Caudal fin more or less symmetrical (holocercal). No large bony plates on the body. Snout normal. **3.**

3. One dorsal fin, or if two, then the posterior one small and fleshy, without rays (the adipose fin). Pelvic fins, where present, approximately midway between pectoral fins and anus. Pneumatic duct between swimbladder and oesophagus. **4.**

 Two dorsal fins, or if only one, then either this is divided into two distinct parts (the anterior one being very spiny or replaced by isolated sharp spines) or the body is greatly flattened with both eyes on one side of the head. Pelvic fins just below or only slightly posterior to the pectoral fins. No pneumatic duct between swimbladder and oesophagus. **13.**

4. Barbels present on the head, the largest pair longer than the pectoral fins. Dorsal fin with less than 8 rays. Scales absent. **SILURIDAE (p.238)**

 Barbels absent on head, or if present then much shorter than the pectoral fins. Dorsal fin with more than 8 rays. Scales present (though very small in two families). **5.**

5. Two dorsal fins, the posterior one fleshy without rays (adipose). **6.**
One dorsal fin. **9.**

6. Scales relatively small, more than 100 along lateral line. Red pigment often present in skin and flesh. **SALMONIDAE (p.98)**
Scales relatively large, less than 100 along lateral line. Red pigment rarely present in skin or flesh (which is white). **7.**

7. Lateral line complete almost to caudal fin. Teeth absent or poorly developed. Pelvic axillary process present. **8.**
Lateral line present only for about the first ten scales. Teeth well developed. Pelvic axillary process absent. **OSMERIDAE (p.163).**

8. Dorsal fin large with more than 20 rays, its depressed length much greater than that of the head. Large black pigment spots normally present in the skin. Small teeth present. **THYMALLIDAE (p.158).**
Dorsal fin normal with less than 20 rays, its depressed length never greater than that of the head. Large black pigment spots never present in the skin, though small black chromatophores may be common. **COREGONIDAE (p.145).**

9(5)*. Dorsal fin distinct from caudal fin. Pelvic fins present. Body not extremely elongate. **10.**
Dorsal fin continuous with caudal and anal fins. Pelvic fins absent. Body extremely elongate. **ANGUILLIDAE (p.241).**

10. Scales on the ventral surface keeled. Lateral line absent. Large elongate scales over the inner part of the caudal fin. **CLUPEIDAE (p.93).**
Scales on the ventral surface not keeled. Lateral line present. No elongate scales over the inner part of the caudal fin. **11.**

11. Head elongate; mouth very large with well developed teeth. Dorsal fin mostly posterior to the anus. Scales present on head. **ESOCIDAE (p.167).**
Head normal; mouth moderate or small, with teeth absent or poorly developed. Dorsal fin entirely or mostly anterior to the anus. Scales absent on head. **12.**

12. Less than five barbels on the head. Mouth normal. Scales usually distinct on body. **CYPRINIDAE (p.177).**
More than five barbels on head. Mouth small and ventral (inferior). Scales on body indistinct. **COBITIDAE (p.230).**

13(3). Two dorsal fins, or if one then it is divided into two parts, the anterior part being very spiny. Body never greatly flattened or with isolated sharp spines. **14.**
One dorsal fin. Body either greatly flattened or with a row of dorsal spines. **20.**

14. Head with a single barbel below the mouth and one small barbel beside each nostril. Anal fin with more than 60 rays. **GADIDAE (p.262).**
Head without barbels. Anal fin with less than 60 rays. **15.**

15. Well developed scales over most of the body. Anterior dorsal fin rays rigid. **16.**

Scales absent over most of the body. Anterior dorsal fin rays flexible. **COTTIDAE (p.304).**

16. Lateral line absent. Less than five sharp spines in the anterior dorsal fin. Dorsal fins widely separated, the distance between them always exceeding the length of the longest dorsal ray. **MUGILIDAE (p.296).**

Lateral line present. More than five spiny rays in the anterior dorsal fin. Dorsal fins continuous or close together, the distance between them always much less than the length of the longest dorsal ray. **17.**

17. Two or fewer anal spines present. Either less than or more than nine or ten spiny rays in the first dorsal fin. **18.**

Three or more anal spines present; nine or ten spiny rays in the first dorsal fin. **19.**

18. Two anal spines present. Tail fin forked. More than ten spiny rays in the dorsal fin. Pelvic fins not joined medially. **PERCIDAE (p.279).**

Anal spines absent. Tail fin rounded. Less than nine spiny rays in the first dorsal fin. Pelvic fins joined medially., **GOBIIDAE (p.293).**

19(17). Second dorsal fin with one spiny ray anteriorly. Less than 70 scales along the lateral line. Anal fin convex. **CENTRARCHIDAE (p.270).**

Second dorsal fin with three spiny rays anteriorly. More than 70 scales along the lateral line. Anal fin concave. **SERRANIDAE (p.266).**

20(13). Three or more strong spines anterior to the dorsal fin. Body not dorso-ventrally flattened, eyes on either side of the head, pelvic fins with less than three rays. **GASTEROSTEIDAE (p.250).**

No spines anterior to the dorsal fin. Body extremely flattened with both eyes on one side of the head (usually the right). Pelvic fins with more than three rays. **PLEURONECTIDAE (p.308).**

7

Lampreys

The lampreys (family Petromyzonidae – meaning literally 'stone suckers') belong to a small but important group known as Agnatha – literally 'jawless' fishes – the most primitive of all living vertebrate animals. Thus they are quite distinct from all the other fish in the British Isles which have their upper jaws fixed closely to the skull and hinged lower jaws which oppose them. The lampreys, in contrast, have no lower jaw and the mouth is surrounded by a round sucker-like disc within which, in the adults, are strong, horny, rasping teeth. These vary in shape, size, position and number among the species, and are an important aid in identification. Lampreys occur in the temperate zones of both the northern and southern hemispheres. Fossils are available from the late Silurian and Devonian periods, some 450 million years ago.

Lampreys have several other very characteristic features. They are always eel-like in shape, but have neither paired fins nor scales. They have no bones – all the skeletal structures being made up of strong, but flexible, cartilage. There is only one nostril, situated on top of the head, just in front of the eyes – the latter rarely being functional or even visible in the young. The gills open directly to each side of the head (i.e. there is no gill cover or operculum) forming a row of seven gill pores behind each eye. Adult lampreys have two dorsal fins, which are often continuous with the elongated tail fin.

Most species of lamprey have a similar life cycle, which involves the migration of adults upstream into rivers to reach the spawning areas – normally stony or gravelly stretches of running water. There they spawn in pairs or groups, laying eggs in crude nests – shallow depressions previously created by lifting away small stones with their suckers. These stones surround and sometimes cover and protect the eggs, while the nest itself may often be

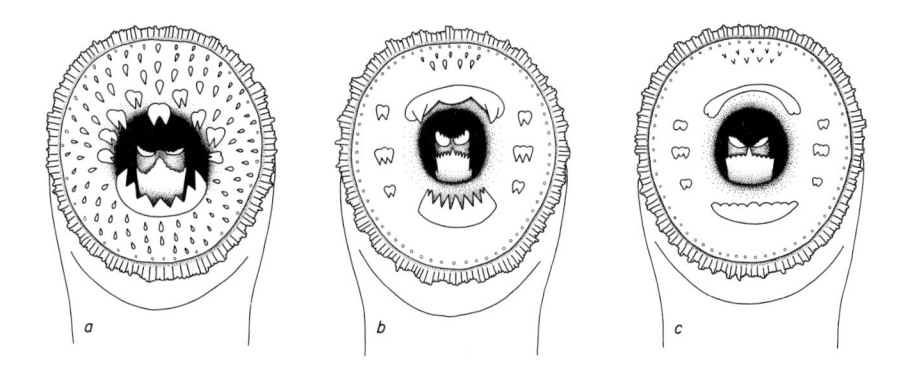

Fig. 26 Mouth structure of adult lampreys: a, Sea Lamprey; b, River Lamprey; c, Brook Lamprey (from Maitland 1972b).

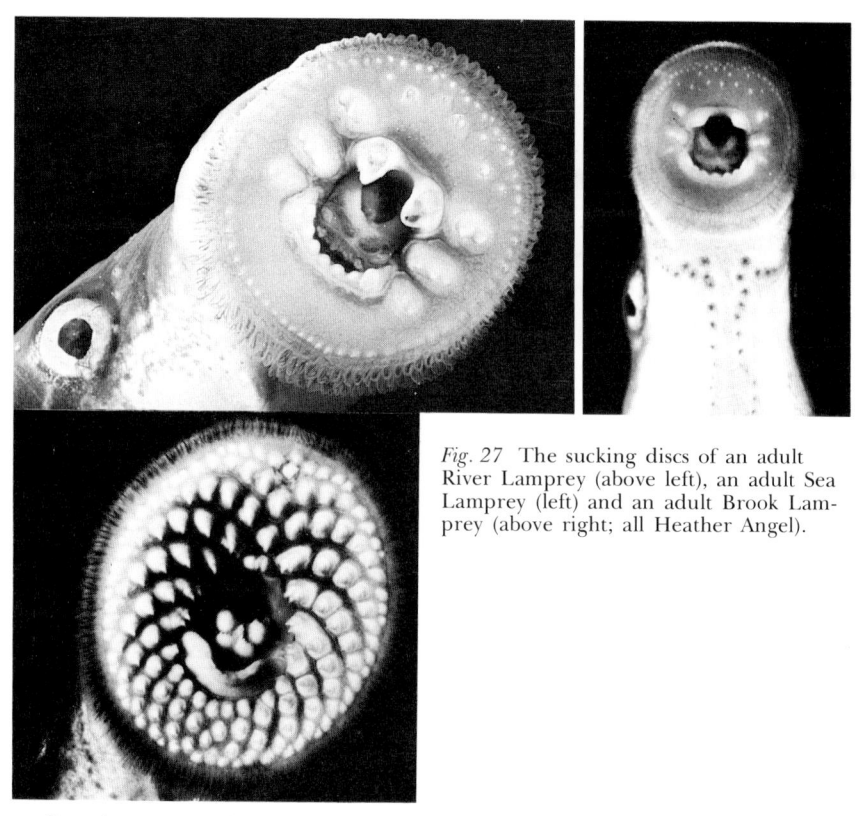

Fig. 27 The sucking discs of an adult River Lamprey (above left), an adult Sea Lamprey (left) and an adult Brook Lamprey (above right; all Heather Angel).

under a large stone, log or clump of vegetation. Frequently, however, the nest is in the open in shallow water and the spawning adults are very vulnerable to predators. After hatching, the young elongate larvae, known as ammocoetes, swim or are washed downstream by the current to areas of sandy silt in still water, where they burrow and spend the next few years in tunnels. They are blind, the sucker is incomplete and the teeth are undeveloped. These ammocoetes feed by creating a current which draws organic particles (coated with bacteria) and minute plants (such as diatoms) into the pharynx. There they become entwined in a slimy mucus string which is then swallowed by the larva.

The metamorphosis from larva to adult is a dramatic change which takes place in a relatively short time – usually a few weeks – after several years of larval development. The rim of the mouth (previously in the form of an oral hood) develops into a full sucker, inside which are the rasping teeth; the skin becomes much more silvery and opaque except over the eyes, where it clears to give the lamprey proper vision for the first time. The lampreys then migrate, usually downstream away from the nursery areas.

Some species of lamprey, such as the Brook Lamprey, never feed as adults – after metamorphosing they spawn and then die – but most are parasitic on various other fish, which they attack, either in large freshwater lakes and rivers or in the sea, where most of the adult life is spent. They attach to the sides of fish and rasp away the skin, eating it and the body fluids and muscle underneath. The prey may never recover from such an attack (especially if the body cavity is penetrated) and in some waters lampreys are serious pests of commercial fish stocks. The most famous example of this is in the Great Lakes of North America, where canalisation gave the Sea Lamprey access, for the first time, to the upper lakes. Various commercial fish stocks there became seriously depleted, particularly the American Lake Charr *Salvelinus namaycush*, whose populations collapsed in a dramatic way. On reaching sexual maturity, the adult lampreys migrate back to their spawning streams. All species seem to die after spawning.

Identification

The ease of identification of lampreys in the British Isles differs between the ammocoete larvae, which are difficult to identify, and the adults, which are much easier and usually distinguishable on size alone. The following key has proved useful.

1. Teeth absent, sucker incomplete. Eyes indistinct and opaque. Branchial groove present. Skin transparent, dull on the underside. **AMMOCOETE LARVAE, 2.**
   Teeth present, sucker incomplete. Eyes clearly visible. Branchial groove absent. Skin opaque, usually silvery white on underside. **ADULTS, 3.**

2. Obvious areas of dark pigment cells on oral hood and base of caudal fin. More than 60 trunk myomeres. **SEA LAMPREY**

   No distinct pigmentation on oral hood or caudal fin. Less than 60 trunk myomeres. **RIVER OR BROOK LAMPREY**

It is not possible under most circumstances to distinguish the larvae of these two species with certainty. Larvae more than 12cm in length are likely to be Brook Lampreys.

3. Teeth on the oral disc close together in radiating rows; supraoral dental plate with two large teeth. Back and sides with marbled pattern. Length at spawning usually 45–90cm. **SEA LAMPREY**

   Teeth on oral disc widely spaced and not in radiating rows; supraoral dental plate with, at most, one small tooth. Back and sides of uniform colour. Length at spawning less than 45cm. **4.**

4. Infraoral lamina with 7–10 cusps. Most teeth strong and sharp. Dorsal fins separate. Length at spawning usually 25–40cm and always more than 17cm. **RIVER LAMPREY**

   Infraoral lamina with 5–9 cusps. All teeth weak and blunt. Dorsal fins connected or almost so. Length at spawning usually 10–15cm and always less than 17cm. **BROOK LAMPREY**

Sea Lamprey *Petromyzon marinus* Linnaeus 1758
Marine Lamprey, Lamprey Eel

The Sea Lamprey is by far the largest of the British lampreys and may reach a length of 100cm and a weight of 2.5kg. The normal adult length is around 50cm. There are no angling records.

The body is very long and cylindrical, except at the tail where it is laterally

Table 7 Food of Sea Lamprey ammocoetes: diatom assemblages found free-living in midwater and in the guts of small (33–35mm) and large (70–72mm) ammocoete larvae in the Snyder-Deadhorse Creek, Michigan, United States (after Manion 1967), as percentage number.

Diatom	Midwater	Large Larvae	Small Larvae
Synedra	45.4	46.6	22.2
Fragilaria	24.3	8.7	14.4
Navicula	11.5	19.1	32.9
Gomphonema	6.1	11.9	13.0
Meridion	7.7	7.1	8.2
Cocconeis	3.7	3.7	6.0
Cymbella	0.6	1.1	1.3
Amphora	0.3	0.3	0.2
Achnanthes	0.0	0.0	0.4
Tabellaria	0.0	0.2	0.1
Surirella	0.2	0.3	0.1
Eunotia	0.0	0.1	0.1
Diploneis	0.1	0.3	0.3
Pinnularia	0.1	0.1	0.5
Amphipleura	0.0	0.0	0.1
Stauroneis	0.0	0.2	0.1
Cyclotella	0.0	0.3	0.1
Neidium	0.0	0.3	0.1
Hantzschia	0.0	0.0	0.2
Rhopalodia	0.0	0.0	0.2
NUMBER OF FISH EXAMINED	–	10	10

compressed. The overhung (inferior) mouth has the form of a large circular sucker frilled with extensions of the skin known as fimbriae. When closed, the mouth has the form of a slit, but when open for attachment it forms an oval sucking disc whose diameter is greater than that of the head or pharynx behind. Inside the mouth are numerous hard sharp teeth arranged in concentric rows. Above and around the tongue the teeth are especially large and bicuspid; below the tongue is a huge multiple transverse tooth with up to ten cusps. The tongue itself has several large complex teeth.

The eyes are of moderate size and positioned on each side of the head just behind the single nostril and in front of the seven pairs of gill openings. The two dorsal fins are distinctly separate in the young, but much closer in the adults. The first of these (the lower) originates just behind the middle of the body; the second (which is slightly higher) terminates just in front of the small tail fin. There are no paired fins. The skin is smooth and scaleless. There are 67–74 distinct muscle blocks (myomeres) along the body, but there is no lateral line and no vertebrae – the entire skeleton being cartilaginous.

At spawning time, the males develop a distinct ridge along the back, whilst the females have a pronounced fold of skin behind the vent.

Fig. 28 A Sea Lamprey (from Maitland 1972b).

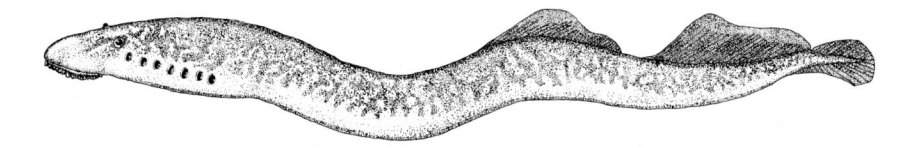

Colour varies greatly with age. The ammocoete larvae are dark greyish-brown above and a light grey below. Occasionally specimens are found which are lacking in pigment and these have a yellowish-gold appearance. Newly metamorphosed animals are a slaty grey-blue above changing gradually to a metallic bluish on the sides to a pale white on the belly. In adults, the main body colour is brownish-grey (paler ventrally) with extensive black mottling. The body colour lightens to a golden brown (almost orange) at spawning time.

The Sea Lamprey is a native anadromous species occurring over much of the Atlantic coastal area of western and northern Europe (from northern Norway to the western Mediterranean) and eastern North America, and in estuaries and easily accessible rivers in these regions. In the British Isles it is absent from northern rivers (i.e. it does not appear to occur north of the Great Glen of Scotland) and has become extinct in a number of southern ones due to pollution and engineering barriers. There are several land-locked populations in North America, but in the British Isles the only site where the species is known to feed in fresh water is Loch Lomond.

The ammocoetes are usually found in silty sands in running water, though in some places they may occur in silt and gravel beds in large lakes (e.g. Loch Lomond). Where suitable substrates are present they occur in streams and rivers upstream as far as the adults are able to migrate; they are stopped by high waterfalls or weirs, dams and severe pollution. The habitat occupied by the larvae of all lampreys seems to be very similar and indeed in the British Isles, Sea, River and Brook Lampreys may often be found together at the same sites.

Several research workers have measured the conditions at places occupied by the ammocoetes in an attempt to define their habitat precisely. The optimum particle size of the beds of sediment in which they occur is said to be 0.18–0.38mm, and to include clay, silt and sand fractions. Shade (which appears to be related to the types of micro-organisms on the surface) and water velocity appear to be important factors connected to the suitability of sites. Normally, suitable sites are found only in some parts of each river system and in some rivers there may be none at all. In British streams, most populations occur where the average stream gradients are 1.9–5.7m/km. Lampreys are rarely found where gradients exceed 7.8m/km. Within the stretches of suitable gradient, adequate sites are often found in conditions of slowing current, where deposition of sand and silt occurs (e.g. in eddies, backwaters, behind obstructions or at the edges of streams).

Relatively little is known about the precise habitats occupied by adult Sea Lampreys. Though adults are sometimes caught at sea, the precise conditions in which they occur have not been described, nor is it certain which fish are the main host species. Most adults found in fresh water are either migrating upstream to spawn or dying after spawning. Habitat seems only to be important in relation to their ability to get to the spawning beds. Just before spawning they may be found in calmer water above the spawning areas or below protecting obstructions, etc. The nests are normally built in areas of flowing shallow water among sand and gravel of varying particle size.

The Sea Lamprey usually spawns in late May or June in British rivers, when the water temperature reaches at least 15°C. Normally, males appear on the nesting sites first and are apparently highly attractive to females, possibly by the secretion of an olfactory sex attractant. The numbers of eggs produced by the females in some populations have been estimated by research workers and average about 172,000 per female. The eggs are small 0.80–1.25mm in diameter) and an opaque white colour when laid.

After hatching, larvae leave the nest and drift downstream, distributing themselves among suitable silt beds. The duration of larval life varies but averages about five years. The age of larvae has mainly been calculated from length frequency analysis, for there is no known method of ageing them. Metamorphosis to the adult form takes place between July and September and the process usually takes a few weeks. The time of the main migration downstream seems to vary from river to river and relatively little is known about them after they reach the sea, where they have been found in both shallow coastal and deep off-shore waters. The spawning migration in Europe usually takes place in April and May, when the adults start to migrate back into fresh water.

There is little evidence for any differences in the food or feeding habits of the ammocoete stage of the three British species of lamprey. All appear to feed from within their burrows on fine particulate matter, mainly micro-organisms, desmids and diatoms in particular. In addition, various unicellular animals including ciliates, euglenoids and rhizopods have been found in ammocoete guts in some numbers. The role of detritus as food is uncertain, but large amounts appear to be eaten during the summer months. Most of the food taken in by the larvae comes from superficial sediments in the vicinity of the larval burrows. The system of ciliated tracts in the pharynx, used as a means of transporting food on strands of mucus towards the intestine, is complex.

After metamorphosis and the downstream migration to the sea, the adults feed on fish there, but detailed evidence on their feeding habits is fragmentary (except in the specialised case of the purely freshwater populations in North America, which have been intensively studied). They seem to feed on a wide variety of marine and anadromous fishes, including Sturgeon, Herring, Salmon, Cod and Haddock. Salmon and Sea Trout entering rivers often bear fresh scars attributable to the attacks by this species.

The mortality rates in ammocoete populations are probably rather low and consistent throughout the larval period. Apart from the effects of fluctuating physical factors, especially during the embryonic period, it is known that the larvae are eaten by Eels, sticklebacks and other fish as well as several different birds (e.g. Herons). Losses may be particularly high during the dispersal from the nest to the ammocoete silt beds and a high mortality probably occurs at metamorphosis. Only a few parasites have been recorded from lampreys and nothing is known about their effect on the host.

There are a number of records of birds and mammals attacking adult Sea Lampreys, especially at spawning time. The species, though a pest in North America, is commercially important in a number of countries in Europe (e.g. Spain and Poland). Humans must be considered as the most serious threat to the species in view of these fisheries, the extensive use of lampricides in North America and the serious effects of pollution and barriers to upstream migration in many rivers.

The larvae live well in aquaria provided they have a suitable substrate in which to burrow and are fed regularly on fine particulate foods (e.g. a sus-

Table 8 Food of adult River Lampreys in Loch Lomond (after Maitland 1980), as percentage of food organisms showing evidence of attack, and in the Forth Estuary, Scotland, (after Maitland *et al.* 1984), as percentage occurrence in the guts of lampreys.

	Loch Lomond	Forth Estuary
Fish		
Brown Trout	6	–
Powan	45	–
Roach	5	–
Fish scales*	–	100
Fish bones	–	100
Fish skin	–	100
Fish muscle	–	100
NUMBER OF FISH EXAMINED	467	25

pension of yeast). However, because of the burrowing habit they are rarely seen. Eventually they metamorphose and start to swim freely about the tank and are easily visible. None of the adults caught in our rivers will feed, for they are all sexually mature and intent on spawning. However, they have very substantial food reserves at this time and will live for many months under suitable cool water conditions. They can easily be induced to spawn in aquaria if they are given suitable gravel and a reasonable artificial current.

River Lamprey *Lampetra fluviatilis* (Linnaeus 1784) Juneba, Lamper Eel, Lampern, Nine-eyed Eel, Nine Eyes, Seven Eyes, Stone Grig

Of the three British lampreys, the River Lamprey is intermediate in size between the large Sea Lamprey and the small Brook Lamprey. The average adult length is around 30cm with a corresponding weight of some 60g, but specimens over 40cm can be found and the unusual race in Loch Lomond (see below) is often less than 20cm. There are no angling records.

Young River Lampreys (ammocoetes) prior to metamorphosis are usually a dull grey-brown in colour and indistinguishable from the ammocoetes of Brook Lampreys. However, they metamorphose at a smaller size (9–12cm) when they become very silvery along the sides and belly darkening to grey on the back. During their feeding stage in the sea, they retain this silvery colour but as the time to return to fresh water to spawn draws near, they lose the silvery sheen and become darker all over. The back (which is not mottled like the Sea Lamprey) is a uniform dark olive to dark grey and this changes to a brownish-yellow on the sides gradually lightening ventrally. The fins are mainly dark brown. The large eye has a golden iris, flecked with brown.

The River Lamprey is easily distinguished from the Sea Lamprey on the basis of size and colouration, and the nature of the teeth inside the mouth is

Fig. 29 A River Lamprey (from Maitland 1972b).

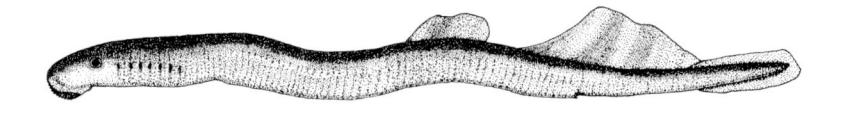

also quite different. However, the general body shape of the two species is similar. Thus the River Lamprey has a long streamlined eel-like body with two dorsal fins which are separate from each other, though the second is continuous with the tail fin. There are no paired fins and the seven gill openings on each side of the head are obvious and easily serve to distinguish this fish from the Eel, which has only one small opening on each side, just in front of the paired pectoral fins. The body is slimy and lampreys, like Eels, are difficult to hold when alive.

River Lampreys are found only in western Europe where they range from southern Norway to the western Mediterranean in coastal waters and estuaries and in accessible rivers. The species is mainly anadromous but there are a few land-locked non-migratory populations isolated from the sea in Finland, Russia and Scotland.

The ammocoetes of River Lampreys occur in silt beds in many rivers in the British Isles from the Great Glen southwards. Occasionally they are found in suitable silts in large lakes. They are absent from a number of rivers because of pollution or obstacles which the adults cannot surmount during the spawning migration – these may be natural waterfalls or artificial dams, etc. River Lampreys often occur in association with the other two British lampreys but occasionally (e.g. as in one small stream in the English Lake District) they may, for reasons unknown, occur as pure populations.

Once the type of silt bed in which the larvae are likely to occur has been recognised it is usually rather easy to determine whether or not ammocoetes are present. It is particularly simple for the fishery biologist who, armed with an electric fishing machine, can simply attract them from their burrows by turning on the current – once in the water near the electrodes the larvae are stunned and easily netted. However, the observant naturalist can simply lift some of the silt on to the river bank and, if present, larvae will soon be seen wriggling out of the silt and back into the river. Needless to say, having watched them all return to the river and burrow quickly into the silt there, the naturalist should see that the mud on the river bank is returned.

After metamorphosis, the young River Lampreys can still burrow but their main purpose seems to be to descend downstream to the sea, usually during spring. In the estuaries of our major rivers they can be found in some numbers and they spend 1–2 years here feeding on a variety of estuarine fish, but particularly Herring, Sprat and Flounders. They often inflict extensive damage on these hosts by rasping away large amounts of flesh from the back. The lampreys themselves are not attractive at this time, for they have a very bloated appearance due to the entire gut being full of blood and fish flesh.

The ancient Romans much esteemed lamprey, but because it has no scales it was forbidden to Jews, along with other scaleless fish. River Lampreys are of considerable commercial value in parts of Europe, and in both Sweden and Finland there are major fisheries for them using mainly basket traps during the upstream spawning migration. After capture, the lampreys are heavily salted to remove the slimy mucus and then grilled or smoked and taken to the fish markets, where they are bought as a delicacy. One of the authors has eaten them in several parts of Finland, and in some places they are so popular that there are grill houses which sell nothing but hot grilled River Lampreys, more or less the equivalent of fish and chip shops in Great Britain! Substantial fisheries did at one time exist for this species on some large British rivers (e.g. the Severn), and indeed it was from a surfeit of this species (possibly in the form of the lamprey pie that the citizens of Gloucester annually presented to the sovereign) that both Henry I and King John were supposed to have died! However, it is no longer of any importance in the British Isles.

Brook Lamprey *Lampetra planeri* (Bloch 1784) Mud Lamprey, Pride

The Brook Lamprey is the smallest of the British lampreys and matures at a length of some 13–15cm. Some populations are known where the adults may be much smaller than this, e.g. on Skye adults spawning in the small burns there may be less than 10cm. At some sites they may be larger. For instance in the River Endrick which flows into Loch Lomond adults may reach 16cm and occasionally even 17cm in length.

The larvae of this species are virtually indistinguishable from those of the River Lamprey except when nearing metamorphosis. The adults are small eel-like fishes with two dorsal fins, usually touching both each other and the tail fin. There are no paired fins. The eyes, which are covered by opaque skin in the larvae, are large and bright in the adults. Characteristically, the teeth are blunt and much less developed than those of the two predacious species. The maxillary plate is wide but there are no lower labial teeth; the mandibular plate has 5–9 blunt teeth.

The ammocoetes are semi-translucent and mainly dull grey-brown in colour, though a 'golden' form does appear from time to time, with very much reduced pigment. After metamorphosis they are much more silvery, especially along the sides and belly. The back remains dark grey-brown.

Lampetra planeri is a purely freshwater species occurring in streams and occasionally in lakes in north-west Europe, especially in basins associated with the North and Baltic Seas. It occurs over much of the British Isles, but is absent from most of Scotland north of the Great Glen, including the northern and all but a few of the Western Isles.

The ammocoete larvae, like those of other lampreys, occur in suitable silt beds, mainly in running water but sometimes in large numbers in silt banks in large lakes. Large larvae can be found in considerable numbers in Loch Ness for instance. The Brook Lamprey is the most abundant and widespread of the British lampreys and is often found in the absence of the other two species, for example above a pollution or physical barrier which prevents the anadromous species reaching that part of the river.

This species does not feed as an adult and so other fish evoke no response. The larvae have light-sensitive cells in the skin and are negatively phototactic, for the most part remaining sedentary within their burrows. However, if disturbed they will swim around rapidly until they find suitable silt in which to burrow. They are capable of completely disappearing into sand in just a

Fig. 30 A Brook Lamprey (from Maitland 1972b).

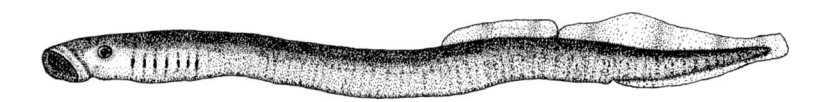

Fig. 31 A group of spawning Brook Lampreys (Heather Angel).

few seconds. As spawning time approaches the metamorphosed adults move out from the silts and start to migrate upstream (often in large numbers) till they reach suitable spawning grounds. These are areas of small stones and gravel in flowing water where the current is present but not too strong. Very characteristically they spawn at the lower ends of pools just where the water is starting to break up into a riffle.

The spawning season of this species in British rivers starts when the water temperatures reach 10–11°C. There is a clear relationship between water temperature and the number of animals at spawning sites, numbers declining as the temperature drops. The nest, which may be constructed by up to a dozen or more adults, is normally an oval depression about 20–40cm across and 2–10cm deep. The actual spawning act is similar to that of other lampreys, though the Brook Lamprey on account of its small size is less fecund, producing only about 1500 eggs per female. After hatching the young larvae leave the nest and distribute themselves by drifting downstream and burrow-

Table 9 Food of Brook Lamprey ammocoetes in the Highland Water, England (after Moore & Potter 1976), as percentage occurrence.

Stomach contents	Highland Water
Algae	
Achnanthes	13.8
Cymbella	8.9
Eunotia	0.9
Navicula	6.9
Nitzschia	4.6
Pinnularia	15.3
Synedra	4.5
Chlamydomonas	7.2
Detritus	+++
NUMBER OF FISH EXAMINED	?

ing in suitable areas of silty sand. By this time all the adults are dead, for none seems to survive long after spawning.

Lampreys are rarely seen by the general public except at spawning time when they become very obvious. Then, the otherwise cryptic and nocturnal creatures seem to 'throw caution to the winds' and move into shallow clear water in broad daylight to start their complex and fascinating communal nest building activities. Brook Lampreys are the species most often seen, and in April and May they can be readily observed in many thousands of streams in different parts of the country. At this time they are extremely vulnerable and are eaten by considerable numbers of Herons, gulls and sawbill ducks.

Larval life seems to vary considerably in different parts of Europe, but in the British Isles it is about 6–5 years. The larvae are some 3–5mm on hatching and about 12–15cm at metamorphosis, which takes place between July and September, usually simultaneously (i.e. within 3–4 weeks) in any one population. The adults usually migrate upstream after metamorphosis but continue to burrow like ammocoetes or hide under stones during the day. Since they no longer feed, they lose weight (and length) up to spawning time, when the females suddenly become heavier as the eggs take up water.

The larvae feed, like those of other lampreys, by filtering fine organic particles, especially diatoms and other algae as well as protozoans and detritus, from the surface of the silt around the mouths of the burrows in which they spend virtually all their larval years. The ciliary mechanism and the mucus threads involved in the collection of this food form a complex, but very efficient, feeding mechanism. The adults do not feed after metamorphosis.

This species is rarely considered to be of any commercial value. Occasionally anglers use the larvae and sometimes the adults as bait. The larvae will live well in aquaria and though they are not often seen there, since they spend all their time burrowed in the substrate, they can be induced to metamorphose and even spawn if the conditions are right. In this connection the species is an extremely useful one for school laboratory demonstrations.

8
Sturgeon

The sturgeons (Family Acipenseridae) are an extremely interesting and valuable family of primitive large fish which are quite distinct from all other living bony fish. Living sturgeons are similar to fossil ones found in rocks about 100 million years old. They occur only in the northern hemisphere, and the family contains about 25 species. The elongate body has no scales, but has five rows of characteristic bony plates – often an important aid to identification. These plates become smoother with age and in some cases disappear altogether in old fish. The head is covered with hard bony plates. The spinal column is upturned into the dorsal lobe of the tail fin (a condition known as heterocercal) and forms its main support. Internal ossification is incomplete and there is much cartilage instead of bone. The snout is elongate and projects well in front of the ventral mouth, anterior to which are four fleshy barbels. The exact form of these varies among the different species. The jaws are weak but the mouth itself is unusual in being a protrusible tube, adapted for its mode of feeding on bottom-living invertebrates in the sediment. The intestine has a characteristic spiral valve.

Many species are mainly marine, but all spawn in fresh water, usually in twos or threes in suitable stretches of large rivers or sometimes in lakes. The adults are often extremely large fish and not particularly efficient swimmers. The eggs are adhesive and stick to rocks, logs, etc. After hatching, the young migrate into their nursery areas – usually large lakes, the lower reaches of large rivers or, in many species, the sea. There, growth is very slow and it may be up to 15 years before maturity is reached and the fish migrate back to the spawning areas.

Sturgeons have been valued as commercial species for hundreds if not thousands, of years. Their large size, ease of capture and tasty flesh and eggs have led to the development of important fisheries in all parts of the world where they occur. However, their slow rate of growth has rendered them very susceptible to overfishing, and a number of populations has become extinct because of this. Others have disappeared due to major pollution in the lower reaches of rivers which they once frequented. The flesh is eaten fresh or smoked, and in some areas is dried. The roe of all species is used as caviar, prepared by removing the ovaries from ripe females, cleaning them carefully and then packing the eggs in brine. Isinglass is prepared from a material found in the swim bladder and is used for water-proofing, preserving and clearing wine.

Depleted stocks in some areas have led to the development of experimental fish farming with a number of species. The fact that several of these interbreed to produce hybrids has helped this industry (which is now quite successful in Eurasia) by allowing the selection of suitable stocks for farming.

Seven species occur in Europe, but only one of these is found in the British

Isles. Sturgeon are often exhibited in public aquaria and young Sterlets *Acipenser ruthenus* can be bought from time to time in aquarium shops; they make attractive and unusual fish in home aquaria. However, they eventually may grow too large for a normal aquarium and require a large tank or pond.

Common Sturgeon *Acipenser sturio* Linnaeus 1758
Baltic Sturgeon

This enormous fish is really only a vagrant to fresh waters in the British Isles since it never breeds here. It regularly grows to lengths of 1–2m and has been known to reach 3m or more, with weights well over 200kg. One of the largest specimens ever recorded was 3.45m in length and weighed 320kg. The females usually grow to a larger size than the males. There are no angling records.

This fish is virtually unmistakable for any other species found in British waters and has all the family features mentioned above. One of the most characteristic of these is the five rows of hard bony plates along the back and sides of the body, the row on the back having some 9–15 of these plates, the lateral rows about 24–36 plates and the rows on either side of the belly about 9–13 plates. The snout is long and pointed and bears two pairs of barbels hanging down midway between the anterior tip and the mouth. The latter can be partially projected during feeding as a short tube. The dorsal fin has 31–43 rays, the anal fin 22–26. The ventral fin carries a strong spine.

The body surface is soft and scaleless, protection being given by the rows of hard bony plates. The colour is usually a dark bluish-brown on the back lightening down the sides to a pale whitish-yellow ventrally.

The original distribution of this magnificent fish was much wider than at present. In the sea it occurred along the entire coastline of Europe from the North Cape to the Baltic, Mediterranean and Black Seas. A similar species occurs along the Atlantic coast of North America. The Common Sturgeon is no longer common, occurring only occasionally in our seas and breeding in only a few European rivers, notably the Gironde, Guadalquivir and lower Danube. Usually a few are caught each year off British coasts by commercial netsmen, but only very occasionally does one ever venture into fresh water here.

The adults favour the lower reaches of large rivers and the young remain there for some time before descending to the sea. Here, many of them apparently stay in the nearby coastal waters, though others obviously do move about for considerable distances to be caught many hundreds of miles away.

Fig. 32 A Common Sturgeon (from Maitland 1972b).

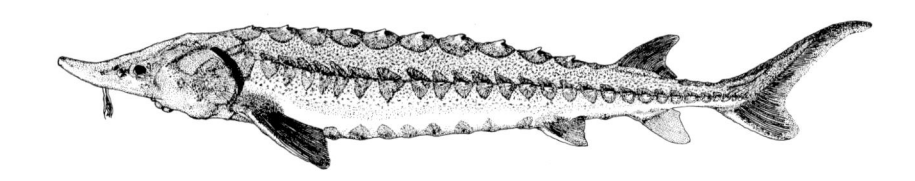

They appear to live mainly over soft sandy or muddy bottoms, to which their feeding mechanism is adapted.

After a number of years in the sea, the maturing adults stop feeding and move back to their natal rivers. They enter these in the early spring and move upstream to the spawning grounds, which take the form of pools where the water is deep (several metres) and flows over a gravel bed. After spawning the adult fish, in poor condition for they have not fed since leaving the sea, drop back down to salt water and start to feed again, many of them dying during the journey.

The actual spawning takes place in early summer and the dark-coloured sticky eggs, about 2–2.5mm in diameter, are laid over the gravel to which they adhere. Females can produce from 800,000–2,400,000 eggs each, depending on size. These hatch in about 3–6 days at water temperatures of some 12–18°C.

Growth is fairly rapid after hatching though it does depend to some extent on local conditions. Most fish reach at least 10cm by the end of their first year and many may reach twice this length. Some start to move down to the sea after this time but most others stay on for another one, sometimes two, years. In the sea growth is steady and fish are usually at least a metre in length when they first start to mature at about 8–12 years of age.

The young Sturgeon feed mainly on bottom invertebrates in their rivers, especially midge larvae and other insects, worms, crustaceans and molluscs. In the sea they feed on the larger worms (including polychaetes), crustaceans and molluscs there, but also take some fish – especially sand-eels and gobies.

The Sturgeon is of little value in the British Isles. By tradition, any caught are supposed to be offered to the reigning monarch but a number of years ago the Comptroller of Her Majesty's Household informed one of the authors that they are rarely accepted. Occasionally they appear on fishmongers' slabs for curiosity value. In July 1933 an angler fishing for Salmon in the River Towy in Wales foul-hooked a huge Sturgeon. The fish eventually beached itself. It was 2.79m in length, 1.49m in girth and weighed 196kg. It was a female and contained 36.3kg of caviar – but it was not accepted by the Royal Household.

On the continent of Europe, however, it is another matter – the flesh of the Sturgeon is highly prized there and even more so its roe, which is processed to make caviar, an extremely valuable commodity supplied to high-class restaurants all over the world. Like lampreys and catfish, sturgeon (including caviar) was at one time banned from the Jewish diet as being 'unclean' because it did not have any scales. The pursuit of this and other species of sturgeon for their valuable roes has been one of the main reasons for the decline in the numbers of all species in recent years. However, the development of sturgeon farms in France and elsewhere, though primarily for the commercial production of caviar, may help in the conservation of this species if the farms are managed wisely. Such farms may help in two ways; firstly by reducing the need to catch many fish from the wild; secondly, by releasing part of the young stock they obtain from wild parents back into the wild again.

9

Shads

The family Clupeidae, many of which are commonly known as herrings and shads, is a large group of pelagic fishes that are found in seas all over the world except the Antarctic. Most species are marine, but some are anadromous and a few live permanently in fresh waters. There are several genera with a total of about 200 species.

Members of the family are mainly small to medium sized fishes with a streamlined laterally compressed body covered by large deciduous, circular, cycloid scales. Unusually, the circuli are arched across the scale rather than arranged in concentric rings as in most cycloid scales. The ventral edge of the belly has characteristic scute-like scales, forming a toothed edge when viewed in profile. The head has large eyes with fleshy eyelids. The mouth is usually terminal and teeth are either small or absent. The many gill rakers lining the back of the pharynx are long and thin and their number is an important character in identification. There is no lateral line.

Most Clupeidae are pelagic in habit and swim around in large shoals near the surface. These may reach enormous numbers, sometimes millions of individual fish. The principal foods of these shoals are the abundant masses of zooplankton which thrive in the richer parts of the sea. The comb-like gill rakers help to separate the plankton from the water – the former being swallowed, the latter passing out through the gills. The fish themselves form a major source of food for larger fish and for enormous seabird colonies in parts of the world.

The large size of the shoals, and the ease with which they may be captured, make this one of the most important commercial families of fish in the world.

Fig. 33 Gills of the shads: a, Allis Shad; b, Twaite Shad (from Maitland 1972b).

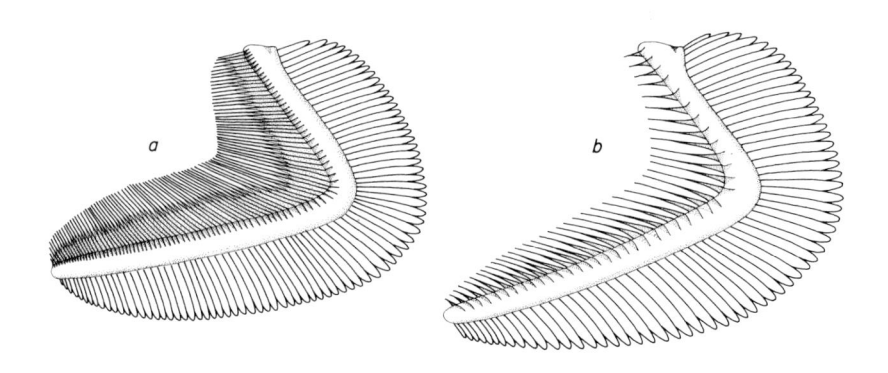

The total world catch is about 30% by weight of all fish caught by humans. The flesh is particularly rich in fats and oils. Recent research has indicated that these oils (and those of other fish) are polyunsaturated and therefore not only healthier as human food, but may actually counteract the ill effects of saturated fats obtained from eating other animals. Fish which cannot be marketed fresh are frozen, pickled or smoked. Fish which are too small for individual consumption are processed to make fish meal or oil.

European Clupeidae are mainly marine, but a few species are found in fresh water throughout their lives, and a number of others enter fresh water either casually or regularly at some time. Only two species in the British Isles can be considered in the latter category.

Identification

The two species of shad found in the British Isles have various distinguishing characteristics which are incorporated in the following key:

1. Main longitudinal row of lateral scales numbering more than 70. More than 60 gill rakers on the first gill arch. **ALLIS SHAD**

   Main longitudinal row of lateral scales numbering less than 70. Less than 60 gill rakers on the first gill arch. **TWAITE SHAD**

Allis Shad *Alosa alosa* (Linnaeus 1758)
Ale Wife, Chad, King of the Herring, May Fish, Shad

This species may be distinguished from the Twaite Shad by the characters given in the above key. This is the larger of the two British shad and commonly grows to a length of about 30–50cm, exceptionally to some 70cm. The present British rod-caught record weighed 2.166kg and was caught off Chesil Beach in Dorset in 1977. Their is no Irish record.This species is now protected in Great Britain under the Wildlife and Countryside Act.

Allis Shad, like most other members of the family, are deep-bodied laterally compressed streamlined fishes. Characteristically they have a well-developed median notch in the upper jaw (into which the lower jaw fits neatly), no vomerine teeth and more than 70 scales laterally. There is no lateral line. The jaws are equal in length and the gill covers have characteristic radiating stri-

Fig. 34 An Allis Shad (from Maitland 1972b).

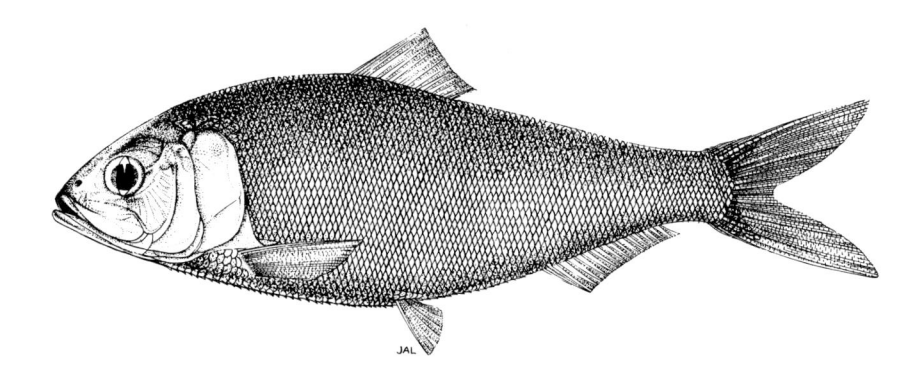

ations on them. The eye has a curious membrane across the front and rear portions. The scales are large and fragile, readily coming away from the fish during handling. These scales are very characteristic of the genus and the radii are transverse instead of radiating from some central focus as in most other fish.

There is a single short dorsal fin with 18–21 rays and medium-sized pectoral, pelvic and anal fins. The caudal fin is well developed and characteristically some groups of scales from the caudal area extend on to it. There are normally 90–120 gill rakers on the first gill arch and this is probably the most specific character to look for, especially when trying to identify young fish.

This fish is found along the coasts of western Europe from southern Norway to Spain and in the Mediterranean eastwards to northern Italy. It occurs mainly in shallow coastal waters and estuaries but during the spawning migration it penetrates the lower reaches of large rivers. It has suffered considerably from pollution, overfishing and river obstructions and is now a rare fish over most of its range.

Mature fish run up from the estuaries into rivers during late spring, thus giving it the name of May Fish in some areas. In some of the larger European rivers it has been known to ascend upstream for several hundred kilometres. Shoals of fish accumulate in suitable pools and spawning takes place there at night. Afterwards the spent adults drop downstream to the sea again, many of them to die there.

The clear eggs (about 4.4mm in diameter) fall to the bottom and remain there in crevices until they hatch some 4–8 days later. The fry are about 10mm on hatching but rapidly grow to 8–14cm after one year. By this time many of them have descended to the sea and the remainder follow during their second year. The adults mature after 3–4 years at about 30–40cm when they start the spawning migration again.

The food of the young fish is mainly bottom-living river invertebrates, especially midge larvae and crustaceans. The adults, feeding in salt water, also rely largely on invertebrates especially planktonic crustaceans (e.g. calanoids and euphausids), but also to some extent on small fish.

Though this fish is highly esteemed for the table in several countries there are few fisheries for it nowadays, largely because it is so rare. However, opinions on its culinary virtues are not universally high and it has been described as a plebeian fish excluded from all 'reputable banquets', and (in Northern Ireland) as the 'bony horseman'. Like many large anadromous species it is particularly vulnerable during the spawning migration both to local fisheries and to the hazards of pollution and obstructions so common now in the large European rivers in which the species was once abundant. It is finally being given special protection in several countries in Europe, and hopefully may recover in at least parts of its former range.

Twaite Shad *Alosa fallax* (Lacepede 1803)
Bony Horseman, Chad, Goureen, Herring Shad, Killarney Shad, May Fish, Queen of the Herring, Shad

Though both are large herring-like fishes, the Twaite Shad is normally rather smaller than the Allis Shad, adult fish usually averaging some 25–40cm with a maximum of about 55cm. The British rod-caught record stands at 1.417kg for two fish – one caught in 1949 near Deal in Kent and the other in 1954 near Torbay in Devon. The most recent notable catch was a fish of 1.247kg caught in 1978 at Garlieston in the Solway Firth. The Irish record stands at 0.907kg for a fish caught near St Mullins in 1985.

The main physical difference between the two British Shad is indicated in the above key. Like the Allis Shad, the Twaite Shad has a transparent membrane across the front and rear parts of the eye, no vomerine teeth and a marked median notch in the upper jaw into which the lower jaw fits, but there are only about 40–60 rakers on the first gill arch and less than 70 lateral scales. The gill covers have a characteristic radial sculpture and, like most other members of the family, the body is rather flattened laterally. There is no lateral line.

The rather short dorsal fin has 18–21 rays, whilst the anal fin has 19–23. There are some 55–59 vertebrae and the ventral scales are characteristically keeled – especially in the region behind the pelvic fins. In colour, the Twaite Shad is usually a dark steely blue along the back which grades into a silver-yellow on the sides and then into a silvery white on the belly. There are usually about 5–10 round dark spots on each side of the back, starting just behind the head and decreasing in size posteriorly.

The Twaite Shad occurs along most of the west coast of Europe, from southern Norway to the eastern Mediterranean Sea and in the lower reaches of the large accessible rivers along these coasts. There are a number of extremely interesting non-migratory populations of this fish in a few of the larger European lakes such as Como, Garda, Iseo, Lugano and Maggiore. In the British Isles, Lough Leane (Killarney) has such a population, which appears to have been isolated here for thousands of years. It is known as the Goureen and was given subspecific recognition by Regan in 1916 as *Alosa fallax killarnensis*. This fish is rather smaller than its marine-based relatives and rarely grows longer than about 25cm.

One of the authors, when hiring a boat to go trout fishing on Lough Leane in Killarney, was surprised to discover that the boat hirers – a family long associated with angling on the lough – did not know about the presence of the Goureen. A similar situation can be encountered in parts of Scotland concerning Arctic Charr, also a shy fish with cryptic habits.

Fig. 35 Twaite Shad (from Maitland 1972b).

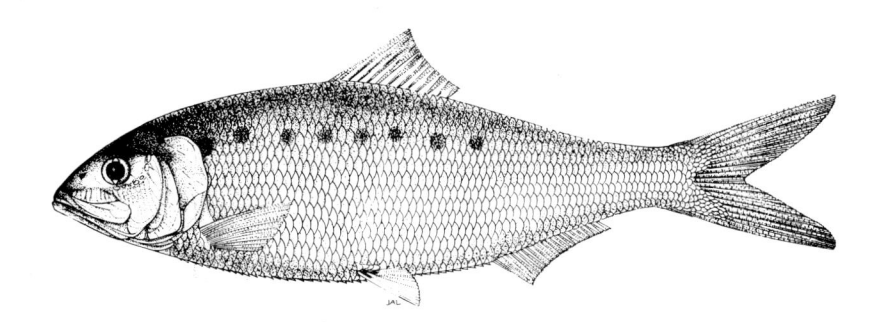

With the exception of these isolated populations in large lakes, the normal habitat of this species is the sea – especially coastal waters off the south-west coast of northern Europe. It has been found at depths down to 100m but it normally occurs in water much shallower than this. The eggs and young are found in the lower reaches of large slow-flowing unpolluted rivers where there is easy access from the sea.

At maturity, the adult fish stop feeding and gather in the estuaries of these rivers in early summer (April and May), thereafter moving upstream to spawn in mid-June in the stretches above the influence of high tide. Usually the males move upstream first, but they are soon joined by the females and spawning takes place in flowing water over stones and gravel among which the eggs sink. The females, depending on their individual size, each produce about 75,000–200,000 eggs. The eggs take about 4–6 days to hatch, and the young drop quickly downstream in the current to the quieter waters of the upper estuary where they start to feed and grow. Small Shad, less than a year old, are found on the screens of the power-stations in the Severn Estuary. The non-migratory populations seem to spawn in or in the vicinity of large rivers entering the lakes, and the young soon find their way into the lake.

Growth in the first year is fairly rapid and they can reach some 5cm in 6 months and 10–15cm after one year. Thereafter, growth is steady and most fish reach about 20–25cm after 2 years and 25–30cm after 3 years. The males start to mature after 3 years and are therefore spawning with older and larger females at first. The females themselves do not start to mature until they are about 5 years old. Full size is usually reached at 8–10 years of age and some fish may live (and grow slowly) for several years beyond this.

The young fish feed mainly on invertebrates, especially estuarine zooplankton, but as they grow they take larger crustaceans of various types (e.g. shrimps and mysids) and also small fish. Adults feed to an appreciable extent on other fish, especially the young of other members of their own family such as Sprat and Herring.

Though it is now much less common than formerly, the species is still fished commercially in some parts of Europe with various types of nets, especially in estuaries during the start of the spawning migration. Some of the catch is smoked before sale. The species is also angled for seasonally in some rivers which still have a reasonable run of fish (e.g. the Rivers Wye and Severn) where it is usually taken on a small metal spoon. A fish of 450g is considered a good specimen. The Goureen is sometimes taken by rod and line in Lough Leane.

10

Salmon, Trout and Charr

The Salmonidae is one of the world's best known families of fish. Although originating in the northern temperate zones of Europe, Asia and North America, their palatability, sporting value and adaptability have resulted in the establishment of members of the family in highland areas of tropical countries where the rivers are sufficiently cool, and in temperate lands in the southern hemisphere. Even where they cannot exist, their products, such as tinned, frozen and smoked salmon – on which major industries may be based – are familiar items.

The life histories of both Atlantic (*Salmo*) and Pacific (*Oncorhynchus*) Salmon have caught the popular imagination – the struggle up-river in the face of all manner of predators and physical barriers, the negotiation of high waterfalls to spawn in the natal stream and finally, in the great majority of cases, death due to exhaustion from their efforts. Following this sacrifice, the return migration of the vulnerable offspring downstream to the ocean begins the cycle all over again.

One of the diagnostic physical features of the Salmonidae is the small fleshy adipose fin situated between the dorsal fin and the tail (though a few other families of fish also have such a fin). Spots, large and small, black, red or yellow are also a characteristic feature, while juvenile fish usually bear 'parr marks' in the form of regular dark blotches ('thumb prints') along their sides.

All the Salmonidae are predatory, feeding on invertebrates and fish, and there is usually a change of emphasis from one type of food to another as the individual grows. Several members of the family are long-lived and there are records of wild Brown Trout *Salmo trutta* and Arctic and Brook Charr *Salvelinus alpinus* and *S. fontinalis* living for more than 22 and 24 years respectively. It is quite normal to find individuals of the Lake Charr *Salvelinus namaycush* of northern North America over 35 years of age.

All the Salmonidae spawn in fresh water, so no member of the family is entirely marine, although a number of species and races spend most of their lives at sea. Some species consist of both anadromous and wholly freshwater (so-called land-locked) races.

All species spawn during the coolest period of the year, usually in running water but sometimes in relatively still water in lakes; in either case they require a clean silt-free bottom for the survival of their eggs and larval stages (alevins). In most stream spawners, a nest – known as a redd – is hollowed out in the gravel by the female, into which her eggs are laid and simultaneously fertilised by the male. The female then fills in the redd, covering the eggs. A feature of the anadromous Salmonidae are 'precocious' male juveniles. These small fish mature before they have reached their sea-going stage and are capable of fertilising the eggs of returned fully grown adult females. With Pacific Salmon, spawning is almost always followed by the

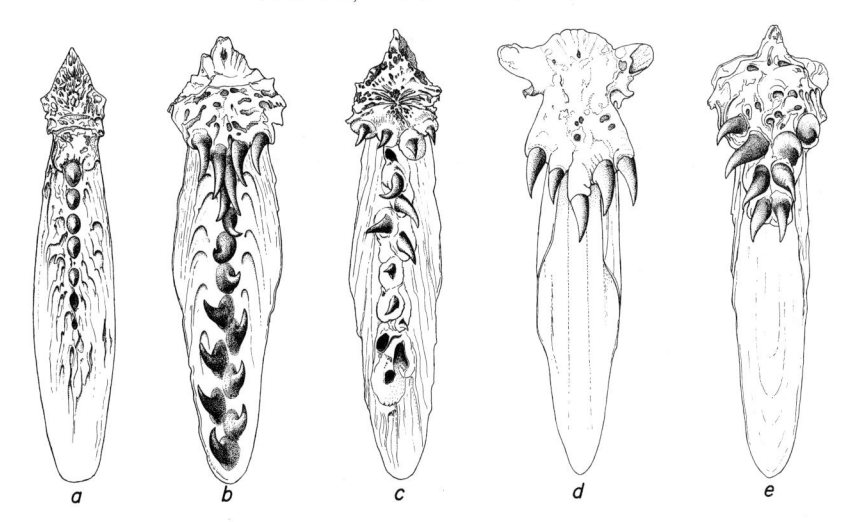

Fig. 36 Vomer bones from adult salmon family: a, Atlantic Salmon; b, Brown Trout; c, Rainbow Trout; d, Arctic Charr; e, Brook Charr (from Maitland 1972b).

death of the adults; with Atlantic Salmon too, almost all the males and the great majority of the females die.

Because of the social and commercial value of salmonids, much scientific research has been carried out on their biology, physiology and behaviour, particularly in relation to their ability to live in both salt and fresh water. In recent years the rapid development of salmon ranching and farming as an important industry has led to increased research on their physiology and genetics.

Identification

The salmonids are widely distributed in clean waters in the British Isles and, because all the species are so similar, their identification is not always easy – especially with small specimens. Experience has shown the authors that many people, including experienced anglers, often have difficulty in identifying these fish accurately. The following key has selected the most important characters of each species and developed them into a dichotomous system to help their accurate identification.

1. More than 12 branched rays in anal fin, which is longer than it is high. Vomer bone long and narrow with weak teeth. **PINK SALMON**

   Less than 12 branched rays in anal fin, which is higher than it is long. **2.**

2. More than 160 scales along lateral line. Vomerine teeth confined to head of vomer, whose shaft is short and toothless. **3.**

   Less than 150 scales along lateral line. Vomerine teeth not confined to head of vomer, whose shaft is long with two rows of teeth. **4.**

3. Hyoid teeth present; 7–13 gill rakers on upper limb of arch. Back mainly uniformly coloured. No black stripe on anal fin.
   ARCTIC CHARR

Hyoid teeth absent; 4–7 gill rakers on upper limb of arch. Back with a strongly marked marbled pattern (vermiculated). Black stripe present on anal fin. **BROOK CHARR**

4(2). More than 160 scales along lateral line. No red spots on body, but a broad pink or red band present along either side. Numerous black spots on body and fins, especially on adipose and tail fins.
RAINBOW TROUT

Less than 130 scales along lateral line. Body may be completely silver but normally has many black and some red spots present; never a broad red band along either side. Black spots on adipose and caudal fins ill-defined or absent. **5.**

5. Length usually less than 15cm. Parr marks (a single line of dark lateral blotches) usually present, or body completely silvery. Tail fin distinctly forked. Juveniles **6.**

   Length usually more than 15cm. Parr marks usually absent (though the body may be well spotted). Tail fin indistinctly or not forked. Adults **9.**

6. Parr marks more or less distinct along sides; numerous spots present, mostly black but some red. Fry & Parr **7.**

   Parr marks indistinct or absent; body almost completely silvery, though a few black spots may be present. Smolts **8.**

7. Parr marks 10–12. A few faint black spots on dorsal fin which has 10–12 rays. Operculum with less than 3 spots. Adipose fin normally brown. Caudal peduncle thin; tail fin with a deep fork and pointed ends. Pectoral fins large, when stretched back often reaching behind level of origin of dorsal fin. Maxilla reaching to about middle of eye.
ATLANTIC SALMON

   Parr marks 9–10. Many definite black spots on dorsal fin, which has 8–10 rays. Operculum with more than 3 black spots. Adipose fin normally red. Caudal peduncle thick; tail fin with a shallow fork and rounded ends. Pectoral fins short, when stretched back not behind level of origin of dorsal fin. Maxilla reaching to mid-way between pupil and rear of eye. **TROUT**

8(6). Dorsal fin with 10–12 rays, 10–13 scales between adipose fin and lateral line. Operculum with less than 3 spots. Caudal peduncle thin; tail fin with deep fork. Pectoral fins large. **ATLANTIC SALMON**

   Dorsal fin with 8–10 rays, 13–16 scales between adipose fin and lateral line. Operculum with more than 3 spots. Caudal peduncle thick; tail fin with shallow fork. Pectoral fins normal. **TROUT**

9(5). Head of vomer bone toothless, shaft poorly toothed with deciduous teeth. Dorsal fin with 10–12 rays, 10–13 scales between adipose fin and lateral line. When pressed to body, last ray of anal fin usually extends about as far as posteriorly as first ray. **ATLANTIC SALMON**

   Head of vomer toothed, shaft also well toothed with persistent teeth. Dorsal fin with 8–10 rays, 13–16 scales between adipose fin and lateral line. When pressed to body, last ray of anal fin does not extend as far posteriorly as first ray. **TROUT**

Fig. 37 An Atlantic Salmon (from Maitland 1972b).

Atlantic Salmon *Salmo salar* Linnaeus 1758 Braddan, Grilse, Springer

The Atlantic Salmon is the largest of our Salmonidae, but its adult size is very variable. Adults returning to fresh water can be as small as 40cm in length, weighing only about 0.9kg, or as large as 125cm and 22.7kg. However, most fish are around 60–75cm and 2.7–4.5kg. The British rod-caught record is for the famous fish caught in 1922 by Miss G. W. Ballantine in the River Tay in Scotland. This magnificent fish weighed 29.029kg. The Irish record is 25.855kg (a fish caught in 1874 on the River Suir) and the world record, for a Salmon caught in Norway in 1925, is 35.89kg.

Sometimes there is confusion between smaller specimens of this species and of Sea Trout, but in Salmon, unlike trout, the maxillary bone usually reaches to about the middle of the eye, occasionally to the hind edge in large specimens; in Trout it reaches well beyond. Also, unlike trout, the head of the vomer bone bears no teeth and the shaft only a few deciduous ones in a single row.

The Salmon has well developed teeth on both upper and lower jaws. The dorsal fin has 10–12 branched rays and there are 8–10 major rays in the anal fin. When this fin is pressed to the body its last ray usually extends at least as far posteriorly as the first ray (with Trout it is the first ray that extends furthest back). There is a distinct bony flesh-covered axillary process at the base of each pelvic fin. There are usually some 15–20 gill rakers and 11 or 12 branchiostegal rays. The body is well covered with cycloid scales, which number 109–130 along the lateral line and 10–13 between the adipose fin and the lateral line. Trout scales are smaller, so they always have a larger number in this position. There are usually some 40–74 pyloric caecae and 57–61 vertebrae.

Occasionally, large silver fish, taken along with adult Salmon, have characteristics between Salmon and trout. These are probably natural hybrids, a small proportion of which occur in many wild populations, for instance it has been shown that there are about 4% in the Lough Neagh (River Bann) system in Northern Ireland. Hybrids that behave like Brown Trout and do not go to sea resemble the latter closely and are hard to identify.

As male, or 'cock' Salmon mature, a pronounced hook, or 'kype', develops on the lower jaw, the tip of which becomes upturned and eventually fits into a corresponding hollow in the upper jaw when the mouth is shut, while the

Fig. 38 Heads of a typical adult female (above) and male (below) Atlantic Salmon near spawning time (Niall Campbell).

whole skull elongates considerably. At this time too, the scales erode, become embedded in the skin and are difficult to remove.

Adult Salmon vary considerably in general shape and they can be short and

Table 10 Food of adult Atlantic Salmon at sea off Norway (after Hansen & Pethon 1985), as percentage occurrence.

Stomach contents	Sea off Norway
Molluscs	
Squid (*Gonatus*)	7.1
Polychaetes	0.7
Crustaceans	
Euphausids	33.8
Amphipods	13.0
Hymenodora	3.9
Various remains	5.2
Fish	
Herring	3.3
Capelin	2.0
Pearl-sides	1.3
Benthosema	11.0
Notoscopelus	0.7
Protomyctophum	0.7
Lantern Fish	0.7
Various Lantern fish	31.8
Notolepis	0.7
Blue Whiting	1.3
Sand eels	0.7
Catfish fry	0.7
Fish remains	30.5
NUMBER OF FISH EXAMINED	154

deep or quite slender. Traditionally some river systems have one type and some the other. The short, thick-set fish is supposed by anglers to be the ideal and it is not uncommon to hear a local angler claim that the lean fish he has just landed is from another, usually neighbouring (and 'inferior') river, and, of course, vice versa!

When fresh-run from the sea both sexes are similar in colour with bright silvery sides and a silvery white belly, though the back may range from brown, through olive-green to dark blue. Previously spawned fish may be quite heavily spotted, especially on the gill covers. As they ripen for spawning in fresh water the pristine 'bar of silver' appearance fades to a bronze-pink. Cock fish colour up considerably, red trout-like spots appearing on the sides over a mottled background of browns, reds and purple – earning it such names as 'Tartan Fish' or 'Kipper'. Their appearance at this stage, including the kype and elongated head, is similar to that of a large old cock Trout, either Brown or Sea, and before advances in scale reading made it possible (i.e. up to the early years of this century), the scales of Salmon and Trout could not be distinguished, and frequent mistakes were made in identification. Even today, similar mistakes can be made before the scales have been examined.

Female, or 'hen', fish also develop spots and a small neat kype and become a dull leaden colour under a purple sheen, again not unlike larger hen Sea Trout.

Fish that survive spawning, 'kelts', the great majority of which are hen fish, become silvery again with black or dark blue backs. Because of their silvery appearance, well-mended kelts are frequently mistaken for fresh-run fish by inexperienced anglers, who are not watching for such signs as the presence of gill maggots in fresh and the (usually) protruding vent in spent fish. However, the distinction is normally clear and looking down on the back of a

Salmon should remove all doubt: with a fresh-run fish the head tapers away from the wide shoulders, with a kelt the back of the head is the widest part of the body.

Salmon fry, between the larval (alevin) and parr stages are difficult to distinguish from Trout of the same size. However, there is one characteristic which becomes more pronounced as the fish grow – the very broad rounded shape of the pectoral fins in the Salmon, which is supposed to give a greater ability than Trout in maintaining themselves in very swift water by 'holding on' to the bottom.

The young Salmon, parr, in fresh water are quite different from the adults and were at one time described as a different species. Characteristically they have a row of 8–12 dark grey to blue thumb-prints or parr marks along the body. Between each of these is a red spot. There may also be a sprinkling of small black or brown spots over the back and the sides and a few red spots below the lateral line. The leading edge of the pectoral and pelvic fins may be white and the adipose fin a leaden colour, rarely appearing brownish or red as in trout.

As the time for their seaward migration approaches, the parr undergo a process of 'smoltification', when the parr marks become masked by a coating of silvery material in the epidermis and the back becomes a brown or greenish-brown. The scales are very easily shed at this time.

The flesh of the young parr and smolts is white but that of fresh-run adults is pink-red ('salmon coloured') and very palatable. As the fish ripens in fresh water both qualities fade away and the flesh of kelts is pale pink to champagne coloured and tasteless. Often it remains like this, so that even mended kelts and fish returning for a second spawning have dull flesh.

The Atlantic Salmon, as its common name implies, is an anadromous species of the north Atlantic and is widely distributed along the Atlantic seaboards of northern Europe and North America, running into most of the suitable clean rivers. There is one natural population in southern Greenland and many in Iceland as well as in rivers flowing into the White and Baltic Seas. It ranges as far south as the north of Portugal in Europe and the northern Atlantic coast of the USA in North America. Some non-migratory (landlocked) populations occur naturally in North America and Scandinavia and there are also similar populations in two lakes in New Zealand, where the species has been introduced from the British Isles and North America. It has also been successfully established in South America, in several Patagonian rivers.

In the British Isles, Salmon are found in nearly all suitable waters where they are not excluded by physical barriers or pollution, and where there are adequate spawning and nursery areas to provide sufficient recruitment of young fish to maintain the population. In suitable habitats, both the young freshwater stages and the returning adults can be abundant. However, due to commercial exploitation (both legal and illegal) in the open sea, off the coasts and in the estuaries and rivers, possibly coupled with an outbreak of disease or intense predator pressure, the number of adults surviving to reach their natal spawning stream may be drastically reduced at times.

The full life cycle of the Salmon has been known for a long time, including the relationship between sea-going smolts and returned adults. As far back as 1653, Isaac Walton referred to the experimental marking of smolts, the re-

Fig. 39 An extreme example of an Atlantic Salmon kelt. This fish was caught in Loch Einich (River Spey system) in August and had probably spawned the previous November. It was alive when captured and measured 63cm in length but weighed only just over 1kg (Fisher Photos).

sults of which he claimed proved that they grew into Salmon and returned to the river in which they were marked. In the British Isles, Salmon normally spawn between late October and early January – although earlier and later instances of spawning are regularly reported. Peak spawning time is usually in November.

After reaching the spawning grounds, the hen fish selects an area of suitably sized gravel or smallish stones in swiftly flowing, usually shallow, water in which to cut her nest or redd. Because of these special requirements for the siting of redds, most spawning takes place in the upper reaches of rivers and their tributaries, but in pollution free, swift flowing rivers, spawning may take place from just above the upper tidal reaches (sometimes even below) all the way upstream, wherever the bed is suitable.

The spawning behaviour of Salmon is well documented. The hen fish, accompanied by the local, dominant, cock fish, cuts out a redd by turning on her side and flexing her body and tail up and down in short bursts of powerful activity. The upwards stroke creates a sucking action lifting the gravel and stones off the bottom to be carried downstream by the current. The larger the hen fish the larger are the stones which are displaced and the deeper the redd. Even a small fish will excavate a hollow 15–20cm deep. During this activity she periodically tests the depth of the depression with an erected anal fin until she is satisfied. Then, stimulated by the cock fish nudging and vibrating beside her, she releases her eggs which drop into the depression, being fertilised at the same time by the sperm released by the male. A high rate of fertilisation is normal. The redd is then filled in by the female – usually by her cutting another depression just upstream, where the spawning act is repeated. Several redds may be excavated, then covered, and a large and conspicuous area of clean-looking gravel may be turned over before spawning has been completed.

During all this activity the cock fish regularly chases away all intruders, including other cock fish as well as Salmon parr and small Trout, which gather to feed on any eggs which may be washed downstream. Spawning often takes place in water so shallow that the backs of the fish are exposed throughout the whole operation and much splashing can be seen by observers from the bank. All this strenuous activity may take place in water temperatures of less than 1°C, a fact that is of great interest to physiologists, because most cold-blooded animals are inactive at such temperatures. Precociously mature Salmon parr may also be in attendance, releasing their sperm at the same time as the adult cock fish and fertilising some of the eggs. At the same time they eat any eggs that fail to reach the redd. Most of these parr smolt the following spring, but a small proportion may stay on in fresh water as 'adult' parr.

There have been occasional reports of ripe female parr, in Great Britain, France and in Spain, but such fish are usually very uncommon.

After spawning, the hen fish drop downstream into quieter deeper waters and a small proportion of them (the number varying from river to river) may eventually reach the sea to begin feeding again after their long fast and eventually become 'mended kelts'. These may return to spawn some time later, occasionally coming upstream the following summer, but some spend a further winter at sea before returning to fresh water. In exceptional cases a hen fish may survive to spawn several times. However, usually she never fully regains her original maiden condition and she may often be leaner and lighter in weight at subsequent spawnings. Previous spawners make little contribution to the stock in a river and may represent as little as 0.5–3.0% of the season's run in eastern Scottish rivers. This figure may be higher in some shorter west-coast rivers. In Canada, multiple spawners are much more common.

The cock fish usually remain in the vicinity of the spawning grounds for some time and try to mate with other hen fish, but eventually they become very weak and emaciated, and often attacked by fungus. Very few cock kelts ever reach the sea to recover sufficiently to spawn again. For some reason, a number of ripe fish of both sexes fail to spawn, the proportions appearing to vary from year to year. They are a source of annoyance to anglers, for although technically unspawned and therefore 'clean' fish they are not worth eating and of no value. They are often referred to as 'rawners' or 'baggots'.

The fecundity of female Salmon can be rather variable, but most fish produce around 1100 eggs per kg of body weight. Eggs of individual fish also vary in size and can range from 5–7mm in diameter. As well as varying from fish to fish the egg size can also vary significantly among different populations. Previously spawned fish do not produce as many eggs as maiden fish, also their eggs may be pale yellow in colour and not the rich orange-red of first time spawners.

In the redd, the embryos develop slowly and hatch in March or April, some 110 days after spawning at temperatures around 4°C. However, the alevins remain in the redd for several weeks more until their substantial yolk sacs have been absorbed. They then emerge from the gravel as fry, usually in early May. The times of hatching and emergence are wholly dependent on the ambient temperatures and can vary from year to year. The newly emerged fry remain in the shallow flowing water over their redds before dispersing gradually. Paradoxically, the food supply in a typical Salmon spawning stream is poor, particularly so in early spring, and initially the mortality

Table 11 Food of young Salmon and Trout from the River Bran (after Mills 1964), as percentage occurrence and the River Endrick, Scotland (after Maitland 1965), as percentage bulk.

Stomach contents	River Bran Salmon	River Bran Trout	River Endrick Salmon	River Endrick Trout
Molluscs	2	3	8	1
Worms	–	–	2	2
Crustaceans	1	1	1	13
Insects				
Mayfly larvae	36	15	56	17
Stonefly larvae	40	17	7	9
Beetle larvae & adults	7	11	2	3
Caddis larvae	45	38	11	10
Midge larvae & pupae	30	16	10	8
Blackfly larvae	10	6	4	1
Others	3	10	2	3
Adult aquatic insects	10	10	–	3
Other invertebrates	–	–	1	–
Fish				
Salmon	1	5	–	–
Terrestrial organisms	6	30	7	40
NUMBER OF FISH EXAMINED	297	514	110	120

among fry is very high. The strongest individuals occupy the best feeding stations, displacing the weaker ones downstream, where the great majority perish. Possibly over 90% of the current year's fry die within their first few months of life. From the evolutionary aspect, this ruthless weeding out of fry may be essential to maintain the genetic health of the stock. It also, in normal circumstances, makes nonsense of the common and wasteful practice of stocking rivers with Salmon fry in the hope of increasing the numbers of adults returning. All this is likely to do is to aggravate the lack of food and result in no net gain in the numbers of fry surviving, more likely the reverse. Only in streams which have been depopulated by some catastrophe or which are inaccessible to adult Salmon is this measure normally justified.

The growth of fry to the parr stage is slow in most rivers and normally 2–3 years elapse before the latter are ready to become smolts and make their way to the sea – usually at lengths of 12–16cm, though smolt size can actually vary from 10–20cm. During their growth phase, the parr have become well dispersed throughout the river, tending to occupy the riffles and runs, rather than the pools and quieter stretches favoured by Trout. Their food consists largely of aquatic insect larvae, but during the summer months, especially in windy weather, aerial and terrestrial insects falling onto the water surface become important. If there are lakes in the river system, some parr may well make their way into these and occupy the littoral zone along the shore, provided that there are not too many predatory fish or competitors. In some situations, parr will move upstream to find good feeding stations. In the richer sections of a river, or where individuals have found a particularly good feeding station, parr may reach the smolt stage within one year. At the other extreme, in high, cold tributaries, parr may still be only 4cm or less a year after they have emerged from the gravel. In such habitats, parr, if they do not drop downstream, may be 4–6 year-olds before they smoltify.

Although smolting normally takes place between April and June, a small number may reach this stage in the autumn and drop downstream. A minor downstream migration of parr from the upper tributaries may also take place at this time, as the first stage of a general smolt migration the following spring. The physiological mechanisms of smolting and migration to the sea have attracted considerable attention from researchers. In most cases, smolts undergo a gradual change from fresh to salt water in the estuary, but there are a number of rivers which plunge directly to the sea. Here, both Salmon and Sea Trout smolts seem none the worse for the abrupt change of environment.

It is not imperative for the survival of a smolt that it reaches salt water. Where juvenile Salmon have been prevented from migration downstream by a dam or even by being placed as fry in a lake with no exit, if the feeding is good, both sexes will grow and eventually develop mature gonads. By this time they closely resemble Brown Trout in appearance.

It is thought likely that when smolts reach the sea they remain to a large extent in their original shoals throughout sea life, the survivors then returning together to their natal rivers. This makes the stocks of individual rivers particularly vulnerable to the current large-scale fishing methods in the sea, such as drift netting with many kilometres of net set per boat. However, evidence from the operation of floating long lines off the Faeroes suggests that at this stage Salmon seem to be feeding as individuals.

Once in the sea and feeding, growth is very fast and Salmon returning to the fresh water after one winter in the sea (now known as grilse) average around 3.5kg. This average may vary considerably during the season from small fish early on, to substantial fish of well over 4.5kg later on, depending on the length of time spent feeding in the sea. In rivers which have substantial runs of multi-sea-winter fish, most grilse are males, but in smaller grilse rivers, the sex ratio may be more even. Salmon returning to fresh water after two or more winters in the sea make up the bulk of the so-called 'spring fish', much sought after by anglers to whom they are particularly vulnerable (because they spend so long in the river) and valuable (because they are normally large).

Typically, spring fish vary considerably in size from river to river – depending on the ratio of two to three sea-winter fish. Thus, in some they may not be much larger than the grilse there, while in others they may be several times the weight of the average grilse. The first of the spring fish may enter their river in the late autumn and in some years a substantial stock may have built up in fresh water by the time the official angling season opens early in the following year. However, their main runs take place normally in the late winter and early spring. Later running, two sea-winter, fish are usually referred to as 'summer fish'; again a small proportion of these may have spent three or even four winters in the sea, providing the largest individual Salmon of all – up to 14kg or even more in weight. This run of summer fish into the river may continue until late autumn, the fresh-run 'autumn fish' – a dullish silver in colour – arriving almost ripe to spawn. Thus Salmon due to spawn the coming winter and those not due to spawn until the following one may be in the river at the same time. In fact, in our large rivers, fresh-run fish may be present in variable numbers all the year round. Fish entering fresh water during the cold months may make little actual progress upstream except during spells of mild weather.

In small rivers, virtually the entire run of returning adults may be grilse, which appear from midsummer onwards. A few previous spawners and the occasional two sea-winter fish may be present. By tradition, according to a practice which originates from the marketing side of the salmon industry, any fish over 2.7kg is classed as a Salmon and those under this weight as grilse. This has often lead to a misapprehension about the nature of the stock a river contains, and most angling record books have columns for 'grilse' and 'salmon' respectively, based on some arbitrary distinction. As a result, salmon fishery owners may be under the impression that there is a substantial run of 'salmon' in their rivers, when, in fact, nearly all the fish are grilse, for by the end of the summer, the latter may have attained a weight of 6kg or even more. Recent investigations, based on extensive scale reading, have shown that, although this may not always have been the case, grilse are currently the dominant form of returning adult Salmon throughout the British Isles.

No definite relationship between the number of years of juvenile freshwater life and the time spent in the sea has been demonstrated. However, it can be said that the longer a young Salmon has spent in the river before migrating to the sea, the earlier will it return within its sea age group.

Some kelts may still be seen in the upper reaches of river systems in midsummer or even later – especially where there are lakes and reservoirs. This could mean that they may have been in fresh water for around 18 months without feeding. The fact that Salmon do not feed in fresh water, yet readily take artificial and natural baits, has always puzzled anglers and others. However, it should be realised that the technique of a salmon angler is to place the lure or bait, worms or fresh prawns for instance, right on the 'salmon's nose'. In other words, Salmon, unlike Sea Trout, do not cruise about looking for food in fresh water. Very occasionally, exceptional feeding behaviour has been recorded; for example there are two instances of fresh-run Salmon caught in Loch Tay with Arctic Charr in their stomachs. In the most recent case, a 12.7kg spring fish was found to contain a Charr of 0.34kg.

The average age of most adult Salmon in the British Isles is some 3–5 years, i.e. 2–3 juvenile years in fresh water plus 1–2 years in the sea. In exceptional cases, eight-year-old fish can occur, while some individuals at the extreme northern limit of their range could be even older. While in the sea, Salmon travel great distances, many migrating to feeding grounds at the edge of the Arctic Ocean and along the east and west coasts of Greenland, where Salmon from North America, the British Isles and Scandinavia mingle. They appear to concentrate in sea areas where the surface temperature is between 4 and 8°C. Their methods of navigation to these feeding grounds and then back to their natal rivers are not yet clearly understood, but it is thought that at least three elements are involved–the use of currents in the open sea, odours (known as pheromones) and other chemicals in the water on approaching the home coast, and finally, from the river mouth upstream, both visual and pheromonal/chemical cues. It has been shown that Salmon do not have a genetic link with the river of their birth and that their ability to return to it at maturity depends entirely on the sequential imprinting of various cues that they received on their way downstream, through the estuary and out to sea as juveniles.

Homing accuracy is not quite 100% and very occasionally adult Salmon, marked as parr or smolts, are found at spawning time in rivers other than their natal ones. Also at times, returning adults, apparently frustrated by not being able to ascend their home river because of very low water levels, or for some other reason, cruise patiently in shoals off the river mouth for a considerable time but eventually move off to find another river which it is possible to ascend. On maturing, Salmon which have been experimentally deprived of their olfactory senses somehow still locate fresh water and will run up any convenient river. Possibly they follow other, unimpaired Salmon.

The food of Salmon at sea consists of pelagic crustaceans such as euphausid shrimps, prawns, small squid and a wide variety of other fish such as sandeels *Ammodytes*, Sprats *Sprattus sprattus*, Herring *Clupea harengus*, lantern fish (Myctophidae) and, in the far north, Capelin *Mallotus villosus*. The presence of some of the food organisms indicates that the feeding range of Salmon extends down to 300m, although most feeding seems to take place in the surface layers. The principal baits used by long-line fishermen are Sprats, fished at depths of 3–5m.

Mortality at sea due to predation is high. Salmon fall prey to seals, whales and large fish such as sharks and tuna, and, especially during their early stages at sea, Saithe *Pollachius virens* and Pollack *Pollachius pollachius*. In fresh water, young Salmon are also subject to predation pressure from Otters and in recent years from Mink, as well as from several species of birds, such as Herons, Cormorants, mergansers and Goosanders and from predatory fish such as large Trout and Pike. Returned adult Salmon are also preyed upon by Otters, though Otters main food seems to consist of young salmonids and Eels. In fresh water, and probably at sea, humans are a major predator of adult Salmon.

Salmon are hosts to many parasites, both external and internal, the most familiar are the copepods known as 'sea lice' and 'gill maggots'. Sea lice become attached to their host at sea and drop off in fresh water within about 3–5 days – thus their presence is an indication that their host is fresh-run. Gill maggots on the other hand become attached to their host while in fresh water, but can survive in sea water and may be present on a Salmon throughout its adult life.

Salmon are also subject to a number of often fatal bacterial and viral infections. Furunculosis is a familiar example of the former and quickly kills fresh-run adults, in certain conditions reaching epidemic proportions – as can the viral infection UDN (Ulcerated Dermal Necrosis), which has been endemic in many rivers in the British Isles since 1967. Mass mortalities of Salmon and Sea Trout resulted from the early outbreaks of this disease. Its presence is indicated by lesions on the nose and between the eyes of the fish, the skin below the lesion becoming etched away leaving a shallow pit. These pits become infected by the conspicuous fungus *Saprolegnia*, which then may invade back along the body causing a fatal secondary infection. The irrational jumping behaviour of infected fish is a sign of the disease. After an outbreak of UDN, some fish may be found which have what appear to be healed lesions, suggesting that the disease may not invariably be fatal. As the severity of outbreaks of most diseases appears to be related to the density of Salmon, some authorities fear that the current trend of buying off coastal and river nets by angling interests may lead to severe disease problems in rivers, especially during low water conditions.

Medieval laws regulating salmon exploitation demonstrate the value of this resource and the early respect that humans have held for this 'King of Fish' from early times. Its size, food value and anadromous habit made it ideal as a source of food for primitive humans, using simple devices to harvest this dependable crop. Ancient trapping devices can still be seen in some rivers, such as the weir at the mouth of the River Liffey in Dublin, which was there at least as far back as 1014AD. However, the life cycle of anadromous fishes is always at risk when rivers are used for other purposes, such as power, water supply and the disposal of sewage. Thus, since the Industrial Revolution in Europe and its counterpart in North America, very many populations of Salmon have been exterminated as the vital link between the sea and the spawning and nursery areas became severed. In later times, however, efforts have been made in some countries to ensure that developments do not totally disrupt the movement of Salmon in rivers, and fish passes or 'salmon ladders' have been installed in many recent barriers to allow fish to move up and down stream. In addition, the laws relating to pollution control have been strengthened and many rivers are becoming cleaner as a result. The recent natural return of the Salmon to the River Clyde after an absence of more than 100 years (because of pollution) is a very welcome sign.

Atlantic Salmon also provide anglers with the 'King of Sport' and throughout its range, except where owned by the state, salmon-fishing rights have high values and may be leased at high rents or change hands for immense sums. However, the formidable pressure groups representing angler interests are of benefit to the Salmon in a society which still otherwise puts quick profit before the future of a long-term natural resource. The future of commercial salmon fishing in estuaries and around the coasts of the British Isles, once a highly profitable industry, may well be in the balance due to the continuing rapid expansion of salmon farming. Salmon, somewhat surprisingly, have taken well to a quiet life in floating cages in the sea, eating dried food pellets. Eventually, farmed-salmon production may lead to a phasing out of all but the most economic wild salmon fisheries.

Brown Trout *Salmo trutta* Linnaeus 1758
Trout (Brown): Breck, Brook Trout, Brownie, Bull Trout, Burn Trout, Ferox, Gillaroo, Lake Trout, Slob Trout, Sonaghen, Yellow Trout
Trout (Sea): Black Tail, Bull Trout, Covichie, Finnock, Fordwich Trout, Grey Trout, Herling, Lammasman, Mort, Peal, Phinnock, Round Tail, Salmon Trout, Scurf, Sewen, Sprod, Truff, White Trout, Whiting, Whitling, Yellow Fin

The enormous variety of form of this species is exemplified by the large number of local names used. Trout with anadromous habits (Sea Trout) and those which are not anadromous (Brown Trout) are here treated as the same species, although they are awarded subspecific status by some authorities as *Salmo trutta trutta* and *Salmo trutta fario* respectively. Trout must be one of the most familiar of British native freshwater fishes. Apart from the probability of encountering the living, freshly dead or cooked organism throughout the country, the Trout motif embellishes a wide range of common household items such as biscuit tins, calendars, plastic mantelpiece ornaments, etc. To many its shape, elongate, streamlined and laterally compressed, typifies the salmon family.

The length of fully grown wild Trout of both sexes can range from a few

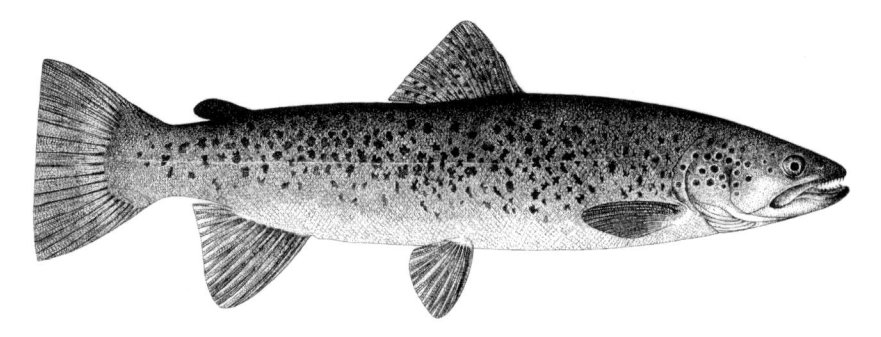

Fig. 40 Brown Trout (from Maitland 1972b).

centimetres to over 95cm, but the size encountered most commonly is around 26– 42cm, the weight equivalents being approximately 226–900g. The British record rod-caught Brown Trout (caught in Loch Quoich, Inverness in 1978) weighed 8.87kg. The Irish record for a lake Brown Trout is 11.85kg (Lough Ennel in 1894) and for a river Brown Trout is 9.07kg (River Shannon in 1957). Larger Trout have been reported from both Britain and Ireland in the past. In some cases these were shown to have been large Salmon in spawning dress while there is uncertainty about most of the others. However, in Britain, it is certain that at least one Trout larger than the present record has been caught. A 'slob' Trout of 13.6kg was taken in the outflow

Fig. 41 Brown Trout from one water showing the variation in spotting (Niall Campbell).

from the Loch of Stenness in Orkney in 1889, but as it was caught on a set line it is not considered to be an angling record. An examination of scales taken from its preserved skin revealed that it was 13 years old.

The world record for a Brown Trout stands at 16.3kg for a fish caught in a lake in Patagonia in 1952, while a Trout of 25kg (aged at 17 years) was found when a lake in Yugoslavia was drained in 1968.

Sea Trout too can attain a large size. The British rod-caught record stands at 10.2kg for a fish caught in the River Leven in 1989. The Irish Sea Trout record stands at 7.42kg for a fish caught in the Shimna River in 1983. However, in recent years a number of large Sea Trout have been taken around the British Isles in nets or found dead, and weights of 10.9–12.7kg have been recorded.

Brown Trout are not likely to be confused with any other fish, except that 'red' salmon have been taken for large ferox Trout and large Sea Trout are not infrequently confused with Salmon and vice versa. In Trout the maxillary bone extends backwards at least to the level of the posterior margin of the eye. The head and shaft of the vomer bone are toothed and the palatine bone and tongue also carry teeth. There are strong teeth on the upper and lower jaws. An important salmonid diagnostic feature, the adipose fin, is, of course, present and usually red or orange tipped. There are 12–15 major rays in the dorsal fin, 13–15 in the pectoral fins, 9–10 in the pelvic fins and 9–12 branched rays in the anal fin. When this fin is pressed back against the body, its last ray (i.e. the one nearest the body in this position) does not extend as far back as the first ray. As with Salmon, there is a bony flesh-covered axillary process at the base of the pelvic fin.

Trout scales are noticeably smaller than those of Salmon so there can be up to 130 scales along the lateral line and 13–16 scales, counted diagonally downwards and forwards, from the front of the dorsal fin to the lateral line. There are 30–61 pyloric caecae and 56–61 vertebrae. Fourteen to 17 gill rakers are present and usually 10 branchiostegals. As noted in the discussion on Salmon, there are occasional occurrences of hybrid fish with characteristics intermediate between Trout and Salmon.

Like Salmon, the male Trout at spawning time develops a hook or kype at the end of the lower jaw, but unlike Salmon, he may live for many years and spawn several times so that this feature becomes progressively more and more pronounced. As with Salmon, the shape of both Sea Trout and Brown Trout is variable. In some populations individuals are typically slender, often with large fins, while at the other extreme in different waters they may be short and thick set. Old male Brown Trout have a tendency to develop large heads with slim bodies tapering away to the tail. Such individuals are often described, usually wrongly, as 'cannibals'.

The colouration and marking of Brown Trout is subject to great variation, even within the same population. Young individuals may often be quite silvery, but after becoming mature spotting usually increases progressively with age in both sexes, while the background colour becomes darker and may be brown-yellow or nearly black. Spotting is also very variable, both in form and density, and there are innumerable combinations of large and small spots, red and black ones, some of which may be encircled by light to dark haloes. The dorsal and adipose fins may bear spots, but if any spotting is present on the caudal fin this is usually restricted to the uppermost part. In occasional

Fig. 42 An adult Sea Trout (Niall Campbell).

populations individuals are found with the whole of the caudal fin heavily spotted and in such individuals the whole head may be heavily spotted too (Plate 10).

The overall colour impression of the fish may be brown, yellow, black or silver or, under water, green. In parts of the British Isles, Brown Trout are referred to as Yellow Trout by local anglers. Some populations occur where the Brown Trout are pure silver, with a few small black spots, just like fresh-run Sea Trout, while at the other extreme, there are populations of Trout with large tightly packed spots making the fish look black. Very rarely, lake populations are encountered where all the individuals of both sexes are virtually identically marked regardless of size or age. The authors know of two such populations of 'golden' and 'grey' Trout respectively in the north of Scotland. These populations could be of considerable interest from the genetic point of view, as their study might throw some light on the post-glacial colonisation by the now land-locked Trout of our inland waters.

At spawning time the markings and background colouration of the male intensify. The belly may become sooty grey merging into amber orange flanks. Most male ferox Trout develop this colouration. Unfortunately, with all trout, and indeed with most fish, the subtle colouration of the living fish fades in a few minutes after death so that photographs usually provide a poor record of the living colour unless taken immediately on capture.

Sea Trout, 'bars of silver' when young and fresh in from the sea, also develop black and brown spotting with age. This is particularly conspicuous when the fish is viewed under water. By the time the male is ready to spawn, he may be indistinguishable from a male Brown Trout, although some authorities claim that the presence of black 'X' spots is diagnostic of Sea Trout. Though that certainly may be the case in some areas, there are also populations of Brown Trout in inland waters that also bear such markings. The female Sea Trout at spawning time assumes a dull leaden colour, but her straight-edged tail and typical square shape distinguish her from a hen Salmon. After spawning, Sea Trout kelts quickly regain their silvery appearance and may be so 'well-mended' that anglers catching them on their way back to the sea have difficulty in distinguishing them from fresh-run fish.

The fry and parr stages of Sea Trout and Brown Trout are indistinguishable and although Sea Trout smolts en route for the sea are coated with easily shed silvery scales, so too may the equivalent stage of some Brown Trout that inhabit large inland lakes. The latter move down from their nursery streams to the lakes at about the same time as Sea Trout smolts are also dropping downstream towards the sea. Like Salmon parr, Trout parr may also bear parr marks alternating with red spots, but the spotting of the two species differs in other ways, as is indicated in the dichotomous key above.

The flesh colour of Trout ranges from white through champagne to a rich orange-pink. The flesh of young freshly run Sea Trout is deeply coloured, but as the fish ages it may become much paler. That of Brown Trout from habitats where there is a good supply of crustacean food is also deeply coloured, as is the flesh of well conditioned ferox Trout – although the latter are almost exclusively piscivorous. The essential crustacean pigment is obtained from the flesh and stomach contents of their plankton-eating prey – small Trout and Charr. The palatability of Trout flesh usually increases in proportion to the depth of its colouration, but while some white-fleshed Trout can be most palatable, intermediates never seem to be.

Trout are abundant in many waters but can be scarce or even absent in habitats where there are numerous predatory fish, particularly Pike. However, even here a sparse Trout population can sometimes be maintained by recruitment from inflowing streams inaccessible to the predators. Sea Trout, once abundant in the fresh waters and coastal areas of the British Isles, have become scarcer in some districts in recent years and in many waters are now unfortunately rather rare. There are probably several reasons for their general decline, and certainly the different phases of their life cycle make them especially vulnerable to different forms of pollution and fishing.

All native Trout populations in the British Isles are descended from early, post-glacial colonisation by anadromous trout, which established populations that now appear quite distinct – some of them being still largely anadromous, others completely non-anadromous. A range of intermediate populations exist. Being for centuries regarded as a highly desirable fish, Trout (from both anadromous and non-anadromous populations) have been widely redistributed by humans and they are now found throughout the length and breadth of the British Isles wherever the water quality is high and there are not too many predacious fish. Where there are no spawning facilities, populations are often maintained by anglers by introductions from fish farms or from the wild. Sea Trout occupy all accessible rivers and often the estuaries of inaccessible ones too, which they use as feeding grounds. It is thought that, like Salmon, many if not most streams and rivers possess discrete populations of Sea Trout.

The Brown Trout, which is native to Europe and western Asia, has been introduced widely throughout the world, including the southern hemisphere, where anadromous populations have become established in Tasmania, New Zealand, the Falkland Islands and southern South America, as well as in some tropical countries where high-altitude streams and lakes offer suitably cool conditions.

Trout spawn mainly from mid-October to mid-December, but earlier dates have been recorded, while in some populations, spawning may be extended into late January or even early February. However, the peak of spawning activity takes place during the latter part of October until mid-November. In many places a rise in the water level of the tributary streams is necessary to entice and allow ripe fish to reach their spawning grounds, and thus the time of spawning can vary considerably from year to year. The ideal situation for redd excavation is clean deep gravel in pure fast-flowing water, usually at the downstream exit of a pool. However, a degree of spawning success can be achieved by using apparently unsuitable substrate such as a peat bottom with only a thin layer of gravel. Occasionally Trout are found spawning in the shallow water of lakes, particularly off gravelly spits where, when there is a strong wind, river conditions may be closely simulated. Some Trout populations inhabiting high-altitude lakes, where there are no inflowing streams, survive in this way. Sea Trout tend to use the lower tributaries of river systems for spawning, but there are exceptions to this; for example, small numbers of Sea Trout spawn far upstream in tributaries of the Rivers Tay and Tweed, 65–80km from the sea.

As with Salmon, the site of the Trout redd is carefully selected and excavated by the female with a male or males in attendance, and covered over again after the eggs are laid. Where the whole process of spawning has been observed in artificial stream sections it appeared that the female selected the site for the redd at a point where water flowed through the gravel at the tail of a pool. No doubt in a busy spawning stream, the chance fertilisation by drifting sperm from males spawning upstream can take place and where both Sea Trout and Brown Trout are present cross fertilisation does occur.

The males are first to appear on the spawning grounds. In both Sea and Brown Trout it is known that a large proportion of individuals return to the stream where they lived as juveniles for their first and subsequent spawnings. Trout are attracted upstream to their spawning grounds off the main river or a lake by a rise in the water flow. They do not usually run upstream during the height of the spate, but when it is abating. After spawning, the females drop back downstream while some of the males remain to mate with the females of successive runs. As the spawning season progresses, runs of both sexes take place, even when tributary streams are low. The spawning period is a time of high mortality – apart from being easy prey to predators, many Trout die from exhaustion while the fungus *Saprolegnia* fatally infects areas of the body damaged by fighting or by struggling upstream over rough obstacles. Trout are under great stress at this time and potentially dangerous pathogens that they may be carrying (e.g. furunculosis), may gain a hold, usually with fatal results.

Sea Trout kelts normally drop back to the estuary fairly promptly and rapidly recover condition if the food supply is adequate. Unlike Salmon, a significant proportion of both Sea and Brown Trout live to spawn several times. Some ripe females do not spawn completely or even partially and consequently can be found with mature eggs inside the body cavities – sometimes also the empty skins of eggs from previous seasons, the contents having been resorbed. Such fish are known as 'baggots'. Trout sometimes miss out a spawning; while this is a rare occurrence with Brown Trout it is not uncommon with Sea Trout.

Trout produce from 1100 to 1700 eggs per kg of body weight and the rate of successful fertilisation is very high. The diameter of the eggs, which are yellow to orange-yellow in colour, is 4–5mm. In females from populations of exceptionally small individuals, the eggs remain about the same size, e.g. a fully ripe female only 10.7cm in length from a roadside ditch in Argyll contained 31 eggs, 3.9mm in diameter. The ripe males from this site ranged from 6.7–11.2cm in length.

Some time after hatching, when the yolk sac has been almost completely resorbed, Trout fry emerge from the gravel and can be seen hovering over the site of their redd. The time between hatching and emergence from the redd varies according to the ambient temperature (e.g. 97 days at 4.7°C, 148 days at 2°C) so that fry may be emerging from mid-March to early May, depending on the region. As with Salmon fry, Trout fry then gradually disperse, the stronger individuals occupying the best feeding stations while the weaker ones drop downstream, the great majority to perish during the first few months from starvation and predation by larger fish and birds. Paradoxically, suitable food for small fish is scarce at this time of year, the main items of their diet being small mayfly and midge larvae. Later in the spring, and increasingly during summer, small terrestrial insects that fall into the stream become important.

In lake populations, some fry drop downstream and reach the lake within a short time of emerging. This can happen if the spawning stream is temporary in nature, perhaps flowing from autumn to spring only. Fry that spend most of their first year in the lake grow noticeably faster than those remaining in the natal stream. However, in general, both Sea Trout and Brown Trout may spend up to five years (but usually only 1–3 years) in their nursery streams before migrating down to the sea or to a lake or large river respectively.

Along the west coast of Scotland, where small streams flow into sheltered bays, it is not uncommon to find the current season's Trout fry under stones and seaweed in the tidal zone, thus spending part of each day in sea water as the tide ebbs and flows. There is no way of telling whether these fry are actually Sea or Brown Trout, but it is likely that some of them contribute to the population of inshore living Trout that are characteristic of sea lochs and termed by anglers 'slob' Trout. Slob Trout also occur in estuaries (the word 'slob' originating from an Irish term for estuarine mud).

In river systems with Sea Trout populations, a downstream migration of silvery smolts takes place each spring. The smolts have usually spent two to three years in fresh water (although smolts of one, four, five and six years of age are also known) and their shoals mingle with those of migrating Salmon smolts. Throughout the British Isles, smolt age appears to increase with latitude. Sea Trout smolts are usually 15–22cm in length and more robust than Salmon smolts. They have brown or yellow backs and yellow fins. A similar downstream migration of Trout 'smolts' takes place where substantial streams flow into large lakes but these young remain in the lake, often growing to a very large size.

Unlike Salmon smolts, not all Sea Trout smolts migrate out into the open sea; some stay in the estuary, some move into shallow coastal waters, while Sea Trout from east-coast rivers may cross the North Sea to Scandinavia and others set off on long migrations far out to the open sea. In fact, there is no real demarcation between the distribution of Sea Trout and Brown Trout for a continuum of Trout types occupies habitats from the source of a river through lakes, through estuaries into coastal waters and out into the open sea.

A proportion of Sea Trout smolts spend only a few weeks or months in the estuary or nearby coastal waters before returning to fresh water, and after midsummer, large shoals of these young Sea Trout, known by many local names (e.g. Finnock, Whitling, Peal, Harling, etc.) are found in the lower reaches of their natal rivers and lakes. They are very vulnerable to anglers and large inroads can be made into their numbers at this stage by greedy fishermen. A small proportion of both sexes of these Finnock are mature and lose their pristine silvery appearance as the summer progresses; the younger the average smolt age, the greater the proportion that mature as Finnock. However, the great majority do not mature and retain their fresh-run appearance, spending the summer, autumn and following winter in fresh water (apparently in a state of semi-starvation) returning to the sea the following spring. In the mean time, the smolts that did not become Finnock have been growing rapidly in the sea. Most of these fish return to fresh water after one winter in the sea, but the time of return is variable: in some systems, fresh-run Sea Trout appear in early spring, but the main runs are usually after midsummer. The rate of growth varies markedly among districts, e.g. after two years at sea, River Tweed Sea Trout may reach a size comparable to that of Salmon. Once in the river, adult Sea Trout are largely nocturnal in their behaviour. During low-water conditions, the clear pools appear to be devoid of larger fish but as dusk approaches Sea Trout appear, often leaping spectacularly. In lakes, however, they are often active during daylight as well, particularly in the autumn.

The factors involved in making a Trout go to sea or not have been the subject of much debate, particularly since the mid-1960s when the decline in Sea Trout catches in a number of areas became noticeable. However, only comparatively recently has any significant research been focused on this

Fig. 43 Part of Loch Sloy and its hydroelectric dam, showing the extensive areas of exposed shore, which is devoid of plant and animal life, when the water is drawn down (Peter Maitland).

Fig. 44 Releasing trout fry into a high-altitude loch as part of a stocking density experiment (Niall Campbell).

topic. While there must be an underlying genetic component involved, it seems to be environmental conditions, directly or indirectly, which decide the migratory strategy which an individual Trout will adopt. Some facts have emerged from research, e.g. most sea-going fish are female – in one system studied, the female to male ratio in migrating smolts over four years was 2.71:1, 4.5:1, 2.33:1 and 2.94:1. In another system, resident Trout showed a ratio of males to females of 6:1; these males were seen breeding with Sea Trout females and the conclusion arrived at was that they were all the progeny of Sea Trout parents.

It is possible that because the greater reproductive-energy needs of females may be difficult to fulfil in some fresh waters, they move to the richer environment of the sea. This problem is of less concern to males. The management of Sea Trout waters for the benefit of anglers would seem therefore to be more a matter of managing environmental factors (once these have been identified) than of artificial breeding and stocking.

Like other salmonids, Trout show a great plasticity, which allows them to flourish in a very wide range of habitats by adjusting optimum size, rate of growth, age of maturity and feeding behaviour to fit the particular habitat.

Fig. 45 Top, A large ferox Brown Trout from Sutherland, shown with two normal adult trout from the same loch (Niall Campbell); *bottom*, A very large Brown Trout caught by one of the authors in Loch Faskally in 1962. At the time this was the British rod-caught record fish and weighed 8.05kg. It was sixteen years old (Niall Campbell).

The relationship between age and size is particularly flexible. As noted above, populations of mature Trout of little more than 10cm in length and less than three years of age can be found while at the other end of the scale there are individuals of 95cm or more at ages of 20 years or greater.

As a general rule the growth rate of Trout is a function of the relative amount and quality of food available to each individual. Small food organisms suit small fish, but there is an optimum size of food organism for most sizes of Trout up to a certain limit. Trout gather their food organisms individually so that to collect a stomach full of small organisms will probably cost the fish a relatively high output of energy: e.g. one adult stickleback is equivalent in weight to about 110 middle-sized midge larvae, all of which would have to be collected individually. In many places, Trout are small because their only food organisms are small. Much larger organisms may be available too but the Trout are never large enough to swallow them. For example, in a small upland loch containing Trout less than 225gm in average weight, one of the authors introduced Three-spined Sticklebacks. These flourished and in sub-

Fig. 46 Loch Garry (Inverness), home of ferox Trout and Arctic Charr, showing the wave-washed exposed shoreline (Peter Maitland).

sequent years the Trout grew noticeably larger, reaching a size when they could prey on the plentiful supply of toads, frogs and newts that appeared each spring. As result, within a few years, Trout of 1.8kg in weight were being caught (often with toads or frogs in their stomachs). Here, sticklebacks filled the size gap between small invertebrates and amphibians. Obviously, other factors affecting the growth rate of Trout are involved in such situations apart from the size and availability of food (e.g. space and genetic characteristics), but quantity and quality of food do seem to be of major importance.

In the Scottish Highlands after World War II, many streams and lochs were impounded (along with their fish populations) to make hydro-electric reservoirs. In these, dramatic increases in the rates of growth and sizes of Trout were observed. Many of the original Trout populations consisted of tiny fish, useless for angling purposes. However, about two years after flooding, the average size of many of the fish had risen to 1.5kg or more. Not only did the young Trout show a great response to the abundance of drowned terrestrial organisms, as might have been expected, but older fish (some around 8–10 years of age) also showed rapid increases in growth rates – demonstrating that fish can grow throughout their lives, not only during the early years.

The physical and chemical nature of lakes and rivers appears to have no direct influence on the growth rates of Trout in them, except perhaps where conditions are so acid as to prevent the hatching of eggs. Observations on the effects of a number of factors affecting fry survival has been made on a wide range of lochs, representing virtually all natural Trout habitats in Scotland. High-altitude lochs (i.e, those at more than 610m above sea level), acid and alkaline lochs, all produced fast-or slow-growing Trout according to the

Table 12 Food of Brown Trout in the River Liffey in Ireland at Straffan and at Ballysmuttan (after Frost 1939), Llyn Tegid in Wales (after Graham & Jones 1960) and Loch Tummel in Scotland (after Campbell 1963), as percentage occurrence.

Stomach contents	R Liffey Straffan	R Liffey Ballysmuttan	Llyn Tegid	Loch Tummel
Molluscs				
Snails & limpets	18	2	9	7
Worms	3	7	5	–
Crustaceans				
Bythotrephes	–	–	7	–
Other cladocerans	–	–	–	3
Ostracods	–	–	1	–
Water louse	10	–	1	17
Freshwater shrimp	16	–	2	12
Crayfish	11	–	–	–
Insects				
Mayfly larvae	70	60	3	19
Mayfly adults	46	24	–	–
Stonefly larvae	18	63	6	11
Stonefly adults	18	21	–	2
Aquatic bugs	4	4	–	6
Beetle larvae & adults	35	51	5	18
Alderfly larvae	–	–	5	4
Caddis all stages	68	81	31	35
Cranefly larvae	–	–	5	–
Midges all stages	64	53	21	41
Blackfly larvae	39	37	–	–
Other insects	64	43	–	–
Other invertebrates	14	17	–	–
Fish				
Salmon (smolts)	–	–	–	4
Trout	–	–	1	–
Roach	–	–	1	–
Minnow	–	–	1	–
Perch	–	–	–	9
Unidentified fish	8	1	6	–
Fish eggs	–	–	9	–
Other vertebrates				
Frogs & Toads	–	–	–	10
Newts	–	–	–	11
Terrestrial organisms				
Insects	24	28	47	24
Spiders	10	20	8	–
Anglers' maggots	–	–	3	–
Detritus	–	–	–	–
NUMBER OF FISH EXAMINED	228	349	389	140

relative abundance and quality of the food supply and to the productivity of the spawning grounds.

A special study has been made by one of the authors of the very large, almost wholly piscivorous 'ferox' trout, found in the large deep oligotrophic lochs of Scotland. Similar Trout are found also in some English lakes in Cumbria, in Llyn Tegid in Wales and in the large loughs of Ireland, both rich and poor. Characteristically, in Britain, these fish grow slowly for about the first third of their life span, feeding on a predominantly invertebrate diet. On reaching a critical length, they switch to a fish diet, with a resulting spectacular increase in growth rate. In Scotland, ferox fish occur only in lochs over a certain size (100ha) that also contain Arctic Charr, and it is likely that the latter species is their main item of diet. In the richer Irish loughs the picture is somewhat different, for here ferox seem to grow rapidly throughout their lives, and although attaining the same eventual size as Scottish ferox, their

Table 13 The main food of Trout, Perch and Pike in Loch Tummel, Scotland (after Campbell 1955) at two periods of the year (A: April–September; B: October–March), as percentage occurrence.

Stomach contents	Trout A	Trout B	Perch A	Perch B	Pike A	Pike B
Molluscs						
Snails	6.8	1.4	–	16.6	–	–
Worms	–	–	–	–	–	–
Leeches	–	–	14.2	–	–	–
Crustaceans						
Cladocerans	4.1	1.4	16.0	–	–.	
Water louse	1.2	35.8	54.0	25.0	14.2	
Freshwater shrimp	7.0	16.0	11.0	16.6	6.6	14.6
Insects						
Mayfly larvae	21.9	16.1	25.0	–	14.2	–
Stoneflies (all stages)	9.6	19.3	3.0	–	–	–
Aquatic bugs	8.2	4.4	–	–	–	–
Beetles (all stages)	13.6	22.5	–	8.3	–	–
Caddis (all stages)	36.9	41.9	39.9	33.3	6.6	–
Midges (all stages)	57.5	19.3	40.4	8.3	39.0	–
Other invertebrates						
Fish						
Perch fry	12.3	4.4	16.6	8.3	14.2	–
Trout	–	–	–	–	14.2	14.2
Salmon smolts	6.2	–	–	–	–	–
Other vertebrates						
Frogs & Toads	4.1	16.5	–	–	6.1	45.0
Newts	5.4	11.9	–	–	–	–
Terrestrial organisms	–	–	50.0	12.5	6.6	14.2
NUMBER OF FISH EXAMINED	73	62	35	12	15	7

life span is noticeably shorter. Due to their large size, full-grown ferox probably breed only with each other, thus enhancing genetic characteristics such as longevity, late maturity and piscivorous feeding behaviour. Electrophoretic studies of enzyme loci have shown that the ferox of Lough Melvin in Fermanagh, as well as two other types of Brown Trout, the 'Sonaghen' and 'Gillaroo', are each genetically distinct and form reproductively isolated populations. In Norway it has been demonstrated by experiments that piscivorous feeding behaviour can be an inherited characteristic. Rate of growth, age at maturity and length of life are also partly genetically controlled.

Populations of 'stunted' trout, so typical of upland peaty waters, usually mature at two or three years of age (with a proportion of the males maturing at 1+ years) and have life spans of only three or four years. However, early maturity and a short life span are also typical of populations of Trout inhabiting rich alkaline waters. Slow-growing, late-maturing Trout (i.e. spawning for the first time at 4+ years or more) are characteristic of large oligotrophic lakes. In such lakes, however, a wide range of relationships between age and size occurs, e.g. Trout that have passed one year in the nursery stream before migrating to the lake often grow faster and mature sooner than Trout that have spent two, three or more years in their natal stream. Generally, the longer the period spent before migration, the slower the subsequent growth and later maturity, but this complex relationship between environment and genetics is not yet fully understood.

Trout are catholic feeders and their voraciousness is well known. The great bulk of their diet throughout the seasons, however, consists of aquatic bottom-dwelling and midwater invertebrates, although from about midsummer

Table 14 Food of Sea Trout in the marine Lochs Etive and Eil, Argyll, Scotland (after Pemberton 1976b), as percentage occurrence.

Stomach contents	Lochs Etive & Eil
Algae	3.9*
Molluscs	+
Worms	
Polychaetes	6.7
Crustaceans	
Isopods	9.5
Amphipods	33.5
Mysids	4.3
Insects	14.2
Fish	
Clupeids	16.8
Sandeels	11.5
Others**	2.7
Terrestrial	
Beetle adults	8.9
Detritus	3.9*
NUMBER OF FISH EXAMINED	1277

*This percentage shared between these items.
**Other fish eaten included European Eel, Whiting, Saithe, Cod, Two-spot Goby, Sand Goby, Snake Blenny, Viviparous Blenny, Sand Smelt, Short-spined Sea Scorpion, Lumpsucker and Flounder.

until autumn invertebrates of terrestrial origin which fall or are blown on to the water surface may dominate. In lakes, Trout patrol territories in search of food, while in streams their feeding strategy is to occupy and hold the best feeding station that their rank in the local hierarchy allows, and wait for food organisms to drift past in the water column or on the surface. They also pick up nearby food off the bottom. In spite of their well-known cannibal tendencies (much exploited by anglers using fish-like lures or dead fish baits), Trout other than ferox take surprisingly few small fish, even though the latter may be in abundance. Generally, the larger the Trout the more likely it is to feed on other fish. Certain species of small fishes appear to be more easily caught by Trout than others. Sticklebacks and Perch fry, for instance, can be important, while Minnows are seldom found in Trout stomachs (although fresh Minnow is a good bait). Minnows do, however, become readily available during early summer, when they gather into tight shoals to spawn in shallow water, and individual Trout may be found with stomachs bulging with them. It may well be that some Trout develop better techniques for catching small fish than the rest of their brethren.

The range of food organisms taken by Trout is very wide. Larger aquatic organisms taken include frogs, toads, newts, crayfish and a range of small fish including even fingerling Pike, while during spates or over newly flooded land, small rodents, shrews and unfledged birds can be added to this list. Trout are usually most attracted by moving objects, but during the 'hungry' time of the year, after spawning and until spring, when food is normally in short supply, quite large inanimate objects may be taken. The authors have seen stones, pieces of wood and on one occasion a coal clinker being taken. It is at this time too that Trout will occasionally pick up a motionless metal lure off the bottom.

Although in most cases Trout locate their prey by sight, they can also use their sense of smell and can detect the turbulence another organism creates while moving through the water. Fresh baits such as maggots, worms and small fish are taken by Trout at depths well beyond the penetration of light. These baits are also effective in shallow water during the darkest of nights. Recent research has involved the gill netting of Trout at depths of up to 30m. Some of these contained fresh Arctic Charr in their stomachs. Deep trolling in lakes using a metal lure is also an effective way of catching large ferox trout, although the large odourless metal lure is moving through water well beyond the limit of light penetration. It is likely, therefore, that in our largest lakes there may be populations of large Trout living mostly in complete or semi-darkness, feeding on shoals of Charr and, in some situations, Powan.

The food of Trout in the sea seems to consist mainly of small fish such as sand-eels and members of the cod and herring families; locally, Smelt and elvers are eaten as well as marine worms, molluscs and crustaceans. Trout caught at sea or in estuaries usually have their stomachs packed with these items. Finnock and small Sea Trout feed like Brown Trout in fresh water, but larger individuals behave more like Salmon – though unlike Salmon, it is common to find a few small invertebrates in their stomachs (usually terrestrial insects taken from the surface and small aquatic invertebrates such as midge larvae and pupae). Occasionally fish are found, but the small bulk taken cannot be of much value and Sea Trout in fresh water lose condition. Because of their increased level of activity at night, larger Sea Trout become vulnerable to anglers then and, due to their habit of taking small invertebrates from the surface, large Sea Trout in lakes are also vulnerable to fly fishing and in particular to 'dapping' – when a large dry fly or real insect on a hook is bounced over the surface by using a long rod and blow line operated from a boat.

Trout are subject at times to large internal and external parasite burdens. The most conspicuous of the latter are sea lice (*Lepeophtheirus*), crustacean copepod parasites which infest Sea and slob Trout, and all anadromous Trout carry them during their first few days in fresh water. Brown Trout in small ponds may be carriers of a close relative, the freshwater fish louse (*Argulus*), and usually also contain a variety of internal parasites in and around the stomach, on the gills and in the muscle of the body itself. A fluke (*Diplostomulum*) infects the eye and may affect the fishes' vision. The most common parasites of all are cestode tapeworms such as *Diphyllobothrium* and *Eubothrium*, and nematode round worms such as *Eustrongylides*. The latter are thin, wire-like orange worms which have a distressing habit of emerging from their cysts in the flesh of the fish while being cooked.

All these parasitic worms enter the fish as larval forms present in food organisms, and are mostly carried by planktonic crustaceans, freshwater shrimps and small fish, principally sticklebacks. Some of these internal parasites may accumulate within the Trout host, as further larval stages or as adults, depending on their life cycles, and in older Trout may reach such a density that the tissue built up around the alimentary canal restricts the passage of food. This situation appears most common in Trout in rich lakes, where there is a large selection of potential invertebrate hosts and small infected fish available to the trout. In fact, it has been suggested that the life span of Trout in some populations may be limited by the build up and accumulation of the internal parasite burden while, conversely, the occurrence of very old and large Trout (e.g. ferox) in certain lakes may only be possible due to a low infection rate by parasites.

Trout, particularly Sea Trout, are susceptible to Ulcerated Dermal Necrosis (UDN) and this and the typically associated secondary infection by fungus caused a very heavy mortality during the late 1960s when this disease was new and rampant throughout the country. Furunculosis kills fresh-run Sea Trout (and Salmon) and can reach epidemic levels under certain conditions when river flow is low and the temperature high. Brown Trout, although they may also be killed by this bacterial infection, can carry the disease which may not manifest itself externally until the individual becomes stressed, as for instance at spawning time.

Trout are preyed on by a wide range of predators in both fresh water and in the sea. Apart from cannibalism and predation by other fishes such as Pike, and sometimes Eels, Trout are taken by sawbill ducks, Herons, Cormorants, Black-throated Divers, terns and gulls. Large and small Trout fall prey to Otters and to Mink, while at spawning time adult Trout stranded in small streams are easy prey for many predators, and even Foxes make the most of this opportunity. At sea, especially in bays, estuaries and sea lochs, Common and Grey Seals make considerable inroads into Sea Trout stocks. However, humans are directly or indirectly the main enemies of Trout, through intensive angling and netting pressure (both legal and illegal) as well as pollution, etc. Sea Trout angling is an important local money earner in the more isolated parts of the country while the profitability of some marginal Salmon netting stations may hinge on the number of Sea Trout also taken. Due to the fact that, unlike Salmon, Sea Trout may return to fresh water to spawn many times, their population structure is particularly vulnerable to heavy cropping.

Brown Trout were once farmed on a large scale, primarily for stocking angling waters, but in recent years they have been largely displaced by Rainbow Trout for both this purpose and for the table. A few farms, however, still produce substantial numbers for stocking purposes – often for 'put and take' fisheries.

Rainbow Trout *Oncorhynchus mykiss* (Walbaum 1792)
Steelhead Trout, Kamloops Trout

The Rainbow Trout is native to the Pacific coast of North America, from Alaska south to north-west Mexico. It is found mainly in the river systems that drain the coastal ranges and the Rocky Mountains west to the Pacific Ocean. There are many varieties of the Rainbow Trout including the well known ones such as Steelhead Trout (which parallels the behaviour of our Sea Trout) and Kamloops Trout. Their taxonomic relationships are not yet clear, however. They are closely related to the other 'black-spotted trouts' such as Cutthroat Trout *Oncorhynchus clarki* and the exotic Golden Trout *O. aguabonita* and Gila Trout *O. gilae*, all natives of south-western North America. Over to the eastern coast of the Pacific Ocean a similar trout is found in Kamchatka and the neighbouring mainland.

Because of their fine sporting qualities and food value, Rainbow Trout have been widely redistributed throughout North America and much of the rest of the world, including the southern hemisphere. They were successfully introduced to the British Isles and to Europe towards the end of the last

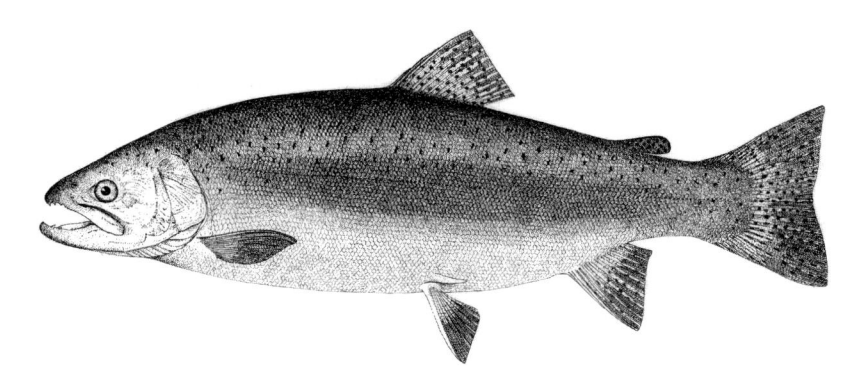

Fig. 47 Rainbow Trout (from Maitland 1972b).

century. Consignments of eggs were sent to Europe in 1882, and from there to England in 1884 and on to Ireland and Scotland in 1888. However, in spite of their very wide distribution within the British Isles for more than a century, only in a few cases has the species established itself to form self-sustaining populations. The vast majority of populations are maintained only by the regular introduction of hatchery-reared fish.

In shape, Rainbow Trout in the British Isles are rather more thick set than the native Brown Trout, and are easily distinguished from the latter by the iridescent pink to red band that runs along each side of the body to the end of the caudal peduncle – i.e. the rainbow. Also they have no red spots, but instead many black ones on both body and fins, including the adipose and tail fins. Usually too, they are more silvery than the average Brown Trout, but individuals, especially the older ones, can be as dark as Brown Trout. The scales are small, with 15–16 from the adipose fin forwards and downwards to the lateral line, which has some 100–150 scales along its length. The dorsal fin has 10–12 rays, the pectoral fins 11–17, the pelvic fins 9–10 and the anal fin 8–12 rays. There are 27–80 pyloric caecae and 60–66 vertebrae, but both these characters are variable and related to the length of the individual and its rate of development respectively.

There is no 'average' size for Rainbow Trout in the British Isles, due to the fact that nearly all populations are artificially maintained and therefore size is dependent on the size of fish when introduced and the stocking density. On the whole, fishery managers aim to produce a Rainbow Trout for the angler of around 340–680gm when stocking 'natural' fisheries (i.e. those into which small Rainbow Trout are introduced and allowed to grow) with hatchery-produced fingerlings. However, due to the tremendous increase in the scale of the Rainbow Trout farming industry, fish of all sizes up to some 9kg can be purchased for stocking, making the catching of 'trophy' Rainbow Trout rather a pointless achievement. A high proportion of the large Rainbow Trout used for stocking angling waters are elderly, retired broodstock and the objective seems to be to put them into a fishery and then angle for them before they die of old age or starvation. Sometimes they may be surreptitiously fed to eke out their life span and maintain some degree of condition.

Naturally hatched Rainbow Trout, which may occasionally turn up in the wild, are silvery little fish, bluish green dorsally and bearing 5–10 widely spaced oval parr marks along their sides as well as a smattering of small black spots. Their dorsal and anal fins have whitish-yellow to orange tips and the adipose fin is edged with black. They should not be easily confused with Brown Trout of the same size.

The teeth, as in Brown Trout, are well developed on both jaws and are present on both the head and the shaft of the vomer bone. When ripening sexually, the head of the male elongates and the background colour of the body becomes darker, contrasting strongly with the increased brightness of the pink-red bands along the sides.

Within the British Isles, Rainbow Trout have been widely distributed to provide sport for anglers. For this purpose, they are a better investment financially than Brown Trout, for Rainbow Trout are more easily captured than Brown Trout. Also, in recent years, hatchery-produced Brown Trout have been difficult to obtain, whereas almost anywhere in the country there is a convenient Rainbow Trout farm with stock for sale. An increased distribution of Rainbow Trout has also occurred as a result of escapes from both inland freshwater farms and marine pens. The authors spoke to one Rainbow Trout farmer recently who admitted that about 2000 fish escaped each year from his floating cages into the loch and river in which the cages were situated. When Rainbow Trout escape from sea pens (or are dumped in the sea for some reason) many seem to move quickly to the nearest estuary and ascend into fresh water. Although there are regular reports of Rainbow Trout being caught in coastal waters or in estuaries, there is no evidence so far of runs of Steelhead Trout becoming established.

Out of the many thousands of waters in the British Isles in which Rainbow Trout have been stocked over the last century, only in about six instances have self-sustaining populations arisen, although there are a number of other waters where they have spawned once or twice after introduction, but then died out. Rainbow Trout are notorious for escaping from waters into which they have been introduced, and elaborate devices are sometimes installed across lake outflows to prevent this.

The last investigation into the breeding status of Rainbow Trout in the British Isles was carried out in 1971. The findings suggested that the situation had not changed much since the previous study in the 1940s. The more recent study found that while at some 40 sites spawning had taken place, at only five were the populations self-sustaining. Two of these sites were in north-west Ireland and three in the southern half of England. Since then, however, a probably self-propagating population has been found in Scotland in a hill lochan in west Inverness-shire. Of the six breeding populations that are now known, two occur in low pH acid waters and four in high pH alkaline habitats.

The reasons why Rainbow Trout do not establish populations in the British Isles are not clear. It has been suggested that they establish more readily in mineral-rich eutrophic waters such as those in England where self-sustaining populations occur. However, one of the permanent populations in Ireland, at Lough Shure, Aranmore, and the only one in Scotland are both in acid mineral-poor waters. It is believed essential for them to have running water for spawning and this would preclude them from establishing in lakes without

Table 15 Food of Rainbow Trout in Llyn Alaw, Wales (after Hunt & O'Hara 1973) between October and February, as percentage volume.

Stomach contents	Llyn Alaw
Algae	15.0*
Macrophytes	15.0*
Molluscs	
Snails	+
Worms	+
Leeches	+
Crustaceans	
Water louse	3.6
Freshwater shrimp	65.0
Insects	
Aquatic bugs	11.2
Beetle adults	0.7
Caddis larvae	+
Midge larvae	0.8
Other insects	+
Fish	
Trout eggs	3.4
Terrestrial spiders	+
Detritus	15.0*
NUMBER OF FISH EXAMINED	38

*This value is shared among the items indicated.

an adequate inflow or outflow. Also, it is thought that the newly hatched fry are at a disadvantage in spawning and nursery streams shared with Brown Trout, where the latter hatch earlier and are therefore established territorially and thus provide too strong competition for the later emerged Rainbow Trout. In their native waters and in most countries where they have been introduced, Rainbow Trout populations are established in a very wide range of habitats, some very cold in winter, others at the upper limit of their temperature tolerance (c. 24°C) in summer, in both mineral rich and poor waters.

In their native waters in North America, Rainbow Trout spawn from March to August, the main period being from mid-April to late June. However, there are also winter spawning populations which breed from late December until early spring. In the British Isles, Rainbow Trout seem to be mainly early spring spawners, from February to March; at the Lake of Menteith, in central Scotland, the species was recorded as spawning in an inflowing stream on 26 March. These eggs hatched on 30 April. The orange-yellow eggs (some 3–5mm in diameter) are laid in a redd in the usual salmonid manner. Females produce about 1760–2640 eggs per kilogram of body weight. Their reproductive behaviour as a whole seems to be similar to that of Brown Trout.

Rainbow Trout seem to be most successful in their native habitats at summer temperatures around 21°C, but lake-living fish can stand higher temperatures than this if they are able to retreat at times to cooler, well-oxygenated waters. In the British Isles, Rainbow Trout have been found to be most active at 16°C. They grow more rapidly than Brown Trout, but overstocking leads to populations of stunted individuals. In lakes with mixed populations of Brown and Rainbow Trout, the fact that the latter show better catch returns is probably due to the fact that they are easier to catch, perhaps because they are less cautious than Brown Trout. This seems to be true for these species in all countries where they are both angled.

The food and feeding behaviour of Rainbow Trout is similar to that of Brown Trout. However, in one study of the winter food and feeding behaviour of Rainbow Trout living alongside Brown Trout in a lake, the former were found to be feeding more actively all winter and to have fuller stomachs than the latter. Most of the food of these Rainbow Trout was shrimps, water lice and water boatmen, but there was also some vegetable matter.

In large lakes outside the British Isles, a proportion of the population of Rainbow Trout may become ferox, like some Brown Trout, and reach a large size on a piscivorous diet. The world record Rainbow Trout is claimed to be a 19.10kg fish from Alaska, while in New Zealand (where they are not, of course, native) fish up to 9.5kg have been taken. The British rod-caught record at the moment is for a fish of 9.645kg caught in Loch Awe in 1986. This was probably an escapee from a local cage farm in the loch. There is no Irish record for this species. Anadromous Steelhead Trout can reach over 120cm in length and 16kg in weight.

The age of Rainbow Trout can usually be determined fairly readily from scale reading. In the British Isles, the species lives for only three or four years on average and in their native waters a similar life expectancy seems normal. The anadromous form, however, often lives for 6–8 years of age. It is often stated that genuine wild Rainbow Trout are much stronger and more successful in the wild than hatchery-produced ones and one of the authors, who has angled for indigenous specimens in British Columbia and naturalised fish in New Zealand, whole-heartedly agrees.

The parasites of Rainbow Trout are similar in many respects to those of Brown Trout. However, they seem particularly susceptible to the eye fluke, *Diplostomulum*, probably because they are mainly hatchery reared and living in crowded conditions where it is easy to pick up a large parasite burden before being released into the wild. Badly infected individuals assume an overall dark colour and swim blindly, close to the surface of the water. This makes them readily available to fish-eating birds (which are necessary secondary hosts in the life cycle), particularly in Scotland, where they are eaten by Ospreys, thus improving the chances of breeding success for both bird and fluke.

In spite of their lack of breeding success in the wild, there is no doubt that

Fig. 48 The first Pink Salmon caught in the British Isles, netted at Montrose in 1960 (Niall Campbell).

Table 16 Food of Pink Salmon in the north-eastern Pacific Ocean: juveniles (after Manzer 1969), as percentage number; adults (after LeBrasseur 1965), as percentage weight.

Stomach contents	Juveniles	Adults
Molluscs		
Gastropods	+	4
Squids	–	7
Crustaceans		
Ostracods	+	–
Copepods	31	1
Cirripedes	6	–
Isopods	+	–
Mysids	+	–
Euphausids	–	12
Cumaceans	+	–
Amphipods	1	7
Decapods	4	–
Insects	1	–
Other invertebrates		
Larvacea	40	–
Arrow-worms	+	–
Fish	5	66
NUMBER OF FISH EXAMINED	573	182

Rainbow Trout will continue to be a common species in the British Isles. Their ease of domestication, high conversion rate of food to flesh and sporting qualities and palatability will ensure their survival.

Pink Salmon *Oncorhynchus gorbuscha* (Walbaum 1792)
Humpback Salmon

The Pink Salmon is one of the five species of Pacific salmon of the genus *Oncorhynchus* which are native to the western rivers of North America, flowing into the Pacific Ocean. The Pink Salmon is one of three of these species which have been introduced by Russian fisheries workers to rivers entering the White Sea and therefore given access to the North Atlantic Ocean. Since the early 1960s, a number of individual fish of this species have been taken around the coasts of the British Isles and the species may now be considered as a vagrant here, even though there is no established population (cf. Sturgeon).

Pink Salmon are now well established in the White Sea area and provide a useful commercial fishery for the USSR. A few breeding populations have now apparently become established in some Norwegian rivers, while some stray fish have turned up in Iceland. The first specimen in British waters, which was seen by the authors, was caught in July 1960 in coastal nets set just south of Aberdeen. It was a fully mature male, 52.1cm in length and 1.8kg in weight, and its appearance caused some consternation, for its heavily spotted tail indicated that it was a Pacific salmonid. However, its other features did not fit with the provisional identification as a Steelhead Trout – the most likely species to turn up since so many Rainbow Trout were being moved around the country. Subsequent detailed examination confirmed that it was actually a Pink Salmon, presumed from the White Sea area. A few others were taken in the following years, but none has turned up for several years now. As a result, however, of recent introductions of this species to the rivers of the White Sea area, some further occurrences might be expected here in the next decade.

Adult Pink Salmon are some 43–61cm in length; a 50cm fish weighs about 1.7kg. The shape is typically salmonid – streamlined and laterally flattened. The mouth is large and terminal. There are well developed teeth on both jaws, on the head and shaft of the vomer bone, on the palatine bone and on the tongue. There are 24–35 gill rakers and 9–15 branchiostegals. The body is well covered with large cycloid scales, which number 147–205 along the lateral line. The pyloric caecae range in number from 95–224 and there are 63–72 vertebrae. There are 10–15 rays in the dorsal fin, 13–19 in the anal fin and 9–11 in the pectoral fins.

The colour of the adults is steel blue to blue-green along the back, grading into silver along the sides and white on the belly. There are large black spots above the lateral line and on the dorsal, adipose and tail fins. The young fish are also greenish with silvery sides but lack parr marks and spots. As the males ripen they develop a kype and the typical 'Pacific' hooked snout, with a gaping mouth and a huge hump in front of the dorsal fin. Much of the body takes on an overall pink hue, except the head and anterior ventral surface, which become a grey-green. The shape of the ripening female does not change too much, but she also becomes very pink with a grey head.

Two other species of Pacific salmon have been successfully introduced to waters in Europe outside the British Isles – the Chum Salmon *Oncorhynchus keta* and the Coho Salmon *Oncorhynchus kisutch* – and it is likely that both of them will make their way to British waters in future years – indeed Coho Salmon have already been recorded in the Channel Islands.

Chum Salmon have been introduced to the rivers of the White Sea area by the USSR but so far none has followed the Pink Salmon to the shores of the British Isles. Some Chum Salmon have been caught, however, by commercial netsmen off the Norwegian coast, and their status has been difficult to ascertain, for the fresh-run fish can easily be mistaken for Atlantic Salmon.

Coho Salmon have been considered of value for cage rearing at fish farms and stock have been taken into northern France for this purpose. Considerable numbers have escaped and young wild Coho have been recorded from rivers in Normandy and Brittany. Indeed, this species is already registered on the British rod-caught record lists and the record stands for a fish of 681gm caught in the sea at St Sampsons, Guernsey in the Channel Islands. As the young stages of this species are considered to be aggressive and predatory towards other young fish, their establishment in European salmonid waters might well have an adverse effect. As a result, a licence to import Coho Salmon into the British Isles a number of years ago caused considerable controversy and was granted on condition that the fish were kept for experimental purposes only, in tanks or ponds from which they could not escape alive into the wild. It is believed that all this stock has now been destroyed.

Arctic Charr *Salvelinus alpinus* (Linnaeus 1758)
Alpine Charr, Char, Charr, Cuddy, Red-bellied Trout, Red Waimb

The spellings for this species of 'Char' or 'Charr' are both acceptable, but the latter – derived from the Gaelic 'tarr' meaning belly (one Gaelic name for the Charr is Tarr-dhearg, meaning red bellied; the Welsh equivalent is Torgoch, meaning red belly) – is the more authentic. Although occurring quite widely in Ireland and northern Scotland, and very locally in south-west Scotland, north- west England and north Wales, the Charr is not a familiar fish to most

Fig. 49 Arctic Charr (from Maitland 1972b).

people and when encountered is often regarded as a curiosity – 'An ice age relict'. In fact, it occurs in quite large numbers in some lakes, probably outnumbering the Trout population where they co-exist, as they usually do. However, due to its cryptic habits it is seldom seen, even by anglers. Relatively little research has been carried out on Arctic Charr in the British Isles, except for the population in Windermere in Cumbria, one of the few places where there has also been a traditional local fishery for many years – originally based on supplying fish for the local 'Potted Charr' industry. However, there has been considerable interest in the species in recent years and it is now being studied and angled for in several other waters. In other parts of the Charr's range it is a useful species; in arctic areas it is a most valuable fish for consumption by both humans and dogs.

Charr seem to fascinate the people who become involved with them and the International Society of Arctic Charr Fanatics is a serious body of scientists established in 1980 to study and promote all aspects of this lovely fish. ISACF organises workshops in a different Charr country every two years, where scientists from the Charr nations meet to discuss current research and conservation and to catch and eat the species. The Arctic Charr, as well as being spectacularly beautiful, is a peaceful fish and, in spite of frequently living in habitats which are extremely remote from humans, can be tamed rapidly and may be taking food from the hand within a few weeks of captivity. In contrast to trout, they do not easily panic in a tank or pond (where they will co-exist with goldfish and other pond species) but swim calmly around in shoals. The association of Charr with some of the most isolated and extremely northerly regions of the world seems to add to their mystique.

In shape, Arctic Charr resemble slender trout, but their background colour and markings are quite distinctive. Like all Charrs (*Salvelinus*) this species does not possess any dark spots, but normally has yellow, cream, pink, red or orange spots on a background ranging from bluish-grey to greenish-brown. The lower half of the sides and the belly are variable in colour and may range from dull pink to bright vermilion. The males are immediately recognisable by their more intense colouration in this area, while the females are sometimes drab and those from dark habitats may even look darkly silver – rather like mature Sea Trout finnock. The belly fins of the males are usually orange to red with a white leading edge, whereas those of females are pale yellowish. Like trout, Charr are subject to wide variation, so

Fig. 50 A young Arctic Charr from Ennerdale Water (William Howes).

such so that the British populations were previously split into at least 15 different species. Though it is accepted that there are a number of distinct local races, all the populations are now considered to be one species – *Salvelinus alpinus*.

The body is slim and streamlined with some lateral flattening. One of the main diagnostic features of the Arctic Charr is the presence of teeth on the head of the vomer bone but none on the shaft. Some hyoid teeth are present but not on the centre of the palate. The gill rakers are well developed – as is appropriate to their commonly planktonic diet – there are 7–13 on the upper arch and 12–19 on the lower arch.

The dorsal fin has 12–15 rays, the pectoral fins 9–11 rays and the anal fin 10–13 rays. The number of pyloric caecae ranges from 28–44, and the number of vertebrae from 59–63. The body is well covered with very small scales, which range in number along the lateral line from 190–240. There are 19–22 scales diagonally forward from the adipose fin to the lateral line.

Young Arctic Charr are a silvery monochrome with 10–18 large grey parr marks along each side. Young and adults of this species can be distinguished from the American Brook Charr, the only other Charr occurring in the British Isles, as they lack the conspicuous dark vermiculate patterning which the latter species has along the back and sides as well as on the upper and lower lobes of the tail fin.

In the British Isles all populations of Arctic Charr are non-anadromous. The adults vary in size but are usually rather small, typically about 20–25cm in length (85–170gm in weight), but in some lakes they may regularly reach over 35cm and 600gm. Some exceptionally large Charr have been recorded recently from the vicinity of floating fish-farm cages in Scottish lochs, where their diet is boosted by the large amounts of waste food pellets available to them. The authors have seen fish of over 1kg netted in these situations. The record fish for a number of years was from Loch Insh, then a new record was established for this species by a fish weighing 1.502kg, caught in 1985 in Loch Earn followed by a fish weighing 2.18kg, caught in 1987 in Loch Garry, Inverness. These records have been beaten several times subsequently – all by Charr taken in the viciniy of fish cages. The present record stands at over 3kg, for a fish caught in 1990 in Loch Arkaig.

The Arctic Charr is a holarctic species occurring all round the northern hemisphere, and in the northern parts of its range forms mixed anadromous

Fig. 51 Loch Sionascaig, Inverpolly National Nature Reserve, where an original community of Trout (both normal and ferox) and Arctic Charr occurs (Rob Tweddle).

and non-anadromous populations (comparable to Brown and Sea Trout) where the sea-going Charr can reach a large size. The world rod-caught record stands at 13.46kg for a fish taken in a river in the North West Territories of Canada. Large freshwater Charr can also occur in large lakes in Scandinavia and in the alpine lakes of central Europe, where ferox individuals have reached over 80cm in length and 10kg in weight.

In the British Isles, Arctic Charr have the reputation of being found only in large deep oligotrophic lakes lying in glaciated basins – which fits in with their ice-age image. Though this is often the case, there are also many populations living in shallow biologically rich habitats, as is commonly the case in Ireland. In Scotland, of 85 Charr lochs investigated by the authors, 43 (52%) had an average depth of 15m and 7 (8%) less than 5m. Arctic Charr are not limited in their distribution by having to live in particularly cold lakes and appear to thrive in much the same upper ranges as Brown Trout. However, there is some experimental evidence that they are able to thrive relatively better than other salmonids in very cold conditions. One of the authors has reared Arctic Charr in an aquarium without aeration or water circulation where the temperature at times peaked to 20°C. In North America, Arctic Charr are known to live at summer water temperatures of 20°C and in swift running water even as high as 23.8°C. The pelagic behaviour of Charr in lakes is probably due more as a result of having to compete with the more aggressive Brown Trout and other competitors and predator species than having to find deep cool water.

Table 17 Food of Arctic Charr in Loch Fada (where Trout are present) and in Loch Meallt (where Trout are absent), both in Scotland, as percentage occurrence (after Campbell 1982).

Stomach contents	Loch Fada	Loch Meallt
Zooplankton	77	4
Midwater & surface insects	18	20
Bottom invertebrates	6	72
Fish (sticklebacks)	–	8
NUMBER OF FISH EXAMINED	25	94

Table 18 Food of Arctic Charr in seven lakes in Cumbria, England (after Frost 1977), as percentage occurrence. A. Windermere B. Coniston Water C. Crummock Water D. Ennerdale Water E. Wastwater F. Thirlmere G. Haweswater.

Stomach contents	A	B	C	D	E	F	G
Macrophytes	3	–	–	5	–	–	–
Molluscs							
Pea shells	3	–	–	–	–	–	–
Crustaceans							
Daphnia	40	78	97	–	–	13	23
Bythotrephes	33	87	55	4	–	3	27
Leptodora	22	9	3	13	–	–	–
Bosmina	3	–	52	48	37	20	–
Other cladocerans	2	–	3	9	–	17	18
Ostracods	1	–	–	–	–	–	–
Diaptomus	3	–	–	–	–	7	–
Cyclops	–	–	16	–	6	37	–
Other copepods	2	–	–	–	–	23	9
Mysis	–	–	–	9	–	–	–
Freshwater shrimp	5	–	–	–	–	–	–
Insects							
Chaoborid l & p	13	–	–	–	–	–	–
Midge larvae & p	21	4	–	9	19	66	73
Other insect larvae	4	4	–	–	6	–	4
Other invertebrates	1	4	–	–	–	13	4
Fish	1	–	–	19	–	–	–
Charr eggs	26	–	–	5	12	–	–
Other vertebrates	–	–	–	–	–	–	–
Terrestrial organisms	2	–	–	–	12	43	4
Detritus	1	–	–	–	–	–	–
NUMBER OF FISH EXAMINED	818	25	41	109	76	48	23

There are no true river populations of Arctic Charr in the British Isles, but they are found in streams running into charr lakes (e.g. Loch Insh) and at times some fish move into or are washed over dams and weirs into flowing water at spawning time. However, in north-west Scotland, there is one instance at least of Charr of less than 1 year in age having been found in a stream flowing into the loch in which the parents had spawned.

There are very few records from the British Isles (three that the authors know of) where Charr have been intentionally redistributed by humans. This is not perhaps surprising, as to begin with it would be difficult to obtain and transport living Charr, and secondly there would be little material value in establishing them in new waters. However, in at least two other waters in Scotland new Charr populations have been unintentionally established by local hydro-electric developments.

Spawning normally takes place from late September to December, but there is also the well known instance of the charr population in Windermere, one part of which spawns in the autumn, the other in the spring (February and March). So little research has been carried out on Charr in the British Isles that there could well be other localities where there are both autumn and spring spawners. In lakes, spawning takes place over gravel and stones, normally in fairly shallow water near the shore or on a submerged reef. In Windermere, the autumn spawners use shallow water, 1–3m deep, but the spring spawners use much deeper water at some 20–30m. A third part of the population migrates up an inflowing river to spawn in November and December. The water temperatures at the time of winter spawning are 6–9°C and during the spring spawning, 4–6°C.

The spawning behaviour is typically salmonid, whether in still or flowing water, and the female clears the bottom of loose debris and excavates a redd at a selected site by turning on her side and sweeping her tail fin up and down. This is done within a territory that a mature male has established and is defending. In the British Isles, males usually mature at 2+ years of age, but occasionally at 1+ years, whereas the females are usually 3+ years old at first spawning. Data on fecundity from one population in a Scottish loch suggested that the relationship between the size (length or weight) of the female and the number of eggs produced was poor, but that a fish of 250gm might be expected to produce 400–600 eggs. The eggs are amber in colour and comparatively large – some 4–5mm in diameter.

The ageing of Charr by scale reading is not such a comparatively straightforward task as with Salmon or trout. The technique is normally used in conjunction with the examination of otoliths, and sometimes the latter technique alone is relied upon. It was found with Windermere Charr that scales were satisfactory for calculating their age and growth with the proviso that care

Fig. 52 Examples of the two races of Arctic Charr in Loch Rannoch: three of the pelagic race above, and three of the benthic race below. The bottom fish had just eaten a small Charr (Andy Walker).

Table 19 The food of the pelagic and benthic races of Arctic Charr in Loch Rannoch, Scotland (after Walker et al. 1988), as percentage occurrence.

Stomach contents	Pelagic	Benthic
Molluscs		
Pea shells	–	12.6
Worms	–	1.9
Crustaceans		
Cladocerans	95.4	1.0
Insects		
Mayfly larvae	–	1.9
Stonefly larvae	1.1	–
Beetles	0.5	2.5
Alderfly larvae	–	1.0
Caddis larvae	–	37.6
Midge larvae & pupae	1.9	5.7
Fish	–	3.6*
Terrestrial organisms	0.6	–
Unidentified	0.7	10.7
NUMBER OF FISH EXAMINED	98	95

* includes 0+ Charr

had to be taken with the spring spawning fish, some of whose fry grew so poorly during their first summer that scales were not formed until the following summer. Thus, evidence of the first year of life is lost and their age is underestimated by one year. The same situation is true with young Salmon and Trout living in high cold streams in the highlands. It was also found with some of the older Windermere Charr that annuli at the edge of the scales could be lost through erosion at spawning time, and otoliths were found to be useful in checking the age of such fish.

Arctic Charr can, however, grow rapidly during their first year of life, which is spent in a lake, and equals or surpasses that of Trout in the same system. Growth is noticeably slower after this, however. The optimum temperature for charr growth appears to be from 12–16°C, which is also the optimum for Brown Trout. Most charr populations are dominated by fish of the 3, 4 and 5 year classes and the maximum age is usually 7–10 years. In Loch Rannoch, where it has been shown recently that there are two races of Charr – one a benthic form, the other pelagic in habit – the growth of the pelagic form is initially faster, but after the fourth year the benthic form starts to grow faster and most of the larger Charr in the loch belong to this group.

Arctic Charr have the reputation of living an exclusively plankton-feeding pelagic life in lakes and they are certainly well equipped to do so with their well-developed gill rakers. These help Charr to feed rapidly on plankton where it is thick and can be taken in easily. This is in contrast to trout, which have to use up much more energy in taking in each plankter individually. However, they are by no means entirely pelagic. Out of 15 Scottish charr populations investigated by the authors, six were found at the time of sampling to be feeding exclusively on planktonic crustaceans, while in a further six lochs these food organisms dominated or co-dominated along with benthic organisms. In three, Charr were found to be feeding almost exclusively on benthic invertebrates, especially molluscs and caddis larvae. All the fish examined were adults.

Some Charr are piscivorous and in one loch eat, not only adult sticklebacks, but also prey upon the egg clumps in stickleback nests. Here, these two species are the only fish present – one of the very few sites in the British Isles where Charr exist in the absence of Trout – and behave like them, feeding on the sticklebacks and benthos and apparently ignoring the plankton there. In Loch Rannoch, with its two races of Charr, small Charr have been found in the stomachs of the benthic group, a situation reminiscent of some charr populations elsewhere in Europe and in North America where ferox-type Charr prey on populations of small stunted Charr. In Windermere, Charr eat some of their own eggs at spawning time. Virtually nothing is known about the food or feeding habits of juvenile Charr in the British Isles, but plankton is assumed to be a major part of their diet.

Anglers catch Charr on a variety of baits and methods of presentation. They may be taken by deep trolling with metal lures or by deep ledgered baits such as maggots and worms. They may also be taken at the surface on a wet fly, particularly in the evening or during the night. In many lochs, the site of shoals of Charr 'dimpling' (i.e. taking small adult insects at the surface) on calm evenings is a familiar sight. Few anglers fish specifically for Charr, but the numbers of such fishermen are increasing steadily. Charr flesh is most palatable, and they are often more easily caught than Trout once the technique suiting a particular habitat is mastered.

Charr are preyed on by other fish, principally large ferox Brown Trout, with which they normally co-exist, and Pike and Perch – the latter two species being common predators in Irish and English charr waters. It appears now that benthic Charr may also be significant predators of young Charr in some habitats. Brown Trout and Eels take the eggs of spawning Charr in Windermere, where Goldeneye ducks are also recorded as predators of charr eggs. Charr seem particularly susceptible to predation by Pike, a recent alien species in many charr waters, and a number of charr populations may have become extinct following the introduction of this voracious species, which is still being thoughtlessly moved about by humans. Charr are also very sensitive to pollution, another factor that has led to their extinction in a number of waters over the last two centuries.

Netting experience suggests that the odour of Charr may be attractive to some predators, such as Eels and trout. It is common to find Eels attacking and eating Charr caught in a gill net whilst ignoring Trout caught in the same net. Dead, fresh Charr are also a favoured bait for large Trout when fished in deep water, below the limit of light penetration. In Loch Doon recently, one of the authors found that the stomachs of all the Brown Trout caught along with spawning Charr were full of charr eggs.

On the whole, Charr are fairly free from parasites. One ectoparasite found in a few populations is the gill copepod *Salmincola edwardsii*, which occurs on the gills and in the gill cavity. The protozoan *Henneguya* occurs in some Charr and forms small pale cysts at the base of the tail. The parasitic tapeworm *Diphyllobothrium* also occurs in some Charr, encysted on the surface of the viscera.

Charr have been relatively little exploited by humans in the British Isles. The English Lake District fish have been caught for centuries and used as a basis for a small-scale local luxury food market, but in other parts of the country they seem only to have been harvested at their spawning time, when they are most vulnerable, and sold locally. Few anglers have bothered to fish for Charr until recently, but due to the pressures on other species, Charr are becoming increasingly regarded as an attractive alternative quarry, particularly since the British Record (Rod-caught) Fish Committee has accepted Charr as a trophy fish. It is likely therefore that in the future, the presence of Charr may be a significant attraction to angling tourists in northern Scotland and possibly in Ireland too. Attempts are at present being made in Scotland to establish a system of cropping the Charr in some large lochs, as is commonly done in Norway, as a crofter industry in a region where other natural resources are few.

Brook Charr *Salvelinus fontinalis* (Mitchill 1815)
American Brook Trout, Aurora Trout, Brookie, Fontinalis, Mud Trout, Speckled Trout

For a long time after its introduction to the British Isles, towards the end of the last century, this colourful salmonid from North America was called the American Brook Trout or sometimes by its specific name 'Fontinalis'. However, it is really a Charr and this fact has become increasingly recognised in recent years. A native of eastern Canada and the east coast of the USA as far south as the State of Georgia, it is found in river systems draining to the Atlantic Ocean, where it is most often called the Speckled or Eastern Brook Trout. However, it has now been widely redistributed throughout North America and to many other parts of the world also. It was introduced to the British Isles in 1868, some time before its compatriot the Rainbow Trout, as well as to most of Europe, including Scandinavia, before the end of the last century. There are now established populations in Europe, Asia, Australasia, southern Africa and South America.

In its native environment there are anadromous and non-anadromous races of the Brook Charr and not long after it was introduced to the British Isles there were reports of specimens being caught in bays and estuaries around the coast. However, there have been no such reports in recent times, probably because it is no longer so widely distributed, its popularity as a sport fish apparently declining in the face of competition from the more dashing Rainbow Trout. However, gradually more and more self-propagating populations of Brook Charr have become established and there are now more of

Fig. 53 Brook Charr (from Maitland 1972b).

Table 20 Food of Brook Charr in long-established populations in two Scottish lochs (+ = present, + + = common, + + + = abundant) (original data).

Stomach contents	Loch 1	Loch 2
Macrophytes	+	–
Molluscs		
Pea shells	–	+
Insects		
Aquatic bugs	–	+
Caddis larvae	+ +	+ +
Caddis adults	+	–
Midge pupae	–	+ +
Fish		
Brook Charr	–	+
Other vertebrates		
Frog tadpoles & young	+ + +	–
Terrestrial organisms		
Dragonfly adults	–	+
Ichneumon adults	–	+
Beetle adults	–	+ +
Diptera adults	+	+ +
Unidentified insects	–	+ + +
NUMBER OF FISH EXAMINED	4	9

Table 21 Food of Brook Charr and Rainbow Trout in Castle Lake, California, United States (after Wurtsbaugh et al. 1975), as percentage weight.

Stomach contents	Brook Charr	Rainbow Trout
Molluscs		
Snails	0.2	–
Crustaceans		
Cladocerans	13.6	15.7
Ostracods	0.8	–
Copepods	2.3	15.0
Insects		
Mayfly larvae	58.5	64.4
Dragonfly larvae	0.6	–
Beetle larvae & pupae	0.3	–
Caddis larvae	1.2	1.0
Midge larvae & pupae	9.8	4.0
Terrestrial organisms	12.7	14.9
NUMBER OF FISH EXAMINED	293	136

these than there are of Rainbow Trout. Some of these populations have easy access to the sea, but there is no evidence that there is any anadromous tendency nowadays.

Brook Charr have well developed teeth in the upper and lower jaws, but elsewhere on the head of the vomer bone only. Gill raker numbers vary from 14–22, pyloric caecae from 23–40 and vertebrae from 57–62. There are normally 10–14 major rays on the dorsal fin and 8–10 on the pelvic fins, alongside the base of which is a distinct, fleshy, pelvic axillary process. The pectoral fins have 11–14 soft branched rays and the anal fin 9–14 rays. The streamlined body is well covered in small cycloid scales, of which there are some 122–240 along the lateral line. The flesh colour ranges from white to a deep pink.

The Brook Charr is typically salmonid in shape but more thick set than the Arctic Charr or even the Brown Trout. It can be easily distinguished from the former by the alternate light and dark wavy lines – vermiculations – forming a marbled pattern on its back and on the dorsal and tail fins. It has many more cream to greenish-yellow spots along its flanks than the Arctic Charr and these spots mix with red ones encircled by blue haloes. To the angler a rising Brook Charr gives a greenish impression whereas an Arctic Charr gives a pinkish-bronze one. The Brook Charr is a really beautiful fish and the authors have known hardened anglers who were jubilant after landing a large brilliant male of the species, and quite unable to bring themselves to deliver the *coup de grace*! The belly fins of mature male Brook Charr are bright red-orange with white leading edges backed by a narrow black strip. The lower flank of the fish is also a bright red-orange grading into a sooty belly. The male also develops a pronounced kype. The females are much paler, but very delicately marked. Sea-running Brook Charr (the 'Sea Trout' of eastern Canada) are overall silvery, but with some red spots showing through the silver. Young Brook Charr are greenish and well vermiculated and are not likely to be confused with any other young salmonids in the British Isles.

Brook Charr spawn about the same time as most populations of Arctic Charr, beginning often at the end of September. As with many other salmonids an area of clean gravel is selected for redd cutting. This can be in a lake (often where a spring is welling up) or in a stream into which the fish have migrated just previously. However, many populations in this country seem to use quite muddy streams for spawning. At spawning time, both sexes become very aggressive towards intruding rivals or potential egg predators. The eggs are quite large, from 3.5–5.0mm in diameter and yellowish-orange in colour. The fecundity of females varies greatly and may range from just 100 eggs for a small female 14.5cm in length to 5000 for a large female of 55.8cm. At 4.4°C the eggs take about 109 days to hatch and at the same temperature the fry start to emerge from the gravel and begin feeding after a further 60 days. Scales start to appear on the fry when they reach a length of some 5cm.

Maturity is usually reached after three years but, as with other salmonids, is variable and to some extent dependent on growth rate. In a loch lightly stocked by one of the authors with Brook Charr fry, the males matured at 1+ years with lengths ranging from 18 to 21cm, indicating a relatively fast rate of growth. They are reputed to be a short-lived fish, similar to Rainbow Trout, and in their native habitat seldom live longer than five years and apparently never beyond eight years of age. However, exceptional populations do occur, and in one high-altitude lake in California (with no spawning facilities) where the species had been introduced, and which has ice cover for eight months of the year, individuals of 24+ years were found.

There is little biological information on wild Brook Charr in the British Isles, though one of the authors has studied two self-sustaining populations inhabiting hill lochs on the west coast of Scotland. There, investigations revealed that in one of the lochs, spawning must take place within the loch itself while in a second, the inflowing and outflowing streams evidently serve as both spawning and nursery areas. In the first loch, small shoals of Brook Charr, all under one year of age, were seen cruising swiftly over the littoral area taking surface insects. A feature of this loch was the abundance of frog tadpoles (which were in an advanced state of metamorphosis) and newly metamorphosed frogs. The stomach contents of adult Brook Charr consisted

Fig. 54 An unusual hybrid: a cross between Brown Trout and Brook Charr, sometimes known as Zebra or Tiger Trout (William Howes).

almost exclusively of tadpoles and small frogs, along with a few caddis pupae. By contrast, no tadpoles were ever found in the stomachs of Brown Trout in lochs in northern Scotland during studies covering a span of 18 years – although adult frogs were commonly found in the trout stomachs each spring. Larval stages (plerocercoids) of the cestode tapeworm *Diphyllobothrium* were found in the gut of one fish.

In the second loch, where the average size of the Brook Charr was much less, and the density of fish much higher, the stomach contained benthic invertebrates, ranging from the pea cockle, *Pisidium*, to emerging midge pupae. Adult terrestrial insects were also found. In one stomach the remains of a less than one year old Brook Charr, about 60mm in length, were found. Again, by contrast, small Brown Trout are very rarely found in the stomachs of normal loch-living Brown Trout.

The age and rate of growth of Brook Charr from these lochs has also been studied. Considering the situation and chemical poverty of the lochs, the rate of growth of the Brook Charr is exceptional, particularly in the first two years. Clearly they are well suited to west highland conditions.

Although there are more established populations of Brook Charr in the British Isles than of Rainbow Trout, it cannot be claimed that the former species naturalises successfully in this country. Of the eight established populations known to the authors, five are in lochs with no stream spawning grounds and the remaining three in lochs where the only streams are small muddy ones. None of these lochs contains Brown Trout, although one of them does have Arctic Charr and some non-predatory coarse fish. It appears that Brook Charr can maintain populations better than Brown Trout in lochs with poor spawning facilities, and also that they are more likely to become established in the absence of Trout and other fish (although there are, of course, situations where the two species live together and they may even hybridise).

Thus, Brook Charr can grow well in the British Isles and should reach weights of 340–450gm in three years, even in poor waters, as long as the stocking density it not too high. They seem particularly suitable for stocking lakes or ponds that are not suitable for Brown or Rainbow Trout. They will thrive in small, shallow, sheltered muddy or peaty ponds, and will rise to an artificial fly in conditions when it is unlikely that a normal Brown Trout would be so tricked! Wild Brook Charr can grow up to 45cm and the British rod-caught record stood at 1.1kg, until specially fattened fish were available and placed in 'put and take' fisheries. The present rod-caught record stands at 2.65kg for a fish caught in 1981 at the Avington Fishery in Hampshire. In North America, the record stands at 6.57kg for a fish taken in the Nipigon River in Ontario.

Brook Charr show the characteristic salmonid quality of great plasticity of form and behaviour in relation to environment. They can flourish as populations of tiny individuals in small streams, or behave like Salmon, migrating downstream to large lakes or coastal waters to feed and reach a size of several kilograms before returning to fresh water to spawn. Like all salmonids they require cool, well-oxygenated water, though they can survive up to 25°C. However, they are normally found well below 20°C and prefer around 13–16°C. They show peak activity and food consumption at just above 13°C. Their feeding habits and behaviour are similar in many ways to those of Brown Trout, and like trout, they can locate their food even in waters of very poor visibility. In one shallow peaty loch known to one of the authors, where visibility was only a few centimetres, Brook Charr and Brown Trout feed almost exclusively on the bottom on the water slater *Asellus*.

There is likely always to be a limited interest from anglers in Brook Charr and most of the breeding populations seem to survive partly because of their remoteness. This is a very vulnerable species and populations could well disappear as a result of the introduction of trout, or of predatory fish such as Pike or Perch. Although not a native fish they are an interesting and attractive species and unlikely to do any harm to our native fish fauna.

11

Whitefish

The whitefishes (family Coregonidae) are a temperate, northern hemisphere family found in cool, clean waters in northern Europe, Asia and North America. Their classification is complicated and often controversial but currently there are thought to be three genera and about 20–30 species. The difficulty encountered in assigning members of the family to any particular species results from the great variety of form. This relates to the particular environments in which each population lives, where the diagnostic features on which they have been classified may become modified. Similar difficulties are also encountered in the classification of the Salmonidae, to which the Coregonidae are closely related.

In appearance, coregonids are typically salmonid in form and background colouration, but they have very large scales and do not have any colour, patterning or spots. They also resemble salmonids in ecological requirements and behaviour, in that they need a cool, unpolluted environment and include wholly freshwater and anadromous populations, the latter particularly in the northern areas of their range.

In large lakes, where they feed mostly on pelagic and/or benthic invertebrates, they usually occur in large shoals and can be the basis of very important commercial fisheries. Their white flesh is excellent in texture and in flavour. In North America, several species provide anglers with sport and have been widely redistributed for this purpose and also for commercial exploitation in the USSR. The Omul of Lake Baikal is a whitefish and it is heavily exploited there for food and sport. No whitefish has been introduced into southern hemisphere waters. Whitefish populations are sensitive to over-exploitation and pollution, and several large populations have 'crashed' in recent times, including that of the famous Omul. In 1971, a seven-year moratorium on the netting of this fish was pronounced by the USSR. A number of populations in other parts of the world have become extinct.

Spawning takes place in the winter when eggs are laid over clean gravel and stones in shallow water, to hatch in the spring. In one genus, *Stenodus* – the 'Inconnu' of rivers flowing to the Arctic Ocean – individuals grow, atypically, to a very large size (up to 130cm), have a large underhung mouth and are fish eaters. The existing populations of whitefishes in the British Isles are thought to have originated, like those of Trout and Arctic Charr, from anadromous ancestors which migrated into fresh waters after the last glaciation.

Identification

Because of the great variety of form found in the members of this family their identification in the many parts of the northern hemisphere is often a matter of some difficulty. The situation is made even more difficult in some places, such as the alpine lakes of Europe, where new species have been introduced and hybridised with the local species to such an extent that both the original types have disappeared and left a single new 'race' in possession of the habitat. However, there are so few populations in the British Isles and all conform rather closely to the expected type that there should really be no difficulty in separating the four species involved. It should be remembered that one of these, the Houting, is a brackish water vagrant species, which is now extinct in British waters. For the sake of completeness, and with the hope that it might one day return, it is included in the following key, which presents the main distinguishing characteristics of the four species.

1. Snout conical and elongated in front. Distance between the front edge of the eye and tip of the snout more than twice the diameter of the eye. **HOUTING**

   Snout not produced in front. Distance between the front edge of the eye and tip of snout less than twice the diameter of the eye. **2.**

2. Upper jaw terminal, mouth inferior. Thirteen or more rays in the anal fin. Less than 65 gill rakers. **POWAN**

   Lower jaw terminal or both jaws the same length. Less than 13 rays in the anal fin. More than 65 gill rakers. **3.**

3. Lower jaw terminal, mouth superior. Less than 85 gill rakers. **VENDACE**

   Both jaws of equal length. More than 85 gill rakers. **POLLAN**

Houting *Coregonus oxyrinchus* (Linnaeus 1758) Hautin, Sea Whitefish

This species is closely related to the Powan *Coregonus lavaretus* and many believe that it is really just an anadromous race of that species. The normal adult length is some 25–35cm but fish of up to 50cm, weighing over 2kg, have been recorded. There are no angling records for this species in the British Isles.

Like most other members of the genus this species is very variable in form, but one of the most characteristic features is the well developed snout, which projects above the inferior mouth. The latter is rather small and toothless. These features separate it immediately from the only other similar fish which might occur in the same habitats, the Smelt. Though both are rather silvery salmonid-like fish with adipose fins, the latter has a large superior mouth with well developed teeth.

The body is streamlined and flattened laterally and is well covered with silvery scales of which there are some 80–90 along the well developed lateral line. The medium-sized dorsal fin has 12–15 rays and the anal fin some 12–15. There are some 27–44 gill rakers and 53–60 vertebrae. Like the others in the family, the Houting is a dark bluish-green along the back which grades into silvery grey along the sides and eventually into a creamy white on the belly. The dorsal fins and tail are rather darker than the other fins.

Though some other species do go into brackish water in the Baltic this is the only truly anadromous whitefish in European waters. Its numbers have undergone a severe decline during this century, probably as a result of overfishing and the impact of pollution and barriers in most of the rivers in which it was formerly abundant, such as the Rhine, Weser and Elbe. It is primarily

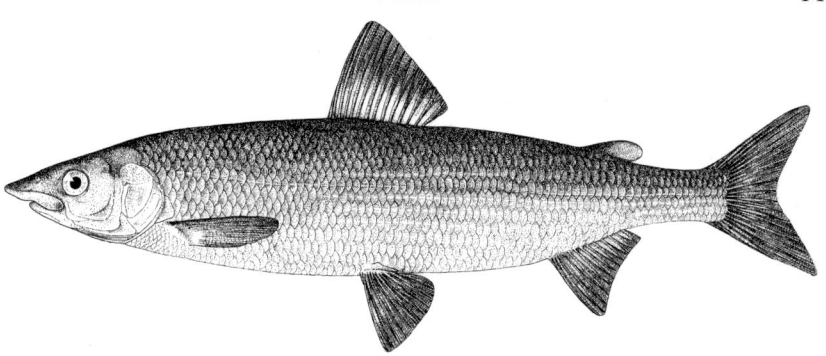

Fig. 55 Houting (from Maitland 1972b).

a fish of the eastern North Sea and especially the Baltic, where it was at one time abundant but now occurs in only a few rivers.

In the British Isles it, like the Sturgeon, has only been known as a vagrant, but at one time it was taken quite regularly along the south-east coast of England and occasionally in estuaries there, such as those of the Colne and Medway. With the great reduction in numbers in its breeding areas its distribution has contracted and no specimens have been seen in Great Britain for many decades.

The Houting is typically an estuarine species and rarely occurs in the open sea. Thus, the low salinity waters of the Baltic suit it perfectly. Here it occurs in a unique assembly of freshwater and marine fishes, which are able to form

Fig. 56 The River Vida in Denmark, one of the few places left in Europe where the Houting still occurs. Formerly not uncommon off the south-east coast of England, it has not been seen there for many decades (Jorgen Dahl).

Fig. 57 Several Houting, photographed in Scandinavia. This species has not been seen in Britain for several decades (Jorgen Dahl).

a brackish water community halfway between their respective normal chemical environments. Thus, as well as Houting, these waters contain Roach and Perch on the one hand and Cod and Plaice on the other.

The Houting has never been known to spawn in the British Isles and so can really only be regarded as a vagrant here. In those areas of the North Sea further east, where it still occurs, shoals assemble each autumn at the mouths of rivers and move upstream to spawn. This takes place from October to December over gravel in running water when the yellow eggs (2–9mm in diameter) are produced. These sink to the bottom and, being slightly adhesive, attach themselves to the small stones there, often falling between the crevices where they are protected from predators of various kinds.

Little is known about the age and growth of this species. The young appear to move downstream into brackish water and spend most of their lives there, only returning to fresh water when they are mature and ready to spawn.

The food virtually throughout life consists almost entirely of zooplankton of various kinds, especially crustaceans such as copepods and small shrimps. Larger fish, though they do rely to some extent on benthic invertebrates, again feed mainly on crustaceans.

Though once a valuable commercial species, which was caught in large numbers in drift nets and traps, especially in upper estuaries and the lower reaches of rivers during the spawning run, its numbers are now so reduced that it is only fished in a few places around the Baltic Sea.

Fig. 58 Powan (from Maitland 1972b).

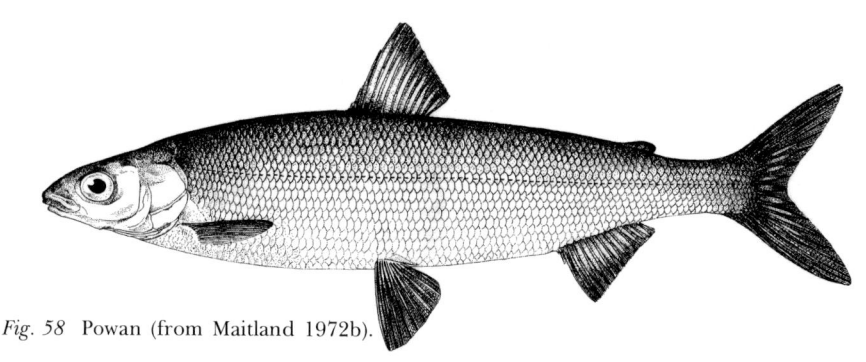

Powan *Coregonus lavaretus* (Linnaeus 1758)
Freshwater Herring, Guiniad, Gwyniad, Schelly, Skelly

The adult size of Powan is normally some 30–35cm (300–400gm), but in some European lakes fish up to 70cm (8kg) have been recorded. The present British rod-caught record is for a fish of 950gm caught in 1986 in Haweswater (Cumbria). It is now illegal to catch this species in Great Britain without a permit.

The body is well built, elongate and laterally compressed. The head is small, as is the mouth, which is inferior in position and has no teeth. There are 25–39 thin gill rakers on the first gill arch. The body is covered by large cycloid scales of which there are 84–100 along the lateral line. The scales can be used for age determination.

The dorsal fin is short, with 3–4 spiny rays followed by 9–13 branched rays. The adipose fin is large and fleshy whilst the paired fins are well developed. The anal fin has 3–4 spiny rays anteriorly, then 11–14 branched rays. The tail fin is large with a well marked fork. Both in Loch Lomond and in Ullswater a small percentage have a supernumerary pelvic fin located between the two normal pelvics.

The head and back are dark bluish-grey which grades to greenish-grey along the sides and eventually to a silvery whitish-yellow on the belly. The iris of the eye is white. There are no significant spots, though sometimes fine black specks are evident. The single fins (dorsal, adipose, anal and tail) are mainly dark, whereas the paired fins are darkened only towards their tips.

The Powan is widespread across much of north-west Russia, Finland and Sweden. It occurs also in several other countries (Norway, Switzerland, Germany, Poland and France) but only in certain areas – usually in mountainous alpine lakes. In the British Isles it is a relatively rare fish with a scattered distribution. It occurs in Lochs Lomond and Eck in Scotland, in Ullswater, Haweswater and Red Tarn in England (where it is known locally as Schelly – a reference to its large scales) and in Llyn Tegid in Wales (called here the Gwyniad – a reference to its whiteness).

Typically, Powan occur in relatively large deep lakes with clear well-oxygenated water. During daylight outside the breeding season adult fish stay in relatively deep water – on the bottom if they are in the littoral areas or at depths of 20–30m if in deeper water. At dusk they rise into shallower water, often coming right up to the surface and in to the edge in littoral areas. At dawn a reverse migration takes place. Occasionally, fish are found in rivers associated with lakes. For example, there is an old record of Gwyniad being found in the River Dee some distance downstream from Llyn Tegid.

Near spawning time the fish move much nearer to the shores of the lake and shoal over the sub-littoral areas there. At these times fish may often get washed ashore and stranded, sometimes in considerable numbers. Thus, in January 1966 large numbers of Schelly were washed ashore in Gowbarrow Bay in Ullswater after a strong easterly wind had been blowing. A similar event occurred in January 1967, on another shore, after a strong southerly gale.

Spawning takes place during winter, usually starting in late December and finishing in early February. At dusk the adult males come on to the spawning grounds, which are characteristically gravelly shallows off headlands or offshore reefs. They shoal there in large numbers and spawn with those females which move in each night as they become ripe. The fertilised eggs fall to the bottom and, being slightly adhesive, lodge between the crevices among the stones and gravel. The eggs are some 2–3mm in diameter and pale yellow in colour. The fecundity of the females varies with size, but they usually each lay 2000–11,000 eggs. Very large females may have up to 24,000 eggs. Incubation takes about 90–100 days (340–420 day-degrees) at winter temperatures in the lake, the optimum temperature being some 6°C or less. Once, a hermaphrodite Powan was found in Loch Lomond with ripe and functional testis and ovary.

The young are some 9–11mm at hatching and have a small yolk sac. However, they are strong swimmers and immediately move off into the pelagic areas, where they spend much of the rest of their lives. In captivity they become quite tame and do not react to movements outside their tanks, readily taking food from the bottom. Growth is variable but in favourable lakes the young can reach lengths of 10–12cm after one year and 15–20cm after two. After two years they may start to mature and usually have an adult length of 25–35cm at 3–5 years of age. Most fish die after six or seven years, but some live to nine years.

Powan feed mainly on zooplankton (especially crustaceans) when they are young. As they grow they start to feed more on bottom invertebrates (e.g. midge larvae, molluscs), though still relying a great deal on plankton – especially during the summer months. At spawning time, many of them eat considerable numbers of their own eggs. In Llyn Tegid, Gwyniad concentrate on bottom fauna from December to July, changing to midwater and surface feeding during the rest of the year.

The Powan is a very important commercial species in most of the countries in which it occurs – Great Britain being the exception to this. It is caught in traps, seine nets and gill nets and is especially vulnerable at spawning time, when it migrates and masses on spawning grounds in great numbers. In Great Britain it has no commercial or sporting significance, other than to a few specialist anglers at the lakes concerned, who used ledgered maggots fished on the bottom in deep water before the species became legally protected. Occasionally, they are taken on fly by trout anglers. One of the authors caught a substantial Powan on a dry fly simulating an adult caddis in a Swedish lake. At the time, he thought he was casting over rising trout! During both World Wars, however, it was fished commercially in Lochs Lomond

Table 22 Food of Powan in Loch Lomond, Scotland (after Slack et al. 1957) as percentage volume and (of Gwyniad) in Llyn Tegid, Wales (after Haram & Jones 1971), as percentage occurrence.

Stomach contents	Loch Lomond	Llyn Tegid
Molluscs	6	71
Leeches	–	1
Crustaceans		
Cladocerans	59	5
Cladoceran eggs	–	16
Ostracods	–	67
Copepods	18	19
Water louse	6	5
Insects		
Mayfly larvae	1	2
Stonefly larvae	–	1
Aquatic bugs	2	7
Beetle larvae & pupae	1	2
Caddis larvae	–	1
Midge larvae & pupae	7	76
Other invertebrates	1	7
Fish		
Powan (Gwyniad) eggs	–	1
Terrestrial organisms	1	1
Detritus	–	81
NUMBER OF FISH EXAMINED	385	725

and Eck and several hundred thousand fish were taken at this time. The flesh of Powan is white and oily with a good flavour.

Powan have a variety of parasites and even a unique one of their own: some years ago a new species of protozoan myxosporidian parasite, *Henneguya tegidensis*, was described from Gwyniad in Llyn Tegid. It occurred there in about 5% of the fish examined, producing intramuscular cysts causing swellings on the body. Several other parasites, including tapeworms and trematodes, are known to occur commonly in Powan in Loch Lomond.

In Loch Lomond too, Powan have a number of predators, one of the most important of these being Pike, which prey on them especially during their spawning period when they are very vulnerable in shallow water. Fewer Powan are eaten by Pike during the summer months, but they are then attacked in large numbers by River Lampreys, which leave characteristic oval flesh wounds along the backs. Usually about 30% of adult Powan in the Loch carry the scars of such wounds. The ferox trout of Loch Lomond were once referred to as 'Powan eaters'.

Powan eggs too have many predators, including adult Powan themselves. In some areas large caddis larvae have been shown to be significant predators. A new threat may be that of Ruffe, which have recently been introduced to Loch Lomond and are already abundant there, being one of the commonest species. In some parts of Russia this fish is regarded as having a major role in depressing the production of whitefish, because of the large numbers of eggs which it eats. A recent examination of the stomachs of many Ruffe caught in Loch Lomond during the spawning season of Powan (January) confirmed that Powan eggs are a major item of Ruffe diet at this time. It seems likely therefore that they will depress the numbers of Powan in the loch.

Vendace *Coregonus albula* (Linnaeus 1758)
Cisco, Cumberland Vendace, Lochmaben Vendace

The Vendace is normally regarded as a small to medium-sized fish, but its size can be very variable between populations, some of which can be quite stunted, with fish maturing in their first year at 10–12cm. The normal adult size is some 20–25cm (100–150gm), but in some European lakes it may reach a length of 35cm (500gm). Exceptionally large specimens of 45cm (1kg) have been reported from Lake Ladoga in Russia. This fish does not appear on the British rod-caught record list, presumably because of its rarity and the fact that it practically never takes bait – being very much a plankton feeder. It is now illegal to capture it without a permit.

The body of the Vendace is streamlined and laterally compressed. The head is rather small and pointed, with a superior mouth in which there are no teeth. The leading lower jaw is very characteristic and this feature alone distinguishes the Vendace from all other members of this family in Europe. There are 36–52 gill rakers. The body is covered by relatively large simple cycloid scales, of which there are some 70–90 along the lateral line. There are 55–60 vertebrae.

The dorsal fin is set midway along the back and is short with 3–4 spiny rays followed by 8–9 branched rays. The adipose fin is well developed and midway between dorsal fin and tail. The paired fins and anal fin are of the normal salmonid size and type, the latter having 3–4 spiny rays followed by 10–13 branched rays. The caudal fin is well developed and deeply forked.

The head and back of the Vendace are a dark greenish-blue grading to a silvery green along the sides and eventually to a whitish-silver on the belly. There are no spots. All the fins are rather transparent but darkened near the tips.

The Vendace occurs in many lakes in north-west Europe, from northern Scandinavia and north-west Russia in the north to Bavaria further south, and from the English Lake District in the west to western Russia in the east. Though this is mainly a lake species, some populations also occur in the Baltic Sea, migrating into fresh water to spawn. In the British Isles it has been known from only four lakes. Two of these are in Scotland (where it is called the Lochmaben Vendace and was formerly described as a distinct species and subspecies – *Coregonus vandesius vandesius*), and two are in England (the Cumberland Vendace – *Coregonus vandesius gracilior*).

The population in the Castle Loch, Lochmaben is certainly extinct and

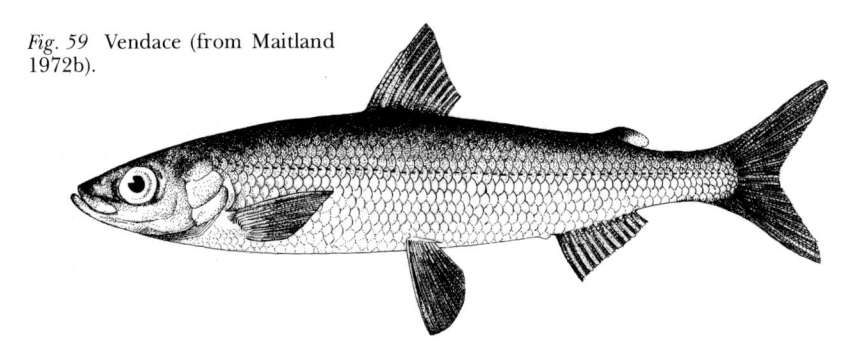

Fig. 59 Vendace (from Maitland 1972b).

Fig. 60 An adult Vendace from Bassenthwaite Lake (Peter Maitland)

none has been recorded since shortly after a new sewage works was opened there in 1911. The species was thought to be extinct also at one time in the Mill Loch, Lochmaben but specimens were caught there by one of the authors in 1966 and in subsequent years. None has been seen for more than a decade, however, and it seems likely that the species is now extinct there too.

In Cumbria the species occurs in much larger lakes – Bassenthwaite Lake and Derwentwater – and may be secure there in the short term. It was found to be common in both lakes in 1966 and since then specimens have been taken in other years.

The Vendace, over its whole range, seems to occur in lakes of any size from a hectare or so upwards. These lakes are often quite rich and are rarely exceedingly oligotrophic. Depth seems to be not too important, though probably several metres is needed, giving freedom from heat stress and lack of oxygen during the summer, as well as protection against potentially fatal chill during the winter. Strong competition and/or predation from Pike, Perch, Roach and other species is probably very harmful unless a good deep/open water niche is available. The size of individual populations seems to fluctuate greatly from time to time for reasons which are unknown.

The Vendace is a delicate pelagic fish which lives mainly in shoals in the open water offshore areas among the plankton. It remains in deeper (dimly lit) water during the day rising to the surface at dusk to feed, then descending at dawn.

Spawning is over gravelly/stony shores during winter, probably late November into December, though the actual timing is likely to vary from site to site (and perhaps from year to year) by a week or so. The mature males gather early on the spawning areas and as females ripen they join the males and spawn together in midwater, the fertilised eggs dropping down into crevices among the stones and gravel. The fecundity of females varies with size, and ranges from 1500 to 5000 eggs per adult female. Exceptionally large females from some Russian lakes have contained over 20,000 eggs. The eggs are some 1.5–1.8mm in diameter and yellowish in colour. The incubation period varies with temperature, but is normally 90–120 days at 1.4°C.

The young possess a small yolk sac on hatching but, like other whitefish, they are free and able swimmers immediately. They are normally some 7–9mm in length but soon start to grow rapidly as the surface waters of their

Table 23 Food of Vendace in Lake Vanern, Sweden in 1972 and 1973 (after Nilsson 1979), as percentage occurrence.

Stomach contents	1972	1973
Crustaceans		
Bosmina	26.4	11.9
Daphnia	15.5	4.4
Limnosida	14.5	14.4
Bythotrephes	42.7	30.6
Leptodora	1.8	0.6
Eurytemora	3.6	7.5
Heterocope	4.5	5.6
Diaptomus/Cyclops	6.4	15.6
Insects		
Midge larvae & pupae	0.9	1.9
Terrestrial organisms	0.9	5.0
NUMBER OF FISH EXAMINED	?	?

lake warm up and zooplankton becomes available. At the end of the first year they reach a length of 8–10cm. After two years they may be 14–18cm, at which time many are mature and growth slows, so that most adults only reach some 20–25cm, even after five or six years, which is the normal length of life.

After absorbing their yolk sac over the first few days of life, the Vendace fry start to feed on small plankton (mainly crustaceans), and zooplankton forms their main diet throughout life. They may supplement it from time to time with benthic animals, which appear in the water column (e.g. midge larvae and pupae), or terrestrial insects which are trapped on the surface, and some eggs may be eaten at spawning time.

The Vendace is an important commercial species in some parts of Europe where it is caught mainly in gill nets, but sometimes in traps and seine nets where there are migrations at spawning time. Its flesh is white and rich in oils, thus making it good eating. It is sometimes smoked and small specimens may even be eaten raw. One of the authors has vivid recollections of sitting in a farmhouse kitchen in Finland, after saying how much he was looking forward to his first taste of Vendace, then crunching his way through an entire raw fish and attempting to look as though he was enjoying it as much as his host apparently genuinely did!

The species is so rare in the British Isles that at present it has no commercial or sporting value. However, in times past it was an important fish at Lochmaben, where an annual festival was arranged each summer by two local 'Vendace Clubs', during which Vendace were caught in fine gill nets and then cooked and eaten outdoors while athletic contests took place.

Pollan *Coregonus autumnalis* (Pallas 1776)
Arctic Cisco, Cunn, Omul

Up until a few years ago, the taxonomic status of this species was very uncertain. Superficially, the Pollan seemed to be intermediate between the Powan and the Vendace and some workers suggested that it was probably the former species, whereas others suggested it was closer to the latter. For example, the mouth of the Pollan is terminal whereas that of the Powan is inferior and that of the Vendace superior.

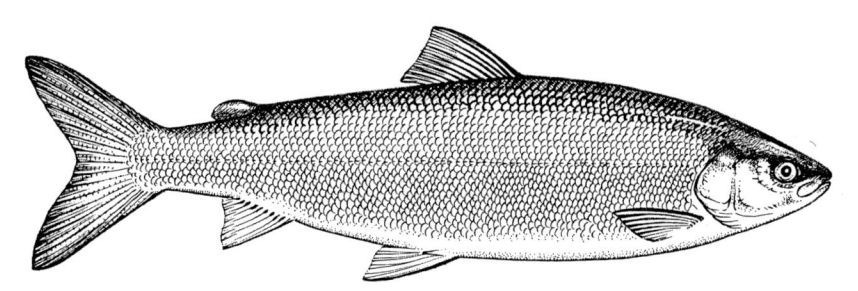

Fig. 61 Pollan.

A Polish taxonomist, studying the detail of the bones of the Pollan, suggested that it was actually neither of the two common British species but an entirely different species – *Coregonus autumnalis* – which is found nowhere else in western Europe and otherwise occurs only in eastern Europe, Asia and western North America. This finding was not fully accepted until biochemical tests, using modern electrophoretic techniques, were used to show that the Pollan does indeed appear to be the same fish as the Arctic Cisco, *Coregonus autumnalis*.

In Ireland, the Pollan usually reaches an adult size of some 30–35cm (350–450g), though occasionally larger specimens are recorded. There is no British rod-caught record at the moment, this category standing open. In Canada, fish as long as 46cm (1.4kg) have been recorded, but weights of up to 2.5kg have been reported from Siberian waters.

The body is elongate and laterally compressed – but less so than in either the Powan or the Vendace. The head is rather small and the mouth is terminal with upper and lower jaws of equal length. There is a small cluster of teeth on the tongue.

There are 41–48 slender gill rakers, 8 or 9 branchiostegal rays and 64–67 vertebrae. The body is well covered by large cycloid scales, of which there are 82–110 along the lateral line. The scales can be used for age determination – but often with difficulty in older fish.

The dorsal fin has 3–4 spiny rays followed by 10–12 branched rays. The adipose fin is well developed. The pectoral fins have 14–17 branched rays and the pelvic fins (each of which has a distinct axillary process) have 11–12 rays. The anal fin has 3–4 spiny rays, followed by 12–14 branched rays. The tail fin is well developed and deeply forked.

The head and back are a dark silvery brownish-green, which grades into silver along the sides and into silvery white along the belly. The dorsal, adipose and tail fins are mainly dark grey and the pectoral fins are slightly pigmented. There is virtually no pigmentation on the pelvic and anal fins.

The Pollan occurs in coastal areas and in the lower reaches of arctic rivers in north-eastern Europe, Asia and north-western North America – from the White Sea to Alaska and the North West Territories. Its occurrence in Ireland is surprising and well outside the rest of its world range. There are no logical explanations for its occurrence there. It is found in several large lakes, including Lough Neagh, upper and lower Lough Erne, and the Shannon lakes – Lough Ree and Lough Derg.

Although it is anadromous throughout most of its northern range, the Irish populations are all non-migratory and purely freshwater. However, for a few years after the establishment of a power-station on the short River Erne, between lower Lough Erne and the estuary, Pollan were taken in salmon nets used in the estuary. An examination of these fish showed that their rate of growth increased in the estuary where invertebrates (especially *Crangon*) dominated their diet. This incident would suggest that Pollan still retain the potential to become, at least locally, an anadromous species. All the lakes in which it occurs are large and relatively clean and deep – although Lough Neagh has undergone considerable eutrophication in recent years.

Spawning takes place in the lake, over beds of gravel and stones in relatively shallow water. As with other members of the family at spawning, the eggs fall down into spaces between the stones. The fecundity of the Irish fish is somewhat uncertain, but probably some 2000–8000 eggs per female. However, some of the larger females in Canada have been recorded as carrying over 90,000 eggs. The eggs are about 2mm in diameter and yellowish in colour.

The young hatch about March with a small yolk sac, but are immediately pelagic. They grow to a length of about 10–12cm in the first year and 15–20cm after two years, when they start to mature. They are fully adult at 3–4 years of age when they are mostly 25–30cm. They normally live for 5–7 years, but occasionally to 9 or 10 years.

After the yolk sac is absorbed, the young fish feed on small zooplankton and later on larger zooplankton, especially crustaceans supplemented by other larger invertebrates which appear in the water column, such as midge larvae and pupae. They start to feed on bottom invertebrates as they get older, including the semi-pelagic crustacean *Mysis*, which occurs in these Irish lakes, sometimes in abundance. At spawning time they may eat large numbers of their own eggs.

Fig. 62 Adult Pollan from Lough Neagh (Andrew Ferguson).

Table 24 Stomach contents of young Pollan in Lough Neagh, Northern Ireland, in relation to mean length (after Wilson 1984), as percentage occurrence.

	Jun	Jul	Aug	Nov	Dec	Apr
Mean length (mm)	48	65	76	130	121	135
Crustaceans						
Daphnia	7	–	57	–	–	–
Bythotrephes	–	–	57	–	–	–
Ostracods	–	25	–	–	–	–
Cyclops	71	50	29	–	–	–
Freshwater shrimp	–	–	–	16	45	–
Mysis	–	–	–	–	18	31
Insects						
Midge larvae & pupae	57	50	14	–	72	69
Other invertebrates	4	–	14	–	–	–
NUMBER OF FISH EXAMINED	14	4	14	6	11	13

The Pollan is the only member of the family for which there is an important commercial fishery. This has taken place for many years in Lough Neagh, and to a lesser extent in the other Irish loughs, and Pollan are regularly for sale in the Belfast and some of the other Irish fish markets. Some were even exported to northern England. They are caught mainly by seine and gill nets. In Lough Neagh they are sometimes used to bait long-lines set for yellow eels by commercial fishermen. The Pollan is of no sporting importance in Ireland. In both Siberia and Canada, this species is an important commercial species and fished extensively by native people, especially during the summer spawning migration from the sea.

12

Grayling

The grayling family Thymallidae consists of only one genus, *Thymallus*, of six species, whose distribution is confined to the temperate and arctic zones of Europe, Asia and North America. They occur in most systems that drain to the Arctic Ocean. There is one species in Europe. Their habitat is cool swift-flowing streams and deep cold lakes.

A characteristic of the family is the faint smell from their palatable flesh (first commented on by the ancient Greeks and which inspired St Ambrose of Milan to call this the 'flower of fish'), which has been likened to that of the herb thyme, hence the origin of the scientific name of the family and the genus. Other characteristics are the high and colourful dorsal fin and the presence of an adipose fin. The latter indicates that they are classified within the same taxonomic order as the salmonid fishes, with whom they usually co-exist. They tend to occur in shoals and on occasions large numbers can be caught by angling. In arctic regions, grayling were at one time cropped in large numbers to provide food for dogs.

Grayling *Thymallus thymallus* (Linnaeus 1758) Umber, Umber Fish

The average adult length of Grayling is about 30cm, with a weight of some 350gm. However, in favourable circumstances this fish can grow up to 50cm in length (1kg), and there have been very large fish of about 60cm (2.3kg) reported. The present British rod-caught record stands at 1.644kg, for a fish caught in 1983 in the River Allen, Dorset.

The Grayling, clearly a member of the salmonid group, is a graceful fish with its long streamlined body, spectacular dorsal and well developed adipose fins. The mouth is small and slightly inferior, and there are small fine teeth present on the upper jaw and on the head of the vomer bone. There

Fig. 63 Grayling (from Maitland 1972b).

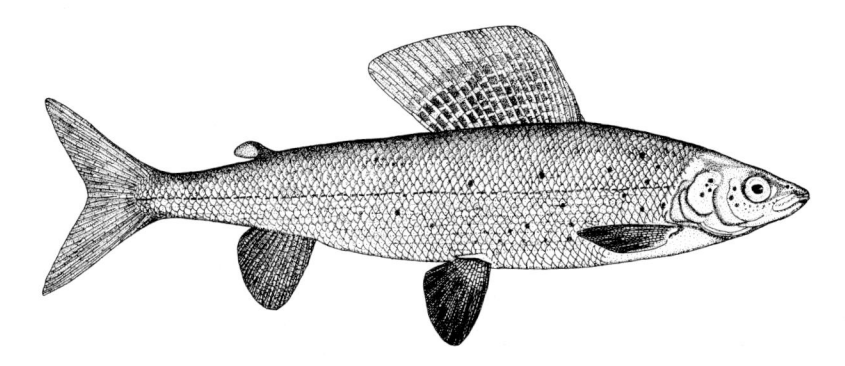

Fig. 64 An example of a stuffed and mounted specimen Grayling (William Howes).

are 21–29 gill rakers on the first arch. The head is rather pointed and the slim body is laterally compressed. The pupil of the eye sometimes appears deep blue and pear-shaped.

Apart from the smell of its flesh, the characteristic feature of the Grayling is the very large dorsal fin, which is both long and high, and is particularly large in the male. It has 4–7 spiny rays and 17–24 long branched rays, the height of the last ray being just as long as that of the middle ray. The base of the dorsal fin is much longer than the head length. The other fins are more normal in size, the anal fin having 2–4 spiny rays and 10–15 branched rays.

The body is well covered by medium-sized cycloid scales, which have a characteristic shape with convoluted anterior edges, and are arranged in very obvious longitudinal rows along the body. There are 74–96 of these scales along the lateral line. The scales can be used for age determination.

In colour, the Grayling has a rather silvery appearance; it is dull grey on the head and along the back grading to a greyish-green on the sides and silvery white on the belly. A number of clearly defined large black spots occur irregularly on the anterior part of the body – these spots are very variable within the species but always remain the same on a particular fish, so that experienced observers can soon identify individual fish within a river, once the pattern of each has been recognised. A similar situation exists with Pike. The young fish, silvery as early post-alevins, soon develop typical salmonid parr marks along the sides, which disappear after one year. The characteristic Grayling dorsal fin is already evident in fry of around 2.5cm. The sides of the body have a number of faint longitudinal violet stripes which darken at spawning time to give a purplish iridescence to the fish. The dorsal fin is well marked with 4–5 rows of reddish black spots on the fin membrane, which are particularly accentuated at spawning time. The free edge of the dorsal fin also develops a reddish margin at this time.

The Grayling is a native of north-western Europe, including Great Britain,

Fig. 65 A lively young Grayling (Heather Angel).

and occurs in suitable habitats from the Arctic Ocean in the north to southern France in the south, and from Wales in the west almost to the Black Sea in the east. It is absent from a number of European countries including Ireland, Iceland, Spain, Portugal and Italy. It has also disappeared from several river systems in which it was formerly abundant, for it is extremely sensitive to pollution of various kinds. In Britain, its early post-glacial distribution was limited to the river systems of eastern and south-eastern England, but now it is common over much of England and Wales, as well as southern Scotland, where it was introduced successfully during the nineteenth century. It now occurs as far north as the Clyde on the west coast and the Tay on the east coast. Although absent from Ireland, a clandestine attempt to introduce it there was thwarted by the quick action of the authorities.

Essentially a river fish, though it does occur in some lakes (e.g. Llyn Tegid), the Grayling occurs mainly in clean, well-oxygenated fast-flowing streams and rivers, but it can thrive at oxygen concentrations at which trout are beginning to feel uncomfortable. In an experimental situation where Grayling were presented with a temperature gradient, they selected water at 18°C. In some parts of Europe, it is so characteristic of some waters – where the bottom is stony and gravelly in the riffles, and the pools are clean and deep – that they are defined in river classification terms as 'grayling reaches'. In some parts of the Baltic – as with several other species which are normally found only in fresh water – it occurs in brackish water. Yet it has shown no tendency to move around the British Isles via brackish water along the coasts.

Where it is common, the Grayling may occur in small shoals. Those fish living in lakes or in the slower-flowing parts of some rivers migrate into fas-

Table 25 Food of Grayling in the River Tweed, Scotland (after Radforth 1940), as percentage number in the River Lugg, England (after Hellawell 1971), as percentage volume and of very young Grayling in the River Frome, England (after Scott 1985), as percentage number.

Stomach contents	River Tweed	River Lugg	River Frome
Algae	–	0.1	–
Macrophytes	+	0.2	–
Molluscs			
Snails	0.2	1.5	–
Pea shells	–	0.1	–
Worms	–	0.1	–
Leeches	–	0.2	+
Crustaceans			
Cladocerans	–	–	++
Ostracods	0.1	–	–
Copepods	–	–	+
Water louse	–	1.0	+
Freshwater shrimp	0.1	18.8	+
Insects			
Mayfly larvae	15.8	6.7	2.0
Stonefly larvae	0.3	0.1	+
Aquatic bugs	1.0	0.2	+
Beetle larvae & adults	12.7	3.8	+
Caddis larvae	1.2	0.1	++
Midge larvae & pupae	58.9	3.5	80.5
Blackfly larvae & pupae	2.4	15.1	1.0
Adult flies	5.1	6.0	8.5
Others	0.1	0.7	++
Other invertebrates	0.2	–	–
Fish			
Fish eggs	–	1.7	–
Dace larvae	–	–	+
Terrestrial organisms			
Insects	3.0	8.8	+
Spiders	0.1	0.1	–
Anglers' Maggots	–	7.4	–
Detritus	+	15.0	–
NUMBER OF FISH EXAMINED	57	253	37

++ in less than 20% of guts
++ in less than 5% of guts

ter-flowing tributaries near spawning time. The display of the males to the females (and in aggression to other males) at spawning time is very colourful and spectacular.

Spawning usually takes place just when river temperatures reach 4°C and are starting to rise in the spring, usually from March to May. The eggs are laid in gravelly shallows where there is some current, and spawning occurs in pairs immediately after the female has cut a redd in the gravel, in territory guarded by the male, in typical salmonid fashion. These eggs are covered up by fresh gravel deposited from further digging activity just upstream. If there is no suitable bottom in the vicinity, Grayling will migrate to find it. Spawning takes place during the latter part of the day, when the water temperature is at its highest. If the water temperature drops, spawning may halt for some days until it rises again.

The fecundity of each female depends very much on her size and may range from 600 eggs in small fish to over 10,000 eggs in large fish. The eggs are about 3–4mm in diameter and yellowish in colour. Incubation takes some

3–4 weeks (180–200 day-degrees) depending on local temperatures. Eggs are eaten by various fish in the vicinity, including the Grayling themselves. After spawning, adults of both sexes are in poor condition until late summer or early autumn.

The young fish hatch at about 10–12mm and have a small yolk sac. Growth rate is variable according to habitat but young fish showing average growth are normally 8–12cm at the end of their first year and 17–20cm after two years – often growing more rapidly than the trout with which they co-exist. They then start to mature at 2–3 years and growth slows somewhat, most fish reaching 23–30cm after three years and, in good conditions, 30–35cm after four years. They live for 6–9 years on average.

When the yolk sac has been absorbed, the young fry feed in shoals (sometimes along with Minnows of similar size) on very small bottom-dwelling invertebrates (e.g. crustaceans and midge larvae). They continue to rely on a wide range of bottom-dwelling fauna throughout life, but particularly crustaceans, midge and caddis larvae. Stomachs nearly always contain some sand, gravel and vegetable debris. In some situations they may take terrestrial insects which have blown on to the surface, and during summer they may concentrate on surface food, including adult aquatic and terrestrial insects. Unlike trout, which usually lie just below the surface when taking adult insects, Grayling characteristically swim steeply up from the bottom each time to take the insect, returning steeply to the bottom again afterwards. Occasionally they eat the eggs of other fish including salmonids at spawning time and even small fish; in these situations Grayling grow very large. They feed actively during the winter and can be angled during cold frosty weather.

When in captivity, Grayling take some time to learn to eat large food items such as whole earthworms. Because stone-cased caddis larvae often figure largely in their diet in the wild, the stomach and alimentary tract may be stuffed with rough grit. This may possibly be the explanation of the ancient belief that Grayling fed on gold. Isaac Walton passes on the information that Grayling fat mixed with honey has medicinal properties against redness or swarthiness, or anything that 'breeds in the eye'.

The Grayling has a good reputation as a table fish in some parts of Europe, but it must be eaten very fresh. It is not caught commercially in Great Britain but is a popular fish with anglers in some areas, especially during winter when the season for salmon and trout is closed. Conversely, it is regarded by some game anglers as a pest in salmonid waters, mainly on the grounds of competition and egg-eating. It also tends to come rather more readily to the fly than trout–to the annoyance of trout anglers. Anglers usually catch Grayling by 'trotting' a small float and a single weighted maggot downstream, though at times a wet or dry fly is very effective. In fact, some dry-fly purists consider Grayling fishing superior to that of trout. The two species are not mutually exclusive and an angler may take a trout followed by a Grayling with the next cast. Grayling are occasionally taken (usually accidentally) by spinning.

In Britain, the Grayling Society was established in 1978 and it produces a journal devoted to Grayling fishing and biology. In France Grayling are regarded sufficiently highly to be reared in hatcheries for subsequent stream stocking, in situations where the stock has been affected by hydro-electric schemes or other developments.

13
Smelt

The smelt family Osmeridae occurs throughout the northern hemisphere, where various species are marine, anadromous or freshwater in habit. There are six genera with ten species in the Atlantic, Arctic and Pacific Oceans and their basins. All members of the family are small, silvery, slender fish with elongate laterally compressed bodies and large mouths. They have well developed teeth and a conspicuous adipose fin indicating affinity with the salmonids. However, unlike the salmonids, they do not have a pointed pelvic axillary process nor are they spotted or coloured. The scales are thin and cycloid and the lateral line is well developed, though incomplete in length. During the breeding season the males (and very rarely, the females) may develop tubercles on the head, body and fins.

Most smelts are popular food fish and have a characteristic odour, similar to fresh cucumber. In some countries they are caught in enormous numbers, and they have been introduced to some large lakes to provide commercial fisheries.

There is only one species of smelt found in the British Isles and any fish from fresh water correctly identified as belonging to the family Osmeridae must belong to this species.

Smelt *Osmerus eperlanus* (Linnaeus 1758)
Sparling

The Smelt, or Sparling as it is often called in Scotland, is a small to medium sized fish whose adult size varies greatly according to habitat. The normal range in length is 10–20cm but the fish can sometimes reach 30cm. A fish about 15cm long weighs some 30g. In general, fish from non-migratory freshwater populations are much smaller than those which have lived in the sea. The present British rod-caught record stands at 191gm for a Smelt caught near Fleetwood in 1981. There is no Irish record.

A small rather slender fish with large scales and eyes, a projecting lower jaw and obvious teeth on both jaws, the Smelt can sometimes be confused with the various *Coregonus* species (Powan, Vendace and Pollan) – which have small mouths and no teeth – and with salmonid smolts which have small scales and at least a few spots of some kind. In addition to the teeth on both jaws, there are teeth on the tongue and on the vomer bone. Like the salmonids and coregonids it has a fleshy adipose fin between the dorsal fin (which has 9–12 rays) and the caudal fin. The paired fins are moderately developed as is the anal fin with 12–16 rays.

There are some 60–70 lateral scales and the lateral line itself is incomplete. There are 55–62 vertebrae and usually 26–32 gill rakers. Live fish are somewhat translucent in appearance and have a very characteristic cucumber-like smell. In colour the top of the head and back are a rather variable dark grey-

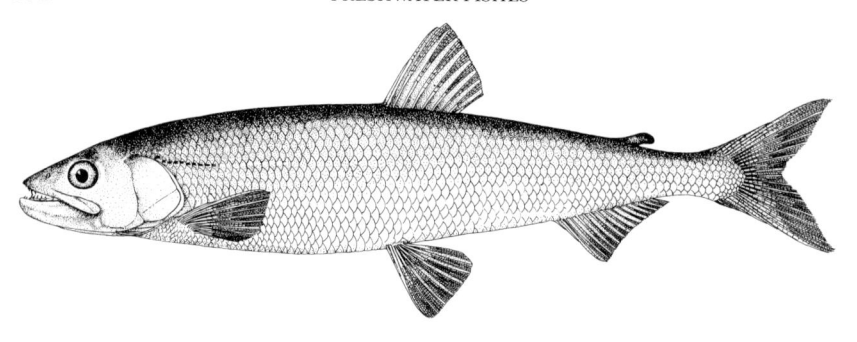

Fig. 66 Smelt (from Maitland 1972b).

green which shades into a silvery green stripe along each side and a silvery white colour below.

The Smelt occurs from southern Norway around the western coast of Europe (including the Baltic Sea) to north-west Spain. It is found in coastal waters and estuaries and migrates into large clean rivers at spawning time. The species is tolerant of wide salinity changes and there are several non-migratory purely freshwater populations in large freshwater lakes in Finland, Sweden and Norway. The Romans were supposed to have cultivated Smelt in freshwater ponds. The sole freshwater population in the British Isles, in Rostherne Mere in Cheshire, became extinct in the 1920s, probably as a result of eutrophication.

This fish clearly favours clean estuaries except at spawning time and though it has the salinity tolerance noted above it is apparently very susceptible to pollution and perhaps other pressures created by humans. Many estuaries which formerly had large populations lost them as pollution increased and the species is much less common than formerly. However, its return to waters such as the River Thames as they become cleaner is a welcome sign and one which it is hoped will be repeated on other rivers.

On reaching maturity, adults migrate up the estuaries and into the lower reaches of rivers in March and April. Usually the run in each river occupies only a few days, but during that time the spawning activity becomes furious and the sticky eggs attach themselves to everything on the river bed – gravel, stones, weed and sticks. Sometimes the river level drops subsequently and leaves many eggs stranded to dry out. The adults are very vulnerable to all kinds of predators (including human ones) at this time and occasionally become so excited during the actual spawning that they swim right out of the water and strand themselves on dry land.

Each female lays about 10,000–40,000 pale-yellow eggs (0.9mm in diameter) and these hatch in about 20–35 days according to the local temperature. The eggs are often laid in quite fast-flowing water and the young are swept quickly down into the upper estuary where they start to feed. Though there is considerable mortality among the adults during spawning, many do manage to return to the sea where they recover to grow further and spawn again in subsequent years. Lake populations of this species usually spawn in or near the mouths of rivers entering the lake or along suitable shores.

Table 26 Main food of Smelt in the Lena River, Russia (after Pirozhnikov 1955), as percentage number and in Lake Vanern, Sweden (after Nilsson 1979), as percentage occurrence.

Stomach contents	Lena River	Lake Vanern
Crustaceans		
Cladocerans	+	27.3
Copepods	+	34.5
Mysids	67.3	3.6
Amphipods	11.4	–
Insects	–	3.6
Fish	+	0.9
NUMBER OF FISH EXAMINED	?	?

Growth is a very variable process in this species according to local conditions. In suitable estuaries the young may reach 10cm by the end of the first year and some 15cm by the third year, which is usually when they start to breed. They may live for several years beyond this, reaching lengths of about 20cm at six years of age. The males are usually smaller than the females and average weights are about 28 and 36gm respectively.

Smelt fry are very small at first and feed on minute zooplankton, probably mainly protozoans and rotifers. As they grow they take larger planktonic crustaceans and some bottom-dwelling animals and eventually they become quite voracious predators taking larger crustaceans (shrimps and mysids) and young fish, such as Sprat, Herring, Whiting and gobies.

There are still several commercial fisheries for Smelt in the British Isles, which rely mainly on their vulnerability during the short spawning run to catch them (sometimes in enormous numbers) in traps and nets. Only two

Fig. 67 Left, Stripping adult Smelt of eggs on the River Cree as part of a conservation project (Peter Hutchinson); *Right*, Eggs of Smelt left high and dry as the water level drops (Peter Hutchinson).

populations are known to remain in Scotland, yet both are the subject of fisheries. On the River Cree in some years up to six tonnes of Smelt are taken from the spawning run – probably a high percentage of the population there and undoubtedly a threat to its existence. In some parts of Europe they are caught in the estuaries in drift nets and trawls and they are sold either fresh or smoked. The authors can verify that they are delicious to eat.

14

Pike

The pike family, Esocidae, is distributed throughout most of Europe and temperate regions of Asia and North America, and consists of one genus and five species. Only one species occurs in Europe. They all live in lakes and slow-flowing rivers and, in the case of European Pike only, in the low salinity waters of the Baltic and Caspian Seas. The elongate body, large head and huge mouth, filled with long very sharp teeth, coupled with their legendary boldness and ferocity are features responsible for their sinister image as the 'freshwater shark'. Many exaggerated tales exist concerning their great size and age and insatiable appetite for other fish and any other small form of animal life that comes their way.

In North America, some species have been redistributed for angling and fish control purposes, but fortunately they have not reached the southern hemisphere. They spawn in the early spring, distributing their adhesive eggs over vegetation in shallow water. A large number of small eggs are produced by each female. A larval stage possessing an adhesive attachment organ follows hatching and at this time the small fish are very vulnerable to a range of hazards, both physical (e.g. changing water levels) and biological (e.g. predation).

In many parts of their range, their flesh is highly esteemed and priced, while in others they are regarded as pests that consume large quantities of more desirable fish. The largest species, the North American Muskellunge (*Esox masquinongy*) has been recorded weighing over 50kg and the European Pike (*Esox lucius*) at just over half that weight.

There is only one species of pike occurring in the British Isles (and indeed throughout the whole of Europe) and so any fish identified from the family key as belonging to the Esocidae must be this species.

Pike *Esox lucius* Linnaeus 1758
Gad, Gedd, Jack, Luce, Pickerel

The name Pike derives aptly from the shape of this fish, with its long near cylindrical body and long duck-billed snout. Its mouth is large and wide and armed with rows of needle-sharp teeth angled backward, making the escape of prey (and the removal of fish hooks) very difficult.

The Pike is one of our largest freshwater fishes, but there is a great deal of variation in adult size. In general, adult individuals range from 40–100cm and 2–14kg. The present British and Irish rod-caught records are 19.05 and 19.09kg respectively; the former for a fish caught in 1985 in the Thurne system in Norfolk, the latter (of almost identical weight) caught in the River Barrow in 1964. Larger fish have been reported caught in nets or found dead. It is reported (in the Irish Times of 23 April 1987) that there is a stuffed Pike on display in a shop in Enniskillen which weighed 22.6–24.5kg when pitch forked out of Lough Erne in the late 1920s. Among Pike anglers there is an interesting belief that the very largest specimen fish are most likely to be found in systems which also have salmon. The reason is thought to be that the maximum size in Pike can only be attained where there is a good supply of large fish to prey on. Adult salmon have been found inside large Pike, and even where fresh-run salmon are too large for Pike to catch and swallow, there is always a plentiful supply of weakened kelts.

Characteristically, Pike have large sickle-shaped teeth, hinged behind, on the head of the long vomer and pads of teeth on the tongue, while the lower jaws each bear five or six long strong canines, unequal in size and attached firmly to the jaw bone. All the teeth are set backwards, making the escape of prey difficult and also facilitating swallowing. The sharpness and set of these large teeth make Pike the only freshwater fish in the British Isles where anglers, to be sure of landing them, need to use a length of fine metal trace between the line and the lure. There are no teeth on the maxillary bones. The lower jaw, as in many piscivorous fish, is longer than the upper one, accentuating the Pike's predatory appearance and in accord with its sinister reputation.

The eyes are set close together (with only one eye diameter between them) and are placed high and forward in the head, thus giving good binocular vision, as befits a predator that hunts by sight. There are many more rod cells than cone cells in the retina, allowing greater visual acuity, and a yellow cornea acts as a light filter, reducing glare in bright conditions.

The single dorsal fin is set well back on the body, above the anal fin, and has 13–15 rays. The pectoral fins have 13–15 rays, the pelvic fins 9–10 rays, the anal fin 12–14 rays and the caudal fin 18–19 rays. The gill rakers are few in number and are really only short stumps. The strong scales are large and cycloid and set deep into the tough skin. The buried portions of the scales are lobed and there are 105–130 scales along the lateral line. There are no pyloric caecae and the swimbladder is connected to the short oesophagus, which leads to a simple pouch-like stomach and thence to a short intestine – an alimentary tract typical of carnivorous fish. There are 57–65 vertebrae. An interesting anatomical feature of Pike is the presence of numerous fine Y-shaped intermuscular bones within the flesh which are not connected to the vertebral column. These reduce its culinary value.

The colour of Pike is very variable and is affected to some extent by size and habitat. Very young Pike are pale green and rather conspicuous, but they soon darken and display the typical banded effect when seen from above. In adults, the upper head and back are dark olive-brown to green, grading on the flanks to pale green with oval yellow patches, which usually form 14–15 broken or solid sub-vertical bands that curve forwards ventrally. This disruptive colour pattern is ideal for concealment among vegetation. The belly is a pale creamy yellow, sometimes dotted with pale-orange spots. The dorsal, anal and caudal fins are dark brownish with reddish-yellow to orange mottling. The pectoral and pelvic fins are usually rather pale. The pattern of markings of Pike of 50cm or more have been shown to be specific to individual fish and can be used for identifying at a later date without tagging and marking.

The Pike is widely distributed throughout much of Europe, Asia and North America (where it is known as the Northern Pike to distinguish it from other

Fig. 68 Pike (from Maitland, 1972b).

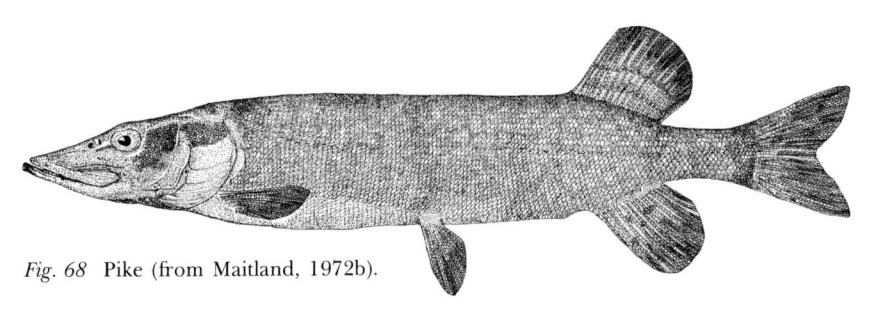

members of the family occurring there). It occurs in lakes and slow-flowing stretches of streams and rivers and is also found in parts of the Baltic Sea where the salinity is less than 10%. Its oxygen demand is comparatively low and so it can survive in habitats where there may be some degree of pollution, providing the oxygen level does not fall below 5.7mg/l. It can stand very cold conditions, but water temperatures above 29°C are fatal. It is probably the most widely distributed piscivorous fish in the northern hemisphere.

In the British Isles, the Pike was one of the indigenous species left in southeast England after the last ice age. However, the very high price of Pike flesh in medieval times (due to scarcity) led many early writers to believe that the species had been recently introduced and was not yet widely established. Over the centuries it has been widely redistributed over much of Great Britain and was introduced to Ireland (probably during the fifteenth century) where it is now widespread (though formerly known by the Gaelic term 'gaill iasc' meaning foreign fish), except in the north-west and south-east coastal areas. In Scotland it is less common in the Highlands, very rare in the northwest, and absent from the northern isles and the Hebrides, with the exception of one population on Islay. In recent years, its distribution has been rashly extended by coarse anglers indifferent to its impact on native fish communities. Much of our information on the natural history of Pike has come from investigations carried out over the last 30 years in Eire, where the importance of this non-indigenous species as a welcome asset and/or a dangerous liability has stimulated research by the Inland Fisheries Trust and latterly by the Central Fisheries Board.

The genetic constitution of samples of Pike from North America, Scandinavia, the Netherlands, England and Ireland has been investigated biochemically and results suggest that, in the case of Irish and English Pike, the phenomenon known as the 'founder effect' has taken place. This occurs when new populations of animals are established from a small number of colonisers, giving a rather narrow genetic variability. These results are comparable with the hypothesis that the distribution of Pike in the British Isles has progressively been moved north and west, away from the native area of south-east England. New waters were probably stocked with a few individuals only due to the difficulty of transport in early times. Such effects will also, of course, be found in some cases of natural transport such as the adhesive eggs on weed on birds' feet, etc., where only a few fish at a time are likely to be transferred.

Pike spawn from February to May, depending on which part of the country,

Fig. 69 A large specimen Pike (William Howes).

when the water temperature is rising and between 4 and 11°C. This is a period when Pike may make long migrations from feeding areas to spawning grounds, behaviour which is exploited by fishery managers wishing to control Pike numbers in salmonid waters, as they are then particularly vulnerable to gill netting. Males arrive at the spawning grounds first, selecting shallow areas of water with thick vegetation, or, if the water level is high, flooded terrestrial vegetation is also very suitable to spawn over. The young fish spawn first and the spawning act itself is usually very vigorous with one or more males and a female rolling over in excitement. The eggs and sperm are liberated when their vents are in close proximity, with a rapid vibration of their bodies which at times break the surface. Eggs are scattered more or less at random, aided by the activity of the spawning pair stirring the water. The eggs are reddish-brown to brownish, some 2.3–3.0mm in diameter, and adhere to the vegetation. Usually a very high proportion of them are fertilised. Spawning takes place at regular intervals and at times may extend over several days. The females are fairly fecund and produce 9000–20,000 eggs per kg of body weight.

The eggs require 150–155 day-degrees for hatching, a period of between 10 and 30 days (usually around 15), depending on water temperatures. A fragile larva emerges which, attaches itself to the vegetation by means of adhesive glands in the head. After about 6–10 days the yolk sac is used up and the free-swimming larva has a length of 6–8mm. This is a period of high mortality, during which perhaps over 90% of the larvae are destroyed. Apart from being predated by various fish and large insect larvae, a fall in water level can have fatal consequences, as the adhesive larvae cannot escape.

Once free-swimming, the fry start to grow very rapidly, feeding first on zooplankton, but are soon large enough to take insect larvae. Within one month a pikelet can be 4cm in length. By the time they are a year old they are 8–10cm in length and fish have become an important item in their diet. A rapid growth rate is maintained for the first two years of life, during which an estimated daily intake of about 3–5% of body weight is required. In Ireland it has been observed that Pike usually grow faster in lakes than in rivers, and that 15 years of age is usually the maximum reached. Irish data include a Pike of 23kg which was only 8 years old – in contrast to another of 11kg which was 14 years old.

Female Pike may live longer and grow larger than males, and few of the latter ever exceed 4–5kg. As a result, in some habitats, male Pike may be an important item in the diet of large females. Some male Pike are mature at 2+ years of age and all are mature at 4+ years. Females mature at 3+ years or 4+ years. Age is usually determined from the annual growth zones found on the opercular bones, though the scales are also useful sometimes, as with most other fish. The pattern of scale growth varies so much from water to water that the pattern of the first year's growth must be known before a scale can be interpreted. This can be done by collecting very small Pike, measuring their length and collecting the scales, to be matched against the early growth pattern shown on the scales of older fish from the same water.

Pike tend to inhabit the shallower parts of lakes or slow-flowing rivers. They are not territorial. As they grow, Pike become increasingly piscivorous, reaching the top of the food chain in most communities in which they occur. They adopt a solitary and fairly sedentary way of life, concealing themselves until their prey (often another smaller Pike) is within striking distance, or stalking it stealthily before making a rapid rush forward to seize it. They will not pursue an intended victim very far if they miss, but will retire and wait for another. Unlike most freshwater species, except salmonids, Pike will feed at very low winter water temperatures, often hardly above 0°C.

Pike are equipped with very sensitive sense organs, particularly those distributed as open pits over the head region. These are part of the lateral-line system and enable the Pike to detect prey before it may be in sight and also help the Pike to orientate itself in the direction of the prey. Experiments with blind Pike have shown that they are able to sense and seize fish that pass close by, but Pike do not appear to feed to any extent during darkness, although they are reputed to feed during bright moonlight.

Pike populations are sometimes found in atypical habitats, e.g. high moor-

Fig. 70 A young Pike (Heather Angel).

land lakes, having been introduced into lakes with high population densities of small trout, with the objective of reducing the numbers so that the size of the remaining trout would increase and become more attractive to anglers. Sometimes the two species have managed to co-exist, with the trout much larger but very much fewer in numbers. Often, however, Pike have completely eliminated the trout, and in such situations, have had to depend mainly on a diet of invertebrates and each other. Quite large Pike (1.4–2.3kg) may be found with stomachs solidly packed with invertebrates, such as freshwater shrimps or water lice. Beyond a certain size or where the invertebrate fauna is poor, Pike depend upon cannibalism for survival, and their population structure resembles that of a very flat pyramid with a wide base, i.e. there are a few large Pike supported by a large number of small young Pike, themselves feeding on invertebrates.

In a 26.3ha moorland loch in Scotland which contained only Pike, and which was poisoned in the autumn to allow restocking with trout, virtually all the Pike were collected and examined. There were 2078 altogether, weighing 140.9kg, which represented a standing stock of 5.3kg per ha. The largest Pike was a female weighing 7kg and the next two largest were both females of 9 years of age, each some 70cm in length. The great majority of the Pike (1867) were between 10 and 15cm (i.e. mostly 0+ fish). Age groups three years old or more to eight years old or more, but less than nine, consisted of only 98 fish in total. Females in all age groups had grown faster than the males. There were some mature fish of both sexes in their third year, but none in their second year. Invertebrates, mostly freshwater shrimps, were an important food of Pike up to 50cm in length, whereas frogs and smaller Pike made up the bulk of the diet of larger fish. Many of the stomachs (38%) were empty – a common finding with Pike sampled in all kinds of habitat.

Even where apparently ample numbers of suitable prey fish are present, quite large Pike may still take considerable invertebrate food: for instance, of 33 Pike (average length 59.3cm) from Loch Tummel in Perthshire, 18% contained freshwater shrimps or lice, 28% midge larvae or pupae, 21% frogs or toads and 23% fish (trout or Perch). However, in many other situations Pike are almost entirely piscivorous on reaching about 50cm.

Table 27 Food of Pike in the River Frome and the River Stour, England (after Mann 1982) and in the Dubh Lochan and Loch Lomond, Scotland (after Shafi & Maitland 1971a), as percentage number.

Stomach contents	R Frome	R Stour	Dubh Lochan	L Lomond
Worms	–	2	–	–
Crustaceans				
Water louse	–	–	–	20
Freshwater shrimp	2	–	–	–
Crayfish	–	1	–	–
Insects				
Mayfly larvae	–	7	41	–
Dragonfly larvae	–	–	9	–
Beetles	–	–	9	–
Caddis larvae	2	1	–	–
Others	2	–	3	–
Fish				
Trout	2	–	–	20
Powan	–	–	–	43
Pike	–	1	1	1
Gudgeon	–	2	–	–
Bleak	–	1	–	–
Minnow	42	35	–	–
Roach	8	18	–	4
Chub	–	1	–	–
Dace	14	12	–	–
Stone Loach	2	2	–	–
Eel	6	4	–	–
Three-spined Stickleback	–	2	–	4
Perch	–	–	41	5
Bullhead	–	2	–	–
Flounder	8	–	–	–
Unidentified	10	15	–	3
Other vertebrates				
Mallard	–	1	–	–
Water Vole	2	–	–	–
NUMBER OF FISH EXAMINED	36	177	22	193

Table 28 Some examples of the weights (kg) of fish eaten by Pike in Irish waters (after Toner 1959b).

Pike Weight	Prey & Its Weight		% Pike's Body Weight
1.36	Trout	0.45	33
1.81	Trout	0.56	31
2.26	Trout	0.91	40
4.53	Trout	1.36	30
6.40	Pike	3.20	50

Adult Pike will try to eat any animal, alive or dead, that is not too big to swallow – indeed Pike are sometimes found dead, apparently choked by an extra large food item. A Pike of 6.3kg has been known to swallow a Pike of 3.2kg. As well as fish, which are swallowed head-first and are usually the main food, they take small mammals (including Brown Rats, Water Voles and Water Shrews), amphibians (Pike are one of the few predators of adult Common Toads), crayfish and waterfowl. In fact it is believed that they can make serious inroads into wildfowl populations by taking their young, or in some habitats even the adults, as in the case of Moorhens and Dabchicks. If a prey fish is too long to be swallowed completely, the Pike will swim around with

FRESHWATER FISHES

Table 29 Food of Pike of different lengths in Loch Choin, Scotland, where Pike were the only fish present (after Munro 1957), as percentage occurrence.

Stomach contents	\multicolumn{7}{c}{Pike Lengths in mm}						
	96–199	200–299	300–399	400–499	500–599	600–699	700–960
Molluscs							
Pea Shells	0.6	6.2	15.9	23.1	–	–	–
Crustaceans							
Eurycercus	0.6	–	–	–	–	–	–
Freshwater shrimp	83.8	72.6	58.7	43.6	2.8	20.0	–
Insects							
Mayfly larvae	6.3	1.8	–	–	–	–	–
Aquatic bugs	–	–	1.6	5.1	–	–	–
Beetles	1.3	–	–	5.1	–	–.	–
Alderfly larvae	1.3	2.6	–	5.1	–	–	–
Caddis larvae	1.3	1.8	4.8	15.4	–	–	–
Cranefly larvae	–	–	–	–	–	20.0	–
Fish							
Pike	–	4.4	41.3	53.8	68.6	100.0	100.0
Other vertebrates							
Frogs	–	0.9	1.6	12.8	22.8	40.0	33.3
Newts	–	0.9	–	–	–	–	–
NOS EXAMINED	160	113	63	39	35	5	3

the tail of the former protruding from its mouth while the front end is being digested.

Prey does not have to be moving to attract Pike, for, as anglers know, a dead fish is a most successful bait, especially a silvery one. The same Pike can be repeatedly taken on this type of bait, but soon appears to become aware of the dangers of an artificial spinning lure. They are bold fish and their lack of fear is well known to anglers; for example, it is not uncommon for a Pike to be hooked and lost and then to take the same bait again immediately. It has also been known for a Pike to seize a fish being played by an angler and for the Pike to hang on so tenaciously that it eventually became played out and could be landed without even being hooked. At such times they have just started to feed again following a period of digestion and fasting after their last large meal, a characteristic of Pike feeding behaviour. The conversion rate of food to body weight is about 5 or 6:1 but sometimes as high as 2:1. The annual intake of food for a Pike around 2kg in weight has been calculated at some 21kg.

Within the last few years, the authors have learned of two occasions when a Pike has grabbed a hand trailing over the side of a boat and of another occasion when a dog was attacked while it was wading.

Probably the main predators of Pike are other Pike, although during the larval stage they are subject to a very high (sometimes 95%) mortality inflicted by invertebrates such as dragonfly and beetle larvae. Occasionally the 'Man bites Dog' situation arises when young Pike are taken by large trout. In recent years in Scotland, the re-established Osprey has become a locally important predator of Pike up to 35cm in length.

The presence of Pike is a particularly important factor in any fish community. They eat large numbers of small fish of all kinds – though they do have apparent preferences for certain species – and affect the population dynamics of almost all the species involved. Many of the coarse fish species favoured by anglers, which are often very prolific, cannot attain a satisfactory

Fig. 71 An adult Pike along with two Mallard ducklings found in its stomach (Niall Campbell).

average size unless their numbers are controlled by Pike, while at the same time the damage they can do to a productive trout fishery can be immense. In one Irish lough, in one year, it was calculated that 1170 Pike destroyed 51.5 tonnes of Brown Trout.

Where trout are present, they are the preferred item of Pike diet, though this may be because they are more easily available for some reason. There is, however, an important relationship between the size of a Pike and its prey. Larger Pike have a preference for a prey about 45% of their own body length. In Windermere, Pike of 61–71cm in length take mostly trout of 28–35cm, whereas the smaller Pike take mainly Minnows and Perch. This aspect of Pike feeding behaviour makes the outcome of their introductions as an angling improvement measure rather uncertain. As Pike grow they feed on larger and larger fish and soon come into competition with the angler for the best fish. A possible way of counteracting this would be for fishery managers to regularly cull the larger Pike leaving only the small ones to deal with the smaller prey species.

To many anglers, especially those in England and Wales, Pike are the ultimate quarry, while Irish Pike waters attract tourist anglers from many parts of Britain and Europe. They are regarded as sporting fish and fight well on a light tackle, often jumping a number of times. The initial runs of a large Pike on being hooked may be much faster and longer than those of a salmon. In many waters they are returned after weighing and thus become increasingly wily, consequently making their recapture a great angling achievement. In salmonid waters, in contrast, they are regarded as evil vermin and are controlled if at all possible by angling, netting, long lines, poisoning and electric fishing.

The flesh of Pike is off-white in colour and has a distinctive flavour. It is considered unpalatable in most of the British Isles, but elsewhere is treated as a great delicacy and can be a very expensive fish to buy. They are also favoured in some countries, where they are cropped commercially, because they are converters of small useless fish species into well-flavoured Pike flesh. The intramuscular bones are a nuisance when eating large fish but can be ignored in small fish by determined diners. Large amounts of Pike are consumed in North America and Europe where they are of considerable commercial value. There are many, often complicated, recipes for its culinary use. The fat content of average Pike flesh has been estimated at 0.7%, which compares with fresh salmon at 17.8%. The farming of Pike takes place in parts of Europe.

Pike make interesting fish in aquaria and can grow quite rapidly if given enough food. If inadequate food is given they rarely stunt like other fish but become emaciated and die. Captive Pike become quite tame but they must only be kept with fish of their own size.

15

Carps

The family Cyprinidae, which includes the carps, minnows, barbels and similar species, is a large and variable group of fish native to most parts of the world except South America and Australasia. They are all freshwater species and only a few are able to venture occasionally into brackish water (e.g. Roach in the Baltic Sea). This is the largest fish family in the world with some 275 genera and about 2000 species. It is the dominant family in European fresh waters in terms of numbers of species.

Cyprinidae may be small to large fishes of quite a range of shapes. The mouth is variable in size and position but never possesses teeth on the jaws. These are replaced functionally by pharyngeal bones with 1–3 rows of teeth which grind against a pair of horny pads on the opposite side of the pharynx. One or two pairs of sensory barbels are often present just beside the corners of the mouth. The fins are moderately developed and usually soft-rayed, except for the spiny stiffened leading rays (i.e. the hard rays) of the dorsal and anal fins in a few species. The body is usually well covered with cycloid scales and in most fish a lateral line is present. The sexes are often different in appearance during the spawning season, the males becoming brightly coloured with well developed tubercles on the head, body and fins; the shape, position and number of these tubercles are useful aids to species identification.

The sense of smell of many members of the family (e.g. Carp, Crucian Carp and Goldfish) is very highly developed and the olfactory cells in the nose alone may number some 270 million. This gives them a sense of smell about twice as good as salmonids (but still short of that of the Eel or the Danube Catfish). In crude terms, the olfactory senses of carps are two million times keener than those of humans. Thus, the sense of smell to these fish is its main contact with the environment – a very important factor to fish living in turbid water or feeding in the dark.

As might be expected from the large number of species, the Cyprinidae show considerable differences in habit and habitat, and occupy a variety of ecological niches in fresh waters. Most species feed on invertebrates and only occasionally on fish. A number are omnivorous, feeding on both invertebrates and plants. A few species are entirely herbivorous, and such fish have proved to be important to humans in two ways – as efficient producers of fish flesh and as potential biological control agents in waters where algae or higher plants have become a problem.

There are 80 species in Europe and 16 of these occur in the British Isles. Many are kept in public aquaria and they are also good subjects for private cold-water and tropical aquaria, particularly species such as the Bitterling, which have particularly interesting breeding habits. A number of the larger species are important commercially in Europe (in both wild fisheries and fish

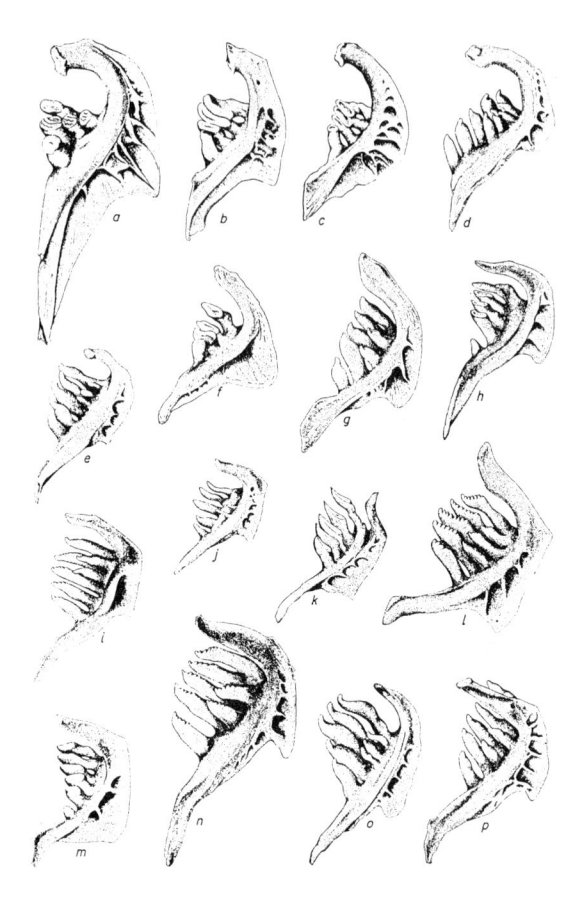

Fig. 72 Pharyngeal bones from the carp family: a, Common Carp; b, Crucian Carp; c, Goldfish; d, Barbel; e, Gudgeon; f, Tench; g, Silver Bream; h, Common Bream; i, Bleak; j, Minnow; k, Bitterling; l, Rudd; m, Roach; n, Chub; o, Orfe; p, Dace (from Maitland 1972b).

farms) and various species form the basis of important sport fisheries all over Europe, including the British Isles.

Identification

The members of this family which occur in the British Isles are relatively easy to distinguish one from another with the exception perhaps of a couple of paired species (e.g. Roach and Rudd, Common Bream and Silver Bream) which are superficially rather similar. However, it is among this family that most hybrids between species are found in the wild and so, where real difficulties are encountered in identifying a specimen, this possibility should be taken into account. Also, an ever increasing number of foreign species from this family are being made available in the British Isles through aquarium and pond suppliers, and it is more than likely that these may be found in the wild, as escapees, casual releases or even as newly established populations. Among the species concerned here at the moment are the Grass Carp *Ctenopharyngodon idella*, Silver Carp *Hypophthalmichthys molitrix* and Fathead Minnow *Pimephales promelas*. Hybrids and potential new resident species are not included in the key below which covers only those Cyprinidae known to be established in the British Isles at the moment. However, because it is being stocked in an increasing number of waters throughout the country, a short account of the Grass Carp is given at the end of this chapter.

1. Barbels present on head. **2.**

   Barbels absent on head. **5.**

2. Dorsal fin with more than 15 rays. Less than 40 scales along the lateral line. Pharyngeal teeth 1.1.3:3.1.1 **COMMON CARP**

   Dorsal fin with less than 15 rays. More than 40 scales along lateral line. Pharyngeal teeth not 1.1.3:3.1.1. **3.**

3. More than 60 scales along lateral line. Dorsal fin convex. Pharyngeal teeth in one row. **TENCH**

   Less than 60 scales along lateral line. Dorsal fin concave. Pharyngeal teeth in two or three rows. **4.**

4. Four barbels on head. More than 50 scales along lateral line. Pharyngeal teeth in three rows. **BARBEL**

   Two barbels on head. Less than 50 scales along lateral line. Pharyngeal teeth in two rows. **GUDGEON**

5(1). Less than 15 rays in anal fin. **6.**

   More than 15 rays in anal fin. **14.**

6. More than 14 rays in dorsal fin. Less than 35 scales along lateral line. Pharyngeal teeth 4.4. **7.**

   Less than 12 rays in dorsal fin. More than 35 scales along lateral line. Pharyngeal teeth other than 4.4. **8.**

7. More than 31 scales along lateral line. Less than 34 gill rakers on first gill arch. First dorsal ray feeble, weakly serrated. Dorsal fin convex. **CRUCIAN CARP**

   Less than 31 scales along lateral line. More than 34 gill rakers on first gill arch. First dorsal spine strong, coarsely serrated. Dorsal fin concave. **GOLDFISH**

8(6). Less than 39 scales along lateral series. Less than 14 rays in pectoral fin. Lateral line short, confined to first 6 scales. **BITTERLING**

   More than 39 scales along lateral line. More than 14 rays in pectoral fin. Lateral line extending at least to middle of body, and usually to tail. **9.**

9. More than 80 scales along lateral line, which is usually incomplete behind middle of body. Tubules of lateral line extending to free edges of scales. **MINNOW**

   Less than 60 scales along lateral line, which is always complete. Tubules of lateral line not extending to free edge of scales. **10.**

10. More than 54 scales along lateral line; 9–10 scales between dorsal fin and lateral line; 5–6 scales between anal fin and lateral line. **ORFE**

    Less than 54 scales along lateral line; 7–8 scales between dorsal fin and lateral line; 3–4 scales between anal fin and lateral line. **11.**

11. Less than 13 rays in anal fin. Length of body more than 3–5 times its maximum depth. 44–53 scales along lateral line. Pharyngeal teeth: 2.5:5.2. **12.**

More than 11 rays in anal fin. Length of body less than 3–5 times its maximum depth. 40–45 scales along lateral line. Pharyngeal teeth not 2.5:5.2. **13.**

12. Less than 47 scales along lateral line. Anal and dorsal fins straight or slightly convex. Caudal fin fork shallow. **CHUB**

    More than 46 scales along lateral line. Anal and dorsal fins concave. Caudal fin deeply forked. **DACE**

13(11). Scales along lateral line 42–45. Front of dorsal fin above or very slightly behind base of pelvic fins. One row of pharyngeal teeth (5:5 or 6:6) on which pectination is weak or absent. **ROACH**

    Scales along lateral line 40–43. Front of dorsal fin distinctly behind base of pelvic fins. Two rows of pharyngeal teeth (3.5:5.3) on which the pectination is strong. **RUDD**

14(5). Length of body more than 4 times its maximum depth. 20–23 rays in anal fin. Less than 5 scales between anal fin and lateral line. **BLEAK**

    Length of body less than 3 times its maximum depth. 22–31 rays in anal fin. More than 4 scales between anal fin and lateral line. **15.**

15. Less than 50 scales along lateral line. Less than 27 rays in anal fin. 8–11 scales between dorsal fin and lateral line. Distance between tip of snout and eye usually less than or equal to diameter of eye.
    SILVER BREAM

    More than 49 scales along lateral line. More than 25 rays in anal fin. 11–15 scales between dorsal fin and lateral line. Distance between tip of snout and eye usually more than diameter of eye.
    COMMON BREAM

Common Carp *Cyprinus carpio* Linnaeus 1758
Koi, Leather Carp, Mirror Carp

This well-known fish has been cultivated and moved around the world for many hundreds of years. Adults usually reach lengths of 40–50cm and weights of 2– 3kg, but much larger fish can occur and fish of up to 30kg at over 40 years of age have been recorded from Europe. The present British rod-caught record stands at 19.957kg for a fish caught in 1952 in Redmire Pool, Hereford. The Irish record is 11.28kg for a carp caught in 1987 in The Lough, Cork, and the world record was claimed in 1985 for a carp of 26.22kg caught in the Potomac River, Washington, USA.

The Common Carp is a sturdy fish with a laterally compressed stream lined body which is usually well covered by large cycloid scales, of which there are some 35–39 along the lateral line. Old fish may become very deep and much less stream lined. Characteristically, the head carries two pairs of barbels on the upper lip, the posterior pair, in the angles of the mouth, being the longer. The pharyngeal teeth are in three rows and rather flattened with slight grooves.

The scaling of this species, like its colour, shows some variation and several

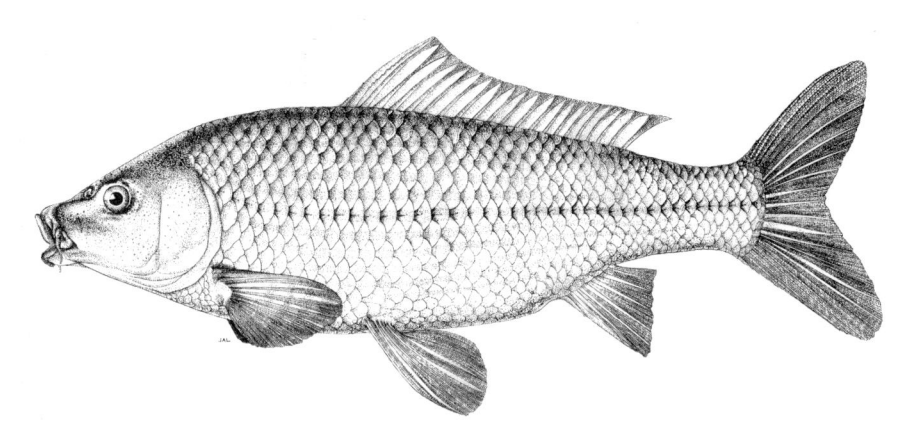

Fig. 73 Common Carp (from Maitland 1972b).

varieties have been bred with different scale patterns. These range from the standard wild form, which is completely scaled ('King Carp'), through a form which has only a single row of very large plate-like scales along the lateral line ('Mirror Carp'), to a completely scaleless form ('Leather Carp'). All of these forms and variations of them can now be found in the wild in the British Isles.

The dorsal fin is long and bears anteriorly, as one of 3–4 spines, a serrated spine followed by 17–22 branched rays. The pectoral fins have 14–17 soft rays and the pelvics, which are thoracic in position just below the origin of the dorsal fin, have 8–9 soft rays. The anal fin has 3 small hard rays followed

Fig. 74 A fine specimen of an adult Common Carp (Dietrich Burkel).

by 4–6 soft rays and there are some 19–21 soft branched rays in the caudal fin. There are 36–38 vertebrae and 21–29 gill rakers on the first arch.

In colour, the upper head and back are usually olive-brown to olive grey which becomes lighter on the sides, with a yellowish tinge. The belly is a dull yellowish-brown. The dorsal fin is usually a dark olive-green but the other fins are a lighter greeny brown, sometimes with a reddish tinge. Small Common Carp may be confused with Crucian Carp, wild Goldfish or Common Bream. In domesticated forms a complete range of colour varieties, mixtures and patterns has been bred for ornamental (pond) purposes. These range from silver ('ghost') and pure white individuals through yellow, orange, red and brown to blue and black and an amazing range of mixtures of these – the 'Koi' Carp. Under ultra-violet light, these may be strongly iridescent.

The Common Carp was originally an Asian fish found only in the warm temperate band from Manchuria to the Black Sea. Because of its importance as a food fish it has been widely introduced and is now found in all the major continents and most parts of the world where the summers are warm enough to induce spawning and allow adequate growth of the young. It is widespread throughout central and southern Europe and is found in most parts of the southern half of the British Isles including Ireland and the Channel Islands, where it arrived during the fifteenth or sixteenth centuries. In Scotland a number of populations do occur but it is likely that the species is reaching its northern limit here and, as in Ireland, can only breed successfully during warmer than average summers. However, carp are very hardy fish and transport well, having a low oxygen demand, a high temperature tolerance and the ability to survive out of water for a considerable time. These factors have no doubt been helpful to its wide dispersion, especially in ancient times.

The preferred habitats of the Common Carp are rich ponds and lakes, canals and slow-flowing rivers where there is an abundance of aquatic vegetation. It can sometimes be found in large numbers and though the young move around together it is not really a shoaling fish. Its tolerance of low oxygen concentrations (it can thrive at levels as low as 0.7mg/l) allow it to inhabit very rich waters where the decomposition of organic matter is rapid. The higher the water temperature the more active carp are.

Spawning takes place in spring and late summer when the water temperature reaches at least 18°C. Mature fish move into the shallows at this time and start to swim around in small groups, ripe females often being accompanied and 'driven' by several males, which push and nudge the female as they become more excited. During the actual spawning the fish become quite frantic and rush to the surface over weed beds creating considerable disturbance and noise, and the species, which is otherwise very wary and often difficult to observe, becomes very obvious to the onlooker at this time. The eggs and sperm are released together during the spawning act and the former, being adhesive, stick to the leaves of plants near the surface. Carp sperm can remain active for about five minutes – a comparatively long time compared to many other fish. By comparison, the active period for trout is just over 30 seconds, and for Burbot, two minutes.

The females are very fecund and, according to size, can produce from 40,000 eggs (a female of 40cm) to well over 2,000,000 eggs (a female of 85cm). The eggs are a clear yellow colour and some 1.2–1.5mm in diameter.

Table 30 Food of Common Carp in South Platte and St Vrain Rivers and Goosequill Pond, Colorado, United States (after Ede & Carlson 1977), as percentage volume.

Stomach contents	South Platte R	St Vrain R	Goosequill P
Macrophytes			
Plants	21.1	38.2	16.2
Seeds	5.0	21.5	5.6
Worms	+	0.1	+
Crustaceans			
Plankton	+	+	0.6
Amphipods	0.1	0.5	–
Crayfish	–	–	43.6
Insects			
Mayfly larvae	0.1	0.1	+
Dragonfly larvae	0.3	0.2	4.2
Caddis larvae	0.4	–	–
Midge larvae	7.8	3.3	4.6
Blackfly larvae	0.2	1.4	–
Fly pupae	2.8	1.1	0.8
Other invertebrates	0.1	1.8	+
Fish	1.9	1.8	+
Terrestrial organisms	4.8	2.5	–
Detritus	55.5	29.9	23.6
NUMBER OF FISH EXAMINED	105	207	204

They take 3–7 days to hatch according to water temperature. On hatching, the larvae sink towards the bottom, but are able to become attached by their mouths to the leaves of aquatic plants, where they remain for a few days before making their way to the surface. At this stage they are vulnerable to predation from a wide range of invertebrates including predatory plankters such as *Polyphemus*. As carp have a permanent duct connecting the swimbladder to the gut, the larvae must swim up to the surface within 14 days to inflate the swimbladder by gulping in air.

The young are quite small (4–6mm) when they hatch but soon grow rapidly if temperatures are high, so that they may be 10–15cm at the end of one year and 20–25cm by the time they are two years old. They start to mature during their third or fourth years when they have reached lengths of 30–40cm and may live, on average, for 10–15 years – often much longer in captivity. The British rod-caught record Common Carp was 15 years old, but lived a further 20 years in captivity. They can be aged by scale examination.

The preferred water temperature seems to be in the lower thirties centigrade (although it would practically never experience this in the British Isles) and, during the winter, carp retire to deep water where they remain in a torpid state. For it to overwinter safely it has been shown that a carp must build up a significant fat reserve: a fish at the beginning of winter with a condition factor (obtained from a formula relating the length and weight of a fish and thereby expressing its 'plumpness' in a single figure) of less than 2.9 may not survive. Overwinter mortality of carp has been observed in Britain as a result of a long, cold winter.

The acute sensitivity of carp to even a small rise in the ambient water temperature was dramatically demonstrated during the mild winter of 1987–88 in England when water temperatures in ponds and lakes rose to over 7°C. Many specimen carp were taken by anglers – a previously unheard of winter event – and the angling column of a national newspaper reported that about a dozen carp of 13.6kg or over had been caught during January. It would appear that, once roused from their normal winter torpor, the carp had to start looking for food to meet an increase in their metabolic demand.

Carp are truly omnivorous feeders and will eat a wide variety of food items, digestion of these being considerably helped by the action of the pharyngeal teeth, which grind up tough or solid items. Carp do not have a stomach (or associated pyloric caecae), the oesophagus merely emptying into the expanded upper intestine, which acts as a 'crop'. The young feed mainly on small crustaceans of different kinds which occur in the plankton and among weeds, but as they grow they start to feed more and more on the bottom on benthic invertebrates, especially midge larvae, crustaceans and molluscs. They often do this by sucking in quantities of mud from the bottom and then expelling it, subsequently taking in the invertebrates they have disturbed by this action. The extensible tubular mouth is capable of penetrating some distance into bottom muds and silts which are stirred up as a consequence, often increasing water turbidity. As a result, they have often been responsible for considerable alteration of habitat, clear weedy waters becoming turbid and weedless as the mud is regularly stirred up and light for the growing plants is eliminated. For this reason, anglers and conservationists have regretted their introduction to many areas. This has been particularly the case in North America, where one of the authors got into trouble for innocently releasing a large carp that he caught in a Canadian river.

The Common Carp has been cultivated for over 2000 years and is of considerable importance commercially in many countries, especially those far from the sea, where sea fish are unobtainable. In early times, the eggs of carp were used as a substitute for Sturgeon caviar by Jews as, according to the Old Testament, Sturgeon (and other scaleless fish) were unclean and thus genuine caviar was not 'kosher'. It is caught commercially in the wild but is also reared in enormous numbers in special ponds. It is also a very important sport fish, and its wily nature, potentially large size and fighting qualities when hooked have made it a sought after species by anglers, who will fish for it throughout the night. Isaac Walton called the carp the 'river fox' – a tribute to its wiliness.

Its popularity as an aquarium and especially a pond fish has also given it a considerable commercial importance in this field, especially in the British Isles with the enormous recent popularity of the keeping of Koi Carp. These are now widely available in a large range of sizes, colours and prices (which can vary from one or two pounds to several thousand for a single fish!).

Crucian Carp *Carassius carassius* (Linnaeus 1758)
Crowger, Gibel Carp, Prussian Carp

This deep-bodied fish is superficially very similar to the 'uncoloured' Goldfish, but whereas in the latter the spines in the dorsal and anal fins are both deeply serrated, in the Crucian Carp these spines are only very lightly serrated. The Crucian Carp varies considerably in its size at maturity. In some populations the majority of the adult individuals are only 5–10cm in length, whereas elsewhere it may commonly grow to 20–30cm. Under ideal conditions it has been known to grow to 50cm in length and 2kg in weight. The British rod-caught record stands at 2.565kg for a specimen caught in 1976 at a lake near King's Lynn in Norfolk.

The body is typically very deep and laterally compressed, and large fish

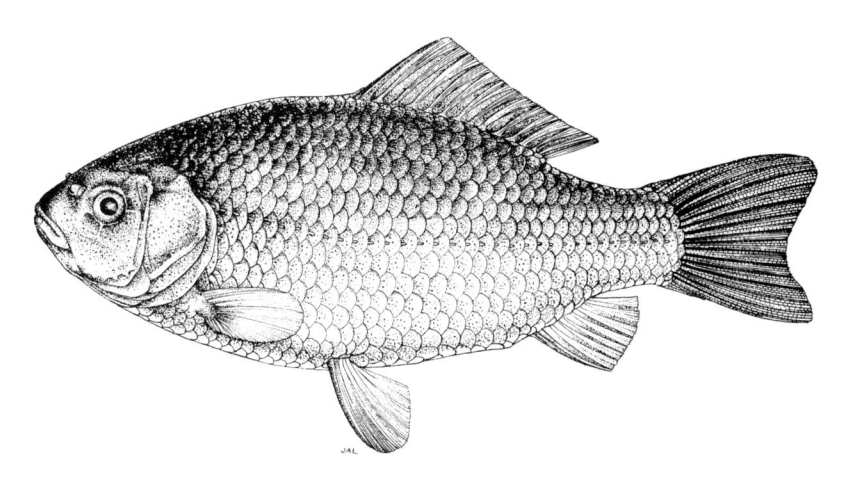

Fig. 75 Crucian Carp (from Maitland 1972b).

often have a 'hump-backed' appearance. In some populations, however, the body is less deep and much closer in shape to that of the Goldfish. The head is small and the mouth terminal with no barbels. Common Carp and Crucian Carp hybrids have small barbels, usually only one pair. There are 26–31 gill rakers on the first gill arch and 4 narrow and smooth pharyngeal teeth on each side. The body is covered with large cycloid scales which do not extend on to the head and of which there are 31–36 along the lateral line.

The dorsal fin is long and usually convex above with 3–4 spines anteriorly, the third of which is lightly serrated, and 14–21 soft branched rays posteriorly. The much shorter anal fin has 2–3 anterior spines, of which the last is lightly serrated, and 6–8 soft rays posteriorly.

Fig. 76 Two young Crucian Carp (William Howes).

In colour, the Crucian Carp is mainly an olive-green to golden-green on the upper head and body grading to a lighter brassy green on the sides and dull brown on the belly. The dorsal and caudal fins are brownish, whilst the pectoral, pelvic and anal fins are a dull reddish-brown. Young fish may have a dark mark at the base of the tail.

This species is native to west, central and eastern Europe as well as much of central Asia, but it has been introduced to a number of countries outside this area. In the British Isles it is native to south-eastern England and is quite common and widespread there. It has been redistributed to the north and west of this (including the Channel Islands) but its occurrence in these parts of the country is patchy and it becomes increasingly rare to the north and west. Only one established population is known to the authors in Scotland for instance and it is absent from Ireland (into which its importation is banned).

The Crucian Carp favours small rich ponds and lakes in lowland areas where there is abundant weed growth, though it may occasionally be found in slow-flowing rivers and canals. It requires reasonable summer water temperatures (in excess of 20°C for several weeks) for successful spawning and growth of the fry, but is more tolerant of stagnation and poor oxygen conditions in both summer and winter than most other species.

Adult fish become sexually active during early summer, when the females fatten and the males develop nuptial tubercles. Ripe females are actively pursued by one or more males and spawning takes place near the surface in thick weed beds, the eggs and sperm being released simultaneously during orgasmic shuddering, when the pair are usually just at the surface. Fecundity of the females depends very much on size and may range from 10,000–300,000 eggs per fish. The eggs, which are a clear pale yellow and 1.4–1.7mm in diameter, are adhesive and stick readily to the vegetation. They hatch in 5–10 days at water temperatures of 15–25°C, requiring approximately 100 day-degrees for development.

The young are about 4mm on hatching and growth is very variable depending on temperature and habitat. However, under favourable conditions they can reach 5cm after one year and 10–15cm after two years. They usually mature after 3–4 years and may live for up to 10 years on average, though specimens older than this are not uncommon and in captivity the species may live for several decades.

The young, after absorbing the yolk sac (this may take 1–2 days) feed on protozoans and small crustaceans in the plankton and among the weeds. As they mature they may eat some plants but rely mainly on benthic invertebrates, especially worms, molluscs, crustaceans and various insects (midge larvae especially).

The Crucian Carp is of considerable value in parts of Eastern Europe where it is cultured in ponds and cropped in the wild using traps and seines. It is especially valuable in situations where mild pollution or eutrophication create low oxygen conditions during summer or winter, which would be inimical to most other species. Though the Crucian Carp is less favoured as a food fish than the Common Carp, hybrids of the two species perform well in some situations and are cultivated from time to time. The Crucian Carp is also a popular sport fish in some areas proving, like the Common Carp, a wily fish which presents a challenge to the angler. It is an attractive aquarium and pond fish and becomes tame rapidly.

Fig. 77 A young Goldfish (Heather Angel).

Goldfish *Carassius auratus* (Linnaeus 1758)
Gibel Carp, Comet, Shubunkin, Veiltail and numerous other varietal names

Most Goldfish, especially those kept in aquaria, do not grow to a large size and lengths of 10–15cm are common in adult fish. However, given good conditions and space in large ornamental ponds or in the wild, the species can grow up to 30cm in length and 1kg in weight. For some reason, there is no rod-caught record for this species, though it is regularly caught by anglers but often confused with the Crucian Carp. Specimens over 40cm in length have been reported from Asia.

In shape, the body can be very variable but is usually rather deep and laterally compressed. It is normally less deep than the Crucian Carp, with

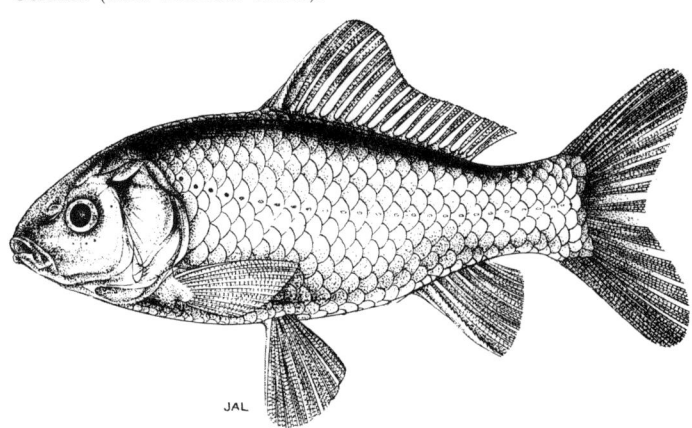

Fig. 78 Goldfish (from Maitland 1972b).

which it is often confused, but in the Goldfish the strongest anterior spines in the dorsal and anal fins are always deeply serrated (only slightly so in the Crucian Carp) and the anal fin usually has only 5 soft rays (usually 7 in the Crucian Carp). There are no barbels at the mouth and the first gill arch has 35–48 gill rakers. There are 4 pharyngeal teeth on either side, all of them narrow and smooth-edged. The body is covered with large cycloid scales of which there are 28–33 along the lateral line. There are some 29–31 vertebrae. The dorsal fin, which is usually concave along its free edge, is long with 3–4 anterior spines and 15–19 soft rays posteriorly. The anal fin has 2–3 anterior spines and 5–6 soft rays. The caudal fin is more deeply notched than in the Crucian Carp.

Most young Goldfish are similar in colour, which is mainly a dull olive greenish-brown, sometimes with a yellowish tinge. As they grow, however, remarkable colour changes can take place. In the wild, most fish darken to be olive-green on the upper head and back, lightening somewhat on the sides to a dull yellowish-green on the belly. In captive aquarium and pond-bred stocks, however, the fish may rapidly change to any one of a number of colours, including white, yellow, gold, red, blue or black or any combination of these with a variety of patterns. It is largely due to these lovely colours that the fish is so popular as a pet.

This species was originally native to Asia and parts of eastern Europe. However, it has been introduced and has established itself in many parts of the world and now occurs widely throughout the warmer parts of Europe. In the British Isles, where it first appeared in the late seventeenth century, it is common in most parts of England, but there appear to be only a few isolated populations in suitable ponds in the Channel Islands (Jersey), Wales, Scotland and Ireland.

Goldfish prefer rich weedy ponds and canals, where there is plenty of cover and the bottom is muddy. They occur in rivers only in very slow-flowing lowland situations and rarely have large populations there. They are frequently found in artificial situations, especially ornamental ponds in parks and on large estates, where their ancestors were no doubt introduced for their attractive colours. In such situations the entire population may have reverted to the 'wild' colour, for the golden and other light coloured forms are very vulnerable to Herons and other predators. Goldfish are among the most temperature tolerant of all fishes – they can survive low temperatures of around 0°C and high temperatures of up to 40°C.

Spawning only takes place in warm weather (usually June and July) when water temperatures have reached 15–20°C and these temperatures have to be retained for several weeks if the young are to make sufficient growth to survive their first winter. As the mature fish ripen the females swell and the males develop nuptial tubercles on the face and gill covers. Ripe females are each followed and nuzzled by one or more ripe males and this 'driving' becomes more and more vigourous until eventually eggs and sperm are liberated together near the surface among weed when the spawning act reaches its climax. This performance is repeated many times during the day until the female is spent. Fecundity varies very much according to size and can range from 6000–380,000 eggs per female. The eggs are a clear yellow colour some 1.5mm in diameter and stick to the vegetation, mostly in warm positions near the surface. Development takes 3–8 days depending on temperature.

One very notable feature about the reproduction of this species is the fact that in a few places the entire population can consist of females. For instance, in lowland ox-bow ponds in Russia samples of as many as 600 fish all proved to be female. However, the scientists studying them demonstrated that, in the absence of males, these fish spawned readily in the wild with other members of the carp family, with which they co-existed (e.g. Common Carp and Crucian Carp). The sperm of these latter males, though unable to fertilise the Goldfish egg, stimulated it to start dividing so that it developed into a young fish genetically identical to its mother, and of course another female. This type of reproduction, producing clones of identical genetic make-up is called gynogenesis and is very rare among fish species.

The young fish are some 4–6mm on hatching and subsequent growth is very dependent on water temperatures. In northern situations they may reach only 2– 3cm by the winter and rarely survive, but further south they may be 10cm after one year and 15cm after two. They are normally mature in their third or fourth years and can live for up to ten years in the wild, often much longer in captivity.

The young fish feed almost entirely on protozoans and small crustaceans in the weed and plankton, but as they grow they become mainly bottom feeders and browsers, eating some plant material but mainly relying on benthic invertebrates such as worms, molluscs, crustaceans and insects (e.g. midge larvae).

Goldfish are of little commercial importance as food and only in a few places are they of interest to anglers. However, they are a major species for aquaria and ponds and there is an enormous international trade in this fish. Many hundreds of thousands are moved annually from warmer areas in the south of both North America and Europe, where the species is easy to breed and rear, to the cooler areas further north. There is also a bewildering variety

Fig. 79 A large specimen Barbel from the River Avon in Hampshire (William Howes).

of exotic, often highly distorted forms, originally developed in China and Japan, with spherical bodies, telescopic and bubble eyes, lion heads, double veil and fan tails and so on. Superimposed on these shapes are many colouring patterns, and the keeping and breeding of these forms is popular in many parts of the world.

Barbel *Barbus barbus* (Linnaeus 1758)
Adult Barbel are usually some 40–60cm in length and 1–2kg in weight, but the species can grow up to 100cm in length and reach a weight of 8kg in very favourable waters. The present British rod-caught record is for a fish of 6.237kg caught in the River Avon in Hampshire in 1962, although larger specimens have actually been caught in England – for example, an 8.13kg fish caught out of season in the River Avon by a salmon angler.

The Barbel is characterised, as its name suggests, by the possession of two pairs of long fleshy barbels on the equally fleshy upper lip, one pair (the smaller) just in front of the snout, the other at the rear angles of the mouth. The mouth is placed ventrally back from the snout. The pointed pharyngeal teeth end in short hooks and are in three rows, 5+3+2 on each side. There are usually about 17 gill rakers on the first arch. The body, evolved for active swimming, is long and rounded with very little lateral flattening, although it is rather flat along the belly. The body is covered in medium-sized cycloid scales of which there are 55–65 along the lateral line. The exposed edge of the scales, which are normally rather deeply embedded, is typically rather pointed.

The dorsal fin is high and convex on its free edge, originating just behind the mid-point of the body and with the strongest of its anterior 3–4 spines serrated behind, followed by 7–9 soft branched rays. The anal fin is long and when laid flat against the body almost reaches the origin of the tail fin. It has three spiny rays anteriorly followed by five soft rays.

In colour, the Barbel is usually a brownish-green on the head and back which grades to a golden-brown on the sides and then to creamy white on the belly. The fins are a dull yellowish-green, sometimes with an orange tinge.

The Barbel does not occur in northern Europe but is found from western France across central Europe to the Black Sea. In the British Isles, it was formerly confined to the east and south-east of England but has been redistributed by angling interests to several river systems such as the Medway, the Severn and the Bristol Avon. It is absent from Ireland and Scotland.

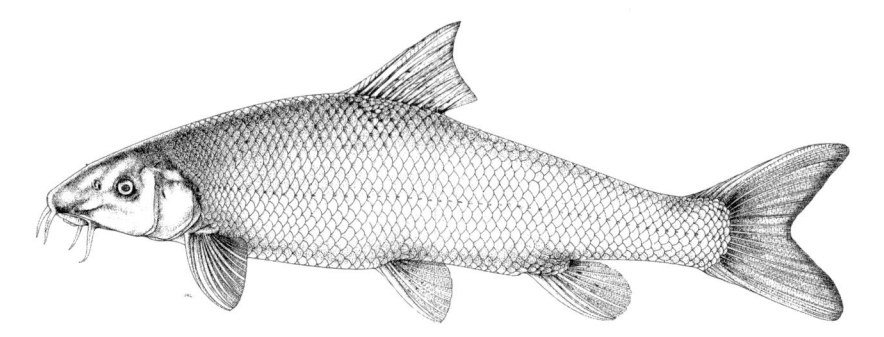

Fig. 80 Barbel (from Maitland 1972b).

The Barbel is a bottom-living fish which occurs usually in the lowland reaches of large clean rivers, where there are stretches of clean gravel and weed beds. It is a very good swimmer and may also be found in other favourable parts of rivers, especially where deep pools offer some protection during the day. Fast water, by weirs and bridges, are among its favourite haunts. It tends to occur in considerable numbers in such habitats, often forming schools during the daytime resting period.

Spawning takes place in May and June or even into July, when adult fish may move upstream and congregate in large numbers near the spawning grounds, which are over clean gravel and among open weed beds in flowing water. The males have by this time developed prominent facial tubercles, which extend in rows on to their backs, and they chase the females until mating is achieved. Some authorities say that a rough redd is prepared. Each female can carry from 3000–30,000 eggs depending on her size. The eggs are liberated into the water and fertilised immediately by the sperm which the males (often more than one male may accompany a female) release at the same time. They are yellow, some 2– 2.5mm in diameter, sticky, and adhere to weed and to the gravel. Development varies with water temperature, but normally takes some 10–15 days.

After hatching, the young fish, which are about 7–8mm in length, drift downstream into quiet shallow stretches of water where they begin feeding after the yolk sac has been absorbed. In good habitats the young fish may reach some 10cm after one year and 15–20cm after two years. They mature normally at about 4–5 years of age, the males usually about a year earlier than the females and correspondingly often smaller.

The fry start to feed on small crustaceans and insect larvae and as they grow they move to larger invertebrates including worms, crustaceans, molluscs (both snails and mussels), and mayfly and midge larvae. Large Barbel will take small fish when they can. They feed mainly at dusk and during the night, moving back at dawn to sheltered resting places under banks or in the vicinity of weed beds. During the winter, Barbel withdraw into deeper water and become relatively inactive.

In a few parts of Europe the Barbel is caught commercially, especially during the spawning migration when it may be taken in large numbers by traps and seines. The flesh is highly regarded in these areas, though bony, but the roe (and possibly even the flesh during the spawning period) is poisonous, causing severe stomach disorders. However, the Barbel is primarily an angler's fish and is respected for its cunning and valued for its fighting qualities in the British Isles, where it is of no commercial importance.

Gudgeon *Gobio gobio* (Linnaeus 1758)

The Gudgeon is a small fish, usually maturing in the British Isles at about 12–15cm, although fish of up to 20cm and over 220gm have been recorded. The British rod-caught record is for a fish of 120gm caught in 1977 at a fish pond at Ebbw Vale in Wales.

This is a distinctive fish and unlikely to be mistaken for any other except when very small when it could be confused with small Barbel or Stone Loach. The body is elongate and rounded with only slight ventral flattening and some lateral compression towards the tail. There is a single pair of long barbels, one situated in the posterior corner of each side of the ventral mouth,

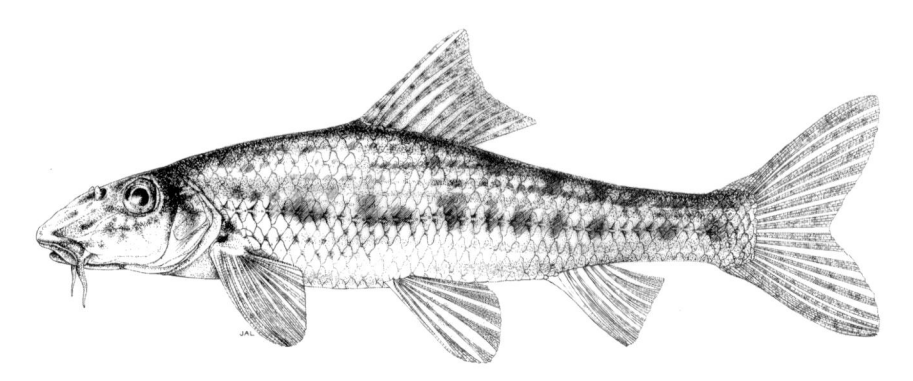

Fig. 81 Gudgeon (from Maitland 1972b).

whose lips are thick. The pharyngeal teeth (5+2+3) are in two rows on either side. The body is well covered in medium-sized cycloid scales of which there are 38–44 along the well-developed lateral line. The sensory neuromast organs of the lateral line are exposed and very sensitive. The scales can be used for age determination.

The dorsal fin has 3 spiny rays followed by 5–7 soft rays. The anal fin has 3 spiny rays followed by 6–7 soft rays. Both these fins have rather narrow bases.

In colour the upper head and back are an olive-brown with some dark spotting, grading to a lighter brown on the sides and a dull whitish-yellow on the belly. Often, there is a silvery bluish tinge over the body. Along each side is an irregular line of dark blotches and the dorsal, anal and tail fin also have an irregular patterning of small dark marks.

Fig. 82 An adult Gudgeon (Heather Angel).

Top, Plate 1 River Muick, Scotland

Middle left, Plate 2 A batch of Bullhead eggs attached to the underside of a stone from Embercombe, Exmoor (Nature Conservancy)

Middle right, Plate 3 Alevins of the Atlantic Salmon (Department of Agriculture & Fisheries for Scotland)

Bottom, Plate 4 Atlantic Salmon spawning in shallow water in November (Niall Campbell)

Top, Plate 5 Two fine adult Brook Trout from a Tayside loch (Niall Campbell)

Bottom, Plate 6 North Third Reservoir near Stirling (Peter Maitland)

Top, Plate 7 A Gwyniad from Llyn Tegid (John Haram)

Middle, Plate 8 A male Three-spined Stickleback from Lindean Reservoir (Andrew Buckham)

Bottom, Plate 9 Adult Goureen – the landlocked Twaite Shad of Lough Leane (Niall O'Maoileidigh)

Plate 10 Examples of the colour variation found in just one species – the Brown Trout. The fish depicted here are typical of local races whose distinctive appearances are influenced by their genetic background (Robin Ade). *a-f*: A series of six Brown Trout from just two burns in south-west Scotland showing the great variety in colour and markings which may occur quite locally. *g*, The Gillaroo, distinguished by its marbled flanks, is a famous angling fish of Irish limestone lochs. *h*, The Sonachan is one of three forms (the others are the Gillaroo and the Ferox) found in Lough Melvin. Each is distinctive in appearance and in its spawning sites and feeding grounds within the loch. *i*, The Golden Trout inhabits a chain of lochs in the northern highlands of Scotland and is believed to be a remnant of an ancient stock of trout which

colonised fresh waters soon after the retreat of the ice cap. j, The Croispol Silver Trout – resembling a fresh-run Sea Trout, this northern Scottish race lacks the colours and markings common to most freshwater stocks (though spots gradually become more obvious with age). k, Grey Trout. The small mouth and distinctive shape and colour are characteristic of these Trout from Ross-shire, which may have a similar history to the Golden Trout. l, Ferox Trout. A large male (5.9kg) from Loch Garry, Inverness. The Ferox Trout of Scottish lochs are known for their large size and great age. Old males retain the hooked jaw all the year round. m, Ferox Trout. A typical well-spotted female (3.6kg) from Loch Ericht in the central highlands. Females retain the normal head proportions.

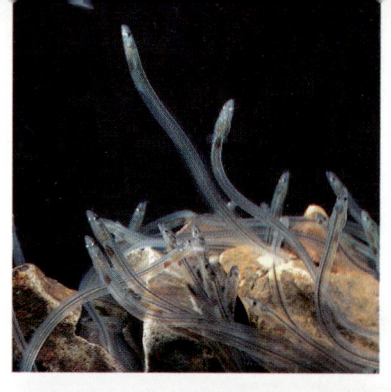

Top, Plate 11 Transparent elvers of the Eel showing gills, heart and backbone (Heather Angel)

Middle top, Plate 12 A Sturgeon taken off the Scottish coast near Ayr (Dietrich Burkel)

Middle bottom, Plate 13 A young Pike (Andrew Buckham)

Bottom, Plate 14 Two fine specimens of Tench (Dietrich Burkel)

Top, Plate 15 A Ruffe from the River Endrick (Andrew Buckham)

Middle, Plate 16 A Gudgeon from the River Endrick (Andrew Buckham)

Bottom, Plate 17 The River Devon near Alva (Peter Maitland)

Top, Plate 18 A juvenile Arctic Charr reared from eggs from Loch Doon (Peter Maitland)

Middle top, Plate 19 An adult Roach (Niall Campbell)

Middle bottom, Plate 20 An adult Grayling (Niall Campbell)

Bottom, Plate 21 Two fresh run spring Atlantic Salmon from the River Tummel (Niall Campbell)

Table 31 Food of Gudgeon in the River Cam, England (after Hartley 1948), as percentage number.

Stomach contents	River Cam
Molluscs	
Snails	5.9
Pea shells	0.1
Worms	0.1
Crustaceans	
Cladocerans	4.3
Ostracods	1.7
Copepods	4.5
Freshwater shrimp	8.8
Insects	
Mayfly larvae	5.3
Beetle larvae & adults	0.6
Caddis larvae	1.1
Midge larvae & pupae	53.4
Blackfly larvae & pupae	11.9
Other fly larvae	0.3
NUMBER OF FISH EXAMINED	372

Like the Barbel, the Gudgeon is mainly absent from northern and southern Europe, but is common in a broad area of the continent from western France to Asia and across to China and the Pacific coast. In the British Isles, although presumed native only to the south-east of England, it has now become widely dispersed (often due to introduction by humans – usually as unused live bait). It is common throughout most of lowland England and Wales as well as parts of Scotland as far north, on the east coast, as the River Don and, on the west coast, as the River Endrick where it is abundant, although it was introduced only about a decade ago by coarse fishermen. It is common in most parts of Ireland.

The Gudgeon is largely a fish of running water and only occasionally occurs in lakes. It prefers fairly fast-running water with a clean bottom of sand and gravel, with some weed beds to provide cover. Here, large schools may build up during the summer months. Its oxygen requirements are similar to those of Grayling and Bullhead. It also occurs in slower-flowing lowland systems in lesser numbers, and there it tends to move into deeper waters during the winter when feeding activity declines.

Reproduction takes place in May and June when the water temperature is around 14°C. The males develop tubercles on the head and front of the body. Spawning takes place in shallow flowing water among plants and gravel, to which the opaque, greyish-yellow eggs, some 1.4–1.8mm in diameter, stick in small groups after they have been laid and fertilised. Each female spawns several times in succession, often with several different males until she is spent, having laid about 1000–3000 eggs in total. The eggs hatch in 10–20 days depending on local water temperatures. After hatching, the larvae drift downstream to slightly quieter water, usually along the edge of the river, where they absorb the yolk sac and start to feed within 5–6 days.

The larvae are only about 4–5mm on hatching and by the end of their first summer may have grown to a length of 5cm. After two years they may have reached 10cm and by their third year they are mature at 12cm or more. By this time, most females are slightly larger than males of the same age. Most fish live for 4–5 years and some may reach 7 or 8 years of age. In an Irish river a proportion of both sexes mature at 2+ years of age, around 7–8cm in length. No size difference between males and females has been noted.

The fry feed mainly on small crustaceans in open water or among weed. As they grow they start to feed more and more on the bottom but still rely largely on invertebrates there, especially oligochaete worms, crustaceans, molluscs and insect larvae. Filamentous algae and fish eggs are sometimes eaten.

The Gudgeon is of little importance commercially, although it is esteemed in some parts of France for the table. Elsewhere, including the British Isles, it is only occasionally angled, but is used mainly as bait for other fish. In some waters, Gudgeon are an important food for large predators such as trout and Pike, hence their value as live bait. The recent extensions of its distribution in Scotland are partly as a result of Gudgeon being carried about by anglers for use as live bait and then tipped into the water at the end of the day's fishing. It is an attractive aquarium fish and will live for many years in a mixed temperate aquarium along with other peaceful species like Minnow and Stone Loach.

Tench *Tinca tinca* (Linnaeus 1758) Doctor Fish

Most mature Tench in the British Isles are about 25–35cm, though the species can grow as large as 70cm in length and 8kg in weight in favourable waters in Europe. The present British rod-caught record stands at 5.689kg for a fish caught in 1985 at Wilstone Reservoir in Hertfordshire and this is now presumably the world record, beating the previous Swedish Tench of just over 4.5kg. Although heavier Tench have been caught in England, these were rejected as candidates for record status due to the fact that they were suffering from an abnormal condition termed 'dropsy' when the abdomen becomes much extended with accumulated fluid and the fish unnaturally heavy. The Irish record stands at 3.55kg.

The Tench is a distinctive fish with a short stocky, rather laterally compressed body, a deep caudal peduncle and rounded outlines. The mouth is terminal and rather small, but with a small barbel set posteriorly at each side. There are normally four or five pharyngeal teeth on each side, the tips of which are slightly expanded and bear a small hook. The body is covered with small elongate cycloid scales, deeply set in the skin, which is coated in thick

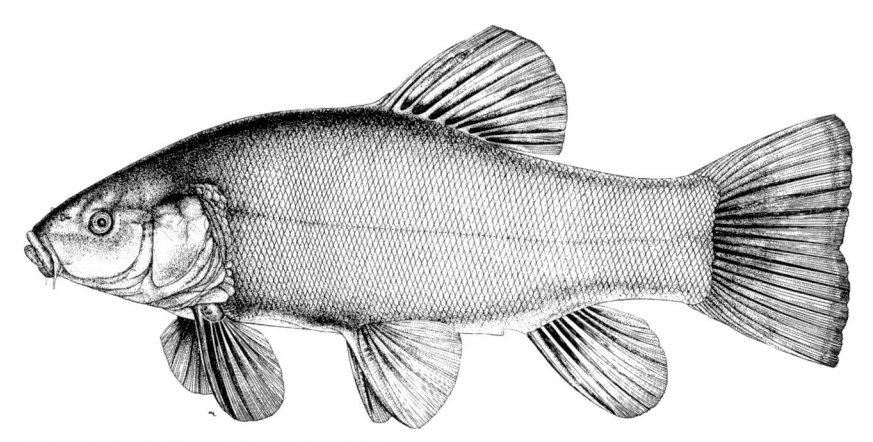

Fig. 83 Tench (from Maitland 1972b).

mucus and therefore very slimy and smooth to the touch. There are 87–120 of these scales along the lateral line. Scales and otoliths may be used for obtaining age and growth data.

All the fins are rather short and very rounded. The dorsal fin has 3 spiny and 10–11 branched rays, the anal fin also has 3 spiny rays anteriorly followed by 8–10 branched rays. The pelvic fins are of particular interest in this species for in the males the second ray is very thickened and the whole fin is much longer – reaching back past the anus. The rays of this fin in the female fish are all normal and the fin does not reach the anus when laid back. Thus, it is possible to recognise the sex of most fish over about 15cm by this feature – something which is not usually easy in most members of this family outside spawning time. Males do not develop tubercles over the head and anterior body, unlike most of the carp family.

The colour is a deep olive green-brown on the head and back, lightening slightly on the sides to dull creamy brown on the belly. The iris of the eye is bright orange-red. The fins are mostly a dark greeny brown. Selective breeding has produced an attractive golden form, which often has dark spots, and is popular for ornamental ponds.

The Tench is widely distributed throughout most of Europe except the north and also occurs right across Asia into China. In the British Isles, like most cyprinids, it is native only to the south-east of England but has been redistributed to many parts of the country so that it is now common in most parts of lowland England, Wales and Ireland and the Channel Islands (Jersey) and is reported from the Scilly Isles. In Scotland it is found in a number of rich lochs in the central belt and a few ponds in other parts of the country, but, as in Ireland, may not spawn every year, owing to its high temperature requirement.

This is a very shy fish and occurs mainly in quiet lowland lakes and very slow-flowing rivers where there is plenty of weed cover and a muddy bottom. It is extremely tolerant of stagnant conditions and appears able to survive in ponds where low oxygen conditions in the heat of summer and under the ice in winter (the oxygen levels may be as low as 0.7mg/l) would eliminate other species. It can stand quite high temperatures of up to some 34°C. It is also very easy to transport around the country, surviving out of water in damp moss or a wet sack for many hours.

Spawning takes place during the summer months, from late June until August, when the water temperature approaches 20°C. This is probably the last British species to spawn in the summer. Each female is driven by two or more males into thick weed beds and the fertilised adhesive eggs stick to the weed near the surface. The spawning act may be repeated a number of times until the female is spent. Each female can produce from 30,000–900,000 eggs depending on her size (i.e. some 125,000 eggs per kg). The greenish-yellow eggs, some 1.3–1.4mm in diameter, take about 3–5 days (75–100 day-degrees) to hatch. The young fry have a simple adhesive organ which enables them to attach to plants and stay among the weed beds until the yolk sac is absorbed (in about 10 days) and they are feeding properly. Tench fry, even though their swim-bladders are inflated within 24–48 hours of hatching, tend to remain inactive much longer than is usual for cyprinid fry, possibly up to a week after hatching. Tench and Crucian Carp are reputed to hybridise freely.

Fig. 84 A young Tench (Heather Angel).

The fry are 4–5mm at hatching but grow steadily if the water temperatures remain high, reaching some 4–8cm (5–10gm) at the end of their first summer, 10–15cm (40–100gm) at the end of their second summer and 20–30cm (200–300gm) at the end of their third summer – by which time most fish are starting to mature. However, in some slow-growing populations in Ireland, both mature males and females of 2+ years and only 12.5cm in length were found. Spawning usually takes place during the third or fourth years and may be repeated every year thereafter. Most fish live for 6–8 years and many much longer, 10–15 years of age being quite common. Individuals as old as 17 years have been recorded.

The fry eat protozoans, rotifers and small crustaceans from the plankton and among the weed beds. As they grow they depend more on bottom invertebrates such as worms, crustaceans, molluscs and insect larvae, especially those of midges, which they hunt mainly at night. They also eat fish eggs when available and regularly take in plant material. Tench are reputed to be able to penetrate some 7cm into the bottom mud – somewhat less than reported for carp. Bubbles rising to the surface are often a sign that Tench are rooting about on the bottom, which they do in a near vertical position. In

Table 32 Stomach contents of Tench of different lengths in Lake Tiberias, Australia, (after Weatherley 1959), as percentage occurrence.

Stomach contents	Tench Lengths in millimetres			
	23–40	41–60	61–100	101+
Algae	57	49	38	15
Molluscs	–	–	9	30
Worms	–	5	11	0
Crustaceans				
Copepods	84	67	64	45
Cladocerans	90	75	81	35
Ostracods	3	34	31	45
Amphipods	59	89	61	55
Insects				
Mayfly larvae	–	–	32	55
Dragonfly larvae	–	–	25	75
Aquatic bugs	–	–	5	5
Midge larvae	32	28	42	40
Other invertebrates				
Water mites	16	10	11	5
NUMBER OF FISH EXAMINED	69	35	26	12

captivity, Tench in their first year actively feed at 10°C. Little feeding, however, goes on during the winter in temperate areas when the fish stay near the bottom in a rather passive state.

There are few commercial fisheries for Tench, but the species is cultured in ponds in some parts of central Europe, yields of 20–80kg per hectare being recorded. The flesh is dark and has a strong flavour but is popular in some countries, e.g. France and Germany, where the standard recipes for carp are also used for Tench. However, it does not suit all tastes, for the Romans abandoned it to the common people, 'who alone feasted on it'. The age-old legend about Tench being the 'doctor fish', whose slime possesses powers of healing for both fellow fish and for humans has been passed from generation to generation and is very well known, and it is apparent that both its slime and its powdered otoliths were used by early physicians. In most places, as in the British Isles, the Tench is more important as a sport fish and it has been introduced as such to other parts of the world, e.g. New Zealand, Australia and North America. It is also a fairly popular aquarium and pond fish, especially in its golden form.

Silver Bream *Blicca bjoerkna* (Linnaeus 1758)
Bream Flat, Tinplate, White Bream

This species is always much smaller than the Common Bream and most adults are about 20–25cm in length and 0.7–1.1kg. In some waters in Europe, specimens as large as 35cm have been recorded but in others growth is poor and the fish mature at a very small size, e.g. 10cm and around 30–50gm. The British rod-caught record was at one time for a fish of 2.04kg (which may not have been a pure Silver Bream), but is at present open. It is believed that specimens of 680 and 878gm, which would qualify for consideration as records, have been caught, but not submitted to the record committee.

Small specimens of Silver Bream and Common Bream might be confused with each other. The Silver Bream is a very deep-bodied, laterally compressed fish, with a rather small head (more rounded in profile than the Common Bream) and no barbels around the mouth, which is semi-inferior

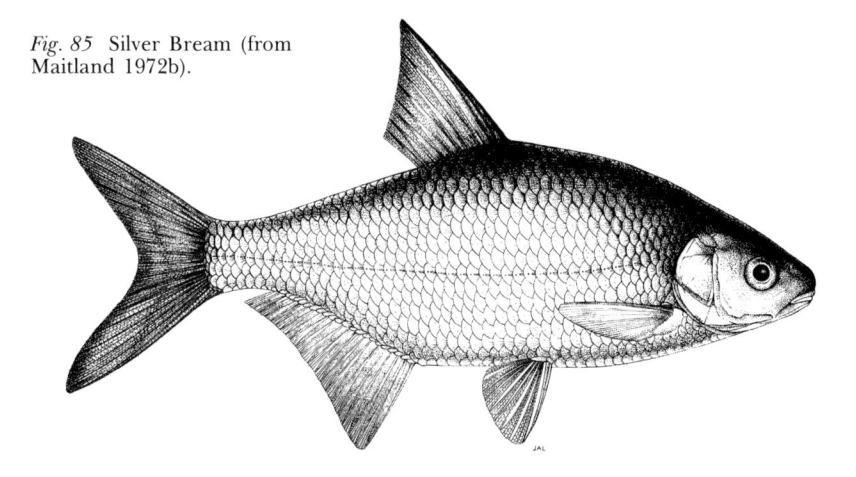

Fig. 85 Silver Bream (from Maitland 1972b).

in position and has rather thick lips. The eye is large and at least as long, or longer than, the length of the snout. The eye of the Silver Bream and a few other fish (e.g. Bream, Ruffe and Pikeperch) has a light-reflecting layer beneath the retina that reflects light back to the rod cells, increasing sensitivity in the normally turbid waters in which they live. The pharyngeal teeth are in two rows on either side, numbering five and two. There are 14–21 gill rakers. Apart from small areas near the head and just behind the pelvic fins, the body is well covered with large cycloid scales, of which there are 43–55 along the lateral line.

The dorsal fin is long with three anterior spiny rays and 8–9 soft rays behind. The pectoral and pelvic fins are rather small but the anal fin (whose origin is characteristically behind the last ray of the dorsal fin) is long and concave along its free edge, with three anterior spiny rays and 21–23 soft rays.

In colour, the dorsal parts of the head and back of the Silver Bream are a dark olive-grey, but this grades quickly into silvery white along the sides and into white on the belly. The dorsal, anal and caudal fins are rather dull grey in colour but the pectoral and pelvic fins are reddish with grey tips.

This species is native to western and central Europe from north-eastern France to the Caspian Sea. In the British Isles it is confined to south-eastern England and its distribution, unlike many other British species, seems to have altered very little over the last few thousand years. However, one specimen recently turned up at Llyn Tegid in Wales, probably released as live bait by anglers, so it seems likely that, as with many other cyprinid species, it will become more widely distributed in future.

The Silver Bream occurs mainly in shallow warm lowland lakes, the slow-flowing lower reaches of large rivers and associated canal systems. It is almost always found in association with weed beds, though in winter it may move into deeper water.

Breeding takes place when water temperatures rise above 15°C in May and June (occasionally in July in colder areas) and at this time the males develop extensive growths of tubercles on the head and front of the body. They then start to drive ripe females around, often in an extremely excited fashion and, as with other members of the family, may be rather obvious to the observer. Spawning occurs in shallow water among thick vegetation, where the sticky light yellow eggs (2mm in diameter) adhere to the weeds near the surface of the water. Spawning may be intermittent and each female will spawn several times before all the eggs are shed; these may number from 15,000 to 110,000, depending on her size. The eggs hatch in about 4–6 days at normal temperatures when the young larvae appear in shoals.

The Silver Bream will hybridise with other members of the carp family such as Bream, Bleak, Rudd and Roach, but these hybrids appear to be sterile. However, they should be remembered when trying to identify fish which have characteristics intermediate between this and other cyprinid species.

The young are only about 4.5–5.0mm when they hatch and growth is reasonably fast at first, some fish reaching almost 9cm at the end of their first year and 12cm by the end of the second. Thereafter growth is rather slower, fish reaching some 15cm after five years. Most males mature after three years and and females after four years. Many fish live up to ten years.

Table 33 Food of Silver Bream in East Anglian waters (after Hartley 1947a), as percentage occurrence.

Stomach contents	East Anglian waters
Algae	0.9
Macrophytes	0.9
Crustaceans	
Cladocerans	48.1
Ostracods	3.8
Copepods	28.3
Freshwater shrimp	0.9
Insects	
Mayfly larvae	0.9
Aquatic bugs	0.9
Midge larvae	6.6
Other insect larvae	1.9
Other invertebrates	0.9
NUMBER OF FISH EXAMINED	106

The young Silver Bream feed on small crustaceans and protozoans at first as well as some algae. As they grow they become more dependent on bottom-living invertebrates and adult fish feed in shoals almost exclusively on benthic crustaceans, molluscs, mayfly and midge larvae as well as a few plants.

In Europe, this species is taken in some commercial fisheries using seine nets and traps, but it usually occurs there as a by-catch with other more desirable species, for its small size and general boniness make it less desirable for the table. In Great Britain and elsewhere in Europe it is caught by anglers, but again they are usually fishing for other species and it is not highly rated as sport fish – indeed it is often considered just a nuisance. Small species are used as live bait.

Common Bream *Abramis brama* (Linnaeus 1758)
Bellows Bream, Bronze Bream, Carp Bream

This is one of the larger members of the carp family in the British Isles and adult fish commonly reach lengths of 30–50cm and weights of 2–3kg. Exceptionally they may reach over 80cm in length and 9kg in weight. The present British rod-caught record is for a fish of 7.427kg caught in 1986 on a private

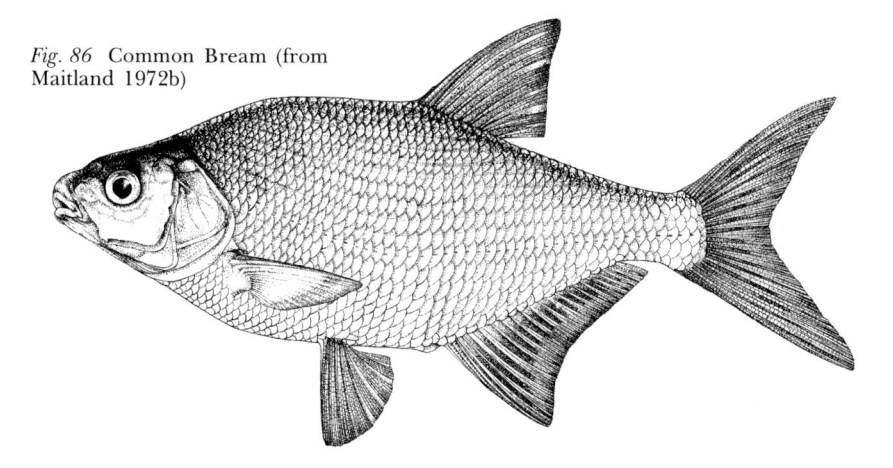

Fig. 86 Common Bream (from Maitland 1972b)

Fig. 87 A large specimen Common Bream (William Howes).

fishery in Staffordshire. The Irish record stands at 5.32kg – a fish taken in the River Blackwater, Monaghan, in 1982.

The Common Bream is an exceptionally deep-bodied fish with strong lateral compression. The head is small and there are no barbels on the slightly inferior mouth, which has thick lips. Like other bottom feeding cyprinids, the mouth can be extended as a feeding tube to suck in mud. The eye is small and its diameter is only about two-thirds of the length of the snout. The pharyngeal teeth are in a single series with five on each side. The back is rather humped and the body is very slimy and covered by large strong cycloid scales which number 51–60 along the lateral line. Scales are used for age determination. The dorsal fin is narrow but high and has three spiny rays followed

Fig. 88 Hybridisation between two members of the carp family in the Castle Loch: Common Bream (above) and Roach (below) with the hybrid in the middle, showing intermediate characters between the two species (Peter Maitland).

by nine soft rays. The pectoral and pelvic fins are rather small, but the anal fin is very long (more than twice the base length of the dorsal fin) with three spiny rays anteriorly and 24–30 soft rays. Its free edge is concave. The tail fin is well developed and deeply forked.

Small Common and Silver Bream can be confused with each other and fin ray and lateral line scale counts may be necessary for accurate identification.

Table 34 Food of Common Bream in the Norfolk Broads (after Hartley 1947a), as percentage occurrence.

Stomach contents	Norfolk Broads
Algae	0.5
Macrophytes	0.1
Molluscs	
Pea shells	0.2
Crustaceans	
Cladocerans	31.0
Ostracods	2.6
Copepods	28.7
Freshwater shrimp	0.3
Insects	
Aquatic bugs	0.2
Alderfly larvae	0.2
Caddis larvae	0.3
Midge larvae & pupae	13.1
Other invertebrates	0.3
Terrestrial organisms	0.3
NUMBER OF FISH EXAMINED	1239

Also, the eye of the Common Bream is set further back in the head than the Silver Bream and is relatively smaller.

In colour, the dorsal part of the head and body are dark brownish-grey graduating to a bronze silver along the sides and yellowish-silver on the belly. The dorsal, anal and caudal fins are a full brownish-grey as are the anterior edges of the pectoral and pelvic fins.

This species occurs across western and central Europe and well into Asia, from western Ireland to Siberia. In the British Isles it is native only to southeastern England, but has been distributed widely across England, including the Channel Islands (Jersey) and Ireland and now occurs also in parts of Wales and southern Scotland.

The Common Bream is a fish of lowland areas and prefers rich, muddy, weedy lakes, reservoirs and slow-flowing rivers and associated canals – also the favoured habitats of Silver Bream, carp and Tench. Its ability to withstand very low levels of oxygen means that it can survive in poor conditions for considerable periods. In some parts of Europe it occurs in slightly brackish waters (in the Baltic Sea) but always migrates back into fresh water to spawn. During the winter, like Silver Bream, carp and Tench, it seeks deeper water and may occur in densely packed shoals sheltering in suitable places, often under ice cover, existing on the fat reserves built up during the summer. No growth takes place during the winter.

Spawning takes place when water temperatures move above 15°C in May and June (sometimes later in cold years) when the mature fish move into shallow warm weedy areas. The males develop numerous small whitish or yellowish breeding tubercles on the head and body at this time and appear to be partly territorial, selecting suitable small territories and defending them against other males. Spawning itself takes place mainly during late evening and the night, when mature males pursue the ripe females into the weed beds, where the eggs are laid and fertilised amidst much splashing. The yellowish eggs, which are about 1.5–2.0mm in diameter, are adhesive and stick to the weeds down to a depth of 3m. Each female may spawn several times over a week or so until all her eggs are laid. The actual number varies with the size of the female, but can range from 90,000–340,000. The young hatch in about 5–10 days depending on water temperature (9–10 days at 12–13°C).

Bream hybridise with a number of other cyprinids. Bream x Roach are probably the commonest of all cyprinid hybrids found in Great Britain, though Bream x Rudd hybrids are very frequent in Ireland.

The fry, which are about 6.0–6.5mm on hatching, stay attached to plants until the yolk sac is fully absorbed in about 7–10 days. They are then just over 8mm in length and start to shoal and feed. Growth seems to be very variable according to local conditions, but some fish reach 7cm in length after one year and 12cm after two years. Growth is steady thereafter and they may reach typical adult sizes of 25–35cm after six or seven years. They start to mature earlier than this, however, usually in the third or fourth year. In Ireland, Bream seem to mature rather later, females at 7–10 years of age at a fork length of 28cm in slow-growing populations, and at 36–37cm in fast-growing situations. It is quite a long-lived species and fish often live for 10–15 years and sometimes for 20 years or more. A Bream of 23 years has been recorded in Ireland.

At first the young feed mainly on small plankton, especially rotifers, protozoans and small crustaceans, but they tend to move to a more benthic diet after a few weeks, for which their extrusible mouth is especially adapted. When feeding the fish work their way along the bottom with a characteristic oblique head-down posture, pushing the tubular mouth into the bottom to detect and expose suitable food items. Molluscs are a particularly important food of large bream, along with freshwater shrimps and slaters. This behaviour often leaves characteristic 'bream pits' on the bottom where an individual fish has stayed for a time feeding on some particularly favoured food items and exposing a hole up to 10cm in diameter and 5cm or so in depth. Their diet includes worms, molluscs, crustaceans and various benthic insects (e.g. caddis, mayfly and midge larvae). A small amount of vegetable matter is eaten in the form of filamentous algae and the leaves of higher plants.

In central and eastern Europe this is an important commercial species and is caught in large numbers in seine nets and traps. In Sweden during the middle of the eighteenth century early fish culture techniques were developed, in which ripe male and female Bream (and Perch) were induced to spawn in containers where the eggs were hatched in large numbers. The flesh is thought by some to be very tasty, though small specimens tend to be rather bony. Others think that the flesh is soft and muddy. Isaac Walton quotes a French proverb, 'He that hath Breams in his pond is able to bid his friends welcome', but adds that Bream are not to everyone's taste. Recently they have begun to appear on fishmongers' slabs in Great Britain. The Common Bream is a popular sporting fish in many areas including the British Isles and is much sought after by specimen anglers in particular. By heavy ground baiting, sizeable shoals can be held in an area while many of their number are caught.

Bleak *Alburnus alburnus* (Linnaeus 1758) Blay

The adult size of this small slender fish is usually some 12–15cm, but in favourable habitats, 18–20cm is attained. Such fish weigh about 40gm. The British rod-caught record is for a fish of 120gm caught in the River Monnow (Monmouth) in 1982.

204   FRESHWATER FISHES

Fig. 89 Top, Bleak (from Maitland 1972b); *Bottom*, An adult Bleak (Heather Angel).

The Bleak has a long slender body which is strongly compressed laterally. The head is small and though the oblique mouth is superior (as befits a surface-feeding fish), with a prominent enclosed lower jaw, its corners do not reach back beyond the front edge of the eyes. The eyes are large. There are 17–22 long gill rakers on the first arch. The pharyngeal teeth are in two rows (2+5) on each side and usually slightly serrated. The body is well covered with large shiny cycloid scales which detach easily, and number 46–53 along the lateral line. Between the pelvic fins and the anal fin there is a sharp scaleless keel. There are 42–45 vertebrae.

The dorsal fin is small and situated well back on the body, nearer the tail than the head, with three anterior spiny rays and 8–9 soft rays. The anal fin is long and has three spiny rays and 16–20 soft rays; its base is much longer than that of the dorsal fin and its first ray is immediately below the last rays of the dorsal fin. This fin and the superior mouth are the main diagnostic features. The pectoral and pelvic fins are small, but the tail is well developed and deeply forked.

The Bleak is a very silvery fish, its name originating from the Anglo-Saxon word 'bloec' meaning shining. In fact, the dorsal part of the head and back are a dark bluish-green, but this quickly grades to silver on the sides and

Table 35 Most important items in the food of Bleak in the Crapina-Jijila Lakes of the Danube system (after Spataru 1967), as percentage occurrence.

Stomach contents	Crapina-Jijila Lakes
Algae	
Anabaena	3.0
Euglena	6.0
Phacus	6.0
Spirogyra	5.2
Maugeotia	3.0
Cosmarium	3.0
Eudorina	2.2
Pandorina	2.2
Cymbella	4.5
Pinnularia	2.2
Macrophytes	16.4
Crustaceans	
Cladocerans	7.5
Copepods	9.7
Insects	
Mayfly larvae	3.0
Beetle larvae & adults	23.1
Caddis larvae	2.2
Cranefly larvae	3.7
Mosquito larvae	3.0
Midge larvae	3.7
Midge pupae	10.4
Midge adults	12.6
Other insects	3.7
Other invertebrates	
Rotifers	2.2
NUMBER OF FISH EXAMINED	268

silvery white on the belly. The fins are mostly a light grey. At spawning time the pelvic and anal fins assume an orange tinge.

The Bleak is found across much of central Europe, from Brittany to the Caspian Sea, but it is absent from both northern and southern Europe. It is absent from Ireland, Scotland and much of Wales but occurs in most parts of England, where it was originally native in the south-east.

Basically a shoaling fish of open surface waters, Bleak are common in many slow-flowing rivers in lowland areas and along the shores of some lakes, where during calm sunny conditions they are conspicuous jumping and rising at the surface to small flies. Their continual activity, according to Isaac Walton, earned them the name of 'River Swallow', while another authority refers to the 'joie de vivre' of the Bleak. Enormous shoals of several million fish have been recorded in some of the larger European rivers. It prefers clear waters and is not associated with vegetation, though in winter it seems to move into deeper water with reduced feeding activity. It occurs in brackish waters in the Baltic Sea.

Reproduction takes place in shallow water in May and June when water temperatures reach above 15°C. The males develop tubercles on the head and anterior body, and drive the females over gravel, small stones and occasional weed growths, to which the eggs stick when they are shed. Each female spawns several times over a few days until all her eggs – usually about 5000–6000 in number – are laid. They are pale yellow in colour and about 1.5–1.6mm in diameter. They hatch in 5–10 days depending on local water temperatures.

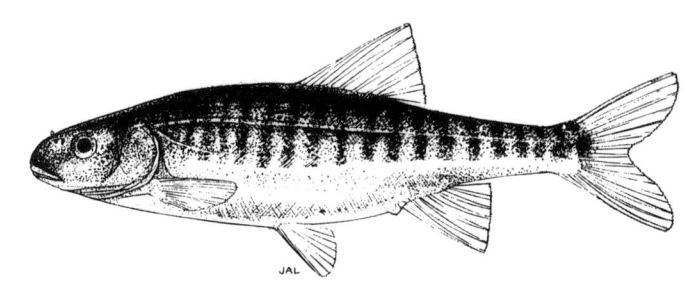

Fig. 90 Minnow (from Maitland, 1972b).

The young are very small on hatching, only about 3–4mm, and grow rather slowly to reach about 3–5cm after one year. They reach about 7–8cm after two years and 10–12cm after three years, by which time they can be mature and start to reproduce. Growth continues thereafter, however, and the fish may live for seven or eight years. Occasionally Bleak will hybridise with other cyprinid fishes such as Roach, Rudd, Dace, Silver Bream and Chub, but the offspring always seem to be infertile.

The young feed on very small invertebrates at first, especially rotifers, protozoans and crustaceans. Later they depend mainly on crustacean plankton and midge pupae as well as terrestrial insects which fall on to the water surface. Occasionally fish eggs and very small fry are eaten.

The Bleak is rarely fished commercially for food, though considered palatable when fried. However, in eastern Europe its scales were used to make pearl essence ('essence d'orient' – for the technique was developed in ancient China) used as a coating for artificial pearls. The attractive silvery crystals of guanine were washed from the Bleak scales and it took several thousand fish to provide just 100gm of essence. Where it is particularly abundant it may be caught in bulk and used for animal feed or fertiliser. Although it is sometimes angled for or caught incidentally during angling competitions, it is really of little interest to anglers (who often consider it to be a nuisance) other than as a bait species and a valuable forage fish for larger species such as Pike and Pikeperch. Some angling authorities recommend young anglers to sharpen their skill by catching Bleak, particularly on very fine tackle and small artificial flies. Thames Bleak used to be preserved in bottles as spinning baits for Pike and salmon anglers.

Minnow *Phoxinus phoxinus* (Linnaeus 1758)
Baggie, Baggit, Banny, Jack Barrel, Jack Sharp, Meaker, Mennet, Mennon, Mennot, Menon, Minim, Minnin, Peer, Penk, Pink, Shadbrid

This small cyprinid, with such a wide variety of common names, matures at lengths of 6–9cm, but in some favourable habitats can grow up to 12cm. It is a familiar fish to all parents of children who catch small fish in nets and bring them home in jam jars. There is no British rod-caught record though Minnows are not infrequently taken by anglers fishing with very fine tackle.

The body is slim and rather round in cross-section with only slight lateral flattening. The snout is blunt and the small mouth is subterminal and has no barbels. There are two rows of pharyngeal teeth on either side (either 2+5 or

Fig. 91 A mixed shoal of Minnows and Bitterling (William Howes).

2+4). The body has rows of very small rather embedded scales along the sides – of which there are 85–100 along the lateral series. There are no scales on the belly. The lateral line itself is incomplete posteriorly. There are 37–42 vertebrae.

All the fins are of medium size and rounded. The dorsal and anal fins have much the same size and shape, the former with three anterior spiny rays and seven soft rays, the latter with three spines and 6–7 soft rays posteriorly. The origin of the anal fin is just below the last rays of the dorsal. The pectoral fins have one spine and 13–15 soft rays whilst the pelvic fins have 1–3 spiny rays and 6–8 soft rays.

The colour of this species is very variable, both inside and outside the breeding season. The normal colouration is an olive greeny brown on the upper head and back and a whitish-grey on the belly. These are separated along each side by a line of colour which can vary from a series of indeterminate dark and gold blotches to a complete black stripe from head to tail fin. During the breeding season the females, which become very fat, retain more or less this colouring, but the males become very spectacular with white flashes at the fins, reddish pectoral and pelvic fins, a black throat, green along the sides and a scarlet belly.

This species is very widespread in fresh waters across virtually the whole of Europe and Asia, from the Atlantic coast of Ireland to the Pacific coast of China. One of the authors has caught them in Lake Baikal. It occurs in brackish water in some parts of the Baltic Sea. In the British Isles, though presumably originally native only to the south-east of England, it is now widespread in England, Wales, Ireland and mainland Scotland – with the exception of the Northern and Western Isles.

The Minnow occurs in a wide range of habitats from small fairly fast- flowing streams to large lowland rivers and from small upland lakes to large lakes and reservoirs. It must have access to clean gravelly areas for spawning – either in running water or on the wave-washed shores of lakes. Its oxygen requirements are only slightly less than those of Trout, Stone Loach and Bullhead, and it begins to suffer stress at oxygen levels less than 7mg/l.

This is a shoaling species which can often occur in enormous numbers, especially in summer when shoals, usually comprising only one year class, move into very shallow water (often only a centimetre or so deep) to feed and sunbathe. It is probable that temperature conditions at these sites are optimal for growth. During winter, most fish move into quieter water and often spend long periods under stones or in thick vegetation in a semi-comatose condition.

They are very inquisitive fish and after being frightened away initially by the appearance of a human will come back to have a better look. If the bottom is disturbed by a stone or net, Minnows quickly come forward to seek any food items that have become exposed. On several occasions when working barefoot in a river, one of the authors has had shoals of Minnows nibbling at his feet and legs! This curiosity often leads to their downfall for a small transparent plastic trap, baited with a piece of bread or other attractant, can catch large numbers of Minnows. Once one fish is inside the others seem to be attracted in even more.

Minnows also appear to be curious of large fish which could be potential predators, and two or three may break away from a shoal to investigate. They can then communicate their fear or apprehension to the rest of the shoal which may immediately flee. Frightened or injured Minnows give off a 'fear' substance from their skins, which quickly warns the rest of the shoal of impending danger. Alarm substances are emitted by many members of the carp family. They seem to be rather non-specific in their action so that an 'alarm'

Table 36 Food of Minnow in the River Cam, England (after Hartley 1948), and in the Altquhur Burn, Scotland (after Maitland 1965), as percentage number (except * = percentage occurrence).

Stomach contents	River Cam	Altquhur Burn
Algae	33*	24*
Macrophytes	11*	–
Molluscs	–	1.2
Worms	–	3.6
Crustaceans		
Cladocerans	4.3	–
Copepods	3.2	0.1
Freshwater shrimp	2.7	3.9
Crayfish	2.2	–
Insects		
Mayfly larvae	3.2	7.2
Stonefly larvae	–	5.3
Aquatic bugs	0.5	–
Beetle larvae	1.2	0.7
Caddis larvae	1.6	5.1
Midge larvae	67.0	47.2
Blackfly larvae	2.2	4.7
Other insects	7.6	4.8
Other invertebrates	3.8	3.3
Terrestrial organisms	–	8.3
NUMBER OF FISH EXAMINED	125	255

raised by one species can be communicated to other cyprinid species in the vicinity. As one author aptly puts it, 'the situation is analogous to the use of similar alarm calls by different species of small birds'.

Reproduction takes place from April to June when water temperatures reach 10°C and more. As they come into breeding condition and the males colour up there is a migration to suitable spawning beds. These may be near by on a clean wave-washed lake shore or where an underground spring upwells through the gravel, or at some distance upstream. Shoals of adult fish often migrate considerable distances at this time, from a lake into an inflow or from a large slow-flowing river or canal into a swifter side tributary. One of the authors has seen them wriggling upstream through wet Willow Moss, with their backs out of the water, when they could be scooped up by the handful.

The males develop very prominent tubercles on the face and pectoral fins and spawning is very much a communal process, with groups of ripe males and females (which sometimes have small tubercles) driving together and releasing their eggs and sperm over clean gravel and stones. The pale yellow eggs, about 1.2–1.5mm in diameter, stick immediately to this substrate. Each female lays some 200–1000 eggs over a day or two and these hatch in 3–6 days at normal temperatures.

The young are only 4–5mm on hatching but take a few days to absorb their yolk sac and start feeding, by which time they are about 7–8mm. Growth is very variable according to local conditions, but after one year most fish are 3–4cm, after two years some 5–6cm and after three years about 6–8cm. They may live, and continue growing at a slower rate, for up to seven or eight years. Maturity in both sexes is usually reached in the second year, though fast-growing individuals may be mature after one year. Mature females are normally larger than males.

Although the main spawning season is spring and early summer, very small Minnows in their first year can be found in the late autumn, suggesting a more protracted spawning season in some places. In nearly all habitats, numbers of small immature Minnows can be found at any time of the year.

The young start to feed on minute foods such as rotifers, protozoans and small crustaceans as well as plant material like diatoms. As they grow they continue to eat a varied diet, taking many crustaceans and bottom invertebrates such as worms and midge larvae, as well as quite a high proportion of plant material – mostly algae. They are truly omnivorous in their feeding behaviour except that, if aquarium observations are valid, they do not take fish flesh – even when hungry. Apart from the plant material, the food of Minnows is very much the same as that of trout, and where they occur in large numbers it seems likely that they must compete with trout for the available food supply. Shoals can often be seen rising to surface food.

Though caught in enormous numbers in seine nets and traps in a few parts of northern Russia for use as fertiliser or animal food, the Minnow is really of no commercial importance in the British Isles or anywhere else in Europe. They are reputed to be palatable when fried like whitebait, and Isaac Walton recommends that they should be beheaded, gutted, washed in salt and then fried with yolk of egg, flowers of Cowslips, Primroses and a little 'Tansy'.

It is widely used by anglers as a bait species (hence its wide redistribution throughout the British Isles) and is an important forage fish for larger species such as Pike and Perch and for many aquatic birds like Herons and Kingfishers. Trout appear to have some difficulty in catching Minnows (compared to the apparent ease with which they catch sticklebacks), especially in lakes – except at spawning time when large numbers of Minnows are eaten at the spawning beds. It is an interesting, peaceful and attractive aquarium fish and very tame individuals have been kept for several years in aquaria by both the authors. Being easy to obtain and keep, it has also been used widely in laboratory experiments, and the early scientific work on fish hearing involved this species.

Bitterling *Rhodeus sericeus* (Bloch 1782) Prussian Carp

This small and particularly interesting species matures at about 5–7cm in length, but occasionally grows to a maximum of about 9cm.

The Bitterling is a deep-bodied little fish which is considerably compressed laterally. The small mouth is slightly oblique and terminal in position. There are no barbels. The head is small. There is one row of pharyngeal teeth on each side. The body is well covered in large cycloid scales which number some 34–39 along the lateral series – although the lateral line itself is very incomplete and is present for only the first five or six scales. Sexually mature females are unique among British fish in developing a long ovipositor at breeding time, which may reach a length of several centimetres.

The dorsal fin, which has three spiny rays and nine or ten soft rays, is high and long, originating just over the pelvic fins and ending above the point halfway along the anal fin. The latter is also large and has three spiny rays and eight or nine soft rays. The paired pectoral and pelvic fins are small but the tail fin is normal in size.

The colouration of the adult Bitterling is somewhat variable according to sex and time of year. Basically, the upper head and back are a greenish silvery grey grading to a bluish-silver on the sides and a silvery white on the belly. There is an iridescent blue-green stripe on each side from about the middle of the body to the tail, on either side of which there may be a short red stripe. The fins are a palish grey with a varying orange tinge. At spawning time, the male colours up brightly, the dorsal and anal fins becoming much redder in colour, while the leading edges of the pelvic fins become a

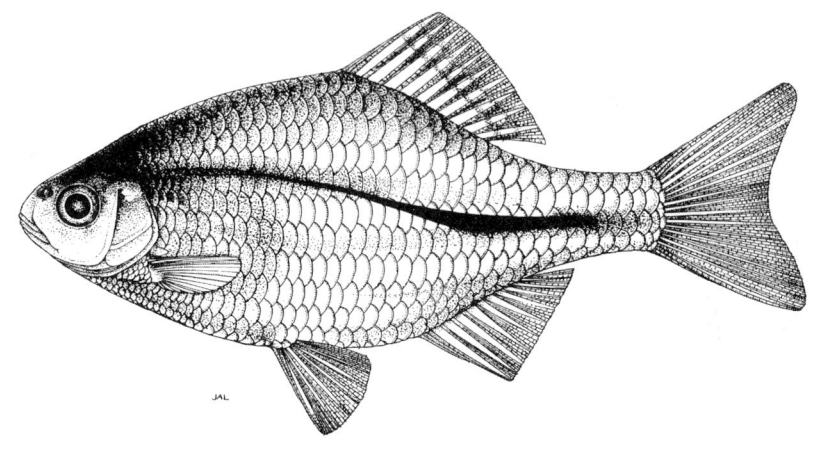

Fig. 92 Bitterling (from Maitland 1972b).

Table 37 The main food of Bitterling in the Crapina-Jijila ponds of the Danube system in Rumania (after Spataru & Gruia 1967), as percentage occurrence.

Stomach contents	Crapina-Jijila ponds
Algae	
Merismopedia	48
Oscillatoria	29
Navicula	76
Cymbella	71
Pinnularia	54
Amphora	51
Gyrosigma	45
Eunotia	37
Cymatopleura	35
Nitzschia	35
Melosira	28
Surirella	27
Synedra	27
Caloneis	23
Fragillaria	22
Cocconeis	20
Rhopalodia	17
Gomphonema	14
Euglena	52
Phacus	27
Cosmarium	36
Oedogonium	31
Scenedesmus	31
NUMBER OF FISH EXAMINED	94

brilliant white and the whole body more iridescent with shades of violet and green predominating. Distinct triangular patches of tubercles develop on each side of the snout and a half circle of the iris becomes red. In captivity, males kept together in the absence of females retain their breeding colouration indefinitely.

This species is native to much of western and central Europe, from France to the Caspian Sea, and to parts of Asia. It is not indigenous to the British Isles, but has been introduced successfully to several ponds in west and south Lancashire and Cheshire, from which it is spreading via the canal systems. It now occurs also in the River Cam, downstream from Cambridge. In the St Helens area it is sometimes referred to as Prussian Carp. An attempt, probably ill-advised, to introduce Bitterling to some of the Lake District lakes appears to have failed.

The preferred habitat of the Bitterling is still or slow-flowing water with plenty of weed growth and a sandy silty bottom where there are freshwater mussels. Thus, it is found in base-rich weedy lowland ponds, canals and slow-moving rivers and can co-exist successfully with native coarse fish, including such predators as Pike and Perch.

The reproductive behaviour and breeding requirements of this fish are unique. During the breeding season, which is from April to June, the brightly coloured male selects a large mussel and defends a territory around it. This territory may move in space if the mussel itself starts to move along the bottom. The male courts passing females and when he is accepted by a ripe female a courtship display starts around the mussel and terminates when the female ovipositor (which momentarily becomes stiff through fluid pressure) is inserted into one of the siphons of the mussel and a few eggs are laid, being fertilised at the same time by the release of milt (which is inhaled by the mussel) from the male, who is always in close attendance. This process is repeated several times until the female is spent, having laid some 40–100 eggs altogether. The eggs, which are pale yellow and relatively large (some 3mm in diameter) remain within the mantle cavity of the mussel, protected there for some 2–3 weeks until they hatch and the young emerge 2–3 days later after their yolk sacs have been absorbed.

The mussel, for its part, produces small larvae known as glochidia, which are passed out of the exhalant siphon and attach themselves to passing fish. After remaining attached to the skin of the fish for some time (and thus being carried away from the parent mussel) the larvae detach themselves and sink to the bottom to begin a normal life.

The fry are about 9–10mm on emergence and grow slowly to reach some 3–4cm after one year. They mature in their second year at around 5–6cm and live for up to five or six years. In the Liverpool area, Bitterling populations appear to fluctuate very considerably in numbers over the years.

The young, being relatively large on emergence, are able to start eating small crustaceans and insect larvae immediately. They also browse on plant material. As they grow they take larger invertebrates, but the diet remains substantially the same.

The Bitterling is of little value commercially as far as food is concerned because of its small size and the fact that its flesh is said to taste bitter. Nor is it of interest to anglers except for use as bait. However, it is an extremely attractive and interesting fish for the aquarium where it may be readily induced to breed. There are many other species found in eastern Asia and increasing numbers of these are being imported into the British Isles for sale in aquarium shops.

Before the present rapid tests for human pregnancy were developed, the Bitterling (like the *Xenopus* toad) was used for the purpose. Females injected with urine from pregnant women protruded their ovipositors, thus indicating a positive test. Large numbers of Bitterling were collected in the Liverpool area over a number of years for this purpose.

Rudd *Scardinius erythrophthalmus* (Linnaeus 1758)
Finscale, Red Eye, Roach, Shallow

The size of adult Rudd in the British Isles is normally some 20–30cm in length and 200–400gm in weight. In particularly favourable habitats the species may grow up to 40cm and 1kg, and very occasionally fish larger than this are encountered. The present British rod-caught record is for a huge fish of 2.097kg caught in 1986 at Pitsford Reservoir in England. The Irish record is 1.4kg – a fish caught in 1959 in Kilglass Lake.

The Rudd is a rather slim but fairly deep-bodied and laterally compressed fish. Large Rudd are decidedly hump-backed. The head is small and the mouth is terminal, but set obliquely and with no barbels. The gill rakers are short and widely spaced with only about 11–12 on the first arch. The pharyngeal teeth, in two rows (5+3) on either side, are strongly serrated. The body is covered in large cycloid scales, of which there are 37–45 along the lateral line. Scales are used for age determination but care is required in determining the first annulus and in recognising subsequent checks or false annuli.

Fig. 93 Rudd (from Maitland 1972b).

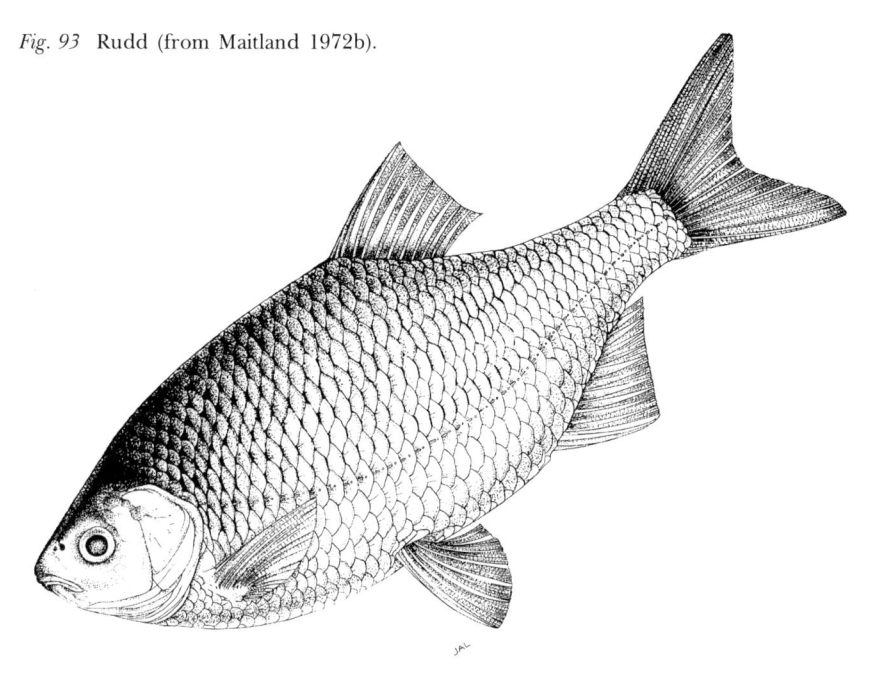

There is a well developed keel between the pelvic fins and the anus. There are 36–39 vertebrae.

Characteristically the origin of the dorsal fin (which is slightly emarginate and has three spiny rays and 8–9 soft rays) is well behind that of the pelvic fins. The anal fin has three spiny rays and 10–11 soft rays. The tips of the pectoral fins almost reach the bases of the pelvic fins. The caudal fin is deeply notched with pointed lobes.

The young Rudd are rather silvery in colour, but the adults are a dark olive-brown on the upper head and back grading to a yellowish-silver on the sides and dull white on the belly. The eye has a beautiful golden-red iris with a red spot above. All the fins have a reddish hue, especially the ventral fins which may be quite strongly red. All colours become intensified at spawning time. Selective breeding has produced a golden form of this species, which is a popular aquarium and pond fish.

Rudd are often confused with Roach, with which they frequently occur. The Rudd can easily be distinguished by the upturned mouth, the position of the dorsal fin, the keel behind the ventral fins and the serrated pharyngeal teeth.

The Rudd occurs throughout much of Europe and western Asia from Ireland in the west to the Aral Sea in the east. In the British Isles, it is native only to south-east England, but has been redistributed by humans so that it is now common in much of Ireland (some confusion exists over its distribution in Ireland due to it being called 'Roach' in some areas), the Midlands and south of England, the Channel Islands (Jersey) and a few places in Wales. There are only two breeding populations known in Scotland – both of them in small lochs in the south-west. In recent years in Ireland, the rapid increase in the

Table 38 Food of Rudd in waters in the Norfolk Broads and Madingley and Fairhill Ponds, Cambridgeshire, England (after Hartley 1947a), as percentage occurrence.

Stomach contents	All sites
Algae	4.6
Macrophytes	0.9
Insects	
Aquatic bugs	1.4
Beetles	9.3
Alderfly larvae	0.5
Caddis larvae	2.3
Midge larvae	1.9
Other insects	6.9
Other invertebrates	0.5
Terrestrial organisms	3.7
NUMBER OF FISH EXAMINED	216

numbers of Roach and the extension of their range appears to have been responsible for a corresponding decline in populations of Rudd.

This species is a shoaling fish, and one of the authors has seen an enormous static shoal of densely packed Rudd (mainly 10–13cm in length) on two occasions during April, congregated in an artificially made inlet entering a small lake in Northern Ireland. The shoal was some 30m long and 2m wide – a conservative estimate put the number of fish at 100,000 plus. This event apparently took place every spring, but did not appear to be connected with feeding or spawning. Rudd occur mainly in rich lowland ponds and lakes, usually where there is an abundance of vegetation. It can stand relatively foul conditions better than some of the species with which it often co-exists. It occurs also in the lower reaches of some lowland rivers. In winter large shoals move to deeper water to await the spring.

Rudd spawn from April to June in southern Britain as the water temperature rises above 15°C, but rather later in Ireland and further north (i.e. late May to early July). Male Rudd mature at three years of age and most females a year later. The males develop a deeper and brighter colouration, though tubercles do not seem to appear on the head and anterior body unlike many cyprinids. They assemble at the spawning grounds and then start to pursue ripe females and drive them, often with much splashing, into weed beds where spawning takes place near the surface. Individual males may eventually spawn with several females. The sticky eggs, which are transparent and colourless or pale yellow in colour and 1.0–1.7mm in diameter, adhere to the weed. The fecundity of the females varies with size and other factors but usually ranges from 90,000–230,000 eggs per female (i.e. some 108,000–211,000 eggs per kg). Hatching depends on the local temperature and may take from 5–10 days.

This species commonly hybridises with other cyprinid species to form intermediate but sterile hybrids. It has been known to do so with Common Bream, Silver Bream, Bleak and Roach.

The young are only 4.5–6.0mm on hatching and adhere by the head to the leaves of weeds for about a week until the swimbladder develops and the yolk sac is fully absorbed. They then start to swim and feed. Growth is very variable thereafter and dependent on local conditions. Some populations in small lakes consist of 'stunted' fish of only 10–15cm which may be many years old, but in favourable waters growth is much faster and fish can be up to 9cm in length after one year, 15cm after two years and 20cm after three years. They are normally mature in the third year but continue to grow slowly thereafter. They may live for at least 17 years. Some studies show that from maturity on females grow faster than males and live longer.

The newly hatched fry feed on very small organisms such as diatoms and other unicellular algae, rotifers, protozoans and crustacean larvae. Rudd, on the whole, are midwater feeders and as they grow, they continue to take some vegetable material in the form of diatoms and other algae, but most of the diet consists of planktonic crustaceans. Later, as adult fish, they take benthic invertebrates such as crustaceans and insect larvae, especially those of caddis and midges, and often adult aquatic and terrestrial insects which have hatched or fallen on to the water surface. Filamentous algae and shoots of fine water plants may assume considerable importance in the diet. Irish investigators question the nutritional value of much of the plant material taken, as much of it appears to be passed out only partially digested. Very occasionally, large Rudd will eat small fish of other species; for instance in Ireland they eat their own fry and Three-spined Sticklebacks. They are rather more active and less cautious in their feeding behaviour than Roach and, as well as being taken by traditional float and bait methods, they may be caught on wet or dry fly or by spinning with small spoons.

Rudd are well known as hosts for 'black spot disease' *Posthodiplostomulum cuticola* and heavy infestations can occur in some lakes. They are also common hosts to the Fish Louse *Argulus*. One of the authors has seen a Rudd population in Northern Ireland where every fish had 5– 12 *Argulus* on its body. Trout placed in this lough soon died, covered with *Argulus*.

Although not fished commercially in the British Isles, Rudd are important in some parts of eastern Europe where they are taken in seine nets and traps. Catches of up to 20 tonnes have been recorded in Russia in a single haul of the net. They are not generally regarded as good eating, however. They are a popular sport fish in many parts of Europe including the British Isles and they are also used as a bait species in fishing for Pike and Pikeperch. Although less common than Roach, they are easier to keep in captivity. The young, especially the golden variety, make very handsome aquarium fish and also do well in the garden pond.

Roach *Rutilus rutilus* (Linnaeus 1758) Braise

The size of Roach in different populations is very variable and dependent on local conditions. In some waters there are huge populations of stunted fish, whereas in other waters where their abundance is less they grow much larger individually. Year class instability seems to be a feature of Roach population dynamics, and stunting may occur periodically as a result of the appearance of an exceptionally strong year class – itself a product of particularly favourable conditions. Conversely, the growth rate of individuals in a normally stunted population may temporarily increase as a result of a large-scale mortality affecting the population. A strong year class can account for as much as half the total population present. Under reasonable conditions, adult Roach are normally some 20–25cm in length and 200–300g in weight. In some waters fish of up to 35cm and 1kg occur, and exceptionally the species has been known to reach over 50cm and about 2kg. The present British rod-

Fig. 94 Top, Roach (from Maitland 1972b); *Bottom,* An adult Roach (Heather Angel).

caught record is for a fish of 1.842kg caught in 1975 in a gravel pit in Nottinghamshire. The Irish record stands at 1.29kg for a fish taken in the River Blackwater in 1970.

Though relatively slim when young, the adult fish is rather deep bodied and laterally compressed with a small head. In stunted fish, the body tends to remain rather slim and does not deepen. The mouth is terminal and slightly oblique and has no barbels. There are normally about ten gill rakers. There is a single row of pharyngeal teeth on each side, usually five, sometimes six in number, and unlike those of Rudd they are not markedly serrated, though the small ones are slightly hooked. The body is well covered by large cycloid scales, which number 42–45 along the lateral line and characteristically have a number of furrows radiating from the centre of the scale over both the exposed and embedded areas. Scales are used for age determination, as are the gill covers (opercular bones). There are 39–43 vertebrae.

Being largely mud swallowers and therefore having to ingest and process large amounts of indigestible material. Roach typically do not have a stomach (or pyloric caecae) but the intestine is very long – around 15 times the length of the fish. With their well-adapted mouths, Roach are able to penetrate some 5cm into the bottom mud, about the same as bream but less than Tench or carp.

The origin of the high dorsal fin, which has three spiny and 9–11 soft rays, is directly above the base of the pelvic fins. The paired pectoral and pelvic fins are rather small, but the anal fins is well developed and has three spiny rays anteriorly followed by 9–11 soft rays. The tail is well developed and deeply forked.

The upper head and back of the Roach is a dark olive greenish brown grading to a silvery brown on the sides and pale white on the belly. The iris of the eye ranges from yellow in small fish to a strong red in adults. The dorsal and tail fins are a dull brownish, but the remaining fins have a reddish tinge, especially the pelvic and anal fins which may be a dark red in some specimens. Roach – especially dead specimens – can easily be mistaken for Rudd, while the quite common Roach × Rudd hybrids may also provide identification difficulties. Roach also hybridise with Common Bream, Silver Bream and Bleak.

The Roach is a common and widely distributed species throughout much of Europe and Asia from Ireland to the west of Siberia in the east. Several subspecies are recognised in different parts of its range. In the British Isles it is common throughout most of England, including the Channel Islands (Jersey), parts of Wales and southern Scotland and now many parts of Ireland, where it is a relatively new introduction but in recent years has extended its range dramatically. This has been attributed to the release by Pike anglers of unused live bait, and by other sport anglers to provide more angling. Other fish species may have suffered as a result of some of these introductions.

The Roach is a shoaling species which is tolerant of a wide range of temperature conditions (up to a maximum of about 38°C) and even some mild pollution. Its oxygen requirement is about the same level as that of Pike and Ruffe, but greater than that of carp or Tench. Consequently, it occurs in a variety of habitats, mainly in lowland areas, ranging from small weedy pools to large clear lakes (e.g. Loch Lomond) and from small streams to the largest lowland rivers (e.g. the River Thames) and often their upper estuaries. It is very common throughout virtually all the canal systems and occurs in slightly brackish water in mainland Europe, in the Baltic, Black and Aral Seas. In winter, large shoals move into deeper water where they feed relatively little until the water starts to warm again in spring. However, one of their sporting virtues is that they are more readily caught than Rudd during the winter (hence one of the motives for spreading them in Ireland – to attract the tourist 'off season'). During the mild winter of 1987–88 specimen Roach were taken throughout the winter.

They are much hunted by Pike and when attacked the shoal of Roach will scatter instantly, diving into thick vegetation for cover. Young Roach are important food for trout, Perch and Pikeperch, as well as of diving birds such as grebes and Kingfishers.

Spawning takes place in April, May and June when the water temperature rises above 12°C. The mature males develop numerous small white tubercles over the head, anterior fins and much of the body and they start to chase ripe females, some of which may also have tubercles. Eventually the fish, often in small groups of one or more females and several males, dash into weed beds where the eggs and sperm are released together, usually near the surface

Table 39 Food of Roach in the River Stour and the River Frome, England (after Mann 1973), as percentage number (except * = percentage occurrence).

Stomach contents	River Stour	River Frome
Algae	11*	18*
Macrophytes	8*	–
Molluscs	20	39
Crustaceans	1	1
Insects		
Mayfly larvae, pupae & adults	4	24
Caddis larvae	25	1
Midge larvae	19	15
Blackfly larvae	12	–
Other invertebrates	7	21
NUMBER OF FISH EXAMINED	347	22

amid much splashing. The eggs, which are pale yellow in colour and 1.0–1.5mm in diameter, are adhesive and stick to the weeds, often in enormous numbers. Each female may lay 5000–200,000 eggs according to size. The eggs hatch in 5–10 days depending on local temperatures and the new fry remain attached to weed for a further few days until the yolk sac is absorbed and they can start to swim freely. In some waters, an intersex condition has been recorded in Roach.

The Roach is often thought of as a still water species, especially in relation to spawning habits. However, in some waters (e.g. the River Endrick in Scotland) there is a mass migration at spawning time into fast-flowing water, where the fish spawn communally over weed beds in some areas. This habit was noted by local people hundreds of years ago, when the Roach (locally called Braise) were caught in some numbers for eating. Immediately after spawning, the weeds in this area are yellow in colour from the enormous numbers of eggs adhering to them. After hatching the young are immediately swept downstream into calmer water.

The fry are some 4.5–6.5mm on hatching but they soon start to grow and under favourable conditions may reach 6–9cm after one year, 9–12cm after two years, 12–15cm after three years (about the maximum length in stunted populations) and so on. The number of days when the temperature is 14°C or above is an important factor in producing good growth in Roach fry. Males usually mature in the second or third years and females in the third or fourth years. Growth continues after maturity is reached, though usually at a slightly slower rate. Fish often live for 10–12 years, with females growing faster and living longer than males.

The young feed on very small invertebrates (e.g. rotifers, protozoans and crustacean larvae) at first along with some vegetable matter (e.g. diatoms). As they grow they move to larger invertebrates, especially planktonic crustaceans and eventually to a diet of a wide variety of bottom-living animals such as worms, molluscs, crustaceans and many species of insect larvae, as well as much detritus, filamentous algae and higher plants. Although much more bottom-feeding than Rudd, Roach will take adult insects from the surface, especially during warm sunny weather.

It has been suggested that the more animal food that there is in the diet, the faster and larger Roach will grow. The most stunted populations are found where detritus is the main source of nutrition. These stunted fish, when moved to richer water where more animal food is available, will respond by increasing their rate of growth markedly. Roach will certainly grow more rapidly where they can feed on molluscs, but do not seem to exploit this food source until they have reached about 15cm in length. There is evidence that while young Roach indiscriminately eat much detritus, older fish are more selective and reject material that cannot be digested.

Roach can be a host to a large range of parasites, both internal and external. At least 53 species have so far been found on or in Roach in the British Isles. The cestode tapeworm *Ligula intestinalis* is a common parasite and can cause heavy mortality in Roach populations. Its life cycle involves two intermediate hosts, initially a planktonic crustacean, then a fish and finally an aquatic bird. The fluke *Diplostomum spathaceum* is also common, where Herring Gulls are among predators of Roach. A common ectoparasite of Roach is the Fish Louse *Argulus foliaceus*.

At Slapton Ley, a large and important sport fishery in Devon, research has suggested that the relative fortunes of Roach and Rudd are linked. Initially the ley was famous for its fine Rudd (and Pike) but after World War II Roach, once scarce and even believed to be absent, have become dominant, although the numbers of both species have fluctuated considerably. There is some overlap in the diet of the two species; Roach are mainly detritus and benthos feeders, while Rudd take much surface food and plant material. Competition at the fry stage is, however, more likely. The fry of both species are plankton feeders, but Roach have the advantage of hatching earlier. In recent years, the ley has also become increasingly eutrophic, a situation that seems likely to benefit Roach more than Rudd.

Roach is considered to be a commercial species in some parts of Europe, where it is caught in seine nets and traps. Though not important as a food fish in the British Isles it is sold in some fish shops from time to time. It is considered by some as the most important and popular of all sporting coarse fish and is much sought after by anglers both as a welcome addition to the bag during competitions and as a specimen fish requiring considerable skill to catch. Isaac Walton called them 'Water Sheep' (in contrast to his term for carp 'Water Fox') on account of their shoaling behaviour and apparent simplicity and foolishness. Possibly the wiliness of large fish in some populations is due to the fact that a great many individuals have been hooked a number of times and released. Walton also reckoned that from the culinary aspect, the best feature of Roach is their spawn. It is an attractive species for the aquarium and pond, but is not so easy to keep as Rudd, nor does it possess a golden variety.

Chub *Leuciscus cephalus* (Linnaeus 1758)
Bottling, Chavender, Chevin, Lob, Loggerhead, Poll, Pollard, Skelly

The Chub is one of the larger cyprinids, with an average adult length of some 30–40cm and a corresponding weight of 500–900gm. Much larger specimens can occur, however, and fish of over 60cm and 4kg have been recorded from central Europe. Although larger fish have been reported unofficially, the present British rod-caught record is for a fish of 3.345kg caught in 1957 in the River Avon in Hampshire.

The body is elongate, but sturdily built and with only slight lateral compression. The head is rather small but very blunt when seen from above

Fig. 95 An adult Chub (Heather Angel).

and with a wide forehead. The mouth is large and terminal, its angle reaching back to the level of the eye. The gill rakers are short and widely spaced and there are 8–11 of them on the first arch. The pharyngeal teeth are hooked and sharp in two rows on each side (5+2). The body is covered with thick cycloid scales, which number 44–46 along the lateral line. These can be used for age and growth studies, though opercular bones are also of use in this context.

The origin of the dorsal fin, which has three spiny rays and 8–9 soft rays, is behind the base of the pelvic fins, and its free edge is characteristically squared. The paired pectoral and pelvic fins are rather small. The anal fin, which has three spiny rays and 7–9 soft rays, is distinctly convex along its free (rear) edge. The tail fin is large and clearly forked.

The basic colour on the head and back is a dark olive greenish grey. This grades to a greenish silver on the sides and eventually to a dull yellowish white on the belly. However, most of the scales on the body have a dark edge

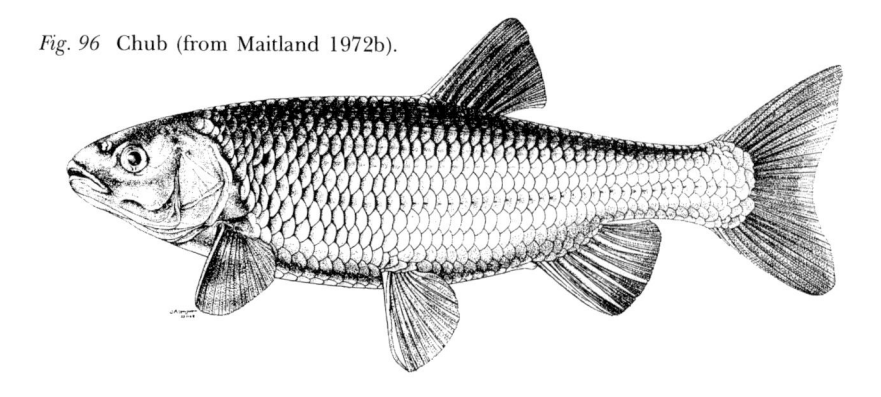

Fig. 96 Chub (from Maitland 1972b).

which gives the whole body a reticulate appearance when seen close up. The fins are mainly a dull grey in colour, but the pelvic and anal fins are usually faintly reddish.

Small Dace and Chub can easily be confused with each other (and sometimes with small Grass Carp), but the concave anal fin of the Dace contrasts with the convex anal fin of the Chub.

The Chub occurs across much of central and southern Europe, from Portugal in the west to the Caspian Sea in the east. In the British Isles it is native to the south-east of England but has dispersed across much of the rest of England and into parts of Wales. It is absent from Ireland and formerly occurred in Scotland only in the Rivers Sark and Annan in the south-west. However, it has recently been introduced to the Clyde catchment and is now found in the River Endrick.

The Chub is mainly a river fish and large shoals occur in the lower and middle reaches of many lowland rivers. Large individuals tend to be more solitary in their habits. It is especially typical of the stretches of mixed habitat found in the middle reaches, where lengths of fast water with stones and gravel alternate with slower pools containing some weed and silt. It is also found in some lakes and in brackish water in the Baltic Sea. In winter it moves into deeper water. However, it can become active again if water temperatures rise, as shown by the large numbers of specimen Chub which were caught in the mild winter of 1987–88.

Spawning takes place from May to June when water temperatures rise above 12°C. The males develop small spawning tubercles and drive ripe fe-

Table 40 Food of Chub in the River Lugg, England, and in the Afon Llynfi, Wales (after Hellawell 1971), as percentage volume.

Stomach contents	River Lugg	Afon Llynfi
Algae	28.3	67.5
Macrophytes	14.6	7.0
Molluscs	0.6	–
Crustaceans		
Crayfish	6.4	–
Insects		
Mayfly larvae	0.1	0.1
Stonefly larvae	0.2	0.4
Beetle larvae	0.1	0.1
Caddis larvae	7.0	9.9
Midge larvae	0.1	0.1
Blackfly larvae & pupae	0.4	0.1
Others	3.8	0.1
Other invertebrates	0.1	0.1
Fish		
Grayling	1.3	–
Minnow	2.7	3.6
Eel	18.3	–
Stickleback	0.1	–
Bullhead	1.8	3.6
Others	4.3	0.9
Other vertebrates		
Frog	1.8	–
Water Vole	0.5	0.1
Terrestrial organisms	2.5	1.9
Other items	0.5	–
Detritus	4.8	2.4
NUMBER OF FISH EXAMINED	416	248

males over suitable areas (usually weed beds) where spawning takes place. Young fish tend to spawn in shoals, whereas there is a tendency for the older, larger fish to spawn in twos and threes. The fecundity of females ranges from 25,000–100,000 eggs depending on size. The eggs are pale yellow, some 0.7–1.2mm in diameter and stick to weeds, stones and gravel. Incubation takes 5–9 days depending on local water temperatures and the young drift into shallow slow-flowing water after hatching.

The Chub, like several other cyprinids, hybridises with other members of the family, and crosses between it and Bleak, Roach and Rudd are not uncommon.

The fry are some 7–8mm on hatching and initial growth is slow, since they only reach 3–4cm at the end of their first year. Thereafter growth is more rapid and they are usually some 10cm at the end of the second year and 15–18cm at the end of the third year. Males start to mature after three or four years (the majority are mature by five years) and females after four or five years (the majority by seven years). By this time they are 20–30cm in length and growth continues after maturity. They normally live for 10–12 years. Females tend to grow faster and live longer than males, although males appear to outnumber females in early age groups.

Initially the small fry feed on minute invertebrates such as rotifers, protozoans, crustaceans and insect larvae. As they grow they gradually change to some plant material and larger invertebrates such as worms, molluscs, crustaceans and various insect larvae. In sunny weather, Chub lie just below the surface among the leaves of floating plants or, more usually, under trees and bushes where insects, berries and seeds are likely to fall. They are very shy and likely to vanish into the depths at the slightest disturbance. Larger Chub eat considerable numbers of small fish, notably their own young, Eels, Dace, Roach, Gudgeon and Minnows. They also eat other quite large organisms such as crayfish, frogs, voles and young water birds as well as some plant material. The most common plant food of Chub in the River Stour in Dorset was the Water Buttercup. The fruits of Mulberry, Elderberry, Bramble and Cherry are traditional baits for Chub.

The Chub is regarded as a very bony fish and is of practically no commercial importance anywhere in Europe. However, it is a popular sporting species and is angled for in many of the countries in which it is found. It has the advantage, from the angler's point of view, of taking artificial spinning lures and particularly wet and dry flies like trout. Isaac Walton and some later writers give involved recipes for cooking Chub in spite of its many small bones and give the impression that the final dish is worth the trouble.

Orfe *Leuciscus idus* (Linnaeus 1758) Ide

Like many other cyprinids the 'average' size of the Orfe depends very much upon its habitat, and fish in a small garden pond, for instance, may mature and spawn at 15–20cm and not grow much beyond that. In the wild, however, they normally grow larger, commonly maturing at 30–40cm in length and 700–1200gm in weight. Exceptionally they may grow much larger than this and fish of up to 100cm and 8kg have been recorded from some parts of eastern Europe. The present British rod-caught record is for a fish of 2.154kg caught in 1986 in a pond at Buxton Towers in north Wales.

Though the young fish are very slim and laterally compressed, the adults

Fig. 97 An adult Orfe (Heather Angel).

are rather thickset in proportion, with a slight humped-back behind the head. The head is quite large and the mouth is broad, terminal and set obliquely. The gill rakers are short and wide-spaced with 10–14 on the first gill arch. There are two rows of pharyngeal teeth (3+5) on either side, which are rather cylindrical with no serrations. The body is covered with large cycloid scales, which number 56–61 along the lateral line. There are 44–45 vertebrae.

The dorsal and anal fins are rather short and the former is situated behind the level of the origin of the pelvic fins. The free edge of the dorsal fin (which has three spiny rays and eight branched rays) is convex whilst that of the anal fin is straight or even slightly concave – a character which distinguishes it from its relative the Chub, where the anal fin has a convex free edge. The anal fin has a longer base than the dorsal fin and three spines anteriorly with nine or ten soft rays behind.

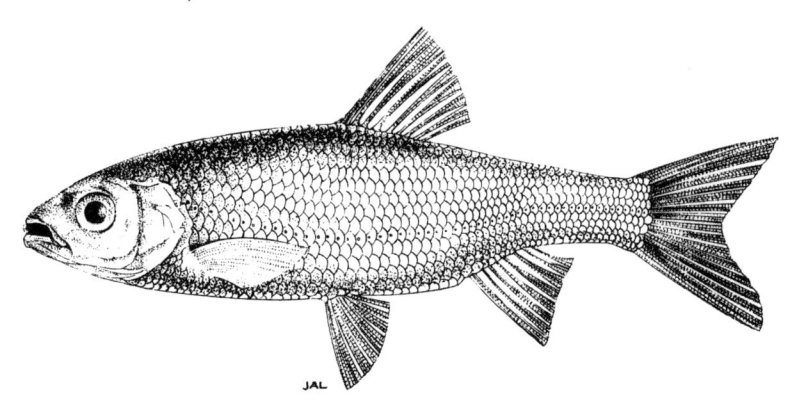

Fig. 98 Orfe (from Maitland 1972b).

The head and back of the Orfe are a dark brownish-grey grading to a silvery grey along the sides. The belly is silvery. The fins are a pale grey, but all of them except the dorsal normally have a reddish tinge. A golden variety has been bred selectively and is a popular and lively fish for aquariums and ponds.

The Orfe is native to much of Europe and Asia occurring naturally from eastern France to Siberia. It has been introduced much more widely, however, and though never native to the British Isles occurs at a number of scattered sites, mainly in southern England and typically in artificial ponds in large gardens and estates where it was originally introduced as an ornamental species.

The favoured habitats of this species are clean slow-flowing rivers and lakes but it also occurs in slightly brackish water in the Baltic Sea. It is a fast-swimming fish, often feeding in shoals near the surface in shallow water though in winter, like many other cyprinids, it seems to retreat to deeper waters.

Spawning takes place mainly in April and May when the water temperatures rise above 10°C. The males develop tubercles on the head and anterior body and start to shoal in the spawning areas in streams or along the stony shores of lakes a few days before the females. When the ripe females appear the males drive them over suitable stones and weed beds and spawning occurs accompanied by much splashing in the shallow water. The pale yellow eggs, 1.6–2.2mm in diameter, are slightly adhesive and stick to stones and weed. Each female may lay from 39,000 to 114,000 eggs, depending on her

Table 41 Food of Orfe in the River Kavlingean, Sweden (after Cala 1971), as percentage number.

Stomach contents	River Kavlingean
Algae	0.9
Macrophytes	12.1
Molluscs	2.4
Worms	4.1
Leeches	0.1
Crustaceans	
Cladocerans	12.8
Ostracods	0.1
Copepods	3.8
Water louse	6.3
Freshwater shrimp	0.3
Insects	
Mayfly larvae	1.1
Dragonfly larvae	0.1
Aquatic bugs	1.0
Beetles	2.8
Caddis larvae	0.7
Midge larvae/pupae/adults	28.3
Blackfly larvae & pupae	5.2
Other insects	7.3
Other invertebrates	0.2
Fish	
Roach & Orfe	0.8
Orfe eggs	0.2
Perch	0.2
Other vertebrates	0.7
Unidentified	2.1
Detritus	5.4
NUMBER OF FISH EXAMINED	1163

size. In streams, the shoals of adults drop back downstream again after spawning. The fry hatch in about 8–16 days depending on local water temperatures. The Orfe will hybridise with other cyprinids in some habitats to produce infertile offspring. None of these seems ever to have been recorded in the British Isles, however.

The young are only 8–10mm at hatching but after absorbing their yolk sacs soon start to grow and may reach 10–12cm after one year and 12–15cm after two years. They mature in their third and fourth years and may live for up to 20 years. The young fry feed mainly on small invertebrates such as protozoans, rotifers and crustacean larvae. Later they feed on larger invertebrates such as molluscs, crustaceans and insect larvae. Large Orfe may become piscivorous and eat other cyprinids such as Roach and Bleak.

The Orfe is still fished commercially in a few places in eastern Europe, where it is taken in nets and traps, particularly during the spawning migration. It has the reputation of being a tasty fish to eat. It is a popular angling species in many countries where it may be taken with both worm and fly, and sometimes by spinner. The golden variety is a popular aquarium and pond fish.

Dace *Leuciscus leuciscus* (Linnaeus 1758) Dare, Dart, Graining

In most habitats, Dace grow to an adult size of 20–25cm and a weight of 150–200gm. Exceptionally, they may reach lengths over 30cm. The present British rod-caught record is for a fish of 574gm caught in 1960 in the Little Ouse, near Thetford in Norfolk. However, larger fish have been reported but not substantiated. The Irish record stands at 510gm for a fish caught in 1966 in the estuary of the Cork Blackwater.

The body is fairly slim and streamlined with some lateral flattening. The head is narrow and small, as is the mouth which is inferior, its posterior angle not reaching back as far as the level of the eye. The gill rakers are wide apart and there are 6–9 on the first gill arch. There are two rows of pharyngeal teeth on either side, usually numbering 5+2, but occasionally 5+3. The body is covered in large cycloid scales which number 45–55 along the lateral line. Scales are used for age and growth determination.

The origin of the narrow-based dorsal fin, which has three spiny rays anteriorly followed by seven soft rays, is above the base of the pelvic fins. Its free edge is concave, as is that of the anal fin, which has three spiny rays and then

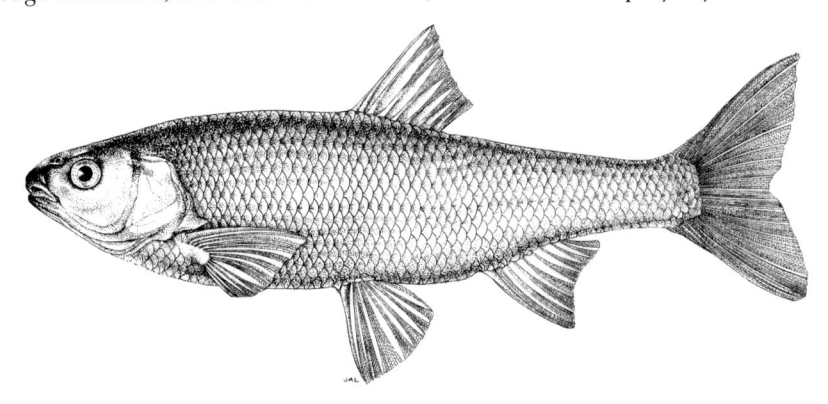

Fig. 99 Dace (from Maitland 1972b).

Fig. 100 Two young Dace (William Howes).

eight soft rays. The caudal fin is quite long and deeply forked. Young Dace and Chub can be distinguished by the shape of their anal fins – concave in the Dace but convex in the Chub.

In colour, the Dace appears mainly to be a silvery fish, but the head and upper body are an olive greenish grey grading into silvery grey along the

Table 42 Food of Dace in the Afon Llynfi, Wales, and in the River Lugg, England (after Hellawell 1974), as percentage volume.

Stomach contents	Afon Llynfi	River Lugg
Algae	36.6	17.0
Macrophytes	0.1	1.1
Protozoans	–	–
Molluscs	1.4	8.1
Worms	0.1	–
Crustaceans		
Water louse	0.5	–
Freshwater shrimp	2.0	2.0
Insects		
Mayfly larvae	3.5	1.6
Stonefly larvae	2.0	0.6
Beetle larvae & adults	2.3	1.8
Caddis larvae	17.8	15.4
Midge larvae & pupae	7.1	4.0
Blackfly larvae & pupae	0.9	16.7
Others	2.1	0.1
Other invertebrates	0.2	–
Fish	–	–
Other vertebrates	–	–
Terrestrial organisms	8.1	14.5
Other items		
Anglers' maggots	–	14.2
Detritus	15.7	3.0
NUMBER OF FISH EXAMINED	409	366

sides and silvery white on the belly. The iris of the eye is distinctly yellowish, often with small dark spots. The fins are a pale grey, but the pectoral, pelvic and anal fins usually have a yellowish-orange tinge.

The Dace is a widespread species across much of Europe and Asia from the Atlantic rivers of southern England and France in the west to Arctic Ocean rivers of Siberia in the east. In the British Isles the species is native to southeast England but it has been redistributed, mainly by live-bait anglers, and is now found over much of England and Wales and the border rivers of southern Scotland. It has recently been moved further north by anglers and is now established in the River Clyde and the River Endrick. Its introduction into southern Ireland was accidental, as was the simultaneous introduction of Roach – two tins of each species, brought over from England as Pike bait, were washed away in a flood on the River Blackwater in County Cork in 1889.

It is of interest to note that during the last century the Dace in northern England was considered a separate species and called the Graining *Leuciscus lancastriensis*. It had obviously reached north-west England (the Mersey system) by that time. The nose of the Graining was described as more rounded than that of the Dace, the scales larger with more radiating lines but fewer scales along the lateral line. The upper parts of the body were pale and drab, tinged with red and separated from the lower part of the body by a well defined line.

The principal habitat of the Dace, which is a shoaling species, is the middle reaches of clean, fast-flowing rivers and streams, largely in lowland areas, but it also occurs in the lower slow-flowing reaches of some rivers and some lakes.

Spawning occurs from February until April and the Dace is our earliest breeding cyprinid. The males develop tubercles all over the head and much of the body, and the maturing fish move upstream to suitable spawning areas – usually shallows below stretches of riffle – the males normally a few days ahead of the females. Spawning takes place over gravelly or stony shallows, often where there is some weed growth, and the yellowish eggs, which are about 1.5–2.0mm in diameter, are deposited in large numbers during the frantic spawning chases of females by the males. The number of eggs laid by each female ranges from 3000–27,000. Incubation takes from 2–3 weeks at 12–15°C.

The young hatch at a length of 7.5–8.0mm and grow fairly rapidly, reaching about 6–8cm at the end of their first year and 10–15cm at the end of their second year. A few of the larger fish mature in their first and second years, but most mature in their third and fourth years, though they keep growing rather more slowly thereafter. They rarely live longer than seven or eight years, with males tending to grow faster than females. Dace are known to hybridise with Bleak, Rudd and bream.

The young fry feed initially on microscopic food such as diatoms, rotifers, protozoans and crustacean larvae. As they grow they eat larger invertebrates such as tubificid worms, molluscs, crustaceans and a range of insect larvae, but during warm weather they are also very active surface feeders and a considerable proportion of their diet consists of terrestrial insects and adult aquatic insects which have fallen or alighted on the water surface. They also eat algae and higher plant fragments. They continue to feed during the winter, when molluscs and caddis larvae form important elements in their diet.

Dace are of little value as a commercial species and are not taken anywhere except as a by-catch when other species are being sought. They are a useful bait species to anglers in certain areas and some anglers fish specifically for them in suitable rivers, where they provide considerable sport to the fly fisherman as they are even faster risers than trout. On the other hand, many game anglers consider them a pest as they may compete with young salmonids in the river, and they are a nuisance when they are persistently caught during angling.

Chinese Grass Carp *Ctenopharyngodon idella* (Valenciennes 1844) Grass Carp, White Amur

One fish which has become quite widespread now in the British Isles (and indeed in many other parts of the world) is the Chinese Grass Carp, often known as the White Amur. This species can grow very large and may reach a length of over 100cm, weighing up to 40kg or more. It is now accepted as an angling species in this country and the present British rod-caught record is for a fish of 7.257kg caught in 1986 in a private lake near Canterbury.

The body is elongate and scaly and slightly flattened along the sides. The head is very wide, especially at the front, and the mouth is slightly inferior. There are no barbels. The pharyngeal bones are in two rows (1.2+4.5) and strongly compressed laterally with the sides deeply folded. There are conspicuous ridges on the gill covers.

The scales are cycloid, darkened at the base and 43–45 along the well developed lateral line. The dorsal fin has three hard spiny rays and seven soft rays, while the anal fin has three spiny rays and eight soft rays. The back is olive-brown, lightening to pale grey on the sides and belly, all with a golden sheen. The fins are all dark grey.

In the identification guide given above, Grass Carp would actually key out to be Goldfish, but the two are easily distinguishable by the pharyngeal teeth (one row in the Goldfish, two rows in the Grass Carp), the lateral scale count (less than 35 and more than 40 respectively) and many other characters, including the cylindrical body shape and large scales of the Grass Carp. In the water it could be mistaken for Chub. In warm climates the Grass Carp often hybridises with the Silver Carp *Hypophthalmichthys molitrix*.

Table 43 Food of young Grass Carp in a pond in Florida in the United States (after Colle et al. 1978), as percentage weight.

Stomach contents	Marion County Pond
Algae	4.8
Macrophytes	
Water Naiad	8.1
Spione Rush	57.0
Arrowhead	20.1
Pondweed	10.1
Molluscs	+
Insects	
Dragonfly larvae	+
Beetle adults	+
Caddis larvae	+
Midge larvae & pupae	+
Terrestrial organisms	+
NUMBER OF FISH EXAMINED	?

Fig. 101 Three young Grass Carp (Heather Angel)

The Grass Carp is native to the middle and lower reaches of the River Amur in Asia. It became an important fish for cultivation in ponds in China and then various other parts of Asia. Gradually it was moved to Europe and to North America and it is now quite widespread in both these continents. It has been introduced to a number of open waters in Great Britain. Like many other cyprinids, it favours rich lakes and slow-flowing rivers.

In its native country and also in a few of the countries to which it has been successfully introduced the Grass Carp spawns in the spring and the pelagic eggs hatch quickly. However, in many temperate countries, due to the low water temperatures, it never matures and so has never been known to breed in the British Isles, nor is it likely to. In such circumstances, the gonads can be brought into condition by hormone injection and the fish then stripped artificially.

One of the important features of this species and a major reason for it being introduced to many areas is the fact that most of its diet consists of higher plants. It browses on these selectively, clearly favouring some species over others, but eventually eating most species if no others are available. In cultivation this means that it can be fed very cheaply on grass clippings and other cheap forms of food, whilst its importance in Britain and North America is that it can be used as a form of biological control to keep down unwanted and troublesome weed growths.

The species has become an important one world-wide both for food and vegetation control. It is used mainly for the latter purpose in Britain, but is also subject now to some angling pressure. It is an attractive aquarium and pond fish and is often available in aquarium shops in this country. One of the authors has successfully kept small specimens in his aquarium.

16

Loaches

The loaches (family Cobitidae) are a group of bottom-living, small, shy and largely nocturnal fishes only found in Europe, North Africa and Asia. In Europe there are three genera and 12 species. They live in the shallows of most types of fresh water, running and standing.

The main characteristics of the Cobitidae are a long sinuous cylindrical body, small eyes and a fleshy, ventrally situated mouth surrounded by a number of barbels. Like the closely related carp family, they possess a single dorsal fin and only pharyngeal teeth.

An unusual feature of the family is that many of its members can swallow air in stagnant conditions, the oxygen being absorbed through the walls of the gut. A result of this adaptation is that some of the species are particularly sensitive to changes in barometric pressure and become very active and restless on the approach of a storm, when atmospheric pressure is falling rapidly. In Europe, one species in particular, the Weather Fish *Misgurnis fossilis*, used to be kept in glass bowls so that its weather-forecasting behaviour could be easily observed. Unlike the drab European loaches, many of the tropical species are very colourful and are popular aquarium fishes.

Identification

The two British species of loach are fairly readily distinguished from one another and the following simple key specifies the particular features to look for.

1. A two-pronged spine present in a small pocket under each eye. Less than 9 rays in the pectoral fins. Barbels similar, all short. **SPINED LOACH**
   Two-pronged spines absent. More than 11 rays in the pectoral fins. Barbels long, one pair slightly longer than the others. **STONE LOACH**

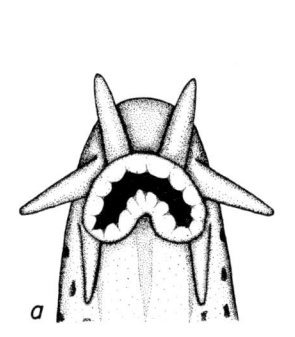

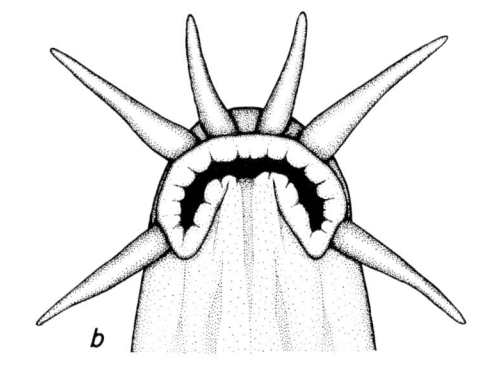

Fig. 102 Mouth and barbels of the loaches: a, Spined Loach; b, Stone Loach (from Maitland 1972b).

Spined Loach *Cobitis taenia* Linnaeus 1758 Groundling

Owing to its cryptic life style and restricted, local, distribution this little fish is seldom encountered unless a special effort (incorporating the use of a fine-mesh net) is made to find it. In the British Isles it is found only in parts of the Midlands and eastern England.

The head is high with a convex profile and, when viewed from above, the body is slender and pointed at each end. The skin of the head extends over the small eyes; all these features additionally distinguish this species from the Stone Loach. The adult fish is usually about 5–10cm in length with a maximum of about 14cm. Females have been shown to grow larger than males. The head and body are laterally compressed and in a pocket below each eye is an erectile double spine (which is very difficult to see in the living fish) – hence its name. Its relative, the Stone Loach, with which it very often co-exists, has no such spine. Around the mouth, which is ventral, are six even-sized barbels on the upper jaw – four in front of the mouth and two directed backwards from its corners. There are 8–10 teeth in a single series on each side of the pharynx. In common with the Stone Loach, the air bladder is enclosed in a bony capsule, and also, like the Stone Loach, it can make use of atmospheric oxygen by gulping air at the surface and absorbing the oxygen through the gut. This is presumably a very valuable asset considering the stagnant nature of some of habitats.

The dorsal fin has 8–10 rays and the pectoral 6–9 (males may have the second ray of these fins thickened). The ventral fin has 6–7 rays, the anal 7–9 and the caudal 13–16. The scales are very small and delicate and do not overlap.

The Spined Loach is an attractive but delicate little fish and after the Nine-spined Stickleback is the smallest freshwater fish in the British Isles. At rest it lies with its head clear of the bottom, unlike the Stone Loach. The body is camouflaged by being well-marked dorsally with an intricate pattern of dark brown to black marbling and with two broken longitudinal rows of 10–19 clearly defined dark-brown spots on a pale, off-white, background. The dorsal and caudal fins bear radiating bands of dark spots, while the pectoral, ventral and anal fins are clear. Apart from the differences in external morphology already referred to it can be distinguished easily from the Stone Loach by the great regularity of its markings.

Spined Loach occur throughout most of Europe except the extreme north. The species also occurs in North Africa and across Asia to Japan. It is indigenous to the British Isles, but its distribution is very local and it is found

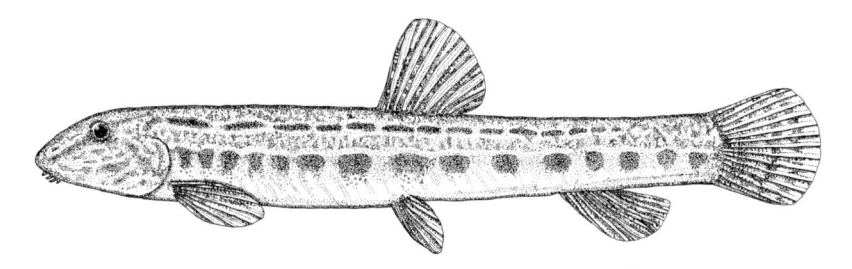

Fig. 103 Spined Loach (from Maitland 1972b).

Fig. 104 An adult Spined Loach (Heather Angel).

in slow-flowing rivers, streams, canals and ditches (occasionally in lakes) in the east Midlands of England, south of the Humber and north of the Thames. Sometimes it occurs in quite small streams along with populations of Minnows, Stone Loach, Bullheads and sticklebacks. Early authorities stated that it also occurred then in Wiltshire and Warwickshire and there are also reports of its occurrence in the north-west Midlands. It has recently been 'rediscovered' in Warwickshire. It is absent from Wales, Scotland and Ireland.

Spawning usually takes place between April and June when adhesive eggs are laid among stones and vegetation in shallow water. The eggs are pale yellow in colour and 0.8mm in diameter, and after spawning they are ignored by the parents. The newly hatched fry take up a bottom-living mode of life almost immediately.

Spined Loach, which are mainly daytime feeders, show a marked increase in feeding activity at dawn. They feed on small bottom-living invertebrates which live on or near the surface of the mud, (e.g. small mayfly and midge larvae), crustaceans (e.g. copepods, chydorids and ostracods) and worms. These are ingested, along with the fine detritus that is constantly being pumped through the buccal cavity. The detritus is ejected through the mouth after the invertebrates have been separated out by, it is thought, being trapped in mucus – which is then swallowed. When not feeding, they bury themselves leaving only their heads exposed. This behaviour is probably the main reason why they are difficult to collect using an ordinary hand net. In aquaria they seem to take longer to settle down than Stone Loach and adopt the habit of remaining buried during the day and foraging at night. However, with increasing water temperature they become more mobile and move about the aquarium taking food which is dropped near them. It appears that their eyes are more recorders of light intensity rather than organs of accurate vision.

As they have no commercial or angling value, apart from occasionally being used as bait in Europe, there has been little incentive to study the Spined Loach intensively and not much is known about their intimate behaviour or their impact on the ecosystem.

Table 44 Food of Spined Loach in the River Great Ouse and gravel pits, Newport Pagnell, England (after Robotham 1977).

Stomach contents	R Great Ouse	Gravel pits
Algae		
Closterium	+	+
Pediastrum	+	–
Cladophora	+	+
Protozoans		
Difflugia	+	+
Arcella	+	+
Molluscs		
Glochidia larvae	+	+
Worms		
Tubifex	+	+
Leeches	–	–
Crustaceans		
Eurycercus	+	–
Graptoleberis	+	+
Acroperus	+	–
Camptocercus	+	–
Alona	+	+
Alonella	+	–
Chydorus	+	+
Pleuroxus	+	–
Bosmina	–	+
Simocephalus	+	–
Ostracods	+	+
Cyclopoid copepods	+	+
Harpacticoid copepods	+	+
Calanoid copepods	–	+
Water louse	+	–
Insects		
Mayfly larvae	+	–
Caddis larvae	+	–
Midge larvae & pupae	+	+
Biting midge larvae	+	–
Rotifers		
Mytilina	+	+
Brachionus	+	+
Keratella	–	+
Detritus	+	+
NUMBER OF FISH EXAMINED	271	106

Stone Loach *Noemacheilus barbatulus* (Linnaeus 1758) Beardie, Colley

Of the two British loaches, the Stone Loach is much better known than its relative the Spined Loach as it is more widely distributed, usually occurs in fair numbers and is easily dislodged from its daytime hiding places under stones and thick aquatic vegetation. It is a fish of some personality that settles down quickly in an aquarium and soon becomes tame, coming out of concealment in the daytime to be fed.

The Stone Loach is a small fish about 7–14cm in length, only occasionally becoming larger than this. Behind the head, with its very small high set eyes, the body is cylindrical, except for a short section near the tail, which is flattened laterally. The mouth is set ventrally, as befits a bottom grubber, with six sensory barbels on the upper jaw – four in front (including the two shortest) and two at the corners – all of which are longer and much more conspicuous than those of the Spined Loach, with which it could be confused initially. The Stone Loach has no spines below the eyes. The body is distinctly slimy and

Fig. 105 An adult Stone Loach showing the well developed nostrils and barbels (Heather Angel)

bears small deep-set scales that do not overlap. The lateral line is clearly visible only along the anterior part of the body. There are 8–10 teeth in single rows along each side of the pharynx but none in the mouth. An anatomical peculiarity of both British loaches is that the air bladder is enclosed in a bony capsule. Age can be determined from their otoliths.

The dorsal fin has 9–12 rays, the pectoral 11–13, the ventral 7 or 8, the anal 7–10 and the caudal 15–19. The pectoral fins in the male are longer and more pointed, but the difference is slight. During the breeding season the males develop minute tubercles on these fins and these are found permanently on all males over 7cm. The patterning of the Stone Loach is very vari-

Fig. 106 Top, Stone Loach (from Maitland 1972b); *Bottom*, Two adult Stone Loach (William Howes)

able and often well defined, forming ideal camouflage when lying among gravel and stones. Young Stone Loach tend to have dark blotches or speckles on a pale background, while the older fish may be heavily blotched with speckled dorsal, anal and caudal fins. Large specimens may be dark olive to dirty yellow-grey.

Stone Loach are found in clean rivers and the littoral zone of lakes throughout west, central and eastern Europe and across Asia to the Pacific Ocean. They also occur in some low-salinity Baltic lagoons. In the British Isles they were originally indigenous to south-east England but since the last ice age they have become widely dispersed throughout the rest of the country except northern Scotland.

This species requires about the same level of dissolved oxygen (10–16mg/l) as salmonids and is thus susceptible to quite low levels of pollution. Their visible discomfort or even death can serve as an 'early warning' of pollution in a stream. Changes in the nature of the river bed (e.g. the deposition of fine mud) can also lead to a decline in the loach population. The European Pond Loach (or Weather Fish), as already mentioned, is well known for its ability to gulp down air and absorb oxygen through the wall of the alimentary canal, which thus acts as an additional respiratory organ when the oxygen level in the water falls. Both British loaches appear to be able to do this too, but to a lesser extent.

Stone Loach spawn from spring to late summer when their yellow eggs, about 0.9–1.0mm in diameter, are shed among gravel and vegetation to which the eggs adhere. They hatch in about 14–16 days at temperatures of some 12–16°C. Egg-laying takes place at intervals during the spawning season. Studies of Stone Loach in the River Frome in Dorset showed that a female of 7.5cm laid 10,000 eggs, at intervals, equivalent to 46% of her initial body weight, between late April and early August.

The newly hatched fry are about 3mm in length and grow rapidly, reaching about 1.5cm in length after some five weeks, when their barbels first become visible. First year Stone Loach may be seen in full daylight during the summer, in small dispersed shoals moving over the bottom. In the Lake District they have been shown to reach over 11cm after five years. Both sexes can mature at one year, and there appears to be a predominance of females in all age groups.

Feeding is most active at dusk or on dull days, when the loach root about on the bottom for food and force the mouth and head into the sand and silt by a vigorous action of the posterior body and tail. In captivity, this characteristic behaviour can be observed easily and they can be seen to detect food at some distance. They are non-visual feeders, often sensing the presence of food by means of their sensitive barbels. Research has shown that, when feeding in small groups, Stone Loach detect and exploit food sources more rapidly and efficiently than when alone. However, when an individual loach detects food and begins rooting about, its activity is sensed by other fish which then converge on the area. Stone Loach of all sizes are often found together under stones and amid thick vegetation, often in the company of Minnows, Bullheads and sticklebacks. The food consists mainly of bottom-living invertebrates; midge larvae, the nymphs of mayflies and stoneflies form a major element in the diet, while worms, crustaceans, caddis larvae, leeches, molluscs and fish eggs are also taken. Feeding activity declines in winter, but in aquaria a small rise in water temperature at this time will induce them to take food.

Stone Loaches have many enemies, particularly trout where they co-exist, but also Eels and large Bullheads, as well as some waterside birds and

Table 45 Food of adult Stone Loach in the Altquhur Burn, Scotland, (after Maitland 1966a), by percentage bulk and 0+ Stone Loach in the River Ouzel, England, (after Hyslop 1982), by percentage number.

Stomach contents	Altquhur Burn	River Ouzel
Algae	–	17.2
Macrophytes	–	0.2
Molluscs		
Snails	–	0.1
Worms		
Lumbriculus	2.8	–
Crustaceans		
Cladocerans	–	0.5
Ostracods	–	26.0
Copepods	0.1	1.3
Canthocamptus	0.4	–
Water louse	–	0.2
Freshwater shrimp	15.8	0.3
Insects		
Mayfly larvae	17.7	6.2
Stonefly larvae	12.3	–
Beetle larvae	0.8	0.1
Caddis larvae	2.8	1.8
Midge larvae & pupae	44.5	19.0
Blackfly larvae & pupae	1.6	32.2
Other fly larvae	0.6	0.6
Other invertebrates	0.6	–
Terrestrial organisms	0.1	–
NUMBER OF FISH EXAMINED	70	308

mammals. The preference shown by trout for loach during angling is one of the reasons for their present distribution, as they became a popular live or dead bait for trout and a spinning bait for salmon (as recommended by Isaac Walton). Many of the older books on angling have accounts of trout fishing with Stone Loach as bait in both Great Britain and Ireland. However, its occurrence in small streams in western Britain not connected with any system which is important for angling remains unexplained.

Not only aquatic predators relish Stone Loach – in some parts of Europe its flesh is esteemed for its distinctive flavour, and attention is given to this aspect of the species by some early authors, including Isaac Walton who, influenced by a report of some 'learned physicians', claimed the loach to be 'grateful to both the palate and stomach of sick persons'. It is also stated that in Europe, in spite of being difficult to transport, Stone Loach were introduced to waters on the estates of great landowners for purely culinary purposes.

17

Catfishes

The family Siluridae, or Old World catfishes, are found in Europe, Africa and Asia. They are immediately recognised by the long barbels or feelers on their upper and lower jaws, the large capacious mouth, small eyes, lack of scales and a small upright dorsal fin.

In the British Isles there is only one species, the Danube Catfish. There are also two species of Ictaluridae (New World catfishes) from North America, the Brown and Black Bullheads *Ictalurus nebulosus* and *I. melas* now established in Europe, but not yet in the British Isles. However, they and a third species, Channel Catfish *I. punctatus*, are commonly sold in aquarium shops in Britain and they may eventually be introduced here from this source.

Many catfish are nocturnal in habit and although they are often thought of as bottom feeders a number of species do feed in midwater and at the surface. They are mainly carnivorous.

Danube Catfish *Silurus glanis* Linnaeus 1758
European Catfish, Sheatfish, Wels

The Danube Catfish is Europe's largest truly freshwater fish and is second in size only to the large anadromous Sturgeon. In its native habitat it can attain a size of 3m, weighing 320kg, and commonly fish from 1–2m weighing 22–36kg are encountered. The British rod-caught record Danube Catfish was taken at Wilstone Reservoir, Tring, in 1970 and weighed 19.73kg, but larger specimens have been seen.

The Danube Catfish is not likely to be confused with any other British freshwater fish (except, when very small, with the very rare – or possibly even extinct – Burbot, q.v.). Its flat head, widely spaced nostrils, small eyes under a transparent skin and the huge mouth, with two very large mobile barbels or feelers on the upper jaw and four short barbels below the protruding lower jaw, together with the tiny dorsal fin, make this fish unmistakable.

Many of the other anatomical features are distinct and of considerable interest. The pupil of the eye is black, the iris white. The two long barbels on the head are supported by extensions of the intermaxillary bones, which allow them great mobility. The upper and lower jaws, the palate and the pharynx bear broad bands of small teeth, incurved and closely set. Behind the head, the body becomes laterally compressed. A short way behind the head

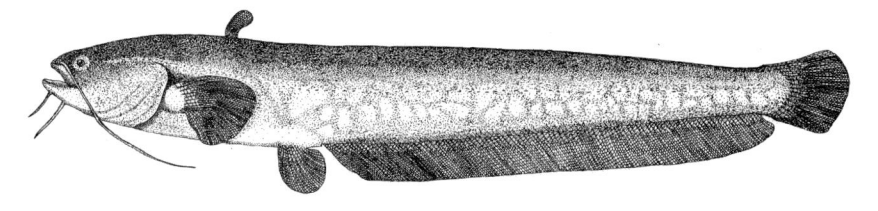

Fig. 107 Danube Catfish (from Maitland 1972b).

is the very short dorsal fin with 3–5 rays. The pectoral fins have 18 rays and the stubby ventral fins, 13. The pectoral fin has a short bony spine, but this is weakly developed – in contrast to other members of the family where the spine is a formidable and sometimes poisonous weapon of defence. The anal fin is long with 75–92 rays. The adipose fin, typical of the North American ictalurid catfishes now established in Europe, is absent.

The soft smooth skin of the Danube Catfish is scaleless and coated in slimy mucus, like an Eel. Out of water it is very shiny. The colouring is rather variable. The head and the back above the lateral line can be black, blue-black, violet, greenish or brownish, sometimes with a reddish or gold sheen. The sides of the body are paler with a dark marbling on a ground of off-white to pale yellow. The whole body is covered to a greater or lesser extent with irregular dark spots. The pigment cells of the skin contain only melanin and its general pattern and colour may take many hours to adapt to a sudden change in background colour. The pectoral fins are usually dark blue at the base and tips and paler in between. The dorsal and ventral fins are yellowish at the base and bluish towards the tips. The anal and caudal fins are greyish-yellow with violet edges. Albino individuals occasionally occur.

Originally, the Danube Catfish occurred in the large muddy rivers and lakes of central and eastern Europe, in the Black and Caspian Seas and in the brackish lagoons of the Baltic, but was not found within the Rhine system or to the west. However, it has been redistributed to some extent within western Europe and was introduced into the British Isles during the latter half of the nineteenth century, when it was put into a limited number of waters in the south-east Midlands of England. Now it appears that its range is once more extending.

The males become mature at two to three years of age, the females at three or four. Spawning takes place from May to July when the water temperature is around 19°C, the male excavating a shallow nest amidst vegetation in shallow water. A large number of pale greenish-yellow eggs, about 3mm in diameter, are laid in this, at a rate of about 30,000 per kilogram of female body weight. Depending on water temperature, they take some 3–10 days to hatch. The nest is guarded by both parents and the fry, around 7mm in length at hatching, are also guarded until the yolk sac has been fully absorbed and they leave the nest. At this stage they are superficially like large tadpoles and grow rapidly, feeding on all kinds of small aquatic invertebrates. They can reach a length of 30cm within their first year. The life span is certainly up to 15 years and may be up to 20–30 years.

Outside the breeding season, Danube Catfish are solitary and mostly nocturnal in habit, remaining concealed in their dens under overhanging banks or submerged objects in deep still water during the day and coming out at night to feed. However, they have been taken during the day by anglers. They are voracious predators and although their main diet is other fish they will take any animal that is not too large for them to swallow. Thus, they have been recorded feeding on large shellfish (e.g. freshwater mussels), mammals, birds (particularly diving ones) and amphibians. Very large Danube Catfish are reputed to have taken dogs – and even children – on occasion. It is said that the two large dorsal feelers on the head which are constantly in motion attract small prey fish in the same way as the first ray of the dorsal fin of the marine Angler Fish (*Lophius*). Small Danube Catfish feed to a large extent on aquatic invertebrates before going on to small fish.

The Danube Catfish is exceptionally sensitive to extra-aquatic sounds and is known to be responsive to frequencies of up to 13,000 per second. This sensitivity is probably due to the fact that the swimbladder, which is linked to the ears by a series of small bones, acts as a very efficient sound amplifier.

This species may grow to an enormous size in its natural environment and it is also farmed to some extent. It is fished for commercially on quite a large scale, with night lines, spears and basket traps, because of its good eating qualities, but it is claimed in some areas that the damage it does to other fisheries cancels this value. As well as having a flesh which is palatable (though rather fatty and indigestible – like 'Pike when young and Sturgeon when old'), their eggs can be used to bulk up the eggs of Sturgeons when making caviar. In addition, the soft strong skin makes leather, the bones and swimbladder a glue and the body fat can be extracted to make lard.

As a sport fish the Danube Catfish is a strong fighter, is highly esteemed and fished for on baited ground lines, though it can be taken on spinning lures. Once landed, it is said, even the largest Danube Catfish will lie quietly on the bank and is easy to transport alive. When disturbed in the water on the other hand it will dash off leaving a cloud of mud.

18

Eels

Eels (family Anguillidae) must be among the most familiar of all freshwater fishes with their almost world-wide distribution – they are found in both the northern and southern hemispheres, and from polar waters to the tropics. They occur in the sea, estuaries, continental rivers, isolated ponds, marshes, ditches and large lakes. The single genus *Anguilla* consists of 16 species, only one of which occurs in Europe.

Their shape and mode of locomotion is characteristic. Unlike the Muraenidae (e.g. the Moray Eel *Muraena helena*) they possess pectoral fins – but pelvic fins are absent. They have very small scales set deep in the skin which is very slimy. Catadromous in life style, they arrive from the sea into fresh water as small juveniles, often penetrating far upstream, and spending many years (often 20–30) feeding and growing until mature, then returning to the sea and migrating far out to traditional breeding areas to spawn and die.

Eels are very catholic in their choice of food, although always carnivorous, consuming invertebrates, fish eggs and fish and other small vertebrates. In many parts of the world eels are the subject of important fisheries. Smoked eel, like smoked salmon, is a universal luxury food.

European Eel *Anguilla anguilla* (Linnaeus 1758)
Astan, Broad-nosed Eel, Bulldog, Eel, Frog-mouth, Glut, Gorb Eel, Grig, Silver Eel, Yellow Eel

The European Eel with its serpentine form and slimy body is unmistakable. The body is cylindrical anteriorly becoming rather flattened posteriorly. The gill openings are only small slits and the eyes too are small and covered by a thick translucent skin. The tubular nostrils protrude just below the eyes. There is a pair of pectoral fins, but unlike most fish there are no pelvic fins. The dorsal, caudal and anal fins are joined into one continuous fin which has over 1000 rays.

The shape of the head was once said to vary with feeding habits, and this gave rise to the recognition of two distinct forms: the sharp or narrow-nosed eel (with the smaller mouth) and the broad-nosed eel, which was said to feed on large organisms. The latter was once referred to as a Grig, Glut or Frog-mouthed Eel and given specific status as *Anguilla latirostris*. These variations were allegedly associated with feeding behaviour only and not with geographic location, sex, age or habitat – though the broad-nosed variety appeared to be more common in estuaries. However, it has now been shown that the great majority of European Eels fall into an intermediate category, with continuous variation between the two extremes.

Lampreys too are serpentine, but can be readily distinguished from eels by their sucker-disc mouth, the lines of gill pores on either side of the head and lack of paired fins. In estuaries and shallow coastal waters in Europe the range of the freshwater eel and Conger Eels *Conger conger* may overlap, although the latter are always said to dominate and can be recognised by the shorter distance between the beginning of the dorsal fin and the head and the fact that the lower jaw does not protrude. In addition, Conger Eels have no scales and very distinctive otoliths.

The scales of the European Eel are transparent, small, narrowly oval and deeply embedded in the skin. They do not appear until the eel is 15–18cm, probably regardless of age. They are laid down as concentric rings of small bony particles and are not ridged by circuli like most other scales of the bony fish. The lateral line is clearly defined and the number of vertebrae may vary from 110–119.

On their return migration to the sea, the fully grown mature male eels are seldom longer than 47cm whereas the females are seldom less. Individuals of around 40–90cm are sizes normally encountered by anglers and commercial fishermen. The British rod-caught record stands at 5.046kg for an eel caught in 1978 at Kingfisher Lake, Hampshire and the Irish record at 2.80kg for a specimen caught in 1979 in Lough Droumenisa, Bantry.

European Eels, during their freshwater or estuarine life, are known as 'yellow eels', but actually vary considerably in colour; when ready for returning to the sea they are called 'silver eels', a fairly accurate description. Eels in fresh water are usually dark brown above the lateral line and yellowish below, but individuals which are pale yellow-amber to dull brown may occur apparently in response to habitat – the yellow individuals occurring where the water is shallow and the bottom sandy. The pupil of the eye is black and the iris orange. On maturation, eels assume a grey or silver-grey colouration and their eyes become much enlarged, in preparation for life in the depths of the oceans.

In Europe, eels are found in all types of fresh waters which are accessible from the sea, and in estuaries and shallow coastal waters. As well as reaching as far north as Iceland, the species occurs around the Mediterranean coasts of North Africa and Asia Minor and in the Black Sea. The distribution of male and female eels often seems to differ, but it is very difficult to sort out what is happening as it is difficult to sex very small eels. It often seems that most eels living in brackish or marine habitats are males and are very small, while most of those in fresh water are female and larger. Unfortunately in the past eels have sometimes been sexed as male because they were very small. It has been postulated by some that eel larvae may be sexually undifferentiated

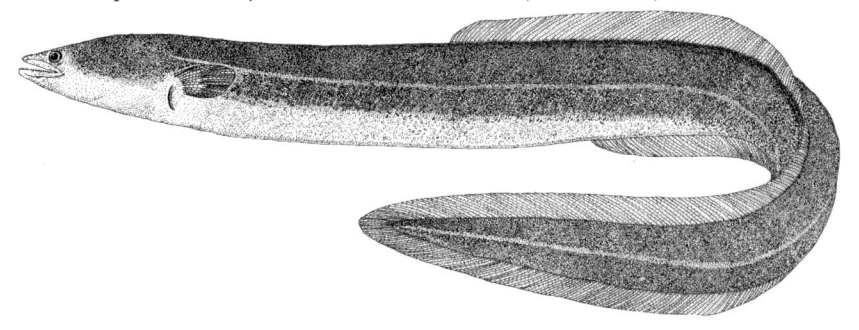

Fig. 108 European Eel (from Maitland 1972b).

and that differentiation only takes place when they reach 23–32cm in length and 5–10 years of age. It was thought that small undifferentiated individuals would develop into males or females according to the environment that they settled in. It has also been observed that where the eel population is dense the majority of individuals are small and male, while where the population density is low, eels are large and female. Female eels tend to remain longer in fresh water than males and continue to migrate further upstream. Thus, they eventually attain a greater size and age than most males. This tendency can also give rise to the impression that in some waters, most eels are female and larger, age for age.

Until the close of the last century, the complicated life history of the freshwater Eel was a mystery and subject to various mythical and magical explanations, e.g. the long hairs from the tail of a stallion were said to turn into eels when dropped into water, or alternatively that they arose by spontaneous generation. However, during the first three decades of the present century, the true story was gradually revealed – one of the great pieces of natural history detection. Even to this day however, no-one has ever seen a spawning eel or knows exactly where they spawn, or how they navigate to reach the spawning grounds.

From late winter to spring, vast numbers of eel larvae, known as elvers, arrive all along the coasts of northern Europe and migrate upstream into all kinds of fresh waters from large rivers and lakes to damp flushes and tiny ponds. At this stage the elvers are around 5–7cm in length and almost transparent (even the vertebrae and blood vessels can be seen through the skin), but with conspicuous black eyes showing. As they make their way upstream, often in dense columns, following the edges of a stream or river, they are preyed upon by various fish (including larger eels) and avian predators. Thus, their seasonal arrival is often advertised by the presence of gulls and other birds lining the waterside and by trout caught bulging with them. All manner of seemingly insurmountable barriers are overcome by these advancing elver hordes, often at great cost to themselves. Dam walls are scaled wherever there are damp areas – though few elvers may actually survive to surmount the crest and continue upstream, the rest becoming desiccated or picked off by birds. On being confronted by a waterfall, they can wriggle around the edges through damp moss and scale wet almost vertical rocks. Water intake systems may be entered and elvers sometimes emerge from cold-water taps in houses, causing some concern. They can even penetrate to small water bodies which have no permanent connection with a stream system, by wriggling through wet vegetation and puddles during rainy periods.

The timing of the annual elver invasion varies from year to year and area to area, but in the British Isles it usually occurs from January to June with a peak around May; some late arrivals can still be seen as late as August, however. The numbers of elvers arriving at the coast also varies considerably from year to year. Obviously they do not all attempt to find their way to the headwaters of each river system but gradually become distributed among most of the suitable waters. In Ireland, elvers initially move only a short way upstream (possibly only 15km or so from the estuary), the further penetration of the inland systems taking place during subsequent years. In Scotland, however, small elvers can be commonly found trying to scale the dam walls of hydro-electric schemes at least 48km above the estuary.

European Eels, of course, are the only freshwater fish that leave the continent to spawn elsewhere. The return migration to the sea takes place after the maturing eels have been in fresh water for a varying number of years. Investigations in Ireland some years ago showed that some eels mature by nine years of age while, in extreme cases, others were still feeding in fresh water after 36 years. (Some Scottish yellow eels have been aged at over 50 years of age.) However, on average, eels from 9–19 years of age form the bulk of the downstream migrants, averaging around 46cm for males and 91cm for females.

In Britain, silver eel males have generally spent some 7–12 years in fresh water and average about 36cm in length, while silver eel females have spent 9–19 years and average around 46cm. The study of eels living in Irish estuaries, mostly males, showed that they appear to mature and migrate before those living in fresh water, mostly females, which mature several years later. Some eels, from 2–9 years of age, were found to be still migrating upstream.

It is during the migration of silver eels that the species is most vulnerable to harvesting by humans. Great numbers, weighing thousands of tonnes, are taken annually in traps and nets set to catch them during their annual rapid passage downstream. Peak movement takes place on dark moonless nights when river levels are high. On reaching salt water, eels lose weight due to osmotic processes which cause water loss until, with the aid of the salt-secreting cells in their gills, they achieve a body salt concentration almost equal to that of marine fishes, and regain weight.

The actual triggering process which sets off the change from yellow to silver eel is still uncertain, but may well have to do with the levels of body fat. For their long journey across the Atlantic Ocean, during which they are believed not to feed, considerable reserves of energy are required. The actual fat content of yellow eels is only about 8%, while that of silver eels is over 30%. The time needed to build up this important reserve to this level must vary very much according to habitat.

From the rivers and estuaries of Europe, European Eels appear to make their way steadily south-west across the Atlantic to the Sargasso Sea, somewhere to the east of the Bahamas and south-west of Bermuda, where they spawn, it is said, at depths of 100–200m, and die. Spawning is thought to take place from February until May. Each female produces several million eggs which are about 1mm in diameter and said to be buoyant, floating about in the sea until they hatch. However, no spawning European Eel, or one about to spawn, has ever been caught or pelagic egg ever found.

The problem of how European Eels navigate has been studied by the tagging of silver eels; recapture data shows that they can cruise at 12km per hour for long periods (e.g. they have been known to cover 1207km in 93 days). One worker has suggested that at the beginning of their migration eels travel near the surface and navigate by the stars, then, on leaving the coastal waters of Europe, they follow a course based on a set angle to the earth's magnetic field. At the last stages, near the actual spawning grounds, smell may be used. (Why this latter sense should not be used more or less from the start, to navigate into and against the Gulf Stream, which transports the larvae in the opposite direction towards Europe, is uncertain.) Birds on their seasonal long-distance migrational flights also use these navigational cues (as well as some others) including, in some species, the olfactory one during the final stages of the journey.

The necessity for eels to make such long and hazardous migrations may have originated during their early evolutionary history, when the relative positions of the continents were different and Europe and America were much closer together (i.e. the Atlantic Ocean was very much smaller).

The smallest European Eel larvae found so far, caught at depths of 90–270m, measured less than 6mm and were still bearing the remains of their yolk sacs. The young, known as leptocephalus larvae, are elongate and flattened laterally, with small pointed heads and relatively large mouths with many teeth. They were originally thought to be a separate species of fish. At this stage they feed mainly on small planktonic animals and within two months of hatching they are 25mm long. Until very recently it was believed that European Eel larvae took 2.5–3 years to drift across the Atlantic from the spawning grounds to the coasts of Europe. This misapprehension arose, apparently, from the faulty analysis of the progressive length/frequency data from the series of samples of larvae collected between the Sargasso Sea and Europe by the pioneer investigators of the 1920s and 1930s. In fact, only one year is involved and not three as believed. This new information fits, of course, data on the velocities of the ocean currents that flow north-eastwards to Europe, moving at speeds of 0.5 to 5 nautical miles per hour, thus enabling a crossing of the Atlantic Ocean in a matter of months. Thus, elvers arriving off the coasts of the British Isles have made the crossing in about 12 months. Divers working in the western approaches have reported seeing glass eels drifting passively towards the coast in a vertical position, with their heads upwards. There is also evidence that eel larvae do not develop fully functional gas-filled swim bladders until they have been in fresh water for several weeks.

During the later stages of the migration, when they are over the edge of the continental shelf, the leptocephalus larvae undergo a metamorphosis into the 'Glass Eel' stage before continuing towards the coasts of Europe. This change involves a reduction in body weight and an alteration in body shape from a leaf-like laterally compressed larva to an elongate slim cylindrical form more suitable for the forthcoming difficult ascent of streams and rivers. As the larvae approach coastal waters, pigmentation starts to develop and they become 'elvers'. However, before starting to embark on their hazardous upstream journey, elvers appear to spend a period of adjustment, possibly about one month, in brackish water. Then, with water temperatures around 9°C they start to swim against the current and set off on their invasion of fresh water.

The eel that is found in the coastal fresh waters of eastern North America and southern Greenland, the American Eel *Anguilla rostrata*, is similar to the European Eel, but has fewer vertebrae (110 or 111) and is rather different in colour and size. It also spawns in the south-western North Atlantic, but apparently further to the south and west of the area presumed to be used by European Eels, although the spawning areas of both species overlap to some extent. Its larvae and elvers drift north-westwards and their journey to the coasts of North America is also completed within one year. The elvers are some 6.0–6.5cm by the time they reach the coast. Some 30 years ago a theory was put forward that there was actually only one species of eel, the larvae of which were all derived from the American spawning stock of adults, and drifted back to the coasts of both North America and Europe. All mature European Eels were presumed to be unable to find their way to the spawning ground and to die in the sea before spawning. This unlikely, but novel, hypothesis created much controversy at the time and a great deal more research ensued. However, circumstantial evidence does not support the theory, which claims that the relatively small external and internal differences between American and European Eels can be explained in terms of the effect of the conditions experienced in early life during their sea migrations. The results of more recent serological and other tests, however, suggest that the two eels are distinct species. The apparent overlapping of the areas of the spawning grounds of the two species in relation to ocean currents can explain to some extent the different routes taken by the larvae after hatching. However, a mixing of larvae does take place and American Eels have been recorded in Denmark. Probably they reach the British Isles, but the task of sorting out the few that do, by laboriously counting the vertebrae of large numbers of eels, has not yet been carried out. The converse may also be true with some European Eels arriving off the coasts of north-east North America.

The age of European Eels is usually determined by an examination of their otoliths, which are leaf-like in shape with a conspicuous shoulder on one side, but in many cases these are difficult to interpret and sometimes only a proportion of the fish in one sample can be aged. Scales have sometimes been used too but this method has even more shortcomings. Scales first appear when the eel has reached a length of 16–18cm, after anything from 2–6 years in fresh water, and appear in succession in different areas of the body. Considerably skill and experience is required to use either method.

Eels flourish in a wide variety of freshwater habitats but probably thrive best of all in rich muddy waters with much aquatic vegetation. It was commonly believed that their ability to live for long periods out of water was due to the filling of their gill pouches with water, but it has been shown that eels with these pouches removed live just as long as those with them intact. It is probable that they are able to absorb oxygen through the skin as long as it is kept damp. Their eyes are kept from drying out by the fact that the outer layer of the cornea is detached from the inner layers. These 'spectacles' protect the eye in a dry environment, while it can still rotate freely beneath.

There is an interesting theory that eels in most of northern Europe are at the northern extremity of their range, as water temperatures, even in summer, are not optimal for the species, while during the winter the low temperatures force eels to be inactive and not to feed. This situation could account for their very slow rate of growth. Farmed eels kept in warm-water effluents, however, grow rapidly throughout the year.

Foraging for food takes place mainly after dusk and their eyes, which contain a high proportion of rod cells with much rhodopsin (a pigment normally associated with marine fishes living at depths), are very sensitive and adapted to this nocturnal hunting behaviour. However, eels can also be seen in hot weather, swimming vigourously around in search of food.

Their sense of smell is very acute, a feature that is exploited by fishermen, whose baited traps can attract eels from a large area by day or night. Being scavengers they are attracted, often in considerable numbers, to dead organisms of various kinds. When feeding on the carcasses of dead fish, they will

EELS 247

Table 46 The main food of Eels in the River Cam and Shepreth Brook, England (after Hartley 1948), Lough Key (after Moriarty 1974), River Erne, Ireland (after Moriarty 1975) and Dubh Lochan, Scotland (after Shafi & Maitland 1972), as percentage occurrence.

Stomach contents	Cam/Shepreth	Lough Key	River Erne	Dubh Lochan
Algae	5*	–	–	–
Macrophytes	5*	–	–	–
Molluscs				
Snails	5	33	29	–
Mussels	–	18	–	–
Worms	1	–	–	–
Leeches	1	–	–	–
Crustaceans				
Water louse	2	47	47	–
Freshwater shrimp	39	4	12	–
Crayfish	43	–	–	–
Others	1	4	–	–
Insects				
Mayfly larvae	17	43	6	9
Alderfly larvae	6	–	–	14
Caddis larvae	6	10	59	–
Midge larvae	4	20	12	4
Blackfly larvae	7	–	–	–
Other insects	5	–	–	–
Fish				
Minnow	2	–	–	–
Gudgeon	3	–	–	–
Stone Loach	2	–	–	–
Perch	–	–	–	24
Three-spined Stickleback	2	–	–	–
Bullhead	2	–	–	–
Unidentified	–	2	65	–
Other vertebrates				
Newts	–	–	–	5
Voles	1	–	–	–
Terrestrial organisms	3	–	–	–
NUMBER OF FISH EXAMINED	108	49	17	22

seize a piece of skin and flesh and then rotate their bodies rapidly tearing off a mouthful to swallow. Sharks and dogfish use the same technique. Smaller eels may be chased away from these carcasses by larger ones and some fighting over possession may take place. Eels are perfectly capable of being cannibal and will attack the body of a dying or newly killed eel, tearing at it in the manner described above.

Some years ago, one of the authors threw the head of a freshly caught Sea Trout into the shallows of a river renowned for its eel population to see, out of curiosity, if it would attract any. Soon a steady progression of eels could be seen homing in on the bait, all approaching from downstream and following a narrow cleft in the bedrock of the river bed. At this point a dead eel, which had an open wound on its side, was placed across the cleft. Eels which had been approaching the bait at some speed halted abruptly a short distance before reaching the dead eel and then edged cautiously up to it before retreating downstream again. Of 27 eels that approached the dead individual, only one swam directly on to the bait. The following year at the same time this experiment was set up again to be photographed. The eels appeared as before, homing in on the bait, but this time all swam past the dead eel, ignoring it. No explanation for this contrasting behaviour is obvious. Later the dead eel was placed beside the bait, whereupon a few eels attacked it, tearing off pieces in the manner described above. Provided that an eel is not ill or injured it appears to be quite incapable of ignoring a morsel of food placed near its head, a behavioural trait also commented upon by Isaac Walton!

The diet of eels is catholic, but the relative proportions of invertebrates to fish taken varies with the size of the individual and from population to population. In Ireland, lake-living eels less than 40cm in length commonly feed mainly on invertebrates including midge larvae, crustaceans (such as the freshwater louse and, perhaps surprisingly, water fleas) and molluscs (e.g. snails, pea shells and mussels). Larger eels take an increasingly large proportion of fish. In other situations, stream-living eels over 20cm take significant numbers of fish, whilst in yet other waters large eels rely mainly on invertebrates, though they will take large animals such as frogs if they get the chance. In estuaries, small Flounders are the fish mostly found in eel stomachs, along with crabs, shrimps and prawns. Many other species of fish (e.g. Rudd and Perch as well as small eels in Lough Corrib) are commonly taken by eels and though there may seem to be different preferences in various areas, availability (in one or more of its many aspects) may be the deciding factor. Again, scent may be important. Eels often attack other fish caught in gill nets and when trout and charr are caught together eels appear to attack only the charr, ignoring the trout. A similar situation has been noticed with Vendace and Perch, where the former may be extensively attacked and damaged in gill nets set overnight, whilst the Perch are ignored.

Investigations of the food of eels in England and Wales have given similar results and confirmed that eels of all sizes live on the range of invertebrates available, though snails seem to be of particular importance. There was less evidence of eels being piscivorous, though larger specimens certainly tended to feed on bottom-living fishes such as Gudgeon, Loach, Bullhead and lampreys (both larvae and adults). In estuaries, Flounders were common items of diet.

In Loch Tummel, a large oligotrophic Scottish loch, eels were found to be feeding extensively on small aquatic worms which live under stones or buried in the substrate – organisms hardly ever found in the stomachs of trout and Perch which co-existed with the eels there. Other items in the diet of eels there included a wide range of invertebrates such as freshwater lice and leeches. It is often claimed that eels do much damage to salmonid stocks by eating their eggs at spawning time. Usually in the British Isles, however, salmonids are spawning at a time when the water temperatures are too low (less than 10°C) for eels to be really active. Feeding mainly halts during the winter and very few eels caught at this time have any traces of food in their stomachs. In one study in Wales no eels at all could be caught by angling methods for examination during the winter months. Predation on the eggs of river-spawning salmonids has not been recorded and that on fry and parr seems to be very restricted. In Windermere, however, eels do at times take the eggs of Arctic Charr during their spawning period of October to March.

On warm still summer nights, eels will push their heads out of the water along suitable shores to seize invertebrates such as emerging caddis flies. In doing so they make a distinct sucking sound as the prey is taken in. This behaviour has also been recorded in the American Eel under similar conditions and the sound described as 'chirping'. During winter, as the water temperatures fall, eels become progressively less active and pass the season relatively moribund, concealed somewhere on the bottom and probably not feeding.

Eels, particularly small ones, have many predators, being a common prey of Herons, Goosanders and Red-breasted Mergansers, as well as other fish such as large eels, Pike and occasionally trout. Eels are often the main food of Otters and they are also eaten by Mink. They are fairly tolerant of pollution of different kinds and are often one of the last fish to disappear as a river deteriorates. In those areas of upland Scotland affected by acid deposition, they are often the only fish left after the others have been eliminated. Eventually, of course, they too disappear with the increasing acidity.

Commercially, eels are one of the most important freshwater fish in Europe and they are caught in enormous numbers in fyke nets and traps of various kinds. All sizes may be cropped by humans. Elvers are trapped in huge numbers, formerly for direct human consumption (as 'elver cakes') but now mostly for stocking ponds and polder lakes for growing on. However, elver-eating competitions still take place in England where, in the spring of 1987, the 'World Eel-Eating Championship' was held in Gloucester and was won by a competitor who swallowed 0.45kg of elvers in 32 seconds. In some places industrial warm water effluents are being used for eel farming – here eels can grow very rapidly for they continue to feed during the winter.

Their flesh is white, firm and with a distinctive flavour, and it has the highest fat content of all our fishes, being over 30% of body weight in silver eels. Their calorific value is considerably higher than that of fresh-run salmon. They may be eaten fresh, pickled or smoked. Fresh eels should never be dropped into a hot frying pan as they will immediately uncurl and 'jump' out – an observation that has given rise to the legend that even when decapitated and gutted they still hang on to life.

European Eels are commonly caught by sport fishermen, but they are not universally popular, for though some anglers specialise in eel fishing, many more abhor them for their snake-like appearance and sliminess and difficulty in handling. When hooked they often twist and turn in such a way as to completely tangle up the line. They are subsequently difficult to unhook and only to be killed with some difficulty. Their powers of survival are legendary among fishermen.

19
Sticklebacks

The sticklebacks (family Gasterosteidae) belong to a group of small prolific fish consisting of five genera and seven species, which are found in a great variety of habitats in the temperate and arctic zones of Europe, Asia and North America. They occur in the sea and in fresh water. One genus, consisting of only one species, is wholly marine, while other species are equally at home in salt or fresh water. Some races are anadromous. Although of little direct economic value they act as useful prey for larger species, converting small organisms into food for exploited predatory species.

With the exception of the marine species – the Sea or Fifteen-spined Stick-

Fig. 109 Morphological variation in Three-spined Sticklebacks (see page 253); left, lateral view of whole fish; right, dorsal view of tail (from Campbell 1985)

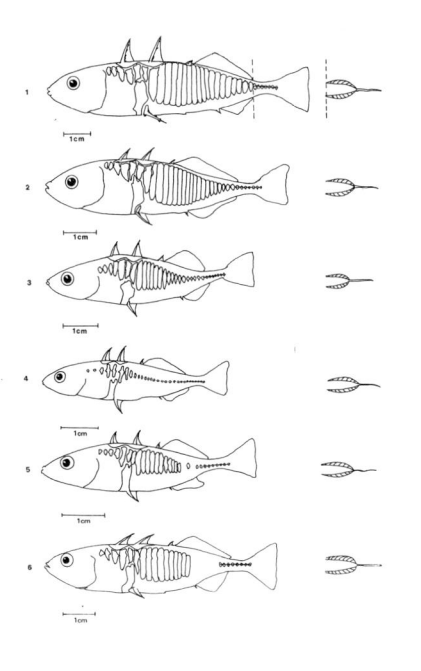

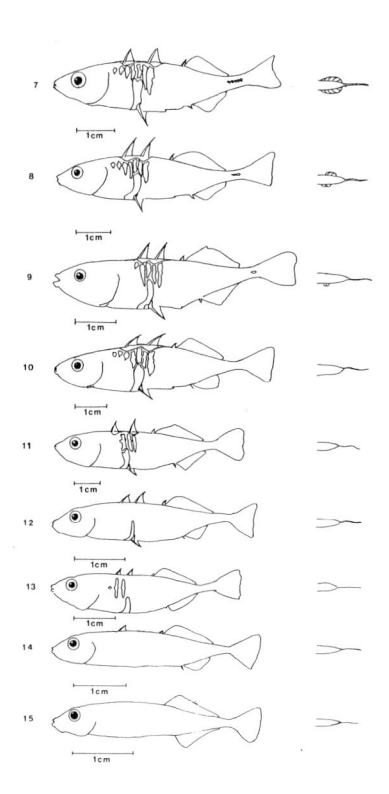

leback *Spinachia spinachia* which has a thin elongate cylindrical body – all sticklebacks are laterally compressed with well developed dorsal and pelvic spines, the characteristic of the family. The mouth is small and adapted for crushing their principally invertebrate diet. The body may be naked or covered by a variable number of bony plates. All species show a characteristic behaviour at spawning time, which involves colouring up and nest building by the males, and the ritualised attraction of the females to persuade them to lay their eggs in the nest. This is followed by a period when the male closely guards the nest and fry.

The family is represented in the British Isles by two species: the Three-spined Stickleback and the Nine-spined Stickleback. Their rigid behaviour patterns and adaptability to captivity have made them one of the most studied of all laboratory animals, while in the field, the wide range of morphological and meristic variation makes them ideal material for study by evolutionary biologists.

Identification

The separation of the two freshwater sticklebacks in the British Isles is a relatively easy matter, as their common names imply. However, variants – and even spineless forms – do occur and the following key serves to formalise the distinctions.

1. Less than five dorsal spines (normally three), the longest about the same height as the dorsal fin. Gill openings narrow, restricted to the sides. Throat of the male vivid red during the breeding season.
   THREE-SPINED STICKLEBACK
   More than six dorsal spines (normally nine), the longest only about half the height of the dorsal fin. Gill openings wide, confluent ventrally. Throat of the male vivid black during the breeding season.
   NINE-SPINED STICKLEBACK

Three-spined Stickleback *Gasterosteus aculeatus* Linnaeus 1758
Baggie Minnow, Barstickle, Doctor, Jack Sharp, Pinkeen, Prickleback, Sprickleback, Stickle, Stickling, Tiddlebat

The Three-spined Stickleback is one of the most widely distributed fish in the British Isles (perhaps only trout and eels are more widespread) and probably one of the most familiar, in spite of its small size. Most adults of this species in inland waters are some 4–7cm in length but in estuaries and in the sea they reach lengths of up to 10cm.

The species is usually slender in outline and laterally compressed, though females about to spawn develop a bulging ventral profile, as do both sexes when infected with a common tapeworm (which may ultimately become as large as the host). After the early fry stage, sticklebacks lose the connection between the oesophagus and the air bladder – i.e. they do not have a permanent pneumatic duct. Vertebrae number from 29–33.

There are no true scales on the body, which may be naked, but normally there is a variable number (1–25) of bony scutes or lateral plates, which line the flanks from just behind the head to the beginning of the caudal peduncle. Along the peduncle, to the beginning of the caudal fin, there may be a further seven or eight small plates, or platelets, expanded laterally to form a

Fig. 110 An adult Three-spined Stickleback (Heather Angel).

static keel. Along the row of lateral plates, including the platelets (or along the skin when plates are absent), is a line of open sensory pits connected to the lateral line canal beneath.

Sticklebacks, as their name suggests, are equipped with stickles or spines. These are formed from modified fin rays. In this species, dorsally there are three spines, the two anterior being much the larger. Behind the spines, 10–14 rays form the posterior or second dorsal fin. Ventrally, there is a single fixed spine as the first ray of the anal fin which has a further 8–11 soft rays. The pelvic fin has one strong spine which can be erected sideways and locked into position, as well as one soft ray. The pectoral fin has 9–10 soft rays and the caudal fin 12. On large sticklebacks, the dorsal and pelvic spines may be noticeably serrated.

Fish with two or four dorsal spines occur occasionally and there are a few populations where individuals have a variable number of very weakly developed spines, from 1–3 in number or sometimes none at all. Such fish usually have few or no lateral plates and very reduced pelvic spines or none at all. So far, in the British Isles, these spine-deficient populations have been found only in northern Scotland and the Western Isles, but they are also known from four limited areas of the western (i.e. Vancouver Island), northwestern (Queen Charlotte Islands and south-west Alaska) and eastern (St Lawrence Gulf) coasts of North America. Plateless forms occur on the west coast of Ireland.

As will be evident, the external features of Three-spined Sticklebacks can vary considerably from the basic form, which has a full complement of well developed lateral plates, spines and caudal keels. It is not known to what extent environmental conditions or geographic situations influence the development of these features. Broadly speaking, however, the marine-living race possesses all these features in a well developed state and is known as the *trachurus* form (formerly called *Gasterosteus trachurus*, the Rough-tailed Stickleback). Inland, in fresh waters, types without keels and with anterior plates only predominate – these are the *gymnurus* or *leiurus* forms (formerly *Gasterosteus gymnurus* or *G. leiurus*, the Smooth-tailed Stickleback).

An intermediate form also occurs, particularly in estuaries, which has anterior plates only (usually more than *leiurus*), but also has caudal keels, although these may not be fully developed or symmetrical. This is the *semiarmatus* form (formerly *Gasterosteus semiarmatus*, the Half-armed Stickleback) which is said to be sea-going, along with *trachurus*, in the southern North Sea and the English Channel. To complicate the situation further, in the British Isles, *trachurus* forms sometimes occur far inland either on their own or along with *leiurus* or *semiarmatus*. Dimorphic populations comprising the latter two forms also occur inland.

So far, in spite of considerable research, the reasons for these variations (i.e. their functional advantages) are not clear – except perhaps in the case of marine forms – for they do not seem to be obvious adaptations to any particular environment or habitat. It is difficult, for instance, to suggest any advantage to a stickleback in being plateless and spineless or what the advantages are in having plates and spines to a fish which is eaten regularly by several different kinds of predators.

It is thought that all these forms have evolved, *in situ*, within the relatively short period since the retreat of the ice cap. This was some 8–10000 years ago, towards the end of the last ice age, when newly formed fresh waters were recolonised from the sea by the anadromous marine-living *trachurus* form, the founding ancestor of the present, non-migratory populations of *leiurus* and the intermediates. An alternative hypothesis has also been put forward, that *trachurus* and *leiurus* forms colonised fresh waters separately, at different times, from isolated glacial refugia, the *leiurus* forms apparently being best suited to inland waters.

Within the British Isles there is a continuum of stickleback variation that ranges from the large, strongly plated and armed marine-living *trachurus* to the small, very rare, totally spineless and plateless form. However, in spite of this wide range of variation, some forms are much more common than others and in Figure 109, numbers 2, 6, 10 and 11 illustrate forms that represent the great majority of sticklebacks found in the British Isles and probably elsewhere. In captivity, inter-morph breeding takes place freely and successfully, but to what extent this happens in the wild in habitats where the various forms co-exist is not known.

Three-spined Sticklebacks vary considerably in colour too. Marine sticklebacks have light olive to grey-green backs and bright silver flanks, while forms living inland tend to have brownish to olive backs with, often, an olive-brown to grey-brown mottling on the flanks, which may form irregular dark vertical bands. The dorsal spines and soft fin rays are pale and translucent and the pelvic spines pale to orange. At spawning times the males assumes the striking colouration that has made the species so well known: his back becomes a conspicuous pale sandy to greenish-yellow or silvery iridescent blue-green, the iris of the eye is a brilliant aquamarine and the throat and anterior flanks are suffused with a brilliant red. Males of spine-deficient populations do not colour so brightly, some barely colouring up at all, although the iris is invariably bright.

The Three-spined Stickleback is found in the sea and in coastal waters and fresh waters throughout the temperate and polar zones of the Old and New

Worlds, but its circumpolar distribution (unlike that of the Nine-spined Stickleback) is interrupted by its absence from parts of the arctic coasts of North America and Asia. In the British Isles, where it was one of the original post-ice age colonisers, it is widely distributed in all types of fresh waters, from weed-choked ditches to large lakes up to about 350m in altitude. Although impassable falls and rapids have presumably been a constraining factor it has been further redistributed by humans, both intentionally and accidentally. It is found too in estuaries, tidal pools, coastal waters and far out in the open sea where it appears to inhabit mainly surface waters – although it has also been found in the stomachs of deep-water fishes.

Spawning normally takes place between March and July, with May and June being the months of peak activity. However, coloured males may sometimes be seen as late as August, possibly either late or failed spawners. Exceptionally one of the authors has observed a coloured male fanning over his nest in mid-October in a pond in the south of England. The actual spawning behaviour has been the subject of a great deal of intensive study, which has produced information basic to an understanding of vertebrate behaviour in general, particularly aspects of aggression, submission and the significance of colour and posture.

At spawning time, males strong enough to hold territories select and clear an area of substrate on which to construct a nest. This is made from any conveniently available material – usually filamentous algae, plant fragments, detritus and sand. This is pushed and pulled by the male (using his mouth) until it takes the form of a low shapeless pile some 5cm across. Where only fine sand or silt is available, the nest may actually take the form of a neatly circular low cone. The parts of the nest are glued together by sticky threads secreted by the kidneys and applied by the male rubbing his ventral region across the surface of the nest from all directions. Subsequently a hole is made through the centre of the nest by the male repeatedly poking his nose into the pile of material. Sometimes only one entrance hole is made but at other times the male pushes himself right through the nest, thus forming a tunnel.

When the nest has been completed, the next phase of the spawning routine begins, and the male embarks on a zig-zag dance sequence in the presence of a ripe female – part of the rigidly ritualised courtship procedure which should eventually result in her following him into or on top of the nest. She then enters the nest, pushing her way through the entrance hole and laying her eggs on the way. The eggs are immediately fertilised by the male, who has been following closely, releasing his sperm with a quivering orgasmic motion. The female then leaves, taking no further part in the procedure while the male tidies up the nest around the egg clumps.

The newly laid eggs are pale translucent yellow in colour and some 1.5mm in diameter. The number laid by each female is usually about 50–100, but a large female is capable of producing up to 450. After a period of rest and feeding a female may spawn again with the same or another male. Textbook illustrations often show the female in the act of spawning with her head protruding at one side of the nest and her tail at the other. This is not always the case though, for where the nest has only one hole she may just press her body over the entrance, laying her eggs partly into the nest. Also, it seems, under aquarium conditions at least, some of the courtship sequence may be by-passed, with an over-ripe female dashing straight on to the nest, which may not even be completed, and laying her eggs attended by a rather 'nonplussed' male who nevertheless usually does manage to fertilise them successfully. The fertilisation of the eggs apparently releases the next stage in the breeding behaviour of the male, when he begins vigourous fanning of the eggs and nest to ensure that they receive an adequate amount of oxygen. Fanning is accomplished by the male going through the motions of swimming rapidly forward, but actually remaining in the same place above the nest by a rapid reversing motion of the pectoral fins. However, he is also on guard at the same time and frequently has to chase off other males or spent females, both potential nest robbers.

The vagaries of the British weather mean that stickleback eggs may vary considerably in their hatching time; 8–14 days is normal, but it may take as long as 20 days. At a constant water temperature of 19°C hatching takes place in 7–8 days. After the young appear, the male intensifies his role as an attentive parent and as well as continuing to fan the nest he picks up any fry which stray away in his mouth and spits them back into the nest. Eventually, when their yolk sacs are absorbed, the fry break out, swimming jerkily to the surface, where they swallow air to inflate their swimbladders and establish their buoyancy in the water. The connection between the oesophagus and the swimbladder disappears shortly afterwards.

Gradually the family of fry shoal away from the nest, sometimes with the male in attendance, though his interest soon begins to wane. Females can be a menace to the young at this time and will feed on them voraciously if not chased away by the male – at times even he may succumb to temptation and eat his own young! He has become rather weak by now and may be displaced territorially by another, unspawned, male. However, in aquaria, and probably sometimes in the wild too, a spawned male may court more females and repeat the process, eventually becoming very emaciated as a result and usually dying. Some males will swallow available food while guarding the nest, whereas others may take it into the mouth but then eject it as though it was one of their own fry, seemingly unable to swallow at this stage.

It is likely that in the British Isles the great majority of inland and estuarine sticklebacks spawn only once in their lives, at 1+ or 2+ years of age, dying afterwards. Their ages can usually be determined from otoliths. The larger marine-living forms may well spawn more than once and are known to live up to four years of age. In aquaria, three years is the common age limit, but a life span of five years has been known. Throughout the world range a maximum age of about four years is normal.

Fast-growing individuals may reach a length of 4.5–5cm after one year, but inland and estuarine populations nearly always include a proportion of small fish around 2.5cm at any time of the year. These may be the progeny of late-spawning parents or just slow growers. In some populations, especially plateless and/or spine-deficient ones, males may mature at around 2.5cm and mature specimens of less than 2cm have been recorded from the Western Isles.

Just as sticklebacks exist in a wide range of habitats, so do their modes of life vary. In weedy ditches, for instance, they may lead a rather solitary life in the thick of the vegetation, feeding on a range of small aquatic invertebrates, including small crustaceans, midge larvae and molluscs. In more open habi-

Table 47 The main food of Three-spined Sticklebacks in the River Birkett and Windermere, both England, and in Easdale Quarry, Scotland (after Hynes 1950), as percentage occurrence and the River Endrick, Scotland (after Maitland 1965), as percentage by bulk.

Stomach contents	R Birkett	Windermere	Easdale Q	R Endrick
Algae	2	–	3	+
Macrophytes	3	+	6	–
Protozoans	+	–	–	–
Molluscs				
Snails	3	–	–	3
Pea shells	2	–	–	–
Worms	6	4	–	3
Crustaceans				
Cladocerans	12	36	–	–
Copepods	20	30	4	+
Ostracods	7	13	–	–
Malacostracans	7	2	56	8
Insects				
Mayfly larvae	+	1	–	22
Stonefly larvae	–	–	–	8
Aquatic bugs	+	–	–	–
Caddis larvae	1	1	–	7
Beetle larvae	+	–	–	5
Blackfly larvae	–	–	–	+
Midge larvae & pupae	15	10	6	42
Other insects	2	–	7	+
Other invertebrates	2	1	–	+
Fish				
Stickleback eggs/young	1	–	4	–
Terrestrial organisms	+	+	+	+
Detritus	3	–	4	–
NUMBER OF FISH EXAMINED	1581	120	55	80

tats they tend to feed in shoals. These may be combined shoals of sticklebacks and Minnows, usually in shallow water near the shore. The distribution of Three-spined and Nine-spined Sticklebacks overlaps in some waters. In artificial situations they can be induced to breed with each other, but produce only infertile offspring; this has not been recorded in the wild, however, where differences in their respective breeding behaviours would make it almost impossible.

In large lakes, both benthic and pelagic living populations may occur, the former feeding on mayfly and caddisfly larvae, midge larvae and pupae, bottom-living crustaceans, worms and small molluscs, and the latter on zooplankton (copepods and cladocerans), midge larvae and pupae and small aerial insects on the surface film. Plant material is also taken to a limited extent, mainly diatoms, but also fragments of other algae and higher plants.

Sticklebacks hunt by sight and have, accordingly, acute powers of vision. This is aided by the retina of the eye having three separate areas concerned with receiving light from different sources, two of them related to underwater sources and one to sources above water. In the scientific literature on sticklebacks there are many references to anadromous behaviour associated with the *trachurus* form. Large-scale seasonal migrations are carried out by sea-living *trachurus* to their inshore estuarine or freshwater breeding grounds, with a return migration of the adult survivors and progeny at the end of the breeding season. These migrations have been observed all along the North Sea coasts of Europe and along the north-eastern and north-western coasts of North America. In the British Isles, however, as well as these truly anadromous populations of *trachurus*, there appear to be many that are more or less static, spending all their time within the same estuary. In an estuary in north-east Scotland a polymorphic population of sticklebacks, comprising *trachurus*, *semiarmatus* and *leiurus* forms, was sampled at monthly intervals for three years. The proportions of the three forms did not vary significantly over this period, thus suggesting apparently that the *trachurus* element was not migratory.

Marine-living sticklebacks do, however, move inshore in the spring to spawn in tidal rock pools, low-salinity tidal pools and estuaries. They usually appear in these places during April and by mid-May large shoals with a progressively increasing proportion of spent females may be encountered offshore. The males return to the sea in late summer, leaving their well-grown fry to spend a few more weeks in the nursery areas before migrating too. Marine *trachurus* can live and breed successfully in pure fresh water as, conversely, can the inland *leiurus* form in full sea water.

Sticklebacks are intermediate hosts to a number of parasites. Probably the most common, and certainly the most conspicuous of these is the large white, worm-like plerocercoid of the tapeworm *Schistocephalus solidus*. Sticklebacks become infected by eating the copepod crustaceans that themselves have been infected by ingesting the tapeworm eggs. These are released into the water from the faeces of a predatory bird, such as a gull, which is the final host – itself having been infected by swallowing an infected, probably disabled or dying, stickleback. In the stickleback, the parasite completely fills the body cavity of the host, eventually killing it; sometimes a very high proportion of the stickleback population is infected. In waters where the infestation level has been high it is common to find the washed-up, dried, empty shells of stickleback carcasses with the body cavities burst open.

Although there is a strong belief that the spines and lateral plates of sticklebacks are protective in function, there is actually little evidence to support this. The erectile spines may in fact be just as valuable or more so to the fish as a means of communication during courtship displays and defence of territory through threat, especially by the male during his nest-guarding phase. Also, in spite of the spines and body armour, sticklebacks are heavily preyed on by a number of predators – avian, mammalian and piscine. It is a valuable food item for Brown Trout and other species in many places, acting as a suitable converter of small invertebrate species into a larger item of food for larger fishes. Stickleback fry also suffer considerable predation from large carnivorous invertebrates such as dragonfly larvae and aquatic beetles, as well as from adult sticklebacks.

Sticklebacks appear to be very tolerant of most types of pollution and in waters which are becoming increasingly polluted they may be the last species to survive. This may be helped by their behaviour; for instance, when in contact with the fish poison, rotenone (derris extract), in a small stream observed by one of the authors, they fled before the poison as it moved downstream, eventually reaching a lake and safety, while small Brown Trout remained and died.

Because of the enormous numbers in which Three-spined Sticklebacks can sometimes occur they have been harvested by humans for a number of purposes including the extraction of oil, as an agricultural fertiliser and as fish meal. As indicated earlier, they have had an important role in science for they make ideal laboratory animals. In fact, the Three-spined Stickleback may well be the most widely studied of all freshwater species of fish. Some of the most basic studies in animal behaviour have been carried out on Sticklebacks – especially during their breeding period.

The ability of all forms of Three-spined Sticklebacks to adapt freely to living and spawning in fresh or salt water has been a stimulus for physiological research into the mechanisms involved in osmotic control. In addition, their great range of morphological and meristic variation is of considerable interest to evolutionary biologists – particularly as these 'adaptations' have taken place over a very short period of time in evolutionary terms and appear to illustrate 'evolution at work'.

Nine-spined Stickleback *Pungitius pungitius* (Linnaeus 1758)
Ten-spined Stickleback

The Nine-spined Stickleback rarely exceeds 5cm in length, many specimens never even attaining this size. In a few exceptional habitats it is said to reach 10cm occasionally. It is, in fact, the smallest freshwater fish in the British Isles.

The body is laterally compressed and more slender than that of its three-spined relative. At first, each species could be confused with the other, but the delicate, slender, caudal peduncle and general greeny-gold colour of the Nine-spined Stickleback are characteristic. It is also known as the Ten-spined Stickleback, but in our experience the great majority of individuals possess nine spines – though the number can vary from 8–12. In fact, individuals with eight dorsal spines are actually commoner than those with ten. The spines are erectile, but much shorter than those of the Three-spined Stickleback, and are offset alternately to the left and right like the teeth of a saw. Posterior to the spines, the dorsal fin has 9–12 soft rays. The pectoral fin has nine or ten soft rays. The pelvic fins have two short erectile spines and 0–2 soft rays, while the anal fin has one very small fixed spine. The caudal fin has 12 or 13 rays.

The lateral line organs are open to the exterior as in the Three-spined Stickleback, and, also common to both species, there is no permanent duct connecting the swimbladder with the oesophagus. There are 32–34 vertebrae.

The body is scaleless and usually naked, but in Europe forms with small lateral plates, usually on the posterior body only, and inconspicuous keels along the caudal peduncle have been recorded in places. In addition, fully plated forms with up to 34 plates occur in Asia and North America. Plateless forms are sometimes classified as *Pungitius pungitius laevis* and plated forms as *Pungitius pungitius pungitius*. Both occur in the British Isles, the former mostly

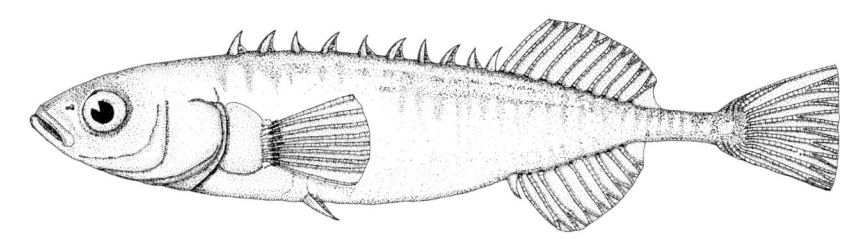

Fig. 111 Nine-spined Stickleback (from Maitland 1972b).

Fig. 112 An adult female Nine-spined Stickleback (Heather Angel).

in the north and west of Scotland and Ireland. A form which is deficient in pelvic spines also occurs, but mainly it seems in the central North American sector of its distribution, though it has been reported in Ireland.

In colour, the back and flanks are usually a greeny-olive gold with dark blotches or bars here and there and also many small dots. The ventral surface is pale. At spawning time, the male develops a sootiness around the head deepening to jet black on the throat and pectoral region, while the pelvic spines become a brilliant white and the rays a pale blue.

The Nine-spined Stickleback has a circumpolar distribution, though it appears to be absent from Iceland. Thus, it is found in the shallow waters of lakes and rivers and in many types of small water bodies in northern, central and eastern Europe, northern Asia and northern North America (including the Pacific coast) often in coastal brackish waters of low salinity.

This species is indigenous to the British Isles where it is not so widespread or common as the Three-spined Stickleback, but it can be abundant locally. The two species often co-exist, but the Nine-spined Stickleback tends to conceal itself in thickly vegetated shallows, often only a few centimetres deep. Due to its lower oxygen requirements, it may be better suited to this type of habitat than the Three-spined Stickleback. In captivity, the two species may hybridise but this does not appear to happen in the wild. In Scotland, the Nine-spined Stickleback is found mostly in low-lying coastal areas on the west side of the country, including the Western Isles and Inner Hebrides. It is very widespread in Ireland and there are many inland populations in central and southern England. It is not as tolerant of saline conditions as the Three-spined Stickleback and does not occur in full sea water around the British Isles, though some North American populations over winter in the sea. However, under laboratory conditions, it can be acclimated to full-strength sea water over a period of several days. It has been suggested that, as in the Three-spined Stickleback, there is a correlation between the presence of lateral plates and keels and a sea going behaviour on the one hand, and between platelessness and a freshwater existence on the other.

Spawning takes place from spring to midsummer in fresh or brackish water. In some waters there may be a pre-spawning migration to suitable spawning habitats. The male constructs a nest made of plant fragments suspended among vegetation, usually near the bottom but occasionally actually on the bottom. In aquaria, the same male has been observed building both

Table 48 Food of Nine-spined Sticklebacks in the River Birkett (after Hynes 1950), as percentage occurrence.

Stomach contents	River Birkett
Algae	+
Macrophytes	1
Molluscs	
Snails	1
Pea shells	3
Others	+
Worms	3
Crustaceans	
Cladocerans	11
Ostracods	7
Copepods	22
Malacostracans	19
Insects	
Mayfly larvae	1
Bugs	+
Beetle larvae	+
Caddis larvae	1
Midge larvae	17
Midge pupae	7
Other insects	1
Other invertebrates	+
Fish	
Stickleback eggs & young	1
Terrestrial organisms	
Spiders	+
Bugs	2
Flies	1
Caterpillars	+
Others	+
Detritus	1
NUMBER OF FISH EXAMINED	656

suspended and bottom nests. The nests may vary in shape and is bound together by sticky secretions as with the Three-spined Stickleback, but unlike the nest of the latter, this one is also glued inside by the male. He does this by exuding a sticky thread posteriorly, catching it in his mouth and pushing his way into the nest with it. Eventually a permanent tunnel is forced through the nest into which the female is induced to enter and lay her eggs. She is attracted by the erratic, zig-zag dance executed by the male in a head-down position. The male then passes through the tunnel, fertilises the eggs and drives the now potentially dangerous female away. Males have also been observed inducing females to spawn before a nest has been built. In this case the nest is constructed afterwards around the fertilised eggs. Usually about 20–30 eggs, each 1.0–1.2mm in diameter, are laid at a time in a single adhesive clump. Each female lays around 80 eggs altogether but not necessarily in the same male's nest. However, a nest may contain a much larger number of eggs than this, sometimes several hundreds, due to several females laying there in succession.

The male guards the nest aggressively, keeping it tidy and fanning regularly to ensure a supply of oxygen to the eggs, which hatch in 6–10 days at normal water temperatures. He then removes the empty egg cases. Fry that fall out of the nest are retrieved by the male, who may then build a 'nursery' for them out of vegetation above the nest.

Abnormal courtship behaviour has been observed when there has been a high density of males at spawning time. Some males that have not become sufficiently dominant to hold a spawning territory assume a 'pseudo-female' role by not colouring up and by competing with females at a nest. They may be courted by a male but may also apparently try to enter the nest and fertilise eggs when the male is spawning with a real female.

A few days after hatching, as with the Three-spined Stickleback, the fry swim erratically to the surface, and if they can pierce the surface film gulp in air to inflate their swimbladders. The connection between the oesophagus and the bladder atrophies shortly afterwards. The fry are relatively small and reach a length of about 0.5–0.75cm after two weeks, when they disperse individually, not remaining in feeding shoals like the fry of Three-spined Sticklebacks. This behavioural difference is very noticeable in aquaria where young Nine-spined Sticklebacks quickly take up individual positions, only bunching when chasing after food items.

The Nine-spined Stickleback is more or less an annual species, usually spawning only once. However, fish of 2–3.5 years of age (as determined from their otoliths) have been found in the wild. Growth virtually ceases when fish become mature at the end of their first year, though some may not mature until their second year. In captivity, they can live for 2–3 years, reaching lengths of 5–7cm.

The diet of this species is similar to that of the Three-spined Stickleback, but rarely includes plant material. It consists mainly of small invertebrates, particularly crustaceans and midge larvae, and, seasonally, the eggs and larvae of its own species.

The main material value of the Nine-spined Stickleback to humans is as a forage species for larger predatory fish, which themselves are harvested commercially or caught by anglers. However, like the Three-spined Stickleback, this species has been harvested commercially when occurring in very large numbers, yielding half a gallon of oil to the 'bushel' (i.e. 61ml per litre). They are subject to heavy predation by birds as well as fish in some habitats. Their behaviour when confronted by a fish predator is said to be rather different from the Three-spined species, for whereas the latter may boldly face up to the attack, the Nine-spined Stickleback will slink away into cover. It is frequently infested by parasites, though believed to be rather less vulnerable to infestations of *Schistocephalus solidus*, the tapeworm so prevalent in populations of the Three-spined Stickleback.

Although they make extremely interesting aquarium fish, especially as a contrast to the Three-spined Stickleback, their use as a laboratory animal has not been as extensive as the latter, although the spine-deficient form of the Nine-spined Stickleback in North America has attracted much interest and research.

20
Cods

The cods (family Gadidae), which includes such well known members as Haddock *Melanogrammus aeglefinus*, Whiting *Merlangius merlangus* and Saithe *Pollachius virens* are almost exclusively marine, playing an important role in the commercial fisheries of the world, principally in the temperate oceans of the northern hemisphere. A few species are found far up into estuaries but very few actually live and breed in fresh water. There is one such species in Europe.

A characteristic of the cods is the barbel growing downwards from the front of the lower jaw. The head is large, as are the eyes, and the mouth has numerous fine teeth. The positioning of the pelvic fins anterior to the pectoral fins is also a distinctive feature.

Burbot *Lota lota* (Linnaeus 1758)
Barbolt, Coney Fish, Eel Pout, Freshwater Cod, Ling, Rabbit Fish

The Burbot, the only freshwater member of the cod family in Europe, strongly resembles a number of marine species including the deep sea Ling *Molva molva* and the coastal and shallow water rocklings, of which there are several species. However, the Burbot is found only in fresh water and is the only fish there to possess the family characteristic of a long single barbel below the chin. In some descriptions of this species in the past the presence of three barbels is mentioned, but there is actually only one, the other two 'barbels' referred to being just raised extensions of the nostrils. The alternative name of Eel Pout implies no connection with the marine pouts – also members of the cod family – but is purely coincidental, pout being a corruption of the Old English term meaning 'fat', i.e. the Fat Eel – a good description of this slimy fish, which squirms like an eel when caught.

Adult Burbot are usually some 30–60cm in length, but in parts of Europe and North America may grow up to 120cm in length and 32kg in weight. In England, most of the Burbot caught in past years were some 30–50cm and 1.3–6kg in weight. There is no rod-caught record, for the species is probably extinct now and also it would be illegal to catch it without a permit from the Nature Conservancy Council.

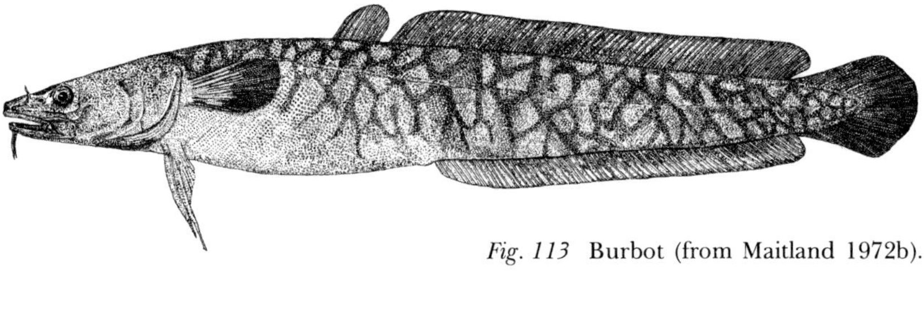

Fig. 113 Burbot (from Maitland 1972b).

The head of the Burbot, with its large mouth and lateral eyes, is flat and the anterior part of the body almost cylindrical becoming laterally compressed near the anus. Burbot could be initially confused with one of the freshwater catfishes, especially the Danube Catfish, but the numerous long barbels of the latter species soon distinguishes them. There are no teeth on the tongue, maxillary or palatine bones, but dense rows of small recurved and pointed teeth on the premaxillary (lower jaw) and vomer bones.

There are two dorsal fins, the first is short with 10–14 rays and the second long (with 60–79 rays) almost reaching to the rounded caudal fin. The anal fin (with 66–70 rays) is also long and stretches ventrally from just posterior of the second dorsal fin to the end of the short caudal peduncle. The pectoral fins have 17–21 rays and the pelvic fins, which are thoracic, and actually slightly anterior to the pectorals, have 5–8 rays. They also possess taste buds and the long first and second rays, which are separated from the fin membrane, are used as feelers. The caudal fin has 36–40 rays.

There are 7–12 gill rakers, 7 or 8 branchiostegals, a long air bladder and 56–63 vertebrae. The number of pyloric caecae varies greatly and ranges from 31–150. The scales, which are very small, are cycloid and deeply buried in the skin.

The colour of the Burbot is appropriate to its habit of remaining concealed until dusk before venturing forth to forage. The head, back, dorsal and caudal fins are yellow-olive to olive-green with dark marbling, the colours and patterning becoming slightly paler on the sides. The marbling is darker and more distinct on young fish. The underside is off-white to yellowish. The flesh is white.

The Burbot has a northern circumpolar distribution and is found in clean lakes and rivers throughout much of northern, west and central Europe and in northern Asia and North America. In the British Isles, where it now has the status of a protected species, its original distribution was restricted to the larger rivers of eastern England from County Durham south to the Great Ouse system, where the last one was recorded in 1972. It has not been seen in this country since then, in spite of a keen watch being maintained, and the fear is that it is now extinct. Its decline and possible extinction may be due to a number of factors including loss of habitat and pollution.

Spawning takes place during the colder parts of the year from November to March, when the water temperatures are from 0.5–4.0°C. Local spawning migrations may take place into suitable spawning habitats – usually shallow water 2–3m in depth with a clean substrate of sand or gravel. Male Burbot are usually first in the area and when the females arrive, spawning (which always occurs at night) is a communal process, up to 20 or so individuals forming a 'writhing ball' and releasing eggs and milt. The fertilised eggs (some 1.2–1.8mm in diameter) are pale yellow and semipelagic. The females are very fecund, each laying about 500,000 eggs per kg of body weight, which means that, like marine Cod, large females can produce millions of eggs at each spawning. Some 200 day-degrees are required for hatching, so that at normal winter temperatures a period of 40–70 days is involved. However, at a steady temperature of 4.4°C the eggs hatch in 4–5 weeks. In European waters the young fry usually appear in the spring. On hatching the larvae float to the surface. They are described as having their heads 'bent queerly downwards' (i.e. like the larvae of their close relative, the Ling).

FRESHWATER FISHES

Table 49 Food of Burbot in Lake Superior, North America (after Bailey 1972), as percentage volume, and in Lake Vanern, Sweden (after Nilsson 1979), as percentage occurrence.

Stomach contents	Lake Superior	Lake Vanern
Molluscs	0.2	–
Crustaceans		
Isopods	+	–
Mysis	21.5	19.1
Pontoporeia	12.1	6.1
Pallasea	–	15.2
Gammaracanthus	–	7.0
Unidentified amphipods	–	2.6
Insects		
Stonefly larvae	+	–
Beetle larvae	+	–
Caddis larvae	+	–
Fly larvae	+	–
Other insects	+	–
Other invertebrates	+	–
Fish		
Charr	4.2	–
Whitefish	10.2	47.0*
Smelt	13.6	47.0*
Stickleback	1.5	–
Trout-perch	0.3	–
Sculpin	16.9	–
Unidentified fish	16.0	47.0*
Fish eggs	2.6	–
Detritus	0.8	–
NUMBER OF FISH EXAMINED	349	?

*This value is shared among the items indicated

Young Burbot grow rapidly, attaining a length of 9–12cm within the first year and 22–23cm by the end of the second. They start to become mature at about 32–34cm, the males usually maturing for the first time when they are 3+ years of age and the females at 4+. They normally live for 10–15 years.

Burbot require clean well-oxygenated water with an oxygen level of 5–7mg/l – rather less than the requirements of trout, Minnow, Stone Loach and Bullhead, with which they often co-exist. They are bottom-dwelling fish, spending the day in concealment under stones, overhanging banks, etc. (behaviour that at one time earned them the names of Coney or Rabbit Fish – terms known to Isaac Walton), emerging in the evening to forage for food. However, they will take food items which happen to come close enough to their hideout in daylight. Their eyes are well adapted to night vision, having a ratio of one cone cell to 240 rod cells (cf. Pike, a daylight predator, with a ratio of 1:9).

Young Burbot feed on invertebrates, especially molluscs, crustaceans (e.g. water lice and small crayfish) and insect larvae, whereas older fish eat other fish and fish spawn, crayfish and frogs. Some authorities regard the presence of Burbot in salmonid waters as very damaging and one in fact goes so far as to advise that they should be eradicated altogether in the nursery reaches of salmon rivers – a factor that should be taken into account should any attempts be made to reintroduce the Burbot to the British Isles. The same authority, however, recommends small Burbot as first class bait for other predatory fishes.

Burbot are very hardy and easy to transport alive. They are popular with ice anglers in Scandinavia and North America, but usually not regarded as a top-class sporting fish elsewhere. They are the basis of several important commercial fisheries in Europe and North America, based on nets, traps and night lines. In England, they were at one time so plentiful in fenland rivers that, as well as being sold in large numbers at local markets, they were sometimes used to feed pigs. Their flesh is very palatable when baked, fried, steamed or stewed – tasting rather like that of the marine Monk Fish *Squatina squatina* – and generally supposed to be highly nutritious. The liver, like that of other members of the cod family, is rich in vitamins A and D and considered a delicacy in some countries when smoked or canned or cooked with the whole fish.

Burbot are easy to keep in aquaria provided an adequate source of live food can be maintained. However, they have a tendency to grow rather large and require larger and larger accommodation. A specimen brought back from Lake Superior in Canada (where it was captured at a length of 3cm) by one of the authors to rear for experimental purposes became hand tame and lived for over 13 years by which time it had reached a length of about 50cm and a weight of 2kg.

Burbot are well known as the intermediate hosts of the huge tapeworm *Diphyllobothrium lateum* which can thrive in the human intestine if the fish is eaten raw or only partially cooked.

21

Bass

The family Serranidae – the sea basses (sometimes called sea perch) – occur in the coastal waters of most seas of the world, both temperate and tropical. Though the majority of the species are marine, a few are found in brackish and sometimes in fresh waters. Some are anadromous. In North America, one anadromous species, the Striped Bass *Dicentrarchus saxatilis* has been successfully established in many fresh waters as a game fish. They are characteristically well built, laterally compressed deep-bodied fish with sharp spiny anterior dorsal fins and ctenoid scales. The mouth has numerous pointed teeth usually arranged in bands. The pre-opercular bone is serrated. Both the dorsal and the anal fins have sharp spiny rays anteriorly and soft rays posteriorly.

All species are very predatory and feed on a variety of bottom invertebrates and fish. They are important commercially and to sport fishermen in many countries. The family contains over 400 species. Only two species enter fresh water regularly in Europe and only one of these occurs around the British Isles.

Sea Bass *Dicentrarchus labrax* (Linnaeus 1758)
Bass, King of the Mullet, Salmon Bass, School Bass, Sea Perch, White Mullet
This attractive large fish matures at a length of around 30–40cm, but specimens much larger than this are common and it can grow up to a length of

Fig. 114 A juvenile Sea Bass (Heather Angel).

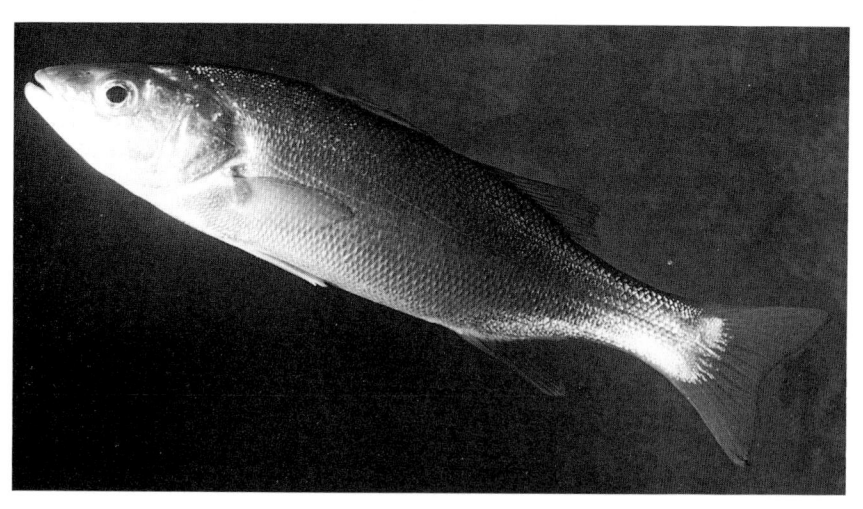

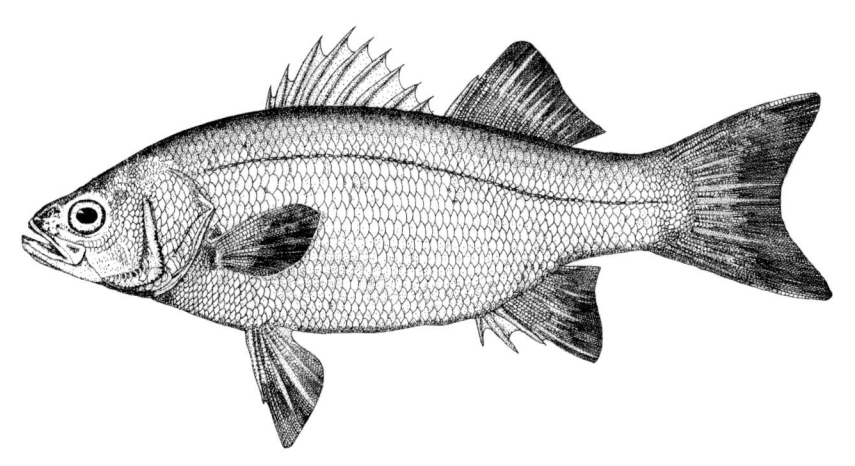

Fig. 115 Sea Bass (from Maitland 1972b).

100cm and a weight of about 9kg. The current British rod-caught record fish was caught off Eddystone Reef in 1975 and weighed 8.334kg. The Irish record stands at 7.75kg for a fish caught in 1977 in Whiting Bay, Ardmore.

The Sea Bass is a strongly built streamlined fish characterised by its two dorsal fins which are quite separate though one is directly behind the other, sometimes almost touching. The head is well developed with a large mouth and eyes and is largely covered by scales. The lower edge of the pre-operculum has a series of downward and forward pointing teeth. The large ctenoid scales are well developed over the whole body and there is a strong lateral line along which are some 66–70 scales. Curiously enough, the scales between the eyes are cycloid. The ctenoid scales can be used for ageing.

The first dorsal fin has eight or nine strong spiny rays while the second fin is softer with one spine followed by 12 or 13 rays. The pectoral and pelvic fins are fairly normal with soft rays but the anal fin has three spines followed by 10–11 soft rays. There are 25–26 vertebrae. Much of the head and back is greyish-green or bluish in colour shading to bright silver along the sides and silvery white on the belly. Small fish are often slightly spotted but these spots disappear in adults except for a dusky patch on each gill cover.

The Sea Bass is mainly a marine species and occurs all along the coastal waters of Europe from southern Norway to Spain and well into the Mediterranean Sea. They occur all round the British Isles but are most common in southern and western areas. As well as inhabiting coastal waters they come into brackish areas and often come well up large estuaries into fresh water and even into the lower reaches of large rivers. First-year bass may be found in estuaries and tidal marsh pools, moving into slightly deeper water during the winter.

Along the coasts they are found in a variety of habitats ranging from sandy and rocky shores to muddy, often highly silted, areas. When they are found offshore at any time it is usually in the vicinity of submerged reefs and they have been caught at depths down to 60m.

They seem to come into very shallow seas and into fresh waters during the summer months, and it is interesting that the species is also attracted to any

Table 50 Food of Sea Bass around Ireland: young, off Youghal; adults, various localities (after Kennedy & Fitzmaurice 1972b), as percentage occurrence.

Stomach contents	Young	Adult
Molluscs	3	2
Worms	9	3
Crustaceans		
Isopods	–	8
Shrimps	88	21
Prawns	–	5
Mysids	34	1
Gammarids	6	–
Corophium	13	–
Crabs	–	66
Other invertebrates	–	1
Fish		
Herring & Sprat	–	8
Sea Trout	–	1
Sand-eels	–	6
Flounder & Plaice	–	15
Brill	–	1
Blenny	–	1
Butterfish	–	1
Sea Stickleback	–	1
Sea Scorpion	–	1
Unidentified fish	3	4
NUMBER OF FISH EXAMINED	32	103

warm-water effluents which may occur in the vicinity. Sea Bass often occur in large schools, which swim very actively during summer seeking out their prey. To some extent the species is a migratory one, often appearing in the North Sea during summer, having moved in from the south-west on a feeding migration. Data from tagging experiments suggest that adults may return to the same summer feeding areas in successive years. Usually the smaller and younger fish appear first to be followed later by larger ones. A reverse migration takes place southwards prior to spawning in the autumn. This takes the fish away from shallow waters and may involve journeys of several hundred kilometres. There is evidence for geographically distinct sub-populations.

The main spawning period of the Sea Bass appears to be from February to May off southern England and perhaps as late as June further north. Ripe fish gather in deep inshore waters and lay large numbers of eggs (200,000–600,000 per kg of female body weight). These are clear (about 1.25–1.5mm in diameter) and pelagic and contain 2–3 yellow oil globules. The early larvae, which are also pelagic, hatch in 4–8 days at a length of about 2mm.

The first post larvae can be found in estuaries in July and August, when they are 15–30mm in length. They reach a length of about 3–5cm by their first autumn and some 16–18cm by the second. They probably start to breed at 4–6 years of age at lengths of about 35–40cm, and they may continue to breed up to the age of 20 years or more. Some fish are known to be long-lived, and specimens of 30 years have been recorded. Females grow slightly faster than males and live longer.

The Sea Bass is entirely carnivorous and the larvae feed on protozoans and small planktonic crustaceans at first. The adults feed mainly on invertebrates (particularly crustaceans) and small fish (especially Herring, Sprat and sand-eels). Squids are another popular item of diet.

The Sea Bass is an important commercial species and usually exploited wherever available, although many previously abundant stocks have now declined. It is also a very popular fish with sea anglers and affords exciting angling in some estuaries and at many places around the costs of the British Isles. In the south-west of Britain and in southern Ireland it is heavily exploited both commercially and by sport anglers, with the result that a minimum size limit of 32cm has been imposed through an EC regulation in 1987. Recent research, however, has indicated that there is good evidence for raising this to 38cm and for the establishment of designated nursery areas where fishing will be illegal or very restricted. Such areas could often be part of more general estuarine or marine nature reserves. It is an extremely good fish to eat with an abundance of firm white flaky flesh and a good flavour. During the winter months it may sell at twice the price of salmon. Young fish usually do well in captivity, in fresh or salt water and are very attractive in aquaria, fed on a diet of live foods.

22
Sunfish

Originating in the fresh waters of North America, the sunfishes of the family Centrarchidae include 10 genera and some 30 species (many of them commonly called bass of different types). A number of these species are now widely distributed within Europe and in other parts of the world, including central and southern Africa, where the Largemouth Bass, originally introduced into impoundments, is now common in many river systems. Six species are known to be established in Europe and two, possibly three, of these occur in the British Isles. Their extensive redistribution by humans is the result of the sporting value and palatability of the larger species and the popularity of the smaller species with aquarists and pondkeepers. Because of their habit of taking prey from just below the surface, sunfish can provide good sport for fly-fishing anglers.

The sunfishes resemble the perches in shape and in possessing a double dorsal fin, the anterior portion of which carries well developed sharp spines, but their scales lack the characteristic roughness of those of perch. Most of the sunfishes are small to medium-sized fish, but the Largemouth Bass can attain a length of over 80cm.

The interesting breeding behaviour of the sunfishes has been well studied. Spawning usually takes place in late spring or early summer, the males excavating a circular hollow in the sand or gravel of the bottom. A period of courtship follows before the eggs are laid in the nest. The male then keeps guard over the nest, fanning the eggs regularly. After hatching, the fry lie in the nest still attended by the male for several days. This parental attention may continue for some time even after the fry have left the nest. Warm-water conditions are essential for good fry survival.

Identification

To people unfamiliar with this family, the species of fish in the Centrarchidae have a superficial similarity which is at first misleading. In fact, as far as the species occurring in the British Isles are concerned, each has several distinguishing characters, which are brought out in the following key.

1. More than 50 scales along the lateral line. Dorsal fins almost separated by a notch. Length of body more than 3 times its greatest length.
 LARGEMOUTH BASS
 Less than 50 scales along the lateral line. Dorsal fins continuous. Length of the body less than 3 times its greatest depth. **2.**

2. Less than 4 spines in the anal fin. Operculum ending in a convex flap which is black in colour. Gill rakers short, the longest shorter than the diameter of the eye. **PUMPKINSEED**
 More than 4 spines in the anal fin. Operculum ending in two flat

points, which are not black. Gill rakers long, the longest longer than
the diameter of the eye. **ROCK BASS**

Largemouth Bass *Micropterus salmoides* (Lacepede 1802)
Black Bass, Green Bass

The Largemouth Bass, sometimes called the Black Bass, is the largest member of the North American sunfish family and probably the most important. It is one of the six species of this family now established in Europe, two, possibly three, of them in the British Isles. It can be readily separated from the other two members of the family by the key given above. It could, of course, be confused with its close relative the Smallmouth Bass *Micropterus dolomieu*, which has also been introduced into the British Isles at various times in the past, but which has not, so far as is known, become established. However, in the Largemouth Bass the jaw extends back to behind the eye, whereas in the Smallmouth Bass it does not extend back further than the middle of the eye.

Although reaching a maximum length of about 83cm and 6.4kg most adult fish are some 20–50cm. The North American and world record for this species stands at 10.1kg. In the British Isles most of the fish seen so far have been between 20 and 38cm.

The body is laterally compressed and shaped rather like that of the Perch, though not so high. There is a protruding lower jaw, as befits such a renowned predator. The teeth, which occur not only on the jaws but also on the palatine and vomer bones, are small, even-sized and numerous and there are similar teeth also on the lower pharynx, arranged in long brush-like pads. The body is well covered with strong ctenoid scales of which there are 60–68 along the lateral line.

The dorsal fins are well developed, the first having 9–10 sharp spines and the second one spine and 12–13 soft rays. The pectoral fins have 13–16 rays and the pelvics, which are thoracic, one spine and 5–6 rays. The anal fin has three spines and 10–11 soft rays and the caudal fin eight rays.

The upper head and back are dark olive and the sides a pale olive-green, often with a yellowish tinge. The belly is whitish. A wide irregular band of single dark blotches runs along the flanks from head to tail. The dorsal and caudal fins are dark green to olive and the anal fin pale green to olive.

The Largemouth Bass is native to North America, where it is found in streams and rivers, ponds and lakes. Because of its fine sporting and eating qualities, the species has been widely introduced to the waters of many tem-

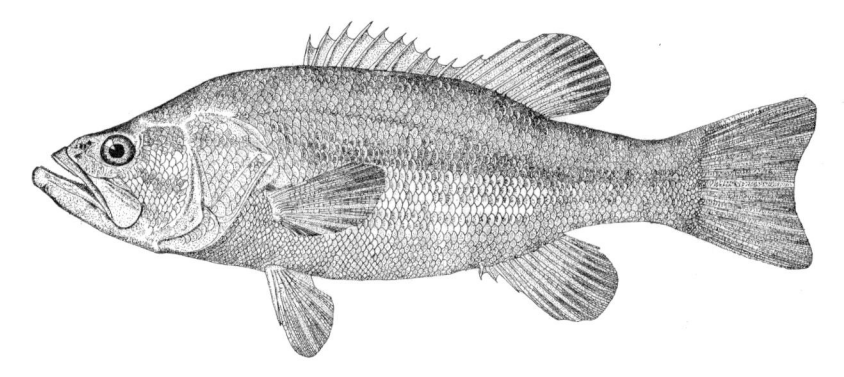

Fig. 116 Largemouth Bass (from Maitland 1972b).

Fig. 117 A Largemouth Bass (Department of Fisheries & Oceans, Canada).

perate and tropical countries where it has often succeeded in establishing itself. It was first introduced to Europe towards the end of the last century and is now firmly established locally in a number of countries in the south. In the British Isles, however, in spite of a series of introductions (often along with the Smallmouth Bass) made in north-west Britain and elsewhere, it is only in the extreme south of England that it is known to have become established, but only at two sites. At one of these sites the subsequent introduction of Pike and Perch may have adversely affected the bass population. At the other site, Largemouth Bass is the only predatory species present and reported to be flourishing. It appears that its early sponsors did not fully appreciate the seasonal high water temperature requirements of both species, needed to ensure successful reproduction and growth of the young.

Spawning takes place from March to July, when the water temperatures reach 16–18°C. A territorial male clears and excavates a nest site about 60–90cm in diameter and, depending on the hardness of the substrate, 3–21cm deep, in some 20–120cm of water. The nest site is usually near the shore in reedy areas or under water lilies in still or very slow-flowing water. The males are very aggressive in defence of their territories and in courtship. The spawning act is repeated many times at short intervals and each female produces some 900–3200 eggs per kg of body weight. The eggs are pale yellow to amber in colour and 1.5–1.7mm in diameter.

The eggs are adhesive and lie at the bottom of the nest, which is guarded and fanned regularly by the male. All other fish, including males and females of his own species, are chased away, though he is not above eating a few of his own eggs from time to time. The eggs hatch in 3–5 days and the emerging fry are about 3mm in length. They stay within the nest until the yolk sac has been absorbed in 6–7 days time, after which they start to swim freely and move about in shoals. At this stage the young bass are pale green in colour and the broods may stay together for several weeks, guarded by the male, who gradually loses interest and deserts them.

Table 51 Food of young Largemouth Bass in Lake Opinicon, Canada (after Keast & Eadie 1985), as percentage volume.

Stomach contents	Small 0+	Large 0+	1+
Crustaceans			
Cladocerans	39	4	2
Copepods	4	1	–
Isopods	–	3	–
Amphipods	7	20	–
Decapods	–	–	18
Insects			
Mayfly larvae	5	36	2
Dragonfly larvae	1	10	3
Caddis larvae	–	–	–
Midge larvae & pupae	17	5	–
Other insects	15	1	1
Fish	12	30	74
NUMBER OF FISH EXAMINED	94	88	95

Little is known about the growth of this species in the British Isles but at one site shoals of young bass can be seen. The average size here is reported to be 15cm, with a maximum length of 40.6cm (1.8kg). In its native environment, young Largemouth Bass may reach 5–12cm by their first autumn. The males mature in 3–4 years and the females in 4–5 years. They can live up to 15 years of age.

Largemouth Bass are voracious predators, eating mostly aquatic invertebrates when young, but soon moving on to large invertebrates such as crayfish and especially to fish, frogs and other large organisms. At one of the British sites the bass co-exist with carp, Roach, Gudgeon and Tench, but appear to prey mostly on Roach (which are also used here as live bait by anglers). To capture their prey the bass lie in ambush at the edge of thick clumps of vegetation or under a log or overhanging bank. They take their

Fig. 118 A Pumpkinseed (Department of Fisheries & Ocean, Canada).

Fig. 119 Pumpkinseed

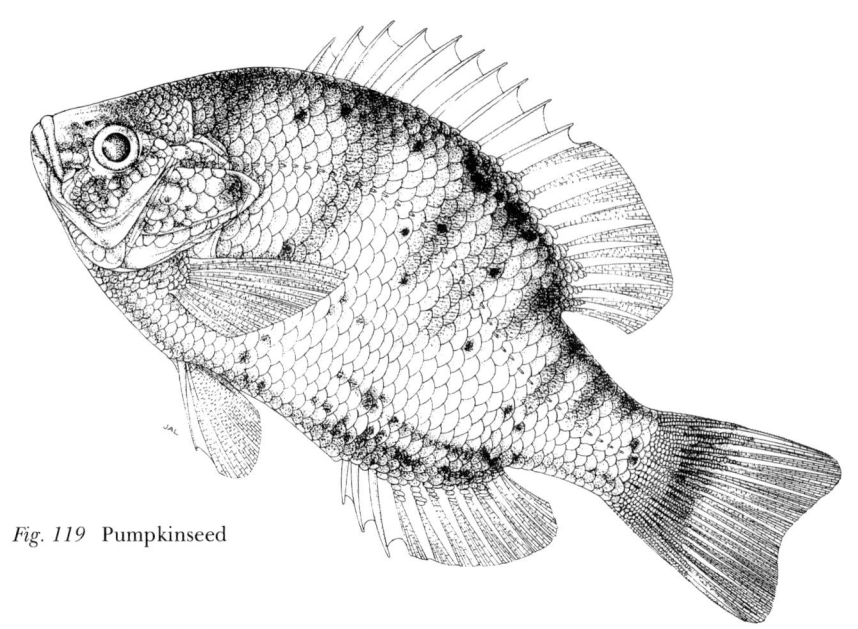

prey (and anglers' lures) by dashing upwards, and this explains the logic behind the use by anglers of the floating plug, which seems to be the most effective way of catching this species. When hooked they fight strongly, often jumping right out of the water.

The flesh is white, flaky and delicious to eat and the combination of this and their sporting quality has resulted in this fish being regarded as an elite angler's fish in many warm countries, where their fisheries are coveted like those for salmonids in cooler climates.

Pumpkinseed *Lepomis gibbosus* (Linnaeus 1758)
Common Sunfish, Sun Bass, Yellow Sunfish

The Pumpkinseed is a colourful little fish which, in its native environment, grows to a length of 15–20cm. Larger individuals do occur, however, and the North American (and world) angling record stands at 520gm. In the British Isles it usually reaches only about 15cm and the British rod-caught record, from Highgate Pond in London in 1977, is currently 74.4gm.

In shape, the body is high and laterally compressed, generally resembling that of a small Perch, but unlike the latter the first and second dorsal fins are joined to make one long fin. The mouth is smaller than that of the Perch and there are patches of sharp, hooked, brush-like teeth on the jaws, with a single row on the vomer bone. There are no palatine teeth, but there are pads of teeth on the lower pharynx.

The dorsal fin consists of two parts, with 9–11 spines anteriorly and 10–11 soft rays posteriorly. The pectoral fins have 12–14 rays and the pelvics, which are thoracic, have one spine anteriorly followed by five soft rays. The anal fin has three spines in front followed by 8–12 soft rays and the caudal fin some 19 soft rays. There are 28 or 29 vertebrae and seven or eight very long py-

Table 52 Food of Pumpkinseed in Lake Opinicon, Canada (after Keast & Walsh 1968), as percentage volume.

Stomach contents	Lake Opinicon
Molluscs	
Snails	2.3
Mussels	5.0
Crustaceans	
Cladocerans	0.7
Ostracods	0.7
Copepods	2.3
Isopods	3.3
Amphipods	7.0
Decapods	2.3
Insects	
Mayfly larvae	1.3
Dragonfly larvae	21.3
Caddis larvae	12.0
Midge larvae & pupae	31.7
Other insects	2.3
Other invertebrates	0.6
NUMBER OF FISH EXAMINED	103

loric caecae. The body is covered in strong ctenoid scales of which there are 35–47 along the lateral line.

The colours are variable, according to age, sex, season and background and are often bright. The upper head and back are greeny bronze or olive merging to dull gold or greeny blue on the sides, overlaid by an even but variable light brown to black freckling, which at times, according to the mood of the fish, forms into a number of vertical bands with some isolated freckles in between. There may be an overall iridescence. The chest and belly are yellow and the gill covers opalescent blue to green with brownish-yellow to orange flecks. The iridescence varies with both light direction and intensity. There is a conspicuous black spot, which may be edged with red, on the rear edge of the brightly coloured gill covers. The colours intensify at spawning times in both sexes, the vertical bands becoming more distinct in males. Young fish are duller and are characterised by having 10–11 conspicuous vertical bands on the almost translucent sides of the body. The black spot on the gill cover is absent, but there is a green iridescent area on the lower gill cover. At this stage they can be confused with Perch, Pikeperch, Ruffe and Largemouth Bass of the same size.

The Pumpkinseed is native to the warm temperate areas of eastern North America, including southern Canada, but was introduced into Europe towards the end of the last century. It is an excellent aquarium and pond fish and it was probably for the latter purpose that it was brought originally to Europe, where it is now firmly and widely established in the warmer areas. Although a popular aquarium fish in the British Isles, it appears currently to be established at only a few sites, all in southern England, but could be present elsewhere for it is being deliberately spread to other waters. It appears that none of the British populations has ever been studied.

Spawning begins when water temperatures reach about 20°C and normally lasts from May to October. The male selects a site in shallow water and hollows out a depression some 10–40cm across (usually about twice the length of the male involved) and 5–30cm deep, depending on the local substrate.

These nests are often in the vicinity of weed beds and a number may be close together. There is considerable courtship display and eventually the couple start a sequence of continuous twisting and repeated spawning in the nest, interrupted periodically by the male chasing off neighbouring males who have come too close. The females, according to size, may produce 600–5000 eggs, which are clear and about 1.0mm in diameter. After spawning, the male guards the nest, fanning it assiduously until the eggs hatch in about 2–5 days. The young lie in the bottom of the nest for a day or so until the yolk sac is absorbed but then disperse and the male loses interest. The male may then use the same nest to raise further broods, mating with the same or different females.

In North America, the young fish may attain a length of 2–8cm by the end of their first summer. A sample of first year Pumpkinseeds collected by one of the authors in October from a lake in north Somerset measured 3–4cm in length. They become mature in 2–3 years and can live up to nine years of age.

The preferred habitat of Pumpkinseeds is areas of thick vegetation in shallow water in lakes or slow-flowing rivers, where they feed on small aquatic invertebrates, small fish and fish eggs.

Because of their well-flavoured flesh, and despite their small size, they are quite an important 'pan fish' in North America, where they are cropped by both anglers and commercial fishermen, using nets and traps. In the English coarse fisheries where they occur they are not popular with anglers, who claim that they attack other species which then become infected with fungus. This aggressive behaviour has been noted by both the authors who have kept adult Pumpkinseeds along with other species in aquaria. However, in spite of their unpopularity they are unfortunately being redistributed in southern England.

In Europe as a whole they have little significance other than as aquarium and pond fish. They certainly make an interesting aquarium fish when kept on their own and can readily be induced to build a nest and spawn in an aquarium.

Fig. 120 A Rock Bass (Department of Fisheries & Oceans, Canada).

SUNFISH

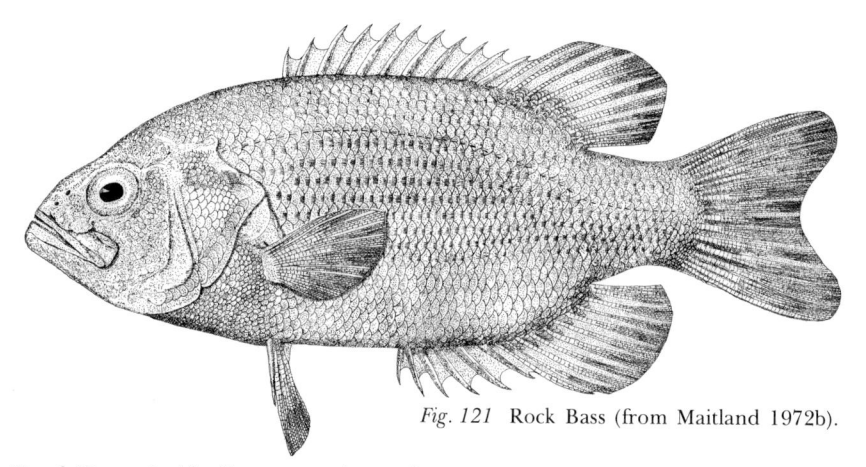

Fig. 121 Rock Bass (from Maitland 1972b).

Rock Bass *Ambloplites rupestris* (Rafinesque-Schmaltz 1817)
Goggle Eye, Redeye Bass

In its native habitats in North America, the Rock Bass reaches maturity at some 15–20cm, but can grow up to 32.5cm, weighing about 1.7kg. The world rod-caught record stands at 1.36kg. When last examined at its only known British site, the largest specimens were about 18cm in length.

In shape, the body is high and markedly flattened laterally – more so than any other members of the family that occur in Europe. Distinguishing features from the other British Centrarchidae are indicated in the above key. The eye is comparatively large with an orange to red iris. There are short fine-pointed teeth on both jaws, and also on the palatine and vomer bones and on the tongue and pharynx.

The first and second parts of the dorsal fin are joined together, the former having 10–12 spines and the latter 10 or 11 soft rays. The pectoral fins have 12–14 rays, whilst the pelvic fins, which are thoracic in position, have one spine and five soft rays. The anal fin has 5–7 (usually six) spines set into a groove, as well as nine or ten soft rays. The caudal fin has 18 rays. The gill rakers are much reduced, with four knob-like rudiments on the upper branch and six on the lower, plus six long gill rakers. The body is well covered by strong ctenoid scales which extend on to the head. There are 39 scales along the lateral line and 29 or 30 vertebrae.

The Rock Bass is not a colourful fish. It is normally greenish-olive to golden-brown on the head, back and sides, with the ventral surface silvery white. The upper parts of the sides bear the darkish blotching or mottling with some, normally indistinct, saddlemarks on the dorsal surface. However, all markings vary in intensity and are most marked at spawning time. The dorsal and caudal fins have brown markings and there is a black blotch of varying intensity at the rear of the operculum.

This species is a native of east and central North America, west of the Appalachian Mountains, but it has been widely redistributed by humans within that continent. In the British Isles there was only one known site where it became established – a disused clay pit in the southern Midlands of England. This population along with several native coarse fish species (including

Table 53 Food of Rock Bass of different lengths in Lake Opinicon, Canada (after Keast & Walsh 1968), as percentage occurrence.

Stomach contents	10–70	Length in millimetres 70–120	120–200
Crustaceans			
Amphipods	30	–	–
Isopods	15	–	–
Crayfish	–	15	++
Insects			
Mayfly larvae	35	35	–
Dragonfly larvae	30	75	++
Caddis larvae	–	35	–
Midge larvae	50	–	–
Other invertebrates	+	–	–
Fish	–	30	–
Terrestrial organisms			
Surface insects	35	–	–
NUMBER OF FISH EXAMINED	?	?	?

Rudd, Roach, Tench and Perch) was flourishing in 1969 but the subsequent unauthorised introductions to predatory Chub and Pike may have led to its extinction. One of the authors failed to find any trace of it in 1987 and local anglers had not seen or heard of it for a number of years. However, it is just possible that the species may still exist there or in other waters if any were transferred in previous years.

In North America, spawning takes place from spring to early summer in still or slow-flowing water, when the water temperatures reach 15–21°C. The male behaves aggressively during courtship and excavates his nest site, which may be as much as 60cm in diameter, on various substrates in shallow water. Other males may nest close by. The adhesive eggs, which are about 2mm in diameter, are laid in clumps. Each female produces between 3000 and 11,000 eggs depending on size, and these may be laid in the nests of several males, while a number of different females may be attracted to lay in the nest of one male. The male guards and fans the nest until hatching and may then continue to guard the fry for a short period.

The eggs hatch in two or three days at water temperatures of about 20°C. The young Rock Bass can reach a size of 2–5cm by the autumn and adults mature in two or three years.

As the name implies, Rock Bass have a preference for deep pools in rocky streams and for shallow areas of lakes where there are rocky areas. They feed on zooplankton and small benthic invertebrates when young, gradually moving to larger invertebrates and small fish (including, at times, their own young) as they grow larger. In North America, they are much sought after by commercial fishermen and anglers.

23

Perch

The perch family (Percidae) consists of six genera and 16 species, 12 of which are found in Europe. The family is distributed widely throughout the northern hemisphere in Europe, Asia and North America. The European Perch has been successfully introduced into Australia and New Zealand. Most of the larger members of the family are familiar to sport and commercial fishermen, particularly the Perch (or Yellow Perch in North America) and Pikeperch, with its close North American relatives the Walleye and Pickerel, and are much sought after. Their flesh is firm, white, flaky and highly palatable.

Some members of the perch family (e.g. the Perch itself) are short and rather thick-set, while others (e.g. Pikeperch) are slim and elongate, but all have the distinctive large sharply spined anterior dorsal fin either separated from or partially joined to a large soft posterior dorsal fin. The body is rough to the touch due to the characteristic large ctenoid scales, which have fine but sharply serrated exposed edges. The opercular bone bears one or more sharp, rear-pointing spiny outgrowths. The mouth is unusually large for the size of the fish and has several rows of teeth. Fishermen have to handle struggling percids with some caution!

The perches are highly predatory in their feeding habits and the larger members of the family are most adept at working as a group, rounding up shoals of small fish which they then catch and eat. Spawning takes place during the spring and summer. In some species, including the Perch, the eggs are laid in long ribbons draped over stones and vegetation.

There is one member of the family which is found regularly in the salt water of the Black and Azov Seas – the Percarina *Percarina demidoffi* – but other species, including Perch and Pikeperch, are found in some places in estuaries and other brackish waters.

Identification

There are three species of this family found within the British Isles and they are readily distinguished from one another by the following key.

1. Dorsal fins separate. More than 9 rays in the anal fin. More than 50 scales along the lateral line. **2.**

    Dorsal fins joined. Less than 9 rays in the anal fin. Less than 50 scales along the lateral line. **RUFFE**

2. Base of the first dorsal fin longer than that of the second. Less than 70 scales along the lateral line. Short teeth only in the mouth. **PERCH**

    Base of the first dorsal fin the same length or shorter than that of the second. More than 70 scales along lateral line. Both long and short teeth present in mouth. **PIKEPERCH**

Perch *Perca fluviatilis* Linnaeus 1758
Barse

The Perch is one of the most familiar and colourful of temperate freshwater fishes. Small Perch could possibly be confused with Ruffe, but the first and second dorsal fins of the Perch are distinctly separate, unlike those of the Ruffe, which are joined to make one fin. Ruffe possess neither the dark vertical bars along the sides nor the dark spot at the rear of the dorsal fin of the Perch, although at times, especially in small specimens, these features may not be very obvious. Of the other percoid fishes in the British Isles, the Pikeperch has separate dorsal fins, but very pale belly fins and an elongate body, while the basses and sunfish have united dorsal fins, the first part always being lower than the second. Detailed ways to separate the three members of the Percidae are given in the key above and in the accompanying illustrations.

The Perch has a deep and laterally compressed body, the maximum depth being just below the beginning of the first dorsal fin. They become progressively and relatively deeper with increasing size and a really large Perch looks almost 'top heavy'; and the term 'fat as Perch' is used by anglers to describe a particularly well conditioned and deep-bodied trout. Structurally, Perch are very advanced fishes, well adapted to life in still or slow-flowing water, but unsuited to living in swift-flowing streams.

The head is small and neat but the gape of the mouth is large. The operculum, which bears scales, ends in a very sharp rear-facing point. The mouth does not extend back as far as the rear of the eye pupil and is edged with many small villiform teeth, which occur also on the dentary, vomer and palatine bones, though the tongue is smooth.

The first dorsal fin has very long sharp 'defensive' spines some 13–17 in number. These make the fish difficult to handle and can inflict quite a deep puncture in the unwary human. However, like the spines of sticklebacks and Ruffe, they do not prevent Perch being a common prey of predatory fish and birds. The second dorsal fin has one or two spines anteriorly followed by 13–17 soft rays. The pectoral fins have 14 rays and the ventral fins, which are thoracic in position, have one spine and five soft rays. The anal fin has two anterior spines and then 8–10 soft rays, while the caudal fin has 17 rays.

The body is well covered with ctenoid scales, which are large and strong and edged with fine spines, giving the fish a rough feeling. There are some 58–68 of these scales along the lateral line and many of them are perforated by the mucus-filled offshoots of the lateral line canal.

There is no connection between the oesophagus and the swimbladder in adults. The stomach is unusual in that it has the form of a large blind ending diverticulum, while there are only three associated pyloric caecae.

The size of adult Perch varies greatly from place to place. In some populations, individuals never attain more than 15cm in length, even after ten or more years of life, while shoals of younger fish of 25–30cm may occur in nearby waters. Populations of stunted Perch are usually those not subjected to pressure from large predatory fish such as Pike, but may also result from the presence of an exceptionally numerous year class, which completely dominates the whole population for a number of years, causing a relative shortage of food and suppressing younger fish. The British rod-caught record stands at 2.523kg for a fish caught in 1985 in a private lake in Kent. The Irish record stands at 2.75kg (caught in Lough Erne in 1946), but even larger fish have been found and some of up to 4.75kg have been recorded from mainland Europe.

The colouration and markings of Perch are variable in that they are subject to rapid changes in intensity according to the emotional state of the individuals. For example, those newly introduced to an aquarium become very pale with their vertical bands hardly discernible, while at the other extreme, wild Perch in the act of pursuing small fish display striking vertical black bands and bright red-orange pelvic, anal and lower caudal fins. This full colouration, unfortunately, rarely seems to persist in captivity. The normal colouration is that the upper head and back are grey to olive-green grading to pale olive on the flanks (sometimes with a silvery sheen), and a yellow-white ventral surface. The vertical bands on the sides, which are so variable in intensity, are 5–8 in number.

The first dorsal fin, with its posterior dark spot, is dark in colour as is the second dorsal and the upper half of the caudal fin – in striking contrast to the brightly coloured pelvic, anal and lower caudal fins. Some populations of rather pale silvery Perch exist. A close-packed shoal of wild Perch, in a bright phase of colouration, is a most impressive sight, when seen through clear water under sunny conditions.

Perch flesh is white, flaky, free from bones and very well flavoured. It is low in fats (c. 1.4%) and high in protein (18.5%) and compares well with that of salmon (17.8, 17.5), trout (0.7, 18.0) and carp (4.8, 15.8) respectively.

Perch occur in lakes and slow-flowing rivers and canals throughout most of Europe as well as in brackish lagoons in the Baltic and in Asia. They have been introduced successfully to Australia and New Zealand. The North American Yellow Perch *Perca flavescens* is very closely related and considered by some to be the same species. The Perch is indigenous to south-eastern England but has been widely redistributed (originally, by humans, for their food value and ease of catching) throughout much of the British Isles, including the Channel Islands and the Isle of Man. However, they have not yet reached the north of Scotland (there is one population in south-east Sutherland), any of the northern isles (Orkney and Shetland), nor the Hebrides,

Fig. 122 Perch (from Maitland 1972b).

except Islay where there is one population. Perch, like Pike, can survive for a long time out of water, especially in cool weather, and this has been an important factor in the history of their redistribution by humans.

Perch spawn in the late spring, when the water temperature is between 10 and 15°C, usually from mid-March until June, with a peak of activity in late April and May. The eggs, which adhere to each other and are enveloped in slime, are usually laid in shallow water, in long white ribbons up to a metre in length, draped over water plants or other submerged objects. Waterlogged tree trunks and submerged branches are favourite sites if weeds are absent. Wire-mesh traps set for Perch during the spawning season down to depths of 5m may become covered with spawn. The males arrive at the spawning area well before the females. When a ripe female arrives, one or more of the males chases her, fertilising her egg ribbon as it is laid. Each female lays about 45,000 eggs per kg of body weight. They are whitish, some 1.5–2.5mm in diameter and take about 120–160 day-degrees to hatch (i.e. 8–16 days at normal water temperatures).

On hatching, the fry, which are about 6.4mm in length, struggle to the surface, where they penetrate the surface film and swallow air in order to inflate the swimbladder. The connection with the oesophagus exists only for a short time and fry which do not succeed in filling the bladder eventually sink and die. An oil globule in the yolk sac increases their buoyancy, but after inflating the swimbladder they can swim normally and embark on a planktonic existence for a short time. Because of their small size they are very vulnerable to predation by other members of the plankton community, including their larger brethren which have hatched out earlier. Thus, the initial mortality can be enormous.

However, initial growth is rapid and they soon start to move around near

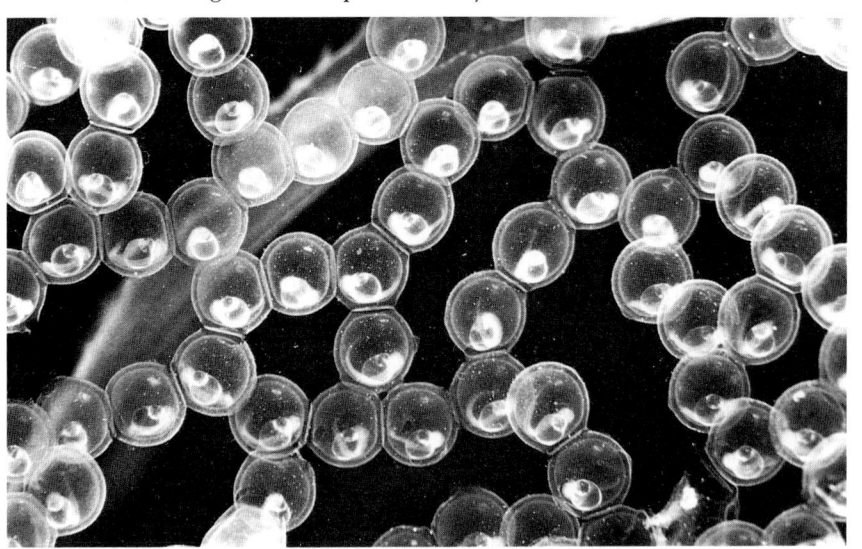

Fig. 123 Part of the egg ribbon of a Perch, magnified to show the young larvae developing within the eggs and a few white dead eggs (Heather Angel).

Fig. 124 A shoal of adult Perch (William Howes).

the surface, sometimes in dense grey shoals, hunting for food and being hunted by larger predatory fish and birds. Once their fins have become fully developed, they move inshore and adopt a more benthic habit, still moving about in shoals but sheltering among marginal vegetation. As autumn approaches and the water temperatures drop, the young fish and adults move offshore into water up to 12–15m deep if this is available. However, solitary individuals are sometimes encountered sheltering under vegetation or stones in shallow water. At this time the level of feeding is reduced.

The growth and survival of young Perch is much affected by temperature. After a long warm summer, the current year class may be very strong, and the reverse is true for cold summers. Thus, there are great variations in year-class strength within Perch populations and the numbers involved may vary by a factor of several hundred from one year to another.

The growth of Perch is very variable according to habitat and other factors. At the end of their first year they may reach 7cm and after two years, 10–12cm. After three years most fish are at least 12–18cm and starting to become mature. Males mature sexually earlier than females, sometimes after one year, but usually after two or three. Most females do not mature until their third or even fourth years and by this time they have started to grow faster than males. A maximum age of about 10–13 years is normal in the wild but in captivity, ages of up to 28 years have been recorded for both sexes. As with trout, the growth rate of Perch can increase as a result of a new and abundant supply of food becoming available – even when they are comparatively old. This has been known to happen when a stream or lake is impounded to form a reservoir and large amounts of terrestrial food (e.g. earthworms) become available.

Perch can be aged, either from the scales or more readily by counting the annual growth zones on the opercular bones, once these have been removed from the fish and cleaned.

Perch have been known to hybridise with Ruffe. When a male Perch is crossed with a female Ruffe the resulting progeny are intermediate in ap-

Table 54 Food of Perch in the Dubh Lochan and Loch Lomond (after Shafi 1969) as percentage by number and in Rostherne Mere (after Goldspink & Goodwin 1979), as percentage points of stomach fullness.

Stomach contents	Dubh Lochan	Loch Lomond	Rostherne Mere
Macrophytes	–	–	2.5
Molluscs			
Snails	–	–	0.2
Pea shells	–	–	0.2
Worms	–	–	–
Leeches	–	–	1.9
Crustaceans			
Cladocerans	36.6	7.0	6.0
Ostracods	–	–	0.2
Copepods	11.9	42.1	1.7
Water louse	0.1	4.0	7.7
Freshwater shrimp	–	–	5.8
Insects			
Stonefly larvae	0.1	0.3	–
Mayfly larvae	30.4	3.2	–
Dragonfly larvae	–	–	3.6
Beetle larvae	0.1	–	1.2
Alderfly larvae	1.1	0.3	9.4
Caddis larvae	0.7	1.6	1.7
Culicid larvae	6.7	–	–
Midge larvae & pupae	12.1	14.3	14.5
Other insects	0.1	–	1.5
Other invertebrates	0.1	–	–
Fish			
Roach	–	–	5.1
Three-spined Stickleback	–	6.8	–
Perch	0.1	–	25.5
Bullhead	–	–	1.0
Unidentified fish	–	0.4	8.0
Other vertebrates	–	–	–
Terrestrial organisms	–	–	2.4
Detritus	–	–	–
NUMBER OF FISH EXAMINED	488	145	821

pearance, having the vertical bars of the Perch and the spotting of the Ruffe. When the reverse cross occurs, the young all look like Ruffe.

Perch forage for food during the day (and, it is said, during moonlight) in roving shoals of fish all about the same size (and sometimes the same sex). Although they are accomplished piscivores from an early age, their diet comprises mainly aquatic invertebrates which they pick off the bottom or from the stems and leaves of aquatic plants. Their main food organisms include leeches (which are ignored by most other fishes), freshwater shrimps and lice, midge and caddis larvae and pupae and small fish. Foods of lesser or only seasonal importance are mayfly larvae and, in oligotrophic waters, stonefly larvae, water boatmen and small bivalve molluscs. Snails do not generally seem to be taken and in a seasonal study of Perch food in Loch Tummel in Scotland they were found in only a small proportion of the fish and then only in winter. At a site in Ireland, it appeared that the presence of crayfish as a food together with a relatively low population density of Perch resulted both in rapid fish growth and, eventually, a large individual size.

Theoretically Perch might appear to be in direct feeding competition with trout, but certainly in larger lakes, trout in summer tend to feed in midwater and at the surface whilst Perch feed mainly on the bottom and among weed.

Like Trout, Perch feeding in the vicinity of inflowing streams take worms, slugs and other terrestrial animals washed down during spates. When attacking smaller fish, Perch show surprising speed and mobility in rounding up and out-manoeuvring their prey – the very reverse of the stalk or ambush technique employed by Pike, or the wild open-mouthed charge of trout. One of the authors spent some time watching Perch in a clear Irish stream preying on Minnows which were shoaling densely in shallow water prior to spawning. A shoal of Perch was hovering in the current some metres away, and every now and then two or three Perch would detach themselves from their shoal and attack the Minnows in a pincer movement, herding the latter into an even denser shoal before pouncing. In captivity, Perch are extremely greedy feeders and seem to have insatiable appetites. In the experience of the authors, young Perch are the only fish that will kill themselves by overeating, given the opportunity! This may occur in the wild too: at Loch Leven, a 1+ Perch of 5.3cm in length was found dead with a 2.5cm Three-spined Stickleback in its gullet.

The feeding activity of Perch is controlled to a great extent by the water temperature, as anglers well know. Hot sunny days are best for fishing, when shoals may congregate at the surface, particularly among or under the leaves of aquatic plants and there they take bait freely. This common experience among anglers seems to conflict with the results of behavioural studies which have shown that Perch are most active at dawn and at dusk, when light intensity is low. However, perhaps the very reason that Perch may be found feeding under overhead plants during the day is that they are seeking low light levels there. At night, Perch shoals break up into smaller groups (in common with many other species of shoaling fish in both fresh and salt waters), which sink to near the bottom and rest there until dawn when they coalesce again into large shoals.

Perch show a relatively poor response to sounds (compared to carps and catfishes for instance), but they are well equipped with large open sensory pores on the head, which help them to detect the presence of prey. Perch, experimentally deprived of vision, can snap accurately at scentless objects moved near the head – just as can Pike. Such an adaptation may help these piscivores to feed in the very turbid water which occurs seasonally in many Perch habitats. Thus, it is possible to angle Perch when there is virtually no visibility by spinning very slowly or jigging a metal spoon lure near the bottom.

Perch are hosts to a considerable number of parasites, some of which are host specific, the rest being shared with other fish species. These parasites include species that infest the exterior of the body, the mouth, gills, eye, intestine and other viscera. Perch are subject to an infectious ulcer disease which may almost eliminate a population in a short time and which can spread rapidly to other populations. During an outbreak of this disease in Windermere a number of years ago it was estimated that over 90% of the population died. This disease, and sometimes other conditions associated with the stress caused at spawning time, can result in the familiar sight of large numbers of Perch being washed up dead on the shores of lakes.

The Perch is an important match and specimen fish for anglers in England, Wales and Ireland, but in Scotland still tends to be considered as vermin (being frequently taken on trout flies) by the largely game-fishing fraternity,

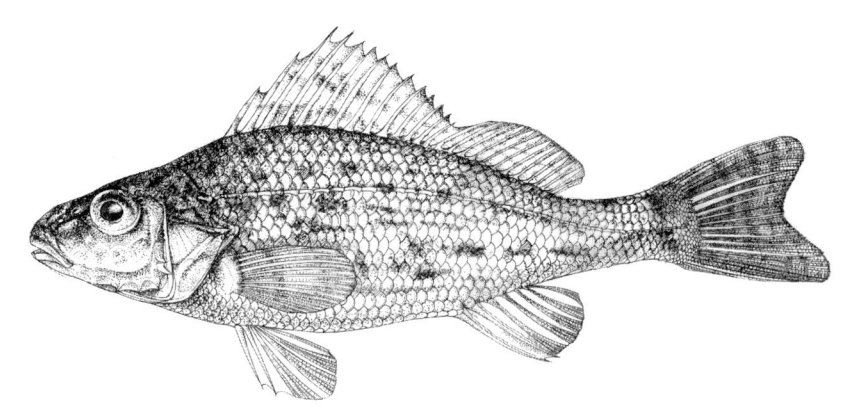

Fig. 125 Ruffe (from Maitland 1972b).

and cast aside in spite of its culinary potential. Filleted and well cooked, the flesh of the Perch is tasty and compares very favourably with that of the best sea fish. In other parts of Europe this is well recognised and there are many varied continental recipes for its preparation.

Perch can be caught in very large numbers around the spawning season because of their habit of entering non-baited traps. These traps are widely used for this species and are made from wire mesh stretched over a heavy-gauge wire frame with a funnel entrance. The largest catches are of the pre-spawning shoals of males. At other times of the year, small numbers may be taken in this way, including females. During World War II, a small fishery was established in Windermere using such traps. The Perch caught were canned and marketed as 'Perchines' to augment the home-produced food supply.

Perch are good aquarium fish, becoming very tame and bold, but any other species sharing their tank should be approximately the same size!

Ruffe *Gymnocephalus cernua* (Linnaeus 1758)
Pope, Ruff

The Ruffe is the smallest member of the perch family in the British Isles, seldom reaching a length of over 15cm except in a few specialised habitats, such as the Baltic Sea where, exceptionally, it may grow up to 50cm in length. The present British rod-caught record is for a fish of 148gm caught in 1980 in a pond at West View Farm in Cumbria.

Although not as high-backed, Ruffe could be initially confused with small faintly coloured Perch, but the first and second dorsal fins of the latter are quite separate whereas those of the Ruffe are joined. In addition, there is no black spot at the rear of the first dorsal fin in the Ruffe as there is in the Perch.

The head is broad and well armoured, the operculum ending in a long rear-pointing spine, while the pre-operculum bears a 'ruffe' of 10–12 rear-pointing spines – possibly the origin of the name of this species (although apparently Pope is the older term). The teeth are villiform and are present on the vomer but not on the palatine bone or the tongue, which is smooth.

Like Perch, Ruffe have only 3 hepatic caecae. The whole body is well covered with strong ctenoid scales which extend on to the head. There are 35–40 of these along the lateral line. There are 35–40 vertebrae.

The first part of the dorsal fin has 11–16 spines whilst the second part has 11–15 soft rays only. The pectoral fins have 13 rays and the pelvic fins, which are thoracic, one spine and 5 rays. The caudal fin has 17 rays.

The Ruffe is by no means as colourful nor as clearly marked as the Perch. The back and sides are sandy to pale brownish green with irregular dark olive brown blotches (reminiscent of those of the Gudgeon), whilst the belly is a pale yellow. The dorsal and caudal fins have broken rows of dark spots on the membranes between the rays. The paired pectoral and pelvic fins are usually a pale brown, but sometimes the former may have a rosy hue.

Ruffe are found in lakes, slow-flowing rivers and canals throughout northern Europe and across central and northern Asia. The species also occurs in the low salinity areas of the Baltic Sea where it reaches its maximum size of 45–50cm and 750gm. They have a lower oxygen requirement than Perch and are thus able to occupy habitats where Perch would be under stress. In the British Isles it is indigenous to eastern and south-eastern England and is common locally, but it has been re-distributed to some extent within the English Midlands and has now reached the lower Severn and Welsh Dee systems. It is absent from Ireland and was too from Scotland until very recently when it became established in Loch Lomond, evidently brought in as a bait by Pike anglers. It is now one of the commonest fish in this loch. It has also appeared recently in south-west Scotland in Loch Ken.

Spawning takes place from March to May, when shoals of Ruffe move into shallow water to lay their eggs in sticky strands which adhere to rocks and

Table 55 Food of Ruffe in the Norfolk Broads, England (after Hartley 1947a) and in Lake Vanern, Sweden (after Nilsson 1979), as percentage occurrence.

Stomach contents	Norfolk Broads	Lake Vanern
Algae	1.0	1.3*
Macrophytes	7.5	1.3*
Molluscs		
Snails	0.5	–
Crustaceans		
Cladocerans	1.0	–
Ostracods	6.4	–
Copepods	13.2	0.9
Water louse	4.9	–
Gammaracanthus	–	3.5
Pallasea	–	9.6
Pontoporeia	–	22.2
Other amphipods	0.5	1.3
Mysis	–	19.1
Insects		
Mayfly larvae	1.5	–
Stonefly larvae	0.5	–
Dragonfly larvae	1.5	–
Beetle larvae & adults	1.5	–
Alderfly larvae	3.9	–
Culicid larvae	3.9	–
Midge larvae	79.4	8.3
Fly pupae	9.3	–
Other invertebrates	–	1.3*
NUMBER OF FISH EXAMINED	204	?

vegetation. The eggs are yellowish white in colour (each yolk sac contains a large oil globule) and 0.5–1.0mm in diameter. Each female can produce 4000–100,000 depending on her size. The eggs hatch in some 8–12 days when water temperatures are between 10 and 15°C.

Ruffe and Perch can hybridise and this appears to occur naturally in some parts of the Danube system. The progeny, however, are sterile.

Newly hatched fry are transparent and 3–4mm in length. By the end of their first year they may reach 3–6cm, and 7–9cm by the end of their second year. Growth then seems to slow and by the time they are four years of age they may only be around 10cm. Very few Ruffe seem to live beyond five years of age. They mature at an early age – males usually in their first or second years and females in their second year.

Ruffe are gregarious fish, often feeding in shoals – though these are rarely as large as some Perch shoals. They are exclusively carnivorous, feeding on bottom-living invertebrates, especially molluscs, crustaceans and insect larvae (notably midge larvae which form a significant proportion of their diet). They take approximately the same range of organisms as Perch, but because of their ability to penetrate deeper into the mud than Perch, Ruffe appear to take a greater proportion of mud-dwelling invertebrates. They also take fish eggs and small fish, and it has been shown in some large Russian lakes that where Ruffe and whitefish (*Coregonus*) occur together, the Ruffe exert a significant control over the production of white fish because of the enormous number of whitefish eggs which they consume. Feeding takes place mainly during the day and at night the Ruffe may lie concealed on the bottom. They feed throughout the winter but at a reduced level.

Ruffe are easily caught by angling with bait such as maggots or worms, but they are not considered to be an important sport fish. Often, small Ruffe and small Perch may be caught at the same time at the same spot. When fishing for Ruffe in the River Neva in Russia, one of the authors baited a three-hooked cast with red caviar, black caviar and worm respectively, but the Ruffe only took the worm! Many anglers consider them to be a great nuisance, taking the bait before a more acceptable species can get to it. As a dead bait they are favoured by Pike anglers. Their flesh is well flavoured, like that of Perch, and there was originally an extensive fishery for Ruffe in the lagoons of the Baltic Sea. This has declined greatly in recent years owing to lack of demand.

Pikeperch *Stizostedion lucioperca* (Linnaeus 1758) Zander

The Pikeperch, now firmly established in England, resembles a much elongated Perch and this almost Pike-like slimness together with its predominately piscivorous diet has earned it both its vernacular name and its specific scientific name. Although a member of the perch family, adults are very unlikely to be confused with the other two British representatives, Perch and Ruffe. However, young Pikeperch could be confused with Ruffe, though the separate dorsal fins of the former should be enough to distinguish them, as shown in the illustration.

In size, adult Pikeperch are some 40–50cm in length, but specimens up to 130cm have been recorded, weighing as much as 15kg. The British rod-caught record stands at 7.8kg for a fish caught in the River Great Ouse in 1977.

Fig. 126 Top, A magnificent specimen Pikeperch (William Howes); *bottom*, Pikeperch (from Maitland 1972b).

Unlike Perch or Ruffe, the mouth of the Pikeperch is armed with large canines as well as many smaller teeth on both jaws. In addition there are large teeth on each side of the palate. There are spines on the pre-operculum and a single rear-facing spine on the operculum. The first and second dorsal fins are separate though very close so as almost to touch, the former having 13–15 spines and the latter 1–2 spines followed by 19–25 soft rays. The pectoral fins have 15 rays, the pelvic fins one spine and five rays and the anal fin two or three spines and 11–13 soft rays. The scales are relatively small and ctenoid and they cover the whole body extending also on to the operculum; there are 80–95 scales along the lateral line and some 45–47 vertebrae.

In colour, the back and flanks of the Pikeperch are greenish-brown or greyish with a gold sheen, with dark-brown, broken vertical bars which may be more intense on the young fish. The ventral surface is silvery white. Both dorsal fins have horizontal rows of irregular black spots and the caudal fin is also spotted. The pelvic, anal and caudal fins are dull and do not have bright reddish tinges like Perch.

290   FRESHWATER FISHES

The original distribution of this species was limited to central and eastern Europe, including Russia. They have been introduced to southern Scandinavia (where they became established in brackish lagoons off the Baltic Sea) and to many other parts of Europe and are now found in slow rivers and rich lowland lakes from the Netherlands to the Caspian Sea. Other closely related species occur in Europe, including sea-going fish in the Black and Caspian Seas.

In North America, the Walleye or Yellow Pickerel *Stizostedium vitreum* is closely related. A small number of this species was introduced into the River Ouse in Bedfordshire in 1925. Nine years later, a large specimen was caught, weighing 5.3kg in the River Delph on the same system. No further specimens were reported and the river became badly polluted, apparently ruling out the possibility of any progeny surviving. This explains the appearance in some record-fish lists of an entry for the British record Walleye. Walleye are easily distinguished from Pikeperch as they have a black spot at the rear of the first dorsal fin where it joins the back. Also, their pectoral and pelvic fins carry markings.

Pikeperch were first introduced into the British Isles from Schleswig-Holstein in 1878. The initial introductions were into ponds without any connections to river systems, as there were some misgivings due to their savage reputation. A second introduction took place in 1910. Subsequent redistributions have taken place from these stocks; their range is still expanding in eastern England and they have recently been reported from sites within the River Severn system.

Just before spawning, which takes place from April to June, there may be a migration from deep water into the shallows. Spawning itself takes place among vegetation (often the stems of emergent plants such as reed (*Phragmites* spp.) or Reedmace (*Typha*) but sometimes over stones and gravel) near the edges of lakes and rivers when the water temperature reaches 12–15°C. The pale-yellow eggs, some 1.0–1.5mm in diameter, are laid singly, not in strings like those of Perch. They are adhesive, sticking to plants, stones and

Fig. 127 An adult Pikeperch (Dietrich Burkel).

Table 56 Food of Pikeperch in East Anglia, England (after Linfield & Rickards 1979), as percentage occurrence.

Stomach contents	East Anglia
Macrophytes	2.3
Molluscs	
Snails	1.1
Mussels	3.4
Crustaceans	
Water louse	2.3
Freshwater shrimp	12.6
Insects	
Dragonfly larvae	1.1
Midge larvae	4.6
Blackfly larvae	1.1
Fish	71.2
NUMBER OF FISH EXAMINED	56

other underwater objects and are guarded by both parents until they hatch in 5–10 days. Female Pikeperch are very prolific egg layers, each producing some 160,000–200,000 eggs per kg of body weight.

The fry measure 5–6mm at hatching and initially remain in shoals. Afterwards they become more solitary. Growth may be very fast during the first year, at the end of which they can attain a length of 30cm, though most fish in England reach only about half this size. Males mature at 2–4 years of age and females at 3–5 years. The maximum life span is usually some 10–13 years.

Adult Pikeperch are principally fish eaters and patrol open water, avoiding dense vegetation, in a solitary way. They feed all the year round, principally at dawn and dusk each day. However, they do not take prey as large as that of Pike of equivalent size, and young fish feed largely on invertebrates, mostly zooplankton. A number of authorities stress that Pikeperch thrive only over a hard clean substrate and that they never thrive over a muddy bottom. However, in most of their habitats the water becomes turbid during the summer, a feature which seems to suit them. They seem to be able to cope with the poor visibility by having specially adapted eyes: there is a layer of colour-sensitive cells underlying the retina which reflects light back through the retina's rod cells, thus increasing sensitivity. One of the authors has caught Pikeperch in a thick algal bloom by jigging with metal spoons.

The flesh of the Pikeperch is relatively free of bones, white, flaky and delicious to eat. As a result, this fish is much sought after by commercial fishermen in Europe and Asia. It is also cultivated in ponds where its fast growth is an advantage. In England it is regarded as an excellent sporting fish, being most vulnerable to natural baits such as small fish (dead or alive) early in the morning or towards dusk. It is likely that its popularity will lead to its becoming more widespread in the British Isles. Anglers will regard this as a mixed blessing, as its presence would result initially in a reduction in the numbers of whatever small prey species were present, such as Roach, Bream, Ruffe, etc. However, this would, in turn, lead to an increased growth rate in these species (due to lowered competition for food) and fewer but larger individuals. Thus, the introduction of the Pikeperch might not suit match anglers fishing for coarse fish, but could suit specimen hunters. The establishment of

Pikeperch in waters hitherto without them usually seems to result in a population explosion of the species, and their impact on the stocks of prey species may be substantial. Eventually, however, the system stabilises at a lower level as a balance is established. The fact that adult Pikeperch prey on their own young is probably an important regulation factor.

24

Gobies

The Gobiidae, commonly called gobies, is a successful family of small fish found in many parts of the world, both temperate and tropical. Most species are marine, but many occur in brackish water and there is a considerable number of freshwater species. These occur in a variety of habitats in both running and standing waters. The well known Mudskipper *Periophthalmus barbarus* of the Far East, which hops over the surface of the mud hunting for food when the tide is out and up into the mangrove roots (i.e. away from water) when danger threatens, is a goby. Because of the close relationships within genera and the small size of many fish, identification may often be difficult. It is further complicated by the fact that there are often considerable differences in colour and size between the sexes.

The main characteristic of the family is that the pelvic fins are very close together and usually united to form a single sucker-like fin. This enables the fish to attach themselves to any smooth, firm object and resist or rest from currents, etc. The body is normally elongate, though often broad and squat anteriorly. The head is large and the lips and cheeks well developed. Sensory papillae and other protuberances are common on the head and often arranged in characteristic patterns useful in identification. The lateral line is either incomplete or absent; there are two well developed dorsal fins; the anal fin is usually similar in size to the second dorsal fin and the caudal fin is rounded.

Often very abundant fish, gobies are usually benthic in habit and common in shallow coastal areas of the sea. A number of species are pelagic. At spawning time, the males become much darker (some species turn pure black), their fins elongate and the shape of the head alters. They build simple nests – usually in the shelter of shells, stones or weed – and guard the adhesive eggs until the larvae emerge and swim away. Many species are short-lived, dying within a year of hatching.

A number of the larger gobies are edible and of commercial importance, particularly in the Black and Caspian Seas. Many species do well in captivity and are kept in aquaria. Altogether in Europe some 22 species occur in fresh water or enter it from time to time during their life histories. Many species occur round the shores of the British Isles and some come into estuaries, but only one of these is regularly found in fresh water in the upper reaches.

Common Goby *Pomatoschistus microps* (Kroyer 1840) Snag

This is one of the smallest of the fishes to be found in fresh water in the British Isles and is mature at a length of 4–5cm. Its maximum length is about 6.5cm.

The Common Goby has the typical family shape – a broad strong head, a short sturdy body and a rounded tapering caudal region. The caudal pe-

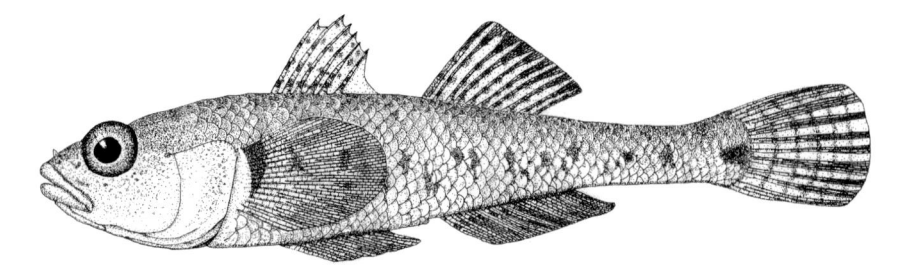

Fig. 128 Common Goby (from Maitland 1972b).

duncle, though narrow, is in fact almost equal in length to the head. Apart from the throat and just behind the head, the body is well covered in scales, which are much smaller at the front than they are behind, and there are some 43–50 scales laterally, although there is no sensory lateral line.

The two well developed dorsal fins are positioned near the middle of the body and are quite separate from each other. The anterior one has 5–6 spiny rays whilst only the first ray of the posterior fin is spiny, the remaining 8–10 being soft and branched. The pectoral fins are large and held laterally, while the pelvic fins, like those of other members of the family, are typically fused to form the sucking disc, which it uses to hold on to smooth surfaces, especially when sheltering under rocks and shells. The anterior membrane of the pelvic fin is characteristically smooth-edged. The anal fin has a leading spiny ray and 8.10 soft branched rays.

The main body colour is usually a light brownish-grey on the back and sides, grading to cream underneath. There is a complex network of darker spots over the upper half of the body (sometimes forming indistinct saddles on the back) and a single row of dark marks along each side, the most conspicuous of which form distinct triangles at the bases of the pectoral fins and the tail fin. Both dorsal fins are lightly spotted. Mature males have a dark spot on the first dorsal fin membrane, a dark throat and dark bars across the body.

The Common Goby is widely distributed along the western coast of Europe, from southern Norway to Portugal, including the whole of the Baltic Sea. It occurs all round the shores of the British Isles, from Shetland to Cornwall.

As its name implies, this is one of the commonest gobies found around the coasts of the British Isles, and though it is basically a marine species it is the only one found regularly in fresh water in the upper reaches of estuaries and in fresh/brackish situations, occurring in small ditches and trickles along the shore. It occurs in a wide range of habitats and though it is mostly abundant in shallow muddy estuarine situations it is also found along sandy shores and in rock pools. Most of the population seems to leave the shallows in winter and moves into the more sheltered deeper waters offshore.

Spawning can occur from April to August, but takes place mostly during May and June. The eggs are normally laid in clumps within the old shell of a bivalve mollusc such as a clam or cockle, though sometimes just underneath suitable stones, and are guarded there by the male until they hatch. The eggs are rather unusual in being oval and are about 0.7–0.9mm in length. Both

Table 57 Food of Common Goby in the Ythan estuary, Scotland (after Healey 1972), as percentage occurrence.

Stomach contents	Ythan estuary
Molluscs	
Snails	15*
Mussels	15*
Worms	3
Crustaceans	
Cladocerans	15*
Copepods	10
Cyprids	13
Corophium	56
Other amphipods	18
Neomysis	9
Crangon	15*
Jaera	19
Insects	
Midge larvae	15*
Fish	
Fish eggs	15*
NUMBER OF FISH EXAMINED	294

sexes may spawn several times over the summer and in favourable conditions the population can build up enormously by the autumn.

Hatching at lengths of 3–4mm, the young fish grow rapidly and may reach lengths of 3–4cm by the end of the summer. They are mostly well grown and often mature by the spring of the following year and usually live for only 1.5–2.5 years.

The young fry feed on protozoans and larval crustaceans and later depend heavily on larger crustaceans of various sorts such as copepods, isopods, gammarids, mysids, etc.

Like most of the small gobies, the Common Goby is of little direct commercial or angling significance, but it is important indirectly as a food source for many larger fish (e.g. flatfish) and is also preyed on by seabirds such as terns. It is easily tamed and is an attractive fish for small aquaria, in which it can sometimes be induced to breed.

25

Mullets

The mullets (family Mugilidae) are very common fish in most oceans, particularly in shallow inshore waters. Many species penetrate brackish and fresh waters, but they usually enter estuaries, lagoons and the lower reaches of rivers for short periods only. There are several genera, with a total of about 100 species found in tropical and temperate waters. Only three species occur around the British Isles.

The mullets are elongate but sturdy fish, whose bodies are only slightly compressed laterally. The mouth is terminal and large, but the teeth are either very small or absent. In some species fleshy eyelids are prominent. The body is covered by large cycloid scales which extend partially on to the head. There is no lateral line. The gill rakers are long and slender. There are two well separated dorsal fins, the anterior being short and supported by 1–5 strong spines, the posterior being longer and supported by softer branched rays. The pectoral fins are set rather high, immediately behind the gill covers.

Mullets are fast-swimming shoaling fish which often come into shallow waters in large numbers to feed, their backs breaking the surface. Much of their food consists of filamentous algae, but invertebrates are also eaten in some numbers. The gut is remarkably long with a powerful muscular gizzard anteriorly, which crushes and breaks up food, subsequently digested in an intestine that may be spiral in form. The air bladder is large.

Spawning takes place in the sea, usually during spring in inshore waters, but relatively little is known about their breeding biology. Mullet fry are exceedingly common along some shores and enter streams in these areas. The adults run into large rivers from time to time.

Though a widespread family, the importance of mullets to humans can vary greatly from place to place. They are angled along some coasts, usually by casting from the shore, but sometimes from boats. Commercially fishermen mostly use traps and seine nets (from which they may escape by spectacular leaping) and catches in some areas may be large – up to 20 million kg per annum in the Mediterranean area. In southern Russia the roe as well as the flesh is important commercially. These species occur around European shores and may enter fresh water from time to time. Few members of this family are suitable for domestic aquaria, but large shoals can make a fine spectacle in a public aquarium.

Identification

Three species of mullet occur round the coasts and estuaries of the British Isles and though they are rather difficult to distinguish from each other when small, the following key should serve to separate maturing and adult individuals.

1. Upper lip thick; its depth greater than a tenth of the head length and more than half the diameter of the eye. No scales present on the lower jaw. **THICK-LIPPED MULLET**

    Upper lip thinner; its depth less than a tenth of the head length and less than half the diameter of the eye. Scales present on the lower jaw.**2.**

2. Scales on the dorsal side of the head extending to the nostrils or beyond. Posterior edge of the pre-orbital bone rounded or truncated vertically. **THIN-LIPPED MULLET**

    Scales on the dorsal side of the head not extending to the nostrils. Posterior edge of the pre-orbital bone truncated obliquely.
    GOLDEN MULLET

Thick-lipped Mullet *Chelon labrosus* (Risso 1826) Grey Mullet

This attractive fast-swimming fish usually reaches a length of some 30–50cm at maturity but can grow up to 90cm. The British rod-caught record was caught in 1979 off Glamorgan in Wales and weighed 6.427kg. The Irish record is 3.45kg and was caught off Killibegs in 1972, but there are probably many fish larger than this yet to be caught.

As its name implies, this species is characterised by its wide swollen upper lip, which is quite unlike that of the other two British species. Underneath this lip are 3–5 short rows of small papillae which increase in number and size as the fish grows. On this lip too are numbers of small closely placed teeth. The edge of the eye is covered with clear adipose tissue.

The body is elongate and very streamlined in shape with only slight lateral compression. It is covered with large cycloid scales that extend on to the head. There are 45–46 of these laterally but there is no lateral line. There are some 24 vertebrae. The two dorsal fins, which are well separated, are small, the first having four spiny rays, the second, 9–10 soft rays. The paired pectoral and pelvic fins are both well developed, the former being set rather high on the body just behind the gill opening. The anal fin has three spiny rays followed by eight or nine soft rays.

In colour, the dorsal surface of the head and the back are a dark greenish grey-blue. This changes to a brilliant silver along the sides which also have six or seven grey bands running from head to tail. Ventrally the fish is pure white.

The Thick-lipped Mullet occurs all along the coast of Europe from western

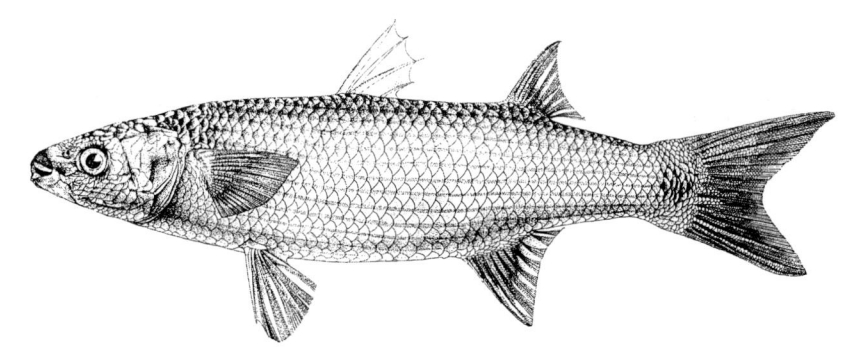

Fig. 129 Thick-lipped Mullet (from Maitland 1972b).

Table 58 Food of Thick-lipped Mullets from various places around the Welsh and southern English coasts (after Hickling 1970), as percentage occurrence.

Stomach contents	Southern coasts
Algae	
Fragilaria	14
Licmorpha	8
Nitzschia	25
Pleurosigma	49
Melosira	27
Other diatoms	14
Amphipleura	31
Ectocarpus	15
Microcoleus	19
Oscillatoria	27
Merismopedia	31
Other blue-green algae	23
Red algae	12
Molluscs	12
Worms	8
Crustaceans	
Ostracods	28
Copepods	60
Amphipods	10
Other crustaceans	26
Other invertebrates	56
Fish	
Fish eggs	28
Detritus	62
NUMBER OF FISH EXAMINED	96

Norway to Spain and all around the Mediterranean and Black Seas. It is probably the commonest of the European mullets.

Mainly in inshore coastal and estuarine species, shoals of Thick-lipped Mullet are common in many bays and inlets and frequently come right up

Fig. 130 Thick-lipped Mullet found trapped in a tidal road culvert in the Outer Hebrides (Niall Campbell).

estuaries almost to the limit of tidal influence. Often very large shoals can be seen from the shore, cruising about in shallow water with their heads and backs periodically breaking the surface. There appears to be a distinct northwards migration during spring, for there is a large increase in numbers of fish around the British coasts in late spring and summer which disappear again in the autumn. However, this may be due partly to the fact that in some waters, at least, the species moves into deeper water for the winter – feeding virtually stopping during this period.

The timing of spawning is very variable according to which part of Europe is concerned. In the Mediterranean it seems to be from December to March, whereas in the Atlantic off Spain, January to April seem to be the commonest months. Detailed information on breeding around the British Isles is scarce but it seems likely that it takes place from June to August, for it is certainly shortly after this that very small young are found in intertidal pools in the southern parts of the British Isles.

The Thick-lipped Mullet seems to spawn in shoals in shallow water and the clear eggs, 1.0mm in diameter, are pelagic and drift in the surface waters until hatching. Growth varies according to latitude, but in southern waters may be very fast, fish often attaining some 15cm after one year and 30cm after three. Most fish start to mature in their third or fourth years and may spawn annually thereafter, often living for ten years or longer, by which time they may have reached a length of 60cm or more.

Mullets are rather unusual in their feeding habits in that, not only are they bottom feeders but they eat principally the growth of diatoms and filamentous algae that form a scum on the substrates of many of the rich shallow waters in which they occur. In browsing on this algae they also take in considerable amounts of the soft mud on which it is growing. They also take many types of invertebrates along with the algae including many molluscs and crustaceans. The young fry feed mainly on crustacean zooplankton. Very large mullets may feed largely on bivalve and gastropod molluscs.

Thick-lipped Mullets are an important commercial fish to various net and trap fisheries in a few places in southern Europe on the Atlantic coast and in many places in the Mediterranean. The white flesh is flaky and most palatable, with a strong flavour of shellfish. The species is a valued sporting fish in some countries but in spite of the fact that it is often present in large shoals it is notoriously difficult to catch by rod and line, due to its food preferences. Plain white bread is a favourite bait. Sometimes frustrated anglers cast over them repeatedly, mistaking them for Sea Trout.

Thick-lipped Mullet can be kept successfully in aquaria. One of the authors once kept a 1+ specimen (caught one spring near Anglesey) in a freshwater aquarium for over a year before presenting it to the Edinburgh Zoo aquarium, where it lived on for several years in a marine tank.

Thin-lipped Mullet *Liza ramada* (Risso 1826) Grey Mullet

This species tends to be smaller than the Thick-lipped Mullet and averages 25–40cm at maturity, with maximum sizes of up to about 60cm and 2.5kg. The British rod-caught record presently stands at 1.599kg for a fish caught in 1983 in Christchurch Estuary, Dorset. There is no Irish record for this species.

As its name implies this species is distinguished from the Thick-lipped Mul-

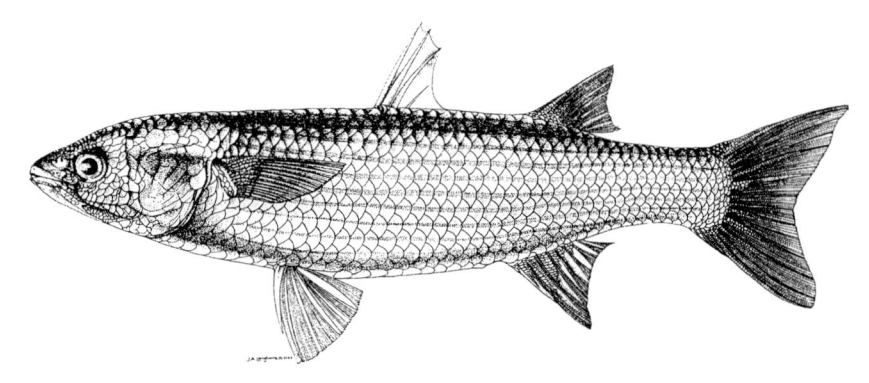

Fig. 131 Thin-lipped Mullet (from Maitland 1972b).

let by its much thinner upper lip (less than half the diameter of the eye), which lacks papillae on the lower margin, and the small bristle-like teeth are restricted to a single row on the edge. Characteristically, the pre-orbital bone is serrated along the lower and front edge, but sinuous at the front and rounded at the corners. There is a narrow adipose eyelid covering part of the eye.

The fins are rather like those of the other mullets except that the pectoral fins are rather short and do not reach the eye when folded forward. The two dorsal fins are well separated, the first having only four spiny rays, the second 8–9 soft rays. The pelvic fins are small and placed well forward, whilst the anal fin has three spiny rays anteriorly followed by 8–9 soft rays. There are 24 vertebrae.

The elongate body is very streamlined and rounded with only slight lateral compression. It is well covered with thick cycloid scales which extend on to the head even as far as the lower jaw. There are 44–46 of these laterally but there is no lateral line.

In colour, the head and back are a dark bluish-grey, which grades to silver along the sides and a creamy white on the belly. Along the sides, running from head to tail, are a series of grey stripes. The fins are usually grey or a greyish-yellow in colour though the anal fin is rather darker and there is a dark spot at the base of the pectoral fin.

This species tends to be much more southern than the Thick-lipped Mullet and does not occur in northern Europe. Its distribution extends from southern Norway and central Scotland along the coasts of the North Sea and the Atlantic south to North Africa and well into the Mediterranean and Black Seas. The Thin-lipped Mullet is only common around the southern coasts of the British Isles, where it is mainly a summer visitor to southern Ireland and the English Channel. It does occur further north of this from time to time but is rare.

Mainly an inshore species, the Thin-lipped Mullet occurs in a variety of shallow-water habitats, including sandy and muddy bays, salt creeks, lagoons and estuaries, where it will penetrate well above the tidal limit and into pure fresh water. Wherever it occurs, it is the commonest mullet in fresh water.

The shoals of fish which appear along the south coasts in summer are assumed to have migrated north from the Bay of Biscay and other places fur-

Fig. 132 A Thin-lipped Mullet (Peter Claridge).

ther south where the species is common. These shoals disappear again in the autumn, presumably migrating back south again. However, as with the Thick-lipped Mullet there is considerable evidence that this species migrates into deep water during the autumn and spends the winter resting there.

Relatively little is known about the reproductive biology of this species though it does breed in British waters. Spawning during the summer months is a communal process among shoals of males and females and the eggs (which are 1.0mm in diameter) are pelagic. They hatch after a few days and the young are planktonic for a short period.

Many features of the age and growth of this species are unknown, but are likely to be similar to other mullets. Maturity appears to be reached after 3–5 years.

The main food consists of benthic algae of various types along with a certain amount of organic mud, which may be ingested inadvertently during feeding. There is also a component of small gastropod and bivalve molluscs, but whether these are preyed on specifically or again just taken accidentally, is uncertain.

Like the other mullets, this species is of considerable commercial and sporting value throughout its range. It is caught commercially by trap nets and by seines, but the species is an extremely wary one and is very skillful at avoiding nets or even leaping over them to freedom at times. Equally, anglers find it extremely difficult to catch in many places even though large shoals may be readily seen offshore cruising around just below the surface.

Golden Mullet *Liza aurata* (Risso 1810) Golden Grey Mullet

This is the least common and the smallest of the mullets found around the British Isles. The average size of mature fish seems to be about 20–30cm, but fish of up to 40cm are not uncommon. Exceptionally it may reach lengths of up to 50cm. The British rod-caught record stands at 1.233kg for a fish caught in 1984 off Alderney in the Channel Islands. There is no Irish record.

The general body shape of the Golden Mullet is close to that of the other grey mullets and it is very similar in appearance to the Thin-lipped Mullet. Thus, the upper lip is narrow (less than half the diameter of the eye) and there are no papillae on its lower surface. However, there are teeth on this lip which are large and well spaced. Other characteristic features of the head include the oblique truncation of the posterior end of the pre-orbital bone, whose lower edge is coarsely serrated. The adipose eyelid is rudimentary.

The two dorsal fins are well separated, the first with four spiny rays and the

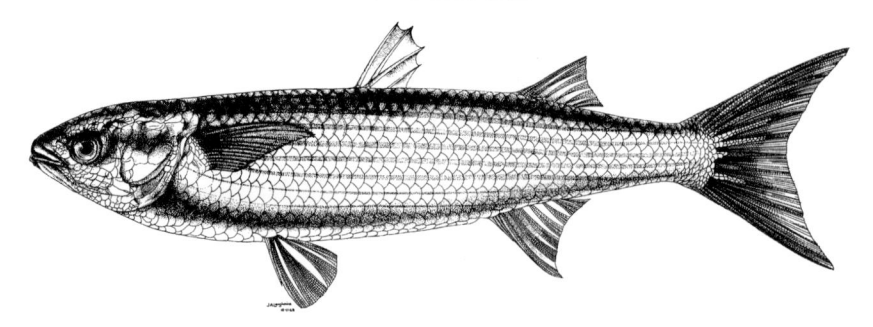

Fig. 133 Golden Mullet (from Maitland 1972b).

second with three spiny rays and 7–9 soft rays. The paired pectoral fins (which are long and reach well beyond the posterior edge of the eye when folded forward) are high on the sides just behind the gill openings, while the pelvic fins are well forward on the belly. The anal fin has three spiny rays anteriorly followed by nine soft rays.

The body is well covered by strong cycloid scales which extend well on to the head. There are 42–47 of these along the lateral series, but, as in other mullets, there is no lateral line. There are 24 vertebrae and 7–9 pyloric caecae.

In colour, the upper part of the head and body are a dark greyish-blue grading to a golden-silver along the sides, which have a series of 6–7 lengthwise greyish-gold stripes. The belly is a creamy white. There are attractive golden spots on the sides of the head and the operculum. The fins are mainly a dull greyish-yellow.

The Golden Mullet occurs along the Atlantic coast of Europe from southern Norway to Spain and further south along the African coast to South Africa. It occurs throughout the Mediterranean and Black Seas and has also been successfully introduced to the Caspian Sea. It is relatively rare around the British Isles especially in northern waters.

Like the other two mullets, the Golden Mullet is a coastal and estuarine species which tends to appear in its northern area of distribution during the summer months only, migrating south or into deeper waters during the autumn and spending the winter there. It often occurs in mixed shoals with either or both of the other British mullets, and like them will penetrate right up beyond the tidal limits of estuaries and into completely fresh water. In southern Europe it is quite common in the lower reaches of some large rivers and the lagoon lakes of their deltas (e.g. the River Danube).

Relatively little is known about the behaviour and ecology of this species in waters around the British Isles and it is presumed by most authorities that its biology here is similar to that of the other two mullet species.

Its reproduction has been studied in the Mediterranean and Black Seas, where it spawns from August to October, usually near the shore. Spawning is a communal process and the shoals of adults lay large numbers of clear pelagic eggs (whose diameter is usually just under 1mm). Juvenile fish also occur among these spawning shoals. These take about 4–6 days to hatch. The females are extremely fecund and each is capable of producing 1,000,000–2,100,000 eggs at each spawning.

The fry are about 3mm on hatching and remain pelagic for some time. Growth is fast, however, and they soon form large shoals, sometimes near the coast but also in offshore waters, and can reach a length of 10cm at the end of their first year and 20cm at the end of their third year. Growth is steady but somewhat slower thereafter, individuals usually reaching their maximum sizes at around ten years of age. The males are mature at 3–4 years and the females at 5–6 years.

Like other mullets, after the fry stage, the Golden Mullet feeds on benthic algae and the invertebrates, especially molluscs, associated with these growths. The stomachs may also contain quantities of mud. There is a tendency for larger fish to contain a high percentage of molluscs.

This species has little commercial importance in northern Europe, but further south and especially in the Mediterranean and Black Seas it is a favoured species and caught in considerable numbers in net and trap fisheries. Occasionally specimens may be caught by rod and line in the British Isles.

26

Sculpins

The sculpins (family Cottidae) are predominantly marine fishes found in northern and arctic regions, where they mostly inhabit shallow coastal waters. However, a few of the 300 or so species live in fresh waters. Three such species are found in Europe.

They are unusual-looking little fish with a squat appearance, large cavernous mouth, opercular spines or 'horns' and mottled skin. Structurally, cottids are very advanced and they are most successful fish in the habitats which they occupy. They are relatively poor swimmers and normally bottom-dwelling, living on invertebrates, fish and fish eggs. In Lake Baikal, in eastern Siberia, there is a beautiful endemic species, the Golomyanka *Comephorus baikalensis*, which is translucent pink with feathery pectoral fins and which leads a bathypelagic life, spending all its time in the deep open waters of this very large lake. Most species are known to guard their eggs in some kind of nest.

The family has no sporting and almost no commercial value and are sometimes considered a pest by anglers. In the British Isles, the only freshwater representative is the Bullhead.

Bullhead *Cottus gobio* Linnaeus 1758 Chabot, Culle, Miller's Thumb, Tom Cull, Tommy Logge

Although, as just indicated, the Bullhead is the only freshwater member of the family found in the British Isles, in appearance it is typically cottid (from the Greek *cottus* meaning head) and very like some of its close marine relatives, which may be found commonly in estuaries. To distinguish it from the estuarine species, it was once called the River Bullhead (the term 'bull' indicating comparative greatness, i.e. Bullrush, Bull Trout, Bull Frog, etc.). The alternative name of Miller's Thumb is said to have originated because of a supposed likeness between the fish and the gnarled and flattened thumb of a grain miller (a product of his constant testing of the flour's texture between his thumb and forefinger as it poured out of the meal spout). Other local names for the Bullhead were Culle (used by Isaac Walton) and Tommy

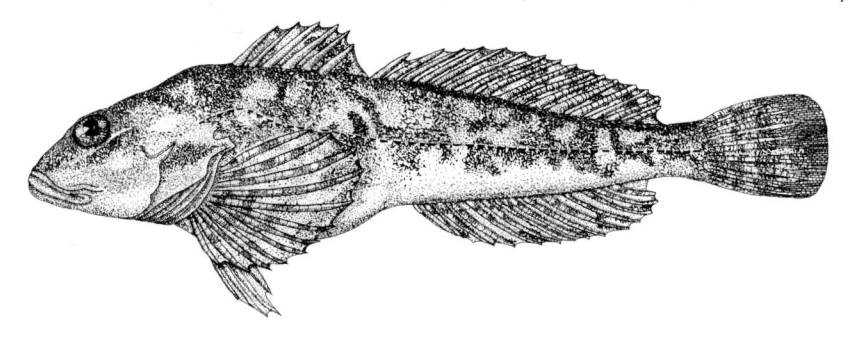

Fig. 134 Bullhead (from Maitland 1972b).

Fig. 135 An adult Bullhead camouflaged on a stony bottom (Heather Angel).

Logge, and all these names suggest that it has long been a familiar fish in spite of its small size. In North America, freshwater bullheads are called sculpins, the Spoonhead Sculpin *Cottus ricei* being a close relation to the British species.

Most mature Bullheads are about 5–10cm in length, but exceptionally they may grow to over 15cm. Females tend to grow larger than males. The British rod-caught record for this species is only 28gm – for a fish caught in 1983 in the Green River, near Guildford, in Surrey.

Generally speaking, Bullheads are not noted for their symmetry or good looks and they are often considered to be an ugly little fish, unmistakable, all head and mouth with a dorso-ventrally flattened tapering body, the widest part of which is across the head and gills and is equivalent to some 25% of the body length. The mouth has a very wide gape, and there are villiform teeth on both jaws as well as on the front of the vomer bone – but there are none on the palatine bone. There is a strong rear-pointing spine at the posterior of the operculum. The comparatively large eyes are situated high on the head, as befits a bottom-living fish, and are unusual in that they have two corneas with a fluid-filled space between. This appears to be an adaptation to their benthic habit in fast-flowing streams and is said to be protection against moving sand particles. It may be this adaptation which causes the pupils to appear pale red in some lights. The Stone Loach has a similar modification.

The skin is very slimy and there are no scales, apart from a row of tubular scale-like structures along the lateral line, 30–35 in number. There is no swimbladder. During the breeding season, the males have marked genital papillae. Adult fish are thought to be able to produce a sound by moving part of the operculum sharply.

There are two dorsal fins; the first is short and has 6–9 spines, the second is long and has 15–18 soft rays. The large pectoral fins have 13 or 14 rays and

Table 59 The food of Bullhead in the River Tees, England (after Crisp 1963) and in the Gogar Burn, Scotland (after Morris 1978), as percentage occurrence.

Stomach contents	River Tees	Gogar Burn
Macrophytes	–	9
Molluscs		
Limpets	–	1
Leeches	–	2
Crustaceans		
Water louse	–	19
Freshwater shrimp	–	9
Insects		
Mayfly larvae	22	15
Stonefly larvae	33	–
Stonefly adults	1	–
Beetle larvae	3	–
Caddis larvae	24	5
Cranefly larvae	–	2
Midge larvae & pupae	42	13
Blackfly larvae	7	4
Fish		
Bullhead eggs & fry	3	–
Terrestrial organisms		
Slugs & worms	3	–
Insects	3	–
Detritus	–	12
NUMBER OF FISH EXAMINED	72	97

the small, thoracic, pelvic fins have 3–5 rays. The anal fin has 12 or 13 rays and the caudal fin some 11 or 12.

The basic colouration of the Bullhead is a dark mottling over a light background, but this varies according to the immediate background on which it is resting, so that it is always well camouflaged. The ventral surface is whitish. At spawning time the male becomes much darker.

The Bullhead occurs across much of Europe, from Cornwall and Brittany in the west to the Caspian Sea in the east. In the British Isles it is indigenous only to south-east England, but it has been fairly widely redistributed since the last ice age and is now found throughout most of England and Wales. It is absent from Ireland and in Scotland is found only in two small parts of the Clyde and Forth catchments.

Spawning takes place from March to June, when the male excavates a small hollow under a suitable stone. A female is then attracted to spawn with him here and a clump of a few hundred pinkish-yellow adhesive eggs, 2–2.5mm in diameter, are attached to the underside of the stone. They are then guarded aggressively by the male and hatch in some 20–30 days depending on water temperature. The newly hatched fry, which the male continues to guard, are about 6–7mm in length and well supplied with a large yolk sac. This is absorbed in 10 or 11 days, by which time the fry are some 9mm in length and start to disperse. Bullheads and sticklebacks are the only native freshwater fish which guard both their eggs and young. They may reach 4–5cm in length after one year, 6cm after two years and 7–9cm or more after three years, by which time they are mature.

Bullheads are exclusively bottom dwellers, resting on their well developed pelvic fins, which are curved outwards ventrally to lie flush with the bottom. They have no swimbladder and live a rather sedentary life under stones or thick weed beds in shallow water. When they are disturbed they move in a short dash, usually downstream, for alternative cover. They occur in a variety of streams and rivers, but usually where the current is fast and the bottom stony. They often inhabit small fast-flowing upland streams where salmonids are the only other fish present. Their oxygen requirements are much the same as those of trout. They occur only occasionally in lakes.

They can be very numerous at times and a small hand net pushed into a bank of vegetation may catch 5–10 Bullheads of all sizes, and often other species as well. A typical Bullhead habitat might also contain high densities of Stone Loach, Minnows and sticklebacks, and some other species, all using the same bank of vegetation for cover.

At dusk, they emerge to look for food. The Bullhead has a reputation, probably much exaggerated, for eating trout eggs and alevins as well as the eggs and young of other fish. Female Bullheads are known to eat their own eggs and fry. In fact, they mainly feed on a wide range of aquatic invertebrates, including molluscs, insect larvae and benthic crustaceans. In artificial circumstances at least, hungry Bullheads may eat quite large fish up to 4 or 5cm in length – sometimes choking in the attempt.

However, Bullheads themselves are important food for trout and many other fish eaters, especially birds such as Kingfishers and Herons. Their distended gills and opercular spines have been known to stick in the throats of these predators, causing their death.

Bullheads make interesting aquarium fish and soon become tame. They may also spawn in captivity, but successful hatching is unlikely unless special conditions of circulating, cool, well-oxygenated water are provided. At one time the 'sweet tasty' flesh of the Bullhead was much esteemed and Isaac Walton and some of the older authorities are enthusiastic about its value as a food.

27

Flatfish

The family Pleuronectidae, commonly known as flatfishes, is a large group of mainly marine fish found in most seas of the world. There are many genera, but only one of these (the genus (*Platichthys*) is catadromous and regularly enters fresh water in the British Isles. As their common name implies, these fish (closely related to percomorph – perch-like – fishes) are strongly compressed, have both eyes on one side and long, well developed, soft-rayed dorsal and anal fins.

This is one of the most distinct families of fishes owing to their flattening and asymmetry. They commence life swimming about normally, but soon, instead of swimming in the normal position they lie and swim on one side, skimming over the bottom. The eye on the lower side gradually moves to the upper side, involving modification of the structure of the head. Interestingly, the eyes can be raised and moved independently, thus increasing the field of vision. The upper side is pigmented while the lower side is usually white. The fish are well known for their rapid adaptation to the colour and patterning of the substrate on which they lie.

Each species comes to lie on either the right or the left side and is said to be dextral or sinistral respectively, depending which side is the upper one. Members of the genus *Platichthys* are usually dextral, but reversal does occur occasionally. Interestingly, the scales on the upper side are mainly ctenoid and those on the lower side are cycloid. Probably cycloid scales, which are smooth, are essential on the undersurface, which is periodically scraping over the bottom.

Flatfishes are carnivorous, feeding on a variety of other animals. Mainly bottom-living fishes in continental inshore waters, they are widely distributed in tropical and temperate seas, with a few species penetrating arctic waters.

Flounder *Platichthys flesus* (Linnaeus 1758) Butt, Fluke

This is the only flatfish in Europe which is regularly found in fresh water and is also abundant in estuaries and around the coasts, where it may well be confused with Plaice *Pleuronectes platessa*, Dab *Limanda limanda* and various other common marine flatfish.

Most mature Flounders are some 20–30cm in length and the species can exceptionally attain a length of 50cm and a weight of 3.5kg. The British rod-caught record stands at 2.593kg for a fish caught in 1956 at Fowey, Cornwall. The Irish record is a Flounder caught near Ballyteigue, Wexford in 1979 and weighing 1.999kg.

The Flounder, like other members of the family, is extremely flattened and lies on one side of the body, the eyes and some other organs having migrated to the other side so that they are uppermost. Most Flounders lie on the left side with the right side uppermost, but reversed animals are quite common,

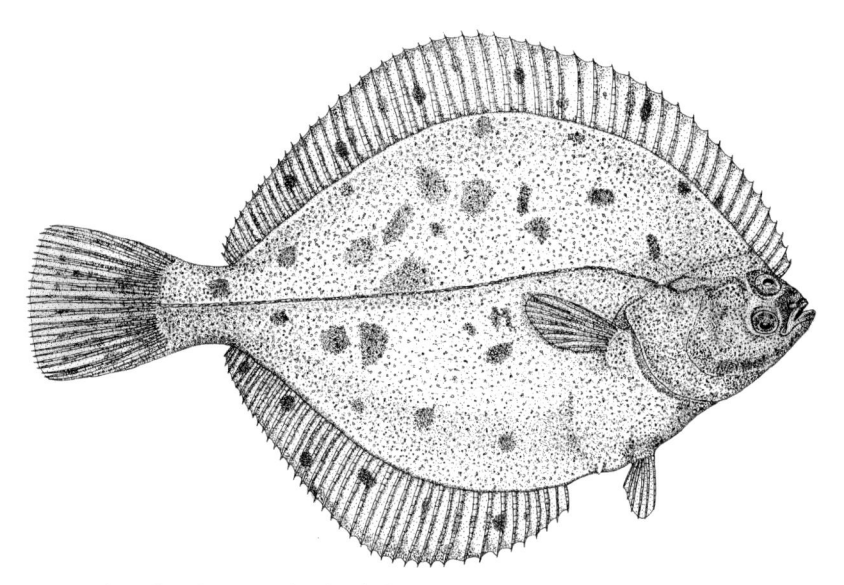

Fig. 136 Flounder (from Maitland 1972b).

where the opposite is true. In normal Flounders, the small terminal mouth is positioned to the right of the eyes. The head is large and flattened and the well developed lateral line curves from it, round the operculum and pectoral fin and then straight down the middle of the body.

The body is covered with small irregularly distributed and shaped scales,

Fig. 137 A young Flounder swimming down on to the bottom (Heather Angel).

Table 60 Food of Flounders in the River Tweed, Scotland (after Radforth 1940), as percentage number.

Stomach contents	River Tweed
Molluscs	
Snails	0.02
Limpets	0.67
Worms	0.74
Leeches	0.01
Crustaceans	
Freshwater shrimp	0.02
Insects	
Mayfly larvae	0.50
Stonefly larvae	0.03
Aquatic bugs	0.01
Beetle larvae	0.35
Caddis larvae	0.19
Midge larvae & pupae	97.33
Blackfly larvae & pupae	0.04
Other invertebrates	0.03
Fish	0.01
NUMBER OF FISH EXAMINED	50

which are characteristically rough on either side of the lateral line especially between it and the pectoral fin, making this area very rough to the touch. The bases of both the dorsal and the ventral fins are also rough and this is one of the simplest ways to identify this species in the field and distinguish it from other flatfish. The dorsal fin has a sharp spine at its base and 52–67 soft rays, whilst the anal fin also has a spine and 35–46 rays. There are 15–22 gill rakers and some 35 vertebrae.

In colour, the upper side (usually the right) is a dull brown with indistinct blotches of greenish-brown or grey and some dull-red spots. The underside (usually the left) is always a pale greyish-white.

The Flounder is a very widely distributed species, occurring in Europe along coastal waters from the White Sea round northern Norway and throughout the North and Baltic Seas to Spain and North Africa and into the Mediterranean and Black Seas. It occurs all round the British Isles in a wide range of habitats but especially on silty, sandy and gravelly bottoms. It is especially common in estuaries and young fish in particular often migrate upstream from the estuaries into fresh water and they may be found in rivers and lakes, sometimes many kilometres from the sea. For instance it is not uncommon to catch this species in Loch Lomond 50km from the sea and living at depths of up to 100m.

At spawning time, mature fish migrate offshore to suitable spawning grounds in April and May and lay their eggs in 25–50m of water. The eggs (about 1mm in diameter) are pelagic initially but lose this buoyancy during development, which takes about 5–8 days at temperatures of 9–12°C. Fecundity is high and females are capable of producing some 400,000–1,000,000 eggs each, depending on size.

The fry are some 2.5–3mm at hatching and are perfectly symmetrical pelagic little fish. As they grow, however, they start to develop asymmetrically and they metamorphose rapidly at 20–30mm to become flattened and bottom living. They grow fairly rapidly in good conditions and can reach a length of 10cm after one year and 15cm after two. Males mature before females at a length of $c.$ 12cm (18cm for females). They usually reach about 25cm after four years and mostly live for 8–10 years, occasionally surviving up to 20 years.

The fry rely on their small yolk sacs for about two days and then feed on zooplankton, especially crustaceans such as copepods and the larvae of crabs. On the bottom they feed on a variety of benthic invertebrates, including worms, crustaceans and molluscs. The young fish often move into fresh water for a year or so, where they feed on tubificid worms, insect larvae and molluscs. It is principally a night-time feeder, and in the sea often undertakes a daily migration up the shore closely following the incoming tide up and then down again as it retreats. It is this habit – during daylight – that makes it such a valuable (and available) prey for Ospreys in Scotland and has partly lead to their concentration as breeding birds around some of the large east-coast estuaries (e.g. Findhorn Bay). It may sometimes swim well off the bottom to take an item of food.

The Flounder is an important commercial species caught in trap nets and seines in several parts of Europe, though it is not rated highly in the British Isles where it is usually a by-catch of some other type of bottom-trawl fishery. It is a popular sport fish and is caught in large numbers by sea anglers all round the soft coasts of the British Isles. It is a delicious fish to eat when fresh, especially when hot smoked.

Though not often kept in aquaria by amateurs, small specimens tame readily and make very attractive additions to suitable freshwater or marine tanks and have the attractive habit of adhering to the glass side by means of the flattened body (thus allowing the pale underside to be examined closely) or almost disappearing on the sandy bottom by a combination of camouflage colouration and burying in the sand.

28
The Future

Distribution Changes
Every year, changes take place in the distribution of freshwater fish in the British Isles, for the situation has never reached equilibrium during the 10,000 years or so since the last ice age. In addition to the slow rate of natural dispersal northwards by many of our native fish species (especially the cyprinids) humans have caused many changes. Few of these have been beneficial to native species, and if things are to improve in the future we must learn from our mistakes. Many of the relevant aspects have been discussed in earlier chapters, but what can be done to rectify them?

Introductions
Many thousands of different introductions involving most of our fish species have been carried out in various parts of the country. Rarely have any of these had a reasoned scientific basis for being carried out, and practically never have the results been monitored. Fortunately, a high proportion of these introductions have been unsuccessful. Certainly some damage to native species has been done by some of them, and there can be few cases where any good has been done – especially as far as our native species are concerned.

In spite of existing legislation, casual introductions continue to occur – sometimes with potentially horrifying consequences. The introduction of Ruffe to Loch Lomond in recent years is an example of this and the even more recent establishment there of Dace and Chub has presented additional threats to the native fish community – especially the endangered Powan and the unique race of River Lamprey there. In recent years too, Pike have been introduced into pristine salmon, trout and charr communities. The lowering of custom barriers within the EEC in 1992 may increase the threat of introduction from the continent.

As well as tightening the legislation to prevent such introductions, we need a change of heart among those involved in carrying out such transfers – in the majority of cases, anglers. With many thousands of lakes and streams in this country, is there any justification at all for moving relatively common species (in the south of the country at least) into additional waters further north, just because they do not occur there? The rare local fish in some of these waters are under enough threats without those posed by the indiscriminate introductions of unwanted species.

Fisheries
The majority of planned introductions taking place at the moment are of sport fish and the usual objective is either to diversify and enhance the existing natural populations or to provide catchable size fish which can be caught immediately – the 'put and take' fishery. Enhancement is very rarely justified

Fig. 138 An adult Rainbow Trout from Clandeboye Lough Co. Down (Niall Campbell).

and in the authors' opinion should never be carried out unless the following questions have been asked. 'Will it do any harm to the existing fish populations and fishery?', 'Is it necessary?' and 'Is it likely to fulfil its objectives?' If these questions were answered honestly, fewer enhancement introductions would be carried out and less damage would be done to our indigenous fish populations.

The popularity of 'put and take' fisheries is undoubtedly increasing, though many find it difficult to understand the satisfaction in catching tame, fat fish which come easily to a lure and may only have been released from the fish farm the day before. There they will have been fed on an expensive pellet diet (much of it consisting of meal made from other fish species to which flesh-colouring agents have been added) and perhaps treated with antibiotics and other medications. Such fish are normally far less attractive than their wild counterparts – often having foreshortened snouts and stunted and worn fins through being kept in close confinement with hundreds of their brethren. In addition to the unreality of the situation, the introduction of such fish can materially damage the native stock through competition for food and space, the introduction of disease and the reduction of the genetic integrity and fitness of the native stock.

An additional problem related to 'put and take' fisheries is that clearly the fish being introduced have been reared somewhere else with all the attendant problems created by fish farms. These include water abstraction, pollution from waste food and faeces, increased demand for industrial fish meal (i.e. more fish will be killed somewhere), introduction of diseases, problems with predators (Herons, Cormorants, Otters, Mink, etc.) attracted to the farm, and impact on native fish from escapees through competition and reduction of genetic integrity. All these factors must be borne in mind when the pros and cons of 'put and take' fisheries are discussed.

Perhaps the answer to these various introductions is to accept that they are going to continue to take place in some waters, but to try to identify waters which are important for various reasons and make sure that no introductions take place there. This would seem to be a reasonable compromise which would ensure that the native stocks will continue in some waters and that these truly wild fish will be available to those anglers who wish to use their skill to pursue them there.

Global Warming

The present distribution and composition of our freshwater (and marine) fish fauna could be radically altered due to the much publicised 'greenhouse effect'. Should this lead to a significant increase in temperatures, as is considered possible by some authorities, the southern part of British Isles may become unsuitable for anadromous salmonids. Consequently Salmon and Sea Trout will be restricted to northern waters – assuming that these do not become too warm also. Populations of Brown Trout might become scarce in the south, as might those Arctic Charr and whitefish in the north.

On the other hand, more members of the carp family would be able to thrive in our northern waters, while Sea Bass and mullets could become familiar fishes in northern estuaries. In the south there would be a temptation for anglers to distribute more widely such exotics as the larger Sunfish and Catfish.

Legislation

The existing legislation in Britain controlling fish introductions has developed on a rather piecemeal basis as a response to a number of emergencies that have arisen in the past. As a result it has a number of deficiencies which need to be remedied if we are to be in full control of the destiny of our native fish populations. One of the biggest loopholes relates to the control of fish coming into the country, for whilst it is difficult to bring in most salmonids in this way, it is relatively easy to import almost any other fish which can be classified as a 'pond or aquarium' species. Thus, many pet shops around the country are at present selling several species which could well establish themselves in the British Isles if introduced, intentionally or unintentionally, into suitable waters. Examples of such fish which could well pose a threat to our native stocks are the Channel Catfish *Ictalurus punctatus* and the Black Bullhead, *Ictalurus melas*.

A simple improvement in the legislation which would help here would be to produce a 'black list' of temperate species of this kind that are likely to cause damage if released in the wild. This could be done relatively easily and cause little inconvenience or financial loss to the importers and suppliers of exotic fish, but the opening of trade within the EEC may prevent any such action from having an effect.

Land Use

One of the most important revolutions in this country which is taking place at present is the pressure for change in land use.

This has been brought about for a variety of reasons, partly financial advantages in planting some crops (e.g conifers) and partly the recent overproduction of foodstuffs. There are likely to be enormous changes in the countryside over the next few decades and these will undoubtedly have effects on our native fish populations. Some of these effects may be good, others bad.

The main trend in the foreseeable future is likely to be a change away from conventional and intensive agriculture towards other forms of land use, particularly forestry and leisure activities. Overall, this is likely to be beneficial to the freshwater environment – especially in the lowland areas, where a reduction in fertilisers, herbicides and pesticides, and less intense drainage, with more ground under both deciduous and coniferous trees should all prove beneficial. In the uplands, however, especially in Wales and Scotland the increasing amounts of blanket coniferous afforestation are already creating problems for fish populations and in some base-poor heavily afforested areas the waters have become acidic and completely fishless. In addition, the development of estate and farm leisure centres is already resulting in the 'enhancement' of ponds and lakes through the introduction of exotics and farmed species for 'put and take' fisheries.

Pollution

Our native fish face a number of problems, some of them common to other forms of wildlife, others more particular to fish. Rivers and to a lesser extent lakes are repositories of enormous amounts of human waste, ranging from toxic industrial chemicals through agricultural slurries and herbicides to domestic sewage. Even aerial pollutants such as sulphur dioxide from powerstation chimneys are eventually washed into water courses as 'acid rain'.

Many rivers have become completely fishless as a result, especially those in the industrial and heavily populated lowland areas of Great Britain. The Rivers Clyde in Scotland and Thames in England are good examples of rivers which formerly had rich and diverse fish populations of some 20–30 species, but which eventually became completely fishless in the lower reaches. Here at one time, not too many years ago, the waters were totally devoid of oxygen and comprised a lethal cocktail of various industrial chemicals.

Other factors have affected fish in various ways. Barriers on rivers, such as weirs or hydro-dams, have blocked the passage of migratory fish to their spawning grounds and so eliminated them. Enrichment from farm fertilisers, overfishing and the introduction of new fish species (many of them from abroad) have all contributed to the decline of fish stocks – especially those of the rarer and more sensitive native species. Fish populations are limited by land boundaries to their immediate water body and thus the whole population is vulnerable to a single incident of toxic spillage or acidification. Where a native species is found in a few waters only – sometimes only one or two (as is now the case with the Vendace) – it is obviously extremely vulnerable and in urgent need of protection.

Over the last two decades there have been very significant advances in combating pollution, thanks to the work of the River Purification Boards in Scotland and the Water Authorities in England and Wales. The trend towards increasingly polluted waters and declining fish populations has largely been reversed and many rivers are now much cleaner than they were 50 or even 100 years ago. Some rivers which were so badly polluted that they became fishless are now clean again and supporting good stocks of fish. The Rivers Clyde and Thames are good examples.

However, the future is less certain, for both the Water Authorities in England and Wales (which have now been privatised) and the River Purification Boards in Scotland are undergoing reorganisation, and it may be that their future structure will make them less efficient at pollution control. There is already considerable evidence that the condition of some rivers in England

and Wales – where the Water Authorities were also responsible for sewage treatment and therefore among the main polluters – is declining, whereas in Scotland the 'River Purification Boards' main role is pollution prevention – while sewage treatment is the responsibility of the local councils. It is clearly highly desirable for these two functions to rest within separate departments if conflicts of interest are not to arise.

Conservation

Both the authors have spent much of their working lives within the field of conservation and feel deeply about it. The conservation of fishes has been sadly neglected until now but there are several indications that this is changing. There is no doubt that public support and feeling behind the conservation movement has strengthened and broadened substantially over the last decade. Many readers of this book are likely to be supportive of wildlife conservation in some form and to have his or her own image of what that means. Natural habitats like meadows and mountains, forests and seashore, rivers and lakes, wildlife like trees and flowers, butterflies and bees, birds and mammals – these are all areas of popular interest and concern. But what about fish, and why conserve them? Do they need it? Are they worth it? The authors believe that the case is strong and would hope that the reader would think so too.

Fish suffer from a bad press! Many are difficult to observe in the wild and so do not have a popular following of field botanists or ornithologists. Instead of being warm and feathery or furry (like birds or bats) they are cold and wet. However, we have noticed that a well stocked and laid-out display in a fishmonger's shop attracts a crowd of window gazers. A good example is the artistic and very varied seafood display in a well-known London store, which continually attracts attention from shoppers and photographers. Most people see fish most commonly as dead objects on a fishmonger's slab or served up in batter with chips. Yet there is substantial interest among some groups of people in living fish. There are reputed to be 3 million anglers in this country, but sadly their main concern is with the species they wish to catch. Indeed, some do harm in a number of ways, such as moving fish around the country and introducing them as predators or competitors to the waters containing rare species. Another major interest group is aquarists, but unfortunately the great majority of these are uninterested in our native fish and are concerned mainly with exotic species.

Yet our native fish species have much of merit and interest. They were among the very first recolonisers after the last ice age along with the first plants and birds. Many are important commercially in some parts of the world. Others (contrary to popular opinion) are colourful and have fascinating life cycles and habits. Several are much easier to observe in the field, if you can be in the right place at the right time, and a number make excellent subjects for aquaria and indeed can often be induced to breed there.

As far as our rarer species are concerned, although all of them do occur in other countries, the British populations have all been isolated for at least 10,000 years and have developed distinct gene pools during that period. This is in contrast to virtually all our birds, which are really just part of the north-west European stock. In some countries, where they are less rare, they

Fig. 139 Stripping eggs from a female Powan at Loch Lomond as part of a conservation project (Peter Maitland).

are valuable commercially. The importance of conserving this resource for the future in virtually all continents and countries is clearly imperative.

The authors consider that about 10 of our native species urgently require specific conservation measures of some kind. Their needs vary greatly. At the worst end of the scale are those species which are probably extinct now in the British Isles. The Burbot formerly occurred in several rivers along the southeast coast of England, but it has not been recorded there for many years now. It seems likely that river pollution has been a major factor in its decline and it is likely that it is now extinct in Britain. Similarly, the Houting used to be a regular visitor to the coastal waters and estuaries in the same area, but because of a dramatic decline in its breeding areas (some of the rivers of Scandinavia) none has been seen for several decades.

The conservation action needed for such species (and others like the Sturgeon) must involve international action and hopefully their eventual re-establishment in this country. The immediate concern in the British Isles must be for species which are still with us but are rare and under very significant threat. Such fish include the Vendace (which occurs in only two lakes), the Powan (which occurs in only six), the Pollan (which occurs only in about four loughs in Ireland) and the Twaite and Allis Shads whose status is still

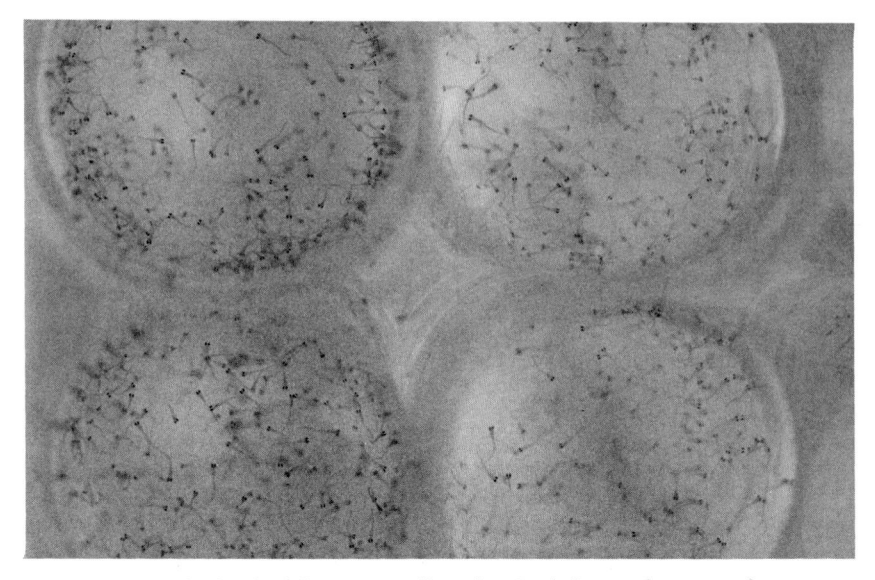

Fig. 140 Powan fry hatched from eggs collected at Loch Lomond as part of a conservation exercise. These jars of young fish are about to be released in another water in the hope of starting a new population there (Peter Maitland).

uncertain but undoubtedly under threat. Here, the local population of Goureen in Ireland is of particular importance.

Finally there are several species which are not immediately threatened, but which have declined significantly this century. We need to learn much more about the threats to such species and about their current status. Within this category are the Arctic Charr, the Smelt and the Spined Loach. Some of these are known to have (or have had) quite distinct races or populations – several of which are now extinct, others of which are struggling for survival.

There is an enormous amount of work to be done in the field of fish conservation and it can probably only be tackled bit by bit. In addition to establishing the status of fish in existing nature reserves and elsewhere, much effort at the moment is going towards identifying the conservation needs of our most endangered species and implementing these immediately, where possible. One of the most positive areas of management lies in the establishment of new populations – either to replace those which have become extinct or to provide an additional safeguard. Any species which is found in only a few waters is believed to be in potential danger and the creation of additional independent stocks is an urgent and worthwhile conservation activity.

The authors believe that this can be done without any threat to the existing stocks. With all the fish concerned it should be possible to obtain substantial numbers of fertilised eggs by catching and stripping adult fish during their spawning period. The adults can then be returned safely to the water if necessary to spawn in future years. Fortunately, most fish produce an enormous excess of eggs and so substantial numbers can be taken at this time without harm. Having identified an appropriate water in which to create a new population this can be initiated by placing the eggs there, or hatching the eggs in a hatchery and introducing the young at various stages of development.

Such a procedure is at present under way with the Powan, supported by the NCC. There are only six populations of the species in the whole of the British Isles – two in Scotland, three in England (where it is known locally as the Schelly) and one in Wales (where it is known as the Gwyniad). The largest population is probably in Loch Lomond and here in recent years one of the authors has netted adult fish from the spawning grounds in January and stripped them to obtain many thousands of fertilised eggs. Some of these were placed immediately in a nearby loch whilst others were taken to the laboratory and hatched, then to be taken for release in the same loch.

The Arctic Charr occurs in only two or three lakes in Wales, a few in England but many more in Ireland and in Scotland – particularly in the north-west. However, it has disappeared from several of its previous waters in England; in southern Scotland, where there were previously at least four populations, only one remains – in Loch Doon in Galloway. The system here is under threat from increasing acidification and part of the current work is to safeguard the stock by creating new populations. Thus, in the autumns of 1986, 1987 and 1988, one of the authors was at Loch Doon and successfully obtained eggs from the adult fish which were spawning at that time. These eggs were hatched under controlled conditions and young fish have been introduced to two large reservoirs in the Scottish Borders.

Work of this type is time-consuming and success cannot always be guaranteed. Additionally, it is quite possible that a new population may not take from a single stocking to a new water. Thus, the Powan and Charr projects will be repeated for several years until evidence of new self-sustaining populations is available. In addition, parallel projects with other fish populations will be initiated to the extent that resources will permit.

One of the most urgent of these projects relates to an extremely interesting small fish called the Vendace. This species formerly occurred in two lochs in Scotland and two in England. Unfortunately, the two Scottish lochs were both very small; in one of them the Vendace disappeared at the turn of this century when a sewage outfall was led into the loch and in the other it appears to have become extinct from various pressures over the last decade. The objective of current work on this species is to identify suitable waters in which new populations may be established and initiate a stocking programme.

In the longer term it is hoped that all the other rare species will be involved in the project and that even the extinct Burbot will be restored to British waters by obtaining stock from waters elsewhere in Europe and reintroducing this attractive fish to some of its old haunts. International cooperation around the North Sea may also favour the restoration of the Houting to its previous densities, so that it too may become again a visitor to our shores.

Some scenarios for the future look bright. There have been enormous strides in pollution control and a number of our worst rivers are now much cleaner. The Rivers Clyde and Thames, mentioned above, are now so much better than 50 years ago that fish have been returning to them in increasing numbers. The final arbiters of water quality are surely the fish themselves and the return of the Atlantic Salmon to the River Clyde after an absence of more than 100 years is a marvellous tribute to decades of work by the local river purification board. These exciting events prove that river pollution is reversible and that recovery can be comparatively rapid.

The authors hope that eventually we will understand much more about the status and requirements of our native species, that all of them will be given much more protection in nature reserves and that their future in these islands will be assured through the re-establishment in previously occupied waters and the creation of additional populations as a form of safeguard. The need is clearly a long-term one. Hopefully, by the end of the century, much ground (really water!) which has been lost will have been recovered and our native fish species will be safe for future generations to use and enjoy in various ways.

Nature Reserves for Fish

There are now many nature reserves of various types and managed by different organisations throughout Great Britain. They have been established for numerous different reasons – some for a unique type of habitat or plant community, many for their ornithological interest and others for the rare flowers or butterflies which occur there. We have no reserves which have been set up especially for their fish and the authors hope that this is something which will be remedied at some time in the future.

Of course, many nature reserves have water bodies on them and most of these contain fish. The exact status of such populations is very uncertain at the moment, and one of the main aspects of present research by one of the authors is to investigate all the National Nature Reserves and find out which fish are there, and thus already given a good measure of protection. Such a baseline is a prime requirement before suggestions can be put forward for any new reserves which may be needed especially for fish conservation.

Research

We know a great deal now about the natural history of most of our fish and much of this has been researched by scientists over the last two decades. However, much remains to be learned, especially, as we have seen above, about our rarer and endangered species. This remains an important area for future research.

However, we are also still extremely ignorant about the population biology of most of our species and the factors controlling their numbers. Information of this kind is vital to the management of our stocks, but unfortunately is difficult to acquire because of the difficulties of obtaining exact counts of entire fish populations and the complexity of factors involved. Nonetheless, some useful studies have already been made and, with the advances in modern technology related to echo sounding, revolutionary new fish counters and new methods of tagging, the future looks bright.

Aquaria

One of the main problems in appreciating the beauty and interest of our native fish is the difficulty of observing them. A number of species can be observed in the field from time to time, especially during their migrations (e.g. salmon and eels) or spawning acts (e.g. lampreys and sticklebacks), but most are difficult to observe and therefore rarely seen. Thus, very few people in the British Isles have ever seen Twaite or Allis Shad, Powan, Vendace, Houting, Pollan or Burbot. An obvious way to remedy this is via aquaria – both public and private. Some excellent marine aquaria have been established as a by-product of the burgeoning aquaculture industry, and these are very well patronised by the public. Certainly, visiting zoos and wildlife parks is the way that most people see many of our native mammals (e.g. Wild Cats, Otters, Pine Martens and Polecats), and there is no reason why this should not also be the case with our native freshwater fish.

Yet there are very few public aquaria or other displays concerning our native fish, and several (in different parts of the country) are surely needed if we wish to demonstrate the variety and interest of our fish fauna. These need not be too expensive nor necessarily aim to include all the British species. They may try to emphasise or explore very local fish, or show some aspects of our commercial species, or demonstrate conservation of our rarer species and so on. It is ironic that it is very much easier to see (and even purchase) a wide variety of exotic fish from many other countries (some of them temperate species which could establish in this country to the detriment of our native fish), but impossible anywhere to see a comprehensive collection of native fish.

In addition to aquarium displays of different kinds there are other means of giving people pleasure and an interest in our fish. For instance, there are many places all over the country where some species can be easily seen at some times of the year. The fish viewing chamber on the salmon ladder over the hydroelectric dam on the River Tummel at Pitlochry is a good example and many thousands of people pass through this each year in the hope of seeing a wild Atlantic Salmon. Why should we not follow the excellent example of ornithologists and create hides and viewing areas in our country parks and some wildlife reserves where the public can see fish in action? Good examples abroad are the Fairy Springs at Rotorua in New Zealand and the Capilano Dam near Vancouver in Canada. At the latter site there is a marvellous display of fish, and uniformed hostesses conduct visitors around. In the British Isles, Sea, River and Brook Lampreys are all obvious at spawning time and their nesting activities and reproductive behaviour are fascinating. At many waterfalls and obstructions salmon and trout can be seen on their spawning migrations and the actual act of their spawning is much easier to observe than most people believe. Minnows and several other members of the carp family gather in large numbers on the spawning beds and can be watched with ease at the right time of year.

Some of the commercial aspects of our freshwater fisheries are also of considerable interest. Of course, there are many anglers throughout the country who spend much of their time in pursuit of various species. However, only in a few places can commercial netting be seen, and only rarely is it ever explained properly to the public. One of the authors was delighted recently to see attractive information notices provided by Highland Regional Council telling the public about Atlantic Salmon – one at a commercial netting station at Bonar Bridge, another at the Shin Falls. There are many other areas of the country where this type of example could be followed.

Fish farms are another area where the interest of the public could be fostered. Indeed many Rainbow Trout farms are already proving an attraction, and thousands of people now visit them each year, usually paying to enter and even to buy the pelleted food on which the fish would be fed anyway by the owner. Fish at various stages of their life cycle can usually be seen on such farms and indeed it is common practice for the adults to be sold on the way out – either fresh or smoked. Such displays should be encouraged and could surely be developed in various parts of the country and for other species.

Following on this theme and another idea which is a developing attraction in many areas for other interests such as castles, gardens and even whisky, why should we not have 'fish trails' around the country? On these trails it could be possible in a day to visit, say, a public aquarium, a fish farm, a place where fish can be seen in the wild (say a waterfall in the autumn or a viewing chamber in a river or lake), a port where fish are landed commercially, a river where commercial netting is being carried out or eel traps, etc. are being emptied and so on. Such trails would undoubtedly boost the tourist potential of any area as well as educate the public about the beauty and value of our native fish and fisheries.

Appendix 1

Distribution Maps

The following maps are all after Maitland (1972a). In each case the page reference refers to the main entry for the species in the chapters. Note that with extinct species (e.g. Houting and Burbot) the former distribution is indicated.

Map 1 Sea Lamprey p.81    *Map 2* River Lamprey p.85    *Map 3* Brook Lamprey p.87

Map 4 Sturgeon p.91    *Map 5* Allis Shad p.94    *Map 6* Twaite Shad p.95

324 FRESHWATER FISHES

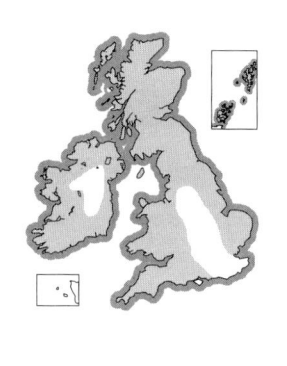

Map 7 Atlantic Salmon p.101

Map 8 Trout p.111

Map 9 Rainbow Trout p.126

Map 10 Pink Salmon p.131

Map 11 Arctic Charr p.132

Map 12 Brook Charr p.140

Map 13 Houting p.146

Map 14 Powan p.149

Map 15 Vendace p.152

APPENDIX 1 325

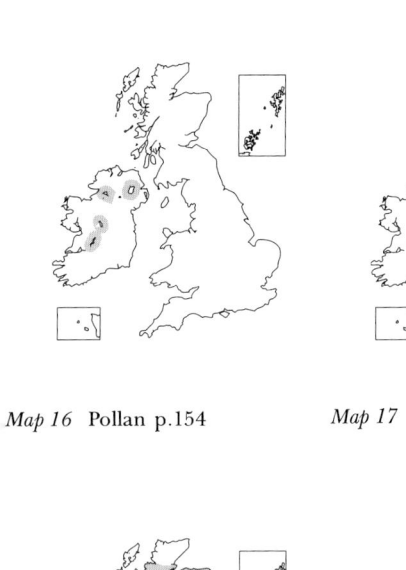

Map 16 Pollan p.154

Map 17 Grayling p.158

Map 18 Smelt p.163

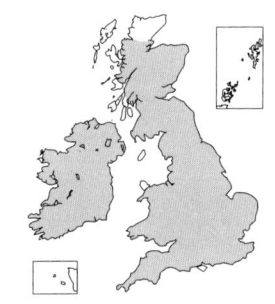

Map 19 Pike p.167

Map 20 Common Carp p.180

Map 21 Crucian Carp p.184

Map 22 Goldfish p.187

Map 23 Barbel p.190

Map 24 Gudgeon p.191

326   FRESHWATER FISHES

Map 25 Tench p.194

Map 26 Silver Bream p.197

Map 27 Common Bream p.199

Map 28 Bleak p.203

Map 29 Minnow p.206

Map 30 Bitterling p.210

Map 31 Rudd p.212

Map 32 Roach p.215

Map 33 Chub p.219

APPENDIX 1 327

Map 34 Orfe p.222

Map 35 Dace p.225

Map 36 Spined Loach p.231

Map 37 Stone Loach p.233

Map 38 Danube Catfish p.238

Map 39 European Eel p.241

Map 40 Three-spined Stickleback p.251

Map 41 Nine-spined Stickleback p.258

Map 42 Burbot p.262

328 FRESHWATER FISHES

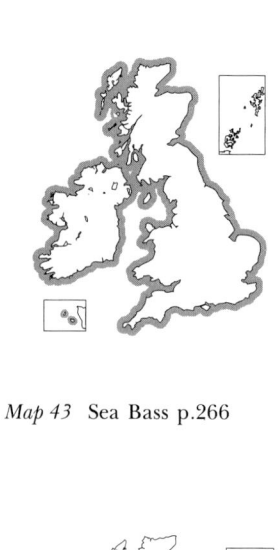

Map 43 Sea Bass p.266

Map 44 Largemouth Bass p.271

Map 45 Pumpkinseed p.274

Map 46 Rock Bass p.277

Map 47 Perch p.280

Map 48 Ruffe p.286

Map 49 Pikeperch p.288

Map 50 Common Goby p.293

Map 51 Thick-lipped Mullet p.297

APPENDIX 1   329

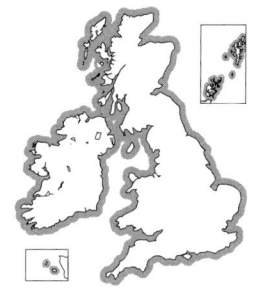

Map 52 Thin-lipped Mullet p.299

Map 53 Golden Mullet p.301

Map 54 Bullhead p.304

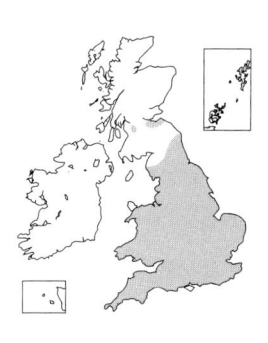

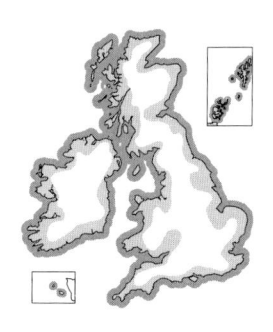

Map 55 Flounder p.308

Appendix 2

The Names of British Freshwater Fishes

Table 1 Some origins for the English names of freshwater fish in the British Isles.

Common name	English origin	Meaning
Lamprey	Lampetra (L)	Stone-sucker
	Lamproie (F)	
Sturgeon	Sturio (L)	Latin name
	Esturgeoun (OE & F)	
Shad	Sceadd (OE)	A herring
	Sgadan (S)	
Allis (Shad)	Alosa (L)	
	Alose (F)	
Twaite (Shad)	Hwit (OE)	White or bright
Salmon	Salire (L)	
	Saumon (F)	
Trout	Trutta (L)	To gnaw (Ancient Greek)
	Truht (OE)	
	Truite (F)	
Rainbow (Trout)	–	Ref. to red band
Pink (Salmon)	–	Ref. to adult colour
Charr	Tarr (S)	Belly
	Tor (W)	Belly
Houting	–	–
Powan	Pollan (I)	Of an inland lake
Vendace	Vandoise (OF)	Dace
Pollan	Pollan (I)	Of an inland lake
Grayling	Gray+Ling (OE)	Ref. to colour
Smelt	Schmelt (Gr)	Ref. to characteristic smell
	Smelt (D)	
Pike	Pike (E)	Shaped like a pike
Carp	Carpa (L)	–
	Carpe (OF)	
Crucian (Carp)	Karausche (Gr)	Ref. to dark colour
	Coracinus (L)	
Goldfish	–	Ref. to colour of domestic form
Barbel	Barbeau (MF)	Bearded
Gudgeon	Gobio (L)	Like a goby
	Gojon (ME)	
	Goujon (F)	
Tench	Tinca (L)	Latin name of fish
	Tanche (MF)	
Bream	Bresme (OF)	Glitter
	Breme (MF)	
	Breme (ME)	
Bleak	Blaec (OE)	Shining
Minnow	Menuise (F)	Small fry
	Mynwe (OE)	
	Mennen (S)	
Bitterling	–	Ref. to taste
Rudd	Ruddy (E)	Colour of eye
Roach	Roche (OF)	–
Chub	Chub (ME)	Possibly chubby = plump
Orfe	Orphus (L)	Latin name of fish
	Orfe (Gr & F)	

Common name	English origin	Meaning
Dace	Dardus (L)	To dart
	Darse (ME)	
Loach	Loche (ME & F)	A slug
Catfish	–	Ref. to feelers on head
Eel	Anguilla (L)	Little snake
	Anguille (F)	
	Ael (OE)	
	Aal (Gr, Du & Da)	
Stickleback	Sticel (OE & ME)	A spine or prick
Burbot	Bourbotte (F)	Bearded
Bass	Barse (ME)	A perch
	Barsch (Gr)	
Pumpkinseed	–	Likeness to seed
Perch	Perca (L)	Pied or spotted
	Perche (F)	Barsch (Gr)
Ruffe	Rough (ME)	Ref. to spiny gill cover
Pikeperch	–	A pike-like perch
Goby	Gobius (L)	Latin name for goby
Mullet	Mullus (L)	Latin name for Mullet
	Molet (ME)	
	Mulet (OF)	
Bullhead	Bull (E)	Large
Flounder	Flynda (ON)	Ref. to movement on bottom
	Flynder (Da)	

Key to symbols: E = English; Da = Danish; Du = Dutch; F = French; Gr = German; I = Irish; L = Latin; (M = Middle); N = Norse; (O = Old); S = Scots; W = Welsh.

Table 2 Gaelic and Welsh names for freshwater fish in the British Isles. As most fish are known by several names an attempt has been made to select the commonest usage for this list.

Common name	Scots Gaelic	Irish Gaelic	Welsh
Sea Lamprey	Creathall-na-mara	Loimpre mhara	Llysywen bendoll y mor
River Lamprey	Creathall-na-h-aibhne	Loimpre abhann	Llysywen bendoll yr afon
Brook Lamprey	Creathall-an-uilt	Loimpre shruthain	Llysywen bendoll y nant
Common Sturgeon	Stirean	Stirean	Stwrsiwn
Allis Shad	Gobhlachan	Sead alosach	Gwangen alis
Twaite Shad	q	Sead fhallacsach	Gwangen twait
Atlantic Salmon	Bradan	Bradan	Eog mor iwerig
Brown Trout	Breac (dubh, etc]	Breac donn	Brithyll
(Sea Trout)	Gealag	Breac geal	Sewen
Rainbow Trout	Breac-dathte	Breac dea-dhathach	Brithyll yr enfys
Pink Salmon	–	–	Eog pinc
Arctic Charr	Tarragan	Ruabhreac	Torgoch yr arctig
Brook Charr	–	–	Torgoch y nant
Houting	–	–	–
Powan	Pollag	–	Gwyniad
Vendace	Pollan	–	–
Pollan	–	Pollan	–
Grayling	Glasag	–	Crothell
Smelt	Dubh-bhreac	Smealt	Morfrithyll
Pike	Geadas	Gailliasc	Penhwyad
Common Carp	Carbh	Carban	Carp
Crucian Carp	–	–	Carp di-farf
Goldfish	Iasg-oir	Iasc orga	Eurbysg
Barbel	Breac-fheusagach	Bronnag	Barfogyn
Gudgeon	Guda	Brannog	Llyfrothen
Tench	Teins	Curaman	Tens
Silver Bream	–	–	Gwrachen wen
Common Bream	Briantadh	Brean	Merfog

Bleak	–	–	Gorwyniad
Minnow	Sgildaimhne	Bodairlin	Pilcyn
Bitterling	–	–	–
Rudd	–	Ruan	Rhuddbysg
Roach	Roisteach	Roiste	Rhufell
Chub	Pluicean	–	Annog
Orfe	Orf	–	Orff
Dace	–	Deas	Darsen
Spined Loach	–	–	–
Stone Loach	Breac beadaidh	Cailleach-rua	Gwrachen farfog
Danube Catfish	–	Cat fionnuisce	Morgath europ
European Eel	Easgann	Eascann	Llysywen
Three-spined Stickleback	Biorag Lodain	Biorach lodain	Doctor coch tri-phigyn
Nine-spined Stickleback	Iasg deilgneach	Garmachan deich gclipe	Brithyll y don naw-phigyn
Burbot	–	–	Llofen
Sea Bass	–	Doingean	Draenogyn y mor
Largemouth Bass	–	–	–
Pumpkinseed	–	–	–
Rock Bass	–	–	–
Perch	Creagag-uisge	Peirse	Draenogyn
Ruffe	–	–	Crychyn
Pikeperch	–	–	Draenogyn penhwyad
Common Goby	Buidhleis	Mac siobhain inbhir	–
Thick-lipped Mullet	Muileid	Millead glas	Hyrddyn gweflog
Thin-lipped Mullet	–	–	Hyrddyn brych
Golden Mullet	–	–	Hyrddyn euraid
Bullhead	Greusaiche	–	Penlletwad
Flounder	Leabag	Leadhbog	Lladen fach

Appendix 3

Growth Curves

The following curves have been selected to indicate typical growth in each species. Unless indicated otherwise, the vertical axes represnet length in millimeters, the horizontal axes age in years.

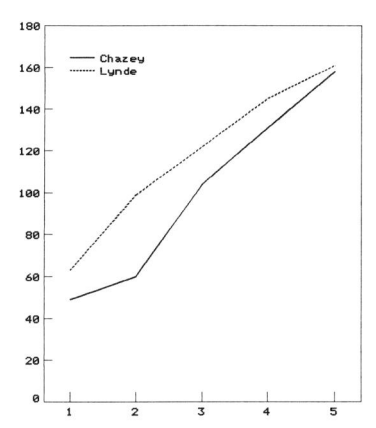

1 Sea Lamprey larvae in the Great Chazey River, USA and Lynde Creek, Canada (after Beamish & Medland 1988).

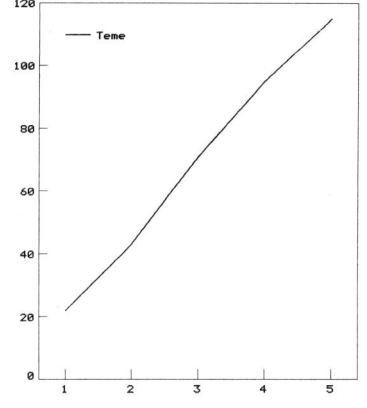

2 River Lamprey larvae to metamorphosis in the River Teme (after Hardisty & Potter 1971).

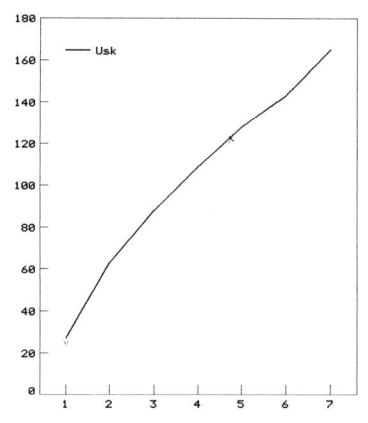

3 Brook Lamprey larvae to metamorphosis in the River Usk (after Hardisty & Huggins 1970).

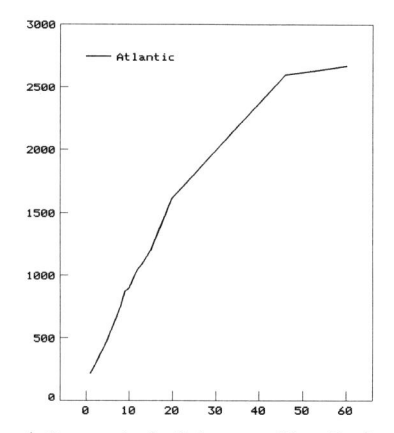

4 Sturgeon in the St Lawrence River, North America (after Magnin 1963). Note: this curve is for the North American population of Sturgeon which some authors consider to be a separate species *Acipenser oxyrhynchus*.

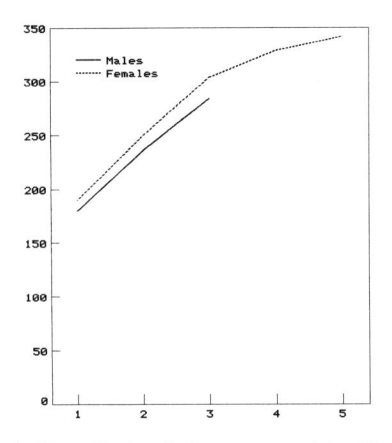

5 Twaite Shad in the Severn estuary (after Claridge & Gardner 1978).

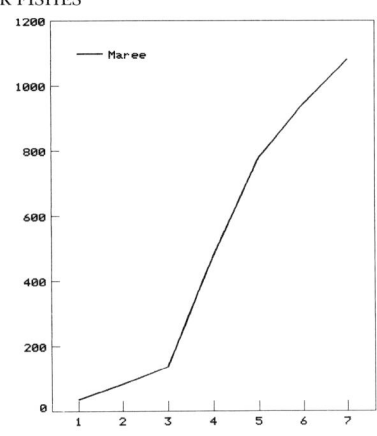

6 Atlantic Salmon from the Loch Maree system (after Nall 1930).

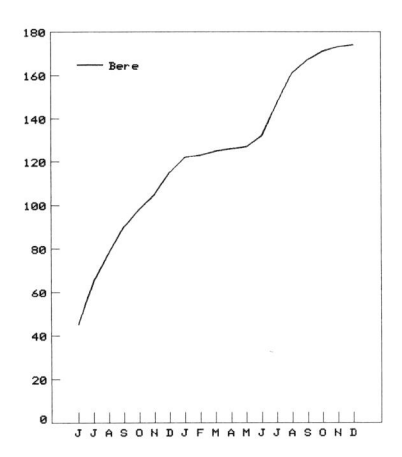

7 Young Atlantic Salmon in the Bere Stream (after Mann 1971).

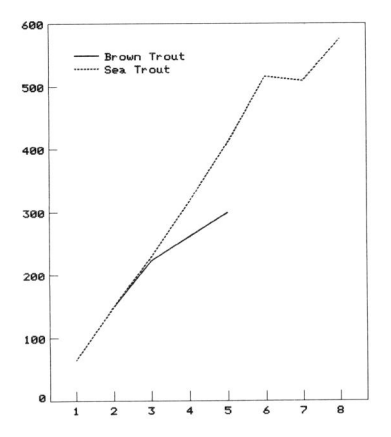

8 Brown and Sea Trout in Loch Kildonan (after Nall 1930 and Campbell 1970).

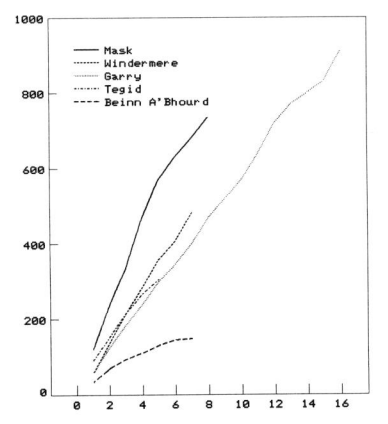

9 Brown Trout in Lough Mask (after Went 1968), Windermere (after Allen 1938), Loch Garry (after Campbell 1979a), Llyn Tegid (after Ball & Jones 1960) and the Dubh Lochainn of Beinn A'Bhourd (Campbell 1971).

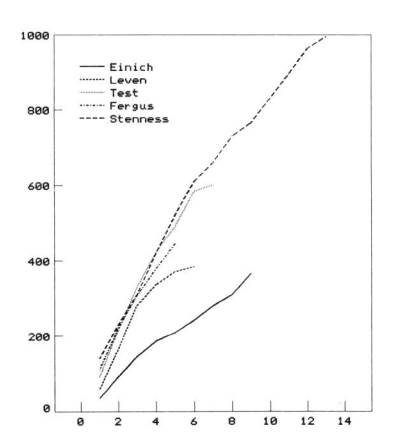

10 Brown Trout in Loch Einich (after Campbell 1971), Loch Leven (after Frost & Brown 1967), River Test (after Gerrish 1935), River Fergus (after Healy 1957) and Loch of Stenness (after Campbell 1979a).

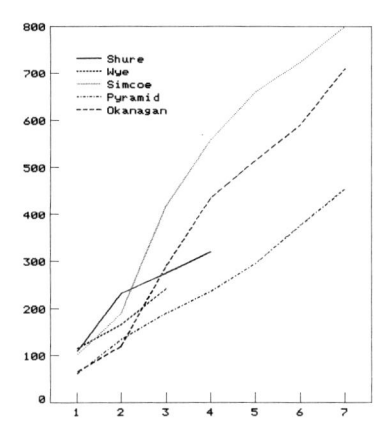

APPENDIX 3   335

11 Rainbow Trout in Lough Shure (after Frost 1940), in the River Wye (after Worthington 1941) and in North America in Lake Simcoe (after MacCrimmon 1956), in Pyramid Lake (after Rawson & Elsey 1950) and in Lake Okanagan (after Clemens et al. 1939).

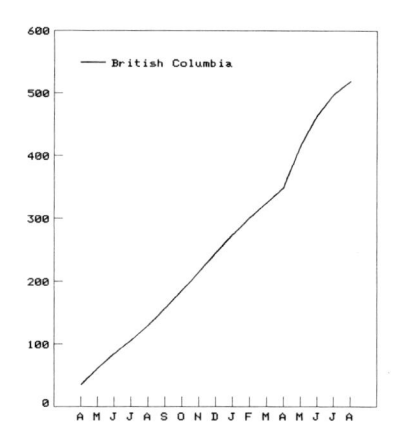

12 Pink Salmon in British Columbia, Canada (after LeBrasseur & Parker, 1964).

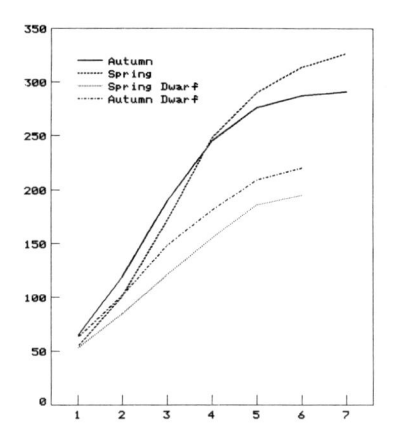

13 Arctic Charr in Windermere (after Frost & Kipling, 1980).

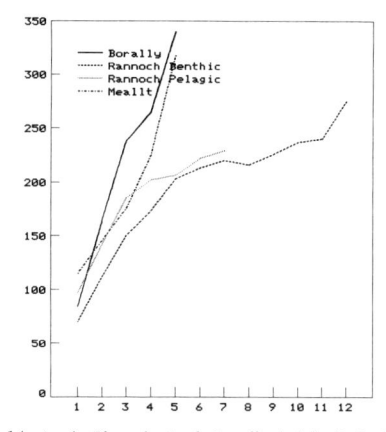

14 Arctic Charr in Loch Borally (original), Loch Rannoch (after Walker, Greer and Gardner, 1988) and Loch Meallt (after Campbell & Williamson, 1983).

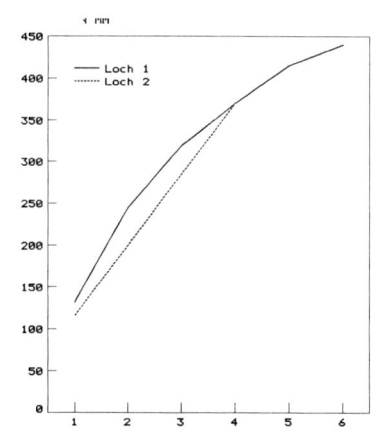

15 Brook Charr in two Scottish lochs (original data).

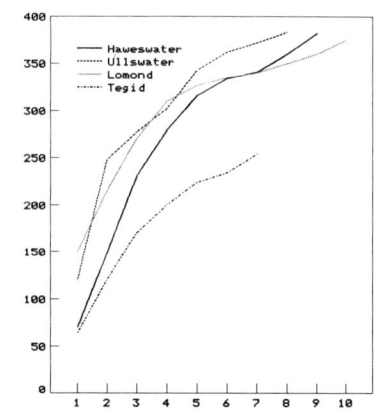

16 Powan in Haweswater and Ullswater (after Bagenal 1970), in Loch Lomond (after Brown 1988) and in Llyn Tegid (after Haram 1968)

336   FRESHWATER FISHES

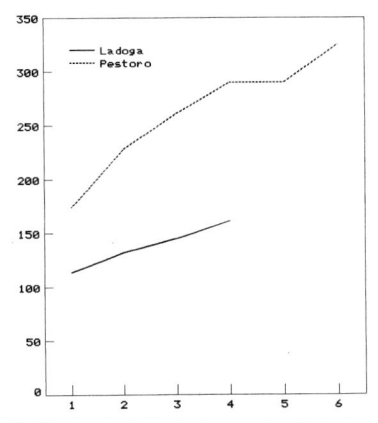

17 Vendace in Lake Ladoga and in Lake Pestoro in Russia (after Berg 1965).

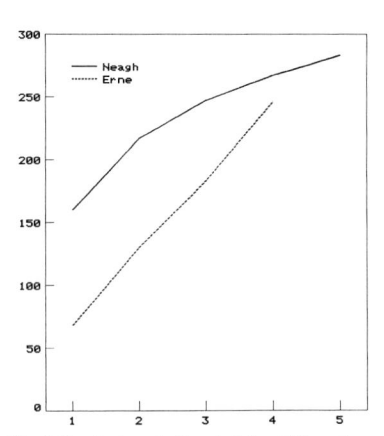

18 Pollan in Lough Neagh (after Wilson & Pitcher 1984) and in Lough Erne (after Twomey 1956).

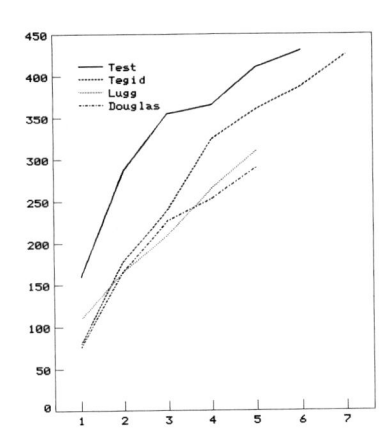

19 Grayling in the River Test (after Hutton 1923), in Llyn Tegid (after Jones 1953), in the River Lugg (after Hellawell 1969) and in the Douglas Water (after Mackay 1970).

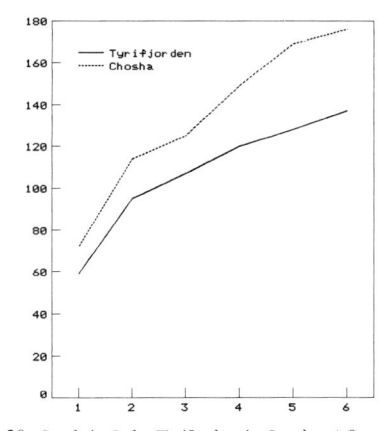

20 Smelt in Lake Tyriforden in Sweden (after Garnas 1982) and in the Chosha Bay area of the White Sea in Russia (after Berg 1965).

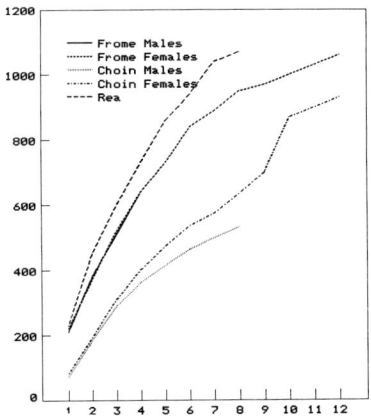

21 Pike in the River Frome (after Mann 1976a), in Loch Choin (after Munro 1957) and in Lough Rea (after Healy 1956).

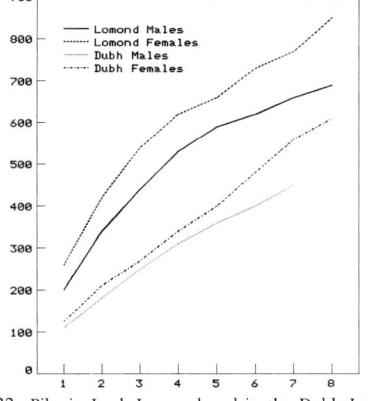

22 Pike in Loch Lomond and in the Dubh Lochan (after Shafi & Maitland 1971a).

APPENDIX 3

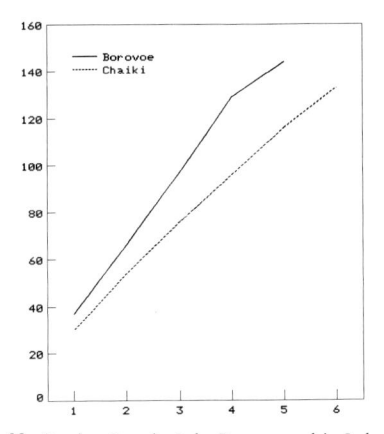

23 Crucian Carp in Lake Borovoe and in Lake Chaiki in Russia (after Berg 1965).

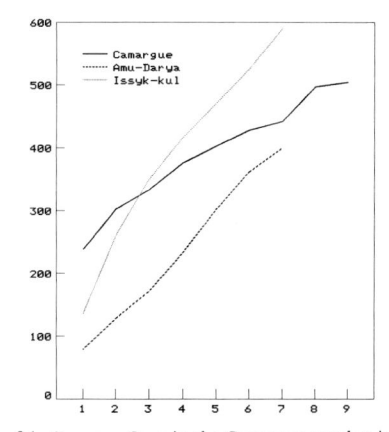

24 Common Carp in the Camargue marshes in France (after Crivelli 1981) and in the Amu-Darya and Issyk-kul in Russia (after Berg 1965).

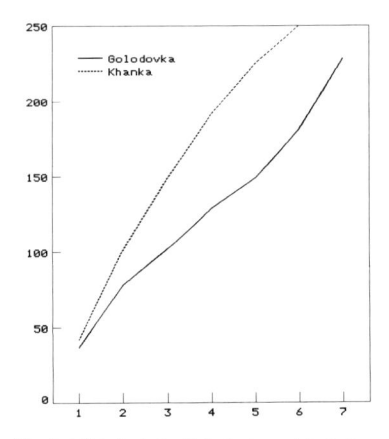

25 Goldfish in Lake Golodovka and in Lake Khanka in Russia (after Berg 1965).

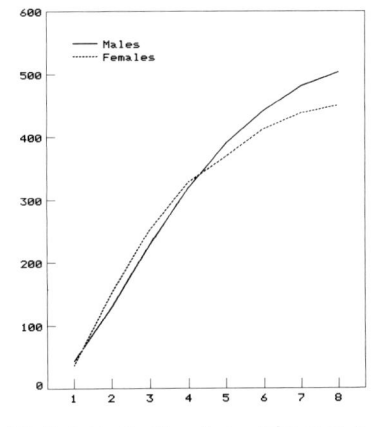

26 Barbel in the River Severn (after Hunt & Jones 1975).

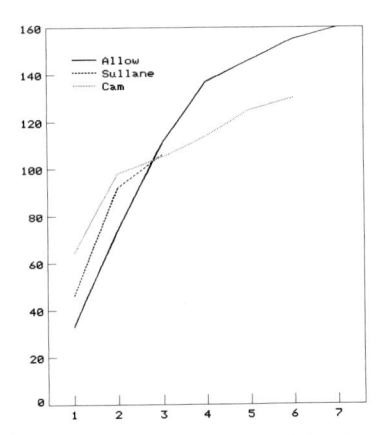

27 Gudgeon in the River Allow and the River Sullane (after Kennedy & Fitzmaurice 1972a) and in the River Cam (after Hartley 1947a).

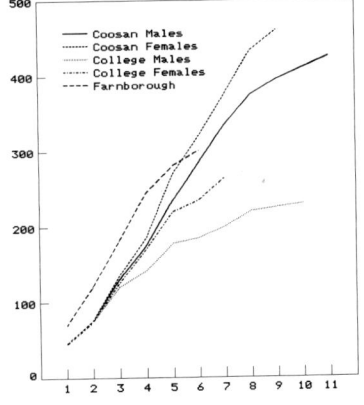

28 Tench in Coosan Lough and in College Lake (after Kennedy & Fitzmaurice 1970) and in Farnborough gravel pit (after Gee 1978).

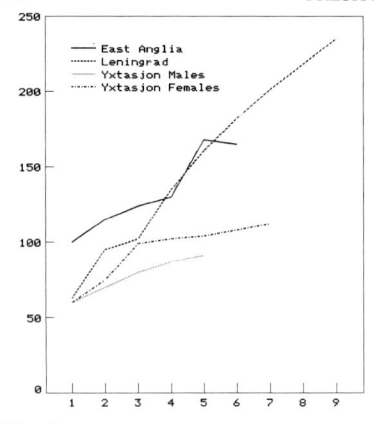

29 Silver Bream in East Anglian waters (after Hartley 1947a), in Leningrad lakes in Russia (after Berg 1965) and in Yxtasjon (after Alm 1922).

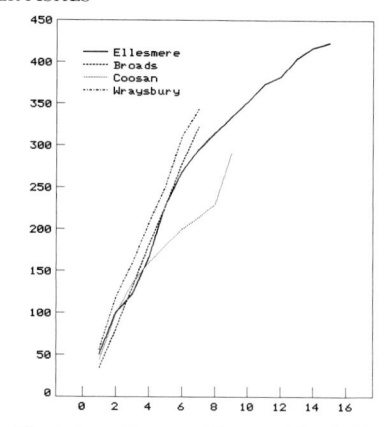

30 Common Bream in Ellesmere (after Goldspink 1981), the Norfolk Broads (after Hartley 1947a), Coosan Lough (after Kennedy & Fitzmaurice 1968a) and Wraysbury gravel pits (after Gee 1978).

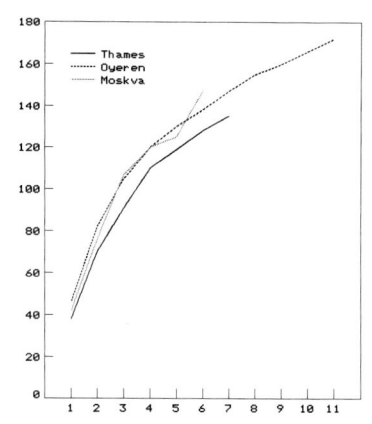

31 Bleak in the River Thames (after Williams 1967), in Lake Oyeren in Norway (after Backe-Hansen 1982) and in the Moskva River in Russia (after Berg 1965).

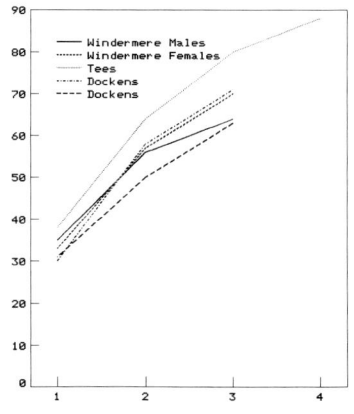

32 Minnow in Windermere (after Frost 1943), in tributaries of the River Tees (after Crisp et al. 1975) and in Docken's Water (after Mann 1971).

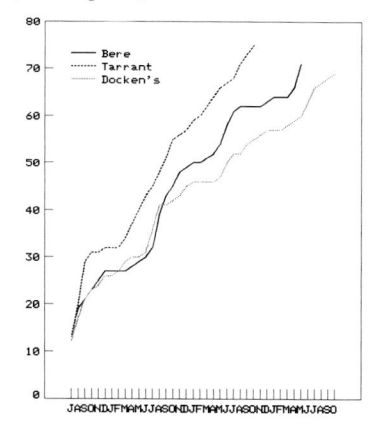

33 Minnow in the Bere Stream, in the River Tarrant and in Docken's Water (after Mann 1971).

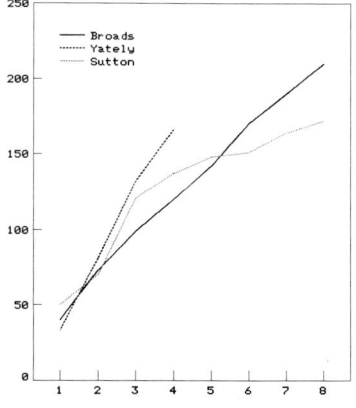

34 Rudd (from Maitland 1972b).

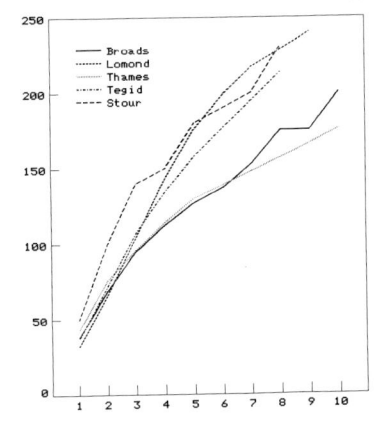

APPENDIX 3

35 Roach in the Norfolk Broads (after Hartley 1947a), Loch Lomond (after Mills 1969), the River Thames (after Williams 1967), Llyn Tegid (after Jones 1953) and the River Stour (after Mann 1971).

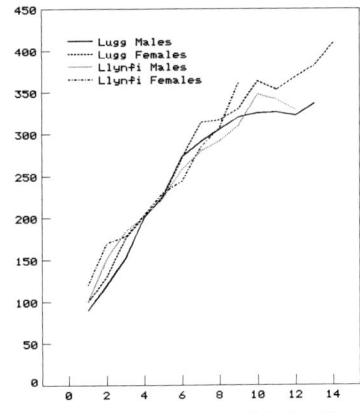

36 Chub in the River Lugg and in the Afon Llynfi (after Hellawell 1971).

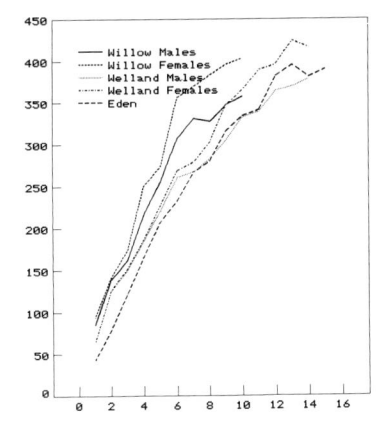

37 Chub in Willow Brook (after Cragg-Hine & Jones 1969), in the River Welland (after Leeming 1967) and in the River Eden (after Hickley & Bailey 1982).

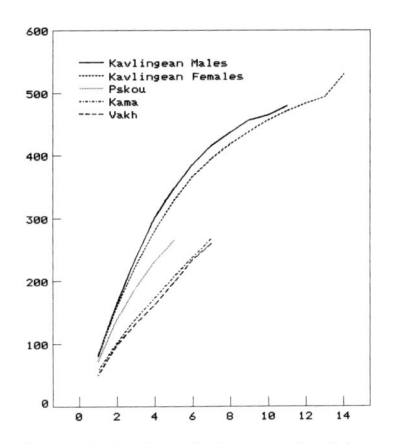

38 Orfe in the River Kavlingean (after Cala 1971), in Lake Pskou and Lake Kama and in the Vakh River in Russia (after Berg 1965).

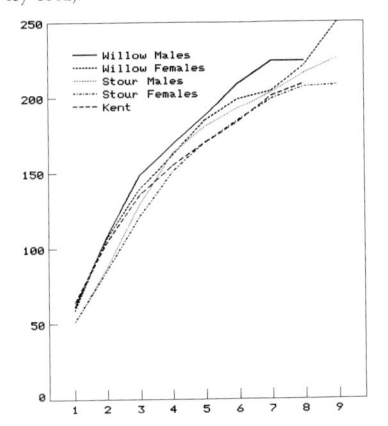

39 Dace in Willow Brook (after Cragg-Hine & Jones 1969), in the River Stour (after Mann 1974) and in the River Kent (after Hickley & Bailey 1982).

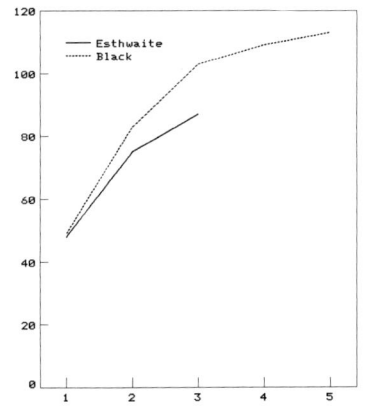

40 Stone Loach in Esthwaite Water and in Black Beck (after Smyly 1955).

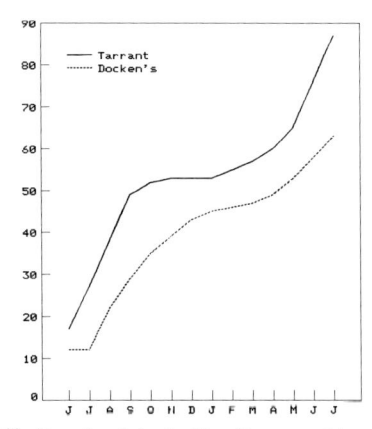

41 Stone Loach in the River Tarrant and in Docken's Water (after Mann 1971).

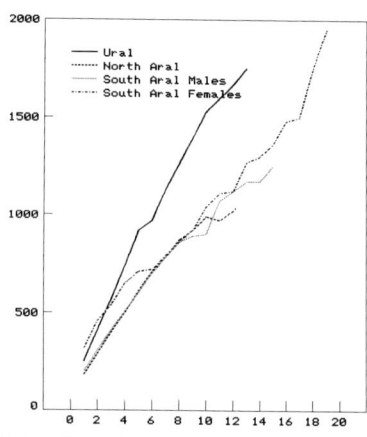

42 Danube Catfish in Russia in the Ural River and in the north and south Aral Sea (after Berg 1965).

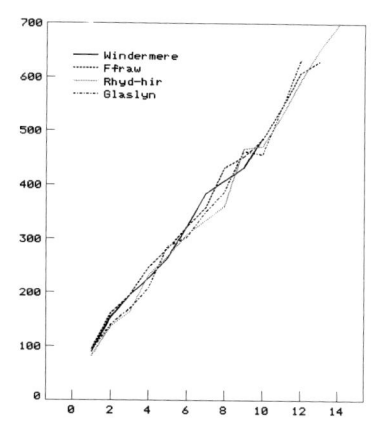

43 European Eel in Windermere (after Frost 1945) and in the Rivers Ffraw, Rhyd-hir and Glaslyn (after Sinha & Jones 1975).

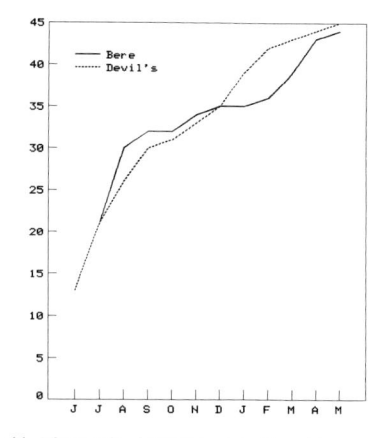

44 Three-spined Stickleback in Bere Stream and in Devil's Brook (after Mann 1971).

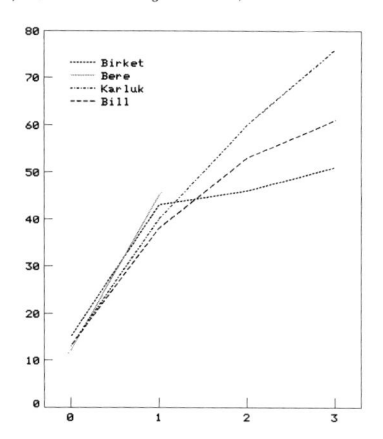

45 Three-spined Stickleback in the River Birket (after Jones & Hynes 1950), in Bere Stream (after Mann 1971), in North America in Karluk Lake (after Greenbank & Nelson 1959) and in Bill Lake (after Coad & Power 1973).

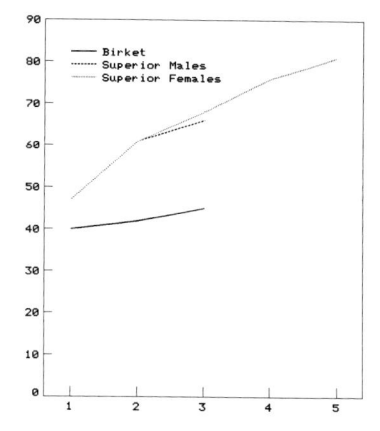

46 Nine-spined Stickleback in the River Birket (after Jones & Hynes 1950) and in Lake Superior in North America (after Griswold & Smith 1973).

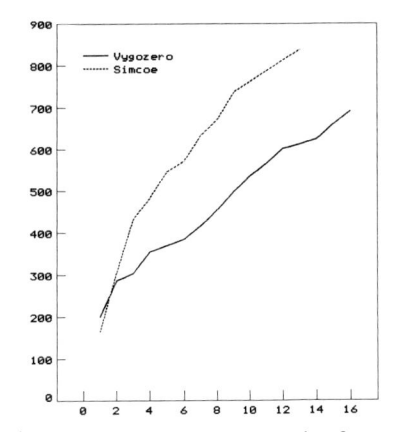

APPENDIX 3

47 Burbot in Lake Vygozero in Russia (after Berg 1965) and in Lake Simcoe in Canada (after MacCrimmon & Devitt 1954).

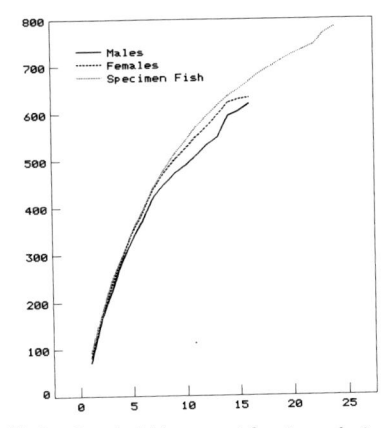

48 Sea Bass in Irish waters (after Kennedy & Fitzmaurice 1972b).

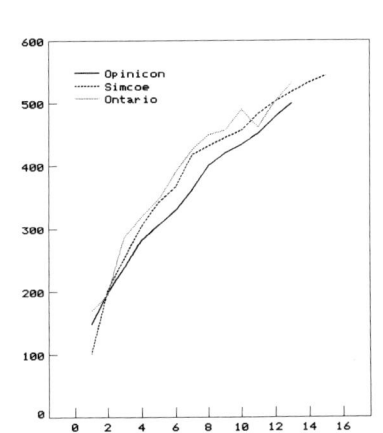

49 Largemouth Bass in Canada: in Lake Opinicon (after Lewis 1965), in Lake Simcoe (after Scott & Crossman 1973) and in various other Ontario waters (after MacKay 1963).

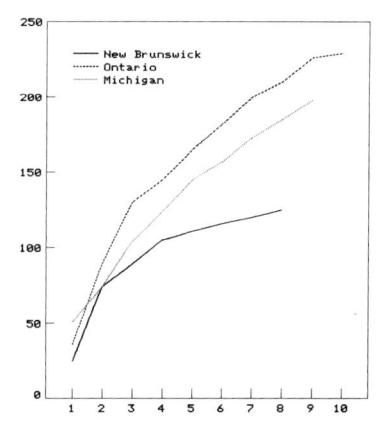

50 Pumpkinseed in North America: in Welch Lake, New Brunswick (after Reid 1930), in various Ontario lakes (after MacKay 1963) and in a pond in Michigan (after Bailey & Lagler 1938).

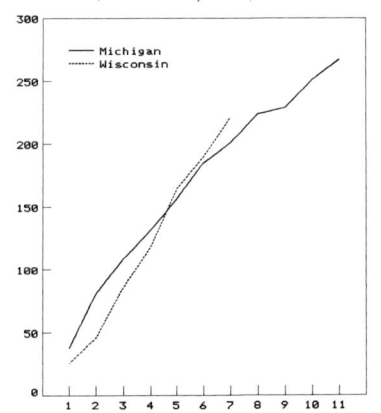

51 Rock Bass in the United States in various lakes in Michigan (after Beckman 1949) and in Wisconsin (after Snow 1969).

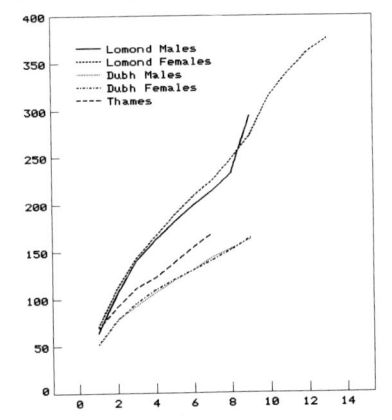

52 Perch in Loch Lomond and in the Dubh Lochan (after Shafi & Maitland 1971b) and in the River Thames (after Williams 1967).

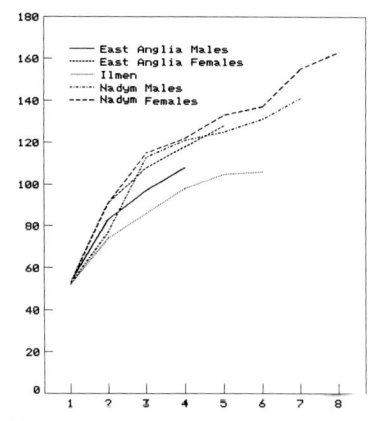

53 Ruffe in waters in East Anglia (after Hartley 1947a) and in Russia in Lake Ilmen (after Fedorova & Vetkasov 1973) and in the Nadim River (after Kolomin 1975).

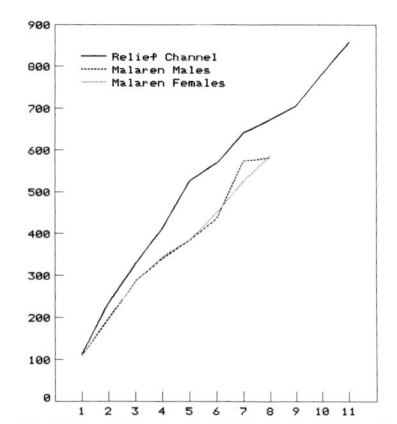

54 Pikeperch in the Relief Channel, East Anglia (after Rickards & Fickling 1979) and in Lake Malaren in Sweden (after Svardson & Molim 1973).

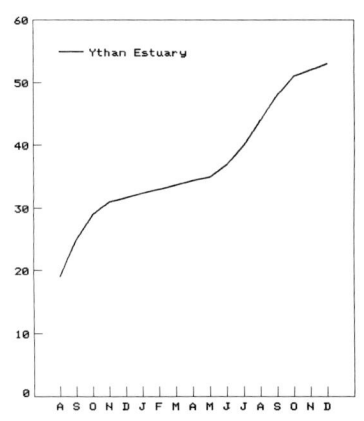

55 Common Goby in the Ythan estuary (after Healey 1972).

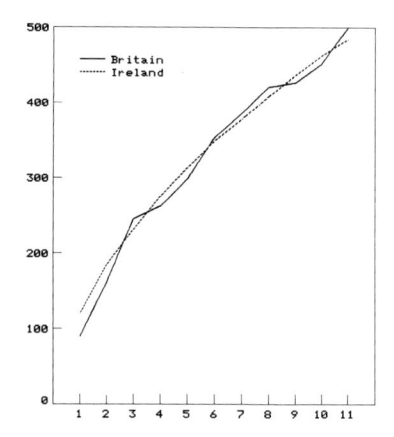

56 Thick-lipped Mullet around southern Britain (after Hickling 1970) and around Ireland (after Kennedy & Fitzmaurice 1969a).

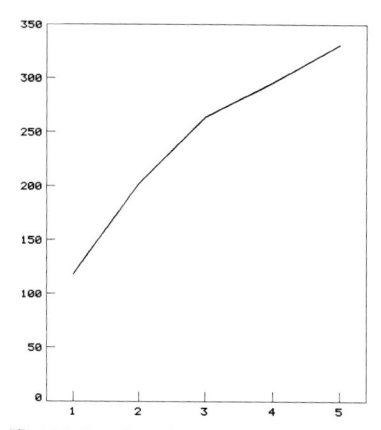

57 Thin-lipped Mullet around southern Britain (after Hickling 1970).

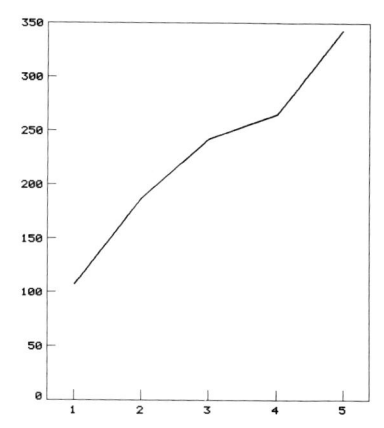

58 Golden Mullet around southern Britain (after Hickling 1970).

APPENDIX 3

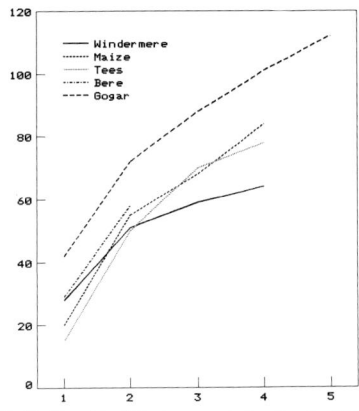

59 Bullhead in Windermere (after Smyly 1957), in Maize Beck and the River Tees (after Crisp et al. 1975), in the Bere Stream (after Mann 1971), in the Gogar Burn (after Clelland 1971).

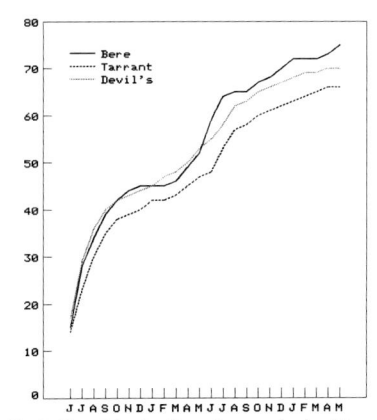

60 Bullhead in the Bere Stream, in the River Tarrant and in Devil's Brook (after Mann 1971).

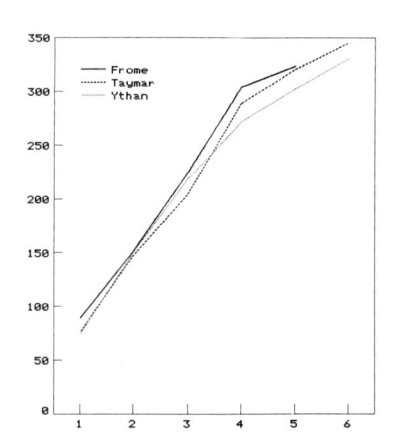

61 Flounder in the River Frome (after Beaumont & Mann 1984), in the Tamar estuary (after Hartley 1940), and in the Ythan estuary (after Summers 1979).

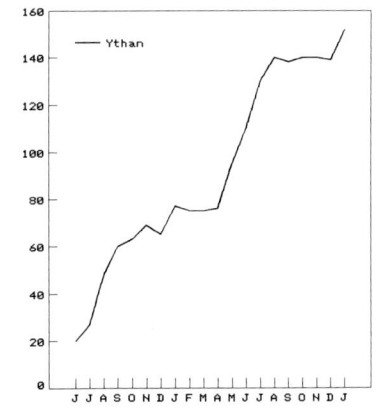

62 Flounder in the Ythan estuary (after Summers 1979).

References

1. Introduction
Alabaster (1963), Badsha & Goldspink (1982), Berg (1965), Berridge (1933), Blaxter (1974), Boyd & Robertson (1988), Brook & Holden (1957), Bull et al., (1981), Campbell & Lack (1985), Farran (1946), Hartley (1948), Heath (1939), Holden (1966), Macan & Worthington (1974), Maitland (1978), Marcy & Galvin (1973), Moule (1852), Pennell (1866), Pycraft (1901), Radcliffe (1921), Regan (1911), Walton (1653), Went (1964)

2. Fish Form and Function
Alexander (1974), Anon (1983, 1985), Everhart et al. (1975), Greenwood (1975), Irish Specimen Fish Committee (1987), Love (1970), National Anglers' Council (1987), Schindler (1957)

3. Investigating Fish
Banks & Irvine (1969), Beach (1978), Braithwaite (1971), Brown & Langford (1975), Chubb (1968), Chubb et al. (1975), Holden & Marsden (1964), Le Cren (1961), Marshall (1965), Mathews (1971), Morrison (1976), North (1980), Stuart (1958), Webb (1976), Young et al. (1972)

4. Distribution and Habitat
Alabaster (1970), Boston & Campbell (1985), Burrough et al. (1979), Campbell & Williamson (1979, 1983), Fitzmaurice (1982), Holden (1959), Jones (1959), Lever (1977), Longfield (1929), Maitland (1969a, 1970, 1972b, 1974, 1977a), Ritchie (1920), Sleaman et al. (1986), Soyer (1853), Varley (1967), Vooran (1972), Went (1979a), Wheeler & Maitland (1973)

5. Fish Conservation
Jenkins (1925), McIntosh (1978), Maitland (1972a, 1974, 1979a, 1985), Maitland & Evans (1986), Maitland & Turner (1987), Mills (1962, 1965), Nature Conservancy Council (1977)

6. Fish Identification
Child & Solomon (1977), Day (1887), Ferguson (1974), Gunther (1880), Gyldenholm (1971), Houghton (1879), Jenkins (1925), MacMahone (1948), Maitland (1972b, 1977b), Malloch (1910), Maxwell (1904), Phillips & Rix (1985), Pincher (1947), Schindler (1957), Scott & Crossman (1973), Terofal (1979), Wheeler (1969), Yarrell (1841)

Sea Lamprey
Applegate (1950), Bardack & Zangerl (1968), Hardisty (1969), Hardisty & Potter (1971), Maitland (1980a), Newth (1930)

River Lamprey
Hardisty (1961b), Hardisty & Potter (1971), Huggins & Thompson (1970), Maitland (1980a, b), Maitland et al. (1984), Morris & Maitland (1987)

Brook Lamprey
Hardisty (1944, 1961a, b), Hardisty & Potter (1971), Huggins & Thompson (1970), Maitland (1980a), Morris & Maitland (1987)

Sturgeon
Harkness & Dymond (1961), Letaconnoux (1961), Wheeler et al. (1975)

Allis Shad
Maitland (1977a), Wheeler et al. (1975)

Twaite Shad
Aprahaimian (1985), Claridge & Gardner (1978), Kennedy (1981), O'Maoileidigh et al. (1988), Trewavas (1938)

Atlantic Salmon
Buck & Hay (1984), Buck & Youngson (1982), Calderwood (1930), Child et al. (1976), Egglishaw (1967), Gardiner (1974), Gardner (1971, 1976), Gee et al. (1978), Hansen & Pethon (1985), Hansen et al. (1987), Havey & Warner (1970), Hawkins & Johnstone (1978), Heggberget & Johnsen (1982), Johnson & Jensen (1986), Johnston (1904), Jones (1959), MacCrimmon & Gots (1979), Malloch (1910), Mills (1964, 1971, 1989), Myers & Hutchings (1987), Netboy (1968), Payne et al. (1971), Pope et al. (1961), Pyefinch (1955), Reddin & Shearer (1987), Sedgwick (1988), Shearer (1972, 1984), Smith (1962, 1964), Solomon & Child (1978), Stasko (1975), Thorpe (1977b, 1987), Thorpe & Morgan (1978), Tytler et al. (1978), Wankowski (1979), Went (1976), Wilkins (1972a,b)

Brown/Sea Trout
Allen (1938), Bagenal (1969a, b), Bagenal et al. (1973), Ball & Jones (1960), Burrough & Kennedy (1978), Calderwood (1930), Campbell (1977), Campbell (1957, 1963, 1971, 1979a), Craig (1982), Crozier & Ferguson (1986), Egglishaw (1967), Elliott (1976), Fahy (1977, 1978), Ferguson & Mason (1981), Frost & Brown (1967), Gardiner (1974), Gerrish (1935), Healy (1957), Hunt & Jones (1972a,b), Hynd (1964), Kennedy (1978), Kennedy & Lie (1976), Kennedy & Strange (1978), Le Cren (1985), MacCrimmon & Marshall (1968), Malloch (1910), Menzies (1936), Milner et al. (1978), Mortensen (1977), Munro & Balmain (1956), Nall (1930), Pemberton (1976a,b), Pratten & Shearer (1983a, b, 1985), Priede & Young (1977), Solomon & Templeton (1976), Stuart (1953, 1957), Thorpe

REFERENCES

(1974a, b), Treasurer (1976), Went (1968, 1979b)

Rainbow Trout
Frost (1940, 1974), Hunt & O'Hara (1973), Kennedy & Strange (1978), Lever (1977), MacCrimmon (1971), Narver (1969), Scott & Crossman (1973), Worthington (1941)

Pink Salmon
Lever (1977), Scott & Crossman (1973), Shearer (1961), Wilimovsky (1962)

Arctic Charr
Andrews & Lear (1956), Barbour (1984), Barbour & Einarsson (1987), Campbell (1979a), Campbell (1982, 1984), Frost (1977), Frost & Kipling (1980), Gardner et al. (1988), Hardie (1940), Henricson (1977), Kipling (1984), Maitland et al. (1984), Moore (1975a, b), Walker et al. (1988), Went (1971)

Brook Charr
Bridges & Mullen (1958), Campbell & Williamson (1983), MacCrimmon & Campbell (1969), Lever (1977), Reimers (1979), Robinson et al. (1976), Scott & Crossman (1973)

Houting
Berg (1965), Maitland (1970, 1972b), Svardson (1956)

Powan
Ausen (1976), Bagenal (1970), Brown (1989), Brown & Scott (1987), Dabrowski et al. (1984), Ellison (1966), Ellison & Cooper (1967), Fuller & Scott (1976), Gervers (1954), Haram & Jones (1971), Maitland (1967a, 1969b, 1970, 1980b, 1982), Nicholas & Jones (1959), Roberts et al. (1970), Scott (1975), Slack et al. (1957)

Vendace
Aass (1972), Dembinski (1971), Jurvelius et al. (1988), Maitland (1966b, c, 1967b, 1970, 1982)

Pollan
Ferguson et al. (1978), McPhail (1966), Twomey (1956), Wilson (1983, 1984), Wilson & Pitcher (1983, 1984)

Grayling
Fabricius & Gustavson (1955), Gerrish (1939), Hellawell (1969, 1971), Hutton (1923), Jones (1953), Mackay (1970), Woolland (1987), Woolland & Jones (1975)

Smelt
Banks (1970), Ellison & Chubb (1968), Hutchinson (1983a,b), Jilek et al. (1979), Naesje et al. (1987)

Pike
Beukema (1970), Bregazzi & Kennedy (1980), Bucke (1971), Fabricius & Gustavson (1958), Fickling (1982), Fitzmaurice (1983b), Healy (1956), Healy & Mulcahy (1980), Kipling & Frost (1969), Longfield (1929), Mann (1976a, 1982), Mulcahy (1970), Munro (1957), Shafi & Maitland (1971a), Svardson (1950),

Toner (1959b), Treasurer (1980)

Common Carp
Beukema & de Vos (1974), Crivelli (1981), Fitzmaurice (1983a), Leeming (1970), Maitland (1964), Stein & Kitchell (1975)

Crucian Carp
Maitland (1977), Marlborough (1966)

Goldfish
Allen (1987), Hervey & Hems (1968), Lever (1977), Maitland (1971)

Barbel
Hancock et al. (1976), Hunt & Jones (1974a,b, 1975)

Gudgeon
Kennedy & Fitzmaurice (1972a), Ladich (1988), Mann (1980)

Tench
Kennedy & Fitzmaurice (1970), Maitland (1977a)

Silver Bream
Hartley (1947a,b), Swinney & Coles (1982)

Common Bream
Bucke (1974), Goldspink (1981), Goldspink & Banks (1971), Hartley (1947a,b), Kennedy & Fitzmaurice (1968), Svardson (1950), Wood & Jordan (1987)

Bleak
Harris & Wheeler (1974), Hartley (1947a,b), Wheeler (1978), Williams (1965)

Minnow
Bibby (1972), Frost (1943), Lein (1981), Levesley & Magurran (1988), Maitland (1965), Pitcher et al. (1986), Rasotoss et al. (1987), Stott & Buckley (1979), Wootton & Mills (1979)

Bitterling
Hardy (1954), Wheeler & Maitland (1973)

Rudd
Brassington & Ferguson (1975), Burrough (1978), Hartley (1947a,b), Kennedy & Fitzmaurice (1974), Svardson (1950), Wheeler (1976)

Roach
Ali (1976, 1979), Broughton & Jones (1978), Burrough (1978), Burrough & Kennedy (1979), Cragg-Hine & Jones (1969), Evans (1978), Goldspink (1978), Hellawell (1971, 1972), Hickley & Bailey (1977), Jafri & Ensor (1979), Kennedy & Burrough (1978), Linfield (1979, 1980), Maitland (1966a), Mann (1973), Sweeting (1976), Wheeler & Easton (1978), Williams (1965), Wilson (1971), Wood & Jordan (1987), Wyatt (1988)

Chubb
Cragg-Hine & Jones (1969), Hickley & Bailey (1982), Mann (1976b), Wheeler & Easton (1978)

Orfe
Lever (1977), Maitland (1977a)

Dace
Cragg-Hine & Jones (1969), Hickley & Bailey (1982), Kennedy (1969), Kennedy & Hine (1969), Mann (1974), Mathews & Williams (1972), Mills (1981, 1982), Williams (1965)

Chinese Carp
Cross (1969, 1970), Edwards (1973), Kilambi & Robinson (1979), Stott & Cross (1973), Van Dyke & Sutton (1977)

Spined Loach
Robotham (1977, 1982a,b)

Stoned Loach
Hyslop (1982), Maitland (1965), Mills *et al.* (1983), Rumpus (1975), Smyly (1955), Street & Hart (1985)

European Catfish
Lever (1977), Maitland (1983), Schindler (1957), Wheeler & Maitland (1973)

European Eel
Bertin (1956), Boetius (1976), Colombo *et al.* (1984), Ezzat & El-Serafy (1977), Kennedy (1984b), Lacey *et al.* (1982), Lacey & Williams (1983), McLeave (1980), Moore & Moore (1976), Moriarty (1973a, b, 1974, 1975, 1978, 1983), Parkhurst (1982a, b, c), Parkhurst & Lythgoe (1982, 1983), Parsons *et al.* (1977), Peters (1976), Sadler (1979), Schmidt (1922), Schoth (1982), Sinha (1969), Sinha & Jones (1975), Tesch (1982), Tucker (1959), Williamson (1987)

Three-spined stickleback
Allen & Wootton (1982), Bell (1974), Campbell (1979b, 1985), Chappell (1969a, b), Giles (1983), Hynes (1950), Jones & Hynes (1950), Lewis *et al.* (1972), Whoriskey *et al.* (1986), Wootton (1973a, b, 1976, 1984), Wootton & Evans (1976), Wootton *et al.* (1978, 1980)

Nine-spined stickleback
Dartnell (1973), Hynes (1950), Jones & Hynes (1950), Lewis *et al.* (1972), McKenzie & Keenleyside (1970), Morris (1952), Solanki & Benjamin (1982), Whoriskey *et al.* (1986), Wootton (1976, 1984)

Burbot
Clemens (1951a, b), Hinkens & Cochrane (1988), Lawler (1963), Marlborough (1970)

Sea bass
Dando & Demir (1985), Holden & Williams (1974), Jackman (1954), Kelley (1979, 1986), Kennedy & Fitzmaurice (1968b, 1972b), Pawson & Pickett (1987), Pawson *et al.* (1987), Thompson & Harrop (1987)

Largemouth bass
Hazen & Esch (1978), Maitland & Price (1969), Mraz *et al.* (1961), Scott & Crossman (1973),

Spoor (1977)

Pumpkinseed
Lever (1977), Scott & Crossman (1973), Wheeler & Maitland (1973)

Rock bass
Hile (1941), Maitland (1977b), Scott (1949)

Perch
Alabaster & Stott (1978), Andrews (1979), Bregazzi & Kennedy (1982), Burrough & Kennedy (1978), Campbell (1955), Coles (1981), Craig (1977, 1987), Craig & Kipling (1983), Goldspink & Goodwin (1979), Guma'a (1982), Jones (1953), Kennedy & Burrough (1977), Lang (1987), Le Cren *et al.* (1967), Pickering & Willoughby (1977), Shafi & Maitland (1971b), Thorpe (1977a), Treasurer (1981), Williams (1965), Willoughby (1970)

Ruffe
Maitland *et al.* (1983), Hartley (1948a, b), Oliva & Vostradovsky (1960), Wheeler (1969)

Pikeperch
Fickling & Lee (1985), Linfield & Rickards (1979), Mansfield (1958), Puke (1952), Rickards & Fickling (1979), Steffens (1960)

Common goby
Al-Hassan *et al.* (1987), Fouda (1979), Fouda & Miller (1979), Miller (1975)

Thick-lipped mullet
Anderson (1982), Erman (1961), Flowerdew & Grove (1980), Hickling (1970), Kennedy & Fitzmaurice (1969a), Reay & Cornell (1988), Romer & McLachlan (1986)

Thin-lipped mullet
Anderson (1982), Hickling (1970), Reay & Cornell (1988)

Golden mullet
Anderson (1982), Reay & Cornell (1988)

Bullhead
Crisp *et al.* (1975), Fox (1978), Hyslop (1982), Morris (1978), Rumpus (1975), Smyly (1957), Western (1971)

Flounder
Beaumont & Mann (1984), Gibson (1972), Jones (1952), Kennedy (1984a), Kislalioglu & Gibson (1977), Moore & Moore (1976), Mulicki (1947), Van Den Broek (1979)

28. The Future
Anderson (1977), Bregazzi *et al.* (1982), Cooper & Wheatley (1981), Crisp *et al.* (1975), Fitter (1959), Harden-Jones (1986), Holt & Talbot (1978), Kennedy (1975), Maitland (1966a, 1982), Maitland *et al.* (1981, 1987), Maitland & Turner (1987), Marshall (1971), Pitcher & Hart (1982), Toner (1959a)

Bibliography

Aass, P. (1972). Age determination and year-class fluctuations of Cisco, *Coregonus albula* L., in the Mjosa hydroelectric reservoir, Norway. *Rep. Inst. Freshw. Res. Drottning*, 52: 5–22.

Alabaster, J. S. (1963). The effect of heated effluents on fish. *Int. J. Air Wat. Pollut.* 7: 541–563.

Alabaster, J. S. (1970). River flow and upstream movement and catch of migratory salmonids. *J. Fish Biol.* 2: 1–13.

Alabaster, J. S. & Stott, B. (1978). Swimming activity of Perch, *Perca fluviatilis* L. *J. Fish Biol.* 12: 587–591.

Alexander, R. M. (1974). *Functional design in fishes.* London: Hutchinson.

Al-Hassan, L. A. J., Webb, C. J., Giama, M. & Miller, P. J. (1987). Phosphoglucose isomerase polymorphism in the Common Goby, *Pomatoschistus microps* (Kroyer) (Teleostei; Gobiidae), around the British Isles. *J. Fish Biol.* 30: 281–298.

Ali, S. S. (1976). The food of Roach, *Rutilus rutilus* (L.) in Llyn Tegid (north Wales). *Sind Univ. Res. J. Sci.* 9: 15–33.

Ali, S. S. (1979). Age, growth and length-weight relationship of the Roach *Rutilus rutilus* (L). in Llyn Tegid, north Wales. *Pak. J. Zool.* 11: 1–19.

Allen, A. (1987). The olfactory world of the Goldfish. *Aquarist & Pondkeeper*, 52.

Allen, J. R. M. & Wootton, R. J. (1982). Age, growth and rate of food consumption in an upland population of the Three-spined Stickleback, *Gasterosteus aculeatus. J. Fish Biol.* 21: 95–106.

Allen, K.R. (1938). Some observations of the biology of the Trout (*Salmo trutta*) in Windermere. *J. Anim. Ecol.* 7: 333–349.

Alm, G. (1922). Bottenfaunen och fiskens biologi i Yxtasjon. *Medd. Land. Styr. Stockh.* 236.

Anderson, L. G. (1977). *The economics of fishery management.* Baltimore: John Hopkins University.

Anderson, M. (1982). The identification of British grey mullets. *J. Fish Biol.* 20: 33–38.

Andrews, C. (1979). Host specificity of the parasite fauna of Perch (*Perca fluviatilis* L.) from the British Isles, with special reference to the study at Llyn Tegid. *J. Fish. Biol.* 15: 195–209.

Andrews, C. W. & Lear, E. (1956). The biology of Arctic Char (*Salvelinus alpinus* L.) in northern Labrador. *J. Fish. Res. Bd. Can.* 13: 843–860.

Anon. (1983). *World record game fishes.* Fort Lauderdale: International Game Fish Association.

Anon. (1985). *World record game fishes.* Fort Lauderdale: International Game Fish Association.

Applegate, V. C. (1950). Natural history of the Sea Lamprey, *Petromyzon marinus*, in Michigan. *US Fish Wild. Serv. Spec. Sci. Rep. Fish.* 55: 1–237.

Aprahamian, M. W. (1985). The effect of the migration of *Alosa fallax fallax* (Lacepede) into fresh water, on branchial and gut parasites. *J. Fish Biol.* 27: 521–532.

Ausen, V. (1976). Age, growth, population size, mortality and yield in the Whitefish (*Coregonus lavaretus* (L.)) of Haugatjern--a eutrophic Norwegian lake. *Norw. J. Zool.* 24: 379–405.

Backe-Hansen, P. (1982). Age determination, growth and maturity of the Bleak *Alburnus alburnus* (L.) (Cyprinidae) in Lake Oyeren, SE Norway. *Fauna Norv.* 3: 31–36.

Badsha, K. S. & Goldspink, C. R. (1982). Preliminary observations on the heavy metal content of four species of fish in NW England. *J. Fish Biol.* 21: 251–267.

Bagenal, T. B. (1969a). The relationship between food supply and fecundity in Brown Trout *Salmo trutta* L. *J. Fish Biol.* 1: 167–182

Bagenal, T. B. (1969b). Relationship between egg size and fry survival in Brown Trout *Salmo trutta* L. *J. Fish Biol.* 1: 349–353.

Bagenal, T. B. (1970). Notes on the biology of the Schelly *Coregonus lavaretus* (L.) in Haweswater and Ullswater. *J. Fish Biol.* 2: 137–154.

Bagenal, T. B., Mackereth, F. J. H. & Heron, J. (1973). The distinction between Brown Trout and Sea Trout by the strontium content of their scales. *J. Fish Biol.* 5: 555–558.

Bailey, M. M. (1972). Age, growth, reproduction and food of the Burbot, *Lota lota* (Linnaeus), in southwestern Lake Superior. *Trans. Amer. Fish. Soc.* 101: 667–674.

Bailey, R. M. & Lagler, K. F. (1938). An analysis of hybridization in a population of stunted sunfishes in New York. *Pap. Mich. Acad. Arts Lett.* 23: 577–606.

Ball, J. N. & Jones, J. W. (1960). On the growth of Brown Trout of Llyn Tegid. *Proc. Zool. Soc. Lond.* 134: 1–41.

Banks, J. A. (1970). Observations on the fish population of Rostherne Mere, Cheshire. *Field Studies.* 3: 375–379.

Banks, J. W. & Irvine, W. (1969). A note on the photography of fish scales, opercular and otoliths using an enlarger. *J. Fish Biol.* 1: 25–26.

Barbour, S. E. (1984). Variation in life history, ecology and resource utilisation by Arctic Charr *Salvelinus alpinus* (L.) in Scotland. Ph.D. Thesis, University of Edinburgh.

Barbour, S. E. & Einarsson, S. M. (1987). Ageing and growth of Charr *Salvelinus alpinus* (L.) from habitat types in Scotland. *Aquacult. Fish. Mgt.* 18: 1–13.

Bardack, D. & Zangerl, R. (1968). First fossil lamprey: a record from the Pennsylvanian of Illinois. *Science*, 162: 1265–1267.

Beach, M. H. (1978). The use of infra-red light and closed circuit TV to validate records from automatic fish counters. *J. Fish Biol.* 13: 639–644.

Beamish, F. W. H. & Medland, T. E. (1988). Age determination for lampreys. *Trans. Amer. Fish Soc.* 113: 63–71.

Beaumont, W. R. C. & Mann, R. H. K. (1984). The age, growth and diet of a freshwater population of the Flounder, *Platichthys flesus* (L.), in southern England. *J. Fish Biol.* 25: 607–616.

Beckman, W. C. (1949). The rate of growth and sex ratio for seven Michigan fishes. *Trans. Amer. Fish Soc.* 76: 63–81.

Bell, M. A. (1974). Reduction and loss of pelvic girdle in Gasterosteus (Pisces): a case of parallel evolution. *Nat. Hist. Mus. Los Ang. City Contr. Sci.* 257: 1–36.

Berg, L. S. (1965). *Freshwater fishes of the USSR and adjacent countries.* Jerusalem: Israel Program for Scientific Translations.

Berridge, W. S. (1933). *All about fish.* London: Harrap.

Bertin, L. (1956). *Eels.* London: Cleaver-Hume.

Beukema, J. J. (1970). Acquired hook avoidance in Pike, *Esox lucius* L., fished with artificial and natural baits. *J. Fish Biol.* 2: 155–160.

Beukema, J. J. & De Vos, G. J. (1974). Experimental tests of a basic assumption of the capture-recapture method in pond populations of Carp *Cyprinius carpio* L. *J. Fish Biol.* 6: 317–329.

Bibby, M. C. (1972). Population biology of the helminth parasites of *Phoxinus phoxinus* (L.), the Minnow, in a Cardiganshire lake. *J. Fish Biol.* 4: 289–300.

Blaxter, J. H. S. (1974). *The early life history of fish.* Oban: Scottish Marine Biological Association.

Boetius, J. (1976). Elvers, *Anguilla anguilla* and *Anguilla rostrata* from two Danish localities. Size, body weight, developmental stage and number of vertebrae related to ascent. *Meddr. Danm. Fisk-og Havunders.* 7: 199–220.

Boston, P. & Campbell, J. M. (1985). *An atlas of Oxfordshire freshwater fishes.* Oxford: Department of Museums.

Boyd, A. & Robertson, R. H. S. (1989). *Facail Teicheolach.* Pitlochry: Resource Use Institute Ltd.

Braithwaite, H. (1971). A sonar fish counter. *J. Fish Biol.* 3: 73–82.

Brassington, R. A. & Ferguson, A. (1975). Electrophoretic identification of Roach (*Rutilus rutilus* L.), Rudd (*Scardinius erythrophthalmus* L.), Bream (*Abramis brama* L.) and their natural hybrids. *J. Fish Biol.* 9: 471–477.

Bregazzi, P. R., Burrough, R. J. & Kennedy, C. R. (1982). The natural history of Slapton Ley Nature Reserve. XIV: The history and management of the fishery. *Field Studies.* 5: 581–589.

Bregazzi, P. R. & Kennedy, C. R. (1980). The biology of Pike, *Esox lucius* L., in a southern eutrophic lake. *J. Fish Biol.* 17: 91–112.

Bregazzi, P. R. & Kennedy, C. R. (1982). The responses of a Perch, *Perca fluviatilis* L., population to eutrophication and associated changes in fish fauna in a small lake. *J. Fish Biol.* 20: 21–31.

Bridges, C. H., & Mullan, J. W. (1958). A compendium of the life history and ecology of the Eastern Brook Trout *Salvelinus fontinalis* (Mitchill). *Mass. Div. Fish Game, Fish. Sect. Fish. Bull.* 23: 1–30.

Brook, A. J. & Holden, A. V. (1957). Fertilisation experiments in Scottish freshwater lochs. 1. Loch Kinardochy. *Freshw. Salm. Fish. Res. Scot.* 17: 1–30.

Broughton, N. M. & Jones, N. V. (1978). An investigation into the growth of 0- group Roach *Rutilus rutilus* (L.) with special reference to temperature. *J. Fish Biol.* 12: 345–358.

Brown, E. A. R. (1989). Growth processes in the two Scottish populations of Powan, *Coregonus lavaretus* (L.). PhD Thesis, University of St Andrews.

Brown, E. A. R. & Scott, D. B. C. (1987). Abnormal pelvic fins in Scottish Powan, *Coregonus lavaretus* (L.) (Salmonidae, Coregoninae). *J. Fish Biol.* 31: 443–444.

Brown, D. J. A. & Langford, T. E. (1975). An assessment of a tow net used to sample coarse fish fry in rivers. *J. Fish Biol.* 8: 533–538.

Buck, R. J. G. & Hay, D. W. (1984). The relation between stock size and progeny of Atlantic Salmon, *Salmo salar* L., in a Scottish stream. *J. Fish Biol.* 23: 1–12.

Buck, R. J. G. & Youngson, A. F. (1982). The downstream migration of precociously mature Atlantic Salmon, *Salmo salar* L. parr in autumn and its relation to the spawning migration of mature adult fish. *J. Fish Biol.* 90: 279 285.

Bucke, D. (1971). The anatomy and histology of the alimentary tract of the carnivorous fish the Pike *Esox lucius* L. *J. Fish Biol.* 3: 421–431.

Bucke, D. (1974). Vertebral anomalies in the common Bream *Abramis brama* (L.), *J. Fish Biol.* 6: 681–682.

Bull, K. R., Dearsley, A. F. & Inskip, M. H. (1981). Growth and mercury content of Roach (*Rutilus rutilus* L.), Perch (*Perca fluviatilis* L.) and Pike (*Esox lucius* L.) living in sewage effluent. *Environ. Poll. A.* 25: 229–240.

Burrough, R. J. (1978). The populations biology of two species of eyefluke, *Diplostomum spathaceum* and *Tylodelphys clavata*, in Roach and Rudd. *J. Fish Biol.* 13: 19–32.

Burrough, R. J., Bregazzi, P. R. & Kennedy, C. R. (1979). Interspecific dominance amongst three species of coarse fish in Slapton Ley, Devon, *J. Fish Biol.* 15: 534–544.

Burrough, R. J. & Kennedy, C. R. (1978). Interaction of Perch (*Perca fluviatilis*) and Brown Trout (*Salmo trutta*). *J. Fish Biol.* 13: 225–230.

Burrough, R. J. & Kennedy, C. R. (1979). The occurrence and natural alleviation of stunting in a population of Roach, *Rutilus rutilus* (L.). *J. Fish Biol.* 15: 93–109.

Cala, P. (1971). On the ecology of the Ide *Idus idus* (L.) in the River Kavlingean, south Sweden. *Ann. Rep. Inst. Freshw. Res. Drottning.* 50: 45–99.

Calderwood, W. L. (1930). *Salmon and Sea Trout.* London: Arnold.

Campbell, B. & Lack, E. (1985). *A dictionary of birds.* Waterhouses: Poyser.

Campbell, J. S. (1977). Spawning characteristics of Brown Trout and Sea Trout *Salmo trutta* L. in Kirk Burn, River Tweed, Scotland, *J. Fish Biol.* 11: 217–230.

Campbell, R. N. (1955). Food and feeding habits of Brown Trout, Perch and other fish in Loch Tummel. *Scott. Nat.* 67: 23–27.

Campbell, R. N. (1957). The effect of flooding on the growth rate of Brown Trout in Loch Tummel. *Freshw. Salm. Fish. Res. Scot.* 14: 1–7.

Campbell, R. N. (1963). Some effects of impoundment on the environment and growth of Brown Trout (*Salmo trutta* L.) in Loch Garry (Inverness-shire). *Sci. Invest. Freshw. Fish. Scot.* 30: 1–27.

Campbell, R. N. (1971). The growth of Brown Trout, *Salmo trutta* L., in northern Scotland with special reference to the improvement of fisheries. *J. Fish Biol.* 3: 1–28.

Campbell, R. N. (1979a). Ferox Trout (*Salmo*

trutta L.) and Charr (*Salvelinus alpinus* (L.)) in Scottish lochs. *J. Fish Biol.* 14: 1–29.
Campbell, R. N. (1979b). Sticklebacks (*Gasterosteus aculeatus* (L.) and *Pungitius pungitius* (L.)) in the Outer Hebrides, Scotland. *Hebrid. Nat.* 3: 8–15.
Campbell, R. N. (1985). Morphological variation in the Three-spined Stickleback (*Gasterosteus aculeatus*) in Scotland. *Behaviour*, 93: 161–168.
Campbell, R. N. & Williamson, R. B. (1979). The fishes of inland waters of the Outer Hebrides, Scotland. *Proc. Roy. Soc. Edin.* 77B, 377–393.
Campbell, R. N. & Williamson, R. B. (1983). Salmon and freshwater fishes of the Inner Hebrides. *Proc. Roy. Soc. Edin.* 83B: 245–265.
Campbell, R. N. B. (1982). The food of Arctic Charr in the presence and absence of Brown Trout. *Glasg. Nat.* 20: 229–235.
Campbell, R. N. B. (1984). Predation by Arctic Charr on the Three-spined Stickleback and its nest in Loch Meallt, Skye. *Glasg. Nat.* 20: 409–413.
Chappell, L. H. (1969a). The parasites of the Three-spined Stickleback *Gasterosteus aculeatus* L. from a Yorkshire pond. I. Seasonal variation of parasite fauna. *J. Fish Biol.* 1: 137–152.
Chappell, L. H. (1969b). The parasites of the Three-spined Stickleback *Gasterosteus aculeatus* L. from a Yorkshire pond. II. Variation of the parasite fauna with sex and size of fish. *J. Fish Biol.* 1: 339–347.
Child, A. R., Burnell, A. M. & Wilkins, N. P. (1976). The existence of two races of Atlantic Salmon (*Salmo salar* L.) in the British Isles. *J. Fish Biol.* 8: 35–43.
Child, A. R. & Solomon, D. J. (1977). Observations on morphological and biochemical features of some cyprinid hybrids. *J. Fish Biol.* 11: 125–132.
Chubb, J. C. (1968). Tapeworms of the genus *Diphyllobothrium* in the British Isles. *Parasitol.* 58: 1–22.
Chubb, J. C., Jones, J. W. & Banks, J. W. (1975). Film and television in fishery research at Llyn Tegid (Bala Lake), Wales. *J. Fish Biol.* 7: 153–157.
Claridge, P. N. & Gardner, D. C. (1978). Growth and movements of the Twaite Shad, *Alosa fallax* (Lacepede) in the Severn Estuary. *J. Fish Biol.* 12: 203–212.
Clelland, B. (1971). An ecological study of a Scottish population of Bullheads. *B.Sc. Thesis, University of Edinburgh.*
Clemens, H. P. (1951a). The food of the Burbot, *Lota lota maculosa* (LeSueur) in Lake Erie. *Trans. Amer. Fish Soc.* 80: 56–66.
Clemens, H. P. (1951b). The growth of the Burbot, *Lota lota maculosa* (LeSueur) in Lake Erie. *Trans. Amer. Fish Soc.* 80: 163–173.
Clemens, W. A., Rawson, D. S. & McHugh, J. L. (1939). A biological survey of Okanagan Lake, British Columbia. *Bull. Fish. Res. Bd. Can.* 1–70.
Coad, B. W. & Power, G. (1973). Observations on the ecology of lacustrine populations of the Three-spined Stickleback *Gasterosteus aculeatus* L. (1758) in the Matamek River system. *Quebec. Nat. Can.* 100: 437–445.
Coles, T. F. (1981). The distribution of Perch, *Perca fluviatilis* L., throughout their first year of life in Llyn Tegid, North Wales. *J. Fish Biol.* 18: 15–21.
Colle, D. E., Shireman, J. V. & Rottmann, R. W. (1978). Food selection by Grass Carp fingerlings in a vegetated pond. *Trans. Amer. Fish Soc.* 107: 149–152.
Colombo, G., Grandi, G. & Ross, R. (1984). Gonad differentiation and body growth in *Anguilla anguilla* L. *J. Fish Biol.* 24: 215–228.
Cooper, M. J. & Wheatley, G. A. (1981). An examination of the fish population in the River Trent, Nottinghamshire using angler catches. *J. Fish Biol.* 19: 539–556.
Cragg-Hine, D. & Jones, J. W. (1969). The growth of Dace *Leuciscus leuciscus* (L.), Roach *Rutilus rutilus* (L.) and Chub *Squalius cephalus* (L.) in Willow Brook, Northamptonshire. *J. Fish Biol.* 1: 59–82.
Craig, J. F. (1977). Seasonal changes in the day and night activity of adult Perch, *Perca fluviatilis* L. *J. Fish Biol.* 11: 161–166.
Craig, J. F. (1982), A note on growth and mortality of Trout, *Salmo trutta* L., in afferent streams of Windermere. *J. Fish Biol.* 20: 423–430.
Craig, J. F. (1987). *The biology of Perch and related fish*. Beckenham: Croom Helm.
Craig, J. F. & Kipling, C. (1983). Reproduction effort versus the environment: case histories of Windermere Perch, *Perca fluviatilis* L., and Pike, *Esox lucius* L. *J. Fish Biol.* 22: 713–727.
Crisp, D. T. (1963). A preliminary survey of Brown Trout (*Salmo trutta* L.) and Bullheads (*Cottus gobio* L.) in high altitude becks. *Salm. Trout Mag.* 167: 45–49.
Crisp, D. T., Mann, R. H. K., & McCormack, J. C. (1975). The populations of fish in the River Tees system on the Moor House National Nature Reserve, Westmorland. *J. Fish Biol.* 7: 573–594.
Crivelli, A. J. (1981). The biology of the Common Carp, *Cyprinus carpio* L., in the Camargue, southern France. *J. Fish Biol.* 18: 271–290.
Cross, D. G. (1969). Aquatic weed control using Grass Carp. *J. Fish Biol.* 1: 27–30.
Cross, D. G. (1970). The tolerance of Grass Carp *Ctenopharyngodon idella* (Val.) to seawater. *J. Fish Biol.* 2: 231–233.
Crozier, W. W. & Ferguson, A. (1986). Electrophoretic examination of the population structure of Brown Trout, *Salmo trutta*. L., from the Lough Neagh catchment, Northern Ireland. *J. Fish Biol.* 28: 459–478.
Cunningham, J. T. (1894). Experiments and observations made at the Plymouth Laboratory. *J. Mar. Biol. Ass.* 3: 247–277.
Dabrowski, K., Kaushik, S. J. & Luquet, P. (1984). Metabolic utilisation of body stores during the early life of Whitefish, *Coregonus lavaretus* L. *J. Fish Biol.* 23: 721–730.
Dando, P. R. & Demir, N. (1985). On the spawning and nursery grounds of Bass, *Dicentrarchus labrax*, in the Plymouth area, *J. Mar. Biol. Ass. UK.* 65: 159–168.
Dartnell, H. J. G. (1973). Parasites of the Nine-spined Stickleback *Pungitius pungitius* (L.) *J. Fish Biol.* 5: 505–510.
Day, F. (1887). *British and Irish Salmonidae*. London: Williams & Norgate.
Dembinski,W. (1971). Vertical distribution of Vendace *Coregonus albula* L. and other pelagic fish species in some Polish lakes. *J. Fish Biol.* 3: 341–357.
Ede, S. & Carlson, C. A. (1977). Food habits of Carp and White Sucker in South Platte and St Vrain Rivers and Goosquill Pond, Weld

County, Colorado. *Trans. Amer. Fish. Soc.* 106: 339–346.
Edwards, D. J. (1973). Aquarium studies on the consumption of small animals by 0-group Grass Carp, *Ctenopharyngodon idella* (Val.) *J. Fish Biol.* 5: 599–606.
Egglishaw, H. J. (1967). The food, growth and population structure of Salmon and Trout in two streams in the Scottish highlands. *Freshw. Salm. Fish. Res. Scot.* 38: 1–32.
Elliott, J. M. (1976). The downstream drifting of eggs of Brown Trout, *Salmo trutta* L. *J. Fish Biol.* 9: 45–50.
Ellison, N. F. (1966). Notes on Lakeland Schelly. *Changing Scene.* 3: 46–53.
Ellison, N. F. & Chubb, J. C. (1968). The Smelt of Rostherne Mere, Cheshire. *Lanc. Ches. Fauna Soc.* 53: 7–16.
Ellison, N. F. & Cooper, J. R. (1967). Further notes on Lakeland Schelly. *Field Naturalist* 12: 3–6.
Erman, F. (1961). On the biology of the Thick-lipped Mullet (*Mugil chelo*). *Rapp. Reun. Comm. Int. Expl. Scient. Mer Medi.* 16: 277–285.
Evans, N. A (1978). The occurrence and life history of *Asymphylodora kubanicum* (Platyhelminthes: Digenea: Monorchidae) in the Worcester-Birmingham Canal, with special reference to the feeding habits of the definitive host, *Rutilus rutilus*. *J. Zool.* 184: 143–153.
Everhart, W. H., Eipper, A. W. & Youngs, W. D. (1975). *Principles of fishery science.* New York: Comstock Press.
Ezzat, A. & El-Sarafy, S. (1977). The migration of elvers of *Anguilla anguilla* L. in the Mex canal, Alexandria, Egypt. *J. Fish Biol.* 11: 249–256.
Fabricius, E. & Gustavson, K. J. (1955). Observations on the spawning behaviour of the Grayling, *Thymallus thymallus* (L.). *Rep. Inst. Freshw. Res. Drottning.* 36: 75–103.
Fabricius, E. & Gustavson, K. J. (1958). Some new observations on the spawning behaviour of the Pike, *Esox lucius* L. *Rep. Inst. Freshw. Res. Drottning.* 39: 23–54.
Fahy, E. (1977). Characteristics of the freshwater occurrence of Sea Trout *Salmo trutta* in Ireland. *J. Fish Biol.* 11: 635–646.
Fahy, E. (1978). Variations in some biological characteristics of British Sea Trout, *Salmo trutta* L. *J. Fish Biol.* 13: 123–138.
Farran, G. P. (1946). Local names of fishes. *Irish Nat. J.* 8: 344–430.
Fedorova, G. V. & Vetkasov, S. A. (1973). The biological characteristics and abundance of the Lake Ilmen Ruffe, *Acerina cernua*. *J. Ichth.* 14: 836–841.
Ferguson, A. (1974). The genetic relationships of the coregonid fishes of Britain and Ireland indicated by electrophoretic analysis of tissue proteins. *J. Fish Biol.* 6: 311–315.
Ferguson, A., Himberg, K. J. M. & Svardson, G. (1978). The systematics of the Irish Pollan (*Coregonus pollan* Thompson): an electrophoretic comparison with other Holarctic Coregoninae. *J. Fish Biol.* 12: 221–233.
Ferguson, A. & Mason, F. M. (1981). Allozyme evidence for reproductively isolated sympatric populations of Brown Trout *Salmo trutta* L. in Lough Melvin, Ireland. *J. Fish Biol.* 18: 629–642.
Fickling, N. J. (1982). The identification of Pike by means of characteristic marks. *Fish Mgmt.* 13: 79–82.
Fickling, N. J. & Lee, R. L. G. (1985). A study of the movements of the Zander, *Lucioperca*

lucioperca L., population of two lowland fisheries. *Aqu. Fish. Mgt.* 16: 377–393.
Fitter, R. S. R. (1959). *The ark in our midst.* London: Collins.
Fitzmaurice, P. (1982). The effects of freshwater fish introductions into Ireland. *EIFAC Symp.* 5: 43.
Fitzmaurice, P. (1983a). Carp (*Cyprinus carpio* L.) in Ireland. *Irish Fish. Invest.* A, 23.
Fitzmaurice, P. (1983b). Some aspects of the biology and management of Pike (*Esox lucius* L.) stocks in Irish fisheries. *J. Life Sci. Roy. Dublin Soc.*
Flowerdew, M. W. & Grove, D. J. (1980). An energy budget for juvenile Thick-lipped Mullet, *Crenimugil labrosus* (Risso). *J. Fish Biol.* 17: 395–410.
Fouda, M. M. (1979). Studies on scale structure in the Common Goby *Pomatoschistus microps* Kroyer. *J. Fish Biol.* 15: 165–172.
Fouda, M. M. & Miller, P. J. (1979). Alkaline phosphatase activity in the skin of the Common Goby, *Pomatoschistus microps*, in relation to cycles in scale and body growth. *J. Fish Biol.* 15: 263–274.
Fox, P. J. (1978). Preliminary observations on different reproduction strategies in the Bullhead (*Cottus gobio* L.) in northern and southern England. *J. Fish Biol.* 12: 5–11.
Frost, W. E. (1939). River Liffey Survey. II. The food consumed by the Brown Trout (*Salmo trutta* L.) in acid and alkaline water. *Proc. Roy. Irish Acad.* 45: 139–206.
Frost, W. E. (1940). Rainbows of a peat lough on Arranmore. *Salm. Trout Mag.* 100: 234–240.
Frost, W. E. (1943). The natural history of the Minnow *Phoxinus phoxinus*. *J. Anim. Ecol.* 12: 139–162.
Frost, W. E. (1945). The age and growth of Eels (*Anguilla anguilla*) from the Windermere catchment area. *J. Anim. Ecol.* 14: 26–36: 106–124.
Frost, W. E. (1974). *A survey of the Rainbow Trout (Salmo gairdneri) in Britain and Ireland.* London: Salmon & Trout Association.
Frost, W. E. (1977). The food of Charr, *Salvelinus willughbii* (Gunther), in Windermere. *J. Fish Biol.* 11: 531–548.
Frost, W. E. & Brown, M. E. (1967). *The Trout.* Collins: London.
Frost, W. E. & Kipling, C. (1980). The growth of Charr, *Salvelinus willughbii*, Gunther, in Windermere. *J. Fish Biol.* 16: 279–290.
Fuller, J. D. & Scott, D. B. C. (1976). The reproductive cycle of *Coregonus lavaretus* (L.) in Loch Lomond, Scotland, in relation to seasonal changes in plasma cortisol concentration. *J. Fish Biol.* 9: 105–117.
Gardiner, W. R. (1974). An electrophoretic method for distinguishing the young fry of Salmon *Salmo salar* (L.) from those of Trout *Salmo trutta* (L.). *J. Fish Biol.* 6: 517–519.
Gardner, A. S., Walker, A. F. & Greer, R. B. (1988). Morphometric analysis of two ecologically distinct forms of Arctic Charr, *Salvelinus alpinus* (L.), in Loch Rannoch, Scotland. *J. Fish Biol.* 32: 901–910.
Gardner, M. L. G. (1971). Recent changes in the movements of adult Salmon in the Tay-Tummel-Garry system, Scotland. *J. Fish Biol.* 3: 83–96.
Gardner, M. L. G. (1976). A review of factors which may influence the sea-age and matur-

ation of Atlantic Salmon *Salmo salar* L. *J. Fish Biol.* 9: 289–327.
Garnas, E. (1982). Growth of different year classes of Smelt *Osmerus eperlanus* L. in Lake Tyrifjorden, Norway. *Fauna Norv.* 3: 1–6.
Gee, A. S. (1978). The distribution and growth of coarse fish in gravel-pit lakes in south-east England. *Freshw. Biol.* 8: 385–394.
Gee, A. S., Milner, N. J. & Hemsworth, R. J. (1978). The production of juvenile Atlantic Salmon, *Salmo salar* in the upper Wye, Wales. *J. Fish Biol.* 13: 439–451.
George, E. L. & Hadley, W. F. (1979). Food and habitat partitioning between Rock Bass (*Ambloplites rupestris*) and Smallmouth Bass (*Micropterus dolomieu*) young of the year. *Trans. Amer. Fish. Soc.* 108: 253–261.
Gerrish, C. S. (1935). Hatchery stock and Trout streams. *Salm. Trout Mag.* 84: 245–254.
Gerrish, C. S. (1936–39). Scales of Avon Trout and Grayling. *Rep. Avon Biol. Res.* 3: 81–95; 4: 44–58; 5: 70–78; 6: 54–59.
Gervers, F. W. K. (1954). A supernumerary pelvic fin in the Powan (*Coregonus clupeoides* Lacepede). *Nature, Lond.* 174: 935.
Gibson, D. L. (1972). Flounder parasites as biological tags. *J. Fish Biol.* 4: 1–10.
Giles, N. (1983). The possible role of environmental calcium levels during the evolution of phenotypic diversity in Outer Hebridean populations of Three-spined Sticklebacks, *Gasterosteus aculeatus*. *J. Zool. Lond.* 199: 535–545.
Goldspink, C. R. (1978). Comparative observations on the growth rate and year class strength of Roach *Rutilus rutilus* L. in two Cheshire lakes, England. *J. Fish Biol.* 12: 421–433.
Goldspink, C. R. (1981). A note on the growth-rate and year-class strength of Bream, *Abramis brama* L., in three eutrophic lakes, England. *J. Fish Biol.* 19: 665–674.
Goldspink, C. R. & Banks, J. W. (1971). A readily recognisable tag for marking Bream *Abramis brama* (L.) *J. Fish Biol.* 3: 407–411.
Goldspink, C. R. & Goodwin, D. A. (1979). A note on age composition, growth rate and food of Perch, *Perca fluviatilis* (L.), in four eutrophic lakes, England. *J. Fish Biol.* 14: 489–505.
Graham, T. T. & Jones, J. W. (1960). The biology of Llyn Tegid Trout 1960. *Proc. Zool. Soc. Lond.* 139: 657–683.
Greenbank, J. & Nelson, P. (1959). Life history of the Three-spine Stickleback *Gasterosteus aculeatus* Linnaeus in Karluk Lake and Bare Lake Kodiak Island, Alaska. *US Fish Wild. Serv. Bull.* 153: 537–559.
Greenwood, P. H. (1975). *A history of fishes*. London: Benn.
Griswold, B. L. & Smith, L. L. (1973). The life history and trophic relationship of the Ninespine Stickleback, *Pungitius pungitius*, in the Apostle Islands area of Lake Superior. *Fish. Bull.* 71: 1039–1060.
Guma'a, S. A. (1982). Retinal development and retinomotor responses in Perch, *Perca fluviatilis* L. *J. Fish Biol.* 20: 611–618.
Gunther, A. C. L. G. (1880). *An introduction to the study of fishes*. Edinburgh: Black.
Gyldenholm, A. D. (1971). Chromosome numbers of fishes. I. *J. Fish Biol.* 3: 479–486.
Hancock, R. S., Jones, J. W. & Shaw, R. (1976). A preliminary report on the spawning behaviour and nature of sexual selection in the

Barbel, *Barbus barbus* (L.). *J. Fish Biol.* 9: 21–28.
Hansen, L. P., Doving, K. B. & Jonsson, B. (1987). Migration of adult Atlantic Salmon with and without olfactory sense, released on the Norwegian coast. *J. Fish Biol.* 30: 713–730.
Hansen, L. P. & Pethon, P. (1985). The food of Atlantic Salmon, *Salmo salar* L., caught by long line in northern Norwegian waters. *J. Fish Biol.* 26: 553–562.
Haram, O. J. (1968). A preliminary investigation of the biology of the Gwyniad (*Coregonus* sp.) of Llyn Tegid. PhD Thesis, University of Liverpool.
Haram, O. J. & Jones, J. W. (1971). Some observations on the food of the Gwyniad, *Coregonus pennantii* Valenciennes of Llyn Tegid (Lake Bala), North Wales. *J. Fish Biol.* 3: 287–295.
Harden-Jones, F. R. (1968). *Fish migration*. London: Arnold.
Hardie, R. P. (1940). *Ferox and Char in the lochs of Scotland*. Edinburgh: Oliver & Boyd.
Hardisty, M. W. (1944). The life-history and growth of the Brook Lamprey (*Lampetra planeri*). *J. Anim. Ecol.* 13: 110–122.
Hardisty, M. W. (1961a). Studies on an isolated spawning population of the Brook Lamprey (*Lampetra planeri*). *J. Anim. Ecol.* 30: 339–355.
Hardisty, M. W. (1961b). The growth of larval lampreys. *J. Anim. Ecol.* 30: 357–371.
Hardisty, M. W. (1969). A comparison of gonadal development in the ammocoetes of the landlocked and anadromous forms of the Sea Lamprey *Petromyzon marinus* L. *J. Fish Biol.* 1: 153–166.
Hardisty, M. W. & Huggins, R. J. (1970). Larval growth in the River Lamprey *Lampetra fluviatilis* L. *J. Zool. Lond.* 161: 549–559.
Hardisty, W. M. & Potter, I. C. (Ed.) (1971). *The biology of the lampreys, Volume I*. New York: Academic Press.
Hardy, E. (1954). The Bitterling in Lancashire. *Salm. Trout Mag.* 142: 548–553.
Harkness, W. J. K. & Dymond, J. R. (1961). *The Lake Sturgeon. The history of its fishery and problems of conservation*. Ontario Dept. Lands Forests, Fish Wildl. Br. 1–121.
Harris, M. T. & Wheeler, A. (1974). Ligula infestation of Bleak *Alburnus alburnus* (L.) in the tidal Thames. *J. Fish Biol.* 6: 181–188.
Hartley, P. H. T. (1940). The Saltash tuck-net fishery and the ecology of some estuarine fishes. *J. Mar. Biol. Ass. UK* 24: 1–68.
Hartley, P. H. T. (1947a). The natural history of some British freshwater fishes. *Proc. Zool. Soc. Lond.* 117: 129–206.
Hartley, P. H. T. (1947b). The coarse fishes of Britain. *Sci. Publ. Freshw. Biol. Ass.* 12: 1–40.
Hartley, P. H. T. 1948. Food and feeding relationships in a community of freshwater fishes. *J. Anim. Ecol.* 17: 1–14.
Havey, K. A. & Warner, K. (1970). The landlocked Salmon (*Salmo salar*). Its life history and management in Maine. *Sport Fish. Inst. Washington*. 1970: 1–129.
Hawkins, A. D. & Johnstone, A. D. F. (1978). The hearing of the Atlantic Salmon, *Salmo salar*. *J. Fish Biol.* 13: 655–673.
Hazen, T. D. & Esch, G. W. (1978). Observations on the ecology of *Clinostomum marginatum* in Largemouth Bass (*Micropterus salmoides*). *J. Fish Biol.* 12: 411–420.
Healey, M. C. (1972). On the population eco-

logy of the Common Goby in the Ythan Estuary. *J. Nat. Hist.* 6: 133–145.
Healy, A. (1956). Pike (*Esox lucius* L.) in three Irish Lakes. *Sci. Proc. Roy. Dublin Soc.* 27: 51–63.
Healy, A. (1957). Brown Trout of the Fergus system Co. Clare, Ireland. *Salm. Trout Mag.* 15: 193–198.
Healy, J. A. & Mulcahy, M. F. (1980). A biochemical genetic analysis of populations of the Northern Pike, *Esox lucius* L., from Europe and North America. *J. Fish Biol.* 17: 317–324.
Heath, A. (1939). *From creel to kitchen: how to cook freshwater fish.* London: Black.
Heggberget, T. G. & Johnsen, B. O. (1982). Infestations by *Gyrodactylus* sp. of Atlantic Salmon, *Salmo salar* L., in Norwegian rivers. *J. Fish Biol.* 21: 15–26.
Hellawell, J. M. (1969). Age determination and growth of the Grayling *Thymallus thymallus* (L.) of the River Lugg, Herefordshire. *J. Fish Biol.* 1: 373–382.
Hellawell, J. M. (1971). The food of Grayling *Thymallus thymallus* (L.) of the River Lugg, Herefordshire. *J. Fish Biol.* 3: 187–197.
Hellawell, J. M. (1972). The growth, reproduction and food of the Roach *Rutilus rutilus* (L.), of the River Lugg, Herefordshire. *J. Fish Biol.* 4: 469–486.
Hellawell, J. M. (1974). The ecology of populations of Dace, *Leuciscus leuciscus* (L.), from two tributaries of the River Wye, Herefordshire, England. *Freshw. Biol.* 4: 577–604.
Henricson, J. (1977). The abundance and distribution of *Diphyllobothrium dendriticum* (Nitzsch) and *D. ditremum* (Creplin) in the Char *Salvelinus alpinus* (L.) in Sweden. *J. Fish Biol.* 11: 231–248.
Hervey, G. F. & Hems, J. (1968). *The goldfish.* London: Faber & Faber.
Hickley, P. & Bailey, R. G. (1977). The effects of cropping on the production of Roach (*Rutilus rutilus* (L.)) in a reservoir intake lagoon. *Fish. Mgt.* 8: 47–51.
Hickley, P. & Bailey, R. G. (1982). Observations on the growth and production of Chub *Leuciscus cephalus* and Dace *Leuciscus leuciscus* in a small lowland river in southeast England, U.K. *Freshwat. Biol.* 12: 167–178.
Hickling, C. F. (1970). A contribution to the natural history of the English Grey Mullets, Pisces Mugilidae. *J. Mar. Biol. Ass. UK.* 50: 609–633.
Hile, R. (1941). Age and growth of the Rock Bass, *Ambloplites rupestris* (Rafinesque), in Nebish Lake, Wisconsin. *Trans. Wis. Sci. Art Lett.* 33: 189–337.
Hinkens, E. & Cochrane, P. A. (1988. Taste buds on pelvic ray fins of the Burbot, *Lota lota* (L.) *J. Fish Biol.* 32:975.
Holden, A. V. (1959). Fertilisation experiments in Scottish freshwater lochs. II. Sutherland 1954. 1. Chemical and botanical observations. *Freshw. Salm. Fish. Res. Scot.* 24: 1–42.
Holden, A. V. (1966). A chemical study of rain and stream waters in the Scottish highlands. *Freshw. Salm. Fish. Res. Scot.* 37: 1–17.
Holden, A. V. & Marsden, K. (1964). Cyanide in Salmon and Brown Trout. *Freshw. Salm. Fish. Res. Scot.* 33: 1–12.
Holden, M. J. & Williams, T. (1974). The biology, movements and population dynamics of Bass *Dicentrarchus labrax* in English waters. *J. Mar. Biol. Ass. UK.* 54: 91–107.
Holt, S. J. & Talbot, L. M. (1978). New principles for the conservation of wild living resources. *Wildl. Monogr.* 59: 1–33.
Houghton, W. (1879). *British freshwater fishes.* London: Mackenzie.
Huggins, R. J. & Thompson, A. (1970). Communal spawning of Brook and River Lampreys, *Lampetra planeri* Bloch and *Lampetra fluviatilis* L. *J. Fish Biol.* 53–54.
Hunt, P. C. & Jones, J. W. (1972a). The food of the Brown Trout in Llyn Alaw, Anglesey, North Wales. *J. Fish Biol.* 4: 333–352.
Hunt, P. C. & Jones, J. W. (1972b). Trout in Llyn Alaw, Anglesey, North Wales. I. Population structure and angling returns. *J. Fish Biol.* 4: 395–408.
Hunt, P. C. & Jones, J. W. (1974a). A population study of Barbel *Barbus barbus* (L.) in the River Severn, England. I Densities. *J. Fish Biol.* 6: 255–267.
Hunt, P. C. & Jones, J. W. (1974b). A population study of Barbel *Barbus barbus* (L.) in the River Severn, England. II Movements. *J. Fish Biol.* 6: 269–278.
Hunt, P. C. & Jones, J. W. (1975). A population study of *Barbus barbus* (L.) in the River Severn, England. III Growth. *J. Fish Biol.* 7: 361–376.
Hunt, P. C. & O'Hara, K. (1973). Overwinter feeding in Rainbow Trout. *J. Fish Biol.* 5: 277–280.
Hutchinson, P. (1983a). Some ecological aspects of the Smelt, *Osmerus eperlanus* (L.), from the River Cree, southwest Scotland. *Proc. Brit. Freshw. Fish. Conf.* 3.
Hutchinson, P. (1983b). A note recording the occurrence of hermaphrodite Smelt, *Osmerus eperlanus* (L.) from the River Thames, England. *J. Fish Biol.* 23: 241–244.
Hutton, J. A. (1923). Something about Grayling scales. *Salm. Trout Mag.* Jan., 3–8.
Hynd, I. J. R. (1964). Large Sea Trout from the Tweed district. *Salm. Trout Mag.* 172: 151–154.
Hynes, H. B. N. (1950). The freshwater sticklebacks (*Gasterosteus aculeatus* and *Pungitius pungitius*), with a review of methods used in studies of the food of fishes. *J. Anim. Ecol.* 19: 36–38.
Hyslop, E. J. (1982). The feeding habits of 0+ Stone Loach, *Noemacheilus barbatulus* (L.) and Bullhead, *Cottus gobio* (L.). *J. Fish Biol.* 21: 157–196.
Irish Specimen Fish Committee. (1987). *Report for year 1987.* Dublin: Irish Specimen Fish Committee.
Jackman, L. A. J. (1954). The early development stages of the Bass *Morone labrax. Proc. Zool. Soc. Lond.* 124: 531–534.
Jafri, S. I. H. & Ensor, D. M. (1979). Occurrence of an intersex condition in the Roach, *Rutilus rutilus* (L.) *J. Fish Biol.* 15: 547–549.
Jenkins, J. T. (1925). *The fishes of the British Isles, both fresh and salt.* London: Warne.
Jilek, R., Cassell, B., Peace, D., Garza, Y., Riley, L. & Stewart, T. (1979). Spawning population dynamics of Smelt *Osmerus mordax. J. Fish Biol.* 15: 31–35.
Johnsen, B. O. & Jensen, A. J. (1986). Infestation of Atlantic Salmon, *Salmo salar*, by *Gyrodactylus salaris* in Norwegian rivers. *J. Fish Biol.* 29: 233–242.
Johnston, H. W. (1904). The scales of Tay Salmon as indicative of age, growth and spawning habits. *Rep. Fish. Bd. Scot.* 23.
Jones, J. W. (1953). Part I. Scales of Roach. Part II. Age and growth of the Trout, Grayling,

Perch and Roach of Llyn Tegid (Bala) and the Roach from the River Birket. *Fish. Invest. Lond.* 5: 1–8.
Jones, J. W. (1959). *The Salmon*. London: Collins.
Jones, J. W. & Hynes, H. B. N. (1950). The age and growth of *Gasterosteus aculeatus*, *Pungitius pungitius* and *Spinachia vulgaris*, as shown by their otoliths. *J. Anim. Ecol.* 19: 59–73.
Jones, N. S. (1952). The bottom fauna and the food of flatfish off the Cumberland coast. *J. Anim. Ecol.* 21: 182–205.
Jurvelius, J., Lindem, T. & Heikkinen, T. (1988). The size of a Vendace, *Coregonus albula* L., stock in a deep lake basin monitored by hydro-acoustic methods. *J. Fish Biol.* 32: 679–68.
Keast, A. & Eadie, J. M. (1985). Growth depensation in year-0 Largemouth Bass: the influence of diet. *Trans. Amer. Fish. Soc.* 114: 204–213.
Keast, A. & Walsh, L. (1968). Daily feeding periodicities, food uptake, and dietary changes with hour of day in young lake fishes. *J. Fish. Res. Bd. Can.* 25: 1133–1144.
Kelley, D. (1979). Bass populations and movements on the west coast of the UK. *J. Mar. Biol. Ass. UK* 59: 889–936.
Kelley, D. (1986). Bass nurseries on the west coast of the UK. *J. Mar. Biol. Ass. UK.* 66: 439–464.
Kennedy, C. R. (1969). Tubificid oligochaetes as food of Dace *Leuciscus leuciscus* (L.) *J. Fish Biol.* 1: 11–15.
Kennedy, C. R. (1975). The natural history of Slapton Ley nature reserve: VIII The parasites of fish, with special reference to their use as a source of information about the aquatic community. *Field Studies.* 4: 177–189.
Kennedy, C. R. (1978). An analysis of the metazoan parasitocoenoses of Brown Trout *Salmo trutta* from British lakes. *J. Fish Biol.* 13: 255–263.
Kennedy, C. R. (1981). The occurrence of *Eubothrium fragile* (Cestoida: Pseudophyllidae) in Twaite Shad, *Alosa fallax* (Lacepede) in the River Severn. *J. Fish Biol.* 19: 171–178.
Kennedy, C. R. (1984a). The status of Flounders, *Platichthys flesus* L., as hosts of the acanthocephalan *Pomphorhynchus laevis* (Muller) and its survival in marine conditions. *J. Fish Biol.* 23: 135–150.
Kennedy, C. R. (1984b). The dynamics of a declining population of the acanthocephalan *Acanthocephalus clavula* in Eels, *Anguilla anguilla*, in a small river. *J. Fish Biol.* 25: 665–677.
Kennedy, C. R. & Burrough, R.J. (1977). The population biology of two species of eyefluke, *Diplostomum gasterostei* and *Tylodelphys elevata* in Perch. *J. Fish Biol.* 11: 619–634.
Kennedy, C. R. & Burrough, R. J. (1981). The establishment and subsequent history of a population of *Ligula intestinalis* in Roach *Rutilus rutilus* (L.). *J. Fish Biol.* 19: 127–128.
Kennedy, C. R. & Hine, P. M. (1969). Population biology of the cestode *Proteocephalus torulosus* (Batsch) in Dace *Leuciscus leuciscus* (L.) of the River Avon. *J. Fish Biol.* 1: 209–219.
Kennedy, C. R. & Lie, S. F. (1976). The distribution and pathogenicity of larvae of *Eustrongylides* (Nematoda) in Brown Trout *Salmo trutta* L. in Fernworthy Reservoir, Devon. *J. Fish Biol.* 8: 293–302.
Kennedy, G. J. A. & Strange, C. D. (1978).

Seven years on—a continuing investigation of salmonid stocks in Lough Erne tributaries. *J. Fish Biol.* 12: 325–330.
Kennedy, M. (1969). Spawning and early development of the Dace *Leuciscus leuciscus* (L.) *J. Fish Biol.* 1: 249–259.
Kennedy, M. & Fitzmaurice, P. (1968a). The biology of the Bream *Abramis abrama* (L.) in Irish waters. *Proc. Roy. Irish Acad.* 67,B: 95–161.
Kennedy, M. & Fitzmaurice, P. (1968b). Occurrence of eggs of Bass *Dicentrarchus labrax* on the southern coasts of Ireland. *J. Mar. Biol. Ass. UK.* 48: 585–592.
Kennedy, M. & Fitzmaurice, P. (1969a). Age and growth of Thick-lipped Grey Mullet *Crenimugil labrosus* in Irish waters. *J. Mar. Biol. Ass. UK.* 49: 683–699.
Kennedy, M. & Fitzmaurice, P. (1969b). Factors affecting the growth of coarse fish. *Proc. Brit. Coarse Fish Conf.* 4.
Kennedy, M. & Fitzmaurice, P. (1970). The biology of Tench *Tinca tinca* (L.) in Irish waters. *Proc. Roy. Irish Acad.* 69,B: 31–64.
Kennedy, M. & Fitzmaurice, P. (1972a). Some aspects of the biology of Gudgeon *Gobio gobio* (L.) in Irish waters. *J. Fish Biol.* 4: 425–440.
Kennedy, M. & Fitzmaurice, P. (1972b). The biology of the Bass, *Dicentrarchus labrax*, in Irish waters. *J. Mar. Biol. Ass. UK.* 52: 557–597.
Kennedy, M. & Fitzmaurice, P. (1974). Biology of Rudd *Scardinius erythrophthalmus* (L.) in Irish waters. *Proc. Roy. Irish Acad.* 74,B: 246–282.
Kilambi, R. V. & Robinson, W. R. (1979). Effects of temperature and stocking density on food consumption and growth of Grass Carp *Ctenopharyngodon idella*, Val. *J. Fish Biol.* 15: 337–342.
Kipling, C. (1984). Some observations on autumn-spawning Charr, *Salvelinus alpinus* L., in Windermere, 1939–1982. *J. Fish Biol.* 23: 229–234.
Kipling, C. & Frost, W. E. (1969). Variations in the fecundity of Pike *Esox lucius* L. in Windermere. *J. Fish Biol.* 1: 221–237.
Kisalioglu, M. & Gibson, R. N. (1977). The feeding relationship of shallow water fishes in a Scottish sea loch. *J. Fish Biol.* 11: 257–266.
Kolomin, Y. M. (1975). The Nadym River Ruffe, *Acerina cernua*. *Scripta Publ. Co.* 1978: 345–349.
Lacey, S. M. & Williams, I. C. (1983). *Epieimeria anguillae* (Leger & Hollande 1922), Dykora & Lom 1981 (Apicomplexa: Eucoccidia) in the European Eel, *Anguilla anguilla* (L.). *J. Fish Biol.* 23: 603–609.
Lacey, S. M., Williams, I. C. & Carpenter, A. C. (1982). A note on the occurrence of the digenetic trematode *Sphaerostoma bramae* (Muller) in the intestine of the European Eel, *Anguilla anguilla* (L.). *J. Fish Biol.* 20: 593–596.
Ladich, F. (1988). Sound production by the Gudgeon, *Gobio gobio* L., a common European freshwater fish (Cyprinidae, Teleostei). *J. Fish Biol.* 32: 707–716.
Lang, C. (1987). Mortality of Perch, *Perca fluviatilis* L., estimated from the size and abundance of egg strands. *J. Fish Biol.* 31: 715–720.
Lawler, G. H. (1963). The biology and taxonomy of the Burbot, *Lota lota*, in Hemming Lake, Manitoba. *J. Fish. Res. Bd. Can.* 20: 417–433.
Lebrasseur, R. J. (1965). Stomach contents of Salmon and Steelhead Trout in the north-

eastern Pacific Ocean. *J. Fish. Res. Bd. Can.* 23: 85–107.

Lebrasseur, R. J. & Parker, R. R. (1964). Growth rate of central British Columbia Pink Salmon (*Oncorhynchus gorbuscha*). *J. Fish. Res. Bd. Can.* 21: 1101–1128.

Le Cren, E. D. (1961). How many fish survive? *Yb. River Bds. Assoc.* 57–64.

Le Cren, E. D. (1985). *The biology of the Sea Trout: summary of a symposium held at Plas Menai, 24–26 October, 1984.* Pitlochry: Atlantic Salmon Trust.

Le Cren, E. D., Kipling, C. & McCormack, J. (1967). A study of the numbers, biomass and year class strengths of Perch (*Perca fluviatilis* L.) in Windermere from 1941–1966. *J. Anim. Ecol.* 46: 281–307.

Leeming, J. B. (1967). The Chub, Bream and other fishes of the Welland. *Proc. Brit. Coarse Fish Conf.* 1: 48–52.

Leeming, J. B. (1970). A note on the occurrence of unusual mortalities amongst Common Carp (*Cyprinus carpio*). *Fish. Mgt.* 1: 9.

Lein, L. (1981). Biology of the Minnow *Phoxinus phoxinus* and its interactions with Brown Trout *Salmo trutta* in Ovre Heimdalsvatn, Norway. *Holarctic Ecology.* 4: 191–200.

Letaconnoux, R. (1961). Frequence et distribution des captures d'esturgeons (*Acipenser sturio*) dans le Golfe de Gascogne. *Rev. Trav. Pech. Marit.* 25: 253–261.

Lever, C. (1977). *The naturalised animals of the British Isles.* London: Hutchinson.

Levesley, P. B. & Magurran, A. E. (1988). Population differences in the reaction of Minnows to alarm substance. *J. Fish Biol.* 32: 699–706.

Lewis, C. (1965). The Largemouth Bass Fishery, Lake Opinicon, Ontario. *MSc. Thesis, University of Kingston.*

Lewis, D. B., Walkey, M. & Dartnell, H. J. G. (1972). Some effects of low oxygen tensions on the distribution of the Three-spined Stickleback *Gasterosteus aculeatus* L. and the Nine-spined Stickleback *Pungitius pungitius* (L.) *J. Fish Biol.* 4: 103–108.

Linfield, R. S. J. (1979a). Changes in the rate of growth in a stunted Roach *Rutilus rutilus* population. *J. Fish Biol.* 15: 275–298.

Linfield, R. S. J. (1979b). Age determination and year class structure in a stunted Roach *Rutilus rutilus* population. *J. Fish Biol.* 14: 73–87.

Linfield, R. S. J. (1980). Ecological changes in a lake fishery and their effects on a stunted Roach *Rutilus rutilus* population. *J. Fish Biol.* 16: 123–144.

Linfield, R. S. J. & Rickards, R. B. (1979). Zander in perspective. *Fish. Mgmt.* 10: 1–16.

Longfield, A. K. (1929). *Anglo-Irish trade in the Sixteenth Century.* London: Routledge.

Love, M. (1970). *The chemical biology of fishes.* London: Academic Press.

Macan, T. T. & Worthington, E. B. (1974). *Life in lakes and rivers.* London: Collins.

MacCrimmon, H. R. (1956). Fishing in Lake Simcoe. *Publ. Ont. Dept. Lands For.* 1: 1–137.

MacCrimmon, H. R. & Devitt, O. E. (1954). Winter studies on the Burbot, *Lota lota lacustris*, of Lake Simcoe, Ontario. *Can. Fish. Cult.* 16: 34–41.

MacCrimmon, H. R. (1971). World distribution of Rainbow Trout (*Salmo gairdneri*) *J. Fish. Res. Bd. Can.* 28: 663–704.

MacCrimmon, H. R. & Campbell, J. S. (1969). World distribution of Brook Trout, *Salvelinus fontinalis*. *J. Fish. Res. Bd. Can.* 26: 1699–1725.

MacCrimmon, H. R. & Gots, B. L. (1979). World distribution of Atlantic Salmon, *Salmo salar*. *J. Fish. Res. Bd. Can.* 36: 422–457.

MacCrimmon, H. R. & Marshall, T. L. (1968). World distribution of Brown Trout, *Salmo trutta*. *J. Fish. Res. Bd. Can.* 25: 2527–2548.

McIntosh, R. (1978). Distribution and food of the Cormorant on the lower reaches of the River Tweed. *Fish Mgt.* 9: 107–113.

Mackay, D. W. (1970). Populations of Trout and Grayling in two Scottish rivers. *J. Fish Biol.* 2: 39–45.

McKenzie, J. A. & Keenleyside, M. H. A. (1970). Reproductive behaviour in Nine-spine Sticklebacks (*Pungitius pungitius* (L.)) in South Bay, Manitoulin Island, Ontario. *Can. J. Zool.* 48: 55–61.

McCleave, J. D. (1980). Swimming performance of the European Eel, *Anguilla anguilla* (L.) elvers. *J. Fish Biol.* 16: 445–452.

MacMahone, A. F. M. (1948). *Fish lore.* Harmondsworth: Pelican.

McPhail, J. D. (1966). The *Coregonus autumnnalis* complex in Alaska and north-western Canada. *J. Fish. Res. Bd. Can.* 23: 141–148.

Magnin, E. (1963). Recherches sur la systematique et la biologie des Acipenserides *Acipenser sturio* L., *Acipenser oxyrhynchus* Mitchill, *Acipenser fulvescens* Raf. *DSc Thesis, University of Paris.*

Maitland, P. S. (1964). A population of Common Carp (*Cyprinus carpio*) in the Loch Lomond district. *Glasg. Nat.* 18: 349–350.

Maitland, P. S. (1965). The feeding relationships of Salmon, Trout, Minnows, Stone Loach and Three-spined Sticklebacks in the River Endrick, Scotland. *J. Anim. Ecol.* 34: 109–133.

Maitland, P. S. (1966a). *The fauna of the River Endrick.* Glasgow: Blackie.

Maitland, P. S. (1966b). Present status of known populations of the Vendace *Coregonus vandesius* Richardson, in Great Britain. *Nature, Lond.* 216–217.

Maitland, P. S. (1966c). The fish fauna of the Castle and Mill Lochs, Lochmaben, with special reference to the Lochmaben Vendace, *Coregonus vandesius* Richardson. *Trans. Dumf. & Gall. Nat. Hist. Antiq. Soc.* 43: 31–48.

Maitland, P. S. (1967a). The artificial fertilisation and rearing of the eggs of *Coregonus clupeoides* Lacepede. *Proc. Roy. Soc. Edin.* 70: 82–106.

Maitland, P. S. (1967b). Echo sounding observations on the Lochmaben Vendace, *Coregonus vandesius* Richardson. *Trans. Dumfr. Gall. Nat. Hist. Antiqu. Soc.* 44: 29–46.

Maitland, P. S. (1969a). A preliminary account of the mapping of the distribution of freshwater fish in the British Isles. *J. Fish Biol.* 1: 45–58.

Maitland, P. S. (1969b). The reproduction and fecundity of the Powan, *Coregonus clupeoides* Lacepede, in Loch Lomond, Scotland. *Proc. Roy. Soc. Edin.* 70,B: 233–264.

Maitland, P. S. (1970). The origin and present distribution of *Coregonus* in the British Isles. *Int. Symp. Biol. Coregonid Fish, Winnipeg.* 1: 99–114.

Maitland, P. S. (1971). A population of coloured Goldfish, *Carassius auratus*, in the Forth and Clyde Canal. *Glasg. Nat.* 18: 565–568.

Maitland, P. S. (1972a). Loch Lomond: man's effects on the salmonid community. *J. Fish. Res. Bd. Can.* 29: 849–860.

Maitland, P. S. (1972b). A key to the freshwater

fishes of the British Isles. *Sci. Publ. Freshw. Biol. Ass.* 27: 1-137.
Maitland, P. S. (1974). The conservation of freshwater fishes in the British Isles. *Biol. Conserv.* 6: 7-14.
Maitland, P. S. (1977a). Freshwater fish in Scotland in the 18th, 19th and 20th centuries. *Biol. Conserv.* 12: 265-277.
Maitland, P. S. (1977b). *Freshwater fish of Britain and Europe.* London: Hamlyn.
Maitland, P. S. (1978). *The biology of fresh waters.* London: Blackie.
Maitland, P. S. (1979a). The status and conservation of rare freshwater fishes in the British Isles. *Proc. Br. Freshw. Fish. Conf.* 1: 237-248.
Maitland, P. S. (1979b). The freshwater fish fauna of the Forth area. *Forth Nat. Hist.* 4: 33-47.
Maitland, P. S. (1980a). Review of the ecology of lampreys in northern Europe. *Can. J. Fish. Aquat. Sci.* 37: 1944-1952.
Maitland, P. S. (1980b). Scarring of Whitefish (*Coregonus lavaretus*) by European River Lamprey (*Lampetra fluviatilis*) in Loch Lomond, Scotland. *Can. J. Fish. Aquat. Sci.* 37: 1981-1988.
Maitland, P. S. (1982). Elusive lake fish. *Living Countryside.* 7: 1672-1673.
Maitland, P. S. (1983). *Catfishes: 'fish with whiskers'*. Living Countryside. 10: 2212-2213.
Maitland, P. S. (1985). Criteria for the selection of important sites for freshwater fish in the British Isles. *Biol. Conserv.* 31: 335-353.
Maitland, P. S. (1986). *Conservation of threatened freshwater fish in Europe.* Report to Council of Europe.
Maitland, P. S., East, K. & Morris, K. H. (1983). Ruffe *Gymnocephalus cernua* (L.), new to Scotland, in Loch Lomond. *Scott. Nat.* 1983: 7-9.
Maitland, P. S. & Evans. D. (1986). The role of captive breeding in the conservation of fish species. *Int. Zoo Yb.* 25: 66-74.
Maitland, P. S., Greer, R. B., Campbell, R. N. & Friend, G. F. (1984). The status of the Arctic Charr, *Salvelinus alpinus* (L.),in Scotland. *Int. Symp. Arctic Charr, Winnipeg.* 1: 193-215.
Maitland, P. S., Lyle, A. A. & Campbell, R. N. B. (1987). *Acidification and fish populations in Scottish lochs.* Grange-over-Sands: Institute of Terrestrial Ecology.
Maitland, P. S., Morris, K. H., East, K., Schoonoord, M. P., Van Der Wal, B. & Potter, I. C. (1984). The estuarine biology of the River Lamprey, *Lampetra fluviatilis*, in the Firth of Forth, Scotland, with particular reference to size composition and feeding. *J. Zool., London.* 203: 211-225.
Maitland, P. S. & Price, C. E. (1969). *Urocleidus principalis*, a North American monogenetic trematode new to the British Isles, probably introduced with the Largemouth Bass *Micropterus salmoides*. *J. Fish. Biol.* 1: 17-18.
Maitland, P. S., Smith, B. D. & Adair, S. M. (1981). The ecology of Scotland's largest lochs: Lomond, Awe, Ness, Morar and Sheil. 9. The fish and fisheries. *Monogr. Biol.* 44: 205-222.
Maitland, P. S. & Turner, A. K. (1987). Angling and wildlife conservation—are they incompatible? *Inst. Terr. Ecol. Symp.* 19: 76-81.
Malloch, P. D. (1910). *Life history of the Salmon, Sea Trout and other freshwater fish.* London: Black.
Manion, P. J. (1967). Diatoms as food of larval Sea Lampreys in a small tributary of northern Lake Michigan. *Trans. Amer. Fish. Soc.* 96: 224-226.
Mann, R. H. K. (1971). The population, growth and production of fish in four small streams in southern England. *J. Anim. Ecol.* 40: 155-190.
Mann, R. H. K. (1973). Observations on the age, growth, reproduction and food of the Roach *Rutilus rutilus* (L.) in two rivers in southern England. *J. Fish Biol.* 5: 707-736.
Mann, R. H. K. (1974). Observations on the age, growth, reproduction and food of the Dace, *Leuciscus leuciscus* (L.) in two rivers in southern England. *J. Fish Biol.* 6: 237-253.
Mann, R. H. K. (1976a). Observations on the age, growth, reproduction and food of the Pike, *Esox lucius* (L.) in two rivers in southern England. *J. Fish Biol.* 8: 179-197.
Mann, R. H. K. (1976b). Observations on the age, growth, reproduction and food of the Chub *Squalius cephalus* (L.) in the River Stour, Dorset. *J. Fish Biol.* 8: 265-288.
Mann, R. H. K. (1980). The growth and reproductive strategy of the Gudgeon *Gobio gobio* (L.) in two hard-water rivers in southern England. *J. Fish Biol.* 17: 163-176.
Mann, R. H. K. (1982). The annual food consumption and prey preferences of Pike (*Esox lucius*) in the River Frome, Dorset. *J. Anim. Ecol.* 51: 81-95.
Mansfield, K. (1958). Pike-perch in England. *Salm. Trout Mag.* 153: 94-98.
Manzer, J. I. (1969). Stomach contents of juvenile Pacific salmon in Chatham Sound and adjacent waters. *J. Fish. Res. Bd. Can.* 26: 2219-2223.
Marcy, B. C. & Galvin, R. C. (1973). Winter-spring sport fishery in the heated discharge of a nuclear power plant. *J. Fish Biol.* 5: 541-548.
Marlborough, D. (1966). The reported distribution of Crucian Carp in Britain, 1954 to 1962. *Naturalist.* 89b: 1-3.
Marlborough, D. (1970). The status of the Burbot, *Lota lota* (L.) (Gadidae) in Britain. *J. Fish Biol.* 2: 217-222.
Marshall, N. B. (1965). *The life of fishes.* London: Weidenfeld & Nicolson.
Marshall, N. B. (1971). *Explorations in the life of fishes.* Cambridge: Harvard University Press.
Mathews, C. P. (1971). Contribution of young fish to total production of fish in the River Thames near Reading. *J. Fish Biol.* 3: 157-180.
Mathews, C. P. & Williams, W. P. (1972). Growth and annual check formation in scales of Dace, *Leuciscus leuciscus*. *J. Fish Biol.* 4: 363-368.
Maxwell, H. C. (1904). *British freshwater fishes.* London: Hutchinson.
Meek, A. (1916). *The migration of fishes.* London: Arnold.
Menzies, W. J. M. (1936). *Sea Trout and Trout.* London: Arnold.
Miller, P. J. (1975). Age structure and life span in the Common Goby *Pomatoschistus microps.* *J. Zool. Lond.* 177: 425-448.
Mills, C. A. (1981). The attachment of Dace, *Leuciscus leuciscus* L., eggs to the spawning substratum and the influence of changes in water current on their survival. *J. Fish Biol.* 19: 129-134.
Mills, C. A. (1982). Factors affecting the survival of Dace, *Leuciscus leuciscus* (L.), in the early

post-hatching period. *J. Fish Biol.* 20: 645–656.

Mills, C. A. Welton, J. S. & Rendle, E. L. (1983). The age, growth and reproduction of the Stone Loach *Noemacheilus barbatulus* (L.) in a Dorset chalk stream. *Freshw. Biol.* 13: 283–292.

Mills, D. H. (1962). The Goosander and Redbreasted Merganser as predators of Salmon in Scottish waters. *Freshw. Salm. Fish. Res. Scot.* 29: 1–10.

Mills, D. H. (1964). The ecology of the young stages of the Atlantic Salmon in the River Bran, Ross-shire. *Freshw. Salm. Fish. Res. Scot.* 32: 1–58.

Mills, D. H. (1965). The distribution and food of the Cormorant in Scottish inland waters. *Freshw. Salm. Fish. Res. Scot.* 35: 1–16.

Mills, D. H. (1969). The growth and population densities of Roach in some Scottish waters. *Proc. Brit. Coarse Fish Conf.* 4: 50–57.

Mills, D. H. (1971). *Salmon and Trout: a resource, its ecology, conservation and management.* Edinburgh: Oliver & Boyd.

Mills, D. H. (1989). *Ecology and Management of Atlantic Salmon.* London: Chapman & Hall

Milner, N. J., Gee, A. S. & Hemsworth, R. J. (1978). The production of Brown Trout, *Salmo trutta* in tributaries of the upper Wye, Wales, *J. Fish Biol.* 13: 599–612.

Moore, J. W. (1975a). Reproductive biology of anadromous Arctic Char, *Salvelinus alpinus* (L.), in the Cumberland Sound area of Baffin Island. *J. Fish Biol.* 7: 143–151.

Moore, J. W. (1975b). Distribution, movements, and mortality of anadromous Arctic Char, *Salvelinus alpinus* L., in the Cumberland Sound area of Baffin Island. *J. Fish Biol.* 7: 339–348.

Moore, J. W. & Moore, I. A. (1976). The basis of food selection in some estuarine fishes. Eels, *Anguilla anguilla* (L.), Whiting, *Merlangus merlangus* (L.), Sprat, *Sprattus sprattus* (L.) and Stickleback, *Gasterosteus aculeatus* L. *J. Fish Biol.* 9: 375–390.

Moore, J. W. & Moore, I. A. (1976). The basis of food selection in Flounders, *Platichthys flesus* (L.), in the Severn Estuary. *J. Fish Biol.* 9: 139–156.

Moore, J. W. & Potter, I. C. (1976). Aspects of feeding and lipid deposition and utilisation in the lampreys, *Lampetra fluviatilis* (L.) and *Lampetra planeri* (Bloch). *J. Anim. Ecol.* 45: 699–712.

Moriarty, C. (1973a). Studies of the Eel, *Anguilla anguilla*, in Ireland: 2. In Lough Conn, Lough Gill and North Cavan Lakes. *Irish Fish. Invest.* 13.

Moriarty, C. (1973b). A technique for examining eel otoliths. *J. Fish Biol.* 5: 183–184.

Moriarty, C. (1974). Studies of the Eel, *Anguilla anguilla* in Ireland: 3. In the Shannon catchment. *Irish Fish Invest.* 14: 1–25.

Moriarty, C. (1975). Studies of the Eel, *Anguilla anguilla* in Ireland: 4. In the Munster Blackwater. *Irish Fish Invest.* 15: 1–14.

Moriarty, C. (1978). *Eels.* Newton Abbot: David & Charles.

Moriarty, C. (1983). Age determination and growth of Eels, *Anguilla anguilla. J. Fish Biol.* 23: 257–264.

Morris, D. (1952). Homosexuality in the Tenspined Stickleback (*Pygosteus pygosteus* L.). *Behaviour.* 4: 233–261.

Morris, K. H. (1978). The food of the Bullhead (*Cottus gobio* L.) in the Gogar Burn, Lothian, Scotland. *Forth Nat. Hist.* 7: 31–44.

Morris, K. H. & Maitland, P. S. (1987). A trap for catching adult lampreys (Petromyzonidae) in running water. *J. Fish Biol.* 31: 513–516.

Morrison, B. (1976). The coarse fish of the Lake of Menteith. *Fish. Mgt.* 7: 89.

Mortensen, E. (1977). Density-dependent mortality of Trout fry (*Salmo trutta* L.) and its relationship to the management of small streams. *J. Fish Biol.* 11: 613–618.

Moule, T. (1852). *The heraldry of fish.* London: Van Voorst.

Mraz, D., Kmiotek, S. & Frankenberger, L. (1961). The Largemouth Bass. Its life history, ecology and management. *Wis. Conc. Dept. Publ.* 232: 1–13.

Mulcahy, M. F. (1970). Blood values in the Pike *Esox lucius* L. *J. Fish Biol.* 2: 203–209.

Mulicki, Z. (1947). The food and feeding habit of the Flounder (*Pleuronectes flesus* L.) in the Gulf of Gdansk. *Arch. Hydrobiol. Ryb.* 13: 221–259.

Munro, W. R. (1957). The Pike of Loch Choin. *Freshw. Salm. Fish. Res. Scot.* 16: 1–16.

Munro, W. R. & Balmain, K. H. (1956). Observations on the spawning runs of Brown Trout in the South Queich, Loch Leven. *Freshw. Salm. Fish. Res. Scot.* 13: 1–17.

Myers, R. R. & Hutchings, J. A. (1987). Mating of anadromous Atlantic Salmon, *Salmo salar* L., with mature male parr. *J. Fish Biol.* 31: 143–146.

Naesje, T. F., Jonsson, B. Klyve, L. & Sandlund, O. T. (1987). Food and growth of age-0 Smelts, *Osmerus eperlanus*, in a Norwegian fjord lake. *J. Fish Biol.* 30: 119–126.

Nall, G. H. (1930). *The life of the Sea Trout.* London: Seeley Service.

Narver, D. W. (1969). Age and size of Steelhead Trout in Babine River, British Columbia. *J. Fish. Res. Bd. Can.* 26: 2754–2760.

National Anglers' Council (1987). *The British record fish lists.* Peterborough: National Anglers' Council.

Nature Conservancy Council. (1977). *A nature conservation review.* Cambridge: University Press.

Netboy, A. (1968). *The Atlantic Salmon. A vanishing species?* London: Faber & Faber.

Newth, H. G. (1930). The feeding of ammocoetes. *Nature, Lond.* 126: 94–95.

Nicholas, W. L. & Jones, J. W. (1959). *Henneguya tegidensis* sp. Nov. (Myxosporidea), from the freshwater fish *Coregonus clupeoides pennantii* (the Gwyniad). *Parasitology.* 49: 1–5.

Nilsson, N. A. (1979). Food and habitat of the fish community of the offshore region of Lake Vanern, Sweden. *Rep. Inst. Freshw. Res. Drottning.* 58: 126–139.

North, E. (1980). The effects of water temperature and flow upon angling success in the River Severn. *Fish. Mgt.* 11: 1–9.

Oliva, O. & Vostradovsky, J. (1960). Contribution to the knowledge of growth of the Pope *Acerina cernua. Cas. Narod. Mus.* 129; 56–63.

O'Maoileidigh, N., Cawdery, S., Bracken, J. J. & Ferguson, A. (1988). Morphometric, meristic character and electrophoretic analyses of two Irish populations of Twaite Shad, *Alosa fallax* (Lacepede). *J. Fish Biol.* 32: 355–366.

Parkhurst, N. W. (1982a). Relation of visual changes to the onset of sexual maturation in the European Eel, *Anguilla anguilla* (L.). *J. Fish Biol.* 21: 127–140.

Parkhurst, N. W. (1982b). Changes in body musculature with sexual maturation in the European Eel, *Anguilla anguilla* (L.). *J. Fish Biol.* 21: 417–428.

Parkhurst, N. W. (1982c). Changes in skin-scale complex with sexual maturation in the European Eel, *Anguilla anguilla* (L.). *J. Fish Biol.* 21: 549–562.

Parkhurst, N. W. & Lythgoe, J. N. (1982). Structure and colour of the integument of the European Eel, *Anguilla anguilla* (L.). *J. Fish Biol.* 21: 279–304.

Parkhurst, N. W. & Lythgoe, J. N. (1983). Changes in vision and olfaction during sexual maturation in the European Eel, *Anguilla anguilla* (L.). *J. Fish Biol.* 23: 229–240.

Parsons, J., Vickers, K. U. & Warden, Y. (1977). Relationship between elver recruitment and changes in the sex ratio of silver Eels, *Anguilla anguilla* L. migrating from Lough Neagh, Northern Ireland. *J. Fish Biol.* 10; 211–230.

Pawson, M. G. & Pickett, G.; D. (1987). The Bass (*Dicentrarchus labrax*) and management of its fishery in England and Wales. Lowestoft: MAFF.

Pawson, M. G., Kelly, D. F. & Pickett, G. D. (1987). The distribution and migrations of Bass, *Dicentrarchus labrax* L., in waters around England and Wales as shown by tagging. *J. Mar. Biol. Ass. UK.* 67: 263–274.

Payne, R. H., Child, A. R. & Forrest, A. (1971). The existence of natural hybrids between European Trout and the Atlantic Salmon. *J. Fish Biol.* 4: 233–236.

Pemberton, R. (1976a). Sea Trout in North Argyll lochs, population, distribution and movements. *J. Fish Biol.* 9: 157–179.

Pemberton, R. (1976b). Sea Trout in North Argyll sea lochs: II. diet. *J. Fish Biol.* 9: 195–208.

Pennell, H. C. (1866). *Fishing gossip*. Edinburgh: Black.

Peters, G. (1976). Seasonal fluctuations in the incidence of epidermal papillomas of the European Eel, *Anguilla anguilla* L. *J. Fish Biol.* 7: 415–422.

Phillips, R. & Rix, M. (1985). *Freshwater fish of Britain, Ireland and Europe*. London: Pan.

Pickering, A. D. & Willoughby, L. G. (1977). Epidermal lesions and fungal infection on the Perch, *Perca fluviatilis* L., in Windermere. *J. Fish Biol.* 11: 349–354.

Pincher, C. (1947). *A study of fishes*. London: Jenkins.

Pirozhnikov, P. L. (1955). Feeding and food relations of fishes in estuarine regions of the Laptev Sea. *Vop. Ikhtiol.* 3: 140–185.

Pitcher, T. J., Green, D. A. & Magurran, A. E. (1986). Dicing with death: predator inspection behaviour in Minnow shoals. *J. Fish Biol.* 28: 439–448.

Pitcher, T. J. & Hart, P. J. B. (1982). *Fisheries ecology*. London: Croom Helm.

Pope, J. A., Mills, D. H. & Shearer, W. M. (1961). The fecundity of Atlantic Salmon (*Salmo salar* Linn.). *Freshw. Salm. Fish. Res. Scot.* 26: 1–12.

Pratten, D. J. & Shearer, W. M. (1983a). Sea Trout of the North Esk. *Fish. Mgmt.* 2: 49–65.

Pratten, D. J. & Shearer, W. M. (1983b). The migrations of North Esk Sea Trout. *Fish. Mgmt.* 2: 99–113.

Pratten, D. J. & Shearer, W. M. (1985). The commercial exploitation of Sea Trout, *Salmo trutta* L. *Aquacult. Fish. Mgmt.* 1: 71–89.

Priede, I. G. & Young, A. H. (1977). The ultrasonic telemetry of cardiac rhythms of wild Brown Trout, *Salmo trutta* L. as an indicator of bio-energetics and behaviour. *J. Fish Biol.* 10: 299–318.

Puke, C. (1952). Pike-perch studies in Lake Vanern. *Rep. Inst. Freshw. Res. Drottning*, 33: 168–178.

Pycraft, W. P. (1901). *The story of fish life*. London: Newnes.

Pyefinch, K. A. (1955). A review of the literature on the biology of the Atlantic Salmon (*Salmo salar* Linn.). *Freshw. Salm. Fish. Res. Scot.* 9: 1–24.

Radcliffe, W. (1921). *Fishing from earliest times*. London: Murray.

Radforth, I. (1940). The food of the Grayling (*Thymallus thymallus*), Flounder (*Platichthys flesus*), Roach (*Rutilus rutilus*) and Gudgeon (*Gobio fluviatilis*), with special reference to the Tweed watershed. *J. Anim. Ecol.* 9: 302–318.

Rasottos, M. B., Cardellini, P. & Marconato, E. (1987). The problem of sexual inversion in the Minnow, *Phoxinus phoxinus*. *J. Fish Biol.* 30: 51–58.

Reay, P. J. & Cornell, V. (1988). Identification of Grey Mullet (Teleostei: Mugilidae) juveniles from British waters. *J. Fish Biol.* 32: 95–100.

Reddin, D. G. & Shearer, W. M. (1987). Sea surface temperature and distribution of Atlantic Salmon in the northwest Atlantic Ocean. *Symp. Amer. Fish. Soc.* 1: 262–275.

Regan, C. T. (1911). *The freshwater fishes of the British Isles*. London: Methuen.

Reid, H. (1930). A study of *Eupotomis gibbosus* (L.) as occurring in the Chamcook Lakes, N. B. *Contr. Can. Biol. Fish.* 5: 457–466.

Reimers, N. (1979). A history of the stunted Brook Trout population in an alpine lake: a lifespan of 24 years. *Calif. Fish Game.* 64: 196–215.

Rickards, R. B. & Fickling N. J. (1979). *Zander*. London: Black.

Ritchie, J. (1920). *The influence of Man on animal life in Scotland*. Cambridge: University Press.

Roberts. R. J., Leckie, J. & Slack, H. D. (1970). Bald spot disease in Powan. *J. Fish Biol.* 2: 103–105.

Robinson, G. D., Dunson, W. A., Wright, J. E. & Mamolito, G. E. (1976). Differences in low pH tolerance among strains of Brook Trout (*Salvelinus fontinalis*). *J. Fish Biol.* 8: 5–17.

Robotham, P. W. J. (1977). Feeding habits and diet in two populations of Spined Loach, *Cobitis taenia* (L.). *Freshw. Biol.* 7: 469–477.

Robotham, P. W. J. (1982a). An analysis of a specialised feeding mechanism of the Spined Loach, *Cobitis taenia* (L.), and a description of the related structures. *J. Fish Biol.* 20: 173–181.

Robotham, P. W. J. (1982b). Infection of the Spined Loach, *Cobitis taenia*, by the digenean, *Allocreadium transversale* (Rud.). *J. Fish Biol.* 21: 699–703.

Romer, G. S. & McLachlan, A. (1986). Mullet grazing on surf diatom accumulations. *J. Fish Biol.* 28: 93–104.

Rumpus, A. E. (1975). The helminth parasites of the Bullhead, *Cottus gobio* (L.), and the Stone Loach, *Noemacheilus barbatulus* (L.) from the River Avon, Hampshire. *J. Fish Biol.* 7: 469–483.

Sadler, K. (1979). Effect of temperature on the growth and survival of the European Eel, *Anguilla anguilla* L. *J. Fish. Biol.* 15: 499–507.

Schindler, O. (1957). *Freshwater fishes.* London: Thames & Hudson.

Schmidt, J. (1922). The breeding places of the Eel. *Trans. Roy. Soc. Lond. B*, 211: 179–208.

Schoth, M. (1982). Taxonomic studies on the 0-group eel larvae (*Anguilla* sp.) caught in the Sargasso Sea in 1979. *Helg. Meers.* 35: 279–287.

Scott, A. (1985). Distribution, growth, and feeding of postemergent Grayling *Thymallus thymallus* in an English river. *Trans. Amer. Fish. Soc.* 114: 525–531.

Scott, D. B. C. (1975). A hermaphrodite specimen of *Coregonus lavaretus* (L.) (Salmoniformes, Salmonidae) from Loch Lomond, Scotland, *J. Fish Biol.* 7: 709.

Scott, D. C. (1949). A study of a stream population of Rock Bass. *Invest. Indiana Lakes Streams.* 3: 169–234.

Scott, W. B. & Crossman, E. J. (1973). *Freshwater fishes of Canada.* Ottawa: Fisheries Research Board of Canada.

Sedgwick, S. D. (1988). *Salmon farming handbook.* Farnham: Fishing News Books.

Shafi, M. (1969). Comparative studies of populations of Perch (*Perca fluviatilis* L.) and Pike (*Esox lucius* L.) in two Scottish lochs. PhD Thesis, University of Glasgow.

Shafi, M. & Maitland, P. S. (1971a). Comparative aspects of the biology of Pike *Esox lucius* in two Scottish lochs. *Proc. Roy. Soc. Edin. B*, 71: 41–60.

Shafi, M. & Maitland, P. S. (1971b). The age and growth of Perch *Perca fluviatilis* in two Scottish lochs. *J. Fish Biol.* 3: 39–57.

Shafi, M. & Maitland, P. S. (1972). Observations on the population of Eels—*Anguilla anguilla* (L.)—in the Dubh Lochan, Rowardennan, Stirlingshire. *Glasg. Nat.* 19: 17–20.

Shearer, W. M. (1961). Pacific Salmon in the North Sea. *New Scient.* 232: 184–186.

Shearer, W. M. (1972). A study of the Atlantic Salmon population in the North Esk 1961–70. MSc Thesis, University of Edinburgh.

Shearer, W. M. (1984). The relationship between both river and sea age and return to home waters in Atlantic Salmon. *Copenhagen: International Council for the Exploration of the Sea.*

Sinha, V. R. P. (1969). A note on the feeding of larger Eels *Anguilla anguilla* (L.). *J. Fish Biol.* 1: 279–284.

Sinha, V. R. P. & Jones, J. W. (1975). *The European Freshwater Eel.* Liverpool: Liverpool University Press.

Slack, H. D., Gervers, F. W. K. & Hamilton, J. D. (1957). The biology of the Powan. *Glasg. Univ. Publ., Studies on Loch Lomond.* 1: 113–127.

Sleaman, D. P., Devoy, R. J. & Woodman, P. C. (1986). The post-glacial colonisation of Ireland. *Occ. Publ. Ir. Biogeog. Soc.* 1: 1–88.

Smith, I. W. (1962). Furunculosis in kelts. *Freshw. Salm. Fish. Res. Scot.* 27: 1–12.

Smith, I. W. (1964). The occurrence and pathology of Dee disease. *Freshw. Salm. Fish. Res. Scot.* 34: 1–12.

Smyly, W. J. P. (1955). On the biology of the Stone-Loach *Noemacheilus barbatulus*. *J. Anim. Ecol.* 24: 167–186.

Smyly, W. J. P. (1957). The life-history of the Bullhead or Miller's Thumb (*Cottus gobio*). *Proc. Zool. Soc. Lond.* 128: 431–453.

Snow, H. E. (1969). Comparative growth of eight species in thirteen northern Wisconsin lakes. *Res. Pap. Dep. Nat. Res., Madison, Wisconsin.* 46: 1–23.

Solanki, T. G. & Benjamin, M. (1982). Changes in the mucus cells of gills, buccal cavity and epidermis of the Nine-spined Stickleback, *Pungitius pungitius* L., induced by transferring to sea water. *J. Fish Biol.* 21: 563–575.

Solomon, D. J. & Child, A. R. (1978). Identification of juvenile natural hybrids between Atlantic Salmon (*Salmo salar* L.) and Trout (*Salmo trutta* L.). *J. Fish Biol.* 12: 499–502.

Solomon, D. J. & Templeton, R. G. (1976). Movements of Brown Trout *Salmo trutta* L. in a chalk stream. *J. Fish Biol.* 9: 411–423.

Soyer, A. (1853). *Pantropheon.* London: Simpkin & Marshall.

Spataru, P. (1967). Locul obletului—*Alburnus alburnus* (Linnaeus 1758) in econimia complexului de Balti Crapina-Jijila (zona inundabili a Dunarii). *Bul. Inst. Cerc. Pro. Pisc.* 26: 68–76.

Spataru, V. P. & Gruia, L. (1967). Die biologische Stellung des Bitterlings—*Rhodeus sericeus amarus*—im Flachseekomplex Carpina-Jijila. *Arch. Hydrobiol. Suppl.* 4: 420–432.

Spoor, W. A. (1977). Oxygen requirements of embryos and larvae of the Large Mouth Bass, *Micropterus salmoides* (Lacepede). *J. Fish Biol.* 11: 77–86.

Stasko, A. B. (1975). Progress of migrating Atlantic Salmon (*Salmo salar*) along an estuary, observed by ultrasonic tracking. *J. Fish Biol.* 7: 329–338.

Steffens, W. (1960). Ernahrung und Wachstum des jungen Zanders (*Lucioperca lucioperca*). *Z. Fisch.* 9: 161–271.

Stein, R. A. & Kitchell, J. F. (1975). Selective predation by Carp (*Cyprinus carpio* L.) on benthic molluscs in Skadar Lake, Yugoslavia, *J. Fish Biol.* 7: 391–399.

Stott, B. & Buckley, B. R. (1979). Avoidance experiments with homing shoals of Minnows, *Phoxinus phoxinus* in a laboratory stream channel. *J. Fish Biol.* 14: 135–146.

Stott, B. & Cross, D. G. (1973). A note on the effect of lowered temperatures on the survival of eggs and fry of the Grass Carp *Ctenopharyngodon idella* (Valenciennes). *J. Fish Biol.* 5: 649–658.

Street, N. E. & Hart, P. J. B. (1985). Group size and patch-location by the Stone Loach, *Noemacheilus barbatulus*, a non-visually foraging predator. *J. Fish Biol.* 27: 785–792.

Stuart, T. A. (1953). Spawning migration, reproduction and young stages of loch Trout (*Salmo trutta* L.). *Freshw. Salm. Fish. Res. Scot.* 5: 1–39.

Stuart, T. A. (1957). The migrations and homing behaviour of Brown Trout (*Salmo trutta* L.). *Freshw. Salm. Fish. Res. Scot.* 18: 1–27.

Stuart, T. A. (1958). Marking and regeneration of fins. *Freshw. Salm. Fish. Res. Scot.* 22: 1–14.

Summers, R. W. (1979). Life cycle and population ecology of the Flounder *Platichthys flesus* (L.) in the Ythan Estuary, Scotland. *J. Nat. Hist.* 13: 703–723.

Svardson, G. (1950). Note on spawning habits of *Leuciscus erythrophthalmus*, *Abramis brama* and *Esox lucius*. *Rep. Inst. Freshw. Res. Drottning.* 29: 102–107.

Svardson, G. (1956). The coregonid problem. VI The palaearctic species and their intergrades. *Rep. Inst. Freshw. Res. Druthing.* 38: 267–356.

Svardson, G. & Molin, G. (1973). The impact of climate on Scandinavian populations of the

Zander, *Stizostedion lucioperca* (L.). *Ann. Rep. Inst. Freshw. Res. Drottn.* 53: 112–139.
Sweeting, R. A. (1976). Studies on *Ligula intestinalis* (L.) effects on a roach population in a gravel pit. *J. Fish Biol.* 9: 515–522.
Swinney, G. N. & Coles, T. F. (1982). Description of two hybrids involving Silver Bream *Blicca bjoerkna* from British UK waters. *J. Fish Biol.* 20: 121–130.
Terofal, F. (1979). *British and European fishes.* London: Chatto & Windus.
Tesch, F. W. (1982). The Sargasso Sea Eel Expedition, 1979. *elg. Mers.* 35: 263–277.
Thompson, B. M. & Harrop, R. T. (1987). The distribution and abundance of Bass (*Dicentrarchus labrax*) eggs and larvae in the English Channel and southern North Sea. *J. Mar. Biol. Ass. UK.* 67: 263–274.
Thorpe, J. E. (1974a). Estimation of the number of Brown Trout *Salmo trutta* (L.) in Loch Leven, Kinross, Scotland. *J. Fish Biol.* 6: 135–152.
Thorpe, J. E. (1974b). The movements of Brown Trout *Salmo trutta* (L.) in Loch Leven, Kinross, Scotland. *J. Fish Biol.* 6: 153–180.
Thorpe, J. E. (1977a). Daily ration of adult Perch, *Perca fluviatilis* L., during summer in Loch Leven, Scotland. *J. Fish Biol.* 11: 55–68.
Thorpe, J. E. (1977b). Bimodal distribution of length of juvenile Atlantic Salmon (*Salmo salar* L.) under artificial rearing conditions. *J. Fish Biol.* 11: 175–184.
Thorpe, J. E. (1987). Smolting versus residency: developmental conflict in salmonids. *Symp. Amer. Fish. Socl.* 1: 244–252.
Thorpe, J. E. & Morgan, R. I. G. (1978). Periodicity in Atlantic Salmon *Salmo salar* L. smolt migration. *J. Fish Biol.* 12: 541–548.
Toner, E. D. (1959a). Predator and prey relationships. *Salm. Trout Mag.* 1959: 104–110.
Toner, E. D. (1959b). Predation by Pike, (*Esox lucius* L.) in three Irish loughs. *Rep. Sea Inl. Fish. Ire.* 25: 1–7.
Treasurer, J. W. (1976). Age, growth and length-weight relationship of Brown Trout *Salmo trutta* (L.) in the Loch of Strathbeg, Aberdeenshire. *J. Fish Biol.* 8: 241–253.
Treasurer, J. W. (1980). The occurrence of duck chicks in the diet of Pike. *North East Scotland Bird Report.* 1979.
Treasurer, J. W. (1981). Some aspects of the reproductive biology of Perch, *Perca fluviatilis* L. Fecundity, maturation and spawning behaviour. *J. Fish Biol.* 18: 729–740.
Trewavas, E. (1938). The Killarney Shad or Goureen (*Alosa fallax killarnensis*). *Proc. Linn. Soc. Lond.* 150: 110–112.
Tucker, D. W. (1959). A new solution to the Atlantic Eel problem. *Nature, Lond.* 183: 495–501.
Twomey, E. (1956). Pollan of Lough Erne. *Ir. Nat. J.* 12: 14–17.
Tytler, P., Thorpe, J. E. & Shearer, W. M. (1978). Ultrasonic tracking of the movements of Atlantic Salmon smolts (*Salmo salar* L.) in the estuaries of two Scottish rivers. *J. Fish Biol.* 12: 575–586.
Van den Broek, W. L. F. (1979). Copepod ectoparasites of *Merlangius merlangus* and *Platichthys flesus*. *J. Fish Biol.* 14: 371–380.
Van Dyke, J. M. & Sutton, J. R. (1977). Digestion of Duckweed (*Lemna* spp.) by the Grass Carp (*Ctenopharyngodon idella*). *J. Fish Biol.* 11: 273–278.

Varley, M. (1967). *British freshwater fishes.* London: Fishing News Books.
Vooran, C. M. (1972). Ecological aspects of the introduction of fish species into natural habitats in Europe, with special reference to the Netherlands. A literature survey. *J. Fish Biol.* 4: 565–584.
Walker, A. F., Greer, R. B. & Gardiner, A. S. (1988). Two ecologically distinct forms of Arctic Charr (*Salvelinus alpinus* (L.)) in Loch Rannoch, Scotland. *Biol. Conserv.* 33: 43–61.
Walton, I. (1653). *The compleat angler.* London: Maurice Clark.
Wankowski, J. W. J. (1979). Morphological limitations, prey size selectivity, and growth response of juvenile Atlantic Salmon, *Salmo salar*. *J. Fish Biol.* 14: 89–100.
Weatherley, A. H. (1959). Some features of the biology of the Tench *Tinca tinca* (Linnaeus) in Tasmania. *J. Anim. Ecol.* 28: 73–87.
Webb, J. B. (1976). *Otter spraint analysis.* Berkshire: Mammal Society.
Went, A. E. J. (1964). Pepper's ghost: alas no more! *Salm. Trout Mag.* 170: 22–24.
Went, A. E. J. (1968). Irish specimen Brown Trout. *Trout Salm.* 13: 21–22.
Went, A. E. J. (1971). The distribution of Irish Char, *Salvelinus alpinus*. *Ir. Fish. Invest. A*, 6: 5–11.
Went, A. E. J. (1976). The recapture of British Salmon in Irish waters. *J. Fish Biol.* 8: 311–316.
Went, A. E. J. (1979a). Historical natural history notes on some Irish fishes. *West. Nat.* 8: 15–26.
Went, A. E. J. (1979b). 'Ferox' Trout, *Salmo trutta* L. of Lough Mask and Corrib. *J. Fish Biol.* 15: 255–262.
Western, J. R. H. (1971). Feeding and digestion in two cottid fishes, the freshwater *Cottus gobio* L. and the marine *Enophrys bubalis* (Euphrasen). *J. Fish Biol.* 3: 225–246.
Wheeler, A. (1969). *The fishes of the British Isles and North West Europe.* London: Macmillan.
Wheeler, A. (1976). On the populations of Roach (*Rutilus rutilus*), Rudd (*Scardinius erythrophthalmus*), and their hybrid in Esthwaite Water, with notes on the distinctions between them. *J. Fish Biol.* 9: 391–400.
Wheeler A. (1977). The origin and distribution of the freshwater fishes of the British Isles. *J. Biology.* 4, 1–24.
Wheeler, A. (1978). Hybrids of Bleak, *Alburnus alburnus*, and Chub, *Leuciscus cephalus* in English rivers. *J. Fish Biol.* 13: 467–473.
Wheeler, A., Blacker, R. W. & Pirie, S. F. (1975). Rare and little-known fishes in British seas in 1970 and 1971. *J. Fish Biol.* 7: 183–202.
Wheeler, A. & Easton, K. (1978). Hybrids of Chub and Roach (*Leuciscus cephalus* and *Rutilus rutilus*) in English rivers. *J. Fish Biol.* 12: 167–171.
Wheeler, A. & Maitland, P. S. (1973). The scarcer freshwater fishes of the British Isles. I. Introduced species. *J. Fish Biol.* 5: 49–68.
Whoriskey, F. G., Fitzgerald, G. J. & Reebs, S. G. (1986). The breeding season population structure of three sympatric, territorial sticklebacks (Pisces: Gasterosteidae). *J. Fish Biol.* 29: 635–648.
Wilkins, N. P. (1972a). Biochemical genetics of the Atlantic Salmon *Salmo salar* L. I. A review of recent studies. *J. Fish Biol.* 4: 487–504.
Wilkins, N. P. (1972b). Biochemical genetics of the Atlantic Salmon *Salmo salar* L. II. The sig-

nificance of recent studies and their application in population identification, *J. Fish Biol.* 4: 505–518.

Wilimovsky, N. J. (1962). *Symposium on Pink Salmon.* Vancouver: University of British Columbia.

Williams, W. P. (1965). The population density of four species of freshwater fish, Roach, Bleak, Dace and Perch in the River Thames at Reading. *J. Anim. Ecol.* 34: 173–185.

Williams, W. P. (1967). The growth and mortality of four species of fish in the River Thames at Reading. *J. Anim. Ecol.* 66: 695–720.

Williamson, G. R. (1987). Vertical drifting position of glass eels, *Anguilla rostrata*, off Newfoundland. *J. Fish Biol.* 31: 587–588.

Willoughby, L. G. (1970). Mycological aspects of a disease of young Perch in Windermere. *J. Fish Biol.* 2: 113–116.

Wilson, J. P. F. (1983). Gear selectivity, mortality and fluctuations in abundance of the Pollan *Coregonus autumnalis pollan* Thompson of Lough Neagh, Ireland. *Proc. R. Ir. Acad. B,* 83: 301–307.

Wilson, J. P. F. (1984). The food of the Pollan, *Coregonus autumnalis pollan* Thompson, in Lough Neagh, Northern Ireland, *J. Fish Biol.* 23: 253–262.

Wilson, J. P. F. & Pitcher, T. J. (1983). The seasonal cycle of condition in the Pollan, *Coregonus autumnalis pollan* Thompson, of Lough Neagh, Northern Ireland. *J. Fish Biol.* 23: 365–370.

Wilson, J. P. F. & Pitcher, T. J. (1984). Age determination and growth of the Pollan, *Coregonus autumnalis pollan* Thompson, of Lough Neagh, Northern Ireland. *J. Fish Biol.* 23: 151–164.

Wilson, R. S. (1971). The decline of a Roach *Rutilus rutilus* (L.) population in Chew Valley Lake. *J. Fish Biol.* 3: 129–137.

Wood, A. B. & Jordan, D. R. (1987). Fertility of Roach x Bream hybrids, *Rutilus rutilus* (L.) x *Abramis brama* (L.), and their identification. *J. Fish Biol.* 30: 249–262.

Woolland, J. V. (1987). Grayling in the Welsh Dee: age and growth. *J. Grayling Soc.* 1987: 33–38.

Woolland, J. V. & Jones, J. W. (1975). Studies on Grayling, *Thymallus thymallus* L., in Llyn Tegid and the upper River Dee, North Wales, *J. Fish Biol.* 7: 749–773.

Wootton, R. J. (1973a). The effect of size of food ration on egg production in the female Three-spined Stickleback, *Gasterosteus aculeatus* L. *J. Fish. Biol.* 5: 89–96.

Wootton, R. J. (1973b). Fecundity of the Three-spined Stickleback, *Gasterosteus aculeatus* (L.) *J. Fish Biol.* 5: 683–688.

Wootton, R. J. (1976). *The biology of the sticklebacks.* London: Academic Press.

Wootton, R. J. (1984). *The functional biology of sticklebacks.* Beckenham: Croom Helm.

Wootton, R. J., Allen, J. R. M. & Cole, S. J. (1980). Energetics of the annual reproductive cycle in female sticklebacks, *Gasterosteus aculeatus* L. *J. Fish Biol.* 17: 387–394.

Wootton, R. J. & Evans, G. W. (1976). Cost of egg production in the Three-spined Stickleback (*Gasterosteus aculeatus* L.) *J. Fish Biol.* 8: 385–395.

Wootton, R. J., Evans, G. W. & Mills, L. (1978). Annual cycle in female Three- spined Sticklebacks (*Gasterosteus aculeatus* L.) from an upland and a lowland population. *J. Fish Biol.* 12: 331–344.

Wootton, R. J. & Mills, L. A. (1979). Annual cycle in female Minnows *Phoxinus phoxinus* (L.) from an upland Welsh lake. *J. Fish Biol.* 14: 607–618.

Worthington, E. B. (1941). Rainbow Trout in Britain. *Salm. Trout Mag.* 100: 241–260; 101: 62–99.

Wurtsbaugh, W. A., Brocksen, R. W. & Goldman, C. R. (1975). Food and distribution of underyearling Brook and Rainbow Trout in Castle Lake, California. *Trans. Amer. Fish. Soc.* 104; 88–95.

Wyatt, R. J. (1988). The cause of extreme year class variation in a population of Roach, *Rutilus rutilus* L., from a eutrophic lake in southern England. *J. Fish Biol.* 32: 409–422.

Yarrell, W. (1841). *A history of British fishes.* London: van Voorst.

Young, A. H., Tytler, P., Holliday, F. G. T. & Macfarlane, A. (1972). A small sonic tag for measurement of locomotor behaviour in fish. *J. Fish Biol.* 4: 57–66.

Index

Abramis brama 12, 199
abstraction 15, 102, 313
acidification 58, 68, 249, 315, 319
acid rain 58, 315
acid waters 121, 128
Acipenseridae 12, 76, 90
Acipenser ruthenus 91
Acipenser sturio 12, 91
adipose fin 98, 158, 163
Adriatic Sea 54
afforestation 59, 315
Afon Llynfi 221, 226, 339
ageing 44, 46
Agnatha 79
alarm substances 208, 209
albinos 239
Alburnus alburnus 12, 203
Ale Wife 94
algae 60
alkaline waters 59, 121, 128
Allis Shad 12, 94
Alpine Charr 132
Alosa alosa 12, 94
  fallax 12, 95
Altquhur Burn 208, 236
Ambloplites rupestris 12, 277
Amenity & Nature Reserves 66
American Brook Trout 140
American Eel 245
ammocoete 80
Ammodytes 110
amphibians 43, 51
anadromy 29, 53, 98, 111, 115, 130, 145, 253, 280, 314
Anglers' Co-operative Association 8
angling 61, 75, 109, 126, 183, 206, 219, 228, 248, 274, 316
Anguilla anguilla 12, 241
  rostrata 245

Anguillidae 12, 77, 241
anti-angling lobby 75
antibiotics 313
aquaria 19, 37, 51, 75, 177, 187, 210, 225, 254, 275, 295, 320
aquarium trade 17, 314
Aral Sea 213, 217, 340
Arctic Charr 12, 132
Arctic Cisco 155
Arctic Ocean 109, 145, 160, 163, 227
Area of Special Scientific Interest 66, 67
Argulus 38, 125, 215, 219
Asellus 144
Astan 241
Atlantic Ocean 104, 131, 163
Atlantic Salmon 12, 101
Aurora Trout 140
Avington Fishery 144

Baggie 206
Baggie Minnow 258
Baggit 206
baggot 106, 116
bait 49, 66, 89, 124, 139, 151, 174, 193, 206, 232, 247, 264
Baltic Sea 54, 87, 104, 146, 152, 164, 202, 239
Baltic Sturgeon 91
Banny 206
Barbel 12, 190
barbels 21, 90, 230, 233, 234, 236, 238 262, 263
Barbolt 262
Barbus barbus 12, 190
barriers 83, 84, 86, 87, 95, 98, 104, 146, 315
Barse 280
Barstickle 251
Bass 12, 266
  Largemouth 12, 271
  Sea 12, 266
  Rock 12, 277
Bassenthwaite Lake 153,

154
Beardie 233
Bellows Bream 199
Bere Stream 340, 343
biological control 235
Bitterling 12, 210
Black Bass 271
Beck 339
Bullhead 14, 238
  Sea 91, 160, 182, 190, 279, 293, 298, 302, 303, 310, 318
  Tail 111
black spot disease 215
Blay 203
Bleak 12, 203
Blicca bjoerkna 12, 197
blood system 26
bones 21, 73, 74
Bony Horseman 95
Bottling 219
Braddan 101
Braise 215
Bream, Common 12, 199
  Silver 12, 197
Bream Flat 197
  pit 203
Breck 111
British Record (Rod-caught) Fish Committee 140
Broad-nosed Eel 241
Bronze Bream 199
Brookie 140
Brook Lamprey 12, 87
  Charr 12, 140
  Trout 111, 140
Brown Bullhead 14, 238
  Trout 12, 111
Brownie 111
Bulldog 241
Bullhead 12, 304
Bull Trout 111
Burbot 12, 262
Burn Trout 111
Butt 308
Buxton Towers 222

Cairngorm Plateau 55
canals 51, 55
Capilano 321
Carassius auratus 12, 187
Carassius carassius 12, 184
Carp, Bream 199
  Chinese Grass 15, 228
  Common 12, 180
  Crucian 12, 184
carps 12, 177
cartilage 79
Caspian Sea 82, 90, 167, 198, 205, 211, 290, 293, 302, 305
Castle Lake 141
Castle Loch 153, 198, 201
catadromy 29, 241, 308, 316
Catfish, Danube 12, 238
catfishes 12, 238
caviar 90, 92, 184, 240, 288
Central Fisheries Board 169
Centrarchidae 12, 78, 270
Chabot 304
Chad 94, 95
chalk streams 56
Channel Catfish 238
Channel Islands 132, 182, 186, 188, 202, 213, 217, 281, 301
Char 132
Charr 12, 98, 132
  Arctic 12, 132
  Brook 12, 140
Chavender 219
Chelon labrosus 12, 297
Chesil Beach 94
Chevin 219
Chinese Grass Carp 15, 228
Chub 12, 219
Chum Salmon 132
Church Street Canal 14
Cisco 152
Clandeboye Lough 313
Clupea 110
Clupeidae 12, 77, 93
Cobitidae 12, 77, 230
Cobitis taenia 12, 231
cods 12, 262
Coho Salmon 132
College Lake 337
Colley 233
Comephorus baikalensis 304

Comet 187
Common Bream 12, 199
  Carp 12, 180
  Goby 12, 293
  Sturgeon 12, 91
  Sunfish 274
Coney Fish 262
cone cells 264
Conger conger 242
Conger Eel 242
Coniston Water 136
conservation 17, 61, 67, 316, 318, 320
Coosan Lough 337, 338
Coregonidae 12, 77, 145
Coregonus albula 12, 152
  autumnalis 12, 155
  lavaretus 12, 149
  oxyrinchus 12, 146
  vandesius 153
Cottidae 12, 78, 304
Cormorants 110, 126, 313
Cottus gobio 12, 304
County Naturalist Trusts 67
Covichie 111
Crapina-Jijila Lakes 205, 211
crayfish 124, 173, 222, 264, 273, 284
Crowger 184
Cruachan Reservoir 57, 60
Crucian Carp 12, 184
Crummock Water 136
Ctenopharyngodon idella 15, 228
Cuddy 132
Culle 304
Cumberland Vendace 152
Cunn 155
Cutthroat Trout 126
Cyprinidae 12, 77, 17
Cyprinus carpio 12, 180
cyclostomes 14

Dab 308
dace 12, 225
dams 16, 86, 103, 109, 243
Danube Catfish 12, 238
Danube Salmon 14
Dare 225
Dart 225
Department of Agriculture (NI) 66
of Agriculture & Fish-

eries for Scotland 64
of the Environment 66,67
of Marine 66
derris extract 257
Derwent Water 153
Devil's Brook 340, 343
diatoms 84
Dicentrarchus labrax 12, 266
Diphyllobothrium 125, 139, 143, 264
Diplostomulum 125, 130, 219
disease 110, 126, 313
Diseases of Fish Act 66
disruptive species 62, 64, 66
distribution 18, 48, 51, 64, 314
divers 62, 126, 139
Docken's water 338, 340
Doctor 251
Doctor Fish 194, 197
Douglas Water 336
drainage 16, 60, 66, 315
dropsy 194
Dubh Lochan 173, 247, 284
Dubh Lochainn of Beinn A'Bhourd 334

Easdale Quarry 256
EC 64, 269, 312, 314
echo sounders 40
Eddystone Reef 267, 273
Eel, European 12, 241
Eel Pout 262
Eels 12, 241
electric fishing 40, 43, 73, 87, 175
electrophoresis 123, 155
Ellesmere 338
elver cakes 249
English Channel 253, 300
Ennerdale Water 136
escapes 313
Esocidae 12, 77, 167
Esox lucius 12, 167
  masquinongy 167
essence d'Orient 206
Esthwaite Water 339
Eubothrium 125
European Catfish 238
  Eel 12, 241
  fish fauna 17, 48
euryhaline 47, 62, 64, 68
Eustrongylides 125

eutrophication 16, 56, 59, 66, 164, 186, 315
extinctions 64, 67, 145, 153, 164, 262, 277, 317
eye fluke 130

Fairhill Pond 215
Fairy Springs 321
fanning 225, 260, 276, 278
Farnborough Gravel Pit 337
Fathead Minnow 178
fat reserves 244
Ferox 111, 114, 120, 122
fertilisers 315
Fifteen-spined Stickleback 250
fin clipping 45
fin rays 71
Findhorn Bay 311
Finnock 111
Finscale 212
fish louse 37
fish anatomy 21
  appeal 61
  archaeology 49
  collecting 73, 74
  cooking 86, 219, 249, 269
  behaviour 28, 256, 259,
  farms 16, 35, 66, 76, 90, 127, 130, 203, 246, 251, 313, 321
  fossil 79, 87, 90
  Gaelic names 72
  habitats 11
  hermaphrodites 150
  importance 11, 19
  lice 38, 215, 219
  measurements 44
  passes 37, 111
  physiology 25, 97, 106, 108
  preservation 43, 73
  scientific names 72
  spearing 240
  threatened species 317
  trails 322
  Welsh names 72
Fisheries Acts 66
  Conservation Board 66
  Society of the British Isles 19
fishing 16, 41, 60, 322
Flatfish 12, 308
Flounder 12, 308

flower of fish 158
fluke 316
food pellets 111, 134, 313
Fordwich Trout 111
forestry 315
founder effect 169
fox 126
Freshwater Biological Association 23
  Cod 268
  Herring 149
  Shark 167
frogs 124, 142, 169
Frog-mouth 241
fungus 106, 116
furunculosis 110, 116, 126

Gad 167
Gadidae 12, 77, 262
Gaill iasc 169
Gambusia affinis 30
Gasterosteidae 12, 78, 250
Gasterosteus aculeatus 12, 251
  gymnurus 253
  leiurus 253
  semiarmatus 253
  trachurus 252
Gedd 167
genetics 51, 53, 62, 107, 109, 114, 120, 122, 127, 169, 316
Gibel Carp 184, 187
Gila Trout 126
Gillaroo 111
gill maggots 103, 110
  rakers 21, 93, 95, 134
gills 69, 75, 93
glacial refugia 259
Glass Eel 250
global warming 314
glochidia 212
Glut 241
gobies 12, 293
Gobiidae 12, 78, 293
Gobio gobio 12, 191
Goby, Common 12, 293
Gogar Burn 306, 343
Goggle Eye 277
Golden Eye ducks 139
ˇGrey Mullet 301
  Mullet 12, 301
  Trout 126
Goldfish 12, 187
Golomyanka 304

Goosanders 110, 249
Goosequill Pond 183
Gorb Eel 241
Goureen 95
Graining 225
gravel pits 68
Grass Carp 228
Grayling 12, 158
Grayling Society 162
Great Lakes of North America 81
Green Bass 271
  River 305
Grey Mullet 297, 299
  Trout 111
Grig 241
Grilse 101
Groundling 231
Gudgeon 12, 191
Guiniad 149
Gulf Stream 244
  of St Lawrence 252
Guppy 14
Gwyniad 149
Gymnocephalus cernua 12, 286
gymnogenesis 189

habitat 11, 13, 15, 55, 58, 64
Haddock 262
Hautin 146
Haweswater 63, 136, 149, 335
Henneguya 139, 151
Henry I 89
herbicides 315
Herling 111
Herons 84, 89, 110, 126, 188, 210, 249, 307, 313
Herring Shad 95
heterocercal tail 90
Highgate Pond 274
Highland Regional Council 321
  Pond 274
  Water 89
homing 109
hooks 41, 75, 167
Houting 12, 146
Hucho hucho 14
Humpback Salmon 131
hybrids 71, 87, 101, 111, 142, 178, 203, 214, 222, 231, 290
hydro dams 315, 321
hydro electricity 51, 54,

60, 121, 136, 162,
  243, 315
Hypophthalmichthys molitrix
  178, 228
ice age 46, 54, 62, 133,
  169, 253, 312, 316
angling 265
cap 253
dams 47
Ictalurus melas 14, 238
  nebulosus 14, 238
  punctatus 238
Ide 222
injuries 76
Inland Fisheries Trust
  169
International Society of
  Arctic Charr Fanatics
  133
introductions 50, 68,
  169, 193, 229, 272, 315
isingglass 90
Isle of Man 282
iris 195, 227, 238, 242,
  253
Islay 281

Jack 167
  Barrel 206
  Sharp 206, 251
James VI 49
Juneba 85

Kamloops trout 126
Karluk Lake 340
kelt 103, 106, 109, 168
Kilglass Lake 217
Killarney Shad 95
King John 87
  of Fish 110
  of the Herring 94
  of the Mullet 266
Kingfishers 210, 217, 307
Kingfisher Lake 242
kipper 103
Koi 180
kype 101, 103, 113, 132,
  142

Lake Charr 98
  Trout 111
Lake Baikal 145, 207,
  304
  Borovoe 337
  Chaiki 337
  Como 96
  Garda 96

Golodovka 337
Ilmen 342
Iseo 96
Kama 339
Khanka 337
Ladoga 336
Lugano 96
Maggiore 96
Malaren 342
Okanagan 335
Opinicon 273, 275,
  278, 341
Oyeren 338
Pestoro 336
Pskov 339
Simcoe 335, 341
Superior 264, 340
Tiberias 196
Tyriforden 336
Vanern 154, 163
Vygozeri 341
Yxtasjon 338
Lake of Menteith 49, 129
Lakes of Killarney 53, 96
Lammasman 111
Lamper Eel 85
Lampern 85
Lamprey, Brook 12, 87
  Eel 81
  River 12, 85
  Sea 12, 81
Lampreys 12, 79
Lampetra fluviatilis 12, 85
  planeri 12, 87
land-locking 53, 64, 68,
  83, 96, 114, 104
Largemouth Bass 12, 271
lateral line 23, 71
Leather carp 180
legislation 64
Leningrad Lakes 338
Lepeophtheirus 123, 125
Lepomis gibbosus 12, 274
leptocephalus 245
Leuciscus cephalus 12, 219
  idus 12, 222
  leuciscus 12, 225
Ligula 219
Limanda limanda 308
limestone 56
Ling 262
Liza aurata 12, 301
  ramada 12, 299
Llyn Alaw 129
Tegid 63, 122, 150,
  160, 198
loaches 12, 230
Loach, Spined 12, 231

Stone 12, 233
Lob 219
Loch Arkaig 134
  Awe 57, 60, 129
  Borally 335
  Choin 174, 336
  Doon 68, 139, 319
  Earn 134
  Eck 53, 62, 149
  Eil 124
  Einich 334
  Etive
  Fada 136
  Faskally 120
  Flemington 57
  Garry 41, 121, 134
  Glashan 54
  Glen Roy 47
  Insh 134, 135
  Ken 287
  Kildonan 334
  Laggan 47
  Leven 40, 52, 118, 285
  Lomond 40, 49, 53,
    63, 73, 83, 149, 173,
    217, 267, 284, 310
  Meallt 136, 335
  Morar 58
  Ness 58, 87
  Quoich 112
  Rannoch 23, 137, 139,
    187, 335
  Roy 47
  Sionascaig 135
  Sloy 118
  of Stenness 110, 112,
    118, 334
  Tay 107, 116
  Trieg 47
  Tummel 122, 123,
    169, 172, 248, 284
Lochmaben Vendace 152
Loggerhead 219
long lines 108, 156, 240
Lota lota 12, 262
Lough Corrib 63, 284
  Derg 156
  Droumenisa 242
  Ennel 112
  Erne 53, 63, 156, 168,
    287, 336
  Key 247
  Leane 63, 64, 96
  Mask 334
  Melvin 123
  Neagh 53, 101, 156,
    157, 336
  Rea 172

FRESHWATER FISHES 365

Ree 156
Shure 128, 335
Luce 168

Madingley Pond 214
Maize Beck 343
Mallotus 110
Marine Lamprey 81
marl streams 56
May Fish 94, 95
Meaker 206
Mediterranean Sea 54, 88, 95, 267, 296, 300, 310
Mennet 206
Mennon 206
Mennot 206
Menon 206
Melanogrammus aeglefinus 262
Merganser 110, 249
Merlangius merlangus 262
Micropterus dolomieu 14, 271
salmoides 12, 271
Mill Loch 153
Miller's Thumb 304
Minim 206
Mink 110, 126, 249, 313
Ministry of Agriculture, Fisheries & Food 64
Minnin 206
Minnow 12, 206
Mirror Carp 180
Misgurnis fossilis 230
Monk Fish 265
Moray Eel 241
morphological variation 251, 253, 254, 258
Mort 111
Mosquito Fish 30
Mud Lamprey 87
Minnow 14
Trout 140
Mudskipper 293
Mugilidae 12, 78, 296
Mullet, Golden 12, 301
Thick-lipped 12, 297
Thin-lipped 12, 299
Mullets 12, 296
Muraena helena 241
Muskellunge 167
Mysis 97, 156

native fish fauna 61, 62, 63, 64
National Nature Reserves 56, 67

National Parks 67
Rivers Authority 65
Nature Conservancy Council 13, 64, 67, 114, 152, 262, 319
Conservation Amenity, Lands & Wildlife Orders 66
Conservation Review 65
nature reserves 66, 318, 320
navigation 29, 109, 244
nematodes 125
nests 29, 33, 83, 138, 234, 251, 260, 272, 293
nets 38, 41, 61, 86, 125, 139, 143, 151, 165, 170, 186, 191,203, 215, 225, 248, 276, 296, 301
night-lines 240, 256
night vision 264
Nine-eyed Eel 85
Nine Eyes 85
Nine-spined Stickleback 12, 258
Noemacheilus barbatulus 12, 233
Norfolk Broads 202, 214, 287, 338, 339
North of Scotland Hydro-Electric Board 57, 60
North Sea 47, 87, 117, 147, 256, 268, 300, 319

Old Statistical Account 48
olfactory sense 110, 177
oligotrophic lakes 56, 135
Omul 155
Oncorhynchus aguabonita 126
clarki 126
gilae 126
gorbuscha 12, 131
keta 132
kisutch 132
mykiss 12, 126
opercular bone 21, 44, 66, 71, 75, 216, 224, 285, 289, 309
Orfe 12, 222
Osmeridae 12, 77, 163
Osmerus eperlanus 12, 163
Osprey 130, 174, 311
otoliths 25, 44, 137, 195, 197, 241, 255,

261, 289
Otters 62, 67, 110, 126, 249, 313, 321, 349
ovipositor 210

Pacific Ocean 126, 131, 163, 193, 207, 241, 255
Pacific salmon 98
pain 75
parasites 110, 125, 130, 132, 151
parr 98, 104
parr-marks 98, 104, 128, 134, 159
pea cockle 143
Peal 111
Peer 206
Penk 206
Percarina demidoffi 279
Perca flavescens 281
fluviatilis 12, 280
Perch 12, 279, 280
Perchines 286
Percidae 12, 78, 279
Periophthalmus barbarus 293
pesticides 315
Petromyzonidae 12, 76, 79
Petromyzon marinus 12, 81
pheromones 109
Phinnock 111
Phoxinus phoxinus 12, 206
Pickerel 167, 279
Pike 12, 167
Pikeperch 12, 288
Pimephelas promelas 178
Pink 206
Pinkeen 251
Pink Salmon 12, 131
Pisces 13
pisciculture 19
Pitsford Reservoir 212
Plaice 146, 308
Planning & Wildlife Acts 64
Platichthys flesus 12, 308
Pleuronectes platessa 308
Pleuronectidae 12, 78, 308
Poecilia reticulata 14
poison 42, 65, 172, 175, 257
Poll 219
Pollachius virens 262
Pollack 110
Pollan 12, 155
Pollard 219

pollution 15, 29, 64, 83, 111, 126, 146, 186, 235, 290, 315
Polyphemus 183
Pomatoschistus microps 12, 293
Pope 286
Potentially Damaging Operations 64
Posthodiplostomulum 215
Powan 12, 22, 149
Powan-eater 152
power stations 97, 156, 323
precocious males 98, 106
Prickleback 251
Pride 87
Prohibition of Introduction of Fish Order 50, 66
Prussian Carp 184, 210
Pumpkinseed 12, 274
Pungitius pungitius 12, 258
  pungitius laevis 258

  pungitius pungitius 258
put-and-take fisheries 76, 126, 312, 315
Pyramid Lake 335

Queen Charlotte Islands 252
Queen of the Herring 95

Rabbit Fish 262
Rainbow Trout 12, 126
rare species 64, 68, 316
rawners 106
redds 35, 98, 105, 115, 137, 142, 161, 191
Redmire Pool 180
Red Tarn 149
reintroductions 67
Red Eye 212
  Waimb 132
Red-bellied Trout 132
Redeye Bass 277
reptiles 51
research 320
retina 168, 198, 256, 291
Rhodeus sericeus 12, 210
River Lamprey 12, 85
River Allen 158
  Amur 233
  Annan 221
  Avon (Bristol) 190
  Avon (Hampshire) 63,

189, 219
Bann 101
Barrow 163, 167
Birket 254, 260, 265, 340
Blackwater (Cork) 225
Blackwater (Monaghan) 202
Cam 193, 208, 211, 247, 337
Clyde 66, 111, 160, 221, 227, 306, 315, 319
Colne 55, 146
Cree 165
Danube 87, 91, 205, 211, 288, 302
Dee (Cheshire) 150, 287
Delph 290
Don 50, 194
Eden 339
Elbe 146
Endrick 52, 59, 87, 107, 193, 218, 221, 237, 256
Erne 247
Fergus 334
Forth 85, 306
Frome 161, 173, 218, 235, 336, 343
Garry 41
Gironde 56, 91
Guadalquivir 91
Humber 46, 65, 232
Kavlingean 224, 339
Lee 14
Lena 165
Leven 113
Liffey 111, 122
Lugg 161, 221, 226, 336, 339
Medway 146, 190
Mersey 65, 227
Monnow 203
Neva 288
Nipigon 144
Ouse, Great 63, 233, 263, 288
Ouse, Little 225, 235, 238
Ouzel 236
Potomac 180
Rhine 46, 56, 146, 239
Sark 221
Severn 56, 63, 87, 97, 190, 287, 290, 337
Shannon 59, 122

Shimna 113
Skealtar 63
South Platte 183
Spey 47
Stour 47, 173, 218, 222
Suir 101
Sullane 337
Tamar 343
Tarrant 338, 340, 343
Tay 13, 101, 114, 116, 160
Tees 306, 338, 343
Test 334, 336
Thames 63, 66, 164, 209, 217, 221, 232, 315, 319, 338, 339, 341
Thurne 167
Towy 92
Tummel 122, 328
Tweed 50, 116, 118, 161, 310
Usk 333
Vida 146
Welland 339
Weser 146
Wye 94, 335
Ythan 295, 342, 343
River Fox 184
Purification Boards 315
Swallow 204
Roach 12, 38, 212, 215
Rock Bass 12, 277
rod cells 264, 291
Rostherne Mere 68, 164
rotenone 43, 257
Round Tail 111
Rudd 12, 212
Ruff 286
Ruffe 12, 152, 286
Rutilus rutilus 12, 215

Saithe 262
Salmincola edwardsii 139
Salmo salar 12, 101
  trutta 12, 111
  trutta fario 111
  trutta trutta 111
Salmon 12, 98
Salmon, Atlantic 12, 101
  Pacific 98
  Pink 12, 131
Salmon Bass 266
  Trout 111
  farming 97
  ladders 109
  ranching
Salmonidae 12, 77, 98

FRESHWATER FISHES 367

Salvelinus alpinus 12, 132
  fontinalis 12, 140
  namaycush 98
sand eels 92, 110, 124,
  268
Saprolegnia 110, 116
Sargasso Sea 244
scales 22, 35, 44, 71, 86,
  102, 132, 141, 185,
  227, 242, 280
Scardinius erythrophthalmus 12, 212
Schelly 149
Schistocephalus 257, 261
School Bass 266
Scottish Wildlife Trust 67
SCUBA diving 17
sculpins 12, 304
Scurf 111
Sea Bass 12, 266
  Lamprey 12, 81
  lice 108, 110, 123, 125
  Perch 266
  Stickleback 250
  Trout 111
  Whitefish 146
seals 76 110, 126
semicircular canals 25, 44
Serranidae 12, 266
Seven Eyes 85
sewage 111, 315, 319
Sewen 111
Shad, Allis 12, 94
  Twaite 12, 95
Shadbrid 206
shads 12, 93
Shallow 212
Shannon Lakes 156
sharks 108, 110, 251
Sheatfish 238
Shepreth Brook 247
Shubunkin 187
Siluridae 12, 76, 238
Silurus glanis 12, 238
Silver Bream 12, 197
  Carp 178, 228
  Eel 241
Sites of Special Scientific
  Interest 13, 55, 64, 67
Skelly 149, 219
Slapton Ley 219
Slob Trout 111
Smallmouth Bass 14, 271
Smelt 12, 163
smolt 29, 104
smoltification 54, 104
Snag 293
Sonaghen 111

Solway Firth 96
Sparling 163
spear gun 17
Speckled Trout 140
Spinachia spinachia 250
Spined Loach 12, 231
Sprickleback 251
Springer 101
Sprod 111
Squatina squatina 265
Steelhead Trout 126
stenohaline 47, 52, 59,
  62, 64
Sterlet 91
Stickle 251
Stickleback, Nine-spined
  12, 258
  Three-spined 12, 251
sticklebacks 12, 121, 250
Stickling 251
Stizostedion lucioperca 12,
  288
  vitreum 14, 290
stocking 49, 107, 126
Stone Grig 85
  Loach 233
Striped Bass 266
sturgeon 12, 90
Sturgeon, Common 12,
  91
Sun Bass 274
Sunfish 12, 270
swim bladder 24, 90,
  231, 235, 245, 251,
  261, 282, 296, 301

tadpoles 142
tagging 38, 44, 75, 104
tapeworms 125
tartan fish 103
teeth 79, 82, 87, 93,
  263, 282, 296, 301, 303
Tench 12, 194
Ten-spined Stickleback
  258
Thick-lipped Mullet, 12,
  297
Thin-lipped Mullet 12,
  299
Thirlmere 136
threatened species 68,
  317
Three-spined Stickleback
  12, 251
Thymallidae 12, 77, 158
Thymallus thymallus 12,
  158
Tiddlebat 251

Tiger Trout 143
Tilapia zillii 14
Tinca tinca 12, 194
Tinplate 197
Tom Culle 304
Tommy Logge 304
toxic chemicals 315
traps 41, 73, 86, 111,
  143, 151, 165, 186,
  191, 203, 217, 240,
  265, 276, 282, 299,
  303, 311, 322
Trout 12, 97, 111
Trout, Brown 12, 111
  Rainbow 12, 126
  Salmon 111
  Sea 111
  Truff 111
tubercles 29, 186, 191,
  202, 205, 209, 221,
  224, 227, 234
Twaite Shad 12, 95
Typha 290

UDN 110, 126
ulcer disease 285
Ullswater 149, 150, 335
Umber 158
Umber Fish 158
Umbra krameri 14

Veiltail 187
Vendace 12, 152
vendace clubs 155

Walleye 14, 279, 290
warm water effluents 14,
  16, 51, 69, 246, 249,
  268
Wastwater 136
Water Authorities 66,
  315, 316
  Buttercup 222
  Fox 219
  Sheep 219
  Slater 144
  velocity 83
waterfowl 62, 173
Weather Fish 230
Wels 238
Welsh Lake 341
West View Farm Lake
  286
whales 110
White Amur 14, 228
  Bream 197
  Mullet 266
  Sea 131, 132, 156, 310

Tailed Eagle 67
Trout 111
whitefish 12, 145
Whiting 111, 262
Whiting Bay 267
Whitling 111,
Wildlife & Countryside
  Act 64, 65, 66
Willow Brook 339

Windermere 133, 136,
  175, 248, 285, 334,
  335, 338, 340, 343
Woodwalton Fen 56
Wraysbury Gravel Pits
  338

Yellow Eel 241
  Fin 111

Perch 281
Pickerel 290
Sunfish 274
Trout 111

Zander 288
Zebra Trout 143
zoos 19